MICHAEL PALIN is a scriptwriter, comedian, novelist, television presenter, actor and playwright. He established his reputation with *Monty Python's Flying Circus* and *Ripping Yarns*. His work also includes several films with Monty Python, as well as *The Missionary*, *A Private Function*, *A Fish Called Wanda*, *American Friends* and *Fierce Creatures*. His television credits include two films for the BBC's *Great Railway Journeys*, the plays *East of Ipswich* and *Number 27*, and Alan Bleasdale's *GBH*.

In 2006 the first volume of his diaries, *1969–1979: The Python Years*, spent several weeks on the bestseller lists. He has also written books to accompany his seven very successful travel series: *Around the World in 80 Days* (an updated edition of which was published in 2008, twenty years later), *Pole to Pole*, *Full Circle*, *Hemingway Adventure*, *Sahara*, *Himalaya* and *New Europe*. Most have been No. 1 bestsellers and *Himalaya* was No. 1 for 11 weeks. He is the author of a number of children's stories, the play *The Weekend* and the novel *Hemingway's Chair*. Visit his website at www. palinstravels.co.uk.

MICHAEL PALIN
DIARIES 1969-1979

The Python Years

WEIDENFELD & NICOLSON

A W&N PAPERBACK

First published in Great Britain in 2006
by Weidenfeld & Nicholson
This paperback edition published in 2007
by Weidenfeld & Nicolson,
an imprint of Orion Books Ltd,
Carmelite House, 50 Victoria Embankment
London EC4Y 0DZ

An Hachette UK company

5 7 9 10 8 6

A CIP catalogue record for this book
is available from the British Library.

ISBN: 978-1-7802-2901-0

Typeset by Input Data Services Ltd,
Bridgwater, Somerset

Printed and bound in Great Britain by Clays Ltd, Elcograf S.p.A.

The Orion Publishing Group's policy is to use papers that
are natural, renewable and recyclable products and
made from wood grown in sustainable forests. The logging
and manufacturing processes are expected to conform to
the environmental regulations of the country of origin.

www.orionbooks.co.uk

For my mother and father

Contents

List of illustrations

1 From the author's private albums
2 John Ferro Sims
3 Drew Mara
4 Carl Samrock
5 Camera Press (Lionel Cherrvault)
6 Edie Baskin

Who's Who in the Diaries 1969–1979

Certain names recur at various points during the diaries. Here is a rough list of those who make regular appearances.

FAMILY

Edward (Ted) Palin born July 1900
Mary Palin (née Ovey) born January 1904
Retired from Sheffield to Reydon, near Southwold, Suffolk in December 1966
Children:
    Angela born 1934, died 1987
    Michael born 1943

Angela married Veryan Herbert in 1958
Children:
    Jeremy, born 1960
    Camilla, born 1962
    Marcus, born 1963

Michael married Helen Gibbins, born 1942, on April 16th, 1966
Children:
    Thomas (Tom), born 1968
    William, born 1970
    Rachel, born 1975

Helen's family:
Father, **Dearman Gibbins,** died 1963
Mother, **Anne Gibbins,** born 1913
Elder sister, **Mary,** born 1940. Married **Edward Burd** in 1964.
    Daughter, **Catherine.**
Younger sister, **Cathy,** born 1945

FRIENDS AND COLLEAGUES

The Stuart-Harris family. Lived next door to the Palins in Sheffield. Father, Charles, was a doctor and became Professor of Medicine at Sheffield University. Mother, Marjorie. Graham, the eldest son, married to Margot, and MP's oldest friend. Daughter Susan is a psychologist and younger son, Robin, also a doctor. Married to Barbara, a New Zealander.

Robert Hewison. Contemporary of MP at Brasenose College Oxford, 1962-5. Fellow cabaret performer and writer. Author of a series of books on modern cultural history, expert on John Ruskin.

Terry Jones. Met MP at Oxford in 1963. First performed together in the Oxford Revue, Edinburgh Festival 1964. Wrote together for television on *The Frost Report*, 1966. Married Alison Telfer, 1969. Children: Sally and Bill.

John Cleese, married to Connie Booth. Separated in mid-1970s.

Eric Idle, married to Lyn Ashley. Separated in mid-1970s.

Terry Gilliam, married to Python make-up supremo Maggie Weston.

Graham Chapman, lived with David Sherlock, later adopted John Tomiczek.

Ian and Anthea Davidson. Met MP at Oxford. Encouraged him to perform in revue and gave him early work at the BBC. A writer and director and occasional Python performer.

Ranji and Rolf Veling. Ranji is a friend from Helen Palin's teaching days. She is Sri Lankan, he is Dutch.

Simon and Phillida Albury. Simon met MP after Oxford in 1965. Television journalist, producer and gospel music fan.

Graeme Garden. Contemporary of Eric Idle at Cambridge. Writer-performer who worked with MP on *Twice a Fortnight* (1967) and *Broaden Your Mind* (1968). First wife Liz and daughter Sally were frequent visitors.

Bill Oddie. Cambridge contemporary of Eric's. Lived nearby. Also worked with MP on *Twice a Fortnight*. Regular source of football tickets.

Tim Brooke-Taylor. Friend and provider of work for MP on *Broaden Your Mind*.

PYTHON'S EXTENDED FAMILY

Ian MacNaughton. Director of TV series and first film *And Now for Something Completely Different.*

Eke Ott. Became the second Mrs MacNaughton.

André Jacquemin. Recording engineer with whom MP went into business as Redwood Studios. Besides being official Python sound genius, André, with partner Dave Howman, wrote and recorded songs for Python and *Ripping Yarns.*

Michael Henshaw. MP's first accountant, from 1966 to 1974.

Anne Henshaw. Michael's wife, who took over Python affairs as de facto manager in 1974.

Barry Took. Marty Feldman's co-writer and the man who helped push Python to the BBC.

Carol Cleveland. Started as glamour girl casting but her talent for well-played, well-timed comedy made her Python's favourite real woman. She appeared in the films and stage shows as well as the TV series.

Neil Innes. Musician. First worked with MP, TJ and Eric I. on *Do Not Adjust Your Set.* Indispensable to the Python stage shows. Neil also appeared in *Monty Python and the Holy Grail* and *Monty Python's Life of Brian* as well as helping Idle create the Rutles.

Hazel Pethig. Costume designer from episode one of the Monty Python TV series through to *Monty Python and the Meaning of Life,* thirteen years later.

Julian Doyle. Editor, cameraman, who could turn his hand to any part of the film-making process. Indispensable part of both Python and Gilliam films.

Geoffrey Strachan. Hugely supportive editor at Methuen who encouraged Python to go into print. Also published the *Ripping Yarn* books.

Tony Stratton-Smith. What Geoffrey Strachan was to Python books, Tony Stratton-Smith was to Python records. Endlessly encouraging founder/proprietor of Charisma Records, who enthusiastically indulged most of Python's whims and even named a racehorse of his 'Monty Python'.

Jill Foster. MP and TJ's agent at Fraser & Dunlop.

John Gledhill. Agent at the Roger Hancock office who looked after Python affairs until 1974.

Mark Forstater. Producer of *Monty Python and the Holy Grail.*

John Goldstone. Producer of *Monty Python and the Holy Grail* and *Monty Python's Life of Brian.*

AT THE BBC

John Howard Davies. Child actor who played Oliver Twist at the age of nine, director of three earliest episodes of *Monty Python*, then Head of Comedy during the later *Ripping Yarns.*

James (Jimmy) Gilbert. Producer/director of *The Frost Report* – MP and TJ's first TV writing break. Head of Comedy in the latter days of Python, then Head of Light Entertainment Department at the time of *Ripping Yarns.*

Duncan Wood. Head of Comedy during first three Python series.

Bill Cotton Jnr. Head of Light Entertainment.

Terry Hughes. Director of the hugely popular Ronnie Barker and Ronnie Corbett series. Producer/director of first three *Ripping Yarns*, until elevated to Head of Variety.

Jim Franklin. Special effects expert on *The Frost Report* who took over the production and direction of the next four *Ripping Yarns* after Terry Hughes was promoted.

Alan J.W. Bell. Produced and directed last two *Ripping Yarns* – 'Golden Gordon' and 'Whinfrey's Last Case'.

Mark Shivas and Richard Broke. Drama producers who backed TJ and MP and encouraged them to write *Secrets* (1973).

IN AMERICA

Nancy Lewis. Publicist for Buddah Records who almost single-handedly fought to get Python accepted in America, and became their US manager.

Ina Lee Meibach. Lawyer in New York who organised Python's battle against ABC TV in 1975.

Al Levinson. Writer, teacher and dramaturge for American Public Theatre who became MP's good friend and regular correspondent in the late 1970s. Lived in New York and Sag Harbor, with his wife Eve.

Lorne Michaels. Producer of *Saturday Night Live*.

1969

Though the first entry of all was April 17th, 1969, I've opened the diary on the first day of Python filming. All the entries were written at my house in Oak Village, north London, except where otherwise noted.

Tuesday, July 8th

Today Bunn Wackett Buzzard Stubble and Boot[1] came into being, with about five minutes of film shot around Ham House. It was exhilarating to wake up to the first day's filming of a new show, especially as the sun was streaming down the village and, despite it being only 7.00, I decided to travel to the BBC on the bus and tube. Sure enough, the clouds came up as I put my foot outside the door, and this April-like weather pattern of showers and sunshine was repeated during the day. We arrived at Ham House about 9.30.

It is a Jacobean house, of pleasing proportions, very restrained, but in a more homely and welcoming way than a classical building. A line of Greco/Roman busts in oval niches along the line of walls leading up to the house give you something to remember it by. We were filming Queen Victoria's slapstick film with Gladstone, and the beautifully kept lawn and flower beds at the back of the house provided just the right kind of formality to play off against.

In the afternoon the changes in light from sudden brightness to dullness caused us to slow down a little, but by 6.00 we had quite a chunk of 'Queen Victoria and Her Gardener' and 'Bicycle Repairman' done, and it had been a very good and encouraging first day's shooting.

1 The name of a fictional forward line from a John Cleese soccer monologue, and the current name for what was later to become *Monty Python's Flying Circus*. Among other titles we tried unsuccessfully to get past the BBC were 'Whither Canada?', 'Ow! It's Colin Plint', 'A Horse, a Spoon and a Bucket', 'The Toad Elevating Moment', 'The Algy Banging Hour' and 'Owl Stretching Time'. Increasingly irritated, the BBC suggested the Flying Circus bit and we eventually compromised by adding the name Monty Python.

Wednesday, July 9th

Arrived at TV Centre by 10.00, and was driven in a BBC car, together with John [Cleese], Graham [Chapman] and Terry [Jones], out beyond Windsor and Eton to a tiny church at Boveney. Dressed to the hilt as a young Scottish nobleman of the Walter Scott era, I was able to cash a cheque at a bank in the Uxbridge Road, without the cashier batting an eyelid.

Thursday, July 10th, Bournemouth

Up at 7.15; Graham C called for me in a mini-cab; we got to Waterloo in plenty of time to catch the 8.30 to Bournemouth. We had breakfast on the train. At Bournemouth we were met by a mini-van and driven to the Durley Dean Hotel, where we were to stay that night. I don't think words can fully convey the depression that swept over me as I entered the Durley Dean. From outside it was bad enough – a five storey red-brick block of indeterminate date, but I should guess 1920s – it looked completely ordinary, if anything institutional. Inside there was firstly a dimness, secondly a pervading smell of gravy and thirdly a total lack of any colour – in the carpets, the lino in the passages, the paintwork in the rooms – everywhere the management had opted for the colour most like stale vomit.

One saw a few guests, mostly elderly, about half of them crippled, wandering about, as if looking for someone to tell them what to do. What with the grey weather, the lack of much to do (it was mainly Terry's 'Changing on the Beach' film) and the gradual realisation that all Bournemouth was as drab and colourless as the Durley Dean, I felt very low all morning.

After lunch we filmed on, collecting crowds of people watching Terry take his trousers down. Graham and I, finishing early, went back to the Durley Dean. The depression I had felt in the morning was lifted slightly by the sun shining into my room, and plenty of hot water for my bath. After that Graham and I drank at the hotel bar until the rest of the unit returned. I made the mistake of telling the barman that Graham was a doctor, and soon he was telling Graham about his insomnia and his sweating and his bad feet.

John C arrived from London and, together with Graham, a lady designer, a lady extra, a focus puller and one or two others, we sampled the nightlife of Bournemouth. We ended up in the Highcliffe Hotel night-club where, for 7/6 each we enjoyed 45 minutes sitting in dimness with a drink, whilst the band had their break. When they arrived back (three middle-aged men, looking like failed Sam Costa,[1] who played 'Fly Me to the Moon' in quite a forgettable way), Graham asked them to play 'Happy Birthday' for John Cleese (it wasn't his birthday at all). But the amplification was so bad that we couldn't hear the announcement and the point of the joke was lost.

Friday, July 11th, Bournemouth

Drive over to Shell Bay, beyond Poole, along a flag-lined route – the Queen is visiting Poole today.

In the afternoon filmed some very bizarre pieces, including the death of Genghis Khan, and two men carrying a donkey past a Butlins redcoat, who later gets hit on the head with a raw chicken by a man from the previous sketch, who borrowed the chicken from a man in a suit of armour. All this we filmed in the 80° sunshine, with a small crowd of holiday-makers watching.

We finished at tea-time and were driven to take our leave of Durley Dean and catch the 5.56 train back to London. On account of an unofficial signalmen's strike, the train took two and a half hours to get to London and left Bournemouth half an hour late. But John, Graham, Terry and myself took a First Class compartment and talked about Shows 4 and 5 and decided that we really had an excellent week filming. Ian Mac[2] is marvellous – the best director to work for and, with a fellow Scots cameraman, Jimmy Balfour, he really gets on with it.

Back in London 9.00 – taxi from Waterloo, end of one of the great days.

Wednesday, July 16th

Filming today in Barnes. The weather continues to be excellent – if anything a little too hot – 80°+ all day.

After lunch we watched Apollo 11 blastoff, on its trip to the moon.

Ended up the afternoon prancing about in mouse-skins for a

---

1 Sam Costa was a heavily moustachioed TV presenter, actor, singer and DJ.
2 Ian MacNaughton produced and directed all the Python TV shows, apart from the first three studio recordings and a few days of film, which were directed by John Howard Davies.

documentary about people who like to dress up as mice. That really made the sweat pour down the chest.

To the many life-changing experiences around this time – fatherhood, quitting smoking, keeping a diary – must be added the alarming discovery that teeth I'd always thought of as glowingly healthy were found to be precariously attached to considerably less healthy gums – a legacy of poor care and too many sweeties in my misspent youth. Treatment involved a series of surgical procedures in which the gum was opened, cleaned up and stitched together again. These were undertaken by Mr Robin Powell, a robust Australian periodontist who once likened it to working on his rockery at home.

Saturday, July 19th

Up early to go to Mr Powell for the fourth and last of my dental operations. I was at his surgery by 9.10. He hadn't arrived, but the nurse sat me down and gave me her *Daily Telegraph* to read. He arrived about ten minutes later, cheerfully announcing that he'd had a late night and a lot of drinks, however he said his hand was steady. It needed to be, for this was the most difficult of all the operations. One tooth was obviously more badly infected than he had expected. I even had to go into the next-door surgery during the operation so that he could use the extra-high-speed drill there. He also took out one of the roots of the tooth, and also a nerve, which gave quite a lot of pain. Mr Powell kept apologising, but I felt at least that I was getting my money's worth. I was finally patched up at 10.10 and drove off to the TV Centre to have a look at the week's rushes

After the rushes, made the final organisational decisions about the Great Picnic, which Gilliam had suggested a couple of days ago and which was now becoming reality. Helen, Thomas[1] and myself, Graham and David,[2] John and Connie, Terry G and his girlfriend and Alison and Terry J set out in our various cars for Henley – loaded with food and wine. It was a very cloudy day, but warm, and along the motorway a patch of sun made us seem less foolish. We drove out to Remenham church, which I had chosen from pot-luck as being a convenient place for an idyllic river-

1 Our son, born in October 1968, so nine months old. The only Python child at the time.
2 David Sherlock, Graham's partner. They'd met in Ibiza in 1966.

side picnic. Everything could at this moment have gone hopelessly wrong – the sky was glowering, it was 2.30 and everyone was getting hungry – but Remenham proved to be just the right kind of place – through a gate and we were walking along a flat bank of pastureland with the Thames flowing beside us. We picnicked opposite Temple Island – ham off the bone, paté, salad, several kinds of cheeses, cherries, apples and strawberries, beer sausage, smoked pork, red and white wine and coffee – it was a wonderful spread. Thomas scavenged amongst the food, and was to be seen eating vast chunks of French bread on and off for about an hour. Everyone, Gilliam especially, became infected by picnic madness and there was a hopping relay race and a lot of fighting. The generous doses of wine numbed any possible after-effects of my gingivectomy.

Thomas stood without holding on today.

Monday, July 21st

At 3.00 this morning I woke Helen, and we both watched as the first live television pictures from the moon showed us a rather indistinct piece of ladder, then a large boot, and finally, at 3.56, Neil Armstrong became the first man to set foot on the lunar surface. He said the ground beneath his feet (I almost wrote 'the earth beneath his feet') was composed mainly of dust – for a moment one felt he was in danger of falling into a kind of quicksand – but soon he was reassuringly prancing about and telling us that the one-sixth gravity conditions were less hazardous than in simulation.

The extraordinary thing about the evening was that, until 3.56 a.m. when Armstrong clambered out of the spaceship and activated the keyhole camera, we had seen no space pictures at all, and yet ITV had somehow contrived to fill ten hours with a programme devoted to the landing.

To bed at 5.00, with the image in my mind of men in spacesuits doing kangaroo hops and long, loping walks on the moon, in front of a strange spidery object, just like the images in my mind after reading Dan Dare in the old *Eagle* comics – only this time it's true. A lot of science fiction is suddenly science fact.

Thursday, July 24th

Met with Ian and the two Terrys at the BBC. We listened to some possible title music – finally selected Sousa's march 'The Liberty Bell' from a

Grenadier Guards LP. There's something about brass band music that appeals to me very strongly. Probably it's all to do with my subliminal desire to march along whistling national songs. It's very difficult to associate brass band music with any class of people. Most enthusiasts perhaps come from north of the Trent working class, but then of course it has high patrician status and support from its part in ceremonial. So in the end it is a brass band march which we've chosen – because it creates such immediate atmosphere and rapport, without it being calculated or satirical or 'fashionable'.

An hour is spent from 5.30–6.30 watching colour pictures of Apollo 11's return to earth. Again how old-fashioned a) the landing (they landed upside down), b) the scrubbing of the spacecraft and the space-suits, in case they are carrying deadly lunar germs, c) the whole business of helicopter rescues, appears. One is almost conscious of the laughter and amazement of viewers in thirty years' time, as they watch film of the first men on the moon returning home.

Friday, August 1st

The days seem to merge one into another without particular distinction. It's tending to feel like that with the writing at the moment. We have four shows completed, but apart from the two weeks' filming in July, there has been no feeling yet of concerted effort on behalf of the show (now, incidentally, renamed *Monty Python's Flying Circus*). Partly because John and Graham have fingers in a lot of other pies – especially their film, *The Rise and Rise of Michael Rimmer*.[1] However, it seems that the next two weeks will be much harder work. At least, there is some kind of urgency. August 30th is our first recording date and we have another week's filming starting on the 18th. Time is getting shorter. But at least it's nothing like the hectic pace which we were starting on this time last year with the first *Frost on Sundays*. Accordingly, I've had much more time at home and, as I write this, I'm in the sitting room with Helen sewing and Thomas being fascinated by the sewing machine.

Terry took Helen and myself and Quick and Ken, Philip John,

---

1 Directed by Kevin Billington, executive producer David Frost, it came out in 1970. Surely the only comedy in which Peter Cook and Harold Pinter appear in the acting credits?

Gerald[1] and a girl from Germany whom Terry and Al had met on holiday in Crete, to the Hiroko Japanese restaurant in Wigmore Street.

Before entering our room we had to remove our shoes. Here Ken and myself made what I expected to be the first of many faux pas. After taking our shoes off, we noticed some oriental style slippers nearby and presumed that we ought to put these on in true Japanese style. Grumbling that they were all too small, we eventually selected two pairs and were tottering to our room when one of the Japanese 'attendants' – it wouldn't be quite right to call them 'waitresses' – stopped us excitedly and told us to take off the shoes. Then we realised the awful truth – that they belonged to people already eating there.

Sunday, August 3rd

John C rang up in the morning to ask if I felt like working in the afternoon, so I ended up in Knightsbridge about 3.00. It's funny, but when one has written in partnership almost exclusively for the last three years, as Terry and I have done, and I suppose John and Graham as well, it requires quite an adjustment to write with somebody different. Terry and I know each other's way of working so well now – exactly what each one does best, what each one thinks, what makes each of us laugh – that when I sat down to write with John there was a moment's awkwardness, slight embarrassment, but it soon loosened up as we embarked on a saga about Hitler (Hilter), Von Ribbentrop (Ron Vibbentrop) and Himmler (Bimmler) being found in a seaside guest house. We do tend to laugh at the same things – and working with John is not difficult – but there are still differences in our respective ways of thinking, not about comedy necessarily, which mean perhaps that the interchange of ideas was a little more cautious than it is with Terry. However, by the time I left, at 7.15, we had almost four minutes' worth of sketch written.

Tuesday, August 5th

Another workday at Eric's.[2] A good morning, but then a rather winey lunch at Pontevecchio in Brompton Road. That is the trouble with

1 Diana Quick and Ken Cranham – actors, friends, neighbours of Terry J, and, at the time, an item. Philip John was a work colleague of TJ's botanist girlfriend Alison Telfer. Gerald was a friend of theirs.
2 Eric Idle.

working at John or Eric's – both are surrounded by a very good selection of restaurants, temptingly easy to go to, especially after a good morning's work, but debilitating and expensive.

Wednesday, August 6th

A thought struck me as I saw a man in an open-necked shirt walking up Oak Village – and that was that, for at least twelve successive years, the first half of August has meant Palin family holidays – either at Sheringham in Norfolk or, later, at Southwold.

I have some wonderful memories of those holidays. Of sitting in the lee of the hill above Sheringham where the golf course was and watching the steam train pulling away towards Weybourne. Of enormous games of tennis on the beach with the Sanders family, of plastic macs and wet days (they do seem to be predominant), of sitting excitedly in the back of the Austin 10 (which we inherited when Granny Ovey[1] died in 1951) and the yearly thrill of seeing a pebble-house, and of seeing the sea for the first time.

Now August 6th has no special significance, it's another working day – but it's a token of the enormous difference between my life and that of my father or most people in the country. I have no fixed timetable. I may go away any time of the year, for any length of time, at little more than two weeks' notice. This degree of unpredictability is beyond the sphere of most people – it is an awful thought how regular people's lives contrive to be.

On this August 6th 1969 I am at home. Terry and I are determined to make this a really productive day, to make up for the semi-productive, rather frustrating Monday and Tuesday. We work on till 8.00, finishing our big 'Them' saga. An 85% success day. Very satisfying – and we really worked well together.

Thursday, August 7th

Drove down to Camberwell Grove (where Terry was living) at lunchtime. Lunched with Terry and D Quick, who has a week's break from filming *Christ Recrucified* for BBC2. In the afternoon we worked rather slowly –

1 My grandmother, Rachel Ovey, from whom we inherited our first fridge as well as our first car.

lots of diversions, e.g. Terry's telescope, which he has bought for his father's birthday, a film which Terry bought that morning, and finally a walk. It seems at last, after almost a year of waiting, that Terry and Alison may have got the house they made an offer for in Grove Park, Camberwell. We walked past it – tall, solidly suburban, in a quiet road on top of the first hill you come to going south from Westminster.

In 1966 my parents (Edward 'Ted' Palin and Mary Palin, née Ovey) retired to the village of Reydon, just outside Southwold in Suffolk. Southwold had already played a big part in my life, for it was on the beach here in 1959 that I first summoned up the courage to talk to a tall, slim, mischievous-looking girl called Helen Gibbins. This led to a holiday romance, which led to marriage, in 1966, and birth of son Thomas (now known to everyone as Tom). The different names I use for my father show, I suppose, how my relationship with him changed as I grew older and the children came along. In these early entries he is, as often as not, 'Daddy', as he had been throughout my childhood, but I was also trying out the more formal (and grown-up) 'Father', and later, seeing him through my children's eyes, he was to become 'Grandfather'.

Sunday, August 10th, Southwold

The weather again very fine and warm, and the lunchtime bathe was once more an enjoyment rather than a challenge. In the afternoon, Daddy and I walked from Potter's Bridge, on the Lowestoft Road, across uncharted fields to the sea at Easton Bavents – the seaward limit of Reydon Smear. Here I bathed again. The sun was shining down, undiluted by any wind, as we walked back through the barley fields to the car, the road smelling of melting tar. In the evening D went to sing his second anthem of the day at S'wold Church – his activities as a chorister seem to be about the only outside activity he can partake in. He can't swim, or pull the bells, or even ride his bicycle. Suddenly, from being very active, he is a spectator. Since his coronary in 1964 he has had confirmed Parkinson's Disease (for which a possible cure, L-Dopa, was mentioned in the *Sunday Times* today), back ailments, etc, etc, and has aged very rapidly.

We ate salmon and drank a bottle of white wine for supper, and afterwards Helen and I walked along the sea front. For the record, it is ten years, almost to the day, that we first met here.

Monday, August 18th

Started off for the TV Centre in some trepidation, for this was the first day's filming, and, in fact, the first day's working, with John Howard Davies, our producer for the first three shows. However, as it turned out, the day could hardly have gone better.

John has an unfortunate manner at first – rather severe and school-prefectish – but he really means very well. He consulted us all the way along the line and took our suggestions and used nearly all of them. He also worked fast and by the end of the day we had done the entire 'Confuse-a-Cat' film, a very complicated item, and we had also finished the 'Superman' film. All this was helped by an excellent location – a back garden in a neat, tidy, completely and utterly 'tamed' piece of the Surrey countryside – Edenfield Gardens, Worcester Park.

Wednesday, August 20th, Southwold

At 8.30, John and Terry, in the Rover, and Eric and myself, in Eric's Alfa Romeo, set off for sun, fun and filming in Suffolk.

Terry and I went round to the Lord Nelson, a pub almost on the cliffs. A step down took us into a warm, low-ceilinged room, which seemed to be mainly full of locals. The barman recognised us from 'Do Not Adjust', so we felt even more at home there. Ended up drinking about three and a half pints each and leaving at ten past eleven in the traditional convivial manner.

Back at the Craighurst (Hotel), Terry giggled so long and loud that Heather, the production secretary, thought I had a woman in my room.

Thursday, August 21st, Southwold

A very plentiful, well-cooked breakfast at the Craighurst, and then out to Covehithe, where we filmed for most of the day. The cliffs are steep and crumbling there and the constant movement of BBC personnel up and down probably speeded coastal erosion by a good few years.

Mother and Father turned up during the morning and appeared as crowd in one of the shots.

In the afternoon heavy dark clouds came up and made filming a little slower. We ended up pushing a dummy newsreader off the harbour wall, and I had to swim out and rescue this drifting newsreader, so it could be used for another shot.

Saturday, August 23rd

Mr Powell looked at my teeth and was very pleased with their progress. In the afternoon I went over to the TV Centre for a dubbing session. Everyone was there, including Terry Gilliam, who has animated some great titles – really encouraging and just right – and Ian MacNaughton, short-haired and violent. He seems now to have dropped all diplomatic approval of John H-D, and is privately cursing him to the skies for not shooting all the film he was supposed to. I think this sounds a little harsh, as the weather was twice as bad with John as with Ian.

Thursday, August 28th

This morning rehearsed in front of the technical boys. Not an encouraging experience. I particularly felt rather too tense whilst going through it.

Watched the final edited film for the first show. A most depressing viewing. The Queen Victoria music was completely wrong, and the Lochinvar film[1] was wrong in almost every respect – editing and shooting most of all.

Terry and I both felt extremely low, but John Howard Davies, relishing, I think, the role of saviour, promised to do all he could to change the music on 'Victoria'. We went off to the bar and who better to meet there than John Bird, in an unusually expansive mood. He greeted us as warmly as when we were doing *A Series of Birds*[2] two years ago. He is somehow so untarnished by clique or cliché or any conditioned reaction, that talking to him can only be entertaining. But one doesn't say much as his *knowledge is infinite*.

1 John C dressed as Rob Roy is seen galloping urgently towards a church where a beautiful girl is about to be married. Cleese arrives in the nick of time – ignores the girl and carries off the bridegroom.
2 A John Bird, John Fortune series, directed by Denis Main Wilson, on to which Terry and myself had been drafted as script editors.

Saturday, August 30th

The first recording day. Fortunately Friday's fears did not show themselves, so acutely. From the start of the first run the crew were laughing heartily – the first really good reaction we've had all week. The sets were good, John kept us moving through at a brisk pace and our fears of Thursday night proved unfounded when 'Lochinvar' got a very loud laugh from the crew. In the afternoon we had two full dress run-throughs, and still had half an hour left of studio time.

As the time got nearer for the show, I had a pint up in the bar and by the time the 'guests' began arriving at 7.30, I felt as relaxed as I have done for days. Tim Brooke-Taylor noted that we seemed very unruffled.

Barry Took[1] won the audience over with his warm-up and, at 8.10, *Monty Python's Flying Circus* was first launched on a small slice of the British public in Studio 6 at the Television Centre. The reception from the start was very good indeed, and everybody rose to it – the performances being the best ever. The stream-of-consciousness links worked well and when, at the end, John and I had to re-do a small section of two Frenchmen talking rubbish, it went even better.

Afterwards there was the usual stifling crush in the bar, the genuine congratulations and the polite congratulations and the significant silences. Our agent, Kenneth Ewing, did not appear to like it – but then he's probably waiting to see what other people think.

About sixteen of us finished the evening at the Palio de Siena in Earl's Court Road, in festive mood. Full of relief.

Sunday, August 31st

The end of August, it feels like the end of the summer, with the weather cool and changeable, the garden looking waterlogged again.

On the Isle of Wight, 150,000 people gathered to hear Bob Dylan – the gutter press are having their work cut out to track down smut in a gathering which seems to be happy and peaceful. 150,000 people and all the violence that the *Mirror* could rake-up was a man getting his head cut on a bottle. It shows how evil papers like the *News of the World* and,

---

1 Co-writer of many shows including *Round the Horne*. Father figure of Python. He pushed our series forward, and lent it an air of respectability at the BBC.

I'm afraid, the *Daily Mirror* are. They have chosen to pick out isolated incidents – a couple making love in a bath of foam, a girl dancing naked – and make them seem like crimes. They are trying their best to indict a young generation, who seem to be setting a triumphant example to the older generation – an example of how to enjoy oneself, something which most Englishmen don't seem really capable of, especially the cynical pressmen of the *News of the World*. It's all very sad.

Saturday, September 6th

Today was the final of the Gillette Cup between Yorkshire and Derbyshire – so for a Sheffielder and a Yorkshireman it was quite an afternoon. As I hurried along St John's Wood Road I wondered to myself whether it would be all over and how empty it would be (brainwashed, perhaps, by the *Daily Mirror*, which had already billed it as an 'undistinguished' contest). But Lord's was actually full. There were, apparently, about 25,000 people there – 3,000 less than at Highbury a couple of hours earlier, but many more than when I went to see the Test Match v the West Indies. Derbyshire were in retreat. 136 for 7 against Yorkshire's 216, with 15 or 20 overs left. But they lasted for an hour, until, shortly before 7.00, the last Derbyshire batsman was caught and the pitch was immediately invaded by happy, beer-filled Yorkshiremen, young boys, vicars and a very few women. Speeches and presentations were made and the MCC Establishment was heartily jeered, and Colin Cowdrey was happily booed as he came forward to present the Man of the Match award. But it was Yorkshire's evening at Lord's, and around the Tavern were gathered those nightmarish faces. Sweaty, splenetic and sour. Not pleasant really.

The diary almost buckles here under the weight of writing, filming and recording as well as learning to be a good father to my son and a good son to my ailing father. My resolve weakens and the 1960s slip away without another entry. How could I miss the creation of the Spanish Inquisition and 'Silly Walks'? To be honest, because at the time neither I, nor any of us, I think, saw Python as a living legend, pushing back the barriers of comedy. We were lightly paid writer-performers trying to make a living in a world where Morecambe and Wise, Steptoe and Son *and* Till Death Us Do Part *were the comedy giants.* Monty Python's Flying Circus *was a fringe show, shouting from the sidelines. It was another job, exhilarating at times, but in the great scheme of things not more or less important than changing nappies or hoping for a lucrative radio voice-over. When I pick up the diary again, we're into the 1970s and times are beginning to change.*

1970

Wednesday, January 14th

Since the last entry, just over four months ago, we have completed the first series – 13 episodes of *Monty Python's Flying Circus*. The press were unanimously in praise of the show – Milton Shulman wrote a major article on it after the BBC mysteriously dropped it for two weeks after the fourth show, Jimmy Thomas of the *Daily Express* attacked *Frost on Sunday* for not realising that Monty Python had changed humour and brought it forward when Frost was trying to put it back, we were favourably compared with *Broaden Your Mind* in the *Telegraph*, have had an article in the *New York Times* and, two days ago, received the final accolade: an appearance on *Late-Night Line-Up*[1]!!

Otherwise reaction has been less uniformly euphoric. Doctor Stuart-Harris – now Sir Charles Stuart-Harris since the New Year's Honours[2] – loves it, and a lot of people say it is the only thing worth watching on television. Ian MacNaughton's mother sits through it in stony silence. Letters of congratulation came from Spike Milligan,[3] Humphrey Burton,[4] to name but two.

Viewing figures averaged out at three million, not bad for 11.10 on Sundays. Practical results are promises of another series, repeats of this series at a popular time, an entry for Montreux, and a possibility of a 90 minute cinema film of the best of the series for showing in the States. This last is the pet project of Victor Lownes, London head of Playboy, who raves about the show and is, at this moment, in Chicago selling it to his boss, Hugh Hefner.

The most gratifying feature of the show's success is the way in which it has created a new viewing habit – the Sunday night late-show. A lot of people have said how they rush home to see it – in Bart's Hospital the large television room is packed – almost as if they are members of a club. The repeats – at popular time – will show us how big the club is!

---

1 Serious BBC2 arts programme, fronted by, among others, Joan Bakewell.
2 Father of Graham, my childhood friend from Sheffield.
3 Spike's 1969 series Q5 had been an inspiration to us. It had been directed by Ian MacNaughton.
4 Head of Arts Programmes at BBC.

Yesterday we went further into negotiations about forming Python Productions Ltd – which now seems to be decided – and next week we will set to work producing a film script for Victor Lownes.

In the morning I took Helen to the Tate's exhibition of Elizabethan portrait painting – called the Elizabethan Image. There were some fine portraits – particularly by Hans Eworth, William Larkin and Nicholas Hilliard – but the subjects were usually titled persons, formally posed, and one longed to see a painter who recorded Elizabethan life on a rather more broad pattern. Two interesting paintings were by Henry VIII's court painters and were blatant and virulent anti-Papal propaganda. One of them showed the Pope being beaten to death by the four apostles, with all his trappings – the rosary, the tray of indulgences, etc – on the ground beside him.

Tuesday, January 20th

The houses around Lismore Circus are fast disappearing – Gospel Oak is being laid waste. I get the feeling that Oak Village is like a trendies' ghetto, hanging on for dear life, until the mighty storm of 'civic redevelopment' is over and we can walk once again in a neighbourhood free of noise and mud and lorries and corrugated iron and intimate little rooms with pink flowered wallpaper suddenly exposed by the bulldozer.[1] It will probably be another two years before there is any semblance of order from all this chaos – by then I'll be 28 and Helen will be 29 and Thomas will be three and going to nursery school.

Monday, February 16th

Terry and I have completed two films for Marty's[2] special – written in reluctance, conceived in duty, they are based on ideas of Marty himself. They're long, but that's about all. Somehow, since Monty Python, it has become difficult to write comedy material for more conventional shows.

---

1 Camden Council had a ten-stage plan for the redevelopment of Gospel Oak. This involved knocking everything down and starting again. Oak Village was stage ten, and because of resolute opposition from residents and media was able to stem the tide. A compulsory purchase order had been dropped in 1968, though hovered as a threat until the early '70s.
2 Marty Feldman, one of the At Last the 1948 Show team, and co-writer, with Barry Took, of much radio comedy. He was now a star in his own right.

Monty Python spoilt us in so far as mad flights of fancy, ludicrous changes of direction, absurd premises and the complete illogicality of writing were the rule rather than the exception. Now we jealously guard this freedom, and writing for anyone else becomes quite oppressive. The compilation of all the last series, plus new links, into the film script 'And Now For Something Completely Different' has been completed and the script should be with Roger Hancock.[1] No further news from Victor Lownes III, under whose patronage the work was done.

The third of our more concrete achievements since the end of Monty Python – now six weeks away – was to write a 10–15 minute script for a trade film for Intertel. We got the job via Graeme Garden and Bill Oddie (veterans in the world of commercials), who were too busy to waste time on it. As a means of income during the lean season it had the advantage of being quick and fairly easy to write, no further obligations, except some acting in it if we wrote ourselves in, and no chance of it clashing with Monty Python.

As we await the final schedule for this Intertel film, Terry is writing his novel, which he won't tell me about because he says it will stop him writing, John is in Dar es Salaam for two weeks, and I am about to start writing Monty Python II, for, as Eric reminded me on the phone today, there are only eleven weeks until we go filming in May, and we are seriously intending to have eleven shows written by then.

The weather recently has been clear, crisp and sunny. Snow fell about four days ago and remains still. We have at last got a fire for the sitting room.

Thomas is as energetic as ever. He helps around the house with devastating results.

Thursday, February 19th, Southwold

At the cottage Thomas was much taken with his new mattress with animals on, but yelled when left to go to sleep. My mother quite obviously thought he ought to be left and that he was just being obtuse, but in fact he merely wanted to see what was at the bottom of the stairs – and once he'd had a look, he went quietly back to sleep. A triumph of reason over discipline.

---

3 Tony Hancock's brother, ran an agency which represented, among others, Eric Idle and Bill Oddie.

Friday, February 20th, Southwold

In the morning we shopped in Southwold, where everyone was going along bent against the wind. But one felt it was a clean, scouring wind, blowing away a winter full of damp and grey and drizzle. Mainly in celebration of this weather, Dad and I decided to go further afield for our afternoon walk. We drove to Minsmere, which is south of Dunwich and renowned for its bird reserve. We parked on the cliffs, for which privilege one normally has to pay 2/-, for these are National Trust cliffs, and have been bought for the nation. But not paid for, apparently.

We walked for almost two hours, with the wind too violent for any conversation – along the beach, where we were protected by the cliffs and there was no wind, only sunshine – and beside the tall bank of reeds that fringes Minsmere Reserve. But we saw not a single bird. The largest feature on the landscape is man-made, and that is the extravagant bulk of Sizewell Nuclear Power Station. But it is obtrusive only because of its sheer size. There is no smoke, no noise, no busy air of the factory about it. It is a silent, brooding presence, totally out of proportion to anything around it.

Friday, March 6th

Began as an ego-boosting day of sorts (two fan letters and a request for autographed photos!) and ended as definitely ego-damaging.

In the afternoon, full of joie de vivre, and encouraged by the warm sunshine, I parked my car in Montpelier Square, and went in search of Benton & Bowles Advertising Agency, where I had been asked to go in order to 'meet a man' about a Maxwell House commercial. I felt fairly buoyant, especially as they had previously asked me to do something, but had been unable to afford my fee (only a miserable £50), and also because Jill[1] had specified that it was not an audition. So I felt good as I crossed the Brompton Road and walked for about 100 yards up Knightsbridge.

Upstairs in the thickly carpeted reception area, the girl at the reception desk is talking to a friend – a Knightsbridge and South Ken trait. She asks me my name and I have to repeat it three times. 'Is Miss Sconce expecting you?' This is my first rebuff. I'm not important

1 Jill Foster, our agent. She worked for Kenneth Ewing at Fraser & Dunlop.

enough for reception to have been given my name in advance. 'Go down to the Lower Ground Floor,' says the girl, 'and Casting Department is on your left.' That's all and back to her friend.

Downstairs I go. No evidence of Jane Sconce or anybody. Through a door I hear the sound of recorded playbacks of voices saying 'Maxwell House – the most exciting sound in coffee today.' I hear another voice from another room: 'All we need is just any out of work actor.' The awfulness of the place and the awfulness of the people make me decide to leave, forget it all, forget this ghastly basement with closed doors. But for some reason I stayed and I found Jane Sconce's office, and she was ever so nice, but really *so* busy, and she took me into this room, and there was a trestle table, two jars of Maxwell House on it, and at one end of the room were four men and a girl, and a camera and a monitor. It was an audition. I tried not to listen as the patronising 'director', or whatever, bombarded me with instructions as to how to deliver my lines, my head swam with that awful feeling of being on the panto stage at the age of seven and how I hoped I wouldn't wet myself. But try as I could, I was unable to avoid reading the script. That was the nadir of this whole sorry enterprise. 'Shake a bottle of powdery coffee and what do you hear? Nothing. But shake a bottle of new Maxwell House and you have the most exciting sound in coffee today.'

I did it quickly and sent it up at the end. The 'director' sharply reproved me for sending it up. At this I attacked for the only time in the afternoon. 'I can't really take it seriously – this is the kind of stuff I spend days writing sketches about.'

But I *did* do it seriously, and I did hurry out without offending any of them, without telling any of them how incredibly cheap and nasty I found the whole set-up.

Sunday, March 8th

I walked over the Heath, which was still snow-covered. The sky was a light grey, but the sun filtered softly through and on the north side of Parliament Hill there were two or three hundred tobogganists and spectators. The spectators ranged across the skyline – like the start of an Indian charge. Sledges were everywhere and half-way up the hill was an ambulance. I walked on to Kenwood House. It never ceases to fill me with some gratitude that at the half-way point of a walk across open grassland and woodland not 20 minutes from the centre of London, one can walk amongst Joshua Reynolds, Gainsboroughs, Romneys, a Turner and a Rembrandt self-portrait.

We watched David Frost 'hosting' the Institute of Television and Film Arts awards at the London Palladium. *Monty Python* was nominated for four awards and won two. A special award for the writing, production and performance of the show, and a Craft Guild award to Terry Gilliam for graphics. But somehow the brusqueness of the programme, and its complete shifting of emphasis away from television and towards Frost and film stars, made the winning of the award quite unexciting.

None of us was invited to the awards ceremony, as the girl who was organising it 'didn't know the names of the writers' of *Monty Python*.

Tuesday, March 10th

At 9.45 I found myself in Mount Place, Mayfair, ringing the bell of Joseph Shaftel, a film producer. The reason for this heavy start to the day was a phone-call from Fraser and Dunlop the night before, asking me to go and meet a casting director for a new Denis Norden-scripted comedy film to be shot in Rome. Apparently my name had been put forward together with those of Graham Chapman and John Cleese; however, still smarting from my experiences at Benton & Bowles, I arrived prepared to be humiliated a little.

But no, all was sweetness and light. I was ushered into a small 'conference' room where sits Denis Norden,[1] who shook my hand and fixed me with his extraordinarily kindly eyes, which made me feel considerably happier about the meeting. He introduced me to a small, shaven-headed American director, who proceeded to send himself up in a most frightening way, and a sleek, immaculate Italian, who I presumed was a co-director.

The conversation turned on a 'Sheffield Wednesday' badge I happened to be wearing, and it suddenly felt as though no one quite knew what they were all there for. Perhaps they were sizing me up. However, it seemed to be taken as read that I was going to do the part – that of a detective's assistant who happens to be an art expert as well – and all the meeting was for was to sound out my availability. Five days' filming in Rome and a day in Florence really made it sound spectacularly attrac-

---

1 In partnership with Frank Muir he had written some of the best radio comedy including *Take It From Here*, one of the few programmes to bring my mother, father and myself together round the wireless.

tive, but it seemed as though May would be the filming date – and by then I would be in the middle of Monty Python filming.

Graham, who had been in before me, was waiting, and we crossed Berkeley Square and went into a coffee house. After coffee, and poached eggs on toast for Graham, we were walking back when I found I'd lost my car keys. The day came to an irritating halt as I scoured Berkeley Square and district staring hard at the pavements and gutters. No luck, I had to go back to Joseph Shaftel's apartment. What must they have thought – Michael Palin back again, with some trumped-up story about losing keys. He must want the part pretty badly.

However, they leapt up and down and were most concerned. The dynamic director, who had previously been doing a passable impression of an imbecile, now surpassed himself, suggesting I look in my pocket. The Italian was quite distraught and was turning the room upside down; only Denis seemed to preserve some sense of proportion. I backed out thanking them profusely, and for all I know they're still looking.

Friday, March 13th

Drove Graham down to Terry's for our first major script meeting for the next Monty Python series. At the moment we have no contract, as we are holding out for a bigger programme budget. The BBC are obviously not used to artists stipulating total budget, but it is something we feel very strongly about, and a stiff letter from Jill Foster was followed by a prompt BBC offer of £4,500 per show plus £25 extra for the writers – a total increase of over £1,000 per show over the last series. (But £4,500 only makes us equal with e.g. *World in Ferment*, *Charley's Grant*.) We are holding out for £5,000.

We spent most of the day reading through. Terry and I had written by far the most and I think this may have niggled John a little. We punctuated the day with an enormous Chinese taken-away lunch. Utter over-indulgence. Large quantities of king-size prawns, sweet and sour pork, beef slices, etc, left at the end. Work-rate cut by half. With one possible exception, the sketches read *before* lunch fared much better than those read after.

Drove up to Abbotsley[1] for the weekend, arriving about 10.00.

1 Abbotsley, near St Neots in Cambridgeshire, home of Helen's mother, Anne Gibbins. Helen's father, a farmer, died in 1963 at the age of 53, from heart complications that would now be dealt with by routine surgery.

Saturday, March 14th, Abbotsley

In the afternoon we went into Cambridge, and whilst Catherine[1] and Helen went to look for clothes, I pushed Thomas in his pram across Trinity Hall Bridge, a quick look at King's College from the Backs, and then we walked along in the direction of Trinity and St John's. The wrought-iron gates of both colleges carried signs banning push-chairs from their grounds, but we eventually found a way in. Thomas was very good as I pushed him past the front of Trinity, alongside garden beds with no spring flowers yet showing, up to the Wren Library, which is half-way through external restoration, and looks like a half-unwrapped present. Coming out of the back door of Trinity was none other than Christopher Isherwood, ex-Cambridge, now living in California. It seemed entirely right that he should be there, and I almost went up and spoke to him. About eight or nine years ago, when I was waiting to go up to Oxford, I read most of his novels, and especially those more obviously autobiographical – *Lions and Shadows, The World in the Evening*, I liked a great deal. I think I found his sensitive, vulnerable and ingenuous hero rather sympathetic.

However, I couldn't remember all this, and the great novelist, the man whose life I felt I had shared those years ago, walked away towards the Backs, and Thomas and I looked at the ducks on the Cam.

Sunday, March 22nd

Today began with a mammoth walk across the Heath in order to tire Thomas out. We took some bread for the ducks, but, alas, another lady was there before us with the same intent, and she lured them all away – so Thomas and I were left throwing large amounts of succulent white bread to a bald-headed coot. On the way back Thomas made the acquaintance of a dark brown cocker spaniel, and I made the acquaintance of its owner, a dark brown Englishman with a Viva Zapata moustache, shades and elegantly effortless brown sweater and trousers. In short, the kind of person who makes one feel slightly overweight and a little shabby. He was a fashion designer, with a journalist wife and two kids, Justin and Sean. Justin was about five, and had a gun with which, he said, 'I'm going to shoot babies.'

---

1 Helen's niece, then four years old.

An afternoon party at Eric's. There, surprisingly enough, Thomas was in his element. For two hours we hardly saw him – he cried only when Marty Feldman a) trod on his hand and b) knocked him over, and for the rest of the time he pottered about, and was seen to be dancing, pinching the book from a serene little girl who sat reading, and thumbing through a book of erotic postcards. A good little party. Black and Tan to drink and I renewed acquaintance with D Jason, H Barclay[1] and Rodney Slater, ex of the Bonzo Dog Band, now a child welfare officer in Modbury Street, Kentish Town.

Tuesday, April 14th

At the BBC there was nowhere to park – the excuse being 'Apollo 13'. In explanation of why 'Apollo 13' should be responsible for filling the BBC car park, Vic, the one-armed gateman, just said 'Apollo 13', in a way which brooked no argument.

In fact it was early this morning that Apollo 13, having just passed the point of no return, had an explosion in one of the oxygen tanks, and this put the Command Module's engine out of action. So this is the first Apollo mission to have gone seriously wrong in space, after a launch which made no headlines because people were just getting used to the smoothness and precision of these first moon missions.

On the way to the BBC I saw a poster for the film *Marooned*[2] – which is a very believable tale about three astronauts stuck in space and the rescue operation to get them back to earth.

The main difference between fiction and fact is that, in the film, another rocket, carrying a never-fully-tested module, is fired to send someone up to save them. There has been not the slightest mention of a possibility of any rescue craft getting to Apollo 13. And this seems to be the most dangerous aspect of the whole, so far glorious, moon landing programme. The Americans have gone all out to get men on the moon as fast as they can, without perhaps consolidating the situation nearer home – e.g. by building space laboratories outside earth's orbit, or by working on a less expensive form of rocket fuel. The result is that, when

---

1 David Jason had been one of the cast of *Do Not Adjust Your Set*, produced by Humphrey Barclay, yet another of the Cambridge comedy mafia, who also produced *The Complete and Utter History of Britain* for Terry and myself in 1968–9.
2 1969 film, directed by John Sturges, starring Gregory Peck and Gene Hackman.

the Apollo astronauts go up, they are out on a limb – if they cannot get back to earth there is no possibility of fetching them.

Back at TV Centre, while Roy Jenkins [Labour Chancellor of the Exchequer] was presenting his fourth Budget to the House of Commons in optimistic circumstances, we were having an equally optimistic meeting with Ian M. He was sober, confident and relaxed. We talked about the BBC's idea of making an album of the best of the first series, the budget for the new series, and ended up with a very convivial drink at the Club.

We all felt very much happier as we drove home. Summer was in the air, and the Budget was fairly harmless, making nothing more expensive and nothing cheaper, but at least I read that the country's trade balance was the most favourable since 1822. Now that does knock the myth of Victorian imperial prosperity on the head. Walked up to the library and back over the Heath.

Thursday, April 16th

At 10.00, cars arrived to take us to the Lyceum Ballroom off the Strand to be presented with our *Weekend* TV awards. We were rushed into the stage door, where a few girls with autograph books obviously thought we were somebody, but none of them were quite sure who. Inside the stage door, steps led down an inhospitable brick staircase to a small room, which was probably a Green Room, full of slightly shabby celebrities and their hangers-on. From the inside of the Lyceum came a heavy, noisy beat and periodic PA announcements for 'Arnold Ridley'.

It was all rather nightmarish, grinning faces loomed up, people pushed through, Eric Morecambe looked cheerful, a dinner-jacketed young man with a vacant expression and an autograph book asked me if I was famous. I said no, I wasn't, but Terry Gilliam was. Gilliam signed Michael Mills'[1] name, the twit then gave the book to me saying, 'Well, could I have yours anyway?' So I signed 'Michael Mills' as well. We all signed 'Michael Mills' throughout the evening.

---

1 Michael Mills, Head of Comedy at the BBC, was the man who green-lighted Python in the summer of 1969. Despite a disastrous meeting at which we could give no satisfactory answers to any of his questions, he came out with the memorable words, 'All right, I'll give you thirteen shows, but that's all!'

Monday, April 20th

Down at Terry's to put together the fifth show of the new series. A mid-morning disappointment – the Rome filming trip, which had always seemed to me too good to be true, has almost collapsed. Virna Lisi, the leading lady, is ill and the schedule is now in disarray. A slim chance that I may be needed before my Monty Python deadline, but I am inclined to write it off. Bad scene. Loss of suntan and at least £300, not to mention experience.

The other four of us, or should I say three and the hovering Chapman (no, that's unkind, and this is a kind diary), the other four of us worked on until 6.45, and completed and read through what I think is one of the best shows to date.

Tuesday, April 21st

An interesting and hard-worked morning giving my voluntary performing services for the Labour Party. Easily the most decisive political act of my life, and almost the only one – though previously I had once voted Labour in the GLC elections. I suppose voting for and supporting Labour is just another painless way of appeasing my social conscience. But it's not much, I cannot see how anyone with a social conscience could vote Conservative. The film which I was doing today had been written by John Cleese, who is now what you might call a committed Labour celebrity – and I mean that in a good sense – somebody who is prepared to *do* something to keep the Conservatives out. At present Labour is increasingly successful in the polls. Two opinion polls out this week actually gave Labour a lead over the Tories for the first time for three years and, in the GLC elections last week, Labour won thirteen seats, their biggest electoral success since they came to power.

Friday, April 24th

Down at Terry's in the morning and for lunch, and from there to the BBC, where we all gathered to watch the playback of two of the last Monty Python series, which were being shown to an American named Dick Senior, who is interested in syndicating them in the States, and an American girl by the name of Pat Casey, who is to be in some way connected with the production of our Playboy-sponsored Python film to be made later in the year.

The first one we were shown was Show 11, and it was painfully slow – the 'Undertakers' and the 'World of History' were two ideas ground underfoot by heavy-handed shooting and editing and also performance. It made us look very amateur and our face was only partly saved by Show 12 – a much better looking show with 'Hilter' and 'Upper Class Twits' providing two of the most remembered items of the series.

Dick Senior seemed a little taken aback, but he was a very intelligent man and could obviously see that there was a cumulative attraction in Monty Python, which an isolated showing could not necessarily convey. Nevertheless, Show 11 is not one to use for sales purposes.

At 5.00 Terry and I arrived at Pinewood Studios to talk to Betty Box and Ralph Thomas about our rewriting *Percy*.[1] After walking for many yards along corridors and up stairs, which one was never sure were entirely real, we arrived at the office which they share. Both of them younger than I imagined. Ralph Thomas seemed the more genuine and pleasant of the two, Betty Box being kind, but hinting at a hard edge beneath. For about one and a half hours we talked and I got the feeling that they were impressed by our criticisms of the screenplay of *Percy*, and anxious for us to rewrite as much as we can in the time. (They start shooting in June and we are filming from May 11th onwards.)

Saturday, May 2nd

By 10.00 was at the Camden Theatre for the recording of a Monty Python LP. The original impetus for this had come from the unaptly named BBC Enterprises, producers of LPs such as *Salute to Steam* and *Keep Fit with Eileen Fowler*.

Straightaway the pattern of the day was established. The record, we were told, was to be done extremely cheaply, we were not going to have it in stereo, we could not afford to pay any copyright for the use of our invaluable music links – so it was all done on an organ, which reduced everything to the level of tatty amateur dramatics.

Spent the morning in the rather attractive Camden Theatre – a fairly

---

1 Screenplay about a penis transplant, eventually filmed, starring Denholm Elliott, Hywel Bennett, Britt Ekland and others. Betty Box, producer, and Ralph Thomas, director, were responsible for a string of Pinewood Studios hits, including *Doctor in the House*.

small theatre, with Atlases supporting enormous mock columns, and a rather luxurious intimacy about the atmosphere – reading through the scripts, briefing the sound effects men. Somehow, one felt, this should have been done sooner.

Helped by Graham Chapman's bottle of scotch, the actual recording, at 4.30 in the afternoon, was really quite enjoyable. Not having cameras to play to, one could judge one's audience, and one's effect on the audience, much more easily. However, the audience was small, most of the sound effects were inaudible and we had never had time to rehearse side two, so there were many things which got little or no response – 'Hilter', 'Nudge-Nudge' and 'Soft Fruit' were especial casualties.

Tuesday, May 5th

My 27th birthday – I bought *The Times Atlas* as my major present – with £3 from Southwold.

Helen bought me a garden chair, which was immediately put to use. This is real garden weather, our patch has been transformed from the quagmire of April, to a firm little lawn with tulips, pansies, wallflowers filling the border, and the clematis and Virginia creeper suddenly springing to life.

A hot 27th birthday – as my mother wrote in her letter, it was a very hot day twenty-seven years ago.

Monday, May 11th, Torquay

Left home around 10 o'clock in the Triumph and, collecting Graham on the way, set out for Torquay and our first two-week filming stretch away from home.

Our hotel, the Gleneagles, was a little out of Torquay, overlooking a beautiful little cove with plenty of trees around. Eric, Lyn[1] and John were already there, sitting beside the pool. The decor was bright and clean and the rooms looked efficient – and there were colours about, instead of the normal standard hotel faded reddish brown.

However, Mr Sinclair, the proprietor, seemed to view us from the start as a colossal inconvenience, and when we arrived back from Brixham, at 12.30, having watched the night filming, he just stood and

1 Lyn Ashley, Eric Idle's wife.

looked at us with a look of self-righteous resentment, of tacit accusation, that I had not seen since my father waited up for me fifteen years ago. Graham tentatively asked for a brandy – the idea was dismissed, and that night, our first in Torquay, we decided to move out of the Gleneagles.[1]

Tuesday, May 12th, Torquay

At 8.00 I walked down to Anstey's Cove below the hotel. It was a dry, fine morning, the sun was in and out, it promised to be a better day. Down by the sea, surrounded by high basalt cliffs, it was tremendously peaceful. The calm of the sea affected me, made me feel relaxed and gave me a great sense of well-being. The sea, waves gently turning over on the shore, is so tranquil compared to the antics of the people who want to get near it – the amusement arcades, the 6d telescopes, the hotels with greasy food, the guest houses with sharp-tongued landladies, the trousers rolled up, the windbreaks, the beach-trays, the sand-filled picnics, the real Devon cream ices, the traffic jams at Exeter, the slacks, the sun oil – all of this endured in order to get near the sea. Two-thirds of the world's surface is water, why should seaside resorts always seem to have so little room?

Back at Gleneagles, I avoided breakfast and Graham, Terry and I asked Mr Sinclair for the bill. He did not seem unduly ruffled, but Mrs Sinclair made our stay even more memorable, by threatening us with a bill for two weeks, even tho' we hadn't stayed.

We checked in for the night at the Osborne, a four-star hotel which is really a converted Georgian terrace overlooking the sea. They were so conditioned to middle-aged and elderly guests that, when I asked at reception for vacancies, she looked at me with some uncertainty and said 'Staff?'

That afternoon we filmed 'Derby Council v. The All Blacks', at Torquay rugby ground, and then in the evening some night-time election sequences at a vast neo-classical mansion in Paignton, which used to belong to the sewing machine millionaire, Singer, who married Isadora Duncan.

Here we filmed until midnight, and arrived wearily back at the

1 Eric and John decided to stay. In John's case a lucrative decision as he later based *Fawlty Towers* on Gleneagles.

darkened Osborne, for sandwiches and late-night drinks and a discussion, later very heated, with Graham about the worth or worthlessness of keeping a diary.

The diary withstood all pressures to end its life. In bed at 3.00.

Wednesday, May 13th, Torquay

After breakfast Terry went off to film at a rubbish dump a piece of Jean-Luc Godard ciné verité involving an exploding lettuce.

It was another hot day and Graham and I, in leisurely fashion, paid our bill and drove round to the Imperial. Here we spent what must rate as one of the most luxurious and effortlessly pleasant mornings of my life. We lay in the sun beside a beautiful heated sea-water pool, and had gin and tonics brought to us.

After a swim and drinks and sunshine, we went into the restaurant, where we ate a most excellent meal, accompanied by a half-bottle of Meursault. After that, we drank Grand Marnier and I smoked a cigar in the lounge.

I hope I never get used to that way of life, I hope I can always enjoy self-indulgence as much as I enjoyed it, that first, sunny perfect morning, at the Imperial.

We drove out to the location and spent the rest of the afternoon playing football dressed as gynaecologists.

Tuesday, May 19th, Torquay

A day on the beach. We start filming 'Scott of the Sahara', an epic film/sketch scheduled for three days. I play Scott, a sort of Kirk Douglas figure swathed in an enormous fur coat with perpetual cigar, looking more like George Burns. John plays the drunken Scottish director James McRettin, Terry plays Oates, Mike, a coloured ex-van-driver with a disconcerting Devonshire accent, plays Bowers and Carol[1] plays Miss Evans. An absurd looking bunch, we set up on Goodrington Sands, a stretch of rather stony sand south of Paignton. Signs saying 'Deck Chairs', 'Beach Trays', 'Ices' abound – this particular stretch of sand has been mercilessly tamed by the holidaymaker.

1 Carol Cleveland, who understood the Python style so well she became almost the seventh member of the team.

It's remarkable how our evening entertainment revolves mainly around food and meals, whereas two or three years ago, when on location for, say, *The Frost Report* at Littlehampton, or *Twice a Fortnight* at Minehead, the first thing we did was see what was on at the pictures. I suspect it's largely the Chapman hedonistic influence, which is also partly to blame for us wasting money at the Imperial.

But then, we are a lot richer than three years ago.

Wednesday, May 20th, Torquay

In the evening, another session with Terry J on *Percy*. Again slow work, stymied by the sheer amount of rewriting needed to make the vacuous last scene work. One good thing about the evening – we discovered the Apollo, a Greek restaurant in the centre of Torquay. The TV is always on, and the kebabs and hummus were excellent. As soon as we ordered kebabs, the proprietor, a large Greek, asked us if we were from London. He said, sadly, that no one from Torquay ever seemed to eat the Greek food – it was always the sausages, chips and peas.

Friday, May 22nd, Torquay

Our last day in Torquay. By a mighty effort of work, from 8.30 to 11.30 on Thursday evening, Terry and I had typed out three-quarters of our *Percy* rewrites (running to twenty-four pages of foolscap) and sent them off to Betty Box.

Today's filming, consisting mainly of short bits and pieces with the milk-float ('Psychiatrists' Dairies') had very much the end-of-term flavour and, by 6.30, John, Connie,[1] Eric, Lyn, Graham and both the make-up girls had started back to London. Terry and I shared a room at the Links Hotel for our last night in Torquay. The Links is where we should have stayed all along – the cost of living there is about 60% lower than the Imperial, but the bed was more comfortable, it's open all night, the bar does not charge extortionate prices, and just in one evening we got to know the manager and his wife and many of the guests, including two hard-drinking Catholic priests.

2 Connie Booth, actress and co-writer of *Fawlty Towers*, married to John Cleese.

Saturday, May 23rd

4.00 a.m. A soft light in the sky, fresh smells, and the far-off sound of a car, then silence again. Shown out of the back door of the Links by a night porter, a quick cup of black coffee and one of last night's sandwiches, then into the car and off to London. Even at 4.30, the roads coming south were very busy, but the Devonshire countryside at 5.00 looked so beautiful that I kept wanting to stop.

Hardly any traffic going my way, but plenty going west as I tore over the Salisbury Plain. Stopped at a lay-by overlooking Stonehenge, and drank more black coffee and ate the remainder of the sandwiches. By 7.45 I was on the outskirts of London. By 8.45, 270 minutes and 214 miles later, I was back home. Thomas was standing on the bathroom stool cleaning his teeth, with no trouser bottoms on. I just cried, I was so pleased to see him.

Sunday, June 7th

Terry and I had to spend the morning working on another of our small-earning sidelines. This time it was a rewrite of a film called 'How to Use a Cheque Book' for the Midland Bank.

Thursday, June 18th

General election day. Ideal polling weather, dry with warm sunshine. Every public opinion poll in the last two months had put Labour clearly ahead – the only possible shadow on the horizon was a 1½% swing to the Tories published in the latest opinion poll – taken *after* the publication of the worst trade figures for over a year, and Britain's exit from the World Cup last Sunday. Nevertheless, everything looked rosy for Labour when I left Julia St at 10.00 to go down to Camberwell.

The morning's work interrupted by the delivery of a large amount of dung. We were sitting writing at Terry's marble-topped table under a tree sheltering us from the sun. All rather Mediterranean. Suddenly the dung-carriers appeared. Fat, ruddy-faced, highly conversational and relentlessly cheerful, they carried their steaming goodies and deposited them at the far end of Terry's garden. As they passed I gleaned that they had come from Reading, that they had started loading at 5 p.m., that one of them was about to go on holiday to

Selsey Bill – his first holiday for seven years. After about twenty-five tubfuls they were gone, but at least they left a sketch behind.[1]

When I turned on the election I heard that in two results there was already a confirmed swing to the Conservatives. I watched until about 2.30, when it was obvious that the opinion polls were wildly wrong – the country had swung markedly to the right. Edward Heath, perhaps more consistently written-off than any Opposition leader since the war, consistently way behind Wilson in popularity, was the new Prime Minister.

My feelings are mixed. What I fear is a shift to the right in the national psyche; there are many good and honest and progressive Conservatives, but there are many, many more who will feel that this election has confirmed their rightness in opposing change, student demonstrations, radicalism of any kind. There are also those who will take the Tory victory as an encouragement to ban immigration (Enoch Powell doubled his majority), bring back hanging, arm the police force, etc, etc.

The Labour government was courageous and humane in abolishing hanging, legalising abortion, reforming the laws against homosexuals, making the legal process of divorce less unpleasant, and banning the sale of arms to South Africa. I am very sad that they are out of power, especially as I fear that it is on this record of progressive reform that they have been ousted.

To bed at 3.00. A long, hot day.

Friday, June 26th

Yesterday we recorded the first of the new Monty Python series. Although there was only about 15 minutes of studio material to record, it had gone remarkably smoothly. There were small problems during the day, but generally there was an optimistic air about the show. None of us had all that much to do, so there was perhaps less tension than usual. We even managed a complete dress run-through, which is almost a luxury compared to some of our hectic recordings in the last series.

The audience was full and, even in our completely straight red-herring opening – the start of a corny pirate film which went on for nearly five minutes – there was a good deal of laughter, just in anticipation. Then John's 'Hungarian Phrase Book' sketch, with exactly the right amount of lunacy and scatology, received a very good reaction.

1 'Book of the Month Club Dung', which found its way into Show 6 of the second series.

Out to the Old Oak Common Club for a rehearsal of Show 3.

A most strange atmosphere at the rehearsal. Ian seemed a good deal less happy than last night; everyone seemed rather quiet and unenthusiastic. Perhaps it's the structure of this particular show, which consists mainly of myself as Cardinal Ximenez and Terry J and Terry G as the two other Cardinals, so the other three members of the cast have comparatively little to do. Perhaps it's also this very dull, oppressive weather. The near-80s temperature of the last month is still here, and the weather is generally overcast and muggy.

Sunday, June 28th

In the morning I pushed Thomas across the Heath to Kenwood House. He loves being taken through the woods and now points excitedly at the trees, and gives bread to the squirrels, who will come right up to the push-chair.

After lunch I went down to the St Pancras Town Hall to rehearse our short Monty Python contribution to a show called 'Oh Hampstead'. The title is, to say the least, equivocal – as it is a charity show, directed by John Neville[1] in order to raise funds for Ben Whitaker, the Labour MP for Hampstead up till ten days ago.

John and I rehearsed 'Pet Shop/Parrot', and Graham and Terry were to do the Minister whose legs fall off. Struck by how very friendly people are when there is the feeling of a cause about. The stage manager and the lady who offered us cups of tea were so matey that it made up for John Neville's slightly detached theatricality.

As we waited to go and perform, we were all taken with unaccustomed nerves. It was live theatre now – no microphones, no retakes, and it brought us up with a jolt. But the audience knew we were giving our services free for the Labour Party – and they'd paid from £2 10s to £10 to watch, so they must have been pretty strong Labourites. Anyway, it went well.

Decided to take up our invitation to Ben Whitaker's after the show party. He lives in a sensibly, modestly furnished Victorian house backing on to Primrose Hill.

I think the party may have been rather foisted on him – he seemed to be opening bottles of white wine with the somewhat pained expression

1 Classically-trained Shakespearean actor and director.

of a man who cannot reconcile the joviality around him, or, indeed, the money he'd spent on the wine, with the fact that he had ten days earlier lost his seat in Parliament, his job as a junior minister, and his chance of political advancement for at least ten years. It would be fairly appalling to be told one could do no more shows for four years and yet for a man of any ambition that's what it must be like. How ungrateful Hampstead has been to Ben Whitaker, I thought, as I shook his limp hand and left his limp party at about 1.00.

Saturday, July 11th

My consumption of food and drink is increasing in direct relation to a) the money I earn and b) the amount of time spent with Graham Chapman, the high priest of hedonism. Terry Gilliam recently gave what seemed a good clue to Graham's attitudes. Terry suggested that Graham, having once made the big decision – and it must have been greater than the decisions most people are called on to make – to profess himself a homosexual, is no longer concerned with making important decisions. He is now concerned with his homosexual relationships and in perpetuating the atmosphere of well-being which good food and drink bring, and in which the relationships thrive. He doesn't want to think too much about himself now, and above all he does not want to have to struggle. He seems to feel that having stated his position he now deserves the good life.

Helen's elder sister Mary, and her husband, Edward, had recently become third-part owners of Roques, a collection of dilapidated farm buildings among the wooded hills of the Lot Valley in France. This was the first of what were to become almost annual summer pilgrimages.

Saturday, August 1st, Roques

I write this by the light of the Lumogaz lamp on the round wooden table in the barn at Roques. Outside the barn it is a still, dark night, behind us a wooded hill rises steeply and, above the trees, the stars, many more than one sees in England. The crickets make a continuous background noise, like an electric fence, small insects land on the paper and have to be pushed away. It is 9.30, Mary and Helen, looking quite preggy now [she had become pregnant again in February], are cooking pork chops over an open fire.

We have been officially on holiday for a week. The last recording was Show 6 on July 23rd. Eric was the first to go, he flew to the south of France on the 24th. On that day the rest of us met Roger Hancock for lunch and formed Monty Python Productions Ltd, on the corner of Dean St and Shaftesbury Avenue, after a convivial, but expensive and badly served meal at Quo Vadis restaurant – where you eat surrounded by photos of the stars, taken at the restaurant. Each photo seems to have caught the victim unawares.

Graham flew to Corfu on the Saturday morning, secure in the knowledge that his extraordinary gamble in trying to write Monty Python and thirteen Ronnie Corbett shows at the same time had been successful, for the simple reason that everyone had done the work for him on Monty Python. In fact on Monday, when John went off to Rome for two days' filming prior to a holiday in Rhodes, Terry and I were, as usual, left to pick up the pieces, tie up the loose ends and make sure that Ian was happy from the writing point of view before we *all* vanished.

We left home in the Austin to drive the 600 miles to Roques. Apart from taking a wrong turn at Tonbridge, which caused our first momentary panic, we arrived at Lydd, on the tip of that monotonous V of reclaimed land which contains Camber Sands and Pontins Holiday Camp, Dungeness Atomic Power Station and its spider's web of power lines, and Lydd Ferry Port.

The buildings of the Ferry Port rather unconvincingly carry the traditional airport jargon – Departure Lounge, Departure Bay, etc, etc – but, when you come to move to the plane, you leave a pleasant English tea room to find that only five cars and eight people are on your flight. A rather old and battered nose-loading plane, proudly bearing the title 'City of Aberdeen', stood on the tarmac. Thomas was fascinated, as he has recently taken to pointing at planes quite vociferously, and to see one at such close range, and then to get on it, and then to take off, was all too much. He kept pointing out of the window at the wing and saying 'Plane?'.

Down below, the last sight of England I remember was a field next to Lydd Airport, which we passed just after take-off, littered with dismembered aircraft.

A delightful journey. The plane never seemed to go above 5,000 feet, it was a clear sunny day and the Palin family made up one third of the total personnel. Very homely – and only 25 minutes before we were flying over the lush dunes and neat holiday houses of Le Touquet.

Le Touquet Airport perpetuated the Trips Round the Bay atmosphere which characterised the whole flight. For some reason or another we didn't have the green insurance card which indemnifies one against third party accidents on the Continent, so, within thirty yards of where we first set foot in France, I parted with 70 Francs (about £5 10s), an auspicious start.

With very little trouble about driving on the right-hand side – at Le Touquet they break you in easily – we drove off towards Rouen, lunched in a field near Crécy, and arrived for the evening at L'Aigle, a town in southern Normandy, where Edward had recommended we stay at the Hotel Dauphin.

On Thursday morning, we had croissants and coffee in bed and left at 9.00 for what we hoped was a straight 350-mile drive through the Loire and Perigord to the Lot.

But things have a way of happening unexpectedly, and we were not fifty yards from the hotel when the exhaust pipe broke in two. The sun was already high in the sky, and my French was not very confident as yet, and it was therefore a most frustrating two hours whilst we waited for a garage to repair the exhaust, gazing imploringly at small enigmatic Frenchmen, watching for the slightest trace of sympathy or urgency.

Eventually it was mended and we left L'Aigle at 11.15. Soon a warning light on the dashboard frightened us enough to turn off the engine and cruise downhill to another garage. We found that this light meant that our oil filter needed to be changed in the next 300 miles, but this was little consolation as we ground our way to the town of Montoire, where we bought bread and lunched in a hot and insect-ridden field. This was the nadir of our journey. We were only about 100 miles from L'Aigle, the car seemed to be cracking up, and the heat was making things even worse. But after lunch Thomas slept for about two and a half hours and we made good time, crossing the Loire at Amboise and reaching La Trémouille, well into Limousin, before stopping for tea. I decided that we might as well press on and try to reach Roques that night.

Roques is an old farmhouse made primarily of local limestone, and looks solid and attractive, with plain wooden roofs and floors. Downstairs there is a kitchen cum eating cum sleeping cum reception room with a large fireplace. Off this is the main bedroom. Stairs ascend to a long room, one half uninhabited, and the other half now inhabited by the Palins. It's rather like a loft, with a dusty wooden floor, but a newly improved roof. Below the ground floor is the washing/bathing room. Again a long room, of which one half is tiled in local red tiles, with a recessed circular shower area and a double basin. At present they are awaiting the attentions of a M. Prunier to connect up the cold water, but hot water is as yet provided either by boiling or by the Baby Burco.

Eating and cooking during this hot, dry weather take place in the barn, which is open on one side and is swathed in early morning sun, which makes breakfast a great meal.

All in all, Roques is solid and simple. One is a long way from telephones and television, there is no water, but there *is* electricity. The silence is frightening, but the satisfaction of the solitariness after London is worth everything.

We eat well here and drink the local wine – and by local, I mean grown one mile away by the small farmer who used to own Roques, M. Lapouge.

Thursday, August 6th, Roques

The hot weather continues. It's now a week since we left London and, apart from one stormy evening, it has been sun and clear skies.

Today I decided to go and visit the local médecin. This was mainly a result of Helen's prompting, and by the continuance of the discomfort which I've been getting every time I pee.

I arrived at his house about 10.00 and his son was lolling about the garden. No sooner had I asked where the doctor was, than the youth motioned me to follow him and leapt on his motorbike. With him and his friend giving me a motorcycle escort, I proceeded in triumph for the 200 yards to the doctor's surgery in the Boulevard Gambetta. Here I waited for nearly an hour and a half until the doctor called me in. His surgery was filled with cigar smoke. I reeled off my carefully prepared speech and all was well until *he* started to question *me*. 'Quand vous *pee-pee*,' he kept insisting, and there was I referring proudly to 'la urine'. He was rather aggressive in the face of my blank incomprehension, and when I came away I had a number of incredibly complicated instructions, which I did not understand, and a consultation fee of 16 Francs – about 25/-.

It was 11.45 and I had with me a sample bottle which I was to fill and take to the chemist. As I drove home, angry at thus wasting a morning, I remembered that the chemist closed at 12.00 for about two hours, so that it would be much better for me to deal with it all before 12.00 than to have to return after lunch. This caused me to take the side road in an attempt to find a quiet, private place to fill my tiny bottle. But the houses were much more prolific than I had hoped and I ended up shielding myself against the car and, with some difficulty, directing my urine into the bottle, the remainder trickling over my hand. This was the end of stage two of my morning of bitter frustration. Stage three began when I found that the medicines prescribed for me at the chemist's totalled 146 Francs, and included four large phials of intramuscular injections – which I had to take to the hospital on the next four days for injection dans 'la fesse' – in the buttock.

The day at last picked up. We'd decided on a sightseeing trip. The drive was pleasant, we were in no hurry, and I was laughing quite happily at my experiences with le médecin. Then fresh trouble broke. Just as we were about to drive up to Domme, the bastide town, there were frightening grating noises from the gearbox. It had finally packed up in three gears. The noise was like a football rattle. I'm sure that the accumulation of tribulations had produced a numbing effect on me, for I felt only a moment's bitter anger, then passed quickly to the state of resignation. We drank an aperitif whilst waiting for a garage to confirm what we already knew. The gearbox, which showed signs of collapse at the beginning of the year, had chosen the small, rather unattractive town of Cenac, 600 miles away from home, for its final death rattles.

Tuesday, August 11th, Roques

At lunchtime Cathy Gib[1] innocently queried whether or not Thomas was on Helen's passport as well as my own, for Helen is taking him back to England. Of course, he was only on my passport. Swift action demanded a phone call to the nearest British Consulate – in this case Bordeaux.

The British Consulate was perturbed at the lack of time to fill in the various forms, so Edward, Mary and myself set off in the Triumph for a totally unscheduled trip to Bordeaux – a 150-mile journey.

1 Cathy Gibbins, Helen's younger sister.

At La Rede, about one hour from Bordeaux, it became obvious that we wouldn't arrive before the Consulate closed at 5.00, so I made another phone call and, after becoming slightly eloquent with a woman who suggested we come along tomorrow morning instead, I eventually received an assurance that someone would be there till 6.00.

So began the last breathless lap. Edward drove manfully and, with the help of a brand-new autoroute just before Bordeaux, we reached the city at 6.00. Directing from the Michelin *Red Guide*, I frantically guided Edward through the Bordeaux rush hour until, at 6.10, we reached the Cours de Verdun. I leapt out, clutching passports, and arrived, dishevelled and breathless, at the Consulate.

There, all was calm. An official, and he was, in every sense of the word, an official, had happily stayed on and, in an atmosphere rather like that of a benevolent but uninspired English master's study after school, I signed the various forms. He proudly produced a number of impressive stamps and, over all this, the last great emergency of a holiday full of emergencies, the Queen gazed down impassively on her tousled subject.

On the way back we ate in Verdelais, just across the wide Garonne from Langan. It was an excellent meal of fish soup (in which I committed the most risible faux pas – tucking in to the red-hot anchovy sauce, which I'd mistaken for the soup itself).

Was heavily bitten in the night and slept badly – only one really good night in twelve.

Sunday, August 23rd

The last week has been spent filming in or around London, ending up at our traditional location – Walton-on-Thames – on Friday. It was less hot this time than in the past – I noticed this because for the last shot of the day I had to stand beside a fairly busy road clad in the It's Man[1] beard and moustache and a bikini. Next to me was John Cleese, also in a bikini.

---

1 The It's Man was a cross I'd made for myself, by suggesting that at the start of each show a haggard, wild-eyed old man should stagger out of incredibly uncomfortable situations, lurch to camera and with his last breath squeeze out the word 'It's'. I was unanimously chosen to play the part, one of the most consistently uncomfortable in Python.

Saturday, September 19th

Our running feud with the BBC Planners has come to a head, for not only is the new series going out at a time – 10.00 Tuesday – which is also the regional opt-out slot, so Wales, Scotland, Ireland, the Midlands and the South don't *see* M Python, but there is to be a break after three episodes when Python will be replaced by 'Horse of the Year Show'.

Our only positive reaction in this matter was to write a very gently worded letter to Paul Fox[1] expressing our disappointment. Last Wednesday we were visited at rehearsal by Huw Wheldon, managing director of BBC TV. It was obviously a peacemaking mission – an attempt to cheer up the lads on the shop floor – an exercise in labour relations. But in his favour it must be said that he *did* come, he avoided being patronising or pompous, he *had* arranged for us to see Paul Fox next week, and he *had* rung the *Radio Times* editor to ensure some more publicity.

We were all extremely deferential, but the visit made us all feel a little better – I suppose we were disarmed by the mere fact of such a deity deigning to notice us, let alone enthuse over the programme, and it does make us feel in quite a strong position for next week's meeting with Paul Fox.

Sunday, 20th September

Terry arrived at 1.00, and together we went up to Graham Chapman's to prepare our material for a charity show – in which we are doing 30 minutes. It's in aid of Medical Aid for Vietnam – which J Cleese refers to as 'Grenades … er … Elastoplast for the Vietcong'. But officially the proceeds from this evening's show will go to providing medical aid for those civilians involved in the war in Vietnam, who do not receive US aid. I think this is a very humane cause, and I believe that the Vietnam war is an international tragedy, in which one can no longer talk of the right side or the wrong side, or the right solution or the wrong solution, but one can at the very least help *all* the thousands of civilians who are dying or injured. If I really thought that the money I helped to raise was being spent on killing people, I would not have done the show, but I trust Hanoi – certainly as much as I trust the Americans, if not more.

1 Controller, BBC1.

We ate an excellent roast beef and Yorkshire lunch at Graham's, rehearsed rather frantically – we are still looking for scripts to learn the words *from* – and set off in Terry's car along the gleaming new Westway to the Questors Theatre at Ealing.

The feeling, as we worked through the lighting plot with Ray Jenkins, a TV writer who asked us to take part, was very much like the Etceteras' Sunday revues, which I produced at Oxford in 1964 and 1965. 'Light stage left, light stage right', 'cross-fade', 'blackout', etc, etc. The adrenaline was flowing healthily as we waited to go on for our first spot at the start of the show.

But the first we knew about the show having started was a hissed urgent voice on the intercom, 'Monty Python – you are two minutes late on, we are waiting for you.'

One or two people were starting a slow handclap as we reached the wings. We launched into the familiar 'Tide',[1] then the interview with the Minister whose leg drops off, a monologue called 'Co-Ed' and finally 'Working Class Culture'. By the time we'd finished we had won the audience back, but immediately all the good was undone, as the group who were to follow us – 'Humblebums'[2] – did not know they were supposed to be on, and were obviously going to take some time to set up their amplifiers, speakers, etc. There was no compere to explain to the audience, just an awkward silence. We eventually leapt into the breach, did a few silly walks and whatever quickies we could remember.

The Humblebums were from Glasgow – and played rather gentle, attractive songs, there was an African group beating out some ethnic melodies which came nearest of everything to taking the roof off the place, and top of the bill was the classical guitarist John Williams – who was not only a fantastic guitarist, but a beaut guy. He was, I must add, a Monty Python fan, so there was a good deal of mutual admiration.

We taxied home at 11.30 feeling very happy and pleased we had done the evening and, who knows, we might have helped someone somewhere to put a rifle ... er ... bandage on ...

1 A sketch from the Oxford days, which involved an enthusiastic foreign salesman extolling the virtues of Tide, apparently unaware that it's a washing powder. He eventually pours some into a bowl, produces a spoon and, with a big smile, eats it. Horrible to perform as, for some reason, I never got round to substituting the washing powder for something edible.
2 A Scottish folk-singing duo, one of whom was Gerry Rafferty and the other, Billy Connolly.

Thursday, September 24th

At 6.30 we all trooped up to the sixth floor for our meeting with Paul Fox, Controller of Programmes, BBC1. A slightly comic entrance. We knocked tentatively at his door and went in, nobody was in the ante-office, everything was tidied up and deserted. We had been standing some moments in the outer office feeling a little disorientated when Paul Fox's door opened and this bulky man with a generous nose and large ears appeared, Paul Fox, no less. He was clearly more nervous than we were – but then he was in a fairly indefensible position, and there *were* six of us.

Inside he poured us drinks and there was the usual difficulty over seats – offices just aren't built to accommodate the Monty Python team.

Fox started by explaining why MP went out at 10.10 on a Tuesday night. Two things I felt were wrong here. One was his premise that it wasn't a pre-nine o'clock show, although I would reckon 8.30 would be its ideal time, judging from the reactions of my ten-year-old nephew Jeremy, his six-year-old brother Marcus,[1] and the large teenage section of the audience at the shows.

But Fox was conciliatory throughout. He sugared the pill with prom-ises of a repeat of eight episodes of Series 1 immediately following our present series and, next year, a total repeat of Series 2 at a national time. He clearly realised that he had underestimated Monty Python, but his apologetic manner did encourage us to talk freely with him about some of our other complaints, e.g. lack of any BBC publicity for the new series, the removal of our invaluable researcher, the budget (which he hotly defended as being above average for LE [Light Entertainment]: moot point) and the two-week break in our transmission after the first three shows. Obviously we could not get him to change his mind, but we came away from his office after one and a half hours and several drinks feeling optimistic that we had at least said everything we wanted to say, he had been friendly and one hopes he was also receptive.

Back home in a cab.

---

1 Jeremy, Marcus and Camilla, the children of my sister Angela and her husband, Veryan Herbert.

Sunday, September 27th

No papers for the last week owing to some strike by the delivery people – but this morning I felt the need for some Sunday reading, so I drove down to Fleet Street and bought an *Observer* and *Times* from a man in Ludgate Circus. A lot of people milling about in Fleet Street – looking out for lone newspaper sellers, or calling at the *Daily Express* building – the only paper which seemed to have a stock of copies at its office.

4.15. Visited National Film Theatre with Simon Albury to see *Arthur Penn 1922* – a documentary about the director of *Left-Handed Gun, Bonnie and Clyde, The Chase, Little Big Man* and a great number of Broadway theatre successes, especially *The Miracle Worker*.

The first film, about and starring Vladimir Nabokov, was a small gem – mainly because Nabokov himself is such a character. He manages to get away with an opinionated arrogance, partly because he is obviously not taking himself too seriously, but mainly because of his facility with words – which in the film he denies, saying that he failed to inherit his father's gifts of description and fluency – he has a beautifully dry humour, wonderful pieces of observation, and an overriding good nature which quite make up for his pedantry. I once read many of his books, the film made me want to read more – especially his autobiography *Speak, Memory*.

Sunday, October 18th, Abbotsley

After breakfast Thomas and I go on a long walk around the village. In the field opposite Manor Farm, the two great carthorses have just been fed. The man who feeds them tells me he has worked the land at Abbotsley since 1926. Then tractors cost £120, now they're £1,120, but the carthorses' days are over. What it took a single-furrow horse-drawn plough to do in a fortnight, a five- or ten-furrow tractor can now do in a day. He doesn't seem to have regrets, but he loves the horses – he says that when you had an eager team of horses, they kept at the plough from seven o'clock till three, with no lunch, until they got tired.

Monday, October 19th, Southwold

Left Abbotsley at 11.00 and drove over to Southwold, leaving Helen and Thomas to stay at Church Farm. The Suffolk countryside seems to be at its best in autumn, and the drive was beautiful. We ate lunch together, and then Father and I drove into Southwold and walked along the sea front. It was cool and sunny, and practically deserted – the season seems well-finished. Saw welcome additions to the Southwold scene – two Adnams drays, with big dray-horses. They have only just been introduced – to deal with local deliveries, apparently to save the money on lorries. I must say they add to Southwold's atmosphere – it's a town that absorbs progress and innovation in only very limited amounts and this technologically retrogressive step is quite in character.

Tuesday, October 20th, Southwold

During this afternoon the weather turned suddenly and dramatically from the reflective, gentle calm of a sunny autumn morning, to an angry sky, N.W. wind and driving rain. At the harbour, the sea was as high as I've seen it, with breakers crashing against the harbour wall. As I write this diary in bed, the wind is still strong outside, but the heavy rain has stopped.

Tonight we ate liver and kidneys, with a bottle of St Estèphe, and watched Monty Python. One of my favourite shows – with the bishop film and the poet-reader, the Gumby announcements and the strange chemist's sketch. Went to sleep with the comforting sound of the wind buffeting the windows.

Wednesday, October 21st

The *Punch*[1] lunch, to which we had been invited by Miles Kington (a friend of Terry's at Oxford, and mine as well in London), is a traditional affair. Originally it consisted of the contributors only, who met, once a week, to discuss subjects for the political cartoon. It is carried on now as a meeting-place for journalists, humorists and writers generally, who may be regulars on *Punch*, or prospective contributors.

We assembled with the other guests for pre-lunch drinks – names I have known so well for so long became faces – Norman Mansbridge, E H Shepherd, the appallingly unfunny David Langdon. I met the editor, William Davis, an economics journalist, probably late thirties, possibly describable as a 'whizz-kid'. His humour I find very ponderous – he nearly

---

1 A quintessentially British humorous and satirical magazine which first came out in 1841 and ran for 150 years. With readership declining from a peak of 175,000 to some 8,000, it was finally closed in 2002.

always has a serious political or topical point to put over, and yet, because he is editing *Punch*, it is given an ill-fitting and tenuous humorous context. When Davis attempts politics and humour, humour loses – unlike Norman Shrapnel of *The Guardian* or, to a lesser extent, Alan Watkins of the *New Statesman*, who seem to mix the two well.

We were shown in to lunch. About twenty or twenty-five of us around a large table; on the walls of this dining cum conference room were framed covers of old *Punches*, photographs of the staff past and present, famous framed cartoons, etc, etc. I sat next to Miles on my right and Vincent Mulchrone on my left. Mulchrone is a well-known feature writer on the *Daily Mail*. A very amiable man, with a North Country accent (I really expected him to be Irish), he was exceedingly self-effacing and seemed more keen to talk about moving house than his journalistic adventures.

At the end of the meal, as we drank coffee and brandy and smoked cigars, Davis hammered on the table and the traditional scavenging of ideas began. It was very reminiscent of *Frost Report* conferences four years ago. It was ironic that the man who provided most of the ideas for *Punch*'s Christmas edition was John Wells – a regular contributor and ex-editor of *Private Eye*, the magazine which has probably done more harm to *Punch*'s circulation than any other. Terry and I also suggested quite a number of ideas, as did B.A. 'Freddie' Young – *Punch* contributor and theatre critic of the *Financial Times*. But he was the only one of the 'older' generation who seemed to be on the wavelength of most of the suggestions. Others, including *Punch*'s film critic, Richard Mallett, who must be the only living critic older than the medium he writes about, nodded rather wearily and drank their brandy.

Thursday, October 22nd

Took a taxi to the Playboy Club in Park Lane, for a party to celebrate starting production on the film.

Inside, the Playboy Club is a taste wilderness. The bunny girls are a real affront to style, desire, everything. They stand around in these ugly costumes which press their breasts out and grasp their buttocks – so that they look like Michelin Men. The bare shoulders are quite pleasant, but the costume's brutal and unsexy and the bunnies seem to have been drained of character, they are either sickly sweet or rather brusquely military.

The evening was not unpleasant – spoke for a while to Dudley Moore, and even Eric Sykes patted me on the arm and said how much he enjoyed the show. I left at 9.00 and by 12.00 I was back in Southwold, having caught the 9.30 train to Ipswich and driven on from there. To go from the Playboy Club to the east Suffolk coast in four hours is as big a change of environment as you're likely to get in England.

Monday, October 26th

Today we started filming *And Now For Something Completely Different*. I got up at 7.00, after having woken at intervals during the night. It was pitch dark outside. It brought back memories of *The Complete and Utter History* filming – almost exactly two years ago. But instead of having to drive out to a location in my own car, I was picked up in an enormously comfortable black Humber Imperial and driven, in the company of Graham and Terry, to our location in Holloway. It was a school gymnasium where we were filming the 'Soft Fruit' sketch, but when we reached the location I felt a sudden, nervous tightening of the stomach, as I saw a line of caravans parked by the side of the road – and opposite them a large white caterer's lorry and lighting generator.

Terry and I were sharing a caravan. It was very spacious and comfortable, with a dressing room and a kitchen in it. We all sat around the table before filming began, joking about this new luxury, like schoolboys in a new form room.

We were on the set by 8.30, changed and ready to film. The 35mm camera was another impressive sign that this was a film, as were the many people whose sole job seemed to be to look after us, give us calls when we were required, fetch us coffee if we wanted it, and generally keep us sweet. But our mirth was great when we saw a man struggling to stick an 'Eric Idle' sign on the back of a picnic chair. Did we really all have chairs with our name on? Yes we really did and, by the end of an eleven and a half hour-day, with only a half-hour break at lunch, I realised that the caravan, the chairs and the ever-helpful production assistants were there to help us work harder, and they were vital. To have a place to relax in after a take, without having to worry about finding out what is happening next, is a luxury we never had on television filming.

The crew seem, without exception, to be kind, friendly and efficient. Ian seems happy and confident; in short, it is a very enjoyable and impressive first day. We have finished the 'Soft Fruit' sketch[1] – which is about four minutes of film.

Finally, to sink back into a car and be driven home is a wonderful load off one's mind.

Saturday, October 31st

We have finished a week's filming now. In retrospect, Monday was our best day in terms of output, but we filmed at a steady rate throughout the week. On Wednesday we started a week's location shooting at Black Park – an expanse of pine forest, silver-birch copses, open grassland and beech-covered lakeside, which happens to be just next door to Pinewood Studios. By Friday we had shot the 'Lumberjack Song', the 'How Not to be Seen' opening and most of the 'Joke' film. Morale in the unit is very high.

Tuesday, November 3rd

In the evening Helen and I went down to the Open Space Theatre in Tottenham Court Road, to see The Scaffold show.[2] The Open Space is what its name implies, and very little else. We were late and just outside the entrance doors we met [Roger] McGough and Mike McGear dressed in neo-Gestapo uniforms waiting to go on. Brief handshake, but the feeling that we'd cheated by meeting them.

As it turned out the show was about love and sex and permissiveness – a variety of sketches apparently about the danger of a sexual revolution – when sex becomes an order, when permissiveness is not only approved of but essential, but without feeling and without emotion – destroying both the romantic young lover and the mackintosh-clad old man.

It is quite a common statement nowadays that sex kills love, and it is often put forward by the wrong people for the wrong reasons, but I felt a sympathy for McGough's writing – I don't particularly like aggressive sexual attitudes, the Danish porno fairs, the *Oh! Calcutta* celebrations of

1 In which John plays a crazed RSM teaching a bunch of squaddies how to defend themselves against bananas and various other forms of soft fruit.
2 A group, formed in 1963 in Liverpool, performing sketches, poems and songs and comprising John Gorman, Roger McGough and Mike McCartney, Paul's brother, who appeared under the pseudonym Mike McGear.

the sexual act, the 'frank, outspoken article' and the 'frank, outspoken interview' with the latest 'sexologist'. But all this seems to me infinitely preferable to repression of sex and illiberal or intolerant attitudes being accepted as 'morally correct'. The public discussion of sex must, I feel, help more than hinder, encourage rather than depress – and I'm not sure whether McGough would ultimately agree with this.

Saturday, November 7th

Slight scare this evening. After spending the late afternoon painting Thomas's room, Helen had quite severe contraction pains. We were due to eat out at Paul Collins' that evening, picking up Simon and Jenny Hawkesworth[1] on the way. At 7.45 there was panic. I was finishing the painting, Helen was worrying about imminent childbirth and Simon and Jenny were waiting for us to collect them. However, Helen was reassured by a phone call to Dr Graham Chapman, and we bundled Thomas into the car and arrived at Paul's house in Barnes about 8.45.

Helen did *not* have a baby.

Sunday, November 8th

I do seem to play a lot of seedy, unsuccessful and unhygienic little men. After washing my hair and shaving at 7.00 in the morning I am driven to work and immediately my hair is caked down with grease and my face given a week's growth of beard.

Ken Shabby[2] was especially revolting, with an awful open sore just below the nose. But Terry J (who has seen the rushes) is worried that it was shot with too much emphasis on Shabby and not enough wide shots to create the joke – which is the relationship of this ghastly suppurating apparition to the elegant and tasteful surroundings.

---

1 All three were friends from Oxford. Paul and Simon were both barristers and Jenny, née Lewis, a singer and poet.
2 Shabby, a disgusting man with a pet goat, who appeals to the father of a beautiful upper-class girl (Connie Booth) for her hand in marriage, but spoils his chances by, among other things, gobbing on the carpet.

Monday, November 9th

We are filming now at the empty, recently sold A1 Dairy in Whetstone High Street. The immediate significance of filming in Whetstone is that, for once, it favours those who live in North London – i.e. G Chapman and myself – who have long since had to leave earlier than anyone else to reach locations in Ealing, Walton-on-Thames and points south. Now we reap an additional benefit of Hampstead living – half an hour extra in bed – and when I am being collected at 7.30 each day, in darkness, the half hour is very welcome.

The dairy premises are so far excellent for our sketches – for they have the same rather dreary atmosphere of failure which characters like Scribbler and Mr Anchovy and the marriage guidance man are born from.

It takes a long time to set up the lights and to lay the track for the first shot. My hair is greased heavily and parted in the middle. It lies clamped to my head like a bathing hat.

Once the first shot is done, progress becomes faster. From the performance point of view, I enjoy the security of being able to do a performance several times and, with the sketch actually done in sections, one is not so worried about remembering words. I enjoyed one take particularly – I felt I was working hard on it and my concentration never dropped.

Thursday, November 12th

Shooting at a pet shop in the Caledonian Road. It's a grey, wet, messy day and this particular part of the Caledonian Road is a grey, wet, messy part of the world. In the pet shop there is scarcely room to move, but the angel fish and the guppies and the parrots and the kittens and the guinea pigs seem to be unconcerned by the barrage of light – and the continuous discordant voices. The shop is still open as we rehearse. One poor customer is afraid to come in, and stands at the door, asking rather nervously for two pounds of Fido. 'Two pounds of Fido,' the cry goes up, and the message is passed by raucous shouts to the lady proprietor. 'That's 15/-,' she says. '15/-,' everyone starts to shout.

We're finished by 5.30. Outside the shop is a little boy whose father, he tells us, is coming out of the nick soon.

'What'll you do when he comes out?'

'Kill him.'

'Why?'

'I hate him.'

'Why do you hate him?'

'He's a ponce.'

All this cheerfully, as if discussing what kind of fish fingers he likes best. As I walk back to the caravan a battered-looking couple argue viciously in a doorway.

Home for a bath and a change of clothes, and then out for the evening to the Warner Rendezvous – a new theatre opening with *The Rise and Rise of Michael Rimmer*, which was written by Peter Cook, John Cleese, Graham Chapman and Kevin Billington, the director. Graham, David and I walked round the back of the crowd into the foyer. It was full of people – not obvious first-nighters, and not an inordinate amount of stars. Peter Cook and Denholm Elliott were standing with their ladies, flashing smiles. As we walked down into the lower foyer, Peter looked up towards us and said in a funny voice, 'Oh, they're all here.'

The seats in the cinema were certainly comfortable, and there were little surprises, like Lord George-Brown[1] and his wife arriving, which reminded us that it was no ordinary night at the movies, but a premiere – Sparkle! Sparkle!

Rimmer with its built-in topical appeal, very funny moments, good performances, is still a second-rate movie – ephemeral enjoyment which makes no special impression and says nothing new, apart perhaps from one very memorable scene when the Prime Minister goes on a prestige visit to Washington for personal talks, and takes his place at the end of a long corridor full of potentates, including the Pope, who each move up one place as the President sees them.

After the film we went with Graham to a party at Les Ambassadeurs, a club in Park Lane. Lord George-Brown came in and stood with his wife rather gloomily until Graham and Terry went over to talk to them. Terry afterwards said that Lady Brown was very bitter about politics and was bemoaning what it did to people.

Terry Gilliam and I collected some food and talked for a while to Arthur Lowe[2] and his wife. Arthur Lowe's performance was about the best in the

---

1 Labour Foreign Secretary in 1966. Resigned in 1968 after differences with the Prime Minister, Harold Wilson. Liked a drink.

2 Later the legendary Captain Mainwaring in *Dad's Army*.

film, and it had been rather scandalously cut down. Beside Peter Cook's wooden smoothness, perhaps Lowe's performance was too good.

I ended the evening with an ominous feeling of impending drunkenness. I remember walking unsteadily up the stairs from Les Ambassadeurs, to be treated by the doorman to phrases such as the over-solicitous 'I'll get your coat, sir', and the downright abusive 'Not *driving*, are we sir?'

Friday, November 13th

After a busy day filming the remains of 'Upper Class Twit of the Year' in fine, sunny weather, arrived home with Terry and together we joined the rest of Monty Python at Chez Victor restaurant in Wardour Street at 8.30, for a paid meal – i.e. we had been hired by an ad agency to have some ideas about a new Guinness commercial.

My first impression was surprise at the number of advertising people present. A representative of the film production company, a director of commercials, an agency man, a product representative and two or three more.

We drank – I carefully, for my stomach was still recovering from Thursday night at Les Ambassadeurs – and, at about 9.00, sat down to our meal. There were various sinister preparations which tended to make me withdraw into silence, e.g. tape recorders and microphones hung around, a type-written sheet with their basic idea for the commercial, and muttered messages between the admen about how best to let us all have our say. Added to which, Messrs Jones and Gilliam led off with ideas of such enthusiastic vehemence that I retreated even more deeply into my shell. After some quiche lorraine and halfway through my liver, I began to lose this feeling of silent panic, and, as the ideas got away from the rather restricting basis which the agency had imposed, I found myself enjoying the whole business much more. Graham C, however, who isn't particularly talkative or assertive, found it all too much and, with a brief word in my ear, departed at about 10.00.

Thursday, November 19th

At 6.00 I was awakened from a deep and satiated slumber – Helen said she felt stronger contractions, but was unsure whether to ring the hospital. Went to sleep again.

At 6.30 woke to hear Helen expressing dissatisfaction with the telephone – it was out of order and she was trying to ring the hospital; the
contractions were stronger than ever.

Thomas was crying and outside the rain was beating down the village
in heavy waves. I felt grim – but got up, dressed, went over to Edward and
Jayne's[1] and got them out of bed to use their phone. When I got back
Helen's contractions were quite severe – she was in favour of getting an
ambulance – but I bundled her and Thomas into the car and set off
through the rain for UCH [University College Hospital]. Arrived there at
7.00. No porter in reception, didn't know where the labour ward was, and
Helen was leaning against a trolley in considerable pain. Eventually a
porter appeared and all he could do was reprimand me for parking on an
ambulance place. Left Helen in the lift with him and went back to the car.
Drove Thomas over to Camden Town and left him at Mary's, then arrived
back at the hospital at about 7.45. Fortunately it was a day in which I only
had one shot to film. At 8.00 I rang the location, and was able to get out of
that one shot so, by incredible coincidence, I had the day off.

I settled down in the waiting room and snoozed. At 8.45 I began to
feel very hungry – I'd been up for two and a half hours. I found a nurse
and, with breakfast in mind, asked her what state Mrs Palin was in. The
nurse giggled a little and said 'She's delivered.' A little boy – 6lb 12oz.

There Helen was – in a very modern delivery room – looking for all
the world as if she'd just been to the shops and back. Hair neat and
unsweaty, face a healthy, unruffled pink. Apparently she had given birth
in the admissions room just after 8.00 – she had been bathed and was
being put in a wheelchair to go up to the delivery room, when she had to
tell them that the baby's head was sticking out. The doctor was off
having breakfast, so two nurses delivered the child.

After tea at Mary's I visited Helen at 6.30. William, or Matthew as he
then was, was small, wrinkled and wizened. When I touched him his
face creased into a look of bitter discomfort and annoyance, but I really
loved him.

Friday, November 20th

Back to filming. Unsettled, mainly wet weather set the schedule back,
but I enjoyed the day – it was somehow less bewildering than yesterday.

1 Edward and Jayne Arnott, neighbours.

At lunchtime I bought ten bottles of wine and we all celebrated William's birth. Eric was appalled by the name William and felt Matthew much less boring. Terry was the opposite.

It's funny, but I have doubts about Matthew – as Terry said, it's 'Hampstead children with page-boy haircuts'. Happy with William.

Monday, December 7th

As I lay, half-awake, watching William being fed, the lights all went out. It was the first power-cut I can remember since the days we lived in Sheffield, caused this time by a work-to-rule of the electricity supply workers. Our lights were out for two hours. Apparently they were switching off selected areas in rotation. The work-to-rule is now three days old, and we have had five power-cuts, the longest being three hours yesterday afternoon.

Tuesday, December 8th

A Python cast lunch at fashionable Parkes restaurant in Beauchamp Place.

At our luncheon – I had lamb which was mainly very expensive – we talked about the future. It seems that all of us are prepared to start work on another TV series next November, except for John. He claims to want a year off to read and absorb knowledge, and possibly travel, and generally improve his mind, and yet he has accepted a commission to write at least six of a new series of Doctor in Love for London Weekend, a series which has apparently plumbed new depths of ordinariness. So, I have a feeling that John will be only too keen to write another series of Monty Python in twelve months' time.

Graham will be writing some more shows for Ronnie Corbett. Eric is quite keen to work on the screenplay of a film idea suggested by Ian – about bank-robbers marooned on Skye – but I fear I may have dampened his spirits rather heavily, by showing less than enthusiasm for it as a Python idea.

Terry Gilliam is writing cartoons for Marty, and then, we hope, directing a half-hour script on which Terry and I started work this morning.

Wednesday, December 9th

I wasn't required on the last day of shooting, but a car collected me in the evening and took me down to Greenwich for the end-of-film party at the Admiral Hardy.

Everyone was smiling, embracing, promising, exaggerating, confessing and forgetting in the manner of business parties – and show business parties especially. It had been a happy film, because each day made people laugh, but if it had been made in a time of full employment, when producers and production managers had to pay a crew well to keep it, our film would have been in trouble, for the relationships between the cheese-paring producers and the hard-working crew were at times near breaking point – only the precarious employment situation in the film industry kept some of the men at work.

This evening the power-cut in the Hampstead area caught us in the sauna at the squash club. Total darkness descended as I was about to leave the shower, clutching my towel. Candles were soon provided, but I dread to think how some of the members might have taken advantage of the total darkness.

Thursday, December 10th

Rung by the BBC and asked if I would like a three-day trip to Munich with Ian at the beginning of next week – to discuss possibility of a co-production between Monty Python and fellow funsters from Bavarian TV.

This evening I repaired to Devonshire Place to have some more dental surgery – the first for almost a year, at the hands of Mr Powell. It was only one tooth which required treatment, and Mr Powell's new surgery is so comfortable that it's a pleasure to lie there. Whilst he was working on it, he called in a colleague who was most impressed by my condition. 'I've never seen that before,' he told Powell, gazing at my mouth – I felt a surge of pride in these rotten old teeth, and am fully expecting to be visited at home by reporters from *Dental World*.

Was seized with desire to sit in a cinema and, after a quick meal, went up to the Haverstock Hill Odeon to see John Boorman's *Leo the Last*. However, some 30 minutes into the film, at a point when it looked as though it could suddenly become interesting, the lights failed. The dreaded power-cuts, which had only yesterday left me blind and naked in the sauna baths, had struck again.

Tuesday, December 15th

In the evening we go round to Graham Chapman's for food, drink and Monty Python No. 12. It is the first time that Helen and I and William have been out in the evening since W's birth. Plenty of time to reflect on this, as I carry William up five flights of bare concrete stairs to the Chapman penthouse.

It was really an evening for Python authors and their wives/lovers – and it worked very well; there was a happy and relaxed atmosphere. However, for some reason John was unable to come. Graham was obviously very disappointed – but it is difficult to tell what he is thinking on evenings like this. He is so busy in the kitchen preparing food. We eventually eat, ravenous, at 10.45, after which he seems to pace about in a most unsettled way. It is strange that someone who takes so much pride and care in producing such excellent food has absolutely no idea how to serve it. The delicious meal of lamb, stuffed with salmon, was served with all the style and elegance of an army kitchen. But the company was good and the drink was abundant, and the show – which was the first one of this new series that we recorded – had edited together well, and was especially good because of the diversity of ideas: the false 'Black Eagle' pirate opening, the dirty phrase book, the paintings going on strike in the National Gallery. Terry Gilliam's 2001-style animations, the Ypres sketch with its false starts, the over-acting hospital, were just a few of them. By general consent, one of the best shows we've done.

Sunday, December 20th

I got ready for the third successive drinking evening – this time it was the BBC Light Entertainment Group who were the hosts.

The only remarkable thing about an evening which is really only any night in the BBC Club – with slightly better food – was the attitude of the Programme Controllers. An article in *The Times* on December 16th had detailed, fairly prominently, the continuing saga of Python's mistreatment by the BBC Programme Planners. Stanley Reynolds was the author, Terry Jones his chief informant, and about 80% of his article was correct and true (which is high by journalistic standards).

David Attenborough, who is, I believe, Assistant Controller of

Programmes,[1] edged his way over to me quite early in the evening and began some rather nervously jocose banter. 'I feel I ought to come and talk to you – being one of those responsible for the repression of Monty Python.' But he made the point that the programme had done extremely well as a result of the BBC's treatment – which is an argument one cannot deny, and any altruistic feelings for the viewer in regions that don't get Python, must always be tempered with the knowledge that it's because of them we get assured repeats, and the extra loot which accompanies them.

Paul Fox, on the other hand, seemed genuinely aggrieved – not that he questioned our grounds for complaint, he seemed chiefly appalled that Stanley Reynolds had got the story. 'That drunken, etc, etc,' muttered Fox, standing in the middle of the hospitality suite, like a great wounded bear.

Monday, December 21st

In the afternoon collected the new car – a Simca 1100 GLS. A five-door estate in the best functional French tradition. At least, when I picked it up at the garage, it was clean and sparkling and looked absolutely brand new. When I bought the Austin Countryman three and a half years ago, it looked as though it had been standing in the rain for several weeks. So this, at least, was a good start to the justification of my decision to buy French rather than English.

Thursday, December 31st

1970 drew to a close in bitterly cold weather. Apart from some dubbing still to do on the film, Monty Python is finished – we spent almost a year on one thirteen-week series and six weeks making a film – now it remains to be discussed as to whether or when we do another series. In December Terry and I have almost completed a 30-minute TV show for Terry Gilliam to direct but, apart from this, and the possibility of more Python, the future is tantalisingly empty. John, Eric and Graham all seem to have gone back to writing for other people – Marty, Ronnie Barker, in John's case *Doctor at Large* – all of which is sad, for we have achieved a big success with our own show and yet only Terry and I seem

---

1 In fact, he was Director of Programmes.

to be progressing on from Python, rather than helping other shows to emulate it, and we are earning less money for our troubles.

We spent the last hours of 1970 down at Camberwell, where Terry and Alison served up a truly epic meal – antipasta, salmon, pheasant, delicious chocolate mousse, cheese, two kinds of wine and a menu!

So 1970 went out with a well-satisfied belch.

1971

Friday, January 8th, Glasgow

Caught the 10.05 'Royal Scot' express at Euston. Terry, Alison and I were travelling to Glasgow to see the production of our 'Aladdin' pantomime at the Citizens Theatre. It was a dull, rather misty day as we tore through the Midlands towards Crewe.

Eating a meal on a train is one of the great pleasures of life. How else could you have soup with Wigan all around you, steak and kidney pie as the expanse of the Irish Sea approached nearly to the window, and coffee with the fells and crags of the desolate Lake District on either side?

Our rooms had been booked in the Central Hotel, which adjoins the station. It is a railway hotel, built in monumentally impressive proportions in the great age of railway expansion. The walls were about three foot thick, with about fifteen foot width to play with on each step of the mighty staircase. After leaving our bags, we decided to walk in the direction of the Citizens Theatre.

We never did reach the Citizens, but we did find a bar, with very old brown, varnished tables and a wooden floor, and we did meet three shabby men, one of whom told us at great length why he was an alcoholic, and then asked for one of our empty whisky glasses. With elaborate furtiveness the rather sad-eyed, younger man of the three took the glass towards his flies, unbuttoning his coat at the same time. I watched amazed, and then a little relieved, as he produced a surreptitious bottle of what looked like sherry and filled the alcoholic's glass with it.

We walked back to the hotel, bathed, and took a taxi across the river to the Citizens Theatre where *Aladdin* by Michael Palin and Terry Jones was the first pantomime the Gorbals had seen for years.

The theatre is a neat size, with a circle and a balcony. We were met at the door, and ushered into the Manager's office. The Artistic Director, Giles Havergal,[1] we learnt, was in Tangier. After seeing the pantomime, we understood why. None of the cast seemed to be able to act too well – they certainly didn't seem to be enjoying it – and, despite the enthusiastic

---

1 Who first commissioned the panto for the Palace Theatre, Watford.

support of the kids, they hurtled through it. What few gems of wit there
are in the script were lost for ever, and the creation of atmosphere, which
is perhaps something the script does best, was spoilt by the speed and
incomprehension of the line delivery. The principal boy had been taken ill
and the girl playing her looked marvellous, but acted like a Canadian
redwood. The love scene with the princess was one of the most
embarrassing things I've ever witnessed – combining, as it did, her
extraordinary lack of acting ability and the princess's extraordinary lack
of charm.

Afterwards we met Phil McCall, the Widow Twankey of the pantomime. He regarded us cautiously at first, as though he felt rather
guilty about the way the pantomime had been done – but when he
realised that we didn't hate every minute of it, he became quite friendly,
and we went next door, to the Close Theatre Club – a student-run club
with a bar and home-made food. We ate plates of chilli and drank a
bottle of scotch, which Phil McCall produced, surreptitiously, from his
coat. We parted on very convivial terms, and walked back across the
bridge to our hotel.

In one of the huge high-ceilinged rooms, we watched the Marx
brothers film *Duck Soup* on TV.

Sank, happily, into bed at about 1.00.

*Around this time Python morphed into a stage show. Tentatively at first,
but it was the start of something that was to snowball from the West End
to Broadway and eventually to the Hollywood Bowl.*

Sunday, January 31st, Coventry

As Terry and I walked through the deserted, rain-soaked streets of
Coventry at 11.45 at night, for the first ever Python stage show, it was
amazing, exciting and rather frightening to turn the corner and see the
Belgrade Theatre seething with people like bees round a honeypot. Here
in this silent, sleeping city was a busy, bustling theatreful of people –
nearly 1,000 of them. From behind stage one could hear just how enthusiastic they were – there was shouting and cheering before anything had
happened. There were ten men dressed as 'Gumbies' in the front row of
the circle.

When, at 12.00, the house lights faded, John entered as the Spanish narrator in the 'Llama sketch', and there was a mighty cheer and pro-longed applause. As soon as Gumby came on for 'Flower Arrangement', the show ground to a halt again with almost hysterical cheering greeting each line (a good example of the 'primitive' style in comedy). For the first half of the show there was a vocal majority killing lines, laughs and all attempts at timing. After a while they seemed to tire themselves out, and one had the satisfaction of hearing people laugh at jokes and words, rather than cheering each character who came on, at random throughout the sketch.

We finished at about 1.30 a.m. but the audience refused to leave – even after the auditorium lights had been on for some time. If any of us so much as put a head around the curtain there was wild applause. After two or three minutes of this, John went out and spoke to them like the good headmaster he is – thanking them for being a wonderful audience and adding savagely 'Now will you *please* go home.' This they enjoyed even more – and it must have been over five minutes after the end that they at last stopped applauding.

It was a strange kind of hysteria for a comedy show to create – one can't imagine it happening to previous 'cult' shows like *Beyond the Fringe* or *TW3* – perhaps it is because Monty Python itself is less con-trolled and contrived than these shows. We have created characters which we ourselves find hysterical, why should we then be surprised that an audience reacts in the same way?

We walked back to the hotel at 2.30 a.m. – with half a dozen grown men with knotted handkerchiefs over their heads disappearing down the road in front of us.

Monday, February 1st, Coventry

After breakfast at a café across from the hotel – called, believe it or not, 'The Gay Gannet' – Terry and I drove off in the Simca to revisit my old school at Shrewsbury.

Terry is such a good companion – his insatiable sense of wonder and discovery added immeasurably to the enjoyment of seeing the school again. I showed Terry the studies, stone passages and stark bedrooms, which had virtually been my life for five so-called 'formative' years. They hadn't changed much, except that the studies seemed to have no restric-tions on decoration – every *one* seemed to be decorated with rich cur-tains, colours, and huge photos of Mick Jagger. The only really sensuous study in my time was John Ravenscroft's (now John Peel, the Radio One intellectual). On the notice board was a rule about women in studies – *women in studies!* An unthinkable sacrilege ten years ago.

In the school buildings there was even more exciting evidence that sacrilege had been, and was being committed throughout the school. On every landing, and on seemingly every spare piece of wall, in what had been dull passages and dark corridors, there were paintings done by the boys. One of them, on the same dour landing I must have passed thousands of times, on my way to the History Library, breathlessly late, on this same landing was a large canvas depicting a clothed youth on a bed, with three ladies around him, wearing only black stockings, suspenders and pants, revealing their crotches provocatively. Presumably it was intended to represent the schoolboy's dream – but to hang this dream in the school buildings seemed to be the best thing that had happened to Shrewsbury since Philip Sidney.[1]

Wednesday, February 3rd, Southwold

Father is now on L-Dopa, a new breakthrough in the treatment of Parkinson's Disease. It is still very expensive (each pill costs about 18/-), but his shaking seems very much better. His movements, and especially his grasp, are becoming more impaired, Mummy now has to help with things like tying shoelaces and buttoning awkward buttons. He takes about three-quarters of an hour to get up, shave and dress.

We went for a walk along Southwold front, in the gathering dusk. There was an exceptionally beautiful sunset – so many shades, from rich deep red to delicate pale pink. We drove on to the Common for a while and watched it.

Wednesday, February 10th

We lunched today at the BBC, Kensington House, and talked with the producers of *The Car versus the People*, a documentary in which we have sadly become involved. The lunch was quite pleasant – little was decided, though much was said, but we did meet Bill Tidy, one of the funniest cartoonists in the country. In fact, it is very, very rarely that a

1 1554–86. Complete Renaissance man and along with Charles Darwin and the founders of *Private Eye*, among the most famous old boys.

Tidy cartoon doesn't raise at least a titter in me. He's a Yorkshireman, beer-drinking and unaffectedly open and straightforward. He carries around with him the convivial atmosphere of a local pub on a Friday night – evident in the way he leans back in his chair and the way he tells stories. He seems to be getting enormous pleasure out of life. He has, it turns out, a child who is either ill or handicapped, and one is enormously glad for the child's sake that it has him as a father.

After our lunch grinds to an inconclusive halt at 3.00, we make our way over to TV Centre to appear on *Ask Aspel* – a show, compered by clean-shaven, charming, man for all seasons Michael Aspel. The idea is to play clips from BBC programmes which children have requested. Apparently they have a request for some Monty Python clip almost every week – giving the lie perhaps to Paul Fox's confident assertion that Monty Python would never work in a pre-nine o'clock slot.

Monday, February 15th

Decimal Day. Today, not only our old currency, but a small portion of our everyday language dies for ever and is replaced. In looking back, this day will perhaps appear as just another step away from the archaic obstinacies that set Britain apart from other countries of the world, and a step which should have been taken much earlier.

Funnily enough, I find myself resenting the new decimal coinage far less than the postal codes (which I fear will one day replace towns with numbers – and after towns streets, and after streets …?), or the all-figure telephone numbers which dealt one mighty blow to local feeling in London and, in the process, made it practically impossible to remember phone numbers.[1]

But the decimal coinage system seems to clarify, rather than confuse. I have no sentimental regrets at the passing of the threepenny bit, or the half-crown, only slight irritation that the sixpence – an old coin – should be incorporated into this new system, even temporarily, and also that for some inexplicable reason a number of smaller shops are still working in pounds, shillings and pence.

---

1 Our own area code changed from GULliver to the soulless 485.

Wednesday, February 17th

At 3.00 I arrive at the studios of Advision to do a voice-over for a Chesswood creamed mushroom commercial. It is the first of about half a dozen voice-over offers which has come to anything – which is pleasing because, of all the pride-swallowing things one does for money, voice-overs are the least painful. They generally take up only an hour or so of one's time, your face does not appear to link you with any product and the money is useful but modest enough to allay any guilt feelings about selling out.

There was the usual gaggle of advertising men present and, judging by the subtlety and intellectual complexity of the advert, six reasonably intelligent wombats could have done the job just as well.

Sunday, February 28th

I had been feeling guilty for some weeks that I had made no effort to follow up my decision to have William christened at St Martin's, the local church standing amongst the rubble of the Gospel Oak rebuilding scheme. And today I took the snap decision to go. I was literally summoned by bells. It was a strange feeling going into a church I did not know for a service that I did not really believe in, but once inside I couldn't help a feeling of warmth and security. Outside there were wars and road accidents and murders, striptease clubs and battered babies and frayed tempers and unhappy marriages and people contemplating suicide and bad jokes and *The Golden Shot*, but once in St Martin's there was peace. Surely people go to church not to involve themselves in the world's problems but to escape from them. And surprisingly also, here in the middle of devastated Kentish Town, was a large, unusually designed stone building, with polished pews and shining brass and a vicar and faithful people gathered. Though rationally I would find it difficult to justify my participation, I nevertheless was glad I went. In a funny way, I was really moved by the faith of the fifteen old ladies, four men, a choir (black and white) who were there with me. But seeing the vicar afterwards I felt a fraud.

Friday, March 5th

In the evening, a sneak preview of *And Now For Something Completely Different*. It is on at the Granada, Harrow, with [Gore Vidal's] *Myra*

Breckinridge. The manager is there to meet us when we arrive at the cinema. We are led upstairs and seated on the left-hand side of the circle, about six rows from the front. The whole idea of showing us ceremoniously to these seats is rather ludicrous, as the place is virtually empty.

Then the curtains draw back and there is our film. I found it dragged heavily and parts of it were downright dull. But my judgement is probably coloured by seeing most of it before – several times. I still feel sad that we didn't write more original material.

Sunday, March 14th

Python's success has resulted in a number of offers – e.g. a Python Christmas book (Methuen), three separate record contracts (Decca, Tony Stratton-Smith[1] and good old BBC Enterprises, who despite themselves appear to have sold over 10,000 of our first LP), merchandising T-shirts, West End shows for Bernard Delfont, etc, etc.

Terry and I and T Gilliam feel very much that we are in danger of losing sight of the wood for the trees. Python is a half-hour TV show and cannot easily be anything else. Any transformation of this show onto record, or onto the stage, will inevitably lose something from the original. The alternatives are therefore to put out these weaker substitute Pythons and make money from very little work, or else to work hard to make everything Python is involved in new, original, critical and silly. This requires a great deal of effort and, as all of us are at the moment employed on other pressing projects, no one seems willing to expend it. So we stumble on, with no great sense of direction. Like the record and the film, we have already stumbled into unsatisfactory compromises. I think there are a great many ahead.

We now have John Gledhill – of the Roger Hancock office – acting as the organiser and agent for Python Productions. It is going to be a hell of a job. Today we talked about notepaper!!

Some kind of sanity has prevailed, in that John C, after being reluctant to do any more TV Pythons, is gradually becoming one of the staunchest advocates of a new series, to be made in the autumn.

---

1 Racehorse owner, John Betjeman fan and general bon vivant, Tony started Charisma Records. He died, much missed by all, in 1987.

Monday, March 29th

Today, more filming for the May Day show,[1] including one gag involving John and myself – in the Grimsby Fish-Slapping dance – which ends up with my being knocked about eight feet into the cold, green, insalubrious waters of the Thames. However, once the waiting is over, this kind of stunt is quite pleasurable – it should almost certainly look funny and you are immediately fished out, undressed and given brandy, which is better treatment than most people who fall in the river could expect. Also you experience this pleasant feeling that, just by jumping into the river, you have justified your existence for that day, and can relax into a state of quiet euphoria.

Friday, April 23rd, St Andrews

The rain poured down all day. Terry rang and said that he and Alison had decided to go up to St Andrews (for our cabaret with John)[2] at lunchtime. As I had to wait until six o'clock for a dubbing session, I booked myself on to the flight to Edinburgh.

I was met by a cab driver who was to take me to St Andrews. We drove north, over the Forth Road Bridge and up to Kinross on the motorway. This then petered out, and the roads were narrower, more silent, with occasional holes, filled with deep puddles. What with the driving rain, the wind and the increasing remoteness of the area, it was, as the cab driver remarked, 'real Dracula weather'.

We arrived at St Andrews at 2.30. The hotel was beside the sea and, although I couldn't see the waves, their noise was quite deafening. I paid the cab driver £10, and he set off back to Edinburgh.

In the hotel I had the following conversation with an obliging night porter:

Night Porter: 'Would you like a cup of tea?'
Traveller: 'Well, that would be nice – but have you anything stronger?'
Porter: 'No, no, can't do that, sorry, not now.'

---

1 An attempt to produce a Euro-comedy link-up to mark May Day. We were chosen to provide the British segment, for which we created a number of very silly traditional dances.
2 John was always getting offered cabaret engagements, and he preferred to do them with Terry and myself than on his own. They paid quite well. He gave them up after being savagely heckled by London University medical students.

Traveller:	'Oh, dear.'
Porter:	'Would you like a glass of beer?'
Traveller:	'Yes, that would be fine.'
Porter:	'Righto.'
Traveller:	'There's not the slightest chance of a drop of scotch?'
Porter:	'A beer and a scotch?'
Traveller:	'Yes, please.'
Porter:	'Righto.'

Saturday, April 24th, St Andrews

My eight o'clock alarm call with newspapers arrived at 7.30, without newspapers. I drank a cup of tea and read a little, then lounged in the bath and pondered rather gloomily on the amount of work that lay ahead today.

At 2.30 we turned up at the Younger Hall, whose interior was as cold and inhospitable as the exterior. The most obvious problem we were going to have to face was the acoustics. One's voice simply died about half-way into the auditorium, unless we spoke at full blast. With long sketches such as 'World Forum', 'Lumberjack Song', 'I Don't Go Out Much Nowadays' monologue,[1] 'Gambolputty', 'Pet Shop' and gross and noisy ones like 'Shabby' and 'Gumby Flower Arranging' to do, this didn't bode well for two performances.

There was no time to eat, and hardly any to drink, before the first show. As usual the house was packed and the audience consistently appreciative. But it isn't a performance I shall remember with much pride. In the back of my mind throughout was the spectre of a second performance, and the gradual deterioration of my voice as I strained and shouted my way through. The 'Lumberjack Song' was a disaster. John, as the Colonel, came on and stopped it once, and we all trailed off and then had another bash – only slightly less distinguished than the first. My long monologue, 'I Don't Go Out Much', was delivered badly and without much confidence.

From the very start of the second performance it was obvious that they were a noisier, more appreciative audience – many of them little

---

1 A monologue I wrote for the 1965 Oxford Revue at Edinburgh. I always preferred to write and create characters rather than jokes *per se*, and this depended very much on performance.

short of ecstatic. I know I used them disgracefully, with shouting, grins, nods, ad-libs, etc. But it was amazing how much more impact every item had. For about 80 minutes it was almost five laughs a minute – 'I Don't Go Out Much' went down as successfully as it used to in Edinburgh – thus justifying Terry's faith in it (I don't think *I* would have put it in the show). All in all, this was one of the great performances. I especially enjoyed corpsing John (he maintains I got him five times).

Wednesday, May 12th

Terry and I have been working fairly solidly together – firstly finishing our eight-sketch commitment for *The Two Ronnies*, which has turned out to be the most unrewarding task financially and artistically. The sketches are drawn from us with lavish praise and unrestrained enthusiasm – and yet when we see them on TV they have been changed and coarsened and we are not happy.

But secondly we have been writing our Munich show,[1] which has been like old times, with lots of wild ideas developing.

On May 5th I was 28, and on May 6th at lunchtime we heard that we had come second at the Montreux Festival – winning The Silver Rose. The winner was an Austrian show, which everyone said was exactly like Python and I must say the title – 'Peter Lodynski's Flea-Market Company' – is not entirely dissimilar. But the lesson of Montreux is why did a Python copy defeat a Python original? The answer I fear is that their production and presentation was slick, whereas ours was unforgivably sloppy.

Saturday, May 15th

This morning we were woken by William at 7.15, then, for a short while, peace, until Thomas gets out of his cot about eight o'clock and is to be heard banging around the house in a very busy way.

Eventually he arrives outside our door, and there is some prolonged heavy breathing. He does not, for some reason of his own rather than ours, like to come in before we ask him, and so it depends on how tired

---

1 The brainchild of German producer and Python fan Alfred Biolek, this was to be a show written by and starring the Pythons, speaking German. It was duly recorded at Bavaria Studios in Munich in early July 1971. At least I can now sing 'Lumberjack Song' in German – a great way of clearing crowded ski slopes.

we are as to how much we take advantage of this uncharacteristic docility. But as soon as he is in the bedroom he rapidly starts to organise a book to be read, despite our half-hearted attempts to persuade him that an extra half-hour's sleep would do him the world of good.

Once we have all got up – now seldom later than 8.45 – and had breakfast, I normally take Thomas for a walk, or on Sundays for a more ambitious outing – last week we went on the North London Line to Kew Gardens. This morning Thomas wanted above all else to try the paddling pool in Parliament Hill playground. He was blissfully happy there for about an hour – and we then went on to feed the ducks on Highgate Ponds, returning home via the café for an ice-cream. Thomas is good company now and chats quite fluently. William sleeps the whole way.

Friday, May 21st

Eric is busy on the Monty Python book, but Terry Gilliam is fighting his way through, and perhaps out of, a lucrative 'Marty' [Feldman series] contract. The American TV people will not let Terry use any nudes, or even see the cleavage at the top of a pair of buttocks, and his Christmas card film, which went out in England in a children's programme on Christmas afternoon,[1] has been banned altogether from American TV. Such is television in the land of the free.

Sunday, June 20th

The first day of recording on our second LP in the Marquee studios. It was a good feeling to be working on Sunday in the middle of Soho – and the session is run almost entirely by and for ourselves. Unlike our previous BBC record there is no audience, and we are able to do several takes on each sketch to try and improve on it. This is very beneficial in one way, but I shall be interested to hear whether we need the impetus of a live audience – whether in fact we subconsciously concentrate harder and bring the better performances out of ourselves if we have an immediate soundboard for our antics. There is one very amenable young engineer, and Terry J is producing.

---

1 On *Do Not Adjust Your Set*.

Monday, June 21st

Another day spent in the recording studio in Dean Street. We worked hard, but my doubts about the record began to grow. Firstly, because it contains fewer bankers (i.e. strong, memorable sketches) than the first record. This is partly explained by the fact that the more conventional verbal sketches translate easily onto record, whereas the more complicated, tortuously interwoven sketches of the second series lose more away from their visual context. I am still worried by the lack of a reaction to our recording – but I put this down as much to my own weakness of judgement as anything. More seriously, I wish that everyone had been prepared to put some work into the writing of the record.

Thursday, June 24th

Leaving the studio at 3.15, Terry and I had about two hours to buy assorted props and costumes for a cabaret at the University of East Anglia in the evening. It was a hot day and, to my added frustration, the shops around Camden Town and Hampstead were all closed. I was looking for old coats, berets, scarves, etc, for Ken Shabby – and there is little worse than driving in a hurry on a hot day round closed shops to try and find torn old clothes. However, the Simon Community in Malden Road was open, and proved to be just what was wanted – but there was hardly time to throw the things in a suitcase, with toothbrush and black velvet suit, before the taxi arrived and we were taken off to Liverpool St.

There were thousands more people equally hot and equally hurried, and we only just managed to get seats in the restaurant car. John and Connie arrived with about 20 seconds to go, complete with cage and stuffed parrot.

We rehearsed the cabaret – it was about 50 minutes' worth – and arrived at the ball by about 10.00. We were shown to a cabaret room and a succession of the usual, rather anxious, slight, dishevelled officials came to tell us what was going on.

The University of E. Anglia, like many of the newer English universities, has had a fair amount of publicity for its sit-ins, protests, marches and other symptoms of left-wing radicalism. I was surprised, therefore, that this element seemed to be quite absent from the ball. They appeared to be an audience of exactly the same people who Robert [Hewison] and I performed to at Oxford about seven years ago.

Wednesday, August 4th

Meeting this morning between Charisma Records and John Gledhill, Terry Gilliam and myself to discuss the record cover. Our suggestion was not the easiest thing to sell. A classical record, with everything crossed out rather crudely and 'Another Monty Python record' scribbled in at the top. On the back a 97% authentic spiel about Beethoven and about the finer points of his Second Symphony – but, for those who can bear to read it through, it is gradually infiltrated by tennis references.

Charisma seem almost an ideal record company – or indeed company of any kind. Their offices in Brewer Street are functional, rather than plush, set on three floors above a dirty bookshop. Tony Stratton-Smith, who founded the company, has a tiny office at the top, with two hard wooden benches (giving the little room a rather ecclesiastical feel), a desk, a table, and an interesting selection of moderniana on the walls. They do not seem to have any fixed attitudes to their products, they seem to take decisions with the minimum of fuss and, what's more, they agreed to our record cover – which is quite a risk for any company.

Thursday, August 5th, Southwold

Caught the 8.00 train from Gospel Oak to Broad St. Thomas stood at the door to wave goodbye in his pyjama top – he was very good until I had almost reached the end of the village, when I heard a beseeching shout of 'Kiss! Daddy. Kiss! Kiss!' as I turned the corner.

From Broad Street I walked down to Liverpool Street Station, which, at 9.15 in the morning, is like swimming against a very fierce current – such is the surge of people pouring up the approach that in a momentary flash of panic I wondered if I would ever make it to the station. It was a rather frightening sight – this sea of faces. It was like some clever documentary maker's piece of film illustrating the increasing conformity of people's lives.

Ate breakfast on the train and was met at Darsham Station at 11.30.

Daddy and I walked across the common to the Harbour Inn. The L-Dopa tablets seem to have completely stopped his Parkinsonian trembling – but they cannot disguise his increasing vagueness and the difficulties of keeping up with what is happening around him.

In the evening I walked up the lane towards Frostenden. It was a clear evening and the sun shone on the gold fields of corn through the trees which side the road and straggle the landscape rather haphazardly, not in neat copses or woods like in chalk country. The effect was warm and secure and reassuring. At the same time, in London, Richard Neville[1] was being sentenced to fifteen months' imprisonment for publishing the Schoolkids issue of *Oz*. I can't help feeling that he would have appreciated this countryside for the same reasons that I do – and yet the only way society has of dealing with his imagination and intelligence is to put him away for over a year.

Wednesday, August 11th

Drove down the A3 through the Surrey Green Belt to visit one of Helen's friends from teacher training college – it was looking very green today, and the woodland, with patches of rough heathland emerging from the trees, dispelled the usual feelings of claustrophobia I have when driving through England's most middle-class county.

After lunch I left the women and children and drove the five miles or so into Guildford, a town with many more old and fine buildings than I remember before. I went to what must be one of the largest, and certainly the most haphazard second-hand bookshop in the country – Thorp's. It took me nearly one and a half hours to cast a very cursory glance over about 70% of their stock – shelved in a variety of different little rooms and one big timber-roofed chamber, in such a way that makes one suspect that the disorder is all part of a careful filing system, which takes years to appreciate fully.

I bought a handsome volume of Bulldog Drummond stories. I felt I ought to have an example of this unique genre – the public school, ultra-xenophobic spy story. It makes great reading – everyone is always 'fixing' each other 'with piercing stares'.

At supper I got into conversation with our hosts about the *Oz* sentences. Clearly, and rather disturbingly, their minds were made up – *Oz* and its editors were evils that had been judged guilty, and let it be a lesson to all others who are threatening the moral fibre of our society, and the most alarming thing was that they did not have a clue as to what *Oz* Schoolkids issue was. They automatically thought it was a collection

---

1 The editor of *Oz* magazine asked for teenage schoolkids to put together an edition. The 'schoolkids' produced an issue which put Neville and others in the dock at the Old Bailey, accused of corrupting morals and intending to 'arouse and implant in the minds of those young people lustful and perverted desires'. His long hair was ordered to be forcibly cut.

of obscene material which the editors had written to try and corrupt schoolchildren. They were quite taken aback when I told them that the issue had been written by schoolkids – and that the jury had acquitted them of the charge of corrupting children's morals. They had complete misconceptions about hippies – J said he wouldn't dare get into an argument in case they set on him. They talked about 'London' as a descriptive term for all rather suspect, critical, left-wing, un-British opinions, and implied that it was here in Surrey that the 'English way of life' would be defended to the bitter end.

The four-month gap at this point is the result of that diarist's nightmare, the loss of an almost complete notebook. According to family folklore it was dumped in the rubbish bin by my son William who, at the age of one, had developed a great interest in putting things inside other things. Whatever happened, it never reappeared. Momentarily bereft, I felt like giving up the diary altogether but the loss made me realise that it had become such a part of my life, that it was inconceivable to jettison it. If anything, I compensated by writing more.

Friday, December 24th

Yesterday I found a smart gallery in Crawford Street and ended up spending £45 on a primitive of two cows painted by someone called Beazley in 1881. Actually I didn't know it was a primitive – the cows looked perfectly normal to me – but it's a very in-word in art circles at the moment, and I think it means that commercially I'm onto a good thing. Be that as it may, I'm glad to have the painting, because at last I've found something that I really enjoy looking at – and the serenity of the two cows is quite infectious. In my quest for pictures I went into another art gallery in Crawford Street and spent an uncomfortable few minutes looking round under the baleful eye of a drunk proprietor – and I mean really drunk, full of self-pity, with red, streaming eyes and almost unable to utter a word – whilst across the table sat a young man gazing impassively at him. As I left the owner tried to get me to have a drink with him. I declined and his face dropped as if he had been bitterly hurt.

Saturday, December 25th

A rather fine, sunny morning, and for the first time in our marriage we woke on Christmas morning in our own home.

Thomas saw James across the road, and then they both saw Louise looking out of her window, and soon there was an impromptu gathering of little children comparing presents on the pavement outside our house. The quiet of the day, the sunny morning and the neighbours all talking made me feel very glad – about staying in London, and about living in Oak Village. If it doesn't sound too pedantic, I felt that this was how city life should be.

Monday, December 27th

In the evening I was part of a rather curious function at the Abraxas Squash Club. This took the form of a fancy-dress squash match between Monty Python and the Abraxas staff, with John, Terry and myself representing Python.

Terry was dressed in oversized trousers, John as a ballerina in a tutu, and I had borrowed the wasp's outfit from Hazel [Pethig]. Playing as a wasp may have looked spectacular, but it was in fact rather difficult, as part of the costume consisted of two extra legs, to the end of which – on Helen's suggestion – I had tied two extra pairs of gym shoes. However, when I tried to make a shot, these spare legs would swing round and nudge my aim. In consequence I lost all three games to a man dressed as a savage.

Tuesday, December 28th

To the Odeon Kensington to meet my mother, Angela, Veryan and the three kids and take them to see our film *And Now For Something Completely Different*. It lasted eleven weeks at the Columbia and took nearly £50,000 at that cinema alone (over two thirds of the cost of making the picture). Its one week at Oxford ran into four weeks as a result of the demand, and it was held over for an extra week in Leicester and Liverpool. All of which bodes well for a film which Terry and I thought would be received with jeers.

We all sat in almost solitary state in the 80p seats at the front of the circle. It was a strange feeling – here I was sitting next to my mother, who had only come to films with me as a rare treat when I was young, watching me on the big screen. Unfortunately the tedious repetition of old material in the film hardly swelled my mind with pride.

Friday, December 31st

Harold Nicolson used to sum up his year on December 31st with a few pithy words. It's a sort of diary writer's reward for all those dull July 17ths and October 3rds. (Will I still be keeping my diary on Dec. 31st 1999? Now that's the kind of thought which gives survival a new urgency.)

1971 was my fifth full year in television and certainly on the face of it we have achieved a lot. A TV series, which has reached the sort of national notoriety of *TW3*. 'Monty Python', 'Silly Walks', 'And Now For Something Completely Different', etc, have become household words. The TV series has won several awards during the year, including the Silver Rose of Montreux. The second Monty Python album has sold over 20,000 copies since release in October, and *Monty Python's Big Red Book* completely sold out of both printings within two weeks. It has sold 55,000 copies, and 20,000 more are being printed for February. In London it was top of the bestseller lists. And finally the film which we made a year ago and were so unhappy about, looks like being equally successful.

From all this no one can deny that Monty Python has been the most talked about TV show of 1971 – and here is the supreme irony, for we have not, until this month, recorded any new shows since October 1970.

The split between John and Eric and the rest of us has grown a little recently. It doesn't prevent us all from sharing – and enjoying sharing – most of our attitudes, except for attitudes to work. It's the usual story – John and Eric see Monty Python as a means to an end – money to buy freedom from work. Terry J is completely the opposite and feels that Python is an end in itself – i.e. work which he enjoys doing and which keeps him from the dangerous world of leisure. In between are Graham and myself.

1972

Sunday, January 2nd

In the morning, Rolf, Ranji [Veling] and I went for a long walk on the Heath and talked about Rolf's pet subject – how to simplify life. He feels that the problems of pollution or increasing crime or mental illness are the result of us all wanting and being offered too much.

I'm glad that there are cars and planes and television and washing machines, and I think we cannot suddenly pretend that they have not been invented – but I feel we must control their use, and that they should be used not to dictate but to stimulate. Any urban planning should include an open play area at least twice the size of the car park, instead of the opposite; there should be severe restrictions on cars in central London – but above all, in every area there should be greater encouragements for people to meet and talk – not in official meetings or on two nights a week, but all the time. There should be space indoors and outdoors, where people would want to stop and gather. At the base of every block of flats there should be a big, well-furnished well-equipped coffee shop or restaurant, a big foyer with papers, magazines, books on sale – and even a few fairground attractions. It would mean a radical redirection of funds available for housing, but one quarter of the vast wealth in the hands of private property developers would, I think, help to equalise a system which at present is doomed – the colossal difference in living conditions which is being widened every day as new council estates are built on the cheap – and with them is built boredom, jealousy, repression, anger …

Helen and I drove over to Simon Albury's flat in Ladbroke Grove. Simon was fairly high when we got there, as were David and Stan. Unstoned were most of the wives, David's sister Rosemary, and ourselves. Source of the stuff was R.[1] I drank bourbon and smoked occasionally, and heard riotous tales from Rosemary Dodd about her Cordon Bleu cooking

---

1 Drugs were a source of great interest at the time. It was quite respectable to have experienced them in some shape or form. Simon had worked on a research paper on drug use for the Home Office.

for the nobility. She had worked with the Queen's cousins for some time, and apparently they drank so much that at one meal there was a special footman detailed to stand behind the hostess and hoist her politely up every time she sank beneath the table.

R, as lithe and big-eyed and diffident as ever, suddenly becomes animated. He is smoking his third or fourth joint of the evening (no passing around here – it's R's joint) and telling me of his poetry writings. After a long and serious build-up I was expecting *The Waste Land* at least, but what I got was 'Zim, Zam, Zap, the Zimbabwe is going to Zap you man' – as Simon A remarked, 'Pot never helped anyone.'

Tuesday, January 4th

At Terry's when Amin – a Pakistani from Alison's Botany Department – returned from Pakistan. He was out there throughout the brief India–Pakistan war – in which East Pakistan was finally taken by the Indians on behalf of the Bengalis who live there. It was a short, sharp war, which has resulted in the setting up of the independent state of Bangla-Desh. Amin was bitter about the Pakistani surrender, and his primary reaction seemed to be emotional – hurt national pride, and a desire for revenge – but as he talked it was clear that he also had a secondary, more realistic reaction, which was relief that the war had ended, and the hope that India and Pakistan would now live together. It was a strange sensation, sitting in a comfortable south London sitting room, hearing from someone who only a month before had been living through air-raids, in a country where the old and infirm had come down from the mountains to the 100° desert to fight – clad in furs and skins.

Friday, January 7th

Back into our routine again – a week of dubbing, writing, rehearsing, and recording.

Today there are two major sketches – one with Graham C as Biggles, using generally abusive language, dictating a letter to King Haakon thanking him for the eels, and finding out Algy was a homosexual – the other was a parrot shop type of sketch with John as a customer in a cheese shop, and myself as an obliging assistant, who has none of the cheeses the customer asks for – and John goes through about fifty, before shooting me. Typical of the difference in writing since the first series, is that, no longer content to just write in a cheese shop as the setting, there are throughout the sketch two city gents dancing to balalaika music in a corner of the shop. Our style of humour is becoming more *Goon Show* than revue – we have finally thrown off the formal shackles of the *Frost Report* (where we all cut our teeth), and we now miss very few chances to be illogical and confusing.

Tuesday, January 11th

This evening, in order to cheer ourselves up after a day in which it rained solidly, Helen and I went to see Woody Allen's film *Bananas*, and another comedy *Where's Poppa*[1] at the Essoldo, Maida Vale. Both the films made us hoot and roar with laughter – though neither added up to much – there were just delicious moments of comedy. *Bananas* was rather like a Python show, with the same kind of feverish pace and welter of jokes and joke situations. *Where's Poppa* was another very funny Brooklyn Jewish comedy.

Came back feeling very much better. Read more of Charlie Mingus' autobiography *Beneath the Underdog* – amazed at the speed of the book and the great turns of phrase and styles of speech which Mingus and his Watts friends speak. Conditions may have been bad and Whitey may have been a continuous oppressive force, but they knew how to have a good time – and there's much more spontaneity and honesty and good, plain communication in Mingus' world than there is in our own.

Saturday, January 15th

At home doing odd-jobs for most of the day. In the afternoon a giggly phone-call, and a girl from Roedean, one Lulu Ogley, rang from a phone box with some of her friends. They wanted to know what I was really like!

Lulu spoke rather like Princess Anne, but asked fairly sensible questions, whereas her friend was unable to bring herself to ask whether or not I was married. Last night John Gledhill gave me a phone number from an anonymous girl who wanted to contact me, and a few days back

1 Directed by Carl Reiner (Rob, his son, and director of *Spinal Tap*, appears in a minor role). It starred George Segal and Ruth Gordon.

I received a rather sultry photo from a girl of seventeen. Altogether most disturbing.

Monday, January 31st

At lunchtime I went for a run across the Heath, and had that rare and pleasurable sensation of running in a snowstorm – the snow silencing everything, emphasising isolation, but cooling and soothing at the same time.

The papers and news today are full of Bernadette Devlin's physical attack on Mr Maudling in the Commons.[1] The shooting of thirteen Irish Catholics in Londonderry yesterday has made England the most reviled country in the world. For almost the first time in the whole of their impossible task in Ireland, the troops seem to have been guilty of a serious misjudgement. Now Bernadette shouts loudly and viciously for revenge. It all seems a most unpleasant and violent spiral, but surely now the British government must start to take the Catholics seriously.

Tuesday, February 1st

In the evening we met Terry and Al for a drink at the Lamb in Lamb's Conduit Street, and afterwards they took us out for a meal to a hitherto untried restaurant, La Napoule in North Audley Street.

Terry became very excited and emotional about Ireland and the Londonderry march. He totally blamed the government – on the grounds that they are the ones who hold the position of power, and they are the ones who should be held responsible for any trouble. I argued realistically rather than instinctively that, as the government had rightly or wrongly taken the decision to ban marches, this decision had to be enforced, hence the presence of troops. The marchers must have expected some trouble for they are quite well aware that any march attracts groups of people who want a fight and will do anything they can to provoke one. The soldiers must have panicked and fired at random, but the explosive situation was caused by the stubbornness of the government and the anger of the Catholics.

2 As Reginald Maudling, the Home Secretary, tried to defend the British Army's killing of thirteen civilians on what became known as Bloody Sunday, the MP Bernadette Devlin, 21 years old and the youngest woman ever to be elected to Parliament, crossed the floor of the Commons and punched him in the face.

I am very cautious of people who are absolutely right, especially when they are vehemently so – but the inaction of the government and especially Maudling's statement last night that any yielding to Catholic pressure would be 'surrender', smacks of Lyndon Johnson and Vietnam and makes me angry and frustrated with Heath's unpleasant government.

Thursday, February 3rd

After a morning's work at Camberwell, we drove over to John's for lunch and a chat about possible new additions to the cabaret at Nottingham University. We decided to put in 'Argument' sketch – a quick-fire Cleese/Chapman piece from the new series, and one or two smaller additions such as the 'Silly Ministers' and the 'Time-Check' – 'It's five past nine and nearly time for six past nine. Later on this evening it will be ten o'clock and at 10.30 we join BBC2 in time for 10.33. And don't forget tomorrow, when it'll be 9.20,' etc, etc.

We caught the 4.50 St Pancras to Nottingham train – spread ourselves over a First Class compartment and rehearsed.

Apparently the demand for tickets had been so great that we had been asked to do an extra performance, with about 700 students at each. They were a very good audience, not drunk, intelligent and appreciative. Our performances were a little edgy, as we were doing new material for the first time, but the second house, at 9.15, was much better. We did about 40 minutes each time, and were paid a little less than £200 each for the evening. In between shows we were visited by interviewers from student papers, rag magazines, Radio Nottingham and the revue group – all of whom were ushered into our presence in a carefully supervised way, making one feel like a visiting Head of State. We then travelled the thirty-odd miles to Lincoln, where we were to do our third cabaret of the evening, at the Aquarius Club.

A little side door next to Woolworths led us into this charmless little club, where two of the first people we saw were police, and the other two were bouncers. There seemed to be a general air of anxiety and unease about the management of the club, but I suppose this was their natural manner, in the best Vercotti[1] traditions. We were led upstairs through a very small room so thick with smoke that it felt as though they were

---

1 Luigi and Dino Vercotti, two hugely ineffective Mafiosi, created by Terry J and myself.

doing laboratory tests to see how much humans could take before passing out. As the time for the cabaret drew nearer, we became quite fatalistic about it and decided to tell them from the start that we were unarmed. A minor scuffle broke out nearby, the basins in the gents were full of vomit and there was a general brooding feeling of squalor and suppressed violence. Imagine our great and pleasant surprise when we started the cabaret and, apart from two girls in the very front, they not only listened quietly, but also roared with laughter.

Sunday, February 6th, Southwold

Arrived at Croft Cottage at 9.45. Both parents looked well. It was a dull and rainy day and not one to lure us outside, but I did cycle to Wangford before lunch and afterwards we walked along the sea front at Southwold. It was a heavy sea, with a strong on-shore wind piling up big breakers. We heard later that one man had been drowned and three others miraculously saved when their fishing boat upturned off this very beach a few hours earlier.

At home in the warmth of Croft Cottage, we shut out the miserable day and ate, drank, watched television and talked. The march of civil rights protesters at Newry this afternoon turned out to be entirely peaceful, which was a tremendous relief after last week's shootings in Londonderry. In the news pictures from Newry one could see cameras – still, film and TV – everywhere, waiting for the violence that caught the media unprepared in Londonderry.

Still Mr Heath and this complacent, indolent, arrogant and unfeeling Tory government refuse to try and ease the situation. Talk in the papers of troops being brought in to deal with the miners' strike – altogether I feel disgusted and depressed by the heartlessness of this government towards the underprivileged. From now on I am a fervent socialist. (This could change within a week – ed.)

Thursday, February 10th

Assembled for an all-Python writing meeting at Terry's at 10.00. John sends word that he is ill. Extraordinarily sceptical response. However we work on, and for a laugh decide to write a truly communal sketch. Accordingly all four of us are given a blank sheet of paper and we start to write about two exchanges each before passing on the paper. After

an hour and a half we have four sketches – with some very funny characters and ideas in them. They may all work if interlocked into a four-
sketch mixture. Eric suggested that we all be very naughty and go to
see *Diamonds are Forever*, the latest of the James Bond films at the
Kensington Odeon. After brief and unconvincing heart-searching, we
drive over to Kensington – but, alas, have not been in the cinema for
more than 20 minutes when the film runs down. After a few minutes
there is much clearing of throat, a small light appears in front of the
stage and a manager appears to tell us that we are the victims of a
power cut (this being the first day of cuts following four weeks of government intractability in the face of the miners' claim). For half an
hour there is a brief, British moment of solidarity amongst the beleaguered cinemagoers, but, as we were shirking work anyway, it looked
like a shaft of reprobation from the Great Writer in the sky.

Friday, February 11th

So serious is the emergency that there are now certain areas which three
or four times a week will be designated 'high risk' and liable to up to
eight hours power loss per day. Camberwell must have been one of
them, for we worked by oil lamp-light from 10–12, and from 3 until 5. At
5.00 drove in to Python Prods. offices to meet Alfred Biolek, here on a
five-day flying visit. He told us that the show we made in Germany had
been shown with generally favourable reactions and he wanted us to fly
over for a weekend and discuss plans for a second German-made programme in September.

Home by 7.00 to a darkened house, so I reckon I have spent eleven of
my working hours without electricity today. The news is exceptionally
gloomy. The miners have refused to break and the emergency will last for
at least another two weeks. A nauseating Heath speech on TV and the
awful complacency of Lord Stokes[1] on *Any Questions* moves me to send
£50 to the miners.

Sunday, February 13th

General feeling of utter gloom from reading the papers – the power
emergency, the civil war in Ireland, the imprisonment of anti-Smith

1 Donald Stokes, Chairman of British Leyland Motor Company.

people in Rhodesia, all rather unpleasant. Shinwell,[1] a politician of sixty years' standing, was on the radio saying that this emergency was worse than the General Strike of 1926, because the feeling in the country was more bitter, and it does seem that Heath and the Conservative government – who pledged themselves to 'unite the country' when they were elected – have, by their non-government, succeeded in polarising it more than ever.

Monday, February 14th

Drove down to Terry's and we worked at putting a show together. Driving home has become quite an adventure now, for with the power-cuts I never know which traffic lights will be working and which won't. Street lights have generally been turned off, and when there is a blackout as well it becomes quite eerie. Driving at rush hour round the darkened Elephant and Castle, with hundreds of cars and as much light as a Suffolk lane is a disconcerting experience. But in a way it seems to take some of the urgency and aggression out of driving.

Tuesday, February 15th

At 10.30 Eric arrives and we work together rewriting three film pieces of Eric's for the next six shows. (Terry is having a day at home.) Our next power-cut comes at 3.00, and we carry on working by candlelight, waiting until 6.00 to do our typing. I must confess to quite enjoying this enforced disruption of routine. It appeals also to that yearning, deep in the back of one's subconscious, to be controlled by the elements – it's a form of security against all-powerful technology. The security of having to stop certain activities when the sun fades and the light goes. After all, only three generations of Palins have known electric light – before that stretch back the influences of many, many ancestors who lived in a permanent power-cut.

Saturday, February 19th

The coal strike is over. Yesterday the Wilberforce Court of Enquiry recommended 20% pay-rises for the miners on the grounds that they were

1 Emanuel 'Manny' Shinwell (1884–1986), socialist peer, the longest-lived politician of his times.

a special deserving case. The miners didn't accept immediately and in late-night bargaining with Mr Heath, secured even more concessions. The picketing was called off at 1.00 this morning, and the miners, after a ballot next week, should be back at work at the weekend. They will have been out for eight weeks – and the country, we are constantly told, is losing millions of pounds due to industrial power-cuts. It seems to me that the Wilberforce report has shown the government to be completely and utterly responsible. The miners 'special case' is not something which Wilberforce himself has discovered – it was clear to anyone before the strike started – but the government, faced with either admitting that their incomes policy was unjust, or trying to break the miners, as they did the electricity workers last year, chose to try and break the miners. In the end the miners won – and the weeks of reduced pay and unemployment which they had added to their already unpleasant working conditions, were made worthwhile. I regard my £50 as well spent!

An interesting sidelight to the strike has been the almost uninterrupted rise of the Stock Exchange during the weeks of crisis.

Monday, February 21st

Took a day off from writing to sort out various dull items of household management and run on Hampstead Heath in the drizzle. In the evening Graham Chapman and David and Barry Cryer[1] and his wife Terry came round for a meal. Graham arrived rather drunk and sullen after a bad day's work, and was rather bellicose to start with. At one point he started into a violent tirade against carpets, and how much he hated them. Barry Cryer remains the same – funny, considerate, straightforward and modest, a winning combination, which has been absolutely consistent since he first introduced himself to me at my first *Frost Report* meeting six years ago. He is the perfect antidote to the introverted unpredictability of Graham, and we all had a splendid evening.

Tuesday, February 22nd

The weather is still grey and dismal. At 2.30 the news comes through of an IRA bombing at Aldershot. An officers' mess has been blown up in

1 Barry and Marty Feldman were the two writers who welcomed me when I arrived for the first script meeting on *The Frost Report*. Barry and I and Terry J later wrote and performed for *Late-Night Line-Up*, from which we were eventually sacked.

retaliation for the killings in 'Derry. But the casualties are five cleaning ladies, one military vicar and one civilian.

Wednesday, March 15th

At Bart's Hospital sports ground at Chislehurst we spent the day filming Pasolini's version of the Third Test Match – complete with a nude couple making love during the bowler's run-up. Two extras actually obliged with a fully naked embrace – which must be a Python 'first'. The filming went smoothly, as it has done all this week. John C hasn't been with us, as he dislikes filming so much that he had a special three-day limit written into his contract.

This evening Helen went out to her pottery classes, and Terry J, Terry G and Viv Stanshall came round for a meeting. The reason for this particular combination was that Viv Stanshall (whom we last worked with on *Do Not Adjust Your Set* – and who has since been doing some very weird and imaginative and original pieces for radio, as well as occasional gigs) had been in touch with Terry G to enlist his co-operation in a musical cartoon – ideas by Viv Stanshall, pictures by Terry G.

However, at the moment Gilliam is going through a spell of disillusionment with animations. He no longer enjoys doing them, and claims his ideas have dried up as well. He is much more keen on directing or writing live action, and this he wants to do in collaboration with Terry J and myself. Gilliam felt that the injection of non-Python ideas from Viv might actually get us going on something, instead of just talking. We all got on well, we ate Helen's fantastic pâté, frankfurters and sauerkraut, and drank several bottles of Sancerre.

In the general mood of confidence and optimism which the Loire had generated, we decided to try and find backing for a 90-minute, feature-length film involving the four of us. Watch this column for further exciting developments.

Thursday, March 16th

Another good day's filming, ending with a marvellously chaotic situation at a flyover building site at Denham on the A40. I was narrator in front of the camera, describing how work was going on a new eighteen-level motorway being built by characters from 'Paradise Lost'. So behind me were angels, devils, Adam and Eve, etc, etc. All around us was the deafening noise of huge bulldozers. We were trying to time the take to the moment when the largest of these mighty earth-movers came into shot. So amidst all the dirt and mud and noise you would hear Ian shouting 'Here he comes!' Rick the camera operator shouting 'Move your harp to the left, Graham!' George dashing to take Adam and Eve's dressing gowns off, then the earth-mover would stop and plunge off in another direction, and all the efforts were reversed.

Thursday, April 6th

Almost two years and nine months to the day since we shot our first feet of Python TV film at Ham, we were at Windsor to shoot what is probably our last. On July 8th 1969 we started with Terry dressed as Queen Victoria, and today we finished with myself dressed as an Elizabethan.

Tuesday, April 11th

Terry and I meet Bill Borrows of the ACTT – the film technicians' union – to ask about joining as directors (for our summer film). The union, which five years ago was all powerful, and held the crippling ITV strike in 1968, which got London Weekend off to such a disastrous start, is now on its uppers. There are few films being made in England (only eleven this year) and the union has 70% of its members unemployed. Along with many other unions it has refused to register under the government's Industrial Relations Bill, and it may go under.

So Bill Borrows was indeed pleased to see Python people. *And Now For Something Completely Different* was, after all, a very successful British film – it's breaking box-office records at a cinema in Canada even now. We were given forms to fill in, and it looks as though there will be no trouble.

Saturday, April 15th

Cool, but often sunny – this was the nearest to a spring day we have had since the middle of March. In celebration of it, we went 'en famille' on the train to Kew Gardens.

At the station we have to wait for an hour, as a woman has trapped herself underneath a train. I presume it was a suicide attempt. People go and stare at her, but the ambulance is a long time coming, and the railway officials are in a complete panic. No one knows where the key to the first-aid cupboard is, for instance. Classic English characters emerge in such a situation – a lady, laden with parcels, tells Helen almost regretfully 'I didn't see any blood across the line or anything – I don't think she'd cut her wrists or anything. Why do people do it, that's what I wonder.'

We were on the station for an hour – which says a lot for Thomas and William's patience. Home by 6.30, and Helen and I spent the evening watching the box. I finished E L Doctorow's *Book of Daniel* – a novel about the Rosenbergs (who were executed for treason in the early 1950s anti-commie atmosphere in the US). Written through the eyes of their son Daniel, it is good because it shows how complicated are the various reactions of family and friends to what now seems just a monstrously unfair case. It's full of atmosphere – the Bronx in the 1950s, for instance – and yet another novel which makes me want to go to America. Here I am, nearly 29, and never outside Europe.[1]

Sunday, April 16th

Our sixth wedding anniversary.

We have reached a kind of material plateau at the moment – a house, two cars, two babies. Now we have more time to think about ourselves, and avoid becoming complacent lumps. We go out by ourselves once a week if possible, to a cinema and a meal, and can always go to the country at the weekends if we become really cheesed off. But we're no longer the young savers, or the young home-hunters. We have a lot – the question now is, what are we going to do with it?

I'm fond of Oak Village – with its relative peace from the motor car, and its scale, which enables you to see your neighbours often. Today I sat in the garden and read about rising house prices in the *Sunday Times*. This place is now probably worth £20,000, which is a 70% increase in four years. We are well-off by most people's standards – but we don't really want to move from here, we don't really want a bigger car. Our biggest luxuries are food and drink.

---

1 Rectified two months later, when Terry J and I made our first trip to America for three weeks of sightseeing from New York to New Orleans, the Grand Canyon and San Francisco.

Saturday, April 22nd

Simon Albury turned up unexpectedly in the evening. We've missed his schemes and stories over the last couple of months – but he made a great comeback this evening, firing me once again with great enthusiasm to go to the States. I must say all the omens seem right at the moment. I have the money and the time in the summer, and I only have one year to go until I'm 30 – which, rightly or wrongly, I regard as a psychological turning-point beyond which one can no longer lay claim to youthful enthusiasm. Also Simon will be in New York making three films for *Man Alive* – the BBC programme he now works for. And of course it's convention time in June, when the American election year really starts to hot up. I've always been fascinated by American politics, and I find the idea of attending a convention exciting in itself, as well as giving a point to going to the States.

Thursday, April 27th, Southwold

I lunched on the train to Ipswich. Excellent railway-made steak and kidney pie, washed down with a bottle of Liebfraumilch. The weather began to clear, as I got on to the little diesel train from Ipswich to Darsham, and, by the time it arrived at Darsham at 3.30, the sun was shining on the fresh, clean Suffolk countryside.

My father met me and drove me to Southwold. He seems as slow as usual, but one can't help feeling that he still has a lot of untapped potential for enjoying life. For instance, he had been on a choir outing to see 'The Black and White Minstrel Show' in Norwich, but he and the Vicar left the main party, and went to see *The Go-Between*[1] instead. Ostensibly not the kind of film my father would like at all, but he enjoyed it so much that he wants to see it again. This was very encouraging – and I can't help feeling that, as his old irascibility decreases, and he is forced to take things more slowly, he does enjoy diversion more.

Unfortunately he is still no conversationalist, and, although still interesting and jokey in his own stories, he finds it impossible to follow anyone else's. This is clearly very difficult to live with, and my mother has become sharp and rather quick to reprove him. I can't blame her.

1 Directed by Joseph Losey, script by Harold Pinter. Set in East Anglia, close to Fakenham where my father was born and brought up.

Her mind works so fast and she has for so long lived with someone who shares hardly any of her interests. The sad thing is that both of them suppress each other's potential instead of developing it. My visits are a sort of escape valve for both of them.

Sunday, April 30th

In between showers, I took Thomas and Willy out to the Zoo. The new monkey house is being feverishly finished off in preparation for the Duke of Edinburghal opening on Thursday. It is not completely satisfactory as the glass fronts of the cages tend to reflect the faces of the crowd. Perhaps it's a subtly intended reversal. The gorillas, orang-utans and chimps bask in rather aseptic glory in their new premises. The sea lions were the only animals who really gave us value for our 80p – and the wild boar had new babies, which gave her a bit more box-office appeal. Thomas was most interested in the dead mice in the owls' cages. In fact he seems preoccupied at the moment with dead things. Any animal not actually moving encourages Thomas to ask 'Is it killed?'

Friday, May 5th

Awoke aged 29. It was sad that the early May sunshine had vanished – to be replaced with grey drizzle. I broke my dietary controls on breakfast and ate eggs and bacon and toast.

We drove on to rehearsal at the new BBC Rehearsal Rooms in North Acton. Although in a drably industrial area – with a view from the window as depressing as that from the old London Weekend Rehearsal Rooms in Stonebridge Park – the block is well equipped and still smart. There are all your favourite telly faces Dr Who, John Paul from *Doomwatch*, Harry Worth, etc, etc. For the footballers amongst us, there is a spacious, soft-rubber covered floor, ideal for indoor footy. Eric is going to buy a ball.

Saturday, May 6th, Abbotsley

A quick lunch, and then to Winhills Junior School in St Neots. At 3.00 I had to be one of the judges in the May Queen contest. Helen, her mother, and three parents, Thomas, William and myself sat at a long table in the playground, whilst no less than fifty-seven entrants for the

May Queen competition paraded before us at the top of some steps. It was not a very pleasant experience seeing these 8–11-year-old girls reduced to such nervous wrecks by the combination of the booming PA system and our appraising stares. Also it took a great deal of time, and the wind was now cool and strong. In addition, William kept climbing up the steps towards the girls, and playing to the audience quite appallingly. However, in the end, a girl was selected. Not my particular choice, but she was a bonny, cheerful-looking redhead, with an English-Rose-like honesty about her. It was rather a revelation to be told by a little girl next to me, 'I don't know why you chose 'er – she swears all the time!'

Sunday, May 7th

Got to talking politics with Helen's mother – she is equally shy of arrogant Conservatives and doctrinaire socialists – and she sees the worst of both on her committees.[1] She says how sad it is that party politics mean so much in local government. There are even fewer chances of an independent like herself being elected when the new areas come into force next year.

Thursday, May 25th

The last Python TV recording for at least eighteen months. Our last show contains the 'wee-wee' wine-taster, 'Tudor Jobs' – with a long bit for myself – both sketches which John doesn't like at all, so there is a slight tenseness in the air. It's a very busy last show, with plenty for everyone to do, and only a small amount of film. A fairly smooth day's rehearsal, but it was unusual to see Duncan Wood [Head of Comedy] and Bill Cotton at our final run-through. Apparently they later told Ian that there would have to be cuts in the show. This is the first time they've ever suggested any censorship – in what has been quite an outspoken series. The recording was chequered. Graham was in a very nervous state – he had been worried by his pulse rate, which he said was 108 before the recording – and was drinking as he hasn't done since December and January's recordings, so in one sketch he skidded to a halt, and it was about eight retakes

1 Helen's mother was on the Huntingdon and Cambridgeshire county council as an Independent, specialising in education.

and ten minutes of recording time later that the sketch was eventually completed.

After the show there was hardly time to feel relief or regret, as Python was cleared away for maybe the last time ever. After a drink in the club, we went on to a Python party at the Kalamaris Tavern in Queensway. We crammed into the basement with cameramen, vision mixers, make-up girls, Python people and their hangers-on

Saturday, May 27th

In an attempt to get most of our Python work out of the way before the summer recess at the beginning of June, we worked all yesterday on material for the German show, and this morning there was still no time off, as I had to gather scripts, props, train times, etc for our first foray into mass cabaret – at the Lincoln Pop Festival tomorrow. It is a frustrating business trying to buy simple things like vases to smash. People are so keen to sell you the unbreakable one. I hadn't the heart to tell the man who sold me on the many virtues of plastic flowers – 'they can be cleaned when they get dirty' – that all I wanted them for was to smash them with a wooden mallet.

Sunday, May 28th, Lincoln

Dawned cloudy and grey yet again. But at least the high winds of the past two days have gone. It's still not good weather for open-air pop festivals, and the Sunday papers are full of reports of mud, and tents blowing down and general bad times from Bardney. We took the 10.15 from King's Cross to Lincoln and British Rail did little to dispel the gloom of the morning by keeping the buffet car locked, and not even a cup of coffee available for the whole journey. We read the papers and rehearsed.

At about 4.00 we set out for Bardney, about ten miles east of Lincoln, and the Open-air Pop Festival [the first to be staged in England since the Isle of Wight in 1971].

In many ways this festival is being used as a test case. There is a great deal of opposition from property owners and Tories generally to the festivals – which they see as insanitary occasions catering for insanitary people who want to take all kinds of drugs, fornicate en masse in England's green and pleasant land, and listen to noisy and discordant music. Locals will be terrorised, property laid waste and traditional English rights generally interfered with. So this festival has only been allowed to go on on condition that if there has been unreasonable nuisance caused, its organisers, Stanley Baker[1] and Lord Harlech, are liable to prison sentences.

The first evidence of this mighty gathering, estimated at 50,000 people, was a long traffic jam stretching from the village of Bardney. People later confirmed that the jams were caused by sightseers who had come to 'look at the festival'. Most of the audience clearly couldn't afford cars, and there to prove it was a constant stream of kids walking beside the road making for the site.

The weather had been really bad for the start of the festival, with gales blowing two marquees down on the Friday night. The marquees could not be salvaged as fans had torn them up and used them as protection from the elements. Real Duke of Edinburgh's Award stuff.

It was about 9.15 when we eventually got through the village. As we were supposed to be on at 9.55, and traffic was at a standstill, we walked. Terry especially was becoming most agitated, and in the end we asked a policeman if there was any chance of a police escort or a police car to take us the remaining mile or so up to the site. He managed to get us a lift with two plain-clothes CID officers. The first thing they wanted was our autographs, and then they embarked on as vicious a piece of driving as I've ever seen. Speeding up the side of the column of cars, they drove maliciously hard at the straggling groups of long-haired pedestrians, blaring their horns and giving 'V' signs.

Once at the site we were taken by John Martin, the organiser, to Stanley Baker's caravan to have a drink and last-minute rehearsal. In Baker's caravan there was iced champagne, and Mike Love and Al Jardine of the Beach Boys (who were appearing after us) sitting around. Slade were over-running – we weren't likely to be on until 10.30. I had a second glass of champagne. We seemed to have cleared everyone out of the caravan. Baker looked in occasionally, smiled rather a strained smile, and disappeared into the night.

At last we were called on. It was about 10.45 when we embarked on what was certainly the most spectacular cabaret I've ever done. The whole occasion seemed to be only comprehensible in terms of

1 Rugged Welsh actor who was also a shrewd businessman and founder member, with Lord Harlech (former British ambassador to Washington), of Harlech TV.

comparisons. For instance, here I was doing 'Tide' to 50,000 people, when I first did it nine years ago to about thirty in the Union Cellars at Oxford. Dennis Wilson of the Beach Boys came up to me and shook my hand and congratulated me, when only seven years ago I was packed in the Odeon Hammersmith trying to catch a glimpse of him.

They started with our signature tune, and there was a roar of recognition from the audience. The lights were very bright, so one couldn't really see the audience, and it was difficult to judge the laughs, which came as a distant rumble – like the beginning of an avalanche. There seemed to be more people on the stage behind us than the entire audience we usually get at cabarets. I had the feeling that we had a certain interest above those of the other groups because revue has never really been attempted on this scale before. On either side of the stage were 60 x 40 foot Eidiphor[1] screens with TV pictures of our faces, and the sound was very good. We tried some new material from the third series – and one of the sketches, the Proust competition, lay there. Otherwise the response was pretty good and 'Pet Shop' went tremendously well – with great surges of laughter. At the end we did seem to get a mighty ovation, and there were shouts for more long after John Peel's announcement.

Before we left Bardney, I felt that I really ought to correct my lingering impression of the day as being one big traffic jam, so we went out into the press enclosure to watch the Beach Boys. The stage itself was high above the crowd – the angle of it giving the same sort of impression as the terrace in the Kremlin from which Soviet leaders are always seen saluting. The figures, even from where I was, were tiny, but the huge screens and the sheer power of the sound, made them seem gigantic.

We were driven back to London in a mini-bus, drinking brandy and eating chicken sandwiches, as the first light of dawn appeared over the Hertfordshire hills.

Wednesday, August 2nd

John Gledhill phones with news of the advent of Python in the States. The first commercial manifestation has been the recent release by Buddah Records of our second LP, *Another Monty Python Record*. Already Buddah seem to have scored a minor coup by getting extracts

1 Large-screen television projector devised by Dr Fritz Fischer. Last used in 2000. From the Greek *eido*: image and *phor*: phosphor/light-bearer.

from the LP onto the stereo-sound selection of Pan Am's transatlantic flights. They have also got the 'Spam' song onto *Current*, the first issue of an audio magazine – an LP consisting of interviews with Presley, Manson, Ted Kennedy and other significant Americans. It's only in the experimental stage at the moment, but full marks to Buddah. I think that the curiosity value of this strange LP – coming out of nowhere – might work well for it in the States.

Thursday, August 3rd

My new black Mini was delivered this morning. Don Salvage, who personally brought the car round, has such an unfortunate manner about him when describing the car that I almost assumed it must have been stolen. Especially as when I rang him about buying a Mini automatic, he first of all told me it would take at least three to six months. Then next day he rang to say he could find one immediately.

Monday, August 7th

Visited Mr Powell's surgery at 10.45 for a session with the hygienist. She turned out to be the girl who had been Mr Powell's nurse during my early batch of gingivectomies, so she must have known my mouth as intimately as only a dentist can. I was given a short, but severe introductory talk about the generally poor state of hygiene in my mouth – and the dangers it presented – whilst at the same time being given the sop that I cleaned my teeth 99% more thoroughly than the rest of the filthy British public. But this wasn't enough, as a vivid red mouthwash indicated. It contained some ingredient which showed red wherever there was a bacteria-carrying layer on my teeth. She rubbed my face in it by showing me the offending red patches in a mirror – complete with epicene red lips. I was cleaned up and given two toothbrushes, a reel of dental floss, and red tablets to show whether my cleaning was getting better. Left at 11.30 feeling quite inspired, and determined to fight this battle for dental survival, against all odds.

Saturday, August 12th, Southwold

Sun shone in the morning and tempted us down to the beach. We took the windbreak and an axe, which is Grandfather's traditional instrument for knocking the windbreak into the sand. It may save him money on a mallet, but one does feel rather sinister taking a wife, two small children and an axe down to the beach.

Sunday, August 20th

Mid-morning, Bill Oddie rang to know if I would like a lift to Clapton for another Monty Python XI fixture. The pretence of the Monty Python XI becomes more and more flimsy – in this match we are only represented by Terry and myself. On the way to the ground, Bill tells me how he and the other two 'Goodies' switched on the lights at Morecambe (a quite considerable showbiz accolade). Bill was unashamedly delighted by the fan-worship – especially the drive in an open car along Morecambe front. It's interesting that no one in Python – even John in one of his most philanthropic moods – would ever have agreed to switch on the lights at Morecambe.

At Clapton Orient (once a league team) there was a 2,000 crowd, mainly of young kids. Our XI consisted of Terry, myself and Bill from TV plus Frank Lampard and Harry Cripps (both West Ham professionals) and a Millwall player. Jimmy Hill[1] led the opposition.

Sunday, September 3rd

Today I was to play cricket for the first time for about twelve years, in a village match organised by Alan Hutchison, John [Cleese]'s ex-Reuters friend. Drove Tim Brooke-Taylor and John down to Bordon in Hampshire, about one and three-quarter hours from London. My romantic image of village cricket was punctured slightly when we arrived. There was no rough and tufty village green, surrounded by neat cottages and a welcoming pub. Bordon is an army village, and we had to drive through the camp to get to the ground.

We found ourselves beside a remarkably professional-looking pitch – almost a Test Match wicket. The opposition, Blackmoor Village, were mostly young men in their twenties and early thirties, and looked to have most of the benefits of regular practice. There was no pub, but a pavilion (I think reserved for the officers), which served drinks all

1 Footballer (Brentford, Fulham), administrator (credited with invention of 3 points for a win system) and panellist (*Match of the Day*).

afternoon. Our side, plus hangers on, was clearly Oxbridge-based – there were elegant, sharp-featured, well-kept ladies, and clean-cut, straight-backed men.

We fielded first, and their first wicket pair put on about 80 before we got one of them out. Fielding, once one has got over the stark fear of a very heavy little ball travelling straight towards one, can be a most relaxing business. I bowled an over with two wides, two very good length balls, one of which was hit hard at me, and I made the mistake of pretending to catch it. The ball hit me hard on the little finger, on its way towards the boundary, but I prevented a run because, as the ball hit my finger, it dislodged a flesh-coloured piece of plaster, which fell to the ground, rooting the batsman to his crease in horror.

Tim bowled two overs, which were both very silly – on occasional balls John would run in front of him up to the wicket, then peel off just before Tim bowled. One of the Blackmoor team was out to a blatant throw – but they had us by the short and curlies anyway – so they accepted the comedy with good grace.

Enjoyed seeing Tim again – and it is refreshing to talk to someone of our age and background, outside the Python group. Tim will take on almost any work, and seems untroubled by the search for quality. This means he gets less frustrated, and more money, than we do.

Monday, September 4th

Python reassembled at Terry's after three months off. Everyone seemed happy to be starting again. Eric had had a recurrence of his liver trouble, and was not drinking, and Graham was one and a half hours late.

A cautionary visit from John Gledhill in the late afternoon. He brought us the latest figures for the film – which most of us had been conditioned into thinking was one of the box-office successes of the year. But up to about five months of its release, the net take (after Columbia had creamed off their share) was only $227,000. We do not start to make a penny until it has passed $500,000 and even if it took $1 million, we would still only stand to make £2,000 each. So the film, which John G reckoned had made us into world stars, has still only brought us £1,000 each. This had an amazing effect on the Python group. Suddenly everyone wanted to work. Within half an hour we had agreed on a third LP for the Christmas market, another book for next year, and a film script as soon as possible. No talk of holidays this time.

Thursday, September 14th

A week of great activity. In five days we have assembled a third Python LP to be in the shops for Christmas. Over half the 50–60 minutes' worth of material is new, and, unlike the second LP, everyone has contributed to the writing. Among the new ideas for the record were a 'B' side consisting of four concentric tracks, all starting at different places on the first groove, so that the listener could get any one of four different versions of the 'B' side; also there was an idea for an extra large record cover, two foot square; a 'free' 'Teach Yourself Heath' record included in the LP, which would use actual Heath speeches to analyse his voice, and teach people the best way of reproducing it. The title we settled on was 'A Previous Monty Python Record'.

We met for lunch and a final read-through of material and, at 5.30, André,[1] the engineer who is doing our new LP, came round and we spent a couple of hours going through the script for sound effects and music cues. Fred Tomlinson and his singers[2] and Neil Innes, ex of the Bonzos, had to be contacted about music – but by 8.00 last night the material was in typeable shape and ready to be sent off to John Gledhill.

I took half an hour off for a run on the Heath – a last futile attempt to prepare my system for the onslaught of German hospitality – and then took Helen out for a meal. She had worked hard looking after six writers and two children during the day, as well as ironing and sorting out my clothes for three weeks in Munich.[3] We ate at Abbots in Blenheim Place, St John's Wood – a small restaurant with a large and interesting menu (red mullet, pigeon, etc), but full of a party of visiting American businessmen, and English people on a 'smart' night out. But it did us both good to leave the house for a while, and made it a very happy last evening.

1 André Jacquemin had engineered several sessions with me, going back to 1966. His committed, efficient, no-nonsense skills impressed me and he became Python's engineer of choice.
2 The Fred Tomlinson singers had played, among other things, the original Mounties in 'Lumberjack Song' and the original Vikings singing 'Spam! Wonderful Spam!'
3 Where we were to be based for the second of two Python specials made for Bavarian TV.

Friday, September 15th, Munich

Apart from Graham feeling a little sorry for himself, the six Pythons all seemed on good form on the plane. At the airport we were thoroughly frisked for weapons and the plane had to delay take-off for half an hour whilst the baggage was searched. All these extra precautions were a result of the shootings of the Israeli athletes and the Palestinian guerrillas at the Munich Olympics last week.

As we expected, this year was more businesslike – we spent the afternoon in costume fittings, and it wasn't until the evening that we had time to relax. Alfred [Biolek, our German producer] and Ian had fallen out for some reason, which is not a good start, and Ian and Eke[1] didn't join us for a meal. After the meal, the inevitable Why Not? Club [well-known from our previous Munich filming]. It had been enlarged and repainted, and we were treated to some classic examples of the Why Not's 'see and be seen' philosophy.

Edith, the proprietress, looking even more like a model out of a very high-class shop window, was soon working hard to mix a powerful concoction of celebrities. After a while the words 'Swiss fashion photographer', 'model from Berlin', 'Austrian TV writer', all sounded the same, as the music of Gilbert O'Sullivan blasted out, and one mouthed greetings to shadowy faces in the gloom. Highlight of the evening was when Alfred appeared at my side, in a state of high excitement, to announce that Christine Kaufmann, Germany's leading actress, and ex-wife of Tony Curtis, was not only here tonight, but, and here Alfred became almost uncontrollable, she *loved* Monty Python!! Soon she was brought to our table, and the meeting of the greats took place. She wore her black hair long and unstyled, wore a simple dress, and her face was thin, fine-boned and un-made-up. I liked her at once, but conversation was made doubly difficult by the music, and by her boyfriend, a German disc-jockey, who chattered about the wonders of Python without even a break for commercials. He was clearly the kind of person who was used to being listened to, rather than listening, had an annoying habit of referring to Python as being very popular with 'all the intellectuals'.

After their whirlwind visit, their places were taken by yet another model – this time a real head-turner, with carefully arranged red hair,

---

1 Eke Ott was the sister of Max, who designed the German shows. Ian MacNaughton fell in love with her and she became his second wife.

a rich suntan, and a thin cotton shirt unbuttoned to the waist. Apparently, Thomas[1] assured me, she had been in *Playboy* magazine. I drank the last remains of my white wine. Miss Playboy's photographer escort, meanwhile, had ordered a magnum of Calvados.

Outside it was 1.30 and raining. I walked home with John – wet, shabby, tired, but still just celebrities.

Wednesday, September 20th, Hohenschwangau

Filming in Neuschwanstein Castle. A clear and sunny day. In the distance the sun picks out the snow on the mountains of the Austrian Alps. It's a perfect day for throwing a dummy of John Cleese from the 100ft tower of the castle to the courtyard below. The tourists watch with great interest – an English couple and their young brother-in-law can't believe their luck that they've found Python in Germany. We finish filming by 11.00 and now have a break until 6.00 for we are night-shooting inside the castle. (Apparently we are lucky to have received permission – for the last crew to film here was Visconti's film of King Ludwig, and apparently they had messed the place up a bit, and urinated in the fine Wagnerian interiors, and were generally unlikely to be asked back.)

I was playing Prince Walter, described in the script as 'rather thin and weedy with a long pointed nose, spots, and nasty unpolished plywood teeth'. The make-up man, George, made a superb job of personifying this creature. My own hair was laboriously curled with hot tongs into a silly little fringe, which made me look like an underfed Henry V, and it took almost two hours before I was ready with my long turned-up nose and spots, to leave the Hotel Müller and be driven up to the castle.

A perfect Gothic horror evening – a cool breeze, and a full moon, glimpsed through the trees and occasionally blotted out by scudding clouds. As we drove through the silent and deserted stone archways of the castle, there was but a single light shining high in the dark walls. Ludicrously clad, wearing a silly false nose and carrying a crate of beer for the unit's supper, I was led through echoing passages and through stone-vaulted halls towards the filming.

---

2 Thomas Woitkewitsch, translator of the Python German shows.

Thursday, September 21st, Hohenschwangau

Another fine, sunny day. Into Prince Walter outfit. Sat around outside the hotel thus attired, read Raymond Chandler, wrote postcards and confused the tourists – who start to appear in droves at about 11.30, are everywhere like insects, and like them, disappear in the cool of the evening. Filmed beside a lake. Eric played his guitar, the crate of beer was kept warm in the water of the lake, and Connie Cleese raped me (on film). What more could a man want of the day?

Friday, September 29th, Munich

Only last night did I learn for certain that today we were to do the most complicated sketch of all – the 'Hearing-Aid' sketch – an old *1948 Show* sketch in which I was given joint billing with John. We could only use the shop to do it in after 8.00, so it was a most uneven and awkward day. As we rehearsed Ian took a phone call from his P.A. in England. She had received a note from Duncan Wood in which he ordered another round of cuts in the current *Python* series.

Terry J sees it as part of a plot to keep the BBC out of any major controversies until the charter has been renewed in 1974. Ian MacNaughton feels that he will be out soon anyway, as the LE bosses hardly talk to him now, and he is prepared to fight with us against this decision. Maybe we cannot win, but I feel it is as important as anything not to lie down and accept this censorship. John C, for the record, wants to avoid any confrontation with Bill Cotton and Duncan Wood, he wants a chat over dinner, and a bit of gentle bargaining.

Thomas came in later on in the rehearsal and added to our increasing feeling of paranoia by telling us that Hans Gottchild, the enormous, Hemingway-bearded head of Bavaria TV had been most displeased with the Python rushes, calling them 'dilettante'.

By the time we had filmed as coal miners at the full-scale model of a coalface in the Deutsches Museum, I felt quite exhausted. All I wanted was a sleep, and all I was going to get was an under-rehearsed, complicated five-hour sketch.

As it turned out the evening was not too bad. We worked in long takes, which required great concentration, but made the whole process seem faster. It was about 10.45 that John and I ended the sketch by hurling ourselves out of a very expensive Munich optician's, on to a pile of rugs and cushions.

Saturday, September 30th, Munich

Caught an S-Bahn train to Starnberg, where we are all expected for food and drink at Eke's father's lakeside house.

John C was there, myself, Eric, Terry G, Graham, Roger Last,[1] Terry and Alison. Everyone was in mellow, gentle moods – perhaps just suffering from tiredness. There were no confrontations, explosions, truth games or any other games. Eke had cooked bean soup and delicious pork and garlic, and we mostly sat in the kitchen swapping stories and drinking wine.

Arrived back at the hotel about 12.45, dog-tired, to find that I had been moved out of my room as two time-honoured guests had arrived late in the evening. I was greeted by the manageress and her effusive assistant, who were both a little worried about my reaction – especially as they had done all the moving. I wasn't unduly concerned where I slept, so they must have been quite relieved at my reaction, but then I found that I had been quartered, not in a separate room, but in a small bed in John Cleese's room. This did niggle me, partly because John's room smelt of stale cigarette smoke, and I was feeling quite fragile in the abdominal area, and also because of the attitude of the lady who had arrived for my room. There was no word of apology – she was merely concerned to let me know what an inconvenient day she'd had. I went to bed ruffled. John arrived in a mellow mood about 1.15 and offered me brandy. I remember reacting to this with a slight feeling of nausea.

Sunday, October 1st

Woke at 7.00. Splitting stomach ache, violent diarrhoea. I would have to be in John's room. Tried to make diarrhoea as quiet as possible. Only the evening before we had been laughing over the fantasy of a 'Hotel Noisy', where a high standard of noise was maintained throughout, and here I was, up at sparrow's fart, rocking John's lavatory. John sportingly maintained he heard nothing.

1 Python production assistant. A lovely, soft-spoken man with an interest in Norfolk churches. When we filmed a football match between a team of gynaecologists and Long John Silver impersonators, Roger was the one whom Graham persuaded, in the interests of medical authenticity, to go out and buy eleven vaginal speculums.

Monday, October 2nd

Arrived back after rushes at about 7.45. There was a call waiting for Terry from Midhurst – it was Nigel[1] to say that their mother had been taken to hospital. Terry was immediately on to BEA to book a plane back to England. He was in a rush and a hurry, but seemed to be in control. Al came upstairs and broke down and cried for just a moment – there was no flight back to London tonight from anywhere in Germany.

Thomas [Woitkewitsch] was fortunately here to help, and he started to ring charter flights and private air-hire firms. The irony of the situation was that we had all been invited to Alfred's to watch an Anglo-Dutch comedy show which Thomas had produced. As Terry phoned Chichester Hospital from Alfred's bedroom, the strident shouts from the telly grew louder and more disconcerting. I sat and talked to Graham in the neutral room. He had spoken to the ward sister and she had told both Graham and Terry that her chances of recovery were minimal. Graham argued clearly and reasonably, and yet still sympathetically, that it was not worth Terry's while trying to charter a plane to London in order to see his unconscious mother.

It was about 10.00 when I saw Terry in his room. He was sitting in a wicker chair, he seemed composed, reflective and rather distant. I clasped him around the shoulders. He said he was happy just to 'sit and think about her'. Graham and I left, and went next door to the Klosterl, for a meal with Alfred, Thomas and Justus [our cameraman]. Not a great meal. Back to the hotel at about 11.30.

A note from Al was stuck in my door. 'Terry's mother died at 9.20. He has gone to sleep with the aid of a sleeping pill.'

For a moment I felt a strange stifling surge of sadness. My eyes welled with tears and for a few moments the news hit me really hard.[2]

Wednesday, October 4th, Munich

In the hotel I was waylaid by Madame, offering me a bottle of brandy as recompense for being thrown out of my room last Saturday. I didn't

1 Terry Jones' elder brother. A journalist.
2 I had got to know Terry's mum well in the days when I visited the family home in Claygate, Surrey. She was an endearing lady and we were very fond of each other. Some of Terry's drag roles on Python were uncannily like her, though absolutely *not* Mandy in *The Life of Brian*.

accept it, but did drink a couple of schnapps with her, and listened to her problems – which seem infinite, ranging from lack of sleep to lack of guests. She seems an unhappy lady intent on making herself more unhappy.

Little time for a bath and a dollop of Yardley's Black Label Talc, before being collected by my driver for the last time, and taken to the end-of-filming party at the Alter Wirt Gasthaus in Grunwald. He was in a sharp suit and seemed to be positively sparkling with anticipated pleasure.

NB: An important clue to the somewhat enigmatic character, whose driving has so often filled me with fear – he and his wife perform in blue films. Felt less afraid of him when I heard this.

Thursday, October 5th, Munich

A clear, crisp, cold clinical day. Paid my £40 phone bill. The lady at the hotel shared with Monika[1] this impression of distant suffering – both had an air of melancholy about them. I wonder if this is to do with the German past. Ostensibly, and materially, more people in Germany seem to enjoy better conditions than in England – the economic recovery from the war has been massively successful. I should imagine that the psychological scars must run deeper.

Must read more German novels – for here if anywhere is a chance to try and prove Solzhenitsyn's point that art and literature are the only spiritual ambassadors between countries. Will re-read Gunter Grass's *Tin Drum.*

Flew back to London with John and Eric. John is a good travelling companion in so far as he is nearly always recognised by stewards and stewardesses who pamper him blatantly; and Eric and I were able to catch a little of this reflected blandishment.

Monday, October 9th

Today I am about to earn £850. This is more than Helen earned in a whole year as a professional teacher.

For this £850 I am required to perform two 15-second commercials for Hunky Chunks. The make-up is poor, the studios of TV

1 Our German wardrobe mistress.

International in Whitfield Street are shabby – so why this money? Well firstly because Quaker Oats, the client, make so much profit from selling their foods that they can afford to throw away £850, and secondly because the bait has to be very tempting to make self-respecting human beings, let alone actors, talk about 'The moist, meaty dog-food that contains more concentrated nourishment than canned dog-food.'

So I sold my soul for £850, and was made to squirm for it. The first ad was done outside in the street with me, a crate of dog-food and a camera. Who should come along as I was recording, but David Jason who lives nearby. He and John Cleese (who was working on the same Hunky Chunks series) hid in a doorway and peered out at me in the middle of a take.

Sunday, October 15th

Thomas and I and William returned from a walk on the Heath to find hordes of policemen in about half a dozen assorted vehicles, milling around Richard and Christine's house on the corner of Oak Village. In the middle of the blue helmets was Helen, obviously the centre of some attention. For an awful moment I thought that she was being arrested – an unimaginable irony in view of her obsessionally law-abiding behaviour. However, it turned out that Helen had been alerted by Muriel of the house opposite to a man climbing over the wall of the Guedallas' with a colour TV set *and* stand. It gradually dawned on Helen that the Guedallas were away and also that TV repair men didn't work on Sundays, and anyway they usually tried the front door first before climbing over the back garden wall.

So Helen and Muriel's husband Bob went looking for this character, and took themselves by surprise when they rounded a corner and literally bumped into him. Helen – quite courageously, considering he had an Alsatian dog with him – asked him what he was doing in the Guedallas' house. Declining explanations, he made a run for it and Helen, *not* Bob, made a grab for him. He easily pushed her away and ran off. Bob shouted valiantly after him, 'We've got your identification.' And he was gone.

Helen had already rung the police. They soon descended in droves – local fuzz and Scotland Yard. The unfortunate telly-snatcher didn't stand a chance. He was picked up almost immediately and so were the

TV and the stand. Helen was quite the local hero, and very pleased with herself.

Saturday, October 21st

Dinner across the road with the recently moved-in neighbours, Rod and Ann. Ann (we found out) is the sister of John Sergeant, who was in revue at Oxford two years after me, and with whom I once did some sketch writing about four or five years ago. He acted in the Alan Bennett series *On the Margin* as Bennett's straight man[1] and then left comedy for news – worked at Reuters and now with the BBC as a sound reporter.

Tonight we were reunited. We spent a very enjoyable evening, and I was especially interested in his stories of reporting from Vietnam and Belfast. Vietnam is badly beaten up, but not such a totally flattened country as people make out – the on-the-spot action news film, which the American networks put out as reports from the battlefield, are all taken by South Vietnamese cameramen. In Ireland everyone reads the papers avidly. The IRA leaders are available at all times to talk to newsmen if you know the right number to ring. John was hijacked in his car once by an IRA man who threatened to blow his brains out if he tried to resist.

Monday, October 23rd

At 8.00 I went out to a Gospel Oak meeting. There are quite a number of consultative meetings held in and around Oak Village, as the whole area is being subjected to such massive redevelopment. In 1951 the first redevelopment in Gospel Oak was Barrington Court – by Powell and Moya. It's a long, ten-storey block, but is as good as many present-day functional designs, and better than most. The West Kentish Town development followed in the 1950s – it's not picturesque, but it is low-rise and friendly.

Then a progressive deterioration of architectural standards, which reached its nadir in the appalling block which borders Mansfield Road and is known locally as the Barracks. It is without charm,

---

1 I auditioned for this series myself, but John was judged to be funnier and got the job. Quite rightly. He later, of course, became ITN's political correspondent.

without style, without any beauty whatsoever – it is essentially a mathematical achievement, a result of juggling a lot of people with a little money, stymied as the Camden planners are now by the general abandonment of high-rise blocks.

Some of the new occupants were at the St Martin's Church Hall tonight to hear proposals for Lismore Circus renovation and for the next part of the Gospel Oak scheme.

The meeting was entirely staffed by stereotypes. If one had written a play with these characters in it would have been called facile and uninventive. Mr and Mrs Brick of Kiln Place – a physically formidable pair and both with plenty to say forcibly and clearly. The populist vicar, who couldn't resist occasional semantic jokes; the hard-line Marxist, in a nondescript coat but with a fine, strong, lean face, worn hard and lined in struggles for the proletariat. The woolly-headed liberals, the gentle, embarrassed architect, and even the local hippy, a squatter who berated the platform from the back of the room for being cynical and hypocritical in even having this meeting at all.

Notes that stuck in my mind – a small Andy Capp-like figure telling the platform with a feeling of frustrated sadness, 'Living round here is bloody terrible.' The soft-voiced, inoffensive, architect taking on the wrath of the gathering as well as its repartee. He was talking of how, even when the builders were working, 'Lismore Circus retained its trees, its flowers, even squirrels ...'- 'and rats' came a voice from the audience. The lack of enthusiasm for the plans from the audience was understandable, but very, very sad. For here was an enlightened borough, with a good and humane record, selling something that people didn't want in the most democratic way possible.

Friday, October 27th

An eventful day. Began with a Python meeting at John's to discuss future long-term plans. An interesting thing happened. I had originally told Charisma that we did not want individual writing credits for the two sides of the single ('Eric the Half-Bee' by Eric and John and 'Yangtse Song' by myself and Terry) on the grounds that Python had never before singled out writers' specific contributions. But Eric had told Jim that he wanted his name on the single. So this was the first awkward point that I brought up with John and Eric this morning. Predictably Eric bristled, but with a bitterness that I didn't expect. He wanted his name on the record because he was going to write more songs and this would help him. He lashed out bitterly at what he thought was merely a weak-kneed way of protecting Graham. John, however, agreed with me – that the principle of Python's 'collective responsibility' was more important. Eric went quiet, John went out to make coffee. I felt bad vibrations and tried to think of a compromise. But as suddenly as the storm broke it was over. Eric apologised, said I was absolutely right and that he was being stupid about it – but all this came out in such a way that I felt a warm flood of friendship as well as considerable relief.

After the meeting we all drove over to the BBC to see Duncan Wood and discuss the cuts he proposed in our new series. These cuts involved the excision of whole sketches about a French wine-taster who serves his clients only wee-wee, and an awful City cocktail bar where upper-class twits ask for strange cocktails – one of which, a mallard fizz, involves cutting the head off a live duck. Other cuts included the word 'masturbating' (a contestant in a quiz game gives his hobbies as 'golf, strangling animals and masturbating'), the phrase 'I'm getting pissed tonight' and most of two sketches, one about a Dirty Vicar and the other about the Oscar Wilde Café Royal set, who run short of repartee and at one point liken King Edward VII to a stream of bat's piss. But we were protesting mainly about the volume of the cuts, not particular instances – tho' Terry crusaded violently on behalf of masturbating, launching off at a Kinseyian tangent about the benefits of masturbation. 'I masturbate, you masturbate, we all masturbate!' he enthused. Duncan crossed his legs and pulled hard on his cigarette. Our point was basically why, if we are going out at 10.15 – well after children and family peak viewing – are we suddenly being so heavily censored?

Duncan Wood at first protested that we weren't being heavily censored, that four cuts in the first nine shows wasn't bad (I must say in the first of the series we got away with the line from a judge, 'Screw the Bible, I've got a gay lib meeting at 6.00,' which certainly couldn't be spoken on any other TV service in the world). So he has clearly relented over certain of the cuts he wanted Ian to make. He promised to review Shows 12 and 13 again, with us, so that we could all see what we were talking about.

After the sting had been taken out of the meeting we got to talking about censorship generally – and why the BBC seemed to be suddenly more frightened of causing offence. Genial Duncan chain-smoked and talked in a vague and roundabout way of 'pressures from outside' causing a temporary tighten-up in censorship. Who and what these pressures were was never revealed. There seemed no evidence that there was popular support for BBC censorship – quite the opposite – the most outspoken of BBC progs, *Till Death Us Do Part*, has an audience of nearly 20 million, and Python itself has higher viewing figures than ever (round about 10 million for the first show of the latest series). Duncan was either stalling or genuinely didn't know, but there was a sinister 'I am only obeying orders' tone to his whole attitude.

We parted amicably – he was happy because he had said nothing and got away with it – as Eric said it was like arguing with a piece of wet cod.

Saturday, November 4th

I travel down on the 24 bus – I really prefer public transport these days: it's more restful, cheaper and wonderful entertainment along the way. Bonuses like an early-morning walk through Soho – one of the areas London ought to be proud of for the quality and quantity of its delights. It is, for instance, a much more honest place of enjoyment than Mayfair, with its Rolls-Royces, expensive shops, poor and snobbish restaurants and red lights. This Saturday morning Soho Square was free of cars, people were washing down the pavements outside their restaurants, there was a quiet and leisurely feeling of waking up, and I felt very happy to be in London.

Spent three hours with André, editing and tightening the B side of the new album until it was in a very strong and satisfying shape, then, with Terry and André, walked across Regent Street and into Savile Row, where the Apple Studios are situated in a well-preserved row of Georgian town houses. They seem to be the only place that has the technology to cut our multiple B side.

Down the stairs to the basement. Into a foyer with heavy carpets, two soft sofas and felt covered walls, all in a rather dark, restful plum colour. A big glass-topped coffee table, designed for only the best coffee table books, was littered with copies of the *Daily Mirror*. A flamboyant stainless steel strip was sunk into one wall. Immediate impression on entering the cutting room of being in a Harley Street dentist's consulting room.

At one point, about 7.00, I had just come back into the studios after having a drink when a slight, thin figure walked towards me. The face was familiar, but, before I could register anything, a look of recognition crossed George Harrison's face, and he shook my hand, and went into a paean of praise for Monty Python – with the same exaggerated enthusiasm that I would have lavished on the Beatles had I met them five years ago. He said he couldn't wait to see Python on 35mm, big screen.

Finally left Apple about 8.00 – the cutter, John, promised to have more attempts at the cut over the weekend, but the chances of producing this highly original B side don't seem too rosy.

Tuesday, November 7th

Heard during the afternoon that Apple were unable to cut the three-track B side. Terry took the tapes round to EMI for them to have a go, so we can only cross our fingers. Tonight is American election night, and I invited Simon Albury and his brother Robert round to hear the results and watch the telly special from 12 till 2.00.

Sadly McGovern got wiped out, almost totally, carrying the District of Columbia's three electoral votes, and Massachusetts – who probably voted because of Kennedy anyway. He has been dogged by misfortune in his campaign – mainly the Eagleton affair, but also because Nixon played a crafty, quiet campaign. It was not until this last week that people have really begun to lay into Nixon's record – he was somehow let off the hook by the press, not because they praised, but because they failed to criticise him until too late.

To bed about 2.45.

Wednesday, November 8th

At last an, as yet, uninterrupted day's writing ahead of me, a luxury which hasn't happened for a long time. Thomas leaves for his playgroup at 9.55. Helen takes William out to the shops. All is quiet for a bit – the sun shines in onto my desk, and I feel all's well with the world. But the phone soon starts ringing – EMI cannot do the cut, what shall we do?

Almost an hour is spent ringing round the Pythons to get them to a meeting on Thursday to listen to the record. We decide to cut the B side in mono, which apparently will allow the three-track cut to work. So Apple now have the job again.

Looked at a book of Yoga exercises.

Friday, November 10th

In the evening a pleasant meal with Robert [Hewison]. Delicious beef olives cooked by the maestro. As usual I was impressed and injected with academic enthusiasm by the neat order of Robert's little flat – with its shelfful of Goncourt journals in French, the latest books on Coleridge – of course his great Ruskin collection (Robert is now a B.Litt.).

Monday, November 20th

Arrived back in London after a long weekend in Southwold with Helen, Thomas and William.

Brought two family portraits back home – one of my great-grand-father, Edward Palin, Vicar of Linton, drawn almost a hundred years ago, I guess – a fine looking man – and the other of his wife Brita née Gallagher – she by contrast looks hunched and rather wizened. I should imagine that was drawn nearer the turn of the century. Amazing to think that I have physical genetic links with these remote figures.

I had this wrong. The older lady was not Brita, my great-grandmother, but Caroline Watson, a rich American lady who had adopted Brita when she arrived on a coffin ship in New York in the 1840s, an orphan from the Irish potato famine. I was to discover fuller details from a cousin of my father's (entry for September 30th 1977). It was such a remarkable story that in 1990 Tristram Powell and I made it into a film called American Friends.

Wednesday, November 22nd

Success with Mark Shivas!

Terry and I talked our way into a commission for an hour-long 'Black and Blue' play – with an improvised verbal synopsis which he appeared to be quite pleased with. It required quite a gamble on his part, and we both felt greatly encouraged by his confidence.

Impressed by his modesty and the almost Spartan simplicity of his office. As producer of the highly successful *Six Wives of Henry VIII* series, he must be one of the most sought-after producers in TV and yet he remains in an anonymous, nondescript, austere office in TV Centre. Such are the artistic attractions of working for an organisation such as the Beeb that they tend to cancel out other *dis*-advantages. After seeing Shivas, we visited Ian MacNaughty and then Terry Hughes to whom we delivered a *Two Ronnies* script. Ian MacN – with Eke always at his side like a prowling lion to encourage, goad, solace, and generally keep him healthy – was in his office, but he didn't know for how long. He wants to go freelance next spring, presumably to do another Python film, for we have never made it clear we will be directing it ourselves.

I think perhaps we should now come clean and let him know that there is not much more work for him with Python. He is a much happier man now than he used to be. So any final break will be that bit more difficult.

Monday, December 4th

A very successful Python meeting at John's. Everyone was remarkably direct about future plans and there was a remarkable freedom of pressure on anyone to fit in with others' plans. The basic factor in the future life of Python is that John has had enough of Python TV shows – he doesn't enjoy writing or performing them – the thought of doing any more makes his stomach tighten, so he said. He is the oldest of us, he has done more TV than any of us, and had done twenty-six *Frost Reports* before any of us really started performing. So he's ahead of us in the disillusionment stakes – tho' I cannot agree with him at all about the drudgery of doing TV shows. I find them hard, but exhilarating experiences and I'm still at the stage of appreciating how fantastically lucky I am to have the opportunity to write and perform my own material, on TV, almost free of restrictions. Still, John does not share this view – and will not commit himself to any more Python work after the film next summer.

The next major factor was that Eric and Graham especially were concerned about making some money next year – so far, making a film is the least lucrative thing we've done. To solve this we decided to try and fix up a two- or three-week university tour in April, on the lines of our successful Coventry Festival show a couple of years ago.

Later in the evening, Eric rang me up – still a little worried about where work, therefore loot, was to come from in the next year. I had mentioned my keenness to do some more TV next Christmas and Eric was ringing to lend support to this. Has today seen the first seeds of a new post-Python TV series, without John and possibly without Graham, or will we, as I forecast, find ourselves all together again next December?

It rained all day. I gave up [John Barth's] *The Sot-Weed Factor* on page 440 and started to read Laurie Lee's *Cider with Rosie*, by the fire.

Tuesday, December 5th

Drove to Harrods to see around their own chocolate factory – the first breakthrough in our protracted attempts to gain some first-hand experience of a chocolate factory for our 'Black and Blue' script. Harrods was like an ocean liner in the dark, rainy, wild evening. A Mr Jackson from the confectionery department, white-haired, but probably no more than 50, with a knowing smile and a rather self-deprecating manner, took us into Harrods underground travel network via a Colditz-style entrance behind the butchery department. We walked under Knightsbridge, feeling even more as tho' we were in an ocean liner – only this time in the engine room.

The chocolate factory was small and personal. None of the machines was enormous, and the whole process seemed to be on a human scale. We saw Harrods exclusive after-dinner mints being stuffed into their little bags by middle-aged working-class ladies; presumably to be elegantly extracted by rich and well-perfumed hands in some Kensington salon. Also I was amused to see how the delicate marking was placed on top of each Harrods 'Opera' chocolate. A matronly cockney lady dipped into the liquid chocolate mixture and inscribed these magnificent chocolates with a deft flick of her nose-picking finger. This was the 'hand' in the 'hand-marked' chocolates.

Thursday, December 7th

In the morning I worked up at home, writing on a little further with the 'Black and Blue' script. Terry was returning this morning from Liverpool, where he had been chairing a meeting about 'cooking and cholesterol', so I was on my own.

At 12.30 arrived at TV Centre to see a playback of our controversial Shows 12 and 13, which Duncan Wood and Bill Cotton have told us must be amalgamated into one, on the grounds of their (to them) offensive tastelessness. Today was our last chance to change this decision, for rather than accept their judgement and trim the shows, we had asked at least if we could see again what we were being accused of, and we had asked that Paul Fox might view the shows as well.

This he was doing in an upper room of the BBC at the same time as we were seeing them in a lower room. Both shows had generally scatological themes, but in nearly every case the naughty material was hardly worth making a fuss about, and most of it was less questionable than some of the material in the first two series (viz. the mother-eating sketch). Neither show was our best, but I certainly could see no earthly reason for combining the two and wasting an entire show.

That evening I was very glad to hear from Ian that Fox had felt this way too, and had insisted on far fewer cuts than Wood and Cotton – which goes to prove that either prurience or cowardice, or a mixture of both, are important factors in LE's official judgement. This was the first time we have ever divided the BBC hierarchy – and the appeal to Fox has this time come out to our advantage. I shall be able to approach him in a new light at the BBC LE binge in a couple of weeks.

Tuesday, December 12th

Terry and I are now well into a writing routine and we're making solid progress.

Rosemary rang from the BBC to say they had received a can of real Devon cream addressed to Mr Pither[1] from a dairy in Bovey Tracey!

Drove home via the BBC to collect my cream – it contained a note from the owner of the dairy thanking us for the free publicity for Bovey Tracey in the 'Pither' show, correcting our pronunciation from Bôvey to Burvey Tracey and ending up 'I think you are all mad'.

Sunday, December 17th

Woke up feeling very depressed. I faced yet another Sunday spent working on the script – and I've had hardly any time at home for about two weeks. The Atticus article on Python in the *Sunday Times* transformed depression into mute despair. A terrible photo, and a worthless column, written in pseudo-joke style – all I dreaded – and, what's worse,

---

1 Reg Pither was the bobble-hatted cyclist on a tour of the West Country whom I played in the 'Cycling Tour' episode of Python.

wrongly attributing nearly all the quotes – and I was unlucky enough to be given Graham's! Thus, the remarks I felt least necessary when we gave the interview – like 'Where is John Cleese, anyway?' and 'Make sure you say that John Cleese is the middle-aged one'- were faithfully reported as spoken by me! Also my name at the beginning was spelt Pallin.

Drove down to Terry's to work; he didn't seem to be particularly worried by the article. Graham rang during the morning. Helen told him I was upset, which I don't think I'd have bothered to do. He and I rang John – John appeared to think it was quite humorous.

Arrived about 10.00 at the BBC party – which is very much an establishment affair, and Python have always regarded it with some suspicion. However, with the notable exception of John, Eric and Terry G, we decided to go along this year. In fact Terry was even wearing his black tie. General feeling of warmth and well-being about this year's binge – the food was more imaginative too with ambitious failures like moussaka. Graham C was stalking through the throng, heavily dosed with drink – presumably to cope with the evening – he was wearing a Bill Oddie T-shirt, spelt Bill Addie, and John Tomiczek[1] was wearing one spelt Bill Oddle (sic). 'Who would you like me to insult?' Graham asked unsteadily. Bill Cotton Jnr occasionally looked anxiously in Graham's direction, but I think that most people present had learnt what to expect from past experience, and poor old Gra was unable to pick a fight.

Half-way through the evening Bill Cotton made a farewell speech to David Attenborough. He delivered his paean holding his cigarette behind his back, like someone who wasn't meant to be smoking, but who certainly wasn't going to waste a good cigarette. Attenborough accepted, to rapturous applause, what looked like a BBC litter bin.

Towards the end of the evening Terry and I plucked up enough courage to approach some of the greats – Milligan, the elder statesman, who has had a remarkably successful year, first his autobiography, *Hitler – My Part in his Downfall*, then a mini-*Goon Show* revival – with a special last *Goon Show* recorded in October for the BBC's fifty years anniversary – and patronised by royalty. He remained sitting through most of the evening, with no shortage of visitors and well-wishers and sycophants like ourselves coming over to see him. He walked very obviously in front of Bill Cotton, just as Bill was selling David Attenborough, and was heard to shout irreverently during the speech. Eric Morecambe

1 A young Liverpudlian who Graham and David adopted.

is another one who never dropped his comic persona all evening. If one talked to him, or if one heard him talking to anyone else, he was always doing a routine. He has a very disconcerting habit of suddenly shouting at the top of his voice at someone only a foot away.

Almost exactly true to the pattern of two years ago, one of the last people I spoke to was Eric Sykes, who has a series on Thursday nights,[1] two hours before us, which gets about the same rating. He's very much easier to talk to than someone like Milligan or Morecambe, because he's a gentler character altogether – even when performing. He was very impressed with the 'Pither Cycling Tour', and was generally flattering about my performances.

So at 12.00 the band of Light Entertainment workers disbanded. I was struck by how young we still are compared to most of the people there. Apart from the Goodies and ourselves, nearly all the performers and writers there are in their forties or even fifties.

Wednesday, December 20th

An interesting piece of work could come our way. This morning I was rung by Memorial Enterprises – who have made films like *Charlie Bubbles, If* and *Gumshoe* – in short, some of the best British films of the last few years. Michael Medwin wanted to speak to me. I was quite excited, but it turned out that he wanted to talk over the question of our writing a 20-minute promotional film for the States to put out as advance publicity for *O Lucky Man*, the latest Lindsay Anderson film, with Alan Price and Malcolm McDowell. Alan had suggested that I might have some better ideas for a promo film than Warner Bros' own publicity men.

I met them at the editing rooms of De Lane Lea in Wardour Street. The film was likely to be very prestigious, and clearly they are gambling on a big commercial success. It has been edited down to three and a quarter hours, and is due to be first screened as the official British entry at Cannes. They are a very pleasant group of people – Lindsay, serious and mock-serious by turns, the kind of person who seems to invite you to make jokes about him, Alan, as self-deprecatingly gloomy as ever, and Medwin, very like the cheerful Cockneys he used to play in 1950s British war films – though much less over the top. He was pleased to hear that

---

1 Called simply 'Sykes'.

Helen and I enjoyed *Charlie Bubbles*,[1] he said we were members of a select club – not of those who enjoyed it, but of those who saw it, for somehow it never found favour with the big distributors.

1 Directed by Albert Finney, and starring himself as a hugely successful Mancunian returning to his roots. Co-starred Liza Minnelli. It was written by Shelagh Delaney.

1973

Monday, January 1st

A good start to the New Year – Python has won the Critics' Circle award as the best comedy show of the year; beat Terry at squash; and at 3.00 we had a meeting with Mark Shivas and Richard Broke to hear their verdict on our 'Black and Blue' script, which was favourable. I think they were surprised how over-cautious we were about our ability to write anything longer than sketches. It restores my faith in myself as a writer – not just someone who left university seven years ago, with no real qualifications and a lot of lucky breaks. Terry's eyes are really on direction – it is this urgent desire for complete technical control that is for him the most important aspect of creation, whereas for me the personal satisfaction of having written or performed something well is usually enough – for then my ambition tends to lead away from the editing room and the dubbing theatre to travel abroad, to reading, to being with my family.

Friday, January 5th

9.30 – arrived at De Lane Lea editing rooms in Dean St to see the 3¼ hour version of Lindsay Anderson's new film *O Lucky Man*. It still needed some editing and dubbing to be done, but it was a very impressive film – and tho' some sequences worked better than others, nearly all of it was of a very high standard – in performance and photography and direction and conception, and there were many moments when I felt a very strong and complete sense of involvement.

At the end, as the lights went up in the little viewing theatre, Lindsay appeared through the door of the theatre with Alan. He laughed and said he'd been spying on us from the projection room. I mumbled my appreciation – but had hardly time to get my thoughts together, and felt rather inhibited about saying anything in the presence of so many people intimately concerned with the film.

Terry and I drove over to the Medical Centre in Pentonville Road, for a complete physical check-up in modern computerised conditions – which normally costs £30, but had been given to us free by Alan

Bailey.[1] The relevance of the film suddenly seemed uncannily close. Only an hour ago we had been watching a film which took horrific looks at scientific medicine, and in which the charming smile and the 'Would you come this way please sir?' were usually a prelude to something most sinister. Now here we were, in the clean, aseptic atmosphere of a rich man's clinic, being shown into a small cubicle and asked to strip off down to shoes, socks and pants. Alan fortified us beforehand with a large whisky – he really is the most wonderfully cheerful and reassuring man. The tests included a blood test, a urine test, a very thorough Question and Answer sequence, which worked by pressing buttons, and looking at a screen, the answers being fed straight into a computer. I found the alternative answers fascinating – from 'I have never coughed blood', 'I have coughed blood, but not in the last year', to the appalling and inevitable 'I have coughed blood often in the last year'.

Tuesday, January 9th

Reading my *Daily Mirror*, my eyes fall on an item 'Monty Python Axed'. The story ran that the BBC were stopping Monty Python and were not making any more. It also ran the story of two sketches being cut from the last show, as if to imply that the show had been cut by the Beeb on grounds of indecency. The inaccuracy of the headline, and the fact that it appeared in a paper which boasts on its front page 'Largest European Sale', moved me to ring the *Mirror*. The TV man who had instigated the story was very pally and 'Hello Michael' with me, but I think a little taken aback that I attacked a small news item so bitterly. It was, he said, part of a much longer article which he had written, and the headline had not been composed by him.

However, Jill Foster did ring the BBC and Bill Cotton did send out a press release denying the story. But the *Evening Standard* rang up during the day to say that they noticed some confusion between the *Mirror* story and a Philip Purser interview with me in the *Daily Mail* (implying that Python would go on) and Radio Sheffield sent round a man to do an interview about Python's plans. So I became a minor celebrity for a day – and lost a lot of work time too.

---

1 Graham Chapman's close friend. They'd both studied medicine at Bart's, but Alan went on to practise.

Thursday, January 25th

Met Tony Smith[1] – the man who is probably going to land the first ever Python road tour.

He was a surprise. Longish hair, unkempt, shirt pulled over what must be a beer-belly – a friendly open face, and a total absence of traditional promoter's accoutrements – cigars, sharp suits and big talk. He was quietly confident that a Python tour would be a sell-out. Bannister Promotions have offered us a guarantee of £17,500, but Tony Smith reckons that we could make 21 or 22 grand – on a percentage split with him. I must put this to the rest of the team. Smith has fairly impressive credentials, including recent sell-out tours with The Who and Led Zeppelin.

At 1.15 gave an interview to a Belgian journalist for a radio programme which is featuring the new Python record on one of its shows – which is more than they do here, and the record isn't even for sale in Belgium! I said Mr Heath ought to take his trousers off once a year. The Belgian evidently felt this was quite a risible Eurojoke.

Saturday, January 27th

Winter this year is being very unfriendly to romantics. No snow, let alone a blizzard, winds moderate, weather warm, and now, to cap it all, bright sunshine. At 2.00 we had a Python meeting at John's. We decide to do the Python tour with Tony Smith. We talk about details of performance and dates and places. I find it extraordinary that John can undertake such a violent month of really hard work repeating basically old material – and yet will not countenance doing another series of Python. I suppose it's all a question of time and money. My God, we're getting so mercenary. Eric is almost totally involved in ads. He has been the most successful of us – with his 'Nudge-Nudge' selling Breakaway chocolate, and another ad in the offing. This afternoon he rang me to say that Gibbs toothpaste had approached him to ask if he could set up a five-minute film for their sales conference. It had to be made quickly and fairly cheaply. Eric proposed that we set it up as a package, with the two of us and Terry. It sounded like good experience – it wasn't for general commercial purposes, and it could be rude. What's more, it's work. I accepted on behalf of us both.

1 Not to be confused with Tony Stratton-Smith, whose Charisma label put out our albums.

Thursday, February 1st

To Portman Square for presentation of the Gibbs film script. Waiting outside the office was Rita Allen, of Selling and Sellers Ltd, who is a conference organiser and valiantly trying to appear relevant to this project. She is mid-thirties, with tired eyes, skilfully concealed in a well-made-up face.

In the office Colin Hessian deferentially introduces me to his boss, a Mr Finn. We sit round a rather silly table, and I read the script through – Gumby voices and all. It goes down surprisingly well. Hessian roars with laughter. Finn is clearly worried that we all like it so much, and after some discussion we make some simple changes – in order to give it a happy ending.

There is controversy over the vox-pop 'I only like toothpaste with crab or hake in it'. Finn doesn't like this. Hessian, being a good deal more independent than I would have expected, stands up for it strongly. What a silly discussion – it puts me in mind of Terry and Duncan Wood arguing the virtues of 'masturbating'. Anyway, they accepted the script happily.

Thursday, February 8th

Up at 6.30. Terry is here by 6.45. It's just beginning to get light, but it looks an unpromising day. Heavy drizzle and dark, dull, low clouds. We are hoping to film the entire Elida-Gibbs salesman film today – some six or seven minutes of script. Fortunately we start early, up amongst the faceless 1930s shopping arcades of Colindale, and by 9.20 a longish sound sequence is completed.

We finish shooting about 6.00, with thirty-seven set-ups in the can. During the course of the day, I have been a filthy, coughing tramp, thrown out of a shop, a salesman in glittering white suit who leaps out of the roofs of cars over shop counters and, right at the end of the day, the most difficult thing, a straight-to-camera hard-sell tongue-twister on the virtues of Close-up Green toothpaste. But I think everybody enjoyed the hard work – tho' it was cold and wet, there is no stronger feeling amongst a crew than when each person in it knows that the other person is working flat out. Terry was excellent – but does have a tendency to get over-excited, which is not so good when others are getting over-excited as well. This is just the time for icy calm.

Friday, February 9th

Arrived at Rules [restaurant] about 1.00. In an upstairs room the Pythons, and several people from Methuen, who had worked on the book [*Monty Python's Big Red*]. On the table were individual sugar Gumbies, and a large chocolate 'Spiny Norman',[1] and menus on which each dish was followed by an appropriate review of the *Big Red Book* – trout followed by 'flat, thin and silly', etc. The meal was to celebrate sales of over 100,000 paperbacks. Couldn't get excited or impressed about it, though – it only added to my feelings of guilt. Here we were, being given an enormous and expensive free meal, in honour of us earning large amounts of money. Also I can't help feeling that Python is better employed creating than celebrating. However, it was a chance to overeat.

From the Methuen lunch – feeling full of cigars and brandy, which ought to be Rules' coat of arms – walked back through sunlit Covent Garden. Knowing that the whole area will be redeveloped (keeping odd buildings of 'historical merit'), it's rather like one imagines walking through London in the Blitz. You know what's happening is not going to do the city any good, but you're powerless (almost) to stop it. However, pressure groups of all opinions seem to be more successful now – Piccadilly and Covent Garden have both had big development plans changed by community action and protest. The sad thing is that the basic thinking behind these redevelopment schemes never changes. Blocks (of offices mainly) dominate. Where there was once a gentle elegance and a human scale, there is now concrete and soaring glass. The City of London is rapidly getting to look like a Manhattan skyline, which doesn't worry me so much – but the blocks creeping into the West End are more sinister, for they are forcing a primarily residential area into acres more of hotels, offices and widened roads, and the scale of London's buildings – which are, by and large, reasonably small, friendly and non-monolithic – is every day being lost.

Tuesday, February 13th, Southwold

Took a day and a half's break in Southwold – having time off from immediate commitments. On the train at Liverpool Street – a late start,

1 Mr Gumby wore knotted handkerchiefs on his head and shouted very loudly. Spiny Norman was the giant hedgehog which the gangster Dinsdale Pirhana was convinced was watching him.

but the train tore through Essex to make up time. I ate breakfast and read the paper. Peace, perfect peace.

Met by Mother and Father in the car. Now he doesn't drive long distances. A few weeks ago he had a skid on the way home, and it clearly worries him greatly. He is also very worried about being left at home alone. Apparently he watched a TV programme about Parkinson's Disease, and at the end was almost in tears, and kept telling Ma how lucky he was to have her.

He is now definitely thinking of himself as an invalid, the times when he tries to make out how incredibly active and busy he is are getting fewer. I think he knows now that taking an hour to dress is a long time for an active man. He is aware of his mind and his concentration drifting. He cannot grasp any concept, statement, idea, argument that isn't utterly straightforward.

My mother looked well, I think she is almost happier now that she knows that all she can do for him is just to look after him. When he was fit and well, it must have been more difficult for her to accept that there was hardly any sympathetic contact between them; now he is more an invalid, their relationship is at least clear-cut.

Thursday, March 1st

In the afternoon we went to see Mark Shivas at the BBC. He hopes to have either James Cellan Jones or Ted Kotcheff to direct our 'Black and Blue' script. Talking of the future, he showed considerable interest in the Pythons' second film – and suggested a man called David Puttnam[1] as a source of money. Terry afterwards thought Shivas himself might have been interested in the producer's job. He seems very confident in us – when we mentioned to him about the waiter script which we have been working on, he said he could almost certainly get a 'Play for Today' slot for it – which is the kind of talk we're not yet used to.

Saturday, March 3rd

I went out shopping in Queen's Crescent market before lunch. In many ways it's a sad place – you notice especially old, shuffling ladies,

---

1 Produced *Chariots of Fire*, *The Killing Fields* and *Local Hero*, but his only major credit at this time was *That'll Be the Day* with David Essex.

poorly dressed, with twitching mouths. You hardly ever see them in Hampstead or Belsize Park. These are people who make a complete and utter mockery of 'democracy' and 'equality' – they're the casualties of the primitive rules of competition which run our society, and the welfare state just keeps them alive. That's all.

Take Thomas and William on to Parliament Hill. It's the English cross-country championships, quite a sight. Over 1,000 runners streaming round the Heath. It was like a *Boy's Own* story. David Bedford – the hero who failed at Munich – was leading the field, as he ran lightly down the hill a foot or so away from us.

Behind Bedford trailed hundreds of runners with no hope. Men whose chins were already flecked with white dried spittle, small, bespectacled balding men with shoulders smartly back, lank, long-haired boys striding down the hill like Daddy-Long-Legs. We moved up to the top of the hill to watch the second lap, and Thomas was running all over the place in his little green duffel coat, trying to emulate the runners. The sun came out as they ran around the second time, and the Heath suddenly seemed small as the long line of multi-coloured vests stretched as far as the eye could see. Bedford was pipped in the second lap by a New Zealander. It was an exhilarating feeling to have been present at a big national sporting event, without having to pay any money, squeeze through any turnstiles and sit where one's told.

Sunday, March 4th

My parents have been married forty-two years. I wonder how many of those were happy.

Sitting writing my diary up in the afternoon when there is a noise outside. A parade with banners passes up Lamble Street towards the new blocks at Lismore Circus – a loudspeaker van follows up. It urges non-payment of the extra 85p a week rent, made necessary by the government's Fair Rent Act. Camden was one of the last boroughs in the country to give in to this act. It's good to see someone still fighting – but like a protective hen, I became all at once aware of feeling alarmed at this civil commotion – a momentary fear that these are the voices of the have-nots, and they somehow threaten us, the haves.

Rung up this evening by a girl who is organising a pageant of Labour. A re-affirmation of socialist ideals – largely sponsored by actors such as

Anthony Hopkins, Vanessa Redgrave and others. Heartening to know so many of one's favourite actors are anti-establishment, but I react against her rather vague left-wing patter, and her presumption that so long as anything was anti-Tory it was good. I go along with her most of the way on this – but in the end, rather than argue, or ask her to explain any more, I agree to send £25. All she seemed to want was money. Money to bring coachloads of workers down from the north.

Monday, March 5th

A Python meeting at Terry's. The first time since the third LP in September that we have all contributed to a creative enterprise – in this case the second Python film. It was in many ways like a typical Python working day. Graham arrived late, and Terry made the coffee – and there was the usual indecision over whether to have a small lunch in, or a blow-out at one of Camberwell's few restaurants – we even played touch football on the lawn, for the weather is mild and sunny – a sort of Indian summer at the wrong end of the year. But for me, the most heartening thing of all was the quality and quantity of the writing that Python has done over the last week. John and Graham, writing together apparently untraumatically for once, had produced some very funny material. Eric had a richer selection of ideas – which sparked off a lot of other ideas, and Terry and I had a rag-bag of sketches – more than anyone else, as usual, but with a pretty high acceptance rate. Today we proved that Python can still be as fresh as three years ago, and more prolific.

Thursday, March 8th

Worked at home – as there was a rail strike, and reports of enormous traffic jams. Outside they're pulling down the line of old houses remaining in Lamble Street. There's something compelling about destruction – as tho' it's really more in our nature than building. I decided to make a photographic record of the rebuilding of Lamble Street from start to finish – all on a single three-minute piece of film.

I heard on the lunchtime news that a bomb had been found in a parked car near Scotland Yard – and it was believed to be connected with the Ulster border referendum being held today. It wasn't until the early evening news that I heard that there had been two big explosions in London. A bomb had gone off outside the Old Bailey – over 200 people were injured and one man killed – another had gone off in Whitehall. The impact on the media was tremendous – 'Outrage', 'Belfast comes to London', etc, etc.

Friday, March 9th

Left for Terry's at 11.15, after a good couple of hours' work. London is under siege, or so it feels. Traffic solid around Tottenham Court Rd – partly because of limited rail service owing to the prolonged go-slow and yesterday's total stoppage, and partly (as I discovered as I tried to take a short cut through Fitzroy Square) due to bomb scares. The area around the Post Office Tower had been totally cleared and cordoned off after a caller had said a bomb would go off at 11.30. Nothing went off. Neither did it at Thomas's play school in Kentish Town, which was also evacuated after a scare.

Sunday, March 11th, Abbotsley

Stricken, during the night, with a strange malaise of the bowels. Spent from about ten to three until six o'clock on the lavatory reading much of Norman Collins' *London Belongs to Me*. Spend the morning in bed with the Sunday papers and no breakfast or lunch. Thomas is fascinated and keeps coming up to see if I'm alright – bringing me Lego and finding some medicine for me – and talking ever so sweetly and politely. Gradually the visits become more frequent. He brings Willy along with him. A plateful of four thin pieces of toast (all I wanted for lunch) has only two left on it by the time Thomas has brought it upstairs. Around two o'clock both he and William ended up in my sickbed listening to stories, so I decided that it was no longer worth being ill and got up around three.

Friday, March 23rd

It has been a glorious week of sunny weather. We have been working for three days on the Python film script with maximum productivity. Ideas have been pouring out, and we have had very concentrated, but quite tiring writing sessions. Today at Terry's we sat outside in the sunshine to write, and for the first day this year I caught the sun. Al fresco lunch with wine and a Chapman salad. John busy writing biographies for the press – 'Despite what Michael thinks, he is not good company.'

Thursday, March 29th

At 5.30 we met Mark Shivas at the BBC and went to meet James Cellan Jones, who is to be the director of *Secrets*, our play for the 'Black and Blue' series. We took bets on what he would be like as we drove along the A40. I envisaged him as a rather burly, stocky man, with a loud voice. I was right, except I may have over-emphasised the loudness of his voice, and I didn't know that he'd have no socks on. He may be brilliant, but I didn't feel an awful lot of sympathy for our play, nor an awful lot of knowledge of it and, when Terry asked about writers attending editing, he closed up like a shell. But as we will be on the Monty Python tour when it's rehearsed, filmed and recorded, there is little we can do, so we might as well leave him the play, and see what comes out the other end. I can see embarrassment and disillusionment somewhere along the line, I'm sure.

Friday, March 30th

Mark Shivas rang early to apologise for what he called J C-Jones' 'scratchy' behaviour towards us. Had we not thought he was being like a prima donna? I said it hadn't worried us, but there were one or two points when we felt that he had the wrong end of the stick, and Shivas promised to talk to him. I feel Shivas is on our side rather than his, but this is probably the feeling he gives everyone, which is why he's such a good producer.

Monday, April 16th

Our seventh wedding anniversary, and fourth year of the diary. Over to B&C Records to talk about promotional work for the tour. On the steps of B&C met the beaming and effusive Tony Stratton-Smith – one of those few people who cheers me up whenever I see him. He was especially full of himself today for he has, almost single-handedly, secured Python's first TV foothold in the US – a deal with the Eastern Educational Network to put out the shows, uncut and unabridged. It's not a lucrative deal, but it's a great breakthrough. Tony now has to get two sponsors for the show and has high hopes of Apple, the Beatles' company – George H is very interested.[1]

Back home to write some programme copy for the stage tour. Helen had a good suggestion yesterday. All its pages will be on one big sheet, which can be folded up into a programme, or kept as a poster. Good Python thinking.

Easter Monday, April 23rd

The first official day of the 'First Farewell Tour', but Terry G, Terry J and myself have been working hard on it for about two weeks, collecting the film, writing and creating the programme, making slides, organising the sound tape with André. The much looked forward to holiday, which Helen and I were to take last week, evaporated under intense pressure of work. We left for Abbotsley at lunchtime on Good Friday. Took some champagne to celebrate Helen's mother's election to the new county council[2] as an Independent.

Rehearsals started at 9.30 at the Rainbow Theatre in Finsbury Park. It's a mammoth 3,500-seater theatre, with wildly flamboyant interior. The huge ceiling is studded with twinkling stars and above the proscenium and along the side walls are passageways, alcoves, balconies, in Spanish-Oriental style, with lights in as if for the start of a massive Shakespearean production. It's a magnificent folly – and it seems an obvious target for developers. However, it continues in being as a rock concert theatre – probably helped by the decision of the Albert Hall not to stage any more rock concerts.

Friday, April 27th, Southampton

Woke about 7.00. Slept fitfully until 8.15. Feet sweating, but fairly calm. A bath and breakfast. It was a fine, sunny morning, so we walked to the theatre. In the distance we could see the enormous liners in the docks, and some way ahead, the steel letters on a grid high above the surrounding buildings read 'Gaumont'. Altogether rather an epic place to start the tour. There was an almost tropical feeling – as if we had come 700, not

---

1 In the end, Dusty Springfield made an on-air introduction to Python's first appearance on New York's Channel 13.
2 Due to Boundary Commission recommendations, Huntingdon ceased to be a county and

70 miles south from London. I became aware of blossoms everywhere, of lush chestnuts in bloom, and a warmth in the air, with a healthy sea edge to it.

The sound is clearly going to be a difficult problem, for, in addition to music and sound f/x on tape (now being worked by André), we have film and animation sound from the projector, voice-overs from two off-stage mikes and six radio mikes, all to be mixed and controlled by Dave Jacobs, a short, dark, grey-eyed young guy, who has had about six hours' sleep in the last three days. In fact everyone looks tired, but the adrenaline of an imminent first night keeps everyone going.

Graham was using more than adrenaline to keep him going. He arrived at 10.00, already a little bleary from drink, and violently angry that he had not been told where to meet us. Gradually he calmed down, but unfortunately the damage was done – what everyone feared might happen, but hoped that for once it wouldn't, *did* happen. By 6.00 Graham was very drunk. We finished a dress run-through at 5.15, with many imperfections still not sorted out, and some difficult costume changes keeping us all tense.

The first house was just over half-full and was happy, rather than ecstatic. But it certainly couldn't be compared with the reception we'd had at Coventry. Perhaps most amazingly of all, 'Silly Walks' went by with an almost embarrassing lack of response, and there were many cases of mikes not being switched up, etc, etc. There was only half an hour before the next house, so there was only time for a cup of tea and a sandwich before we gathered on stage for 'Llamas'. John, Eric, Terry G, Terry J and Neil resplendent in their Spanish gear, Carol in her sequinned leotard, and me in an old mac with 'Eat More Pork' written on the back, and my Gumby gear underneath.

As soon as the curtain went up for the second house, the atmosphere was one of wild enthusiasm. Favourite characters – John in the Llama sketch, Gumby, Terry and Graham as Pepperpots, Eric as Nudge-Nudge, and Graham's Colonel and Ken Shabby – were given rounds of applause, and 'Pet Shop' at the end was as self-indulgent in performance, and as hugely popular in reception as it has ever been.

But Graham was far gone. He had missed his entrance in 'Argument' twice, made 'Custard Pie' a dull shadow of its former self, and slowed down many a sketch. Only his own 'Wrestling' had been done really well.

Upstairs in the restaurant of the Dolphin, Graham and Eric reached a point of explosion and Eric threw down his napkin with a rather impetuous flourish and left the restaurant. Later Graham, Eric and John had 'full and frank discussions', in which John told Graham straight out that he had performed very badly in both shows and if he went on like this every night there was no point in him continuing on the tour. For my own part, I feel that Graham's condition was the result of a colossal over-compensation for first-night nerves. He had clearly gone too far in his attempt to relax – maybe now the first night is over he will no longer feel as afraid.

Saturday, April 28th, Brighton

At 10.00 we left Southampton and moved along the south coast to Brighton.

The first house was not brilliant – there were severe sound problems, late cues and sketches which went on too long.

The second house was better, with a big audience response, but again difficulties with sound and film. Helen was there to see it, so was Maggie,[1] Barry Cryer, Ronnie Corbett, etc. Very few congratulations flying around – a sort of tacit approval at best, at worst a positive awkwardness. As I waited outside the theatre after the show, waiting for John G to sort out which cars should take us home, I felt very depressed. I feel that my contribution to the show is not as great as it could be. I feel that we are marking time – regurgitating old material, milking the public in a way Python never has done quite as blatantly. But as Helen, and Carol's hubby Peter, who travelled back with us, said, the audience loved it, and with a few changes it has the makings of a great show. We have already made some cuts – 'Half-a-Bee' song didn't even last two performances – but there are others.

Saturday, May 5th, Birmingham

The tour is now in its second week, and we have done eleven shows already. My voice is getting a little husky and I hope that if I treat it carefully it will last tonight's show at the Hippodrome and three shows in Bristol before two days off in London. And I am, almost as I write, 30 years old. Thirty years old in this Post House, a colourful, but colourless hotel, which could be anywhere in any country. Thirty years old and enjoying all the benefits of standardisation.

1 Maggie Weston, ace make-up artist who became Mrs Gilliam.

Most of the people who stay in these places are businessmen, and that's what I feel is the difference between my being 30 in Birmingham and 20 at Brasenose, and ten at Birkdale[1] – now, for better or worse, I am a part of this standardisation – a money-earning, rate-paying, mortgage-owning man of business. For Python is business – it's no longer an unpredictable, up one year, down the next kind of existence. Python has the magic ingredient, 'market potential', and our books and our records are only on the verge of making as much money as we could want. And yet some of the spontaneity and the excitement has gone as security has crept in and, although I am in a job which still allows me to wear knotted handkerchiefs over my head and have 2,500 people pay to see me do it, I still feel that I am a 30-year-old businessman.

The show went well, tho' my lack of voice is becoming a slight and annoying restriction. At the end of 'Pet Shop' I did the usual 15-second approach to John and, feeling the end of the show only thankful seconds away, said 'D'you want to come back to my place?' Conscious of the laugh being less ecstatic than when my voice was working. But worse was to come. John turned to me and said 'No'. It didn't get much reaction and a combination of disappointment at this rather poor ad-lib and consuming fatigue made me just remain silent, look suitably disappointed and wait for the curtains to close. I really was in no mood for witty extemporisation. But I suddenly became aware that Eric, in a compere's spangly jacket, had come forward to the front of the stage and was talking to the audience. 'Ladies and gentlemen, this evening is a very special evening for one of us here tonight ...' then it became clear ... 'for tonight Michael Palin is 30 years old.' The audience cheered, my mind started racing as I began to go through my options ... Eric was going on ... 'And tonight we've brought along one of Michael's very great friends ...' faces of John and Terry looking at me grinning ... 'one of his most favourite personalities in the world of showbiz ... Mrs Mary Whitehouse!' Neil plays a few chords, and on comes Eric's mother – the spitting image of the good Mrs Whitehouse,[2] bearing a cake with candles. Everyone is looking at me, grins have become grins of anticipation – what will I do? How will I react? Carol Cleveland brought me a bunch of chrysanthemums – and there was the get-out. I found

1 Birkdale Primary School, Sheffield, which I attended from 1948 to 1957.
2 Mary Whitehouse, concerned at the decline in public morals, started the Clean-Up Television Campaign, which became the National Viewers' and Listeners' Association. She never directly attacked Python, but saw the BBC as a den of impropriety.

myself saying 'Ladies and gentlemen, I would like to say how pleased and proud I am to have received this cake from that great shit Mary Whitehouse (cheap, but desperate and it got a good laugh) and all I can say at this moving moment is … (relapse into Gumby voice) … ARRANGE THEM … IN THE CAKE!' And plunge the lovely chrysanthemums into the lovely cake.

I had got out of it, and the audience were clapping and laughing and singing 'Happy Birthday'. I felt not only relief, but great pleasure and thanks that my birthday had actually been made remarkable – as I said to Eric, 'At last there's something to write in my diary.'

I had organised a birthday meal for everyone at Lorenzo's, an Italian restaurant. Food passable, wine and champagne. Sat next to Robert [Hewison], who ten years ago almost single-handedly pushed me into revue performing.

Back at the hotel I remember Neil helping me to my room, where I stripped off and collapsed into bed. Neil, Terry, Eric, Carol and I can't remember who else crowded into the room. We read poems from the *Oxford Book of Twentieth Century Verse*. Neil insisted on spilling wine over my carpet. The last I remember is Neil offering me a joint, which I declined – for my system had had a big enough battering for one day. An enormous card had arrived from André and Dave, someone was eating my chocolates and, about 3.30, my thirtieth birthday ended, and I lay back, utterly exhausted and very, very happy. Thank you Birmingham.

Sunday, May 6th, Bristol

Left for Bristol at midday with our driver, Bill; Eric and John in the other limousine with Sid driving.

As we drove out of Birmingham, we ran into a violent cloudburst on the motorway out of the Midlands. Bill confided to us that he was staying behind Sid because Sid's car wasn't working too well and the brakes were in a very dangerous state. Nevertheless, we were having some trouble keeping up with him. I looked at the clock. We were touching 100. In front Sid was swaying his limousine around like a raft in a storm. I buried my head in Evelyn Waugh's diaries in *The Observer*, or else tried to sleep. I felt doubly glad I was with Bill – but uncomfortably aware that the window was misting over, and yet Bill was blaming the poor visibility on the intensity of the rain. Terry J, behind, suggested he use the demister. Bill didn't know where it was, and Terry and I had to show him.

When we reached Bristol we had to stop and ask some passers-by where the Dragonara Hotel was. Shortly, as we approached a roundabout, there was this brand new brick pile with a huge sign, 'Dragonara', crowning it. I could scarcely believe my eyes as Sid turned into the roundabout and, inches from the sign itself, sped away and off to the left, up a hill and out towards the docks. Bill, after turning on the dual carriageway, drove past both entrances of the hotel and off to the roundabout *to follow Sid.*

Thursday, May 17th, Edinburgh

One of the most vocal and enthusiastic audiences we've had. The usual knot of twenty or thirty autograph hunters outside, and one of them asked me to come and have a coffee and a drink with them. Foolishly I indicated our fat Daimler, and muttered something about the Queen Mother waiting; but then had to sit in the car for a full 15 minutes for John to finish signing. A couple of belligerent Scots looked resentfully at the car, and I thought we were going to have a repetition of Birmingham, where someone spat on the windscreen.

Even when we eventually left, Sid took us steadfastly the wrong way. I have never been on a journey with him when he has gone directly from point A to point B. We drove out along the road to Peebles tonight – and we made the mistake of thinking that it was so clearly *not* the right road that Sid must be at any moment about to turn off. But it was not until I shouted to him 'Is this the Glasgow road, Sid?' that he took action and we veered off to the right. We were now in the middle of a housing estate, with our enormous limousine squeezing its way into a cul-de-sac, some ten miles from our hotel.

The consistency with which Sid goes wrong is such that, as Neil said, the law of averages ceases to apply.

Friday, May 18th, Edinburgh

Neil and Eric very pissed tonight on stage. The unusual spectacle of Eric not quite in control. The difference in his timing showed how crucial timing is. Both his long travel agent monologue and 'Nudge-Nudge', which usually provoke enormous reaction, went by almost unnoticed. Neil was falling about behind stage, in high spirits, and his 'Idiot Song' was wonderfully bad – full of wrong notes. A show to remember, but not necessarily for the right reasons.

Saturday, May 19th, Edinburgh

Did not enjoy the first house particularly. They were not a very voluble audience, and I was anxious about my voice as usual.

The second house much noisier, and managed to get through it – with the voice standing up surprisingly well. Back at the hotel, tired and hungry, to be confronted with 'night service'. Could we have a bottle of champagne, please? Much conferring with manager and his lackeys – then a very smartly dressed young man came to tell us that we could only have drinks available in the 'night store' – this included a selection of dishes limited in quality and quantity, as only the British know how. Of the six items available, four were not available. I ended up with a gin and tonic, a large brandy and a roll and cheese.

Went to bed. Could not get to sleep owing to presence of David Bowie and his acolytes in the hotel. Bowie is currently the hottest touring property in Britain, having recently played to 18,000 in Earl's Court. Tonight Bowie was in Edinburgh – and staying about a couple of doors down on the same floor as myself. They weren't exactly noisy, there were just so many of them. From 2.00 to 3.00 and beyond it was like trying to sleep through the invasion of Poland.

Sunday, May 20th, Edinburgh

At 12.00 sauntered down to the lobby – which was filled with the Bowie party's gear, and Bowie attendants. What a relief from roomfuls of grey suits – this morning it was almost as though squatters had moved in. Tall, gangling men in worn denim moved through the throng like a dozen Jesuses, sharply dressed chicks sat around smoking – everyone wore a relaxed air of confidence – they were, after all, part of the hottest road show in Britain. With our Sunday papers and our conspicuous lack of hangers-on we looked very dull and anonymous.

Outside the hotel was Bowie's splendid personal conveyance, a chunky black and white Dodge Van, which looked like nothing I had ever seen – it was an armoured car, in effect – with thick steel sides and black windows. A stylish version of a Black Maria.

The second house at Glasgow earlier in the day, was, I think, the best performance of the tour so far.

Even the police had come in to watch us. Five or six of them, including two policewomen, sat behind stage and watched the second show, and one of them came on and jumped around during the Idiotting sequence. They managed to find a bottle of whisky for Graham from nowhere.[1] In fact, as they left, they asked us if we wanted 'anything else'.

Monday, May 21st, Leeds

Two more full houses and great enthusiasm again.

Back at the hotel a strange little group was gathered in the lobby, in the middle of which was David Hemmings, a sort of sub-Frostian whizz-kid, who made a whole lot of films after *Blow-up* and became Hollywood material. Also he built up a business called Hemdale, which I suspect is now linked with Frost in some way, who is of course now linked with Slater-Walker, who have just joined with Hambros Bank, and who, as *Private Eye* put it this week, are soon to make a bid for England.

Anyway, David Hemmings was heavily drunk, and Graham Chapman, also heavily drunk, was having quite a verbal battle with our Dave. Graham was lurching about telling Hemmings that he wasn't going to go to bed with him. Around Hemmings were various ladies and battered-looking men, who, it turned out, were all from Yorkshire TV. A feeling of confrontation and combat in the air. As of rival gangs circling each other. Python sitting rather aloof, Hemmings being loud and organising little trials of strength – like picking matchboxes off the floor with your teeth, whilst leaning over an armchair. Eventually the gangs came together, and Hemmings got us involved in a game of American football; he tried one run with the cushion we were using as a ball, and crashed down over a whole tableful of drinks – broken glass everywhere – and it was only after this that the night porter, a man of extreme tolerance, came and cooled things down. Whilst the others were deciding whether to carry on the game outside, I went to bed. It must have been 3.30. Outside a good Yorkshire mist was closing in.

Wednesday, May 23rd

After Leeds a long run down to Norwich, which was our thirty-fourth performance since we started at the Gaumont, Southampton, twenty-seven days before. My parents came to see the show. It was good to see

1 At that time Glasgow was a dry city on Sundays.

my father there. I didn't think he was up to going to the theatre, but it was his own decision.

The first Python stage appearances abroad were on an eccentric tour of Canada. All the team were there, augmented by Neil Innes and Carol Cleveland.

Sunday, June 3rd, Toronto

In Toronto, a small crowd, maybe 150 in all, were waiting outside the customs and, as we came out of the customs hall, there was quite a lot of cheering and shouting. (Apparently our TV show had been out the night before and CBC had added an announcement that we would be at the airport at 6.00.) They were a cheerful rather than a violent crowd. Signed a few autographs and climbed on to an old British bus with an open upper deck, which had been provided for us. CBC had also provided a four-page illustrated news-sheet called 'The Flying Python' and were wearing Gumby T-shirts. There was a lot of effort involved, but somehow the welcome seemed anti-climactic – the fans were not quite vociferous enough, and there was a lot of time spent sitting on top of the bus feeling rather conspicuously spare, before we moved off.

The trip into Toronto was soon cut short when a policeman flagged down the bus and turned us off the motorway for travelling too slowly.

This morning I woke at about 4.30 with a feeling of complete disorientation – it took me some moments to remember that I was in a hotel room, and it was quite a shock to remember that the hotel room was in Toronto. A heavy wave of homesickness came over me – the room was colourless and unfriendly, the hotel was massive and impersonal, and I was going to be away from home in rooms like this for the next three weeks. I switched on TV. In a chintzy set with potted palms, a very well made-up, expensively gowned, 35–40-year-old actress was talking to Kathryn Kuhlman, a frizzy-haired, rather wild looking mother/confessor figure. The actress was telling of how she gave up her life of sleeping pills, and came to know Christ. At moments she tried to cry, but couldn't – it was a grotesque, but quite compulsive exercise in hard-core bad taste. As Kathryn Kuhlman turned to camera to make her final message on God's behalf, piped music soared in, and, as the credits rolled over this programme that had been about giving all up to join Christ, I caught the title 'Miss Kuhlman's gowns by Profil du Monde'. An extraordinary programme – a kind of coffee-table Christianity.

Tuesday, June 5th, Toronto

I switched on the Watergate hearings – and here was instant courtroom drama – the characters seemed to be characters I'd seen before – the Edmund O'Brien figure of Sam Erwin, the chairman, the film star smoothness of Senator Howard Baker, and the star today – Sally Harmony – a somewhat overawed, but quite pretty divorcee, who was trying to explain away her involvement in the bugging. The whole Watergate case has taken up more press and broadcasting time than any other cause célèbre I can remember. The Americans watch it with fascination and they are given all the hearings all day on three channels. There are signs that the coverage is beginning to slacken, however. I think the initial shocks have all been absorbed by now, and unless Nixon is found to be directly involved in the bugging or cover-up of Watergate, the story will not pick up its impetus of two or three weeks ago.

Meanwhile there was Sally Harmony, sweating lightly on her upper lip, being cross-questioned in front of millions. It's so like fiction that there could be a danger that it will become fiction in people's minds.

Wednesday, June 6th, Toronto

After about five hours' sleep last night, I was called at 6.30 to go for an early show interview with CTV – the main alternative channel to CBC. Terry J and Terry G were the only other two whom Tony [Smith] could persuade to do it, and the four of us left the Royal York Hotel at 7.00 in a cab. It was a grey morning, our route took us out of the city centre, and along an expressway with huge apartment blocks on either side. Enormous numbers of new apartments must have been built in the last ten years, and it was all residential – I could see no factories, or even shops, just acres of instant neighbourhoods.

Our interviewer was called Percy. He was a young and fit-looking 50-ish, with a very open friendly face, but we didn't know how serious he would be. As he was in a single shot doing an introduction to camera about how brilliantly zany we all were, I pointed my finger at his speaking mouth, and he bit the end of it. From then on, he almost took over the show. We talked seriously for a moment, then anarchy would break loose, and at one point Percy stood up and flung his coffee mug on to the studio floor, where it shattered. He rugby-tackled Terry Gilliam as we upturned the table on set.

They all seemed to be in the spirit of things by now, and, as the programme neared its end, suggested we do anything we wanted to whilst the girl and the other link man were signing off. So we leapt on the girl in the middle of her final announcement and the show ended with a chase.

Friday, June 8th, Montreal

The performance tonight, at the vast impressive Place des Arts, was nearly sold out – almost 2,500 people there, which I think is the biggest crowd we've played to on the tour. Mind you, we need them – for with the expenses of hotels, etc, we stand to make little more than £1,000 each for this whole Canadian effort. (John G had once estimated it as high as £3,000 each.) However, a good audience and, with the help of a neck mike, my voice is in fair trim for our two shows in Ottawa tomorrow. Two very good reviews of our show last night – one from a heavy, bearded, youngish critic who told me that he thought Python was better on mescalin.

Sunday, June 10th, Ottawa

Talked over the subject of the moment – whether or not to extend our tour to make TV appearances in the States. This was first mooted in Montreal by Nancy Lewis, from Buddah Records in New York, who have been responsible for a great deal of Python promotion in the States and who, apart from the record, are also trying to persuade Columbia to take the wraps off our film. Nancy, who is a very kind, gentle girl, has absolute faith in Monty Python's saleability in the States, and she has fixed up a series of TV interviews – including the *Johnny Carson Show*, and the *Midnight Show*, and film showings and radio interviews. But these will involve staying on in North America for about five days longer. John C and I are very much against this. I know how disappointed Helen would feel, and I desperately want to get back home anyway – having been away, apart from odd days, for nearly two months.

We decide on a compromise decision – i.e. that those who want to go to the States – Graham, Terry and Terry G – should appear on behalf of Python on the TV shows, and John and I would go to San Francisco and leave on the 24th. But during the course of yesterday evening it became clear that only John and I were happy with this arrangement, and the two Terrys especially felt that it was all or none.

As I thought about it, and as I talked to Nancy, who has almost put her job in jeopardy on our behalf (for Buddah are to pay all expenses), the more I realised that I ought to go, for Python's work is not down to one person, and if a majority of the group feel strongly enough that the American publicity is necessary to sell the work we have all done together, then the minority has a strong responsibility. So I agreed to go, and called Helen today and told her the sad news that we would not be returning until the 28th. She took it very well, but it is so difficult to explain satisfactorily when one is four and a half thousand miles away.

John C is vociferously against going. He regards it as an exercise by PR people for PR people – he strongly objects to being forced to do it, and last night, in the bar of the hotel, said straight out to Terry G that he enjoyed the industrial relations films he has been doing, much to our scorn, as being more worthwhile than Python. This saddened me, but at least John was saying what he felt.

That evening we were taken to a British High Commission-sponsored party at an apartment block. Some classic English stereotypes, including a man with a red face and a bow tie who asked me rather peremptorily if I could find him some ginger ale, and then spent the rest of the evening apologising that he hadn't recognised me. He kept coming up and remembering things I had done in the show and how marvellous they were.

Monday, June 11th, Ottawa–Calgary

A long travelling day. Owing to the selective strikes, we didn't leave Ottawa airport until about 12.00, and then had to fly to Toronto to transfer to a plane to Calgary.

On the journey I started talking about Python, the States and the group itself to Graham, and it suddenly became very clear to us that if we all, apart from John, wanted to do another Python series, then we should do one. The reaction in Britain and Canada showed that there was a great demand for a new series, and John had stated his position vis-à-vis Python very clearly on Saturday night at the Chateau Laurier in

Ottawa. Maybe a fourth Python series was born as we flew over the wheatlands of Saskatchewan.

Thursday, June 14th, Calgary–Edmonton

Up at 9.30 to travel to Edmonton. Should be exhausted, but couldn't summon up the energy.

On the plane sat next to John C, and had a good long chat. He is still very anti our trip to the States – now saying that it will be a loss financially, despite Buddah Records taking care of the hotel bills. He hates chat shows, and feels that in doing them Python is going against all its principles.

We landed at Edmonton out of grey skies. Before even going to the hotel, Terry J, Eric, Carol and myself are whisked off to the Edmonton Press Club. When we arrived there, about thirty people were sitting around tables in a dark basement, drinking.

Slowly but surely, it became obvious that we could not get away without some sort of cabaret. Eric and Terry first took the microphone and, after some opening banter, asked for questions. A silence, then one wag chanced his arm. 'I'd like to ask, as there are two of you up there, could one of you get me a Carlsberg.' Laughter. Then Terry and Eric grabbed this unfortunate pressman, pulled him indelicately across the dance floor and poured beer over him. It's quite amazing what Python has become.

Friday, June 15th, Regina, Saskatchewan

We have already cancelled our appearance in Saskatoon, owing to heavy travel costs and very low advance bookings. So we are here in Regina – Ordinary Town Canada, with its wheatmarket and its oil refineries and its RCMP headquarters, for two days, with almost no chance of making a profit.

Slept for two hours in the morning, a sleep broken only by a Tony Smith phone call, after I had been off for ten minutes, asking if I would appear on a lunchtime chat show, being recorded NOW. I told him I wanted my name right at the bottom of the list and, as I was the first person he'd rung, he was able to apply more heavily persuasive methods on the others. After I woke up, I had a shower, and ordered up some hot hors-d'oeuvres and a half-bottle of Chianti and a jug of coffee, watched Terry J, Terry G, and Graham on TV. Terry G very funny, slowly tying his mike lead around himself until he finished the interview totally trussed up and then died.

Saturday, June 16th, Regina, Saskatchewan

Terry and I had a lunchtime drink at the Red Lion Beverage Room, and played shuffleboard together, and then with a local. Canadians, as a whole, are about the most open, friendly people I know. There are none of the guarded, reserved, slightly resentful looks one sometimes receives when trying to meet the English. After lunch I lay on my bed, looked out over Saskatchewan and read *Jane Eyre*. I don't think I have ever felt so rested on the whole tour.

In the evening, a rather poor meal at a dimly lit restaurant called Golfs – it was trying its hardest to be exclusive and smart, and personified the worst aspects of North American snobbishness: 'Would you care to be seated for a cocktail?' Or, when we wanted to eat, 'Oh, indeed, sir, the hostess will come and seek you out.' And, when we were sat at table, 'This is your table for the evening, your waiter will be Randy.' At least that got Graham interested.

Despite the gloomy fears of Tony Smith, the ticket sales at Regina had increased greatly in the last two days, and we had a very respectable 60% house.

Wednesday, June 20th, Vancouver

At last the end of term has arrived. Tonight, in this well-appointed but fairly unexciting town, surrounded by pine-clad mountains, 8,000 miles from England on the edge of the Pacific, we perform *Monty Python's First Farewell Tour* for the forty-ninth and last time. Vancouver has treated us well, with the most extensive publicity coverage so far in Canada, plus more than the usual parties and receptions – and, in a 3,000 seat theatre, one 70% house on Monday, over 80% on Tuesday (when we broke a fifteen-year record at the Queen Elizabeth Theatre – taking $3,000 on the door) and tonight a complete sell-out, with people turned away.

Thursday, June 21st, San Francisco

We caught the 4.00 United Airlines flight to San Francisco via Seattle. The American Customs and Immigration at Vancouver Airport were less than welcoming, and we left Canada, this warm, friendly, straightforward, happily unexciting country, in a morass of red-tape, form-filling and an indefinable feeling of mistrust.

Arrived in San Francisco in the evening. As we drove from the airport it was dull and rather cool, and the cloud hung low over the mountains around the town like duvets hanging out to dry. Our hotel was called the Miyako. The hotel is designed in Japanese style, both inside and out, but this turns out to be compromised in many ways. Only a minority of the rooms are what I'm told is authentically Japanese – i.e. beds which are just light mattresses on the floor – the lobby is run with traditional American Western hotel efficiency – so much so that I witnessed the peculiar sight of a Japanese man trying to check into this Japanese hotel, and being unable to make himself understood.

Saturday, June 23rd, San Francisco

Nancy, Terry J, Neil and I and Eric are driving today down the coast road from SF to LA. We hired a couple of cars, which Buddah paid for, and at 7.00 or thereabouts, made our first stop at Monterey. With my susceptibility to romantic names, I felt we had to see Monterey, but it was rather anti-climactic. The harbour is a good deal less attractive than Brixham, and there was little hint of the magic of the place in the jettyful of seafood parlours, amusement arcades, rotten gift-shops, which sold ashtrays and books by Steinbeck. We drank a beer and set off towards the even more romantic names like Big Sur and Barbary Shore. A pilgrimage from Steinbeck, through Miller and Kerouac to Chandler.

We reach the mountains of Big Sur around 8.00. They are very beautiful – ridge after ridge ending in steep cliffs into the sea. Forested and wooded slopes with strong, clean smells on the edge of the Pacific. But it's slow driving round the promontories, down steeply into the valleys and up round the mountains again, and there are few hotels or restaurants – it being a national park.

We stop about 8.30 at the Big Sur Inn – a remote, low, cottagey building which wouldn't have been out of place in a Beatrix Potter illustration. I went in to ask if we could have a room for the night – and found myself in a comfortable, cheerful pair of dining rooms. Antiques and old furniture were everywhere, but not in a set-up, stylised, decorative way, but just as a haphazard collection, like a crowded Victorian sitting room. They had no rooms or reservations for dinner.

At 1.00 we stopped at the Holiday Inn in Santa Monica. They were full, but told us of a motel which might have vacancies. Suddenly, after resigning ourselves to sleeping en masse in any room we could find, we had five rooms booked at the Vandenburg Motel in Santa Maria.

In the dimly lit bar an ageing lady was playing the piano, spurring on a small and equally ageing group of residents to sing 'Frère Jacques'. The response was patchy. We sat at a table and ordered brandy and white wine. After a while the pianiste signed off with a sad, slightly drunk, speech to the effect that this was her last night here for a while (God knows where she was going to next), and she was looking forward to coming back and entertaining them all again. This received little encouragement from the ten or fifteen people left. I went to bed about 2.00, and put a quarter in the Magic Fingers.[1]

Sunday, June 24th, Los Angeles

In no other city have I seen such enormous hoardings advertising groups and their LPs. Grinning faces of Jack Carson, Andy Williams, John Denver and Diana Ross, a hundred times larger than life, look down on the strip. We passed Dean Martin's restaurant, and, not much further on (across the road from a huge hoarding advertising Led Zeppelin's latest LP *Houses of the Holy* with a strange picture of naked children climbing over what looked like the Giant's Causeway), we found our hotel, the Hyatt Continental. On the side of the marquee it read 'Buddah Records Welcomes Monty Python's Flying Circus'. We were in Hollywood.

Monday, June 25th, Los Angeles

At 2.30 three of the production team of the *Midnight Special* arrived to talk over our spot in the show tomorrow night. They were very American, all slightly paunchy, and wisecracking a lot – but genially. We talked over our prepared programme, which included animation, 'Gumby Flower Arranging', a clip from the 'Silly Olympics' film, 'Nudge-Nudge', 'Children's Story', 'Wrestling' and Neil's 'Big Boots'. (This

---

1 The Magic Fingers Bed Relaxation System was a way of vibrating your bed to lull you comfortably to sleep. A quarter of a dollar would wobble you gently for about five minutes. It always worked for me, until it stopped, whereupon I woke abruptly.

programme, like that for *The Tonight Show*, had to be without John, who flew back to England last Friday.) After going through the details of the show, we had to put on what felt like an audition. A run-through, cold, for these three TV men. Fortunately they laughed a lot, objected to nothing, and we felt greatly encouraged. At one point we asked them what would happen if there was no such laughter from the studio audience. He dismissed our worries lightly. 'We can always sugar it,' he said.

Tuesday, June 26th, Los Angeles

At 5.00 we arrived at NBC Burbank Studios to record our eight-minute slot for the *Midnight Special*. This is a relatively new rock show, which has built up a strong following and goes out at 1.00-2.30 in the morning every week. It's primarily a music show and is taped in gigantic sessions starting at 8.00 in the morning and going on until midnight. There is an informal live audience, who sit around on cushions, and look modish – a cross between campus and St Tropez. When we arrive at the studio Al Green's group are just playing, there's also an English band called 'Foghat', who seem very pleased to see us. It seems like bedlam, with groups wandering around, getting mixed up with other groups.

Sitting in the dressing room, we drink white wine from the store across the road (for there is no bar at NBC) and at 8.00 they are ready to tape us. For some reason there are no monitors in the studio, so the audience cannot see our animation or film clips. A friendly, but not ecstatic reaction.

Wednesday, June 27th, Los Angeles

At 11.00, up to the pool for an hour and a half. Graham's entourage has now swelled to five or six. We have hardly seen him in the last four days. He has been looking for a beach house to rent for a holiday after we've finished here. He found one in Laguna. Graham was an eye-opener in Canada. He drank far less, was much less aggressive and his performing was sure and confident – the best I've ever seen it. Perhaps it was because he was on his own. As soon as he is faced with the extraordinary complexity of his private life it seems to sap his energies totally. His worst performances on the English tour were when John Tomiczek's family were sitting morosely in his dressing room.

A lunchtime meeting in Nancy's room with a man from the *Los Angeles Free Press*, a sort of West Coast Village Voice with a fair smattering of extraordinary small ads – 'Your Penis Longer in 30 Days or Money Back'. 'Men – learn to wrestle with two nude ladies at the Institute of Sexual Intercourse.' We ordered up hors-d'oeuvres and Graham, Terry G, Terry J and I talked about ourselves to a tape recorder once again. Terry J's heart was clearly not in it, and he ended up back in my room watching the Watergate hearings – which he has been following avidly.

At 2.30 we once again drove out on the Hollywood Freeway to the NBC Studios. Whereas the *Midnight Special* has an audience more likely to appreciate Python, the *Tonight Show* is an all-American institution. At one go, Python will be seen by the few aficionados in New York and San Francisco, and also by the Mormons in Salt Lake City, the tobacco farmers of Louisiana and the potato growers of Idaho, the blacks in Harlem and Watts, and possibly even John Dean, President Nixon and Senator Fulbright.

To make things more nerve-racking, it was to be recorded as a live show, with no stops or retakes, for the tape had to be ready an hour or so after recording to be flown to the various parts of the States for transmission the next evening.

A great air of unreality. Here was Python going out to its greatest single audience ever, and to us it was no more than a hastily organised cabaret. We were totally unknown to the audience, and felt like new boys at school. At 6.00 the recording started. This week Joey Bishop, one of F Sinatra's and D Martin's buddies, was hosting the show as regular host Johnny Carson was on holiday. Bishop was on good form, fluent and funny. When it came to our spot he produced our two latest LPs and tried, quite amusingly, to explain the crossed-out Beethoven cover. All good publicity. The sketches went smoothly – tho' our starter, the two Pepperpots[1] talking about soiled budgies, was totally lost.

Friday, June 29th

Arrived home about 10.30. Thomas had stayed away from school to meet me, and we spent the morning unpacking and discovering things like the fact that my two Indian canoes from Banff wouldn't float, or

---

1 Pepperpots was the generic name for the screechy ladies in *Monty Python*. John and Graham coined the name because of their shape.

even rest for a moment on the surface of the water. As Thomas pointed out – the Indians weren't really very good at making canoes.

We spent much of July on holiday near Castiglione della Pescaia in Italy with our friends Ian and Anthea Davidson, their daughter Clemency and a lot of very tiny, very vicious sandflies called serafini.

Friday, August 10th

It's now about two and a half weeks since we flew back from Italy and, during that time, although I've succeeded in avoiding any major work commitments, we seem to have been busier than ever, renewing friendships that have lapsed since April and enjoying, with a sort of revived energy, living in London.

Like yesterday, walking through Bloomsbury, south of the Museum, a neat, compact village of Victorian terraced houses with bookshops and magic shops and an atmosphere of small-time human activity, a well-worn, lived-in feeling. The sun had come out and was shining from a clear sky, suffusing the buildings with a golden glow. Of course, I need hardly say that there are plans to knock this down.

Two weeks ago today, I drove up to Southwold and took the old man to Cambridge for a reunion dinner. I looked after him as carefully as I could, carrying his bag into the college lodge, as if he were a freshman. It was quite a curious reversal of the roles – for his reunion was for all those who had left Cambridge in 1921/22, so around the lodge of Clare's new buildings had gathered a group comprised entirely of 73-year-old men, all a little rusty and unfamiliar with the proceedings, exactly reliving their first days at the college over fifty years ago.

I showed the old man to his room, which was in a far corner of the quad. He was in a room opposite his slightly fitter friend Clive Bemrose, who had undertaken to 'keep an eye on him', though I had noticed that even Clive Bemrose couldn't remember to do his flies up after a pee. I felt very out of place, with my long hair and baggy denims.

In the quad a floppy, fattish, rather shambling man, with a case as tatty as my father's, and a head as bald, asked us the way to Thirkell Quad. My father double-took in surprise, 'Well I never, if it isn't my old best man, Bags Cave.'

Recognition spread less spontaneously across Bags' face, but at last it came. 'Good Lord,' he said to my father, 'Hugh St John Gordon! ... Palin,' he corrected himself. My father didn't seem to notice anything untoward, so pleased was he to encounter Bags. It was Silence and Shallow.

'How are you, old boy?'

'Oh, wilting a little, old boy,' said Bags, sadly, and started talking about hospitals.

Being back in Cambridge transformed and inspired my father in such a way that I could visibly see it doing him some good. He was suddenly in control – he knew where he wanted to walk to, and he remembered Cambridge well. I noticed afterwards that the only time he was a little restless was when we walked around the new buildings at St John's. The joy of Cambridge for him, at his age, is in its lack of change. It doesn't disorientate him as other cities do, for he can still see many, if not all, of his old haunts. We walked around the colleges, drinking in the privileged atmosphere, on a perfect, calm, sunny evening. I think we both felt great enjoyment during the one and a half hour walk, and it left no question in my mind as to whether it was worth bringing him or not.

Two days later, on the 29th of July, it was Angela's 40th and Jeremy's 13th birthday and we went down to Dulwich for lunch. The sun came out for us, and we lay in the garden and drank sherry and I tried to take a few photos, as it was one of the very rare occasions on which the family was all together.

It occurred to me what a polite lot we all are. I can remember Angela's childhood being punctuated with violent rows and shouting matches, I can remember many occasions when I hated my father for his intolerant, irrational rule-making, and his surliness to my friends, but now, with age, we've all mellowed. More optimistically, there doesn't seem to be any repetition in Angela's or my family of the lack of contact between father and children which we experienced.

In the garden after tea, Grandfather[1] sat in a deck chair, increasingly concerned with his lack of bowel movements. Granny, getting a little tired, tried to ignore him, and sat talking to Helen. Jeremy, Marcus and Camilla took Thomas and myself on at football. Veryan was cross at the mess we'd made to the lawn. Angela's chief present was an almost new

---

1 Daddy, Dad, Pa, Father, 'the old man' has, as Thomas and William grow older, morphed into 'Grandfather'.

Citroen 6. The first time she's had a car of her own. (Later in the week it was rammed up the back at some traffic lights.)

Next day I took Grandfather down to the West End and dropped him in the Mall, collecting him later from the dark recesses of 'his club', the Institute of Mechanical Engineers. He appeared to be at a low ebb. He didn't feel like shopping for the coat he had wanted, and said that his wretched condition was definitely slowing him down. With some misgivings I took him to the Barque and Bite, on the Regent's Canal. It was conveniently un-full, and, as it turned out, we ate a really excellent meal. He had melon and a very generous Dover sole, I succumbed to salmon and asparagus quiche and guinea fowl, he drank beer, I had a half-carafe of house wine. He liked the situation and he relaxed a lot during the meal. We had a good chat and I even told him that Helen and I were possibly going to have another baby – something which I wouldn't dare tell any other member of the family.[1] It didn't sink in at all, but it felt good to be in confidence-sharing mood with him. He livened up a lot after lunch, and I took him, Thomas and William to Syon Park for the afternoon.

As I drove out along the M4, I became aware that all three of them were asleep – all nodding gently. After a moment Grandfather woke up and said, à propos of nothing, 'There's a plane.' He kept on about planes and the airport and in the end I asked him directly if he'd rather go to the airport. He jumped at this and, in the heat of mid-afternoon, we found ourselves on top of the Terminal 3 car park, watching the activity. After 20 minutes or so, he said he'd had enough, so we started back. We never did get to Syon.

The next morning, I took him to catch the 11.30 train back to Suffolk. He looked rather tired and had little bounce left, and it was as well he was going back. But I think the four days had in fact done him a great deal of good, in taking his mind off his ailments, real and imagined, and giving him things to do – the trip to Cambridge, the airport, the Barque and Bite, which showed him that he is not yet an invalid. In fact, his capacity to enjoy himself is very strong, but he needs pushing.

On Tuesday, Terry and I played squash in the afternoon, and then went on to the BBC for a meeting with Cotton and Duncan Wood about the future of Python. Cotton restated his position that if we were to do a show without John it should not be called Monty Python – it should try

---

1 And which didn't materialise for another eighteen months!

and be something different, and it should be tried out in an on-air pilot, with a possible series next year. We in turn had bristled at the idea of having to prove ourselves in a pilot, and so it devolved on John C. How involved is he prepared to be in a new series? If he is adamantly against any involvement when Bill rings him, then we shall have to think about alternatives.

Tuesday, August 14th

This evening at 10.05, the first TV play written by Terry and myself went out on BBC2. *Secrets* had been given a blaze of pre-publicity of the sort normally reserved for the Cup Final. Mainly, I think, because it was the first of a new series, with a prestige star, Warren Mitchell, and a prestige producer, Mark Shivas, and a prestige director, James Cellan Jones. But also because it was at last something new in the midsummer wilderness of repeats. Anyway, we had the *Radio Times* cover, several trailers, and nearly every critic wrote it up as the main thing to watch this evening.

Helen and I took the children down to Terry's and watched there. As the show started I felt a tingling nervous expectancy, and, although it was all recorded long ago, I watched it as if it were live, willing the actors on to say the line faster or slower, hiding my head during a grossly over-played scene, laughing with tremendous relief when we all laughed. Many things were too cod and too heavily played, but I felt it looked very professional. Graham rang to say he'd enjoyed it and, about 12.00, Barry Cryer was the only other caller. He liked it, but, I think, with reservations. Whatever happens, I don't think after the enormous publicity build-up the critics will ignore it.

Wednesday, August 15th

I opened the *Daily Mirror* to find the headline on the TV page 'Choc Drop Flop'. I groaned, but reading on was worse. It was a violently unfavourable criticism, savagely attacking the writers but, 'as a favour', not mentioning our names. *The Guardian* had nothing.

I bought the other papers, and the situation seemed worse. Both Peter Black in the *Mail* and Richard Last in the *Telegraph* felt that it was the writers who were at fault. Last compared us with Evelyn Waugh, unfavourably of course, and Black felt we hadn't been very clever. Mind you, as a critic, he can hardly have any credence when he caps his review by saying 'if only Graeme Garden, as the Major in the Monty Python series … could have stopped it'.

James Thomas in the *Express* thought it fell flat and it was not until I read *The Times* that there was any crumb of comfort. At least he thought it was hilarious. For two or so hours, I felt like a hunted man. I didn't even ring Terry, I didn't really want to go out.

About 11.00 Simon A rang. He had seen it with his brother and a friend and they had all found it very funny. His objections were the same as mine – that more realism would have helped, that the overplaying of the slapstick made the tale seem more trivial than it was meant to be – but it hadn't spoilt it for them. His call cheered me up a lot, and from then on the day began to improve – Terry G had liked it, with reservations, Ann across the road had enjoyed it without reservations.

In mid-afternoon Mark Shivas rang. He sounded briskly efficient as he expressed his satisfaction with the way the play had been received. People he had come into contact with all seemed to like it. He said that Peter Black and James Thomas had both arrived ten minutes late for the press showing, and that all the good reviews were from people who had not seen it at the press showing – *The Times* and the *Evening News* and the *Evening Standard* (both of whom liked the play a great deal). Shivas was highly pleased, and to reaffirm his confidence in us, he fixed up a lunch date next week, to talk about our writing another play.

John Junkin[1] rang in the evening, just to thank us for making him fall off his chair.

Wednesday, August 22nd

To Sound Developments Studios in Gloucester Avenue. John and I are doing commercials for Corona lemonade (they must have been some of the first commercials to be made for Capital Radio, the new London commercial radio station, which doesn't start broadcasting for another few weeks). Quite a jolly hour – tried different voices – two very modest and unaggressive ad people.

We drank coffee and stood outside in the sun. John is clearly determined to remain uninvolved in any major Python TV project. He says he is writing with Connie, which is something he always wanted to do, and which gives him the afternoons free! In addition he is doing voice-overs

---

1 Comedy actor and writer. Linked closely with Marty Feldman.

like this one to make quick money. I presume, tho' he doesn't talk about it, that he must be working on his films for industry as well. He was keen on doing another record and on being involved in the next Python film.

When I mentioned rewrites of the film, John hesitated for a moment, then cryptically hinted that he would try and make himself available for this. As the film was written by all of us for all of us, I was a little concerned at his attitude, but it turns out that he is hoping to spend three months in Africa from January to March. This made me inwardly very angry, because he knew the film was around, and he must have realised that there would be more work to do on the script. But that is John all over, he can be incredibly self-centred, and, if he wasn't so charming with it, I would have told him so.

Later in the morning I took a bus down to Whitehall and visited the Inigo Jones exhibition at the Banqueting House. The Banqueting House is one of my favourite London buildings – stylish, elegant and civilised, totally unlike the heavy, neo-classical façades of the Home and Foreign Office across the road. I suppose the key is that Inigo Jones was a Sean Kenny[1] figure – a theatrical designer who spent more time designing fantasy buildings than real ones, and this is perhaps why the Banqueting House has a lightness of style, with ornamentation that looks as tho' it's meant to create exuberance. The Foreign Office and the Home Office were built and designed by Victorian engineers. They are solemn and full of a sense of their own importance.

Graham rang, still very worried about the future. It's all a bit of a bore, but I eventually said I would ring Bill Cotton, and find out whether the series was on or off. Bill, who was quite pleasant, couldn't see why we were all so scornful of a pilot. His diagnosis was that there was pride on both sides, and why didn't we stop being so stiff-necked? Bill said he would talk to Duncan and ring back tomorrow.

Thursday, August 23rd

A shopping trip with Helen. Based in the King's Road area. A very good lunch at the Casserole. Robert used to take me there when we were doing *Hang Down Your Head and Die*[2] in 1964. It was one of the first

1 Sean Kenny, one of the cool young stage designers of the 1960s, died in 1973, aged 41.
2 *Hang Down Your Head and Die*, an Oxford University theatre show about capital punishment. Terry J, Robert and I were in the cast. It came to the Comedy Theatre, London, in 1964, produced by Michael Codron.

London restaurants I went to – one of my first encounters with Sophistication. So it was appropriate that one of the first people I saw on entering was William Donaldson, Esq.,[1] blacklisted theatrical agent and the man who paid me my first ever wages after I left Oxford (£50 for working on *The Love Show*).[2]

Willie looked a little hunted, but was as urbane as ever. 'I was going to say how much I enjoyed your play, Palin' (which he pronounced Par-lin, as always) 'but I thought it would be a little unctuous.'

Helen and I hardly talked, just listened to the table next door where two aggressive ladies from the world of PR were meeting with an Australian publicity man.

'Is he camp?'

'Well ... er ... yes, yes, but not in the way ...'

'He's incredibly religious.'

'Oh, I would so love to go to India.'

Just getting off to sleep when Graham rings (11.20) in his vehement shouting mood to tell me that Marty had had a slight nervous breakdown, and other things which don't interest me at all, especially when I'm standing naked in my office getting my balls cold. But they clearly do mean a lot to Graham, and I am hamstrung by an ever-conciliatory nature. It's at times like that that I wish I was forceful, opinionated and rude.

Friday, August 24th

Took Thomas by bus and train down to Greenwich. We walked around the Cutty Sark for half an hour. Interesting to see the tiny, short bunks which they slept in. The sailors can't all have been four foot long. Then up the river in leisurely style to Westminster. Journey of nearly three-quarters of an hour, tho' skirt-flapping hovercrafts do it in about ten minutes. A gentle and unusual way to see London. Sad to see the rows of wharfs. Free Trade Wharf, Metropolitan Wharf etc – all empty now, as so much of the loading and unloading is done at Tilbury and further down river.

Now it's all a rather eerie, dead world, until you reach Tower Bridge

---

1 He later wrote *The Henry Root Letters*, amongst other things.

2 *The Love Show* was a theatrical documentary about attitudes to sex through the ages. Brainchild of Willie D, who brought in Terry J to write it. Never produced.

and the first of the big new developments, which will eventually change the whole emphasis of this part of the river from trade to housing and leisure. Hotels, marinas, all these things are promised.

Wednesday, August 29th

To Ingmar Bergman's *Cries and Whispers*. A superb piece of film-making – not just technically flawless, but enriched by technique. The acting, as usual with Bergman, was strong, precise and utterly convincing. The placing of the camera, the movement of the camera, the lighting and the extraordinary colours of scarlet, black and white, created the mood and made a not unconventional script and situation into a film of total involvement and great beauty. Both Helen and I were stunned. As we stepped out into the brashness of the Tottenham Court Road, it seemed an unreal, trivial world. Very powerful. If I could make one film like that in my life I would be quite happy to retire.

Saturday, September 1st

Bill Oddie offered me one of his season tickets for Chelsea this afternoon. They were playing Sheffield United, and, although they were unlikely to be classy opponents, at least I could see my team in action.

It was a game which brought bowed heads, groans of despair and mute helplessness to the Chelsea supporters around me. Chelsea, with players of real flair like Hudson and Osgood, after a first 15-minute burst, could do nothing right. Sheffield United, a messy and undynamic side to start with, were made to look like quite classy.

Bill grumbled throughout, in his rather endearing way – the only thing he doesn't seem unhappy about is birdwatching. He's energetic and involved in his work, rather like Terry, he seems thoughtful and very aware. I always think the Goodies must be growing more sophisticated, but then he tells me that they're off to Weymouth to shoot a Goodies and the Beanstalk special.

Monday, September 10th

In the evening I spent nearly an hour on the phone with J Cleese.

We talked over everything – but I feel John wants to get completely out of all Python involvement. What a long way we've come since John's phone calls four and a half years ago when he was trying to set up Python. So much has changed in John. V. interesting. We talk about it all the time.

Tuesday, September 11th

Thomas's first day at school. He was dressed by 8.15 and quite clearly full of excitement. At 9.30 he walked off down the road with Helen, holding his envelope with 48p dinner money in it.

At lunch dropped in at the Monarch in Chalk Farm Road, as today was the last for Nick and Mum, the two who ran the Monarch and made it such a relaxed and friendly pub. A small literary coterie had gathered to pay their last respects. There was Graham, Barry Cryer, Bernard McKenna,[1] Tim Brooke-Taylor, an incredibly effusive John Junkin and myself. I've never been in a group which has taken over a pub as they did today. We sang 'Irish Eyes Are Smiling' at full blast, several times. Tim had a nice story. He said to John C at the radio show on Sunday, 'I hear you're dithering about Python.'

'Er ... not really,' said John.

Thursday, September 13th

The news is of fresh bombings in London yesterday, of the overthrow of the first democratically elected communist government of South America in Chile, of Mr Heath's rosy optimism in the face of an enormous trade deficit.

In the afternoon Terry came here. He thought of 'The Monty Python Matching Tie and Handkerchief' as a title for the new LP. We played squash at 4.30. Just for name-dropping purposes, Al Alvarez[2] was there, extolling the beauties of his villa near Lucca in Italy. I felt like a holiday all over again.

In the evening I gave Graham, John and David and Nancy a lift down to Terry's, where we spent a jolly evening watching old Python shows. I must say, I can't share Terry's enthusiasm for re-viewing of the shows. They seem far too ephemeral to me. Interesting imperfections.

---

1 Comedy writer ('Doctor' series), actor, terrific fan of modern jazz and bullfighting.
2 Al Alvarez (b. 1929) is a poet, critic and poker player. He was a keen squash player too, and most of our conversations took place half-naked in the changing rooms.

Optimistic developments today – it's rumoured that the BBC will offer us seven Python shows next year.

Wednesday, September 19th

Lunchtime meeting at Methuen's to discuss promotion of the *Brand New Bok*. Interesting social differences between the publishing crowd and the B&C Charisma Record crowd. Publishing is white wine and lunches at Rules – Charisma is beer and shorts at the Nellie Dean and afterwards at the Penthouse Club. Today it was all white wine, sandwiches and smiles in the office of David Ross, a small, sharp-faced Scot, who is in charge of their publicity. Advance sales have already totalled 105,000 and the book isn't out until Nov. 1st. There were copies there for all of us. I was pleased with the way it looked – once again the artefact had exalted the material, and I was relieved that the vast amount of sexual content in the writing was arranged so that the book didn't appear totally one-track minded.

One of the great satisfactions of the book was the success of the lifelike dirty fingerprints printed on every dust-jacket. Our publisher Geoffrey Strachan told the story of an elderly lady bookseller from Newbury who refused to believe the fingerprints were put there deliberately. 'In that case I shall sell the books without their jackets,' she said and slammed the phone down so quickly that Geoffrey was unable to warn her that beneath each dust-cover was a mock soft-core magazine, featuring lots of bare-bottomed ladies beneath the title: 'Tits and Bums, A Weekly Look at Church Architecture'.

Saturday, September 22nd

Out early to buy breakfast for Pythons. A sunny morning, a crisp autumnal edge to the air in South End Green. It's funny how autumn seems to have started so punctually. 9.30, Eric arrives – the first time I've seen him since we parted company at Los Angeles Airport on June 28th.

John's here, all smiles – and in fact everyone except Terry G. Orange juice, hot croissants and coffee, then a big read through of material for the new album. A sketch which Graham and I collaborated on yesterday has John and Eric in stitches. But still nothing very exciting. One section of a 'Phone-In' type sketch, which Terry and I wrote, is about the only piece that has everyone rolling about.

Tensions flare at the end of the meeting when Terry, in passing, mentions that Mark Forstater will be fulfilling a kind of producer's function on the film – John reacts strongly, 'Who is this Mark Forstater?' etc, etc.[1] John has a way of making it sound like a headmaster being crossed by a junior pupil, rather than equal partners in a business disagreeing. Terry quite shaken and retires to the kitchen to avoid exploding.

Around 1.30 everyone leaves except Eric, who is in a cheery mood and anxious to find out about future of the group who met this morning. He and I drive down to Camden Town, and buy a kebab at Andy's, then come back here and talk. Eric in a much more obliging and co-operative frame of mind than he has been in the past. He says he is living on no money, and I believe that from anyone who comes from Earl's Court to Gospel Oak by bus at 9.30 in the morning.

Wednesday, September 26th

Terry and I went up to the Flask in Hampstead and had a good air-clearing talk about the future. We both feel now (c.f. flight to Calgary three months ago) that another series of Python for the BBC – with John writing a regulation three and a half minutes per show – is not worth doing, certainly at present, if at all. I was not encouraged enough by the material we wrote for the record to believe that Python has vast untapped resources. I think we may be straining to keep up our standards and, without John, the strain could be too great. On the other hand, Terry and I do have another direction to go in, with a play in commission and another on the stocks. We work fast and economically, and still pretty successfully together. Python it seems is being forced to continue, rather than continuing from the genuine enthusiasm and excitement of the six people who created it.

Monday, October 1st

Sunny and warm. Took Thomas to school. Now he doesn't even need me to come into the playground with him. We cross the road, past the lollipop man, and then Thomas asks me to stay on the corner and runs the

1 Mark Forstater, an American film producer living in London, originally introduced to us by Terry Gilliam.

last twenty yards up to the school gate on his own – with his blanket and his apple.

One of my earliest memories is of the school hall at Birkdale, with my mother saying goodbye and leaving me standing there with my shoe-bag, bitterly unhappy. I must have been Thomas's age, just five. 1948.

Drove up to André's to listen to the tapes of the LP. Some sounded very flat. Terry G, Terry J and myself discuss possibility of an extraneous sound effect running throughout the record (e.g. Indian attacks or a cleaning lady using carpet sweeper, etc) – which could be faded up to enliven some of the less exciting sketches.

Wednesday, October 3rd

A Parents' Meeting at Gospel Oak School. Went in with Christine,[1] met Jean Oddie on the door, she introduced me to Adrian Mitchell and wife.[2] They were all in a long line outside enjoying an illicit cigarette before the meeting began. Meeting attended by 150 or so parents. Headmaster says this is remarkable attendance. He has been asking around other schools and finds that most have less than ten parents along to meetings like this. But Gospel Oak does demonstrate what tremendous differences there can be between schools within the state system.

This school has a nucleus, or perhaps even a majority, of enlightened, liberal, *Guardian*-reading parents, who are concerned about their children and the way they're brought up, to the point of obsession. They not only read books and articles about education, they also write them. It must be one of the most literate, articulate parent groups in the country. The school functions better through this interest – more time can be spent teaching the kids than disciplining them, and everyone seems to benefit all round. But the disparity between Gospel Oak and other schools the Head Teacher mentioned is disturbing – for when people talk of state education as providing equal opportunity for all kids, they are in cloud cuckoo land. I'm just glad Thomas is at Gospel Oak where opportunities are more equal.

1 Christine, a neighbour and the wife of Richard Guedalla, my occasional squash partner.
2 Adrian is a poet, playwright and novelist. His wife Celia started the Ripping Yarns second-hand bookshop, a treasure trove on the Archway Road, north London.

We elect a Parent Manager for the ILEA Manager's board, and then are shown a 20-minute film about child molesters. Quite well-made, I would like Tom to see it. A discussion on the merits of the film afterwards. Lots of articulate women. There must have been upwards of 100 psychiatrists among them.

Monday, October 8th

On Saturday afternoon Thomas's fifth birthday party. Twelve kids altogether.

Sunday spent playing with Thomas's new toys and reading about the Arab-Israeli War, which had broken out that morning with all the inevitability of the sun rising. Took Thomas and Willy up onto Parliament Hill to try and fly his new kite. Heard someone describing to a group of friends some of the jokes from our second German show, which had gone out on BBC2 the night before. Couldn't fly the kite. Packed it up, and walked home ignominiously.

In the evening Hazel and Andrew,[1] Roger Last and Simon Albury round. We watched the start of a new *Frost Programme* series – it was about private education. It started such an animated discussion in the room that we soon ignored the telly and turned it off. Conversation at last killing the art of television.

First day of legal commercial radio. Very dull. Newsreader couldn't read news properly.

Tuesday, October 23rd

At 5.00 into a quite eventful Python meeting. Everybody is present, tho' Graham's about half an hour late. This is the second of our 'chase Gledhill' meetings. Gledhill looks more relaxed and cooler than when I saw him at his Barbican flat a week ago. Then I thought he would crack up within a day or two. Now he seems more confident. He takes control from the start, and offers for discussion a number of fairly unimportant points. Do we want to appear on the *Russell Harty Show*? Everyone says no, apart from Graham. We are into royalties on the second record! £19 each. And who wants to go to Denmark for a two-day publicity trip?

Having cleared these out of the way there is discussion about the

---

1 Hazel Pethig, Python costume designer; Andrew was her partner at the time.

[Michael] Codron[1] offer of six weeks, starting at Christmas, in the Comedy Theatre. Eric and John are very keen. Terry G less keen, myself very anti. For some reason I find myself in the rare position of being out on my own (tho' Terry J, I think, feels the same, but is keeping tactfully quiet to avoid accusations of a block vote). Briefly, I see it as six more weeks of a show which I find very dull, and here we are going to the West End, forsaking our Rainbow/pop following – which, John says, 'scares the shit out of me' – for the £2.50 circle and front stalls audience, with a show that seems to me full of old material – some of it done in the West End before. What has become of Python the innovator? Are we at the end of our creative careers, at the tender ages of 30–32?

Graham arrives, I think a little fortified, and from the stage show the talk goes on to accounts. Graham is the first to attack fiercely. He says we have asked for the accounts for long enough, and John has done nothing – but John G produces an envelope and, with a triumphant smile, reveals – six copies of the company accounts. A breathing space, everyone feels better, Graham looks discomfited. John G follows this up with optimistic details of payments to come within the month. Such is the success of this move, that he manages to get away with the extraordinary revelation that Tony Stratton-Smith does not have the money for the film. Tony's offer, we had been constantly assured, was the one cert. in a changing world. Then I notice the beautifully presented accounts are only for the year up to October 1971! They are two years behind.

At last the attack develops. Gilliam rants and raves and expresses his frustration very forcibly, banging the chair. Eric is very quiet. John C wades in, tho' not ruthlessly. I try to tell John G why we are dissatisfied – that he has for too long been giving us definite optimistic pronouncements which turn out to mean nothing. Graham gets angry again, and John G reacts – cleverly, in retrospect – with injured aggression. He fights back. 'Then why not get yourself another Python manager?' he says, sweeping his glasses off with a flourish. You could have heard a pin drop in Waterloo Place this uncommonly mild October afternoon. John G, unconfronted by a barrage of protests, moves quickly on, but into an area where, for the first time, he commits himself too far – 'Frankly, as far as I am concerned, Python may not be here next year, and I've got

1 Successful West End producer for, among others, Michael Frayn, Harold Pinter, Simon Gray and Alan Ayckbourn. Gave me my first and last West End break in the Oxford Experimental Theatre production of *Hang Down Your Head and Die*, in 1964 when I was 21.

other eggs in the basket which I have to develop as well ...' Still no reaction. He retracts and returns to safer ground, 'In any case, I think this is the only area where I may not have produced the goods.' Here followed the most damning silence of all. We'll see what develops.

I left the meeting feeling pleased with myself for not giving in over the stage show, but with the unhappy feeling that somehow we must do something for the sake of the group. As Terry G says, there is a danger that we should become too purist, and in rejecting everything because it isn't *quite* right, we end up with nothing but principles.

Thursday, October 25th

To the office of Michael White in Duke St, St James's. A successful and fairly prestigious young impresario – *Sleuth*, *Oh Calcutta!* and many other well-known titles on the framed playbills around his office. Pleasant, disarming, unpretentious feel to the offices.

John Goldstone[1] was there and Mark [Forstater], and we started to chat after White had offered us a drink. He and Goldstone seemed to share many of our feelings about what the film should be like. White talked of the 'really good comedy film' which has yet to be made. What he meant was, I think, that our film should not depend on TV for anything more than a sales impetus, it should be a film of merit in itself. Such intelligent interest in our film we haven't encountered before. All in all it was an amicable meeting – but then John Cleese in Cambridge Circus was one of White's prized talents 12 years ago, and Terry has also been in a revue which White backed.

Tuesday, October 30th

Tonight a long phone call from John Cleese. He proposed asking John Goldstone to our Python meeting on Thursday to explain the deal and tell us where and if he thought Mark would fit in. In the end we agreed to ask Mark along first, just to give him a hearing – but even then I was made to feel I had wrung a major concession from John.

---

1 John Goldstone was a film producer brought in by Michael White. I'd first met him at Barry Took's in the days before Python.

Wednesday, October 31st

John Gledhill rang this evening. The clash comes nearer. I told him we were meeting Mark tomorrow. He was taken aback, but recovered. 'He's no negotiator, anyway,' says John. Finally he says, of course, whatever Mark's function, he, Gledhill, will do all the deals. I ring Mark later. Mark wants to do all the deals because he says that Gledhill is very bad at it – and was embarrassing at a meeting with Goldstone recently. So, the collision may come earlier than I thought – perhaps tomorrow. Co-operation, as an option, seems to be receding. It's all a long way from being out there filming and I find it depressing to have to get into this personal tangle. Especially as there is no villain of the piece, no easy target whom we can slander and malign. Both Gledhill and Mark are nice people.

Evening a little brightened by the extraordinary latest news from Washington. Two of the most vital tapes, which Nixon has finally agreed to hand over, do not exist. On a vital John Dean conversation – the machine wasn't working!! The Nixon/Gledhill situations do have a number of parallels. In either case there is a central figure who has far more work and far greater responsibilities than he can cope with, and yet is determined to fight, by some very devious means, rather than relinquish any of this work or any of these responsibilities.

Thursday, November 1st

Surprise, surprise. A cordial, relaxed, totally constructive meeting at John's. All of us present, and Mark as well. Mark explained the film deal, thoroughly and efficiently, and also gave us a run-down on how he would hope to be involved in the film, and how much of a cut he would like.

At 6.00, a party at Methuen's to launch the *Brand New Bok*. No famous names, instead representatives of the printers, blockmakers, binders, etc, who had been involved in actually making the book. During the party Gledhill had very good news about the NFFC,[1] who were only too keen to go ahead with Python, White, Goldstone. John had with him a sheet of Heads of Proposals, which towards the end of

1 National Film Finance Corporation, government-sponsored agency with money to invest in British films.

the party he was getting people to sign. I couldn't take much of it in at that time, but seeing other signatures, and presuming it was merely a contract for story development in order to get the £6,000 front money, I, too, signed.

Monday, November 5th

Another Python meeting chez Cleese. When I arrived there at 1.00 John Gledhill was sitting on the arm of a sofa looking wide-eyed and uncomfortable. Also there were Mark, John C, Eric and Graham. No one seemed to be talking to each other. It was like a morgue. Then Terry J and Gilliam arrived, and we walked up to Tethers for lunch and a chat.

Once in Tethers, Terry J asked Mark to outline his criticisms of the contract which John G had asked us to sign at the book launching party last Thursday night. As Mark ran through the clauses, it was increasingly clear that we were being asked to sign away our copyright on the film – which is tantamount to signing away every bargaining counter Python ever had. Mark will draft a new agreement, with his solicitor, and we will present it to Goldstone later in the week.

Wednesday, November 7th

Met Irene Handl[1] at Studio G today where we were both to do a voice-over. A lovely lady who immediately talks to you as tho' you've been friends for years. If Bill Tidy is the spirit of the Snug Bar personified, then Irene Handl personifies the warmest, most comfortable armchair by the fire.

Monday, November 12th

Esther Rantzen has rung to ask if I will do an interview about the *Brand New Monty Python Bok* on her prog, *Late Night Esther*. I agreed, and found myself leaving home at 11.00 p.m. to go down to the studio. Nervous, I'm afraid, despite many interviews, etc. I still find projecting myself less easy than it used to be – maybe I'm just more self-conscious now. Sit in an ante-room clutching my 'Bok'. The Producer,

---

1 British character actress and author of two bestselling novels, *The Sioux* and *The Gold-Tipped Pfizer*. I'd grown up with her wonderfully distinctive voice on the radio.

small, bearded, bespectacled, appears. He doesn't look like the kind to take risks, so (with some difficulty) I select a fairly inoffensive passage about what to do on meeting the Royal Family.

On the air about 11.45. A dull old prog with lots of stock BBC muzak to put everyone to sleep. Esther doing her bit very well, with great energy considering she had done a radio prog at 9.00 in the morning as well. We have a rather unimpressive chat. Esther reads the extract from the 'Bok' rather badly (afterwards I find this is mainly because the bearded, bespectacled little Producer keeps screaming through her earphones to tell her to stop before she reads anything compromising).

Tuesday, November 13th

Met with Jimmy Gilbert at BBC in the morning.[1] Jimmy very genial, welcoming – very much the feeling of a nostalgic reunion, for all of us, except Gilliam, had helped to keep Jimmy in material for two series of *Frost Reports*. He had only inherited Duncan Wood's office the week before, and it was still in the process of changeover. The walls were bare, a disembowelled record-playing unit lay against one wall, and Jimmy looked far from at home in it.

I'm not sure if he really grasped what we wanted – which was, in effect, a new series of Python, without John, and different in style from the others by being unified, organic half hours, and not just bric-a-brac, loosely slung together. He is going to see Alasdair Milne[2] next week and will put the programme suggestion to him. Quite a substantial part of our future is now in genial Jimmy's hands.

Thursday, November 15th, Southwold

I went up to Southwold on the train to see how the parents were. Found Mother looking fairly chirpy and less tired than when I saw her last. Daddy is slower and less capable each time I see him. However, he still responds to my visits in much the same way – it's obvious that he enjoys them and that he's pleased to see me. But his mind wanders and he is easily distracted, which is making Mother very irritable. I always remember him as an irritable man easily moved to the sharp reproof, happier with the sarcastic

1 He'd just been promoted to Head of Comedy.
2 Managing Director, Television.

put-down, embarrassed by the open compliment. Now, unable to marshal his thoughts and actions very clearly, the tables are turned and he is the victim of another's bottled-up bitterness and impatience.

While I was there we went for a long walk in the cool bracing sea air at Minsmere, with a big red sun sinking behind the bird sanctuary as we walked. He has had more hallucinations recently. He talks about 'When that man was in the kitchen ...' and so on. Recently he locked the door in the evening, in case 'those men' got in. He knows by their accents that they are quite cultured, and they are apparently friendly, but it is frightening that they should be so real to him.

Saturday, November 17th

Ate breakfast on the Ipswich–London train, and read some of Ivan Illich's book *Tools for Conviviality*. In the words of the old cliché, a most thought-provoking book, and very depressing – for he so clearly and radically tackles the problems of 'progress' and social organisation that I was left with a feeling of profound dissatisfaction and yet at the same time helplessness.

His diagnosis – that we have gone too far, too fast, that we are the slaves, not the masters of technology, in short that the contribution an individual can make to society has become so limited and so insignificant – is very clear, but where do we begin to change things? How can we eventually start renouncing what we have in order to go back to a less complicated society but one with greater respect and freedom for the individual? Suddenly I am aware that aggression and greed are not vices which suddenly spring up and are crushed in a war, they are institutionalised in the system we live in.

Back home to complete and utter disorientation. There are men on my roof erecting a corrugated iron temporary roof atop some scaffolding. This new structure towers over our house only marginally less conspicuously than the hand of God actually pointing at the front door. I suppose I felt like the soldier returning from leave in the war only to find his house had gone, except in this case it had grown.

Monday, November 19th

William is three today. The day when he was born now seems so remote. Those were the days when everyone seemed to be having kids. Now everyone seems to have mellowed and settled. After all the excitement we've all calmed down a little. There are not so many babies, there are more little people now.

I took Tom to school, then down to Terry's for another meeting on the film. Some good stuff from Eric – and some of the pieces I'd written at S'wold went down well, which was encouraging. At lunchtime Terry had a shouting match with John which blew up from nowhere, and the intensity of T's outburst took even John by surprise. It was all about T feeling oppressed by John's rather dismissive handling of any suggestion of Terry's. In fact John is trying to be fairly accommodating, but he does tend to dominate the group more than he used to.

In the afternoon he suddenly had to leave and Terry Gilliam had to leave in order to drive John and Graham in to the Centre. Eric went off to see a film, and Terry and I were left with the fag-end of the afternoon and the dirty coffee cups.

Saturday, November 24th

Drove up to Abbotsley at 50 mph as the government had requested. Most people appeared to be observing the unofficial limit.[1] It was rather like being in a slow-motion film.

Tuesday, November 27th

Worked at Terry's in the morning. A very poor session. We both wrote 75% tripe, and seemed unable to summon up excitement or concentration about the film. The most I could manage was a sketch about Galahad having smelly breath.[2] This was the level. But after a lunch of cold spring greens and beans, we decided to call it a day, and went through our mutual morale-boosting act about bad days and good days and the amount we'd done last week, etc, etc. Terry didn't cheer up much until I dragged him into London.

We parked in Leicester Square, then took in one hour of Pasolini's *Canterbury Tales* which Terry G had recommended. Superb recreation of mediaeval England – the kind of style and quality of shooting that we

1 The result of petrol shortages after the Arab-Israeli war.
2 Prompted by my reading out a sketch about a knight using coconuts instead of a horse, we agreed around this time to investigate the King Arthur story as a basis for the new film.

must get in our film, to stop it being just another *Carry On King Arthur*.

Wednesday, November 28th

Met at TG's later. He has been reading various fine-looking books on mediaeval warfare, and found that much of the absurd stuff that has already been written for the *Holy Grail* film has healthy precedents (e.g. taunting one's opponents and, as a last resort, firing dead animals at them during a siege – both quoted as mediaeval tactics by Montgomery). Then over to John's for a script meeting.

Mark F was there. The film deal is still not finalised. Apparently our Fairy Godmother, Michael White, is being quite businesslike with us – his cohort, John Goldstone, wants 12½% and a fee for a job whose function we cannot quite pin down, and Michael White wants his name prominently on the credits, plus various controls and final word on appointment of crew, production staff, editing, etc. So Mark has not signed yet. At the same time, Tony Stratton-Smith has come up with an offer of £45,000 from Pink Floyd, so there are alternative sources giving us a stronger hand against White.

Thursday, November 29th, Bradford

Woken by alarm at 7.00. Collected Graham from Belsize Park, and we got down to King's Cross by 7.30. Joined the rest of the Methuen party for a trip to a literary lunch in Bradford – where we were expected to give some sort of speech, along with Denis Norden, Gyles Brandreth and Leslie Thomas. Breakfast on the train. Jilly Cooper, of the low breasts and alluring smile, was also there.

At Leeds we were met by a coach which took us on to Bradford – a puzzling piece of planning this, as the train went on to Bradford anyway. We drove past a tripe works and into the grey centre of the city, spattered with a light covering of snow. Even since we were last in Bradford for Python filming three years ago, the demolishers have started to attack and replace some of the finest Victorian buildings. The stylish glass and steel curved roof of Victoria Station is going, a marvellous, grimy, black Baroque hall in the centre of the town is being knocked down, and so is an old, fine, stone-walled market. They are being replaced by the usual faceless crap. Four-lane highways and insurance company offices, with no style, or beauty, or sympathy. Our literary lunch was held in one of these new and faceless blocks – the Norfolk Gardens Hotel.

We disembarked from our coach (a funny thought, somehow – a coachload of writers) and were taken into a carpeted ante-room leading to the dining room, where we were given drinks whilst the guests assembled. Mostly ladies, but a number of younger ones who didn't look quite like the hangers and floggers we'd expected.

We started our communal Python speech with Graham doing 'Thank you very much and now some readings from the "Bok"' as a very prolonged mime. Then I got up and read some 'Biggles' in Swedish and then out of the book. Quite rude stuff, I suppose, but no one seemed to worry unduly. Terry read the 'Horace' poem and John finished up by reading a rather disappointingly unfunny piece from the 'Fairy Story'.

Then we sat outside in the ante-room and signed endless copies of the 'Bok'. Jilly Cooper was sitting next to us and, as she wasn't signing as many as we were, Terry passed one lady's Python book to Jilly to sign. The woman grabbed the book back, saying 'I don't want her to sign … I don't agree with her.'

Too rushed to keep a daily diary for the next month, I rounded up the salient events after Christmas.

Friday, December 28th

It's a still, grey, anonymous afternoon.

At the beginning of December I had been working with Terry J down in Camberwell [on the script of what was to become *Monty Python and the Holy Grail*] and had a wearying week travelling as much as possible by public transport, owing to the 'oil crisis' – the 30% cut in Arab supplies to the West which has resulted in near-panic this week at the petrol stations. Many only open for two or three hours a day, and police have had to sort out traffic-jamming queues at many garages. London Transport, with a 30–35% undermanning problem, is no longer as efficient as it used to be, and it's quite common to wait 10 or 15 minutes for an Underground train, on a dusty, dirty platform (Victoria Line excluded). However, I arrived only about 15 minutes late at Tony Stratton-Smith's office. Tony, smiling and benignly jokey as ever, opened a bottle of sparkling wine and detailed his proposals for raising £75,000. £25,000 was to come from Led Zeppelin and £20,000 from Pink Floyd. Tony Stratton himself would make up the last £25,000, and small investors like Michael Wale[1] wanted to put in £2,000. Tony asked one or two routine questions, but altogether his offer seemed a lot more attractive than White–Goldstone. All he wanted for supplying finance was 5% – but Mark, a steady negotiator to the end, got him down to 4½%.

Both Led Zeppelin and Floyd were prepared to write or play theme music for us – an additional bonus, which could boost our chances in the States.

In the second week of December the weather improved – we had long sunny spells and clear skies. The oil panic passed its worst stage, but it was clear that the Arabs, by the simple expedient of controlling the exploitation of their own oil, had at one stroke brought the era of unquestioned expansion to an end. The very suddenness of the effects of the oil cutbacks is amazing. Only a month ago Anthony Barber [Chancellor of the Exchequer] and Heath were telling us that Britain was at last heading for sustained economic growth, and if we all pulled together, an era of prosperity and boom would be on us by the end of '74. On December 12th I was at Belsize Park Post Office collecting petrol rationing coupons – old-fashioned Suez coupons, still bearing the authority of the Minister of Power!

The government of expansion and progress has introduced an Emergency Powers Bill, which bans all display lighting, enveloping London in pre-Christmas gloom. Railways and coal, both despised and run down in the last fifteen years, are now being talked of, together with North Sea oil, as Britain's hope for the future.

The film script was completed on Friday 14th – but still without enough group work on the links and plot scenes. But some very funny writing from all sources – Graham and John in particular were back on form.

On Christmas Eve collected Grandfather and took him to an afternoon carol service at Westminster Abbey. On the way he talks some complete nonsense. Strange non sequiturs, as his mind gropes from subject to subject, forgetting where he began and what he was trying to say. But it clearly is a great source of pleasure to him to sit in the Abbey for an hour. I left him there and drove around Westminster.

1 Journalist and co-writer of *Now!*, the TV pop show produced by TWW in Bristol, on which I spent six months as a presenter in 1965–6.

London was quiet and empty. The lack of public display lighting (except for the Norwegian Christmas tree in Trafalgar Square, which has been given a dispensation for today and Christmas Day), the feeling of impending industrial crisis, only temporarily stemmed by Christmas, the various IRA bomb explosions in the last two weeks, all couldn't help but create a melancholy atmosphere.

I rather liked it actually. I drove into Soho, and drank a coffee and bought the last croissants before Christmas at a little French bakery, and it seemed that people were more ready to smile – were a little more aware of each other, rather than the headlong rush to buy, sell, display, offer, wrap, fill. But I could just be over-romanticising.

Python has been directly hit by the new emergency fuel-saving powers. TV has been ordered to close down at 10.30 and our repeats, scheduled at 11.25, are now presumed cancelled.

1973 is the year which saw the break-up of the Python group. I was unable to accept that it was happening – indeed there were possibly more combined projects in 1973 than in 1972. The *Brand New Bok*, the *First Farewell Tour* from April to June, the *Matching Tie and Handkerchief* LP, the film script. But all these projects were, to a certain extent, Python cashing in on a comfortably receptive market, rather than breaking new ground. The only project of '73 requiring new creative effort was the film – and although much good new material came up, there was nothing like the unified enthusiasm of the first two series. A freshness has gone, and 1974 will see just how we pick up the threads again.

1974

Friday, January 4th

The industrial trouble with the mines and railwaymen has now eclipsed the oil crisis. The government decided on an all-out confrontation with the miners and the railwaymen. Mr Heath's bluff with the three-day week has been called. Now both sides are sweating it out, while the country gets darker and colder.

Met with Graham and John Gledhill at lunchtime. Graham is going to assemble a trial script for Jimmy Gilbert at the BBC to satisfy their need to see what Python may be like without John. A humiliating experience to start the year with. John Gledhill has at last some money from the Canadian tour – £350 each, but JG has managed to get us assurances of £1,500 each for a week at the Theatre Royal, Drury Lane in February.

Left JG's in a hurry to get back home to collect Thomas and take him to the Mermaid to see *Treasure Island*. I wanted to have a pee, but decided to wait till I got home. I must have underestimated the urgency of the situation, because no sooner in the car than I wanted to go desperately. Every traffic light was agony. I drove my Mini like a stunt driver, passing whole traffic jams, overtaking on the inside, outside and middle in my agony to get back. But I made it, rushed in and hung over the lavatory in a cold sweat, eventually being forced to lie on the bathroom floor, still in my long black coat. Thomas was sympathetic. I told him I had a stomach ache and he patted my doubled-up shoulders with kindly consideration and said that he gets stomach aches as well.

We set off at 2.00 and arrived about five minutes late at the Mermaid. An action-packed version of *Treasure Island* played for all it was worth. Enormous explosions, violently realistic stage fights – in one of which young innocent Jim Hawkins knees an evil pirate in the balls – much to the kids' delight.

Tuesday, January 8th

Met Eric and Terry for lunch at Pontevecchio in Old Brompton Road. Eric ordered a bottle of champagne and orange juice and we sipped this whilst waiting for T to arrive. Outside a really angry day, with heavy rain lashed against the windows by gale-force winds. The grimness of the weather rather matched my mood.

Left with the feeling that our futures are distinctly unsettled. Lots of offers, but few which seem to have much sense of direction. We haven't done a new series for eighteen months, and the current repeats are the last time we will have a series of Python on BBC TV, unless Jimmy Gilbert can get the go-ahead for a non-Cleese show. The film is a development, and certainly the best thing we have around, but so far no final word on finance. To spread further despondency, all I needed was a call from J Cleese.

It came in the evening. There had been the suggestion, from his very own lips, when we put the film together in December, that we should spend a week on it in mid-January. Tonight, when I ask him about availability, he tells me that he can only make one and a half days' meetings during January and none at all until the first two weeks of February. This bombshell is dropped quite unapologetically. I swallowed for air and within a moment or two my reaction came – but it wasn't as I expected. It was a reaction of relief rather than anger, a sudden welcome burst of indifference about John and his future and his work. He may come in with us, he may not, but as from this evening I couldn't care less.

Friday, January 11th

Down to Joseph's for a haircut at 1.00. He has just bought his own electricity generator – for unlike food stores, restaurants, cinemas and TV stations, hairdressers are not exempt from the emergency electricity restrictions and can only work half-days. All the lights were switched off, but J was taking advantage of an anomaly in the law which allowed him power to dry the hair of people who had been washed in the morning shift.

Small hints of emergency life around. The *Radio* and *TV Times* are now very slim, with only a couple of pages devoted to indirect programme information. Cardboard boxes and, indeed, packaging of all kinds, are increasingly short. In shops now tins, etc, are packed on a slim cardboard base with polythene wrapped around them.

In the evening Helen and I went to see Marco Ferreri's *La Grande Bouffe* at the Curzon. A stylish, revolting, very funny and very sad film about four men[1] who decide to eat themselves to death. Some of those

1 Played by Marcello Mastroianni, Michel Piccoli, Philippe Noiret and Ugo Tognazzi.

heavy, over-rich meals at restaurants taken to ultimate, absurd lengths. Outrageous but never offensive, never heartless, never cheap. Sad to think that it can't even be given a national certificate and has to be restricted to London viewing.

Monday, January 14th, Southwold

Mother looked encouragingly well on her 70th birthday. She is living testimony to the fact that people can thrive on a difficult life. Her face may have aged, her stoop increased a degree in the thirty years I've known her, but her energy, mental and physical, is barely diminished. It's great that at 70 she seems as likely to survive the next twenty years as myself or Thomas or Willy. There is no hint of age withering her.

I took them out to the Crown Hotel in Framlingham for a celebration lunch. The hotel was warmed by a blazing log fire, the food was good and simple and the main hall of the hotel had as extensive and fine a selection of Tudor beams and timbers as I've seen. Very gemütlich. Afterwards we walked along the battlements of Framlingham Castle. It was a cloudy, but bright and mild day, and the expedition was quite a success.

I left Southwold to get back to London at about 5.00. Heard on the car radio that the latest and maybe the last attempts at conciliation between government and TUC had broken down, and there was to be a full rail strike tomorrow.

Tuesday, January 15th, London

Python meeting at T Gilliam's. We decide to do two weeks at Drury Lane, tho' I have a feeling in my bones that we would have done better to concentrate on one smash-hit week and leave people wanting more, rather than expose ourselves and our material to the spotlight for two weeks.

There was some fairly bitter debate over timing of the film and rewriting. In the end, after the personal differences had been aired, we got down to some fast and efficient business, dates were agreed and there was a very useful hour's discussion of the film. An idea I had for the gradual and increasing involvement of the present day in this otherwise historical film was adopted as a new and better way of ending it, so I felt that I had done a bit of useful work over the last hectic month.

We decide to call our Drury Lane show *Monty Python's First Farewell Tour (repeat)* and overprint it with the words 'NOT CANCELLED'.

Thursday, January 17th

At lunchtime, met Tony Smith, John Gledhill, Terry J, Terry G and André at Drury Lane to have a first look at the theatre in which we will be spending two weeks at the end of February. A gloomy first encounter. In the dark foyer, flanked by dusty, heavy pillars and classical columns, the eye is immediately drawn to a war memorial – to the fallen in two wars.

The approach to the auditorium, the passageways and halls, are furnished and decorated in the grand classical style. Doric columns, porticoes, domes, balustrades and statues of great actors in niches. On the walls flanking the wide and impressive staircases are huge oil paintings. It somehow feels as likely and as suitable a venue for Python as a power station. The size of the auditorium would a year ago have made me laugh and run out straightaway to return Tony's contract, but having rehearsed in the Rainbow, and played the Wilfred Pelletier Theatre in Montreal, both of which hold over 3,000 seats, the wide open spaces of the Theatre Royal (2,200 seats) no longer hold quite the same terror. Nevertheless, the sight of three balconies and innumerable lavishly decorated boxes, and a general air of London opulence and tradition, tightened my stomach a little.

Friday, January 18th

GC and I, at GC's suggestion, went to the BBC to talk to Jimmy, who is vacillating still over a BBC series. Frightfully welcoming and anxiously effusive. He took us to lunch and straightaway brought up the subject of the series. He wanted to check one or two details – just so he could make a clear suggestion to his superiors, he said. From then on he talked as if the series was in the bag.

It seemed as tho' some decision had been made in the Beeb to treat us nicely again, and Graham and I completed a tidy half-day's work on behalf of Python by collecting a list of seven studio recording dates from Jimmy G, which, being in November, would fit in well with our year's schedule.

Suddenly it seems that 1974 could be our busiest and most creative since '71.

JG told us that to date *The Brand New Monty Python Bok* has sold 161,000 copies, and the new record is selling faster than any of the previous ones. Less hopefully, he showed us a decidedly gloomy letter from BBC sales people in New York; despite all Nancy is doing, they do not seem any closer to a US TV sale of the series.

Indeed, one station in New York had, apparently, 'indicated a positive distaste for the program'. But the sales people, who are part of Time-Life Films, have evidently been affected by something like the same masochistic enthusiasm for the programme that Nancy has. At the end of the letter they did say that, for them, selling the programme was becoming rather like a crusade.

Sunday, January 20th

Took the kids for a short walk up to Lismore Circus with Sean[1] (Thomas's godfather) and Simon (Willy's godfather). They rode their bikes for about ten minutes, when a window in Bacton (the tall tower block in the Circus) opened and a vehement old lady shrieked at them to 'go away and play where you live'. I've always felt sorry for old ladies in high-rise blocks of flats, up till now.

Tuesday, January 22nd

The national situation looks depressing. No deal with the miners or with the railwaymen. The restrictions on lighting, TV and the Government's SOS (Switch Off Something) campaign, have now become quite accepted aspects of national life. The three-day week is still in operation.

Thursday, January 24th

I was still talking to the man from Coverite Asphalters on the roof at 11.30 when I remembered I should have been at the Theatre Royal, Drury Lane, for a press party to launch our two-week 'season' at the end of February.

Eventually reached Theatre Royal by cab at 11.55. Monty Python, not over-announced, on the outside. At least we have our name on paper, if not in lights. (When will anyone ever have their name in lights again?) Inside, a box-office without a queue. Up the wide staircase to the Circle

---

1 Sean Duncan, now a judge in Liverpool. We'd been at Shrewsbury and Oxford together.

bar, which is of the proportions of Adam's library at Kenwood House, with four huge Corinthian columns dwarfing a motley collection of about thirty press folk.

Nicholas de Jongh of *The Guardian*, looking tubby and rather windswept, moved amongst us with an uncertain, rather indulgent smile and a notebook, asking us for witty things to say. At least Eric had something reasonable (which appeared next morning in the paper). He was feeding his son Carey at the time, and replied 'It was all right for Oscar Wilde, being gay. He didn't have to feed babies, he had both arms free for being witty.' N de J: 'But Oscar Wilde had children.' EI: 'Trust *The Guardian* to know that.'

Sunday, January 27th, Abbotsley

Today, a pleasant lazy day. Thomas and I made a bonfire, we sawed some wood and played football and went off on an archaeological trip around Abbotsley. Thomas had uncovered pieces of old china in the garden, and pursued this new interest quite keenly during the day. A joint of beef and Yorkshire pud for lunch. I don't think I've ever not enjoyed a Sunday at Abbotsley – it's one of those unchanging, unexceptional, but unfailingly satisfying institutions, when the whole pace of life slows to a comfortable, convivial saunter.

Home at 8.30 to find the plasterer, Bill Berry, at work. Bill Berry is quite a character. He's a tiling man by trade, and is at present relaying a marble floor at London Airport's Terminal One. He's done Buckingham Palace and the National Gallery as well, he told me.

He's always coming out with strange non sequiturs. You'll be talking to him about terrazza tiles and he'll suddenly say 'Croup,' with an air of great finality. You look around bewildered. 'Croup,' he repeats, even more positively, and points at Thomas, 'That's what he's got.'

Friday, February 1st

Drive into town for a meeting with *New Musical Express*, who want us to review the week's new singles for them. Their offices in Long Acre are securely locked, but after much bell-ringing, tall, rangy features editor T Tyler leads me through deserted corridors up to an eyrie high in the building, where various members of *NME* staff sit in candlelit gloom.

They are all fairly cock-a-hoop over press reaction to their Marianne

Faithfull interview, published yesterday, in which Marianne said quite quotable little things about how she'd slept with three of the Stones to find out which one she liked best.

In the evening Helen and I and Mary and Edward went to see Truffaut's *Day for Night* – a film about filming, which left me with the kind of happy escapist pleasure that old Hollywood comedies used to. Afterwards we ate at Rugantino's, where I had brains for the first time. They tasted like roe, soft and spongy. It's funny, one can happily eat a cow's liver or a sheep's kidney, but eating brains seems to encroach on dangerous, mystical and spiritual areas. Like eating roast mind.

Friday, February 8th

An election has been announced for February 28th – depressing news, for the Tories will probably win and they don't deserve to. Heath has been stubborn to the extreme with the miners, who are now to start on a full strike. He was elected on a pledge to create 'one nation' – and he's now whipping up Tory middle-class anti-worker feeling as hard as he can. One of the points of the Tory manifesto is that the government should not pay security benefits to strikers' families. It is as near as Heath has yet gone to outlawing strikes, and is indicative of an across-the-board tightening of controls on personal freedom, which is becoming very sinister. We may not have a 1984 like George Orwell's, but if the Tories have their way we will be a very carefully controlled society indeed. All very sad, especially as Labour and the left are muddle-headed and ideologically dogmatic.

For me it's just head down and keep working. The three-day week does not so far seem to have damaged the country too much. The only real shortage is toilet rolls! But the foreign press make out we are almost in the state we were in in 1940, on the verge of collapse. Heath's propaganda seems to be every bit as effective as Hitler's was.

Monday, February 11th

Into London with Terry J to a meeting with Geoffrey Strachan at Methuen. He had read and liked our material for the *Fegg* book,[1]

---

1 This became *Bert Fegg's Nasty Book for Boys and Girls* (Methuen, 1974), later revised and improved as *Dr Fegg's Encyclopaedia of All World Knowledge* (Methuen, 1984).

would like to commission it – and started talking about size of the book, paper, art director, etc. Drank a Kronenbourg at the Printer's Devil to celebrate the birth of Bert Fegg.

Friday, February 15th

Today Geoffrey rang to say that a board meeting of Methuen had officially approved our book project and he was going to go ahead and commission it. Meanwhile we have had meetings with a cartoonist called Martin Honeysett, who has in the last year drawn some very funny, Python-like cartoons for *Punch* and *Private Eye*. Terry was especially keen for Honeysett to be involved, as he had met him at a *Punch* party and taken a great liking to him. However, it turned out that Martin Honeysett had never met Terry in his life and was pleased, but a little bewildered, to get such an enthusiastic phone call from him. Terry had, in fact, met quite a different cartoonist.

Sunday, March 3rd

We have now completed seven shows at Drury Lane – ending last week with a grand flourish of two shows on Friday and two shows on Saturday. I am chewing pastilles and gargling with honey and lemon three times a day as a result.

The gilded, glittering Drury Lane must have been amazed by the scruffiness of the audience on the first night. Kean and other great British actors of the past would have turned in their graves if they could have seen the front row full of Gumby-knotted handkerchiefs on the opening night on Tuesday.

The reviews have been surprisingly extensive – it takes a second-hand collection of old TV material for critics to start taking Python really seriously. Harold Hobson was greatly impressed and called us true Popular Theatre – and Milton Shulman, perhaps our first critical friend of the TV series, was equally enthusiastic. Despite the fact that it's an old show, already toured in the provinces and Canada, London critics have devoted enormous space to analysing it, even in the grudging *Observer* review (which described Terry and myself as 'virtually indistinguishable' and tending 'to screech a lot').

We're in the fortunate position of not having to rely on reviews to sell our seats. Despite the fact that Drury Lane holds 2,200 people, we are booked solid for two weeks, we have extended our run to four weeks, and at every performance there are apparently touts out the front selling tickets for £5–£10.

Whilst we were Gumbying at Drury Lane, there was an election – one of the most exciting for years, in which Heath failed to frighten the country into massive anti-union protest and came out with fewer seats than Labour. Heath has not yet resigned and, as I write, is busy haggling with the Liberals and others to try and form a coalition. Suddenly British politics have become alive, volatile and exciting.

Monday, March 4th

Into our second week at Drury Lane, and a lot of business to do during the day.

Meet with the Henshaws[1] and Nancy L and Ina [Lee Meibach].[2] There were some sandwiches and white wine. Under discussion was Nancy's official future with Python. At a recent meeting we decided to put Nancy in charge of our new music publishing company, Kay-Gee-Bee Music Ltd, and also to give her control of records and recordings and all future contracts.

Ina waxed lyrical about the future of Python in the States – and rather frightened everyone by talking of a 15% fee for Nancy's work. We still see our roots as an English TV comedy show, and I think we are all wary of the American monster, where everything can be so BIG and success can be so ENORMOUS and so on and so on.

The live show has been a must for pop personalities. Mick Jagger and Bowie have shared a box – rather off-putting, actually, they were right beside the stage – and Ringo has twice been to see it.

Tuesday, March 5th

The Tories finally gave up trying to form an anti-Labour coalition and Wilson is PM again. A great appointment is [Michael] Foot, as Minister of Employment.

---

1 Michael Henshaw had been my accountant since 1966. His wife Anne was helping sort out Python's affairs.
2 Nancy's lawyer in New York.

Friday, March 8th

In the throes of a heavy cold – woke up after a night of sneezing and running nose with an incipient sore throat. And two shows tonight. I really felt low, and very worried that my voice would not survive especially as we do not have another night off until next Tuesday. Rang for an appointment with Doc Freudenberg [my GP], but he was fully booked. I was advised to go along and wait. Rang Terry and cancelled our work plans for the day. Got to the new health centre in Kentish Town and waited there for two hours before seeing Freudenberg. He prescribed penicillin for the sore throat, but was really more interested in how the show was going!

Eventually got home and went to bed about 2.00. Very low ebb. Slept on and off and listened to the radio. Feeling a helpless lump. Down to the theatre at 7.00. Drank lots of hot lemon and was helped by a throat spray. Strangely enough, although it seemed unimaginable to perform two shows when I was lying sneezing in bed this afternoon, once at the theatre it became a job which had to be done. For four hours I almost forgot about the cold, and the combination of theatre lights, leaping about on stage and having to concentrate the mind on acting probably did me more good than a day off.

Friday, March 15th

An easier week, this third one. Tonight is our last show of the week, and we also had Tuesday off. Also the two-shows-an-evening dates are all behind us, so the pressure of the first two weeks has eased considerably. My cold is a lot better and the voice is bearing up well. We have at last completed the Python film script. Terry and I, as usual, did most of the rewriting. It took us a week and a half of very solid work, and today we completed that by deciding formally to cut the 'King Brian the Wild' sequence – the film is now shorter and has more shape.

This morning we met at Terry Gilliam's at 10.30 to read through our rewrites. The BBC had a sound team there. They are anxious to do an *Omnibus* programme on Python. None of us is particularly keen to be subjected to the sort of documentary which we're always sending up, so we were all a bit lukewarm towards the slightly pushy producer who was present at our meeting. A concentrated three-hour session on the film. Little argument, except over the 'Anthrax' sequence, and at 2.00 we had agreed on a final script. All of us, bar John, went to a Chinese restaurant in Belsize Park to celebrate.

Saturday, March 16th

Angela had said that two weeks ago, when she went up to Southwold, Grandfather had deteriorated rapidly.

He was seen last night by a psychiatrist from St Audry's Hospital in Woodbridge, and his condition was serious enough for him to be taken in first thing this morning. He didn't go by ambulance – he went in the car with my mother and a nurse, but it sounds as tho' his brain is now so affected by the Parkinson's that he may never see Croft Cottage again.

I rang my mother this evening. She sounds relieved that he's at last being properly looked after – but even so said she misses him.

Friday, March 22nd

Tonight there are some shouters in, and a drunken group up in a box. The week's audiences have been capacity, apart from Monday and Tuesday, and, rather than become jaded, the show has brightened up a bit, and we're enjoying it more than ever. John has added little embell-ishments to 'Silly Walks' in order to corpse me. Terry and Graham, as the two Pepperpots, have a continuing battle with each other centring around lipstick and names. Graham's lipstick tonight stretched round his mouth, up and over the top of his nose; Terry had a phone number written in lipstick across his chest. They also have fun with names – starting by calling each other comparatively simple medical names (Mrs Scrotum, Mrs Orgasm), they have now become wonderfully obscure – Mrs Vas Deferens – and tonight's masterpiece from Graham was Madame Émission Nocturnelle.

In the 'Custard Pie', when I have to shout 'Hey Fred!' at Terry G, I have varied the names a lot – but none with greater success than 'Hey Onan!'. That was a week ago, and I haven't had so many people laughing on stage since. Tonight, however, I could tell that John C was reacting to the noisy crowd as he usually does, by tensing up, and 'Pet Shop', normally a corpser's delight, was rushed through at quite a lick.

Saturday, March 23rd

Last night tonight.

This was the show that Tony Stratton-Smith was recording, and yet responses to such great favourites as 'Silly Walks' were the worst ever.

Graham was very fuddled through 'Four Yorkshiremen' and in the 'Election' sketch, John forgot a fairly important line and 'Parrot' ended prematurely after I replied 'Yes' instead of 'No' to John's query about the slug, 'Does it talk?' He chased me off the stage claiming afterwards he was too tired for ad-libs.

Champagne and scotch on stage for the company and friends. The stage hands were in sentimental mood and genuinely seemed to have enjoyed the four weeks. By an extraordinary coincidence there is a man who works front of house in the Theatre Royal called Mr Gumby. He was small and middle-aged and looked a bit like what I imagine Richard Goolden looks like as Mole in Toad of Toad Hall. He kept insisting that I call him Leslie, and I realised I was repeatedly calling him Mr Gumby, just to relish the name. Anyway, I got the cast to sign my Gumby handkerchief for him, which will surely confuse him even more.

Tuesday, March 26th, Southwold

Up to Southwold on the train. Met at 11.30 at Darsham by Mother. From Darsham we drove into Wickham Market and had lunch at the White Hart, then drove on to St Audry's Hospital near Bury St Edmunds.

Up anonymous institutional corridors smelling of disinfectant, until we reached the Kenton Ward on the second floor. It was a long room, bigger than I had expected, with high walls. About twenty beds neatly set out. In the first part of the ward the TV was on and about fifteen or sixteen men were slumped in chairs around it. I didn't notice them at first because they didn't react at all as we entered the ward, whilst the three or four nurses and two male attendants sitting at a table beyond a glass partition turned immediately. There was little sign of life from the inmates.

Then I saw my father sitting on the side of his bed. Here was the man who played football with me, who ran along the towpath at Shrewsbury when I rowed in Bumpers, who used to try and teach me to overcome my fear of the sea at Sheringham. He was now sitting on his bed with his head bent, muttering to himself, and picking with helpless hands at the cord of his pyjamas, which were open, exposing his white stomach. He didn't look up as I approached him – he didn't hear as I talked to him. When eventually one of the male nurses came across and, like dealing with a child, firmly but pleasantly did up his pyjamas and put on his dressing gown, he at last looked up. His eyes were heavy and dull, with a film of moisture across them and a rim of white along the lower lids.

George helped him round to a chair and we sat down to talk. 'George,' Daddy explained, was a man 'whose instructions it was best to ignore.' We later found out that 'George' was really called John and clearly he depended on him – but his old cantankerous nature had not wilted entirely. As we sat, he talked almost non-stop. He would start long descriptions about what had happened that morning and the story would wander into flashbacks of the past with an undetectable deftness that many film directors would envy. He was talking about how he had been on the lavatory that morning – and suddenly said that he finished on the loo at 10.47.

'10.47?' we asked.

'Yes, that was the train to Shrewsbury', he went on, 'which they used to drag me on to kicking and screaming.'

He had some strange Pythonesque fantasies in his mind too. Apparently the hospital was run by the Japanese, and last night one of the patients had sat on a 'beautiful' marmalade cat, which had had surgery this morning.

After talking for an hour or so, we were asked down to see Dr Hyde, who is dealing with the case. On the way to his office we passed a line of old padded cells – they looked like stables with strong wooden doors, with a spyhole in each. They were going to be knocked down any time now, said the doctor. He was a tall, thin, wispy-haired 40ish man – the kind of brainy boffin who moves rather nervously, and throws his body around in a slightly uncoordinated fashion. Eminently accessible, he seemed to want to answer all our questions. I guessed afterwards that he was trying to be optimistic. I don't think he holds out much hope for my dad. He has cerebral arterial sclerosis, like having a prolonged stroke, and, although he has made progress since entering St Audry's, the general pattern from now on will be downhill. But how much does my father still know about where he is, and who we are? How seriously should we take his desire to come home? It would be awful if his perception was much clearer than we thought, that it was just his body which had failed him. The doctor was noncommittal, but did say that we should try, in any way, to give him some hope, something to look forward to – perhaps in a week or so we could take him out in the grounds in a wheelchair. He didn't hold out much hope of him ever coming home again.

Wednesday, March 27th, Southwold

The paper full of the Budget details. The *Daily Telegraph* came out in its true colours, saying that this, Healey's first Budget, would hit the managerial classes. I weep for the managerial classes. May they be spared the worst – to sell their second car, to have to change the BMW for an Austin because it uses less petrol. To have to have one instead of two gin and tonics when they get home after a hard day's managing. Grudgingly the *Telegraph* mentions the rise in pensions for old people – the £500m subsidies for basic foodstuffs like bread and milk and meat and fish, the reductions in National Insurance contributions and in income tax for those earning less than £3,000 a year. It sounds to me to be a good, fair, just Budget – an attempt to solve inflation *and* help people who suffer most from it – i.e. those who can't afford one car let alone two, and those who can't afford one gin and tonic, let alone two. Mind you, it's easy to say this from the lofty heights of one who could afford an entire quart of gin every evening.

We got to the hospital at about 6.45. The inmates of the ward were queuing up for a milk drink. The nurses were talking amongst themselves – they obviously try not to mollycoddle the patients too much. My father was on his bed again, away from the others. He was agitated about something and tried straightaway to tell us about it – but his stammer was too bad. His lips couldn't form any sound, they just opened and shut like a fish. We got him up and he walked, with a stick and unaided, around to the chair where we had sat yesterday. Like yesterday, once he was in the chair, he talked a little more fluently. Today his mind was on some sort of meeting there had been in the ward – a man had spoken for three-quarters of an hour – it was some sort of Farmers' Union meeting.

He didn't seem to take a lot in, until we discussed our chat with the doctor yesterday. Then he appeared to know that Easter was in a fortnight, and when I said we would take him out for a drive then, or in a chair around the grounds, he looked up and said quite clearly and emphatically, 'But I want to come home.'

Saturday, April 6th

Ten past seven in the evening, writing the diary out in the garden. In the last week everyone's been coming out of doors again, in the wake of an early blast of summer. Hyacinths, providing a delicate whiff every now and then, are just about on the turn, but they've been out in profusion. Wallflowers of deep yellow and deep red and a single small white daffodil are out at the moment.

After lunch today Eric and Graham came round for what was to have been a Python (less John) meeting re the new TV series.

We have to decide whether or not the VTR dates which Jimmy provided in February are still practical. Things look bleak. The dates were fixed at a time when we were only doing two weeks at Drury Lane instead of four, and we have enormously underestimated the amount of time which the two Terrys will have to spend on the film. They will neither of them be able to concentrate for any length of time on a new TV series until late August – which is when Ian wants all the scripts in. So either Graham, Eric and I write all the scripts, which I think is out of the question, or we make an awkward compromise and start to film one month later, or we put the whole thing off until the spring. Eric, who has a small TV series of his own planned for January '75, is keen to leave the series till the spring of next year.

After our meeting in the sunshine, Eric stayed on here to bath (for his bathroom has been half-demolished by a gas explosion last week! Firemen and police rushed round. Eric said it was rather like a sketch – with firemen drinking cups of tea in the sitting room!) – Helen and I took our relentlessly energetic boys for a long overdue walk to the Heath. Thomas kept finding pieces of china in the huge piles of earth dug up where they're enlarging Parliament Hill running track. Promised to start a museum for him when we got home.

Sunday, April 7th

Rang Terry J. He was of the opinion that it would be impolitic to alienate the BBC by refusing at this stage to do a series it had taken so long to set up. As Terry's attitude was a rather key factor (for he will have to work incredibly hard if he is to contribute much to the series *and* edit the Python film) I was quite heartened. Certainly the most comfortable solution would be to do the series on the dates offered. Terry was more worried about finding a new direction and positive and strong ideas for the series, so I left him to have a think and call me back later. Eric was basically quite easy-going and adaptable, provided he could safeguard his three months in France during the summer.

Monday, April 8th

Tony Stratton-Smith rang in the evening – he had been listening to the *Python Live at Drury Lane* tapes and was enthusing as only Strat can. He wanted to release a live album in June, as the high point of a Python month – a big promotional push to boost sales of all our LPs. Tony reckons this Python month could shift another 80,000 or 90,000 of our records, which, as he says, would keep us off the breadline during the summer! A lucky coup is that *NME* [*New Musical Express*] want to issue 400,000 Python flimsies as a give-away with their paper in late May.

Thursday, April 11th, Southwold

Helen, Angela, Granny and I arrived at St Audry's Hospital at about 4.00. Grandfather was sitting watching TV. He got up when he saw us and seemed to recognise the four of us and be genuinely pleased to see us. He was in day clothes for the first time, and looked 100% better, tho' still a little stooped and his eyes were moist.

Fortunately, due to his much improved state, I was able to talk quite matter-of-factly to him about the problems of getting out. He wants to come back straightaway – he lives in a half real, half fantasy world of telegrams from Granny to say he's coming out, recommendations from the doctor – everything he says is geared to his release from this 'Institution' as he calls it. He has tried to get out twice, and has been discovered by nurses half-way down the stairs. One nurse was treated to a volley of abuse, so she says, when she tried to stop him.

But today he was negotiating tenaciously with me, like an ageing politician trying to strike one last bargain, pull off one last coup.

Easter Sunday, April 14th, Southwold

Drove over to St Audry's after breakfast to bring Grandfather home for the day. (It's nearly a month since he went into hospital.)

Took him some clothes and a box of chocolates for the nurses. They dressed him behind some screens, while I spoke to Mr Smy, the charge nurse. We were talking fairly softly, but when I mentioned to Mr Smy that Grandfather recently had been very confused there was a shout from behind the screen – '*I'm* not confused.'

Sun shining as we drove back to Southwold – the sharp cool wind at least had blown fogs and hazes away and the countryside looked fresh and green. A great day for colours, heavy dark shadows on the pine trees, and a vivid, almost luminous green on some of the fields.

We had a chicken casserole for lunch and he drank a glass of Alsace wine. Afterwards he pottered around the house, looking in all the rooms, trying to make helpful comments, but they generally came out as grumbles. His life is very much geared to his current obsessions, and these obsessions are nearly always anxieties and problems. There seems to be nothing that makes him happy any more. He told me he dislikes all the nurses, and clearly he is finding it very difficult to be told what to do by people who, as he says, 'have an inferiority complex' (a social inferiority complex, he means), which they take out on him. He even said they mutter about Mummy after she's gone because 'she's well-dressed and well-spoken'.

At 6.30, Granny and I drove him back to the hospital.

Monday, April 15th, Southwold

After lunch, built a new piece of fence for Granny, whilst she and Helen sorted through an old chestful of Grandfather's papers. Letters from Shrewsbury home to his parents, old school reports, Indian Railway timetables, dance cards from Poona, with the names of his partners for the evening marked.[1] A fascinating collection – in the Shrewsbury and India days much evidence that he was quite a character, enjoyed life and was sociable: 'always looks as though he has done something wicked, but never has' – school report from Shrewsbury.

His later letters to the head of Edgar Allen's,[2] for instance, complaining that the £1,600 salary he was receiving in 1960 was hardly sufficient for a 'public school-educated, university graduate', have a much more hopeless air about them.

But Thomas and Willy love his old bundles of cheques and Thomas has taken to playing 'bank managers'.

---

1 In the 1920s, soon after qualifying as an engineer, my father spent five years in India on various public works projects including the Sukkur Barrage across the River Indus in what is now Pakistan. He was always very proud of that.
2 The Sheffield steelmaker for whom he spent many years as Export Manager.

Tuesday, April 16th, Southwold

Woke feeling refreshed, then suddenly my heart sank to my stomach as the full weight of work about to descend, the number of small problems, things to be done, things to avoid being done, hit me. A silly reaction, to be so bowled over. It will disappear when I am up and doing things, but the pleasure of being in Suffolk, remote from all phone calls, deals, confrontations, etc, etc, is just beginning to sink in, and I think the sudden realisation that the brief rest was over and that tonight I would be back among the pressures, hit me harder than usual this morning.

We had a superb little lunch, it being our eighth wedding anniversary, with a half-bottle of Bollinger, and delicious freshly caught cod with mushroom sauce.

Drove home via St Audry's where we stopped off to see Grandfather. As I took him back after a short walk to the car park, he mounted the stairs to the ward with a heavy sigh and murmured, 'Here we are ... the via dolorosa,' and he stood at the window, waving, trying to smile as Thomas (unconcerned of course by the fate of his grandfather) and I walked away in the late afternoon sun to our car. It could have been heart-rending, but I am trying to keep the whole thing in proportion, and not become too emotional about his condition. It may seem heartless, but it's the only way, I'm sure.

Monday, April 29th, Ballachulish, Scotland

Sitting down to write this overlooking the broad sweep of Loch Leven. Below me cars are queuing for the Ballachulish ferry, across the water the sun shines through a break in the cloud, pinpointing a small whitewashed group of cottages and emphasising the green of the fields running down to the water's edge. Beyond them the mountains rise into the mist. A tranquil sort of morning. We have been in Scotland a little over twenty-four hours. On Saturday night I said goodbye to Helen and the boys in the usual unsatisfactory way – a rushed meal together – a 'Quick, can you sew on this?' and 'Have you seen my that?' sort of leave-taking. I won't see them again until May 25th. Still, Scotland has been very welcoming, and I feel relaxed and comfortable and invigorated here, after the busy two weeks since we left Southwold.

During that time we rehearsed the film [*Monty Python and the Holy Grail*], inevitably rewrote some of the scenes as we did so. But it came to life during rehearsal – we began to laugh at each other's performances again, and from being rather an albatross of worry round our necks (finance, script, etc, etc) the film became enjoyable and fun.

I'm trying to think how I can begin to chronicle all that happens on this film. Will try a kind of shorthand and see if it works.

Tuesday, April 30th, Ballachulish

First day of filming. Woken at 6.45. Sunshine streaming through the curtains. Into chainmail and red-cross tabard. A difficult day today – the Bridge of Death scene where Eric and I die and Lancelot is arrested by the police. Dangerous too – from what I hear. Difficult decision over Galahad's blond wig. Instead of noble and youthful, I look like I should be serving in a supermarket. End of Galahad as a blond.

Such is the economy on this film that not only do the actors have a mini-bus rather than cars to go to the location, but they also have to drive it.

John (Lancelot) and I (Galahad) driving up through Glencoe in a Budget Rent-a-Van in full chainmail.

Scrambled up to the Gorge of Eternal Peril – this took about 15 minutes of hard climbing.

Camera broke midway through first shot.

The day is hastily rearranged and, from having been busy, but organised, it was now busy and disorganised. The sun disappeared. John Horton's smoke bombs and flames worked superbly. Graham as King Arthur got vertigo and couldn't go across the bridge. He spent the day rather unhappily cold and shaking. Eric and I and John sat around listening to stories from the Mountain Rescue boys about how many people perish on these spectacular mountains each year. Five or six deaths usually.

Terry J comes up to me in the afternoon and says he's 'a bit worried about Terry G's priorities in choice of shots'[1] – we run two and a quarter hours overtime, until nearly 8.00. Everyone in the young unit seems happy enough.

Enjoyed the sight of Hamish MacInnes, head of Mountain Rescue in Glencoe, flinging rubber corpses of knights into the gorge. More terrifying ledges to climb round on tomorrow. I hope Gra's OK.

Back at hotel at 8.30 for large Bell's and a bath. Couldn't really face

---

1 *Monty Python and the Holy Grail* was directed by both Terry Jones and Terry Gilliam.

the four-course hotel meal, so sat in the bar with Eric, drinking scotch and watching card tricks.

But Sunday night was the *most* eventful, when I giggled a great deal over the menu after some very high-quality grass of Eric's, and Graham ended up being seduced by an Aberdeen gentleman on a fishing holiday. Graham resisted evidently, but was well pissed and woke me about 1.00 banging on my door saying he was Ethel de Keyser.[1]

On Monday night he woke me *again* just after I'd dropped off, when I heard him in his room saying 'Betty Marsden!' rather loudly in a variety of silly ways.

Tuesday night, however, he was kind enough to be content with putting a note under my door with 'Best wishes, Betty Marsden'[2] written on it.

Wednesday, May 1st, Ballachulish

At lunchtime still no word that we were needed. Eric and I sit in the quiet, well-kept garden beside the hotel, thinking we're rather like officers at the Craiglockhart Hospital,[3] sitting waiting to recover before being sent back to the Front. Eric says he's Sassoon, and I'm Wilfred Owen – who had 'a bit of a stocky body'.

Lunch with Mark, Eric and John, who is trying to read a book of philosophy and is constantly rather cross – but quite fun. He continually goes on about the 'bovine incompetence' of the waitresses – who are certainly no Einsteins, but good-hearted Scottish mums.

After lunch the unreality continues. Eric and I go round to Ballachulish House to play croquet in the sunshine. Ridiculously idyllic. The Lady of the Manor, a tweedy, rather sharp Englishwoman, appears with an enormously impressive, kilted, very red-faced Scottish laird, who leaves in a large old Lagonda. All too Dr Finlay for words. Eric idly fantasises we may have caught them 'in flagrante'.

After the croquet and a few words with the Lady of Ballachulish, more sitting in the disabled officers' garden. At about 3.30 the call comes. Sir Robin and Sir Lancelot drive their Budget Rent-a-Van up to

1 Ethel de Keyser (1926–2004), South African anti-apartheid campaigner.
2 Betty Marsden (1919–98). Actress on *Round the Horne* and in *Carry On* films. Why Graham chose her name I don't know. She had once expressed a wish to die with a glass of gin in her hand, so maybe that was it.
3 A Victorian pile in Edinburgh where officers were sent for treatment of shell-shock during the First World War.

Glencoe, complete with a message from the producer to say we must stop by 6.00. At about 6.00 we are hanging onto the ledge above the gorge waiting for a long shot of the Bridge of Death. Terry J directs Terry G to get some more dirt on his legs (as the Soothsayer).

Then suddenly John Horton's effects go off, a few flares, firecrackers, smoke bombs, then, surprising everybody, huge mortar blasts which send scorching barrels of fire high into the air – the grass and trees are burning. No one (except John H) knows where the next blast will come from. Gerry Harrison shouts, TJ shouts. John's stand-in races across the bridge with suicidal courage, only to be told to get back again as the camera can't see anything through the smoke.

I think we may have a few more days of difficulty before the film gets together. TG was very unhappy as he sat on the top of the mountain. And Galahad drove the van back.

Rather sad notices around Ballachulish today asking for volunteers to join an army for a scene tomorrow. They're only getting £2 and I think even the Scots will baulk at that.

Cocktail bar – 8.45. Neil [Innes] arrives from London via train, bus and foot. Great rejoicing. Within an hour he's on the piano, spurred on by Eric, and a bearded left-handed Scots accordion player and a guitarist materialise from somewhere and the Ballachulish Hotel resounds with rather raucous sing-along.

Thursday, May 2nd, Ballachulish

Woken by whine of my tape recorder about 1.00. Woken again by Neil plus guitar coming in to sleep in the spare bed in my room about 2.00. Finally woken by loud sneeze at 10.00.

Eric and I have another lazy day at the rest home for officers, while Graham and Terry are finding the Castle Aaargh! We go to the location about 2.00, and they still haven't had a lunch break.

Graham is getting shit poured all over him. He's taking a great deal of punishment in these first few days of filming.

Wonderful chaos round about 4.00. Out on the island the motor boat which drove the wondrous ship in which Arthur and Bedevere reached the Castle Aaargh! broke down and Terry J was left drifting across Loch Leven with the radio communication set. Terry G, in great Errol Flynn style, leapt into another dinghy, pushed it out with a flourish, but failed to make the engine work and was left also drifting about twenty yards out to sea. The whole scene, enacted in front of a motley army of extras, was great entertainment value – and cheered everyone up enormously.

Finally, frenetically, the army shot was completed, and, going into heavy overtime yet again, the day finished about 6.20. Or rather didn't finish, because we then had to drive to Killin on Loch Tay, our next location. Graham and I in the Mini, driving over the most forbidding, lonely landscape in Britain as night fell – rain, mountains on either side, huge black clouds hanging on their summits.

Friday, May 3rd, Killin

At last a chance to see the scenery we drove through last night. We are filming in a cave three or four miles beyond Ardeonaig, and the road winds rather prettily along the side of Loch Tay. From where we are filming – a rather tough ten-minute climb from the road – you can look down the length of Loch Tay and across the other side to the mountains, tipped by Ben Lawers (nearly 4,000 feet). A spectacular location, but soon filled with the flotsam and jetsam of filming – boxes of equipment, tea urns, Land Rovers churning up and down the hill with lights, and wood for the construction team.

A slow day's filming, it seems. Rather a lot of worried faces when we run into overtime again. Hazel especially has hardly had a moment to organise herself and her costumes, and looks completely shattered.

Julian [Doyle] took me aside after filming today as we walked down the hillside and said he was worried that the way things were being shot this week was putting a big strain on the budget (almost the entire £1,000 allowed for overtime was spent in this first week) and there would have to be some compromises by the Terrys somewhere along the line.

So we had a meeting at the Killin Hotel tonight in among the costumes, and the production/direction points of view were put forward. I think Terry G accepted that they would have to simplify the shooting script and perhaps compromise on some of the locations. Terry J was less compromising, but in the end everyone decided that we should postpone final decisions on Hadrian's Wall, etc, for a week, to see if we could catch up. It was also decided not to move to Doune until Monday.[1]

1 Hadrian's Wall was dropped later as being too far away. The Scottish National Trust had vetoed most of our castle locations, deeming the script 'not consistent with the dignity of the fabric of the buildings'. Doune was a privately owned castle.

Saturday, May 4th, Killin

A good day's filming at last. Even John and Eric aren't grumbling, even tho' we go into overtime again. John Horton's rabbit effects are superb. A really vicious white rabbit, which bites Sir Bors' head off. Much of the ground lost over the week is made up. We listen to the Cup Final in between fighting the rabbit – Liverpool beat Newcastle 3–0.

More good rushes in the evening. The boat that takes them across to the Castle Aaargh! looks really magical. It will give the film just the right kind of atmosphere and build-up to make the non-ending work. Terry Bedford's[1] effects, especially his fondness for diffusing the light, work superbly.

I bought drinks for everyone at dinner as it's my birthday tomorrow, then had a couple of smokes with Neil, went for a walk and shouted abuse at a Celtic supporter on a bicycle. Utterly collapsed about 11.00.

Sunday, May 5th, Killin

Thirty-one. A birthday on the road again. Slept until 10 or 11 – at half past eleven a knock on the door. It was Neil, complete with a birthday present – three ducks, a yo-yo and a junior doctor's kit! Downstairs about 12.00. The foyer of the hotel was littered with Python gear. Hazel was working on costumes and the other half of the hotel foyer was full of Make-up's wig boxes. Neil and I decided that it would be best to avoid the Killin Hotel for the day. Drove up into the Ben Lawers National Park. We walked for nearly three hours in total solitude, and managed at last to reach a patch of snow – about 2,600 feet up.

We drove back around Loch Tay – passing on our way the town of Dull – which was exactly as its name suggests. We couldn't even find a shop to buy a postcard with 'Greetings from Dull' – so we stopped for tea at Weem. Tea and scones served by a Scottish lady with a soft, high-pitched voice, in a reverential atmosphere rather more like a funeral parlour than a hotel. Bought Neil a meal at Ardeonaig – where we found Eric, who had been spending the weekend there, away from the rest of the unit. He sent me a silly birthday message on a meringue, which was delivered to the table, and also bought me a bottle of champagne. I was nearly tempted to stay at the Hotel Anthrax, so lulled was I by the meal

1 Director of Photography.

and the wine and the attentions of one of the ladies – but fortunately my 31st birthday passed celibately and Neil and I drove home about 11.30.

Monday, May 6th, Killin

Eric and I dressed as monks (gear that really rather suits us) toiling up to the cave at 8.30. Very clear sky and the sun is already hot. Quite a long piece for me today as the monk who reads the instructions about the Holy Hand Grenade. As the sun is so bright, all the camera angles have to be changed, and the actors, so much fodder in the process of film-making, find themselves standing on a steep slope, precariously perched barefoot on rather slippery mud. All the knights are in the stream down below. Terry J gives me a good piece of direction which makes my perf. more silly and lively. But it is a hard morning's work for everybody. For the first time we see the pages – they are weighed down with very heavy packs and their first movements have to be uphill over rather difficult terrain. Everyone very near the end of their tether – Graham shaking and quivering with suppressed neurotic rage – when lunch break is called at 2.30.

I'm not needed in the afternoon, so go back to the hotel and decide to go off early to Doune. Rang home first, and spoke to Tom, who burst into tears, and all I could hear was his sad pleas that he wanted his Daddy back home. Quite disconcerting and left me feeling very depressed. Then the car wouldn't start. But John C (to whom I had promised a lift) helped me to push it up the main street of Killin to a garage, where a Scottish Jimmy Cagney promised me he would 'charge it for a wee while', as the battery was flat.

JC and I sat on the rocks on the Falls of Killin – those same falls of which Helen had sent me a postcard in 1962, which put us back in touch after a year and turned our little Southwold romance into an Oxford romance as well. Oh, how soppy.

John and I talked about life. I sympathise quite a lot with his urge to be free of the obligations and responsibilities of the Python group – but I feel that John is still tense and unrelaxed with people, which compounds his problems. He has more defences than Fort Knox.

But he was very enjoyable company and, after we collected the car from Mr Cagney, we drove into Doune, stopping at Callander to have a leisurely meal at a sixteenth-century hunting lodge turned into a hotel – full of antiques, old prints, a rather delicate atmosphere. John and I talked about psychoanalysis – John is going to a new man, who he reckons has changed him greatly – told John to try harder to do things which he enjoyed, and not to accept work he didn't enjoy. Hence JC went to Kenya for two months and says he has never since felt the psychosomatic symptoms which he always used to get while working.

And so to Doune at 10.00. This is to be our home for the next two weeks.

Tuesday, May 7th

Up at 7.15, after a rather uncomfortable night. The walls of the room are paper-thin and, tho' I have a spacious double bed, I was continually woken by strange sounds from the pipes and the plumbing – including an irregular dripping noise – rather like a Chinese water torture, which went on all night, and which I could never track down. John and Eric equally disaffected with the Woodside and later today they move out to a hotel in Dunblane which apparently has sauna baths and a swimming pool. But the Woodside has a rather friendly, welcoming atmosphere downstairs which I would be sad to miss. So I decide to stay.

Today we shoot the Camelot musical sequence. A long and busy day for 50 seconds' worth of film. Dancers dressed as knights wrecking Camelot. In the middle of the day Mark has arranged a press call, but as the two Terrys are busy directing, the brunt falls on Eric, Neil, John and myself. The usual questions: who is Monty Python? How did you all get together? Obvious questions maybe, but they drive us potty. Lots of photos – can you all put your heads round the shields? Etc. Eric and Neil try to escape, Colditz style, by walking out of the gate when Mark isn't looking, talking terribly urgently to each other – they made it back to the hotel before being recaptured.

We pass the afternoon with a game of football. Despite the chainmail, some quite good moves. Bill Hagerty of the *Daily Mirror* stays around with a photographer – he is apparently doing a big centre page spread on us. He has a better technique than most journalists. The indirect approach. He just stays around, chats and gets to know us – and only occasionally jots in his notebook. I told him the story of Graham shouting 'Betty Marsden' – which will probably end up on ten million kitchen tables!

Wednesday, May 8th

The first of two and a half days on the Castle Anthrax scene.

Spent the morning being drenched by the Perth and Kinross Fire Brigade. Next time I shall think twice about writing a scene in a raging storm. I start behind camera, and before 'Action!' I am solemnly wetted down by Tommy Raeburn of Props, with a little greenhouse watering can. I then rush up through rain provided by a fireman from behind a bush, to a castle made of cardboard.

Thursday, May 9th

Amazing how much eating one does on filming. If you get up at 7.15 it is nice to have a cup of coffee at least before going over to the Doune Rural Hall (headquarters of the WI) and, with a full breakfast menu available, I am quite often tempted to a kipper or even a piece of toast. Then, at 10.30 on set, there is more coffee and soft, delicious bap rolls with sausages and scrambled egg. Ron Hellard supplies a gargantuan lunch with much pastry and potato, which is also hard to resist. At around 4.00 tea/coffee and cakes (v. good home-made currant buns) and, after a drink back at the hall at the end of the day, and a look at rushes (shown, extraordinarily enough, in the Silver Chalice Bar!), there is a four-course set meal at the hotel. Consumption is about double what one eats at home.

This was the second day on Castle Anthrax. Doune Castle's severe granite halls are now filled with about twenty girls in diaphanous white gowns, shivering against the cold. John C, Eric and I are sitting with Neil on an old bench in the Great Hall, singing old Adam Faith/Cliff Richard hits, in a desperate attempt to combat boredom. The bathing scene takes two hours to set up – the girls giggle a lot, and generally it's about as sexy as a British Legion parade.

We shoot on late – until 7.30 or so – utterly shattered – but Carol C stood up to it remarkably well and was v. funny. Like Neil, she is an honorary Python, and has very little trouble in clicking into our way of doing things.

Friday, May 10th

9.30: In Anthrax Castle again, with Tommy poised with watering can.

'Michael, can you fall about six inches to your left?' after I have crashed onto the stone floor for three rehearsals already.

11.00: Still waiting for the shot. Terry J, who tends to become very Ian MacN-like sometimes – 'Come on, now *quick*, we must get this shot in before 11.25, we really *must*!' Terry G is working away more quietly with the camera crew, checking the shot, putting a candle in foreground here and there. Gerry Harrison, the first assistant director, for all his sometimes alienating head prefect manner, is always very accessible and can get a cup of coffee for shivering actors.

Out in the main courtyard of the castle, a BBC crew from *Film Night* are interviewing Graham C. Quite glad to avoid that sort of thing, really.

'Alright, the generator's been refilled with petrol!'

'Let's go.'

'Come on, we must get this shot in by 12.25!'

We finish Anthrax with a last v. good take, especially from Carol, and that sequence is now finished, and we go out to the front of the castle.

The BBC doggedly film the filming. Cardboard battlements have to be added on to the castle before John does his taunting. 'John! Don't lean too heavily on the battlements, you can see them bending.'

At about 4.30 there are a few distant claps of thunder, the sky turns a fine deep grey – which Terry Bedford is very pleased about – and we get one shot in with this background before an enormous cloudburst empties the field in front of the castle.

The cry of 'It's a wrap!' goes up, and Tommy Props leaps out into the still pouring rain with a look of great exultation and starts to clear up. He particularly has had a fiercely busy week, and no one wants to work late tonight.

Back to the Women's Institute to change, then to the hotel for a drink and rushes. The table I'm sitting on in the Silver Chalice Bar splits right across, and the manager, Mr Ross, is left rather pathetically holding this broken half table when some non-Python guests arrive to check in.

Saturday, May 11th

A rather grey day, with intermittent rain. At the gates of Doune Castle Philip Jenkinson is standing with the *Film Night* crew.

I haven't been chatting with him for long before we have been imperceptibly shuffled into an interviewing position beside a car, and I find myself being filmed at about 11.00 in the morning, the dullness of my replies matching the dullness of the day! After that they move over to a well in the courtyard and interview Graham, who at least managed to get some silly lines in – he deliberately mishears Phil Jenkinson's rather facetious remark about an 'insanity' clause being built into the contract – 'There is an insanitary clause, yes.' Funnily enough, Phil Jenkinson is besotted by Eric Idle's take-offs of him and constantly refers to them.

John is doing the Taunter on some artificial battlements at the back of the castle. He's getting very irritated by TG's direction of his acting. TG tends to communicate by instinct, gesture and feeling, whereas John prefers precise verbal instructions. So TJ has to take over and soothe John down.

Then the shot where live ducks and chickens, as well as dead rabbits, badgers, etc, are flying over the battlements. Small boys are recruited to help catch the chickens as they're flung over. 'Those spotted roosters are fast,' warns Tommy.

A rather jolly day, with much corpsing from John, Eric and myself when Brian McNulty, third assistant director, in rich Glaswegian, reads in John's Taunter's lines for us to react to. How can you react without laughing to a broad Glaswegian saying 'Of course I'm French, why do you think I'm using this outrageous accent?'

Monday, May 13th

The day of the Mud-Eater. Clad in rags, crawling through filthy mud repeatedly and doggedly, in a scene which makes the flagellation scene from *Seventh Seal* look like *Breakfast at Tiffany's*. Extras all supposed to have plague – boils and pustules everywhere. People really do look wretched and, after two hours wallowing in the mud, because the plague village is such a convincing set, reality becomes fantasy and fantasy becomes reality. The camera crew, the scrubbed and well-dressed line of faces looking at us and occasionally turning a big black machine towards us, seems quite unreal, a horrible dream.

At the end of the day I have to eat mud. John Horton prepares a mixture of currants, chocolate instant whip, pieces of fruit cake and cocoa, and pours it out onto a patch of soil from which it is indistinguishable.

That night at dinner the menu began with 'Various effluents' – and I asked Mr Ross rather gruffly what this meant, then saw the rest of the menu – 'Mud cocktail', 'Fillet of sole à la slime', etc, etc. A complete mud menu.

Later in the meal I was presented with a bowl of mud which I dutifully tasted. It turned out to be solid cooking fat coated with chocolate. So the Mud-Eater seems to have passed into the folklore of the film.

Thursday, May 16th

The last three days have been like the start of shooting in Ballachulish. Phoney filming. Sitting waiting to be called. Tranquil mornings at the Woodside. There has been work to do, but none of it very taxing. Twice Graham and I have worked our lines through for the opening scene, and twice it has been postponed. From the end of this week onwards I am going to be in practically every scene, and the only advantage of these lazy days has been a chance to enjoy the sunshine and to keep the journal up to date.

News coverage has been extensive – the *Mirror* had a front page picture of John, and a big double-page centre-spread with a large picture of us all in knights' gear, posed as a football team. A very good 'entertainment' piece by Bill Hagerty. The *Express* had a large, much less interesting, half-page, which made the early editions until they found the *Mirror* had scooped them and was later withdrawn. *Newsweek* had a whole-page feature on Python (tho' mainly John – 'an ex-*Newsweek* staffer'). The *Times* Diary had a short unpleasant piece of gossip – about John hating filming.

Weston Taylor of the *News of the World*, a rather dog-eared, but quite amiable sort of chap, has been hanging around. Eric was very rude to him, mistaking, I think, one individual for a newspaper's policy. But then Eric was also very rude to Andrew Tyler of *NME* who arrived in Killin on May 4th, and tried to interview Eric on the mountainside, with very little success. Perhaps 'very rude' isn't quite fair, but Eric gave him a rather sharp little homily. 'Most of my friends who I know and like have done interviews, and I don't recognise them in the interviews,' he said.

Anyway it turns out that Tyler's one-week sojourn with us turned out to be a largely accurate, amusing, exhaustive and informative account of Python filming. (Copies of the 'Python' issue of *NME* with Mr Gumby plastered on the front and the flimsy record of extracts from *Live at Drury Lane* and the big interview arrived on the set when I was doing the Prince's Room scene. Greeted with much interest by the make-up girls – whom he described as 'sour-faced'. Much mirth from everyone.)

Saturday, May 18th

End of third week's filming. I've had the second longest single speech in the film to do today. A large crowd scene with lots of mutilated extras. Must have done the speech at least fifteen times.

There's a party tonight organised by the camera crew – so I've had a bath – gratefully washing away two days in wig, beard, moustache and heavy make-up, and I'm thinking how much longer I can delay having a drink!

Downstairs – Met one of the crew waiting to go to the party. He looks serious. 'Mike,' he says. 'We work bloody hard out there, and I think we deserve it.'

I'm a little puzzled. 'Deserve ... what, Ron?'

'Women.'

He looks me in the eye like a man who thinks I can give him medical treatment. 'Women ... Mike ... that's what we need.'

Monday, May 20th

Spent a day in the hills above Callander doing a great deal of silly riding.

Strange surreal moment: a wooden cut-out of Camelot, which stood on the top of the hill, and looked utterly three-dimensional and realistic, suddenly blew away.

12.00 midnight: whilst soaking in my bath I hear a distant shout. 'I'm going to bed, but I don't necessarily have to go to bed alo-o-one.' It's Dr Chapman in the passage. He repeats the line three times, like someone selling scrap iron and it recedes along the corridor.

Friday, May 24th

In the hotel room catching up on the diary whilst they film the Historian. A very heavy week for me – with two long speaking parts on Wednesday and Thursday. I am not sure, but I don't feel quite on top of the performances. Something tightens up inside me during a take – the relaxation and control of a rehearsal is lost. Mind you, filming is an appalling process for reducing an actor to the role of machine.

In the Knights of Ni, for instance, I was to do close-ups first. Directly in front of me are a group of anoraked people squatting down, far more preoccupied with their equipment than with me. Someone reads the lines off in a flat voice, which gives you little encouragement. An eyeline keeps you looking at no one at all. Two huge white polystyrene reflectors enclose me on either side – it feels like acting in a sandwich. Then you are about to start and the sound isn't right – and then the sun comes out and that isn't right, as the camera focus has to be adjusted – and during this so much of one's spontaneity and relaxation just drain away.

Yesterday a long day as the Father – for the second day running a part involving heavy make-up, beard, moustache, etc. A great sense of relief when it was finished. Have not done such sustained and exhausting acting as I have this week since the last Python series. Creating new characters suddenly seems an enormous effort.

A little disappointment at the rushes tonight – saw my first appearance as the Father in the wedding scene, and didn't feel I was quite funny enough – but again, all the early close-ups of my speech to the crowd were done cold, without the crowd there, to some arbitrary mark, and it was Terry J's very good idea to make me do another take in close-up right at the end of the day. That, I think, is quite funny.

Monday, May 27th

Helen and the children come up from London. Helen, who is probably pregnant again, is feeling worse in the evening than the morning. The boys stayed up to watch the rushes and see their dad in a lot of strange guises.

Rather pleased to share with Helen and the kids the silly things I've been doing over the last four weeks. It was the Knights of Ni, which people seemed to like quite well.

Tuesday, May 28th

A rather fraught morning. Today we are to shoot Robin and the Singers' encounter with the Three-Headed Knight. But Graham, who is one of the three heads – the other two being myself and Terry – is not back from London. It's a complicated piece of learning, which needs all of us to rehearse it properly, and in the last week or so Graham has lost all his early confidence over lines and can hardly remember even one-line speeches.

Graham, Terry and I huddle into the cab of the camera van to learn the words. (One thing we MUST have on future filming is a caravan or, even better, a Dormobile, which is purely for the actors to use. When there is nowhere to sit, nowhere to relax while they spend one and a half hours setting up the shot, one can get very ratty.)

Anyway, we huddle in the camera van, a magazine of film sticking into my back, a battered little jackdaw beside me in its box (John Welland, the camera operator, found it and is trying to nurse it back to health on Ron Hellard's scrambled egg). I wasn't enjoying myself at all. Graham couldn't get it right.

Finally we are strapped into our Three-Headed Knight costume at about 5.00. All my apprehensions about it were unfulfilled. Graham, with just a little prompting, was fluent and funny, and Terry J was the one who seemed to be physically suffering in the uncomfortable costume. We were released about 6.30!

Wednesday, May 29th

John, dressed as a magician, spent much of the morning on the narrow top of an extremely impressive pinnacle of slate, across the quarry from us.

Twice the cameras turned. Twice John, towering above the green and pleasant vistas of the Trossachs, gave the signal to summon forth mighty explosions. Twice the explosions failed, and John was left on this striking, but lonely, pinnacle. He kept in good form, reciting his old cabaret monologues across the quarry, but it was a hard start to the day for him – and he was cold and subdued by the time he came back.

Once again it was a day where visual effects took the major amount of time, leaving John's quite long passages of dialogue to the later part of the afternoon. John's performance was good, but he had passed the point when it might have become inspired. But then you never know on film.

Thursday, May 30th

God appeared to us in the morning – with the help of John Horton's fireworks. Tom came down to the location and was quite impressed to see my now rather shabby Galahad gear – especially the sword. He and Willy played around with the other kids on the mound leading up to the castle.

Finally called to do the opening sequence of the film at the end of the day. Usual difficulty with 'swirling mist', as it was a totally unmisty day. But beautiful views all around from the castle battlements – rolling green hills stretching into the distance, tranquillity, peace. I will remember standing up on those cardboard reinforced battlements with John, looking round on a view that can't have changed much since Doune Castle was built.

Tomorrow is the last day of filming. Already an end of term atmosphere. Eric left at lunchtime with Lyn and Carey [their son] – to spend a night at Edinburgh on the way home. John will not be seen again after we've finished on the battlements. The WI hall is no longer looking like an over-stocked jumble sale – the majority of the costumes are packed away in their skips, ready to be taken back to London.

Friday, May 31st

The weather seems to have turned at last. Today is cloudy and it's been raining quite hard in the night.

The long and wordy Constitutional Peasants scene. Feel heavy, dull and uninspired – wanting above all else for it to be the end of the day. Arrive at a bleak location in the hills above Callander. Mud is being prepared.

Terry Bedford is angry because Mark has been trying to economise by buying old film-stock. Some of the film which has arrived today is six years old. Terry will not use it – in fact he threw a can into a nearby moorland stream – so we have 1,000 feet on which to do this entire scene. Very little chance of re-takes. Somehow it takes a supreme effort to get the words and the character together. We do the scene in one long master shot and, thank God, we get through it first time without a hitch. Ideally would have liked another take – just to see if any part of the performance would be better, but there is not enough time or enough film. The day gets greyer as it progresses, blending perfectly with our peasants' costumes and mirroring the generally downtrodden air.

Willy and Helen arrive midway through the afternoon. Willy is a little apprehensive of me at first, what with sores on the face, a shock of red hair, blackened teeth and rags, but he stays long enough for doughnuts and milk at tea.

I'm almost too tired to enjoy fully the elation at the end of the day, when the filming, or my part of it anyway, is finally completed. Want to leap up and down, but can't. So I just stand there looking out over the

Scottish hills, all grey and dusky and hazy as evening falls, and feel wonderfully free.

That night, back at the hotel, I had a drink with Tommy Raeburn and
the other chippies and drivers – hard men of films, who nevertheless
reckoned the chances of the film's success to be very good. Roy Smith,
the Art Director, said he wished he had money in it.

Three large gin and tonics and a bottle of red wine floored me early
on, however. As the Rosses finished serving up a special five-course meal
with a jokey 'Holy Grail' menu, complete with 'Mud Sorbet à la Palin', I
began to feel my legs getting wobbly and my vision beginning to swing
out of control and, about 11.30, went up to bed, thirty-two days after we
had first clung to the side of the Gorge of Eternal Peril in Glencoe.

Wednesday, June 5th

Today I talked to Gail at Charisma. She says that 70,000 copies of the
Live at Drury Lane album are being pressed, tho' not at EMI – for the
lady pressers there, whose unofficial censorship we have come up
against before, would not consider dealing with a record containing, as
Gail put it, 'three fucks and a dagger up the clitoris'.

At 4.30 we met at Henshaw's. We talked about various points, including a fund, from our film proceeds, to give most of the main members of
the crew a share in the profits. This was agreed, in principle, to be a good
thing.

Wednesday, June 12th, Southwold

Caught 9.30 train and breakfast to Ipswich.

Father and Mother on the platform at Darsham. At first appearance,
my father, who three months ago seemed quite seriously ill, looks
extremely fit and well. Very sun-tanned and, tho' a little stooped, certainly not the shuffling wreck he had been in St Audry's. His mind seems
stronger. He can understand more, and his recent memory is no longer
so clouded. Also his hallucinations have stopped. All this since he has
been taken off the wonder drug L-Dopa.

After lunch – dressed crab and Adnams beer – I took him for a drive,
which was quite successful. Again impressed by the improvement in his
mental condition (the awful twist being that this improvement makes
him more aware of his physical deterioration).

We visited Benacre Church, Henstead Church and then on to Wenhaston – through sunlit Suffolk lanes, with lush green countryside almost overgrowing the road on either side. Ended up at the Harbour Inn about six – the sky was a perfectly clear azure blue above the sea – Southwold looked clean and brilliant, like a newly unwrapped present.

Monday, June 17th

A damp, musty kind of morning – pools of water on the roofs and roads after the night's rain, which came down after a series of thunderstorms last night. Have just heard on LBC that the Houses of Parliament are burning – a bomb was placed in the kitchens at Westminster Hall and went off at 8.30. There have been five casualties, one serious. The fire-boat is out on the Thames and, according to the news, the fire is still spreading. This must be the biggest propaganda coup of all for the IRA (if it is them), but I think it will rebound heavily – echoes of 1940, when P'ment was last burning, etc, etc.

Occasionally, when these rather traumatic things happen, you imagine for just a moment that this is it – there'll be a national panic, a crisis after which nothing will ever be the same again! But in an instant it all passes. Thomas is at school giving flowers he's brought back from Abbotsley to Mrs McCann, with a look of great pleasure and achievement on his face, Helen is at the doctor's, having an examination for our third child, Mrs B[1] is being relentlessly importuned by William, who is trying to persuade her to stop cleaning the bathroom and buy some sweets for him, and I am about to sit down, reach for the notebook and try and think of ways to make people laugh. So life goes on, and Parliament-burning quickly assumes a perspective.

Monday, June 24th

This morning we saw a rough cut of the film – the first time I've seen the whole lot put together. In its raw state, without dubbing, sound f/x, music and any editing guidance by the two Terrys, it tends to be rather heavy in certain scenes – the Knights of Ni and the opening of Anthrax possibly – but there are set pieces like the Plague Village, the fight with the Rabbit and the Holy Hand Grenade which work very well, even at

1 Lilian Blacknell, neighbour, cleaning lady, baby-sitter and general good sort.

this stage, and the recently filmed Black Knight fight wasn't in, which I hear is also a great set piece.

The only scene which I felt was seriously deficient at this stage is the appearance of the Three-Headed Knight. It just doesn't look imposing enough, and very similar in set-up to the Knights of Ni.

Ended up at the Linguaphone Institute in Oxford Street, where I enrolled for a course of Italian lessons. Rather dog-eared surroundings, but the people there are pleasant and smile a lot and Mr C, my Italian coach, looks convincingly Italian and makes little jokes about his language – 'When you hear an Italian couple having a row, it sounds as if they are singing in an opera' – and little jokes about his own incompetence with the tape recorder – 'I am the only man to have fused a candle' and 'I pressed so many knobs, I eventually got Vatican Radio'. Anyway, he's jolly. But the course he started me on looked so unutterably dull – it was all about being a businessman and leaving briefcases at the airport and meeting secretaries and – oh! – it was so awful I told them I didn't think I could manage to summon up any enthusiasm for it. So he went away and came back with a slightly more difficult course, still heavily business-orientated, but with more general conversational words and phrases.

So I got into my little booth and played with the tape recorder. I hope I can keep this course going. It was a big psychological step to come in off hot and dusty Oxford Street and commit myself to it, but I feel that I must start now if I'm ever going to learn a new language – or at least attempt to become anything less than helpless when I travel.

Wednesday, July 3rd

A grim, grey morning with gusting winds and bursts of rain and general drizzle. Suddenly the sunny days of May and early June seem light-years away. But it's good for application. Started work at 9.15 [on new Python TV series] and by lunchtime had 'The Golden Age of Ballooning' typed and organised into a twenty-nine-page script, which could do as a half-hour on its own. Feel rather pleased, as it is almost entirely my own work.

With this satisfactory morning behind me and even a little sunshine peering through to cheer the day up, I drove over and looked through Drew Smith's[1] black and white stills from the film, and selected a batch.

1 Drew Smith was stills photographer on the *Holy Grail*.

Then up to the Angel at Highgate to meet Graham. As at the Monarch, Graham has developed an almost familial relationship with the people who run the pub, which makes for a very pleasant atmosphere and nearly always a free drink. I looked through the work on the 'Michael Ellis' script which G and I had worked on together. Some good ideas there – and it made me laugh. Also made me aware of the usefulness of co-writing, after my euphoria of the morning! There are just jokes and ideas in the Michael Ellis script which I would never have made as funny if I had been writing it on my own.

Came back to find Thomas not well and asleep under a rug on the sofa. Willy, quite disconcerted by this, was trying hard to feel ill himself, and lay, rather unconvincingly, on the other sofa, under a blanket.

I took W swimming in the end. We spent an hour there. W is a real joy to take around. He talks to everybody, especially men in showers, and gives complete strangers a running commentary on the progress of his latest wee, and how Daddy is wearing trunks, etc.

Thursday, July 11th

Writing with Graham. Started about 11.00, worked until 12.45 then off to the Angel; drank a v. good pint of ale, played a couple of games of bar billiards with Graham, talked, and tried to avoid eating until 2.30. Started work at 3.00 – Graham took a little time to get upstairs and, when he eventually joined me, he muttered happily that 'These French cleaners are so passionate'.

Graham is a very good person to write dialogue with, and has very good silly ideas, but there is a rather uncomfortably undisciplined feeling to the day's work. We manage about two hours in the morning, before he starts getting really fidgety, then two more hours in the afternoon. Whereas Terry and myself, when we have a full day's writing, put in about six and a half solid hours.

Anyway, at 5.35 I remember I have a tutorial with Mr Cammillieri and, going against the rush-hour traffic, make Highgate to Soho Square in 15 minutes. An interesting tutorial. He just spoke Italian to me, but we at least got on to interesting topics. He said he was surprised I was an actor, but not surprised I was a writer. Perché? Well, all the actors he has met are self-centred, constantly play-acting and not genuine. Feel flattered, I suppose.

Sunday, July 14th

My mother rang to say that Father has started to see visions again – this time mice, hamsters and Welsh choirs. She sounded worried enough to suggest that I should try and go up there for a day this week.

But it's a busy week ahead, as Eric is back from France today for two weeks and, by some sort of Herculean effort, we should have most of the six new TV shows mapped out by the time he goes back.

Monday, July 15th

St Swithin's Day, apparently. The weather today should hold for forty days according to the horny adage (as I'm reading *Return of the Native* by T Hardy, I'm full of horny adages). Well, this St Swithin's Day was one of the coldest, wettest and most depressing days of the summer, so things don't look too good.

Graham, looking ravaged and with a hangover you could almost touch, arrived outside Julia St at about 10.30 for a lift down to the 10.00 writing meeting at TJ's. Yesterday had been the eighth anniversary of him and David, and G had had too much. He was fragile for most of the morning and only a large amount of gin revived him at lunchtime!

The 'Ballooning' story, Mr Neutron and, read last, but appreciated most, the Michael Ellis 'Harrods Ant Counter', which I'd put together with GC, and typed up rather uncertainly on Friday, very well received, which was most encouraging.

Thursday, July 18th, Southwold

To Southwold on morning train. Father shuffles more than even a month ago, and walks all the time with shoulders bent and sagging.

I took him out to the Queen's Head at Blyford in the early evening. He grimly hung on to a half-pint of bitter, grasping the handle of the glass doggedly, refusing to let it go. He clearly has few enjoyments left, but the chiefest of them is being at home, and here lies the difficulty. How long can Mother lift him out of the bath, support his dead weight as he gets out of the car? How long can she endure five or six interruptions to her sleep each night, putting his legs back into bed, cleaning up the carpet? How much longer can she dress him and undress him? How long will her mental stamina last in the constant presence of someone who never talks to her?

At least Angela and I are now visiting her more regularly, which cheers her up, and she has extraordinary reserves somewhere which keep her going.

Tuesday, July 23rd

Dreamt that John Cleese had been offered a series of thirty shows by Jimmy Gilbert!

Worked up at Graham's. A poor day. Graham's house, expansive as it is, is unaccountably shabby. There is hardly a working-surface in the place. G in a state of high nervous tension because John [Tomiczek] is out all day, and so is David at the moment (he's working at Covent Garden dressing the Stuttgart Ballet). Meanwhile Towser the pedigree dog is playing havoc ripping the innards out of soft furnishings and has to be kept in the kitchen. Graham keeps on disappearing upstairs. A callow choral-singer from California, called Walter, who is staying at the house, wanders about.

I find myself a cup of coffee and eventually a bit of table space in the 'dining' room, which is a pleasant-sized room, with a fine wooden table, but the whole place is littered with bottles of every conceivable beverage from Kum-Kwat to strange Italian liqueurs. On the floor there are boxfuls of Foster's lager and tonics and ginger ales.

Graham eventually appeared, shaking with nervous effort, poured himself a gin and tonic and gradually subsided. But the rest of the morning was taken up with incessant calls from our publicists, to try and fix up an interview about our new LP. A good half-hour wasted. What happens when publicity takes over the thing you're trying to publicise.

Wednesday, July 24th

At 6.30 a Python business meeting at Henshaws'.

What was the meeting about? Oh, I think, what should we do with the Python fortunes when they really start coming in? A pension fund? An office in Tuscany? How to avoid paying ourselves and the taxman all the money that is going to come in. Is it? I suppose so. After all, *Python Live at Drury Lane* does sound to be the bestseller of all our albums – No. 19 next week, according to Gail at Charisma.

Then Mark talked over publicity for the film. Eric refused to become involved in most of it. A few heated words, but he would insist on this silly point of principle that no interviews ever do anyone any good, and are hateful, degrading, etc, etc.

Thursday, August 1st

Up to Graham's for our script meeting with Ian. G had prepared, or was preparing, in his usual chaotic style, a barbecue lunch to mark the occasion.

After lamb kebabs, tandooried chicken, a Foster's lager and several glasses of red wine, in a hazy August sunshine, we retired indoors to read the scripts.

Ian was drinking scotch with dedicated frequency, inveighing against Terry Gilliam for wanting assistants for his animation, against Jill Foster (his, and our, agent) for some unspecified, but clearly deeply felt reason, us for trying to get shows in that were too long, and so on and so on. We tried to discuss Neil's position with Python, but Ian leapt at Neil with an almost paranoid intensity and the last two hours of the meeting were a pointless waste of time, with Ian at his worst. No longer jolly and charming and ebullient, but confused, aggressive and quite unconstructive.

I left at 7.00 with a deep feeling of frustration that remained with me throughout the evening, despite Neil and Yvonne's excellent company at supper. I began to feel what was the point? Here was a series that only Graham was really keen to do, and yet only Terry and I were writing. Here was a series which we had, for better or worse, fought for from the BBC and, with not a few misgivings, we had asked for Ian only to direct it, and yet Ian comes back at us with a totally unrealistic 'this is my show, you do what I say' attitude. We didn't need to do it for the money – why the hell were we doing it?

With these gloomy thoughts I went to my bed at half past twelve.

Tuesday, August 6th

One of the most satisfying copies of *The Guardian* that has ever come through my letterbox swished onto the mat at 8.00 this morning, bearing front-page news of Nixon's admission that he knew about the Watergate cover-up and personally directed it within five days of the incident. As I drive down to Terry's to write, I remember the day, five and a half years ago, when TJ and I drove out along the A40 on our way to film *The Complete and Utter Histories* and despondently listened to the unbelievable news of Tricky Dicky's elevation to the Presidency. Now I listened to the equally unbelievable news that he had lied blatantly and repeatedly to his supporters, his lawyers, his 'friends', his country and the world, for two years!

Father went into hospital at St Audry's again for a two-week period. He is seeing hamsters everywhere now – they squelch under his feet as he walks in the sitting room. My mother has to carry a bag to put them in. When the doctor arrived the hamsters got up Grandfather's trousers and began to attack his privates. My father, so staid and unimaginative over most of his life, is now becoming quite Pythonic. The hamsters seem to bother more than frighten him, as do the two men who have evidently been in the garage since 1966!

Fraser and Dunlop rang with an offer of £4,000 to do a Stone's Ginger Wine commercial. One day's work. My hands went clammy, and I told Jill I'd think about it. £4,000 for a day's work is the kind of proposition that gives greed a good name.

Thursday, August 8th

For the last two days little but writing (we now have four scripts completed) and Nixon. Only this evening, two days after his self-confessed lying, does it seem that the man has finally got the message, and is probably about to become the first American President to resign in office.

A wonderful galaxy of early Nixon film – the suffocatingly schmaltzy Checkers speech, the effusive endorsements from Frank Sinatra, Gerry Ford and Eisenhower speaking of Nixon as 'a man of integrity' in 1968. But there can have been no TV spectacle as chilling as the replays of Nixon's last three Watergate addresses to the nation – where Nixon looks the world in the eye and lies.

Monday, August 12th

Stop Press: writing my diary at 11.15 when the phone rings. It's Nancy from New York, almost speechless with good news. As from October, the entire Python first series is being screened on American TV by PBS.[1] I

---

1 The Public Broadcasting Service (Channel 13). The only non-commercial channel on US television. It is supported by public subscription.

told Nancy it must be Gerry Ford's doing. Python, which has been going for almost as long as Richard Nixon was President, has finally broken in the States within four days of his resignation.

Sunday, September 1st, Abbotsley

In many ways these last two days have been an extension of last week's summer holiday in the Lot – totally relaxing days spent with the family, away from work and away from too many other people. Worked in the garden, had the best night's sleep for a week, and ended up today astride a tree, half-submerged in the stagnant pond, wearing only my under-pants! I was trying to salvage my appalling attempt at tree-felling, which had propelled the tree straight into the stagnant water.

My Tarzan-like activities were greeted with much mirth by Helen. Willy leant up against the wire and made up songs to sing to himself, and Thomas fussed around like an old hen worrying about me – 'Oh, do be careful, Daddy.' 'Oh, isn't Daddy strong?' 'Oh, Daddy, you're *so* nice,' and other slightly unhelpful observations.

Sunday, September 8th, Exeter

From today we start filming on the fourth Python series. Packed during the morning – took Helen and the boys out for a very pleasant goodbye lunch at Maxwells, and left with the Mini and Terry Jones, about 2.00.

Arrived at 8.30 at the White Hart Hotel in Exeter. An historic inn, with its history quite spectacularly displayed – beams, torture instruments on the walls, cannon, etc. But a fairly cosy, un-smart bar, where Ian, Eke, Graham and John and Douglas (Graham's writer friend from Cambridge)[1] and others all sat.

Thursday, September 12th, Exeter

Today the weather was grey and rather miserable and, owing to a wrongly chosen location, I stood around for two hours in full drag, false eyelashes and all, before shooting for the day was cancelled. Eric and I walked up to the castle, or what remains of it after Cromwell. The weather began to

---

1 Douglas Adams, who later wrote *The Hitchhiker's Guide to the Galaxy*, had recently been asked by Graham to help him on his solo project *Son of Dracula*.

improve and we wandered around some gardens, then, both in rather a silly mood, walked back through the town and stopped at a shop which was prominently displaying ladies' panties with little messages on the front. We went inside. A chunky, middle-aged lady assistant, looking rather like I had done an hour previously, came up to us.

'Oh, she'd love a pair of these,' she said to us.

Eric indicated me, 'No, they're for him.'

I told her I wouldn't be able to get them over my head.

'We're looking for some with the AA sign on them,' said Eric.

She took this quite seriously and helpfully said 'We *did* have some with road signs on.'

'No, it's AA ones we want,' Eric confirmed.

We later bought some dressed crab and ate it with our tea back at the hotel.

Friday, September 27th

Filming aboard HMS *Belfast* moored by the Tower of London. I was to go along there at lunchtime, meet them and prepare for quite a long sketch to be filmed on Westminster Bridge in the afternoon. The rain fell heavily and persistently all morning and I arrived at HMS *Belfast* at about 12.45. 'Oh, the BBC, yes,' said an obliging Petty Officer. 'You know where the bar is, don't you?'

Well, I found the BBC ensconced, incredibly happily, in a warm, busy bar amidships – the only oasis of light and warmth and cheerfulness on board this steel-grey hulk. Terry, with an angelic smile, recommended the rum. Ian was as red-faced as I'd ever seen him on this filming. Outside it still poured. The morning's shot had been completed, but with much laughter amongst the crew of *Belfast* – for Graham was dressed as a Captain in full drag. 'Better keep Les below decks,' and other naval banter was apparently heard.

On from *Belfast*, in heavy drizzle, to our rendezvous point in a car park beside County Hall. When we arrived it was raining heavily again and it was obvious they wouldn't be able to film for a while. However, in the car park there just happened to be an enormous marquee, with '2nd International Festival of Wine' in large letters outside. So I added four glasses of wine to my rum and lagers and, when we actually came to start filming, at about 4.00, beneath the South Bank Lion, I was in an extremely cheery state and ready for anything.

The advantages of being dressed as a policeman are that I was able to stop four lanes of traffic on Westminster Bridge at rush hour, walk across the road, hit Terry, dressed as a lady, grab his armchair and walk back across the road with the cars still respectfully at a standstill!

Disadvantages of being dressed as a PC were that, as I waited for the cue for action, I would be approached by Americans asking where they could find a restaurant where they wouldn't need to wear a tie and harassed motorists asking me where the GLC licensing department was. One old lady approached me, stared hard at my false moustache and said, 'What are you? Real or a fake?'

'Have a guess,' I said

She surveyed my loose moustache and pinned-up hair for a moment, 'You're real.'

Tuesday, October 1st

In the evening we had an investors' preview of *Monty Python and the Holy Grail* at the Hanover Grand.

Tony Stratton-Smith was there, and Ali and Brian Gibbons – the financial wizards behind Charisma. I chatted up Madeline Bell to try and get her to appear as the Ronettes in the next Python record,[1] and there were a lot of beautiful people, presumably Pink Floyd and their wives, and also Maggie Gilliam, Carol Cleveland and Helen, who had never seen the film before.

Mark had to make an announcement before the film explaining that it was not yet finally cut. But the result was even more disastrous than I'd thought. It was one of those evenings when Python flopped. There was some laughter and there was some enjoyment and there was polite applause at the end. Michael White and John Goldstone wouldn't speak to us. White walked out at the end, giving Terry G a brief and non-committal pat on the shoulder.

Undoubtedly the poor quality of the print hadn't helped. A couple of times there were booms in shot which killed the scenes after them. The soundtrack had been so realistically and thoroughly dubbed by Terry G and John Hackney that the slightly gory sequences had a sickening impact which didn't help loosen people up.

1 Madeline Bell, African-American soul singer who had many hits in the UK with the group Blue Mink after making a mark as a backing singer for Dusty Springfield.

I didn't, I must admit, immediately look to technical faults to explain away my acute discomfort through most of the showing. I just felt, looking at it, that there were not enough jokes there. The film was 20% too strong on authenticity and 20% too weak on jokes.

None of the investors seemed anxious to shake us by the hand or even tap us on the shoulder. Only Tony Stratton-Smith came up and was clearly distressed to see us unhappy. He tried everything to jolly us up, for which I'm eternally grateful. The room was too hot, said Tony, the drink wasn't free, the projection was terrible – which in fact it was.

Terry J clearly felt that what was wrong was there was too much animation and too noisy a soundtrack. Both faults of TG. Poor TG. He had to put up with stick from Mark and Michael White later in the evening, and has been working eighteen hours a day on the film.

Helen and I went on to a meal at Rugantinos with Eric and Lyn. Eric had walked out half-way through the viewing.

Wednesday, October 2nd

Spent a most uncomfortable day in a studio jungle at Ealing, trying to portray the almost unparodyable David Attenborough. We got the make-up on, hair pinned up, bladder stuck on and wig over that – but after nearly an hour it wasn't quite right. Then suddenly I made a face that caught Attenborough and made the whole ensemble work. I spent the rest of the day trying, with various degrees of failure, to recapture this expression.

The discomfort of the make-up was nothing, compared to the special effect required to make Attenborough sweat profusely – this consisted of pipes thrust up my trouser legs and under my armpits and connected to the water supply for the studio. Unfortunately, for some reason, the supply wasn't working and I had to stand around in the tubes, anchored to a long rubber pipe for about 30 minutes before I could be reconnected to another studio! When the shot was eventually ready, it was impossible to do a fully practical rehearsal, so I was half-way into a take of a long speech when I felt ice-cold water pouring from my armpits.

From filming, I drove straight to Regent's Park and a Python film meeting. Michael White was the surprise guest – he had come along, he said, to tell us not to be too disheartened about the film. There were things that could be done to save it. It was, in his opinion, far too bloodthirsty, far too unpleasant in its atmosphere; almost every scene, he complained, showed death, disease, dirt or destruction, and his feeling, and the feeling of many people at the showing, was one of profound depression after seeing it.

It was not easy to take the whole White approach as The Word, but several aspects of it rang true.

TG stayed quiet and didn't fight. Graham bristled at every criticism of the violence – he regards it as important, honest, etc, etc. Terry J, like a cat with his hackles up whenever Mark's around, prowled the room, arguing fiercely that it should never have been shown in its unfinished state, that the film we saw on Tuesday was a badly edited cut, full of mistakes, and that anyone who had seen the viewing a month or so ago would realise what damage had been done.

Thursday, October 3rd

A rare day of sunshine – even tho' it was cold. Drove Graham down to Motspur Park, where we were filming a cricket match. Graham still mightily depressed about the reaction to the film. He really does feel that we are in danger of being panicked into drastic alterations to what he considers is one of the best pieces of work we've ever done.

A mournful drink after lunch with Ian, Terry and Graham. Eke has gone back to Germany and Ian has reverted to the spirits, which Eke seemed successfully to divert his mind from. In the afternoon he could hardly stand up and at one point he actually fell backwards over the camera tripod.

Apart from this afternoon, Ian has been a changed man – confident, co-operative and always in control, both of us and the crew.

Saturday, October 5th

At 10.00 down to the Henshaws' for a meeting about the film with Eric, Terry G, TJ, Gra, Mark and John Hackney, the editor.

The meeting, which Terry J had wanted to make very brief (his point being that there was very little to do to the film apart from losing all the 'improvements' made over the last four weeks), lasted solidly from 10.00 until 5.00. Everybody had their say about every part of the film. Eric and Mark won a point over the Three-Headed Knight (which all the rest of us who were actually in England working on the film in the summer thought was disastrous), which is now back in for us to look at. The animation has been cut down (the first time I can remember in all Python history when we have actually chopped any of TG's stuff). Some of Neil's music was thought to be not right, so we are putting on a lot of stock music. We have lost more of the 'Ni' sequence. There was nearly deadlock over reshooting the very important opening joke with the coconuts. Mark clams up on any mention of reshooting and TJ rises accordingly.

Thursday, October 10th

The second election this year. I feel more strongly pro-Labour than I did in February. Then it was a case of voting on the single issue of stopping the country grinding to a halt as a result of E Heath's appalling misjudgement of the 'have-nots' and their strength. Since then the record of the Labour government has been impressive. They actually have held back rising prices, they have kept mortgage rates down, they've cut VAT, they've introduced fairer legislation on the sharing of North Sea Oil revenues and, on the international front, they have been a strongly heard voice in Washington and in the Common Market, and they have actually produced the 'social contract', which seems more than just another economic formula for trying to save the British economy (again) – it is an attempt to use and build on a sense of corporate responsibility among the working classes, which men like Sir Keith Joseph[1] would deny they ever had.

So that's why I once again found myself in the Polling Station at Tom's school, at 9.15 on a wet October morning, voting for Jock Stallard[2] for the second time in a year.

Friday, October 11th

The Labour overall majority is three. Big gains by Scottish Nationalists. The Liberal revival failed again – their share of the vote was down – and the Tories lost about twenty seats.

1 Secretary of State for Social Services in the Heath government. Architect of free-market Conservatism.
2 MP for St Pancras North.

Monday, November 4th

As soon as we got to rehearsal today and started to read through the 'Mr Neutron' script, an almost tangible blanket of gloom fell on everyone. The script was bitty, and rather difficult to read, admittedly – it's a show where we only need ten minutes' studio – but this alone couldn't account for the unprecedentedly dolorous mood around the table. Then I tracked it down – it was emanating from Eric. Eric, who can so often be the life and soul, was very deep into one of his dark, silent moods.

Because Eric was in France for all but two weeks of the entire writing and planning stage of the series, there is very little of his contribution in the series. In a welter of bitterly delivered contradictions, he criticised us for not accepting his half-hour, and at the same time bemoaned the fact that we wrote half-hours at all. He didn't like writing stories, he liked writing revue.

At lunchtime came a fresh jolt from the BBC. In Graham's speech as the Icelandic Honey Week rep – very funny and all recorded – they wanted the lines 'Cold enough to freeze your balls off, freeze the little buggers solid in mid-air' cut from the tape, as well as one 'piss off' (we could keep the other). Jimmy had apparently said very strongly to Ian that 'if and when Python Productions made their own series they could say what they like', but for now they must accept what the BBC say. Censorship in fact. Yes, says Jimmy, it is 'censorship'. We had already burned off most of our frustrated anger at the BBC's decision to omit the word 'condom' from that show. I mean, if condom is considered a bannable word on British TV in 1974, what hope is there!

One of Jimmy's reasons for this fresh bout of anti-sexual censorship is that we are going out at 8.30 on BBC1 when the shows are repeated. So, from lunchtime today, we are faced with an important decision. Do we let the BBC change Python into a soft, inoffensive half-hour of pap, or do we fight to keep its teeth, its offensiveness, its naughtiness? Do we have to conform or disappear?

Came home to cauliflower cheese, a couple of glasses of white wine and a sit by the fire whilst I watched *Panorama* on the World Food Conference in Rome. Within the year one in five of the world's population will suffer from starvation. It's like saying they'll suffer from death.

How small and insignificant it makes the events of today seem – and yet they have left me quite drained.

Tuesday, November 5th

Tom very pleased with himself this morning as he has learnt to tie his shoelaces. He keeps tying and untying them and had to show Mr Jarvis[1] how to do it. Helen later tells me they kept on coming undone as he walked to school.

A few fireworks at the Guedallas', and quick drink, then Robert H came round for the evening.

Robert thinks we ought to stop Python whilst we're still at the top. I think 31 is a little early to quit – but a few more mornings like yesterday could change my mind.

Wednesday, November 6th

Rehearsals a lot more convivial today, but Graham is feeling very low, as in Monday's editing Terry and Ian decided that, in view of the censorship cuts demanded by the BBC, the entire Icelandic Honey Week speech from Show 2 would have to be taken out. The loss of three sentences at the BBC's behest has therefore effectively castrated a funny, absurd, harmless and well-performed little piece.

Anne Henshaw[2] came to the rehearsals to give us some money from the book (which seems set for some good sales again this Christmas – the *Papperbok* is No. 3 in the best-selling lists, below *Watership Down* and Lyall Watson's *Supernature*) and she also showed us a letter from the financial front-man at Charisma, which tried to argue that we were not owed £11,000, but nearer £6,000. This is clearly not true, so the situation there is deteriorating rapidly. Anne is going to keep plugging away at them, but it seems as though Python may find itself in the courts for the first time. What a depressing week it's turning out to be.

Friday, November 8th

Nancy rang from New York to say she was ecstatic about the critical success of the TV show in New York, and especially over a rave review to be published in the prestigious *New York Sunday Times* in a couple of days. Boston and Philadelphia have bought the show.

1 Sam Jarvis, our house-painter.
2 Anne had taken over as our manager from John Gledhill.

'Discover for the first time
the full story of my
great-grandfather, Edward
Palin, who married Brita
Gallagher, an orphan
of the Irish potato
famines of the 1840s.'
(September 30th, 1977)

'Sorted through an old
chestful of Grandfather's
papers ... In the
Shrewsbury and India
days much evidence that
he was quite a character:
"always looks as though
he has done something
wicked but never has" –
school report from
Shrewsbury.'
(April 15th, 1975)

'In 1966 my parents,
Edward "Ted" and
Mary Palin, retired to
a village just outside
Southwold in Suffolk.'

With Ian Davidson at a
Python rehearsal in the
tank-top days, 1970.

Charity football and
experimental beard, 1970.

Pythons at play,
Germany, 1971.

Filming 'Kamikaze Scotsmen' at Norwich Castle, 1971. With Eric Idle and Hazel Pethig.

With 'Auntie' Eric. 'The Cycling Tour', Python, 1972.

'Almost two years and nine months to the day since we shot our first feet of Python film, we were at Windsor to shoot what is probably our last.' With Ian MacNaughton. (April 6th, 1972)

Helen's mother and her
grandsons, Willy and
Tom, Abbotsley, 1972.

Helen's sister,
Cathy, with Tarquin
at Abbotsley.

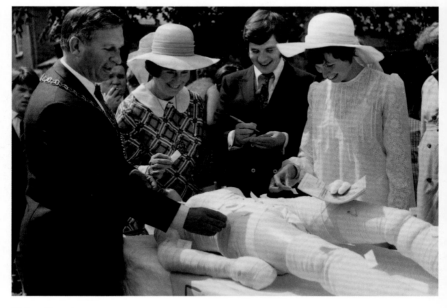

Helen attempts a
circumcision, local
fete, 1972.

Heyday of the flares.
With Tom at home, 1973.

'The longest day and my
father's three-quarter
century.' My mother
had baked him a cake
in his house colours
from Shrewsbury
School.
(June 21st, 1975)

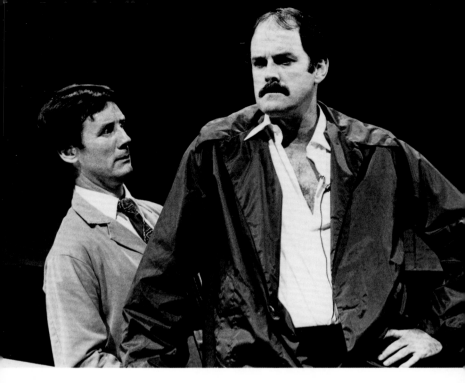

Radio Times

Good taste time

INSIDE: Is Warren Mitchell
about to bite off more
than he can chew? in
Black and Blue Tuesday
BBC2 Colour

SECRETS

'The first TV play
written by Terry and
myself . . . had been given
a blaze of pre-publicity.'
The launch of *Secrets*.
(August 14th, 1973)

'John turned to me
and said "No". The
unconventional end
of the 'Dead Parrot'
sketch on my thirtieth
birthday.
(May 5th, 1973)

'How do you know he's
a producer? He's the
only one who hasn't got
shit all over him.'
Eric, myself (as Mud
Eater) and Mark
Forstater, *Holy Grail*,
1974.

'First day of filming. Graham got vertigo . . . and Eric and I and John sat around listening to stories from the mountain rescue boys about how many people perish on the mountains each year.'
(*Holy Grail*, April 30th, 1974)

'How can you react without laughing to a broad Glaswegian accent saying "Of course I'm French, why do you think I am using this outrageous accent?"'.
(May 11th, 1974)

Graham as the lecturer,
Terry G, Terry J and
myself take up positions
for the 'Custard Pie'
sketch, 1975.

'The Surprise Pie.'
Terry and me at
Drury Lane, 1975.

Saturday, November 9th

Our fifth recording. Graham is round here in a mini-cab at 9.30, catching me with the toast and marmalade fresh in my mouth. But we are round at Eric's by ten to ten, and at the BBC 25 minutes early (a record, I think). Not a great deal of pressure this week as 19 minutes of the show are on film. So it all goes smoothly and unremarkably. For the fireside scene in which the Trapper and Captain Carpenter talk to Teddy Salad, the CIA agent disguised as a dog – John Horton and Richard had excelled themselves – Richard just working the dog with his hand right up its backside was funny enough.

At the end of the dress run-through, Jimmy Gilbert appeared, a little awkward perhaps, but clearly on placatory mission. Great show last week, he said, and apparently the viewing figures – at 5.8 million for Show 1 of the fourth series – were the best on BBC2, apart from *Call My Bluff*!! This doesn't strike me as all that wonderful.

Wednesday, November 13th

After rehearsal today Anne Henshaw came to tell us that Charisma are, in fact, broke. How serious it is we don't know – but at least they admit that we are owed £13,000 and presumably this money increases every time someone buys one of our records.

Thursday, November 14th

Simon A came round. He had been at a union meeting called to talk about the next step in his continuing war against the producer and editor of *World in Action*, who, in their bid to lure Granada reporters up to Manchester, have taken the unprecedented step of threatening to fire those who won't come. It sounds as though a fearless *World in Action* exposé of *World in Action* is required.

SA has been working for the last seven weeks gathering material for a programme on police corruption. He says the information is incredible. Corruption starts early in the Metropolitan Police, when bobbies, in order to be well considered, are judged on the number of arrests they make. According to SA's sources, it is commonplace therefore for vagrants and down-and-outs to be quite falsely charged with trying to break into cars, etc, etc. The corruption at the top is almost institutionalised. One forgets the close social connections between police and the underworld. In many cases there is a mutual respect, in some real friendship – and SA says a man like James Humphries, the recently gaoled Soho 'porn king', was a regular dinner party guest of senior policemen.

Tuesday, November 19th

A clear, sunny morning. London is drying out after a week of heavy rain. The pound at its lowest level ever yesterday, share prices down to 1958 levels, the miners' rejection of a big productivity deal, and another report from the Hudson Institute in Paris, which prophesies that Britain has had it, and in the 1980s there will be a decline in living standards, which will leave us on a level with Spain. Certainly we have already made our mark on Benidorm, so maybe UK and Spain should amalgamate and go into leisure in a big way, and leave the smooth, Tonik-suited executives of Germany and Holland to run our business for us.

Anyway, despite this gloom, life goes on, and Python flourishes. Our third show finally seems to have brought people back to the fold. Both the *Sunday Times* and *The Observer* noted this weekend that the show was back on 'cracking form' (the *Sunday Times*). We recorded our last show on Saturday – to a very receptive audience, which was most encouraging. The BBC, or rather J Gilbert on the phone to G Chapman, have confirmed that they want us to do seven more shows in the spring, and Eric was heard on Saturday night to agree to doing them – provided there are plenty of sketches and not so many storylines.

Friday, November 22nd

The depressing pattern of grey skies, rain and dark days is matched only by the news. In Tunis Arab guerrillas select an unarmed businessman from a plane they have hijacked and, merely to hurry up the business of forcing the release of six of their murdering compatriots, stand the man in the doorway of the plane and shoot him in the back. This evening there are two explosions in Birmingham pubs. Seventeen people are killed. An Irish voice gave an 11 minute warning, but so far the Provisionals have not claimed responsibility.

Saturday, November 23rd

An evening out with Nigel and Jude.[1] We met Nigel at his gallery in Sloane Gardens.

I found his current exhibition quite baffling. Why is it that modern art should make you feel so clumsy for not understanding it? It's a curious feeling of inadequacy to stand and look at a roomful of carefully-hung, expensively-lit objects, which someone considers paying nearly a thousand pounds for, and to find them as meaningful as a tin of anchovies.

But Nigel would probably counter this by saying that he has an exhibition of tins of anchovies opening only next week.

Monday, November 25th

Saw John C for the first time in many weeks – we did a couple of voice-overs together. The first in Studio G, Wardour Street, was a frightfully banal affair for Nairn Cushionfloors. An attractive lady producer, with the usual helpful and precise instructions – 'Can you read it slower, but with more pace?'

'Try the high-pitched, deep voice and don't emphasise the bit about "warm" and "springy".'

'You don't want them emphasised?'

'No, not emphasised, but just strongly delivered.' Etc, etc.

Whilst John and I were involved in this quite appallingly worthless artefact ('Never look a gift horse in the mouth, Mikey,' said John), a pillar box exploded in rush-hour Piccadilly, less than a mile away. All part of the IRA war.

Friday, November 29th

5.30: Arrive at 22 Park Square East [Michael and Anne Henshaw's home] for a Python meeting. Nothing of great interest until we start, in the absence of JC, to discuss 'Next Year'.

Eric: 'Does anyone feel like me that the TV series has been a failure?'

One can almost feel the 'Oh, no, here we go again' ripples spread

---

1 Nigel and Judy Greenwood. Together with elder sister Sarah, they were the three children of my father's sister. Nigel was a couple of years older than me.

round the room. So we are into the area which had surfaced briefly at the Old Oak Club at the beginning of this month and which had submerged, I hoped finally, during the last three weeks. The area of Eric's Doubt. If pushed he will say he regards the series as a near disaster, beneficial to none of us. If one counters with the fact that nearly all the major newspapers have come round to the view that Python without John was worth doing again, Eric retreats into a 'Well, if you believe the press you'll believe anything' attitude.

TG and I are both keen to do another seven. I am decided in my own mind that the last six have been good enough, and well-received enough, to try and complete a further seven – as a group, using TG and Eric more fully and TJ and MP less.

Then, after half an hour or so, Eric is suddenly agreeing, not only to the series, but to a rescheduling of dates taking us up to July. He doesn't look all that happy, but he seems to have agreed. So Python carries on. Then we elect a new Chairman by playing stone and scissors. I win, so Terry G has to be the new Chairman.

I caught up with Eric as we got outside the front door and asked him whether he was really happy about what had been decided. He feels that he no longer gets satisfaction out of Python because it is restricting. His writing and his ideas come up against the T Jones wall and he has no longer the stomach to keep fighting every inch of the way over every inch of material. Also he feels that, with John no longer there, he hasn't an ally. Having unloaded himself of this much, we say goodnight.

Saturday, November 30th

Eric comes round about 3.00. He suggests going for a walk. So, Eric and I set off for the Heath, both of us in thick coats, the watery November sun sinking splendidly as we reach the top of Parliament Hill. It's so like le Carré[1] I have to pinch myself.

Eric goes through his reasons for dissatisfaction. (I learn later from Terry G that Eric is reading Sartre at the moment – he was reading McLuhan a month ago when he was arguing that the content of Python books is quite unimportant compared to the form – and during the filming in Scotland he was reading Machiavelli. TG thinks if we can get

---

1 I was deep into John le Carré's *Tinker, Tailor, Soldier, Spy* and for quite a while tended to see everything through his eyes. And November is a very le-Carré-like month.

at Eric's library cards, we can get at the man!) He feels Python no longer works as a group. The formula is dull, we no longer surprise and shock, we are predictable. But he clearly misses John a great deal. None of us are as good as John or ever will be, he says.

Lynsey de Paul[1] moved today. I shall miss the slightly sexy, exotic atmosphere she gave the street, but not the drunken groups of local morons who try and sing 'No Honestly' outside her house at 11.30 at night.

Sunday, December 1st

Grey, but dry day. Two long phone calls re Python in the morning to TG and TJ. I have an instinctive warmth towards TJ – and yet TG is the only person whom I can now talk to fully and objectively about Monty P.

Mary and Edward [Helen's sister and brother-in-law] come round to supper in the evening. I have a rather good theory that in twenty-five years' time there will be far more countries (far more national divisions) in the world than now. I would like to see Estonia and Latvia as independent nations and Wales and Scotland for that matter. And I think it is going to happen – as people get less and less satisfaction from being part of a large international wodge. Look at the signs – Palestine's representative at the UN, Scottish Nationals with eleven seats in Parliament. In its nastiest form – the IRA.

Tuesday, December 3rd, Brace of Pheasant Inn, Plush, Dorset

I left for Dorset at 12.30 after booking a room in an out-of-the-way six-teenth century thatched inn (thank you, *Good Food Guide*) at Plush, a village fourteen or so miles north of Dorchester in what looked good Hardy and walking country.

My much needed spell of 'time off' had acquired a certain signifi-cance and I left unhappily. Helen upset because of the baby being due in a month or so and my going away – even tho' I know she wanted me to go. If I'd just taken off that morning it would have seemed all far less calculated.

It was a grizzly grey day as the train rattled over Egdon Heath. My

1 Lynsey de Paul. Singer, songwriter, glam rocker and, for a few years, our neighbour. She sang the British Eurovision entry in 1977.

first impression of Dorchester was of seeing schoolboys out of the corner of my eye, nudging each other and pointing at me. One followed me back from the station. So much for getting away from Monty Python. But as soon as I left Dorchester in a cab for Plush, I felt very Sherlock Holmes-ish – the night was dark, I could dimly see the outlines of hills on either side, the road wound crazily and suddenly the taxi had stopped. 'Right, this is it, sir.' Oh, yes, there was a whitewashed thatched house outside, but that was about all. The cab turned and sped off into the dark.

A snug little inn – my room is tiny and I share it with a huge chimney-breast. The pub is well unimproved. A low beamed ceiling and a single bar/dining room which makes for a cheerful communal spirit. An open fire, a landlord with a rather jolly, but loud voice, just returned from a holiday in Tenerife, where he had taken his wife to recuperate from a stroke. She was in hospital at the moment having her kneecaps removed (I couldn't work out whether this was in some way related to the holiday or not).

A rather frail, but florid-faced chap with a fine check sports coat, cavalry twills and a military moustache, came in from the night.

'Hello, Colonel,' says the barman.

'I could ring Roy Mason's bloody neck,' says the Colonel ruefully, tho' not violently, as he eases himself onto the bar stool. (Roy Mason had just announced some almost universally applauded and long-delayed cuts in our defence budget.)

That was rather the tone of the evening. A characteristic I noticed from my vantage point by the fire (where I sat with a large whisky and ice, trying to read *Tinker, Tailor, Soldier, Spy*) is that these country chaps talk only of facts – the size of an aeroplane, the hours of sunshine, the number of pigs so and so has – never feelings, nor impressions and certainly not emotions.

Wednesday, December 4th, Plush

Today I have walked nearly twenty miles over the hills and across the muddy fields of Dorset, I feel deliciously tired, I have had a long soak in a hot bath and in half an hour or so I will don my brown velvet jacket and elegantly clump downstairs for a drink, a read perhaps around the open fire, and then a meal which I know will be excellently cooked, and a bottle of rather expensive wine.

But it's all such a lovely illusion. I know that the maître d'hôtel will greet me with a booming voice when I get downstairs – and there'll be absolutely no chance of me slipping unobtrusively into a seat until everyone in the bar knows where I've been and what I'm drinking. I shall then try to read and yet find it impossible in the confined space of the bar to avoid hearing the rich country voices of the customers airing their rich country views.

Though there have been wonderful things down here – the food and the stunning sunny weather today and striding along the chalk ridges with the sun lighting the valleys – I am looking forward to being in that train pulling into Waterloo at 1.20 tomorrow. Pulling into the jostle and the bomb scares – but pulling into the richness of life which can only come when you have many people doing many different things. Down here, in the heart of an agricultural community, I feel the oppressive weight of years of tradition, convention and orderliness on the people around. I could get used to it, I suppose, but I feel this evening that I am too hopelessly and happily corrupted by the richness of London life ever to be right for Dorset, or vice-versa.

Monday, December 9th

I lit a fire at lunchtime, tho' it's not much less than 50° outside, but Willy wanted to send a letter up the chimney to Father Christmas to ask for a sweet factory.

William is sitting on the floor of my room, looking through old photos of the first four years of his life – like an old man looking back on his memories.

Nothing is expected of me for at least a week. This must be the root cause for the blissful sense of relaxed contentment I feel at the moment – though just having written that fills me with a little apprehension! A twinge of guilt.

Friday, December 20th

Lunchtime at the Angel in Highgate. The jolly lady who runs it has now given five copies of *Bert Fegg's Nasty Book* to people for presents. I had to sign one today. (Later in the afternoon, shopping at W H Smith's in Kensington High Street, I noticed that there were an awful lot of *Bert Fegg* books on the counter. Unsold or there owing to popular demand? I counted nearly fifty in a pile before I became embarrassed and moved away!)

Talked to Douglas Adams about the disappointed reactions he had had to Python series four. He thought the scripts were far better than the shows.

Saturday, December 21st

A great party at Robert Hewison's. Ten or fifteen people in his little room at Fetter Lane. Lunchtime – excellent mulled claret, no one from Python, so little shop talked. Renewed acquaintance with the Walmsleys[1] and enjoyed ourselves enormously.

Nigel told us that a man actually exists somewhere in the labyrinthine bureaucracy of the government, whose sole job it is to scrutinise every new car number to ensure that the combination of letters and numbers do not accidentally spell something rude, misleading or even ambiguous – in *any* language. Nigel, too, laughed when he first heard this, but it was put to him that maybe the government had a duty to protect spinster schoolteachers from the possibility of their driving through Czechoslovakia with 'Want a Good Time?' on their bumpers.

Wednesday, December 25th

On Christmas morning, the four of us had the house to ourselves. The boys played happily, Helen and I sat around and I read some of *A Christmas Carol*. Great stuff. After Hardy I feel myself being drawn, unprotesting, into the nineteenth century world, whose books and authors used to be forced at you from an early age, so I developed an image of Dickens, Jane Austen, George Eliot, as being heavy, worthy and boring. But now I'm acquiring an enormous taste for these same authors, and rediscovered Dickens' *Christmas Carol* (my old Birkdale school copy) with sheer joy.

---

1 Nigel Walmsley and wife Jane. Nigel was at Brasenose with me and went on to run the Post Office for a while. Jane was a journalist and TV presenter.

1975

Wednesday, January 1st

No newspapers, no letters. A bank holiday and all that that entails. All my working urges suddenly evaporate. Everything is still and quiet outside. Decide to treat it in the spirit which Heath intended this holiday when he decided on it for the first time last year. Rang Ian and Anthea [Davidson] and invited them for drinks, rang Robert for his mulled wine recipe and settled down to not working until this afternoon. But, well, one thing led to another. I should have started a play, Ian should have been writing for *The Two Ronnies*, Anthea should have been designing her summer clothes for the shop and Helen should have been having a baby, but somehow twelve and a half hours, four bottles of wine, three or four beers, several games of Scrabble and cribbage and one Indian take-away meal later, we were all still in the sitting room.

As Anthea said, this could be the year we learnt not to work too hard!

Monday, January 6th

A dull, overcast day. A gusting moderate wind sends icy draughts into my eyrie.[1] It takes most of the morning to warm the place up. My brain doesn't seem to warm up at all, and I struggle with an uninteresting idea for a play.

After lunch I take Thomas and Anthony Tackerberry to see *Dr Who and the Daleks* at the Adelphi. The kids are good company – the seriousness and lack of self-consciousness of six-year-olds makes their conversation a delight to listen to. Anthony, having told me his father was a barrister, said to me, 'I know what you are … you're a filmer.' Or the time he'd hit his head on a radiator – 'My *God* it hurt,' he said, with such feeling you almost had to wince. 'It came down my head and down my neck and onto my shirt …' adding, almost as an afterthought, 'the blood.'

Anyway, we arrived early. Parked in the now almost deserted streets

---

1 A new, half-glassed-in extension had been built on top of the house. My first custom-built work-room.

of Covent Garden. The main market buildings are fenced off. I don't know what they're doing in there, but the whole area could be allowed to become a most amenable shopping, eating, walking, living area. At the moment, in the first shock of losing the market that gave it its character and shaped its life, it is eerily quiet – only just breathing.

Wednesday, January 8th

After the excesses of rain and wind in October and November, the weather lately has settled down into a meek routine of still, lifeless, grey days. The IRA New Year truce lasts until January 16th and the total absence of any bomb attacks since the day the truce started shows how well-controlled the IRA is. The feeling in the press is that we have a bad year to come – increasing unemployment, steeply rising prices, etc, etc, but it's as if the worst is over. The nation is now entering a year bad enough to bring out all the Dunkirk spirit, whereas last year it was a year of such sudden and bewildering change that no one knew quite how to react.

Everywhere the talk is of cuts, savings and 'trimming back'. Notable exceptions, of course, being the now blue-eyed coal industry and the railways – five years ago the twin symbols of decline in a world of technological evolution.

Thursday, January 9th

Another sign of the times. The Beatles' company, Beatles Ltd, officially and finally ceased to exist today. The company, which held the Beatles group as such together in various legal obligations, has become increasingly obstructive to their various separate careers. The group haven't played together since 1969. We began when they finished.

Friday, January 10th

By one of those strange coincidences, today was the day that Python and the Beatles came together. In the last two months we've heard that George H has been using 'Lumberjack Song' from the first BBC LP as a curtain raiser to his US stage tour. So it seemed almost predictable that the two groups would be sooner or later involved in some joint venture.

Terry J, Graham and myself on behalf of Python and Neil Aspinall and Derek Taylor[1] on behalf of the Beatles, found ourselves at lunchtime today in a hastily converted office at the Apple Corp's temporary head-quarters in smart St James's, to watch the *Magical Mystery Tour* – the Beatles' TV film made in 1967. At that time I remember the film being slated by the critics and it vanished, swamped by an angry public who doubtless felt the Beatles had let them down by not subscribing to the image of success and glamour which the public had created around them. When it was suggested at a meeting late last year that we should try and put out the *Magical Mystery Tour* as a supporting film to the *Holy Grail*, there was unanimous agreement among the Python group. After several months of checking and cross-checking we finally heard last week that the four Beatles had been consulted and were happy to let the film go out. So today we saw it for the first time since 1967.

Unfortunately it was not an unjustly underrated work. There are some poor and rather messy sequences, it's very obvious when the group is miming to playback and there's a cutesie *Top of the Pops*-type look at Paul during 'Fool on the Hill', which is very tacky and dated. However, it *is* extraordinary still, it is far too impressionistic and odd to be just outdated and many sequences are very successful. It's also quite long – nearly an hour, but all in all we were pleased. It will have great curiosity value and should be complementary to the Python film, because much of it looks like familiar Python territory.

Ringo was suddenly there, talking with Graham and Terry. He was dressed like a British Rail porter, with a black serge waistcoat and black trousers. I noticed his hair was streaked silvery at the sides. He looked rather ashen-faced – the look of a man who needs a holiday.

I was given George Harrison's number by Aspinall, who said he thought George would appreciate a call – he's apparently the all-time Python fan, and it was at his mansion near Henley that they had been last night looking at the last Python TV series.

Later in the evening, fortified (why did I feel I needed fortifying?) with a couple of brandies, I phoned George Hargreaves (as Derek Taylor and Aspinall referred to him). An American girl answered – or rather a girl with an American accent. She sounded bright, but when I said I was from Monty P she positively bubbled over and went off to get GH. George and I chatted for about 20 minutes or so. He adores the shows so much – 'The only sane thing on television' – he wants to be involved in

1 Neil was the closest to a manager the Beatles had at the time; Derek was the press officer.

some kind of way with us in the States. He said he had so many ideas to talk about, but I was a little wary – especially when he told me he envisaged a Harrison-Python road show, with us doing really extraordinary things throughout the show, such as swinging out over the audience on wires, etc. Hold it George, I thought, this is hardly the way to get John Cleese back into showbusiness! But he's clearly an idealist who has warm feelings towards us and it's very flattering to hear one of one's four great heroes of the '60s say he'd 'just like to meet and drink a glass of beer with you, and tell you how much I love you'.

Monday, January 13th

Monday, 13th January was only one and a half hours old when Helen woke me lightly and said she thought we ought to go in. There was no fuss or panic, but the contractions were now at five minute intervals.

At 2.00 we drove through Camden Town and the deserted Hampstead Road in the direction of UCH, over which the GPO Tower flashed its red light, like a twentieth-century Bethlehem.

At about 2.15 I left Helen with the midwife and was shown into the waiting room. A cluster of fathers there – one in a white hospital gown smoking a cigar, who had clearly just become a father, and one other, a nervous-looking man, biting his nails and staring at the floor. The orderly switched the radio on, to loud and raucous strains of *Oliver* or *Mary Poppins*. 'Better to have this than no noise at all,' he said.

Helen began to have major contractions at about 3.00. She counted six of them and on the sixth Sister Whitbread announced that she could see some hair! Excitement – hair! We've never had a baby with hair before. Then a few more pushes. Helen managing really well. Keeping in control. I was telling Helen it had hair – dark hair – when a look of pure, spontaneous joy filled her whole face – 'It's a *girl*!' That was the best moment of all. A great moment – not seeing it was a girl, but seeing Helen's face at the exact second when she saw Rachel for the first time.

Now she was out – the usual greyish-purple colour which so frightened me when Tom was born. Sister Whitbread was cleaning out her nose. She was big, they all said. Helen could not believe it. Her enjoyment was total. It was twelve minutes past three.

Monday, January 27th

Terry Gilliam rang about 9.30 and set off a whole chain of calls which resulted in a total replanning of the year ahead.

TG had seen Ian MacNaughton at Sölden – he had driven over from Munich with Eke to ski with them for a day or two. On the slopes Ian told TG that he was highly dissatisfied with the way the BBC and Fraser and Dunlop (Ian MacN's agent as well as ours) were treating him. He has a job in Israel, which both the BBC and Jill knew about, which would prevent him from working on the Python TV show until May (i.e. until after our filming). So it appears that, if we want Ian to direct our shows, and I think everybody does, we cannot start filming until May. This would mean studio dates running into August, which I know will be unacceptable so, as TG said, the alternative is to put it all off.

I rang off and digested this new situation – and the more I thought about it, the more attractive postponement of the recordings became. TJ was keen and, when I rang Eric, he was not only keen, but as positive about Python as I've heard him in a long while.

Tuesday, February 4th

Good news from New York – Python is top of the PBS Channel 13 ratings there, beating even *Upstairs Downstairs*, which has just won an Emmy and all. Sales to other stations increase – far away places with strange-sounding names – to Pensacola, Florida, to Utica, Illinois, Syracuse, NY, Athens, Georgia and so on. It sounds as though there's been a mistake and we've sold it to Greece.

Thursday, February 6th

We have written a synopsis of the *Holy Grail* for the EMI publicity people. Eric wrote it some time ago and it is extremely funny and totally unrelated to anything that happens in the film. 'Might this not be a bad thing?' says Mark to me over the phone today. EMI are worried that Up North there are critics who often review the film entirely from the synopsis, without ever seeing it; surely therefore we should provide a straight synopsis as well. My mind boggles at asking Python to help incompetent idiots who haven't time to see the film they're talking about.

Monday, February 10th

Mark rang, as he usually does when I'm having an enjoyable evening, this time on a matter of great profundity – the invitations for the Magazine Critics' showing of the *Holy Grail.*

I am so sick of being Python odd-job man, and yet the alternative is to *not* know what's going on in your name – which is infinitely more dangerous. I think of this when Mark rings and it just keeps me from physical violence.

Saturday, February 15th, Southwold

A drizzling, grey morning. We are going to Southwold for the weekend. Manage to pack three kids, carrycot, ourselves and Tom's new bicycle in the Citroen and we arrive, after a slow run, at about 2.45. A late lunch. But at least the weather has improved – it's sunnier and colder than in London. A fresh Suffolk wind off the sea clears the nostrils and freezes the fingers. We are staying at the Swan Hotel.

Funny that, fifteen years ago, when Helen and I first met in Southwold, the Swan Hotel represented the unattainable – the comfort and sophistication which we were never likely to know. Heavy tweed suits, ladies in suede jackets moving between heavy leather armchairs and through finely carved doorways – it was a world miles away from our own.

And now we are here, part of it all, in rooms which are floodlit from outside, with wrought-iron balconies and a view out onto a square that, in scale, feels like Toy Town – a neat, little miniature, into which at any time you expect a Victorian coach and four to appear, with ladies in big bonnets and men with side whiskers.

Wednesday, February 19th

Am now reading Dorothy Wordsworth's Journals, so watch out for hypersensitive observations on the weather. If she were alive now she could totally transform the image of the Meteorological Office. Weather forecasts would become works of art.

Me, myself, personally having always rather keenly felt the changes in atmosphere and attitude which different kinds of weather create, took it as a good omen that today was a sunny, brilliantly sunny, neo-spring morning, for the first gathering of all the Pythons for six months or so.

At any rate, Eric and John were at the Henshaws' when I arrived – both tanned. Eric was back from a week in Tenerife with Barry Cryer, and John from Africa. Anne Henshaw was a good deep skiing brown. I felt like the skinny schoolboy whose mother never lets him go out. Fortunately Mark looked more sallow than usual and Graham when he arrived looked truly dreadful. Pale as if he had just come out from under a stone and hobbling with a broken bone in his foot. He'd done it on a chair. Graham seems to be going through his body breaking every bone at least once.

But there is a good feeling to the group and, when we start to talk about publicity ideas the chemistry works and ideas bubble out in a stream.

When we suggest a 'Dummy Premiere in the presence of Her Royal Highness the Dummy Princess Margaret' – with a car laid on to transport this now famous Python dummy lady to the theatre,[1] and us all lined up shaking hands, Mark says that EMI just wouldn't wear it. Terry J said 'Mark, if you don't feel that you can fight EMI for the things we want, then someone else ought to be doing the job.'

Well, at the end of the meeting, Mark is still doing the job.

This evening dinner at the Henshaws'. A famous bearded playwright is there. Yes, David Mercer himself.[2] Odd to sit opposite a man you have unflatteringly impersonated on TV. Also an American writer called Al Levinson. A sort of Earth Father figure in his fifties, solid, smiling, sensitive, dependable. He shut himself in the kitchen at one point, trying to soothe Rachel's cries on his broad shoulder.

'You're much better looking than you are on television,' he started, before I'd hardly been introduced to him. He was a great fan of the show, and I still get a kind of kick from hearing someone talk about friends in New Jersey who will never miss a Python episode.

Famous Playwright Mercer describes himself as 'a sort of rich man's Alan Bennett'. He delivers this in tones which demand a reaction so we all laugh. I even say 'very good' and retreat as though outclassed by Oscar Wilde on his best form. And then I realise that I laughed because I didn't know what he was talking about and, on reflection, I don't think anyone knew what he was talking about.

1 The life-size Dummy Princess Margaret had been created for the Python TV series and, rather than leave her in the props store, we used her to add a bit of class to the Drury Lane stage show, in which she occupied a box throughout the run.
2 David Mercer, author of *Morgan: a Suitable Case for Treatment*, *The Parachute*, *Let's Murder Vivaldi*, died in 1980, aged 52.

Oh, I nearly forgot the best bit of news today – a letter from Stephen Frears at the BBC, asking if I would be at all interested in taking a part in a new TV version of *Three Men in a Boat* which he is filming in the summer. He is a superb young director,[1] much involved with Alan Bennett, and I hear that Tom Stoppard is writing the adaptation. Given the new Python schedule, I could do it without unduly buggering anyone else up. Am not raising any hopes – but it is the most exciting work prospect since we first talked about Monty Python.

Thursday, February 20th

Another Python meeting. This time to discuss affairs of Python generally and to plan our future in general.

When I arrived, Eric was the only one there, stretched comfortably in a corner of the sofa, wearing what looked very much like a bovver boys outfit, with TUF boots and jeans with rolled-up bottoms.

Good news at the beginning of the meeting – Nancy rang through to say that a US record deal was signed today with Arista Records – we would get an immediate $10,000 advance on *Matching Tie* and *Live at Drury Lane*. So good work there from Nancy, who has also secured her pet consideration on a record contract – $50,000 set aside just for publicity.

It was on the subject of paying off Gledhill[2] that the meeting suddenly and abruptly took off. As I remember it, Graham was on the phone to Jimmy Gilbert to check the autumn TV recording dates, John Cleese was being unusually co-operative and had even indicated that he might consider coming on this publicity tour to the US in March, when Eric suddenly became quite animated, attacking the Terrys and anyone around for being mean with Gledhill. From here Eric went on bitterly to criticise Python for becoming nothing more than a series of meetings, calling us 'capitalists' and ending up by saying 'Why can't we get back to what we enjoyed doing? Why do we have to go through all this?' It was rich dramatic stuff.

Terry J was on his feet – 'Well, if that's how Eric feels, we might as well give up,' and he nearly left there and then. GC and JC looked at each

1 Assistant director on *Charlie Bubbles* in 1967, he had directed Albert Finney in the excellent *Gumshoe* in 1971.
2 John Gledhill had ceased to be our manager as from November 1974.

other in amazement. Only the entirely admirable Anne H managed to cool everything down by giving out cheques for £800 each from Charisma – an advance for the LP made last May!

A selection of letters are read out to the assembled gathering. From CBC Canada – 'We would like the Python group to contribute up to ten minutes of material for a special programme on European Unity. The group can decide –' the reading was interrupted here by farting noises and thumbs-down signs. On to the next.

'Dear Sirs, I am writing on behalf of the Television Department of Aberdeen University ... ' An even louder barrage of farting.

'Dear Monty Python, we are a production company interested in making TV films with Python, George Harrison and Elton John ...' Despite the fact that £36,000 is mentioned in the letter as a possible fee for this never-to-be-repeated offer, it is jeered raucously and I tear the letter up and scatter it over the Henshaws' sitting room. In this symbolic gesture, entirely characteristic of the general irresponsibility of the assembled Pythons, the meeting staggers to an end and we all make our several ways.

Saturday, February 22nd

I suppose this could be said to be the day on which Python finally died. Obviously only time will tell whether this is a hopelessly over-dramatic reaction – but at the time of writing it does feel as though the group has breathed its last after nearly six years of increasingly doddery life.

The conditions of its demise were quite unspectacular. We ate lunch in my sunny work-room and afterwards I took Thomas, Holly and Willy to Little Venice, where, on a housing estate bordering the M4 elevated section, I had seen a big galleon-shaped climbing frame, which I thought they would like. They clambered on it and Tom rode his bicycle round the paths with arrogant confidence. Back in time for *Dr Who*.

I noticed Eric's car outside the house and felt quite pleased. It proved that his mood on Thursday was just a mood, and things must be alright if he could come round to tea.

He'd signed me a copy of his novel *Hello Sailor* and, though he wasn't ebullient, we had a cuppa together and chatted vaguely, and I really had no idea that he had any bad news, or even news, for me. (Helen said she had known something was up as soon as he appeared on the doorstep.) Carey was bashing around. He seems to me a very lively, jolly little fellow with a lust for biscuits. Eric asked when we were going to the States and then said he wanted to talk. We went upstairs to my work-room, trying not to make the occasion seem too momentous – both deliberately playing down our behaviour!

Upstairs, in the now cold room – we didn't bother to put the fire on – Eric told me, again, but finally this time, that he couldn't go on with Python. He'd thought about it a lot over the last few weeks, the decision hadn't come lightly – but he felt that he had to get out or he would, as he put it, 'go mad'. It wasn't just Python, there had been other troubles over the last few weeks – he'd tell me about them 'over a pastis in the summer,' he smiled. He hadn't anything he was going to do – he just wanted to enjoy the experience of 'waking up in the morning, knowing I don't have to do anything'.

I must admit I had slight pinch-of-salt feelings. At my most cynical I felt here is someone who has his own novel, and another virtually commissioned, about to come out, and his own TV series too [*Rutland Weekend Television*], to add to an already short and success-ful radio series, and he is understandably anxious to shed his old Python skin. Eric the loner feels that he has taken all he can from the Python group – he's moving on, like John did. Oh, he did say in passing that if John came back to do a TV series he would come back too. But meantime, he just wanted to take it easy, write his new book, maybe work on a play.

There was nothing I could say but bully for you. I have long since got over feelings of reproach or bitterness towards Eric. Now I feel just bliss-fully liberated from a tiresome duty as one of the Python anchormen – now perhaps I can be selfish as well. The prospect is interesting.

Eric and I parted on good terms. There's no animosity – we'll see him and Lyn and Carey socially – so perhaps in a year, or even six months, we'll all be back in the fold again. But if not ... now that's a really excit-ing prospect ... if not ... this clear and rapidly cooling February evening, as Eric's Volkswagen Beetle clatters off down Oak Village – this evening could be the end of lots of things.

Monday, February 24th

To the Henshaws' for what could be yet another momentous Python meeting.

I'm the first there – Anne H hurries up the stairs with some coffee and says ruefully, 'This is going to be quite a morning, isn't it?' Graham arrives next. He takes the news of Eric's latest decision stoically to say the least. He smiles as if he knew what was going to happen and betrays no outward and visible signs of distress, anger or anxiety whatsoever – apart from taking a beer at 10.30. The two Terrys are equally resigned (TJ had felt this was an almost inevitable sequel to last Thursday's meeting anyway).

The news from America daily lends an extra air of unreality to the situation for, by all accounts, Python is catching on in the States as *the* prestige programme to watch. Nancy rings to say San Francisco has now taken the series, Yale University are doing *every*thing they can to get a print of the first Python film off Columbia, the illustrator of the *Marvel* and *Incredible Hulk* comics wants to do a Python comic. Python is set to become the latest cult amongst the AB readership group, whilst back in little old quaint, provincial London, it has finally run its course, and four of its creators are sitting around deciding who is going to do the cleaning-up before the place is finally locked up for the year – or maybe for ever.

The new book is off for the summer, the TV series is off for the autumn. Touring seems the only hope of getting us together again. But, though I am prepared to ring Geoffrey Strachan and Jimmy Gilbert and all the others whom we are constantly messing about, and tell them it's all off, I do not feel, at this stage, that we can ring Tony S-Smith and change our minds once again over the album of the film. So the four of us agree to put the album together in the next couple of weeks. Eric and John have intimated that they are available to do any voices, but the way I feel at the moment, it's a matter of pride to do it without them.

We lunch together, the four of us, united at this time like a group who have just lost a close relative, at the Villa Bianca in Hampstead. Graham apologised for being late, but he was buying Plasticine and knitting needles. A moment's incomprehension, then GC explains that you make the figures out of Plasticine and stick knitting needles in them.

As if not enough had happened today, Mark rings to say that we haven't got the Casino for our West End opening – we are back to the ABC Bloomsbury, the Scene at the Swiss Centre and the ABC Fulham Road (now four cinemas). TJ is especially furious – he feels that Python will just not work in small cinemas – it will appear to be slow-moving and unfunny – it needs big audiences. Terry speaks on this point with the conviction of an early Christian missionary.

Tuesday, February 25th

At 10.00 Graham and Douglas Adams arrive at Julia Street and, over coffee, we work out select front-of-house photos for all the cinemas (we include one of Tom standing beside a Christmas tree at home) and work out silly captions – then down to Soho to meet Jack Hogarth, head of EMI distribution, to try and put our arguments against an ABC Bloomsbury opening. The receptionist's soft instructions, the carpeted corridor, the name on the door, the secretary in the outer office, and the huge ten-foot desk which Hogarth gets up from, all work their insidious spell. They are the trappings of authority and responsibility. Abandon hope all idealists who enter here. How can you speak on equal terms to a man with forty square feet of polished wood between him and you?

Terry J took the lead, I tried to back him up, and GC said nothing. Not that there is much you can say when Terry is in the form he was today. He was away with guns blazing, and it was a joy to watch.

Hogarth was treated to a pyrotechnic display of Jonesian extravagance … Did *he* know we could pack any cinema anywhere? Did *he* know people had marched in sub-zero temperatures in Toronto to get the series put back on CBC? And so on. We came out with a vague promise by Hogarth to look into it, but for the rest of the day TJ was seething, prowling dangerously like a leopard with a thorn in its bottom.

Thursday, February 27th

The Indian spring continues. As do the phone calls. It took me one and a half hours to make myself a cup of coffee this morning. Every time I got downstairs the phone rang and I had to come up again. Finally drank mid-morning coffee at 1.30!

The film and the film publicity is gathering an almost inexorable impetus. The good news is that EMI have put us into the Casino after all, and the incredible news is that they are simultaneously opening us at the ABC Bloomsbury and ABC Fulham Road. Nat Cohen of EMI now seems to be quite converted to Python and is prepared to give it the full treatment. It shows how fast things are moving – only 48 hours ago we were being told we were lucky to get a cinema like the ABC Bloomsbury at all. Now they are confident in filling 1600 places.

A half-hour call from John Goldstone. He has had a letter back from the censor. The film cannot be given an 'A' (over-fives, accompanied), unless we cut down two gory moments, and lose one 'shit', the words 'oral sex', the entire phrase 'We make castanets of your testicles' and some of King Arthur's repeated 'Jesus Christs'.

I was prepared to trade the 'shit' for the 'oral sex', otherwise we'll settle for an AA (over-fourteens). It's all too silly.

A call from Jill. She has told Jimmy Gilbert at the BBC of our decision to drop the autumn series after all. But Jill tells me that JG is interested in a Michael Palin show to fill the slots he'd reserved. I couldn't quite believe it, but, coming a week after Stephen Frears' *Three Men in a Boat* offer, it makes me feel excited and confident and quite unsure of the future. Too much is happening.

Friday, February 28th

Up to G Chapman's for record writing. A gorgeous morning in Highgate. We listen (TG, TJ, Graham, Douglas and myself) to the tapes of the film. And surprisingly involving it is too.

Plenty of ideas come out for presentation, etc, but the work fizzles to a halt at lunchtime when TG has to go off and strip wallpaper in his new house and Graham and Douglas had obviously pre-arranged a meeting in the pub.

TJ and I both sensed another day was falling apart, but the marvellously warm, almost balmy air of Highgate in this unbelievable February, helped to keep us from becoming depressed. Instead we went to the San Carlo restaurant and, over whitebait, liver and a couple of glasses of wine, we discussed some ideas for future writing projects.

I feel that TJ and I have spent over a year as caretaker to Python, and from today on, I say, over my big cigar[1] and Calvados, Terry and I are going to do our own thing again.

Or do I really mean my own thing? I must say the Stephen Frears and Jimmy Gilbert offers have boosted my confidence and my determination. But I think we both felt better as a result of lunch. TJ is going up to North Yorkshire today for a weekend break with Al, and Helen and I are going to Abbotsley.

The last few hours of the week were typical of this whole mad, frenetic week. Phone calls on every subject under the sun, including an

---

1 I gave up smoking in 1969, but somehow neglected to give up the occasional recreational cigar. Until later in 1975, that is, when my system rebelled against even these.

enquiry via Jill for me to do a short film next week to publicise Mike Oldfield's new single, 'Don Alfonso'. It's all very urgent, etc, etc. Virgin Records sent me a copy of the disc by taxi and, around six o'clock, one Richard Branson rang. I hadn't heard the record, but said I was too busy.

When I did hear it I realised I had made the right decision.

Saturday, March 1st, Abbotsley

Helen's sister Mary, who has exams this coming week, is using my work-room while we're away, and she rings after lunch, while I am out trundling Rachel round the quiet, muddy roads of Abbotsley village, with my mind on nothing in particular, to say that a BBC Radio 4 reporter has been pestering her to find out details of the 'Python break-up'.

Mary had given nothing away. She said she knew none of the Pythons' whereabouts or phone numbers. The reporter, according to Mary, said 'Oh, surely there's a phone book of his beside the phone.'

However, G Chapman had been tracked down and, at 5.30, as I cleaned my car in the drive at Church Farm, out of the radio came the Python theme music, which they then ran down. 'Yes, after five years, Monty Python is no more,' etc, etc. Graham gave an excellently controlled, sensible, low-key interview, which didn't deny the story.

Monday, March 3rd

This morning at GC's, where we are assembled to finish writing the record of the film soundtrack, TJ was very gloomy. He felt that the 'break-up' story was not going to do us any good, and it was his fault that it ever got out in the first place. It turns out that the story first appeared in Saturday's *Sun*, written by Chris Greenwood under the headline 'Python Packs It In', describing an interview 'with Python spokesman Terry Jones'. Poor Terry knows the guy – a friend of his brother's – and couldn't really lie ... but he feels very bad about it today.

A depressing morning's work. Once again Douglas is present, which gives me an irrationally uncomfortable feeling. Is this a Python album or a Python-Adams album? Graham is restless and contributes little ... he has a lunchtime meeting and constant phone calls about future plans, which distract terribly.

Tuesday, March 4th

Down to Soho for a meeting at 11.00 with Stephen Murphy, the film censor. Outside the doorway in sunlit Soho Square are gathered as evil-looking a crew as I've seen outside of *The Godfather*. Terry Jones, looking lean and impish, Gilliam in his absurdly enormous leather coat, which makes him look like a looter, Mark Forstater and John Goldstone, dark and efficient.

We marched in this formidable phalanx into S Murphy's office. It was not unlike a university don's room, there was a fine mahogany table, books around the walls and a bay window, which added a rather medi-aeval feel to the place. From up here Soho Square looked idyllic, like a sunlit university quad.

Murphy has a donnish air, he chain-smokes and has a mischievous face and a slightly uncoordinated physical presence. But he's genial and easy and a wonderful change from the executives of EMI. Of course the censor is not a government watchdog, but a man appointed by the industry to protect itself, so there wasn't a great deal of unseen pressure as there is at the BBC in these sort of discussions. Jolly Mr Murphy claims he has done a great deal for us and, if we want this 'A' certificate (in order to make more money!) we must go a little way with him. So could we lose 'oral sex', 'shit' or any of the 'Jesus Christs'? '"Oral sex" *is* a problem,' he said, very seriously.

Well we came out and, over a coffee in Compton Street, decided that we would agree on changing a couple of Arthur's angry 'Jesus Christs'! TJ eventually came up with a replacement. Arthur should say 'Stephen Murphy'!

TJ and I drive down to Thames studios at Teddington to talk to Verity Lambert, Head of Plays there. Do we want to write a TV play? Anyway, there is an offer open from Thames, which is nice.

We go and have a pint of Young's at a nearby tavern. A well-intentioned demonstration march goes by. 'Evening Classes for Richmond' is on their banners. Some of the rude labourers from the pub go to the door and shout 'Eat babies!!' Much laughter.

As the American bandwagon rolled on, there was an almost insatiable demand for Pythons to help publicise the TV series on PBS and the release of a new record album. The two Terrys, Graham and myself agreed to go over.

Friday, March 7th, Marriott Essex House Hotel, New York

We fly from a grey and drizzling London morning at 12.00 on a TWA jumbo. The plane isn't full, apart from the first class section under the bulbous nose. For us galley slaves back in 'the coach' as they coyly call it in the airline publicity, there is plenty of room to wander and stretch out. Terry J has an early burst of windowitis, and thoroughly disturbs himself as he darts from window to window, seat to seat, seeking the perfect view. The journey is inexorably and crushingly boring. Lunch nasty, brutish and short.

Since we were last in New York City, nearly two years ago, there has been the oil crisis and Watergate, the rise of unemployment, the dire situation in the US car industry and President Ford's drastic economies. But New York is as brash, as bold, as booming as ever.

Once again I was amazed, impressed, excited by the size and grace of these huge soaring steel and glass monsters on either side. Some now are in jet black colours, like huge natural outcrops of granite – not buildings at all. But clustered around the streets at the base of these huge monuments to financial freedom are many small shops and delis, which give New York its life. In a half hour on the street all the cobwebs of that long, dull flight were blown away and I experienced again the sheer delight of walking in New York.

Back to the hotel – drenched. In T Gilliam's room we launched into our first interview – with a guy called Howard Kissel from *Women's Wear Daily*. He looked just like Tiny Tim, he was easy to talk to, had a good sense of humour, and asked intelligent questions.

We walk round the corner to the Russian Tea Room. Clearly a place to be seen. Full of chic, sophisticated New Yorkers, looking over their shoulders all the time to spot the celebrities. Caroline Kennedy, daughter of JFK, was at the table next to ours. Funny that on our first day in NY in '72 Terry and I passed Ted Kennedy in the street. Maybe they just walk around all the time.

TJ flaked out, but I was so high on New York that, despite being over-full of blinis and red wine, I walked around a bit with Michael Winship of PBS. An interesting guy, he had been a member of the Washington press corps during Watergate. He said the night Nixon resigned there was a numb feeling of total paralysis, then, as the helicopter flew off from the White House lawn, a huge burst of festivities broke out. 'The King is Dead', 'Long live the King' atmosphere, he says, was incredible.

Well, this extraordinary day ended about 12.00 (4.00 a.m. British time). G Chapman, who always seems to wander into my life at the end of the day, appeared in the hotel corridor. He was shaking his head in disbelief and seemed anxious to tell me a story of his visit to the City Baths.

I sank into a fitful sleep. Make a mental note not to eat or drink ever again.

Sunday, March 9th, New York

We wandered down with our photographer towards the Park Plaza Hotel. He took a few shots of the four of us standing in front of the ponies and traps which do trips round Central Park. After only about 20 seconds of shots, one of the men sourly grunted about us losing him custom (there was no one for miles anyway) and moved his horse to the other side of the street. Then this generous spirit of animosity was carried on by another horse owner, a young long haired boy, who, somewhat to our amazement, for we had hardly been there for a minute, began to lecture us on the American way of life in general, and paying modelling fees to horse owners on Central Park in particular.

But the final straw, which caused GC and I to laugh all the way to the Plaza Hotel, was when one of the horses took a sudden and very violent lunge at Terry J. The wonderful aggrieved indignation in Terry's voice I'll remember for ever.

'He's bitten a lump out of my coat!'

Sure enough there was a chunk of fur missing from the sleeve of Terry's brand new big, brown shaggy coat.

Over to Channel 13, which is in a small, cramped, but friendly basement a couple of blocks from the UN and on the edge of the East River. In the studio is a small presentation area, in which sits Gene Shalit, a genial Harpo-Marx sort of character. Behind Gene are some thirty or forty people at desks with telephones. Throughout this evening and the next 11 evenings, the programmes of Channel 13 (which include English imports like *Upstairs Downstairs* and *The Ascent of Man*) are interspersed with jolly sales pitches from Gene in which he asks the audience to phone up and pledge money – five, ten dollars, whatever – to keep this non-commercial station going.

Gene Shalit's children are there (his daughter, who can't have been more than fifteen, leaned conspiratorially towards me and whispered softly, 'You know, Python and grass go very well together'), also a few fans (unattractive but keen) and we are all squashed in a small viewing/reception room. Periodically during the five hours we appear with Shalit – at one time answering phones, at another being interviewed.

The general chaotic business of the evening sorts itself out by around 12.00. Two Python shows have gone out on Channel 13 that evening, plus at least half an hour's screen time of ourselves. We later heard that the viewing figures for tonight were the highest Channel 13 ever had.

At the end of the evening, on air, we make a very committed statement about public subscription television and the freedom which it brings. Python, as far as we are concerned, could never have gone out in the States without public broadcasting – fortunately tonight has proved that we now have enough power to enable us to cock a mild snook at the commercial stranglehold on American TV.

Monday, March 10th, New York

A poor night's sleep. I have a nagging sore throat, aches all over and the appalling continuous hum of the air-conditioning outside my window. I feel just … just bad. But this is a promotional tour and physical weakness has no sympathetic hearing.

Today is dominated by a party, to be held at Sardi's restaurant, to launch us as new stars on Clive Davis' Arista label. Nancy has kept phoning, anxiously mentioning the party – there is talk of us changing (into what? We have one suit between us). Anyway, there is generally evident a feeling of rising excitement, as though one of the Main Reasons for our trip is to be fulfilled. We arrive at Arista's offices at 1776 Broadway (which must equal the White House, Pennsylvania Avenue, for *the* all-American address).

Well-dressed girls are at desks everywhere. We are given a beer each and the 'Clive won't be long now's' increase in frequency. At last the moment comes to go into the presence of Him. When I asked if we should kneel, they laughed, but slightly nervously.

The first thing that impressed me about the Great man of the American Recording Business was his office. He had the kind of exaggerated fifteen-foot desk which we write into sketches, and yet you could see he needed it. It was full of papers, letters ready for signing, telephones, intercoms, etc, etc. There seemed to be no acreage which was just added on for show. Around the walls were at least twenty gold discs, pictures of him with his family, citations from the Pope and an embossed certificate for outstanding services to the Jewish community in New York. Huge sofas and beautiful speakers and a washroom attached.

He was evidently concerned about spending money on this launch party without being sure of getting something out of the function – i.e. a little sketch from us, perhaps, a short appearance, a few jokes. He was clearly feeling his way with the Python group. He may be World Expert on Dylan, Sonny and Cher and Blood Sweat and Tears, but one got the feeling he was not yet certain about why he liked Python or why others liked Python. He was at the stage of simply being aware that people did like Python.

Like a fussy mother with new-born chicks, Davis ushered us into the lift. He twinkled, smiled, joked about the pouring rain in Broadway, 'We had it specially imported to make you feel at home', and got us all taxis. Then he bustled us into Sardi's, waiting until we'd all handed in our coats before leading us upstairs. Some 150 folk were assembled.

Clive said a few words, we joked a little and then the 'Thomas Hardy Novel-Writing' track was played. I had to pinch myself to believe it was all happening. Were we really in Sardi's, the renowned Broadway restaurant, with Clive Davis, the renowned record producer, surrounded by a crowd 'ooohing!' and 'aaahing' with uncertain delight as a not brilliant sketch about Thomas Hardy writing a novel was played over a hastily rigged-up record player system? No, it couldn't be true, I'd finally flipped. Then was everything afterwards untrue? Did a stout little lady with a Middle European accent keep badgering me about Swiss rights to Monty Python? Did the wife of Bill Ryan of *Esquire* magazine really claim that *Bert Fegg's Nasty Book* had made her laugh so much it had cured her back pains?

Tuesday, March 11th, New York

Another fitful night's sleep. Terry came in about 10.00 bearing a note from two Python groupies which had been slipped under his door last night. Jones and Palin Ltd were offered a good time in New York, by two fans who were hopelessly in love with us and had waited in the bar for five hours last night.

But we had no time for that sort of stuff. Oh, no, another Herculean day lay ahead. I felt better in my stomach today, and enjoyed a French lunch at a restaurant called Mont St Michel, in the quiet and civilised company of the cravatted John O'Connor of the *New York Times.*

Later, whilst lying flat out, but sleepless on my bed, the phone rang, and one of the co-authoresses of Terry's letter gave me a ring. They were downstairs. But this schedule has ruined me in more ways than one, and I mumbled excuses, saying that I was, well … I was no fun at the moment!

Unfortunately TJ had asked his fan to ring back later and therein lies a grand tale. TJ was back in his room at 12.30 (after a Chinese meal we'd had together with Ina Lee Meibach and others at the Hunan Yin) when the phone rang and the persistent Python groupie told TJ she was in the lobby and would like to see him – but couldn't because 'they' wouldn't let her up to his room. Here TJ, sensing a cause, and especially one against Marriotts, made the wrong move of the evening and went downstairs. True enough, two armed guards stood by the lift and forbad TJ to take this lady up to his room.

I would love to have been a fly on the wall, for TJ, by his own account, went berserk. All the bitterness of the TWA food and the static which afflicted him unmercifully and the noisy air-conditioning, must have poured out at these poor heavily armed men. But they insisted that Terry must pay if they were to let the girl into the room. So they obviously weren't anti-hookers, they were perpetuating a system whereby hookers were OK if Marriotts got a rake-off. So Terry's wrath was well-directed and in the end he defied these thugs and got the girl upstairs. It was only then that he discovered that she was a heavy lady of un-outstanding features and by no means a beautiful princess rescued from the jaws of the dragon. The next morning Terry was therefore full of shame, he said, but the story is such a classic that I think it worthy of this full account.

Wednesday, March 12th, Barclay Hotel, Philadelphia

I never imagined, and certainly from hearing the opinions of Americans on the subject, I was never encouraged to imagine, that Philadelphia would be an improvement on New York. In fact it's like being released from jail. The Amtrak ride from Penn Central in New York is through some of the most dreary, miserable landscape in the world, a vast dumping ground – Manhattan's colostomy bag – but, in just the four hours we've been here, I've felt like a bird released from a cage. Now this may have something to do with the fact that my room looks out over the city and is on the twenty-first floor, rather than the dungeon in the Essex House which looked out on brick wall and more brick wall, but, for instance, I just heard a clock chiming – and I haven't heard that since I left London. There is light and space and air here. But unfortunately there is no time. We have done two newspaper interviews already in our twenty-first-floor suite and are about to go out to dinner ... God! How food terrifies me now ... I just can't wait to not see it. And after that there is a radio inter— I can't go on, I must go and change, my phone is being paged and my door banged on.

Thursday, March 13th, Philadelphia

The morning spent at the Philadelphia PBS TV studios. We recorded some direct, almost sincere, straight-to-camera promos, extolling the thinking man's channel. Then, from somewhere, they conjured up a rather nervously cheerful lady, who was going to interview us. She looked afraid but, on discovering we were nice lads, loosened up. Typical of the refreshingly disorganised set-up – this ten-minute chat suddenly took off when the director snapped his fingers and cried 'Hey, if you give me 15 minutes to get another camera, we could make this a 30-minute special!' And a 30-minute special it became.

Left Philly at 3.45 with fond memories. Arrived in Washington about 5.00. We have a sumptuous suite in the Watergate Complex, overlooking the Potomac. (A dirty river, a lady reporter told me – especially where it flows past the Pentagon, where it is full of used prophylactics.) I go around stuffing my case full of anything marked 'Watergate' – soap, writing paper, even, to Graham's irritation, the room service menu.

Saturday, March 15th, Dallas

We are driven into, or almost into, Dallas, to an incongruous looking fifteen-storey hotel set in the Oak Lawn area – full of attractive weather-boarded houses. We learnt later that these are the only old houses allowed to survive in this rich and developing city. My room at the Stoneleigh Park Hotel is quite stupendous. The bedroom has views on two sides and an eight-foot-wide, beautifully comfortable bed. A bathroom, generously proportioned, is attached, but the star turn is a long sitting-room – forty feet long at least – furnished in the Empire style, with elegant sofas, chaises longues, and Watteau reproductions on the wall.

Drove down to the PBS station, to find ourselves facing a barrage of microphones and reporters, who sat amongst the scenery and props, barring our way to the studio. I have never seen anything like it. Admittedly, most of the microphones belonged to young fresh-faced lads with cheap Philips cassette recorders and none of the mikes had NBC, ABC or CBS News stuck on the end, but this was the first time any of us have ever experienced this saturation coverage. Every word was recorded or written down, questions fell fast, one on top of the other, as did the answers. It could have been awful, but as it was so spontaneous it was exhilarating.

There are a great many people out here who do want to know *all* about Monty Python. It's as genuine, simple and direct as that. And, as a result, the self-consciousness I had always felt about talking about ourselves to English journalists, etc, does not apply here. One can answer directness only with directness.

After the 'press conference' we are moved through into the studio, which is packed, mostly with young people, college kids, and one or two 30–40-ish liberals. I am handed a rather fine stuffed armadillo, as a present from Dallas. This I hang on to throughout the interviews.

The next few hours are all handled very informally. We are in chairs on a podium and are chatted to at regular intervals by Ron Devillier,[1] programme director of the station. A lovely man, comfortably built, soft-voiced, bearded, about 35–40, with a lack of pretension and a great deal of knowledge and intelligence. Ron asks people, as usual, to ring in with pledges of money and buy membership of Channel 13 for a year. The phones ring behind and an army of volunteers answer them.

Graham establishes on the air that he is a supporter of gay causes – and gets a greater number of appreciative and enquiring calls from viewers than anyone else.

During the course of the evening they played no less than three Python shows. It was an orgy of Python – a total immersion in total enthusiasm, that didn't end until after 12.00. Thankfully we disengaged ourselves and, with about ten folk from the station, went to a tatty nearby clapboard house for a quite superb Mexican meal.

---

1 Ron was the man who broke *Monty Python's Flying Circus* on US television. Python's success began not in New York, but in Dallas.

I still had the armadillo with me when I got back to the hotel room and, later that night, frightened myself with it quite considerably when I went for a pee.

Sunday, March 16th, Navarro Hotel, New York

Ron Devillier picked us up at 12.00 and took us for a drive round Dallas. Devillier, clearly no lover of the downtown area – though he lives in Dallas – shows us the Kennedy Memorial, which it took eight years to put up. He says that now it is hard to imagine how much people in Dallas hated President Kennedy and all he stood for. After his assassination, classes of schoolkids cheered and a teacher who tried to give her class a day off in Kennedy's memory was fired.

We eventually found ourselves at the scene of the shooting. What struck me most was the eerie ordinariness of the spot. Possibly I'd expected the area to be razed to the ground, but here we were, on a cool March Sunday, standing on the most famous – the *only* famous – grassy knoll in the world, looking up at the Book Depository windows from which Oswald had fired, and across to the road, narrow by American standards, where Kennedy had been shot. The strongest impression is that Oswald must have been a genius to fire three times accurately from that angle, at a car travelling away from him down a sloping road. Second impression is that the grassy knoll, besides offering a much closer and easier view of the target, was an ideal place for an assassin to escape from. An expanse of open railway land, away from streets, cars, sightseers.

As we walked back to Ron's car and drove down towards the railway bridge, I reflected on how much more far-reaching an event had taken place here than the great and utterly anti-climactic triumph of America – the landing on the moon. The '60s and the '70s are notable for their disasters, not their triumphs.

American Airlines flight to NY. At La Guardia, as I wait for our luggage, with my armadillo's explicit and rather white rear end sticking out from under my arm, a heavily furred and expensively coiffed American lady drawls at me, 'Where d'you get that?' I explained I was given it by some friends in Texas. She obviously couldn't comprehend this … 'Well, I'm from Texas and I wouldn't have given you a thing like *that.*'

We are spared the Essex House Hotel again and stay instead at the

Navarro, also on Central Park South. This is a smart, pleasant hotel, which is mercifully not part of a chain. A comfortable suite – this time on the 12th floor *and* overlooking Central Park.

I have a bath and, feeling greatly refreshed and looking forward to an evening with no interviews, TV phones to answer or any promotional activity of any kind, skip through the *NY Sunday Times*, and then down to the bar to meet Nancy. But the day is not to end totally pleasantly, for Nancy is suddenly recognised by Kit Lambert, manager, or ex-manager, of The Who (whose film *Tommy* opens in NY on Tuesday). He shouts, there is much embracing as of old friends, and he joins us at our table. He is quite obviously in an emotional state. Though he is clearly aware that we are all listening, he seems anxious to hire Nancy to work for him and offers her £1,000 a day. Nancy laughs it politely away and remains noncommittal. But Lambert has an even less tolerable friend, an English accountant, who laughs gratuitously and ingratiatingly at Lambert. He tries to chat up the waitress and makes a thoroughly unpleasant mess of it.

A young boy arrives, sits quietly and eyes the decaying Lambert with a mixture of disappointment and disgust. After a half-hour that seems like a lifetime, the festering and smouldering atmosphere is relieved by the arrival of a girl, who is also English and clearly has the unenviable task of fixing dinner for this frightful threesome. After an hour, they leave. I had warmed to Lambert in the meantime. At least he sounded bright – he reminded me of the hero of Lowry's *Under the Volcano*, with often flashes of a brilliant display of knowledge – of languages, literary references, etc. And so it didn't come as a great surprise to hear from Nancy that he is a brilliant failure. He is suing, or being sued by, The Who, who now clearly try and avoid him. He has a self-destructive urge, which takes the form at present of regular over-indulgence in cocaine and alcohol – and from his face (a handsome face) and general bearing, it looked sadly as though he was doing a good job of it.[1]

Monday, March 17th, New York

Back to promotion with a vengeance today.

A photographer was trying to get some zany photos. 'Could you all lie on the bed as if you're dead, please?' 'No,' was the easiest and most

---

1 Lambert died in 1981, aged 46.

painless reply. Once again we have to go into our spiel about not doing zany pictures. It now sounds like some sort of religious thing – like Jews not eating pork. But in the end we used the armadillo a lot and that seemed to keep him happy.

Down to the bar for lunch and a drink with Rik Hertzberg and friend from the *New Yorker*. We ate looking out over Central Park South and the very well-heeled class of persons passing by. Definitely one of the world's superior sidewalks. At one point a man came in and shook us all by the hand. I don't know who he was, but later he rang, saying he was a film producer and would like to 'talk over some ideas'. While we were thus on display, and chatting very pleasantly (Rik seems the nearest to one of us we've met), they pointed out a man who was apparently well-known in NY for star-spotting. He spends all his time outside hotels approaching people indiscriminately and asking them if they're celebrities. He then takes an autograph off them. Rik guaranteed that if any of us popped out of the elegant revolving door of the Navarro, we would be accosted instantly. We tried it with Terry Jones with total lack of success. Terry even hung around waiting to be recognised. Finally, in some disappointment, Rik buttonholed the star-spotter and said, 'Aren't you going to ask your usual question?' He viewed Terry rather sceptically and then said ... 'OK, can you lend me ten bucks?'

Tuesday, March 25th

Grand Python reunion at the recording studio![1] [Neither Eric nor John had come on the US publicity tour.] All of us, except Terry Gilliam, contributing. John C had written a piece about a Professor of Logic. We recorded it first time. I think John's psychiatrist should be sent a copy. It was a funny piece, largely, but loaded with rather passionless and violent sexual references, which sounded odd, for some reason. But there was a generally convivial atmosphere – and we had an excellent lunch at Cheung-Cheung-Ki, about fifty yards down Wardour Street.

We decided that our next film would be 'Monty Python and the Life of Christ' – with Graham as Christ, and featuring exciting new characters like Ron the Baptist. We also decided with remarkably little fuss that we would all get together to do a six-week stage show in the US next spring.

1 André Jacquemin's new premises in Wardour Street.

Terry and I much brightened this evening, when we go to talk to Helen Dawson of *The Observer*,[1] who had just seen the film on her own. TJ had raced around that morning all in a tizzy trying to prevent her seeing it. Terry has this quite reasonable theory that comedy is best enjoyed with an audience of over 1,000, preferably packed closely together – but from this he has drawn the erroneous conclusion that no one can enjoy comedy *except* in a crowd of over 1,000. Helen Dawson turned out to have loved the film and laughed at all the right places and even at the Knights of Ni! She talked to us for a half-hour or so. She's a lively, capable little lady. Needless to say we both warmed to her! Terry confided that this time last night he had been unhappy because Sheridan Morley[2] had disliked the film. 'Great!' she said, 'If Sheridan Morley didn't like it, you're alright.' And she didn't say it with any malice.

Wednesday, March 26th

To London Weekend Studios for a Saturday morning children's show with Michael Wale and an audience of kids doing the interviews.

They showed two clips of the *Holy Grail* film and then the kids asked questions. First was 'How much do you think John Cleese was missed in the last series?' I went on about how we lacked an authority figure, etc, etc, at the end of which Terry said, 'Well, we really ought to ask you that question.' 'Oh, I didn't think it was half as good without him,' came the smart reply. The last question was from M Wale, who asked us what we thought of the Goodies. Up spoke young Jones and denounced the Goodies publicly for trivialising serious topics and having no values. The interview ended with a Geordie jug band group throwing eggs at us.

Good Friday, March 28th, Southwold

Really quite heavy snow in the village this morning. On the nine o'clock news they were talking of 'treacherous' conditions on the roads around London. But the sun came out and melted everything in a couple of hours. Helen and I left, in separate cars, at about 12.30. She to Abbotsley with the kids and me in the Mini to Southwold for a couple of days, as

1 Soon to marry John Osborne.
2 Son of actor Robert, Oxford contemporary of Terry Jones.

Mother had rung during the week to tell me that Father had had a sharp deterioration in his condition last Tuesday.

Physically, he is fast becoming a write-off and there's a temptation to think that death would be a merciful release – but when I see the twinkle in his watery eye when he struggles to make a joke, or the enjoyment he gets from buying and giving two boxes of chocolates to Mother on Easter morning, or his sad 'Come again, soon' as I leave, I find the 'merciful release' attitude dangerously simple.

Thursday, April 3rd

Today our second film opens in London. An encouragingly good notice in *The Guardian* this morning. Even though they exhorted the team to stay together, they couldn't remember our names: 'Cleese, Idle, Chapman, Graham and Jones'!

Graham and I did a voice-over for Bulmer's Cider in the morning. After the voice-over I dropped in at Anne's. It has taken her and Alison[1] a week to cope with the complications of tickets, parties, dummy Princess Margarets, etc – all the ramifications of a premiere which none of us really wanted, which EMI got cold feet about, and which Mark Forstater has washed his hands of. Anne, finger in the dyke, is single-handedly avoiding disaster tonight.

A very good Alexander Walker review in the *Evening Standard* ('The brightest British comedy in ages') and *Time Out*, who've also enjoyed it, help to cheer us all up, for these two are influential amongst our London audience. In fact there is no bad review today – but there is an unpleasant little piece in the *Daily Mail*. Not a review, but a variation on the Python split-up story, which seems as elusive as the Holy Grail to most papers.

In the foyer, the flabby head of EMI Distribution was trying to be jolly, but was obviously quite worried about the Princess Margaret dummy, which he had heard was to be around after all. He was clearly very nervous about how and where and when we were going to spring this royal embarrassment on them.

Up in the circle bar, the head-nodding, the hand-shaking, the across-room smiles had all begun. There were just so many people to talk to there. I talked to John Peel briefly and Brian McNulty, and Ron Hellard,

---

1 Alison Davies, Anne's assistant, another Python stalwart.

and even my wife. Ten-week old Rachel Mary lay, undisturbed by all this merrymaking, in a corner of the bar.

The film was very well received. Simon A, and André, both of whom were quite severe critics of the showings, both enjoyed the film for the first time tonight.

Afterwards, a party had been laid on in the stalls bar (this entirely due to Anne H and Terry G's initiative) for all the crew (who had not been invited to the later party at the Marquee).

I was particularly touched when Terry Bedford, who has had a good deal of praise in the reviews for his photography, said 'You were great.' I'm so used to being anonymous in Python that it's nice to know someone noticed.

From the Casino we all moved on to the Marquee Club. A party which I hadn't been looking forward to, but which turned out to be excellent, full of nice people and everyone in good spirits. The occasion had really been organised and paid for by Charisma – the company which we all love, but which doesn't actually seem too keen on paying us royalties.

Neil Innes, looking like a Belgian shopkeeper in his Sunday best, is on good form. He and I decide that the time has come to talk to our backers, and we converge on Messrs Page and Plant from Led Zeppelin, who are standing, almost shyly, together. They are great fans of the show – they liked the 'Bicycle Tour' particularly – and apparently many pop groups now carry video cassettes of Python, as an obligatory part of their equipment.

Sunday, April 6th

The popular press, *News of the World*, *Daily* and *Sunday Express*, *Daily Mail*, *The People*, *The Sun*, have given us rave reviews. The *News of the World* even said that the credits on their own were funnier than most comedy films.

Dilys Powell, in the *Sunday Times*, in a much longer review, was soft, kind and unenthusiastic, and *The Observer* joined *Sounds* and the *New Musical Express* in panning us. But I am generally surprised and greatly relieved by the reactions.

Graham rings to tell me that the *Sunday Express* is the latest paper to join in the Python-splitting activities, and that I am quoted this time as saying that John Cleese is interested only in the money, etc, etc. There is a long reply by John in which he says it is 'malicious' to suggest he's only interested in money.

I rang Connie after supper. She sounded quite emotional and said John was very upset, though mainly it seemed with the *Express* reporter who had rung and put words into his mouth, rather than with my alleged 'attacks' on him. John himself rang later and, if it's any satisfaction to the *Sunday Express*, we had the fullest and friendliest chat we've had for ages.

Friday, April 11th

An old-fashioned pub-crawl. Down to Cambridge Circus on the 24 bus, walk along Old Compton Street, past the cinema with its huge and quite grabbing adornment of posters, turn down Dean Street at 5.45 and into the York Minster. Eric, whose suggestion this little jaunt was, rolls along about 6.00, and we split a half bottle of champagne.

From the York Minster we move on up Dean Street to the Nellie Dean, where we find Tony Stratton-Smith, ebullient and highly excited by the first week's figures. *Grail* is No. 3 in London this week, and has grossed nearly £19,000.

I really must try and cut down on this wining and dining, but it's all part of the unnerving transitional world Python is in. Terry G and I admit we spend far more time than is healthy talking, analysing, discussing every aspect of the group and the group's dynamic, but, as Terry says, it's becoming like a drug. We need our daily fix of Python. I know as I sink, heavy-stomached into my bed, that Terry G will ring me over the weekend, and tell me how he thinks Eric's becoming very positive again … and if we can only get rid of Graham … goodnight Vienna … At least we still laugh about it all.

One thing is different this time – whereas before Python in '69 we were only a moderately saleable commodity as a group, and quite unsaleable as individuals, now we have a high reputation and a good name as both. The film's success in the last couple of weeks has helped to prolong Python's life and greatly increase its prestige.

Wednesday, April 17th

This afternoon, I go to the BBC to see Jimmy Gilbert. I have already decided to turn down, on grounds of dangerous lack of time, JG's offer of the six now defunct Python slots next autumn. This didn't seem to deter him. He clearly just wants me to do a show – he isn't really concerned about subject matter and he has a director, Terry Hughes, who wants to work with me.

Terry Hughes, neat, almost over-amiable, smiling, regular-featured – he looks like an advert for suits – has been anxious to do a show with me for two years, and now clearly feels that he has priority over others when JG wants to get a show together around me.

Terry and I talk – me fencing a little to try and find TH's attitudes. He says he wants to do a show which is exciting and experimental. He drops his voice and says, wearily, 'Anything after two and a half years of *Two Ronnies*.'

So … OK, I say, I would be happy with JG's plan to commission one show, which will be the first of a series if it works. Whereas this sort of caution would have driven us mad in Python, or *Do Not Adjust*, now it suits me fine.

With Monty Python and the Holy Grail set to open in New York, we set off across the Atlantic for the second time in a month.

Thursday, April 24th, New York

Eric has been in NY since last Saturday, Terry G since Sunday and Terry J since Tuesday night – and today Graham and I have to leave hot and sunny London to join them. We take off around 12.30.

No one could be found to meet us, so we took a cab from Kennedy. Sadly we seem to have exchanged fine weather for foul. It was grey, glowering and raining as we joined the traffic jams on Van Wyck Expressway and East River Drive. Both of us hungry, so we revived ourselves with large and delicious club sandwiches and beers at the St Moritz Hotel. As we walked back to the Navarro, two girls, one Oriental and spotty, the other American and fat, accosted us. 'Oh, it's you … Oh! We've just been talking to the two Terrys and they were so nice, but Eric just walked past us!'

Friday, April 25th, New York

I was up at 6.00 and in the lobby of the Navarro at 6.30. Met John Goldstone and Eric I there and was driven in a huge, greedy limousine to the ABC *A.M. America* studios. We (the Pythons) were to co-host this nationally networked ABC TV morning show – and it runs for two hours.

At 7.00 the show began, hosted by a lady called Stephanie something or other, an attractive redhead, with a cool, head-of-school-like assurance, but she was playing along well with us. Eric kept holding up cards on which he'd scribbled things like 'Norman Mailer – Ring Your Mother'. Once or twice before an item of serious news – e.g. the fall of Saigon – Stephanie would ask us to refrain from being *too* silly, but generally we were allowed a loose rein.

Eric and I did the first hour of the show, then Graham added to our number and TG and TJ joined at 8.30. Terry G made a rude drawing of a man with slobbering tongue and staring, lust-filled eyes and held it alongside Stephanie's head as she signed off and, as the credits rolled, they actually exhorted us to wreck the studio.

No one seemed to feel it was incongruous that we should be part of a programme which included the latest bulletins on the end of America's longest war, or serious interviews about Reagan's chances in 1976.

We ended up in the Plaza Hotel for breakfast, and drank orange juice and champagne out of the largest, widest glasses I've ever seen. Typical of America, always confusing quantity and quality – to the eternal detriment of the latter.

At 12.00 we rolled up outside a modestly fashionable 'brownstone' with a recently restored front, on one of the streets somewhere in the East 60ths. This is the studio of Richard Avedon – by all accounts One of the World's Leading Photographers and He has chosen to photograph no less than us. Python is to be immortalised in the pages of *Vogue*.

Avedon turns out to be a slight, wiry, dark-skinned, bespectacled man, who could be between 25 and 55. Full of vitality and easy charm.

We are dazed from our efforts in NY and our early appearance on ABC and he must have found us a lifeless lot as he made us coffee. But after ten or 15 minutes of uninspired ideas, he leapt on the suggestion, made by Graham and Terry J, that we should be photographed in the nude. The idea sounded no worse and a lot better than putting on silly costumes or funny faces, so it was resolved. We would keep our shoes and socks on, though, and I would wear my hat.

Avedon – remarkably spry for one who has, by his own account, just worked a 15-hour, non-stop session – took us into his studio, a simple, square room, white-walled, about twenty feet high. Apart from camera equipment, simple lights and photos of Marilyn Monroe and a huge blow-up of A's photo of the Chicago Seven, the place was quite austere.

Soon the Python group were a little naked gaggle and Avedon was busy arranging us in a parody of the sort of beautiful person photo where all is revealed, but nothing is shown. So our little tadgers had to be carefully hidden behind the knee of the man in front, and so on, and every now and then Avedon would look through the viewfinder of his Rolleiflex and shout things like 'Balls! … balls Graham, balls.'

After a few more exhortations like this, GC was heard to mutter, 'Are you *sure* he's the world-famous photographer?'

We dressed, muttering jokily amongst ourselves about how ashamed, how very ashamed, we were of what we had done. The elfin Avedon, busy as ever, talked to us as he scribbled some letter. I couldn't help noticing that the one he was writing began 'Dear Princess Margaret.'

As we walked out into the sunlit street, I felt slightly high and rather relieved, as though I'd been for an exotic medical check-up.

Took a few hours to myself this afternoon. I decided to take a trip out to the Statue of Liberty, as Tom had specially asked me to get some pictures of it. I travelled down by Subway, which is one of NY's finest features – like its telephones. It's noisy, dirty and literally every coach is covered in aerosol drawings – or just simply people's names (crisis of identity of many people in the States, suggested the *New York Times* reporter today – alienation of the individual, etc, etc). But these noisy, dirty Subways are faster, more frequent and more efficient than the London Underground, and I'm very endeared to their ear-shattering clatters and their functional stations thick with the smell of fresh-cooked doughnuts. It's a refreshing break from the carefully tailored world of limousines and hotel suites.

Missed the Statue of Liberty ferry, walked back up Broadway, bought two plastic statues of Laurel and Hardy in a tatty street market on Canal Street, so by the time I reached Gallagher's Bar to see Earl Wilson I was over half an hour late and it was raining.

The place was almost empty but, at a table in the corner, surrounded by photos of jockeys, horses, etc, Graham, Terry J, who had nobly sat in for me, Sue from the public relations agency and the small, neat, elderly and very bemused-looking E Wilson. He seemed to suffer from an unfortunate impediment for a reporter – he couldn't hear a word. Added to this, GC was being quite irresponsible and saying very strange things.

Sue, a PR lady and not a bright soul, just tried to look happy as he shouted for the fourth time in the ear of this hapless columnist, '*Penis!*'

From Gallagher's we took a cab to the offices of Don Rugoff and Cinema 5, the man and the outfit who are distributing our film in the US. He looks a fair shambles. Around 45-ish, thick glasses, a strong face, made permanently grumpy by his habit of pushing his chin into his neck and turning the sides of his mouth down. The rest of his body was mostly stomach, a huge pointed paunch which he pushes in front of him, like some antenna casing. Rugoff's voice, like his general physical presence, is rough and untidy. I liked him a lot.

We excused ourselves about 6.00, and walked back to our suite at the Navarro, where Nancy, or somebody, had organised a cheese and wine party for our friends. I suddenly realised I had had only two hours sleep in the last 36, and Italian white wine wasn't likely to revive me. But the party was quite well attended. All sorts of strange people began arriving, including Martin Scorsese, director of *Mean Streets* and *Alice Doesn't Live Here Any More*, the ubiquitous Jo Durden-Smith[1] and several Rolling Stone staffers. Ed Goodgold,[2] whose company is always good fun, maintains Python has done and will do a lot for the Gentiles in America, who've been until now totally swamped by Jewish comedians and Jewish comedy – Lenny Bruce, Woody Allen, Harvey Kurtzman, Mel Brooks, Carl Reiner, etc, etc.

Sunday, April 27th, New York

We were to be at Cinema II on Third Avenue at 11.00 a.m. to welcome the first crowds and to give out coconuts as people came out. The phone rang and woke me about 9.40. It was John Goldstone. Could we get down to the cinema as quickly as possible; there had been people queuing since 5.30 a.m. and Rugoff had already opened the film, with a special extra 9.30 performance. Time only for a delicious American grapefruit and a quick coffee and into the limousine.

When we reached the cinema there were, indeed, your actual crowds. People queuing right round the block. There was only one way into the cinema and that was through the main entrance – so through the crowds we went.

1 An Oxford contemporary. Like my friend Simon Albury, Jo worked on *World in Action*.
2 Rock group manager (Sha-Na-Na) and colleague of Nancy's at Buddah Records.

Once in the cinema we were taken to a kind of broom cupboard below stairs, where we felt like prisoners. There was coffee and dough-nuts. Rugoff told us we couldn't go out of the theatre, or let ourselves be seen at a window (!) for fear of inciting riots on Third Avenue. 'We've only got one patrolman,' he kept muttering morosely. I think he hoped and expected that there would be riots, but we know our audience quite well – they want to be silly, they want to chat, they want to shake hands, they want you to sign the plaster on their broken arms, but generally speaking they don't want to tear us limb from limb.

But they did fill the cinema all day long and Rugoff was able to claim at the end of the day a house record take of ten and a half thousand dollars. He even had photographers taking pictures of the crowds (which he was later to use in a very good double page *Variety* ad).

Plant and Page from Led Zeppelin came to the 8.00 performance, which brightened things up a little. We greet each other like old friends now. Suddenly someone shouted 'Led Zeppelin!' as we talked and, as the chant grew, we moved discreetly away – for they *can* cause riots.

Monday, April 28th, New York

To see Clive Davis at Arista. He smiled benignly round at us all. Chided us for doing a nude spread in *Vogue*, but not *Playboy*, which is where the market is. The *Matching Tie* album has been out a week and a bit and already he's getting a good demand for it, he says. He even gets us to talk to eighteen countrywide reps, who are at this moment all connected up on a conference line. So we say 'hello' to disembodied voices in LA and Chicago and Davis encourages them to 'break records, to sell records'.

The whole tenor of our discussion today is that of an enlightened headmaster to his star pupils. He's giving us a lot of rope, but he still firmly holds the end.

To a sound studio to record some radio commercials for Don Rugoff. Terry and I manage to write and record three 30-second commercials before Rugoff finally turns up. I've noticed the look in people's eyes when he's around. He seems so harmless and yet he must have a reputa-tion, for there is a look of anticipated fear and anxiety which flashes across people's faces in his presence. I've seen it with Sue, the PR lady, and I saw it again today in the eyes of the girl who was organising this voice-over session. Rugoff grumpily accused people of not doing their job properly. He introduced an air of tension and then accused everyone of not being relaxed. He asked me to do it more upbeat, which was completely wrong, and had to change his mind afterwards. The only light in this hour of greyness was when we played him the three commercials we'd done – and he liked them all. He actually smiled. So everyone relaxes and is happy and Rugoff wins hands down because he is a lovable bastard.

So, on to the party, held in the massage parlour of the Commodore Hotel in honour of Python. As we swept in, high in the sky with our well-nurtured popularity, the photographers looked past us to see if there was anyone famous around. It was a total, unreal, fantasy. Clive Davis ushered me over to meet Andy Warhol. I talked a while to the King of the Beautiful People. Led Zeppelin were there and Jeff Beck and Dick Cavett, but *no* Norman Mailer or John Lennon or anyone *really* interesting!

I just remember Loudon Wainwright III, to whom I was very effusive and gave my address, and the rather lovely dark eyes of one of the masseuses.

Thursday, May 8th, Southwold

A perfect May morning – a slight haze clearing away from the trees and fields in the distance. Cows munching the lush, rain-soaked grass in the sunshine. A nine-hour sleep behind me. I feel as contented as the cows.

Have promised to take Dad to Lowestoft – which we do. He needs someone around all the time, and I have to try and get to his stream of dribble before it hits the newly polished floor of a shop. A wonderful piece of Englishness – there is a new and splendid library in Lowestoft, and here my father would have been really happy. However, on approaching it, we are faced with a notice on the door: 'OPENING OF THE NEW LIBRARY …' – encouraging so far – '… THE LIBRARY WILL BE CLOSED ALL DAY FOR THE OPENING'.

Father had given me an excellent birthday present, conceived, bought and wrapped entirely by himself. It was a big Adnams poster showing all their pubs, and we used it to find ourselves a splendid little place called the Wherry Inn at Geldeston, a little village tucked away a mile or two off the Beccles–Norwich road. A friendly pub in a friendly village; everyone stopping for a chat with each other. We were able to sit out in the sun, on our own, with beer and sandwiches, and Father could droop and dribble to his heart's content and still enjoy himself.

A trip which cheered us all up. And Father is rarely cheerful these days. I went for a walk last night with him, and he told me that he really would like to be 75, and after that he doesn't care.

Tuesday, May 13th

Eric's new show *Rutland Weekend Television* was on for the first time last night. Quite a milestone for Python – the first TV manifestation of the parting of the ways. Not a world-shattering show, but a very palatable half-hour's TV. I didn't feel that Python was being used. Of course there were ideas which Eric would not have written without the influence of five years with Python, but it was still very much his work, his show and his particular kind of humour. Bits went on beyond the cutting stage, some ideas were woolly and it lacked the solid richness of Python, but I enjoyed it and TG, who was watching with me, felt the same. A neat, nice and simple idea too – a TV station with no money. Neil Innes as great as ever, and the camerawork made it seem anything but cheap. GC rang afterwards, he didn't like it. I smell grapes.

Stephen Frears, the director of *Three Men in a Boat*, comes round to see me. He makes the distinction between Pythons and 'actors' and says that the others he will get will be actors. He ends up giving me the script to read and says he thinks of me as Harris. We chatted for an hour or so. He didn't relax me a great deal – he's rather a disconcerting guy, with big, round, slightly poppy eyes, unkempt hair and clothes and a rambling, discursive style of talking which makes it very difficult for me to tell what he's actually saying.

After I'd read it, I rang him back, as he'd asked. He was pleased that I liked the script (Stoppard – very impressive, funny and yet full of period feeling, a sympathetic adaptation of the book, full of love of the Thames Valley). But he rambled a little about getting all the three actors at once, then apportioning parts only after he'd selected all three and played around with their relative ages, physical appearances, etc, etc. So would I mind waiting for a final decision? This confused me, I must say, but all I could say was I was 100% enthusiastic and to be involved as any of the three characters would be tremendous fun. I'm not sure whether he is preparing me for the worst or not.

Helen had made a superb steak and kidney pie with a *Three Men in a Boat* design on it. We ate it with a half-bottle of Bollinger '64!! A little prematurely, perhaps.

Thursday, May 15th

Mid-afternoon and I'm rewriting the last two pages of one of our Crucible plays[1] when Tony Stratton rings. He was having dinner last night with Steve O'Rourke – Pink Floyd's manager. Floyd are very keen to get us on the bill for their prestigious open-air gig at Knebworth in July. We'd said no, but O'Rourke has made us a new offer. For five of us, a half-hour cabaret appearance, £1,000 each in notes, no questions asked, ready at the end of the show. It's like an offer from the underworld.

Cleese rang. The *Sunday Express* have apologised for the article a month or so back in which I apparently accused John of working for money only. They want to give John and me a lunch. John keen on acceptance, which I went along with against my better judgement.

Friday, May 16th

Read *Three Men in a Boat*, as I got a call asking me to go and meet Frears and Tom Stoppard for tea at the Waldorf at 5.00. On re-reading, Harris is really the part I would like (he's the funniest), though I still feel I'm physically wrong.

At the Waldorf at 5.05. Tea is taken in a tall-ceiling lounge, with steps down to a sunken dance floor. Frears and Stoppard are discreetly tucked away on a sofa in the corner. Frears, crumpled and worried-looking, Stoppard, a lean and neatly dressed contrast. Frears introduces me to Stoppard and we make small talk about sharing agents, etc. Tea is ordered. It turns out that Stoppard is very easy-going about the play. Evidently it is Frears who is going through agonies of indecision on the casting. There doesn't seem to be too much worry about myself. Stoppard is complimentary and says virtually do whichever part you like. Much discussion on whether, if I was Harris, I should eat potatoes and drink beer for a month to 'heavy' myself up. I decline a sickly cake, as one passes on a silver tray.

Stoppard a breath of fresh air after Frears' gloomy frownings. He says, when it all boils down to it, filming is about getting together a group of people you like. He quotes Evelyn Waugh, 'The Second World War wasn't bad, provided you were with nice people.'

1 Two short plays commissioned by David Leland from Terry and myself for the Sheffield Crucible's studio.

So the conversation steers away from me, without a decision, and on to who should be J – the other main part. Tim Curry of *Rocky Horror* fame is suggested as having the right public school background. Frears is worried that Tim may be enjoying life too much in Los Angeles. Robert Powell is suggested.[1] They both agree he's brilliant, but Stoppard is doubtful about his looks. 'He's a little Spanish-looking, gypsy-like for J.' So nothing is decided.

Stoppard has to go to a rehearsal of *Travesties* (yet another in his long line of award-winning plays) next door at the Aldwych. As he leaves we shake hands and he says, 'If I next see you in a striped blazer and a boater with a pillow stuffed up your trousers, I'd be very pleased.'

Saturday, May 17th

It's foul weather again. Little sympathy among the gods for Gospel Oak's Nuts in May Festival. Mary and Catherine B [Helen's sister and her daughter] lunch here and we stand in the rain in Lamble Street waiting for the procession to appear. Bedraggled but unbowed, the floats begin to turn the corner from Grafton Road. They vary from flower gardens, to pleasantly unspectacular scenes of nursing life, to a Gothic anti-eviction float from the squatters, with a huge, bloody papier-mâché axe poised above the grinning kids on top of the float. On one a girl dances like the neighbourhood Isadora, long, flowing, rather absurd movements, for she is dressed in army boots and is clearly well stoned. There is a huge carnival traffic jam in Lamble Street as they try to manoeuvre an extra-large float into Lismore Circus. I film some of it. No respite for my identity problem. I am spotted by two girls atop the Inter-Action Art Bus, who wave excitedly. One of them bends down to shout something into the cab. Within moments the loudspeaker booms out 'A big hello to Mr Eric Idle, who you can see is with us today.'

Thursday, May 22nd

Out to lunch at Gay Hussar with John Cleese and the *Sunday Express*.

The *Sunday Express* was represented by an attractive, dark-haired, heavily-pregnant lady called Olga something,[2] who turned out to be a

---

1 Popular actor – *Doomwatch, Jude the Obscure*. Chosen to play Jesus Christ in Zeffirelli's TV mini-series, *Jesus of Nazareth*.
2 Lady Olga Maitland, later a Tory MP.

writer for the Express *Diary* (no, *not* the Express *Dairy*). She tried hard to be nice and understanding, and in return we were models of public school charm and politeness. I'm glad it was just a diary story, because this sweet lady did constantly get the wrong end of the stick, and I would hate to have entrusted her with hard information. But I suppose she will be the first journalist to learn of our plans for a new film – and my part in *Three Men*.

At 6.00 at the Henshaws' for a Python meeting. All present, except Eric, who is in France. Briskly it was decided to set aside Sept/Oct period of 1976 to write a new film and May/June 1977 to film it.

Gilliam is the lone voice of bitter protest against this timetable. He rants and raves about 'leisurely lives' and clearly fears that we are signing ourselves a death warrant. The rest of us accept it. Actually I think what we have decided is quite sensible, though I feel that a year's break would have been better than eighteen months – and he's right, there's no certainty that when the next movie comes out – in New Year 1978 – Python will carry the same impetus which is filling the box offices at the moment.

My dates for *Three Men in a Boat* were confirmed today. They amount to nearly six weeks' work. The fee is a little more than half what I was offered to spend half an hour at the Knebworth concert. C'est showbiz.

Saturday, May 24th

Copy of a letter arrived in the post from Maurice Girodias, famous publisher of the Olympia Press in Paris in the 1950s – the first man to publish *Candy, Lolita, The Ginger Man* and other post-war underground classics which are now school curriculum material. He's a pioneer of total literary freedom and apparently has run into trouble over the last few years (since *Last Exit to Brooklyn*) from Sir Cyril Black.[1] He was served with writs by Sir Cyril after Girodias had, in his own words, 'published under the Ophelia Press imprint a book with the title "Sir Cyril Black", in which a particularly vicious villain carries that noble name'.

Girodias now wants us to appear as witnesses at his trial. He says 'I am sure they (MP) will not be indifferent to my plight since, after all, I have fought many battles in the past which have opened the way to the (relative) freedom of expressive opinion we are now enjoying,' and later

---

[1] A Tory MP and deeply religious, pro-censorship, disciplinarian, temperance campaigner.

slightly fudges the fine moral tone by saying 'such an occasion could be turned into a rather wild occasion for both publicity and fun, rolled into one'. He even says he can apply for a postponement of the trial if we are not available. To be asked to appear at Girodias's trial has the same ring of unreality as being photographed by Richard Avedon.

What do we do? I am utterly opposed to such bigots as Sir Cyril Black; of Girodias I know nothing except his taste in literature, which roughly accords with my own. So support should be given. But three or four days in New York at the end of the week would deal my already limited writing time a severe blow. Also our appearance would be publicised in a way in which we have no control. We need to be absolutely certain ourselves about our dedication to Girodias, our knowledge of the case, and how we feel we can best help.

So I am trying to concentrate on what I do know about – my writing – through which my own views about Sir Cyril Black can, I feel, be better put over than by attending a show trial in New York.

But I feel so weak for not doing anything. I certainly feel Python's name should be linked with this very worthy cause in some way. This difficult moral problem disturbed me more than it ought as I sat on the loo reading the letter before breakfast.

Monday, May 26th

En famille, we drove up to South End Green, briefly surveyed the photo display for *Monty Python and the Holy Grail* playing at the Hampstead Classic this week, then went on to sample the delights of the Bank Holiday Fair on the Heath. Subjected ourselves to the usual gut-gripping violence on Big Wheels, Rotordyne, where you are spun round at colossal force until you stick to the wall, and Whizzers, where you're just hurled around until you feel your stomach is going to come out of the top of your head.

Thursday, May 29th

Yesterday I started on one of the 'atmosphere' pieces for the Jimmy Gilbert show. Set in a boys' school in Edwardian England. I read it to Terry this morning, who enthused greatly – but he's worried that Light Entertainment will do it badly and the 'atmosphere' which it needs may be lost. I am enjoying the writing routine again, though.

Monday, June 2nd

Referendum day is Thursday,[1] and we are alternately told that whatever we say doesn't matter a jot in the great pattern of things (James Cameron in *The Guardian* on Saturday) or that it is the most important decision we will ever make in our lives (most politicians). I am still undecided. In both cases it boils down to having confidence in Britain. Either to stay in Europe and keep up with the fast pace of material progress which undoubtedly have made France and Germany quite attractive places to live in, or to have the confidence to break from the incentive and the protection of Europe and become a one country independent free trader, as in the good old days. Neither decision, I think, involves the downfall of our nation. Once a decision is taken it will all be absorbed into the system and the country will carry on working (or not working) as it always did. For once a major politico-economic issue in Britain has not been debated on purely class lines. Tories mix with Labour, socialists with Monday Clubbers, unionists and bosses on pro and anti platforms. Only the implacable revolutionaries, who see the Common Market as a purely and quite reprehensibly capitalist device, seem to have a unity in the ranks.

I tend towards Cameron's view – though I will probably vote 'No' as a vote against the smugness and complacency of the over-subscribed 'Yes' campaign. I think Britain will survive both decisions – but it will be more exciting, I feel, to watch the consequences of a 'No' vote and, as one of society's little band of jesters, excitement helps my business.

Drove down to Terry's in a torrential storm, with cold winds whipping round the car. We worked steadily on with 'F J Tomkinson's Schooldays' – as the half-hour has now become. It needs consolidating and tightening, which we do bit by bit. As usual the last ten minutes are the most difficult.

Drove home in another storm. Watched a long TV Referendum debate. There ought to be one channel, run as a public service, which broadcasts all parliamentary proceedings, because they are quite involving and, rather than bore the pants off everyone, they may cure our national political apathy, for on major issues like this there are some very good performers about.

1 Harold Wilson's Labour government asked the question 'Do you think the UK should stay in the European Community?' Edward Heath's Tory government had taken us in on January 1st, 1973.

John Goldstone rang to say that the *Grail* has broken records on its opening in Philadelphia and Toronto and that Don Rugoff has plans to transfer it to a new cinema in NY and wants to have a death cart trundled through the streets of NY as an ad. Given Mayor Beame's reported plans to sack 67,000 city workers in order to meet huge unpaid bills, this may be a public service as well as a publicity stunt.

Thursday, June 5th

Today at 10.00 I remembered that our kitchen was to be photographed by the Royal Duke.[1] So there was hasty cleaning of the kitchen, then Helen took Rachel and William off for injections (routine NHS stuff). While she was away, I locked myself out while emptying the waste-paper basket. Managed to enlist the sporty help of Clare Latimer[2] next door, but trod in dog shit in her yard, then nearly castrated myself on our roses and fencing. She laughed and declared it was all very Monty Python. In the end I climbed over the roofs and into my room, just in time to clean the shit off my shoes and welcome the Duke of Gloucester into the kitchen.

Cast my vote in the Referendum. I voted 'Yes' because I was not in the end convinced that the retention of our full sovereignty and the total freedom to make our own decisions, which was the cornerstone of the Noes' case, was jeopardised seriously enough by entering the Market. And I feel that the grey men of Brussels are no worse than the grey men of Whitehall anyway. But I didn't decide on my vote until this morning, when I read the words of one of my favourite gurus, Keith Waterhouse.[3] He would vote 'Yes' he thought, but without great enthusiasm for the Referendum or the way its campaign has been conducted, because of the attractions of the European quality of life! And he concludes, 'I may be naïve in hoping that remaining in Europe will make us more European, but after a thousand years of insularity from which have evolved the bingo parlour, carbonised beer and *Crossroads*, I am inclined to give it a whirl.'[4]

---

1 The Duke of Gloucester was a partner in Hunt Thompson – for whom my brother-in-law worked as an architect. They designed a number of improvements to the house.
2 Clare Latimer, our neighbour for many years. Now a celebrated caterer and food writer.
3 *Daily Mirror* columnist, novelist and playwright – *Billy Liar, Jeffrey Bernard Is Unwell*.
4 67 per cent said yes. Of the administrative regions, the only rejections were in Shetland and the Western Isles.

Tuesday, June 10th

The hot weather continues. Spent yesterday and most of today working on the last quarter of the Palin Show script. Quite pleased with progress – at least there is now an ending.

Midway through the afternoon, drove over to TV Centre to have my hair shorn unmercifully.

With my new short back and sides, drove over to Cosprops in Regent's Park Road to try on the blazers, striped swimsuits, etc, for *Three Men*. Stephen Moore (George)[1] and Stephen Frears and I went for a drink afterwards. Moore is a delightfully easy-going, affable bloke, very good company. Frears is very endearing in his scruffy, self-deprecating way. I like them both a great deal.

Wednesday, June 11th

The first-time writer, director and all three Men in the Boat get together. The place, the airless, featureless cell of room BO 55 at the TV Centre. Present today, narrow Tom Stoppard, eyes sparkling. 'How are *you* today, Michael?' Rather quiet, frazzled, detached producer – Rosemary Hill. She looks anxious. Two large PAs – one of whom I later discover is Jack Hawkins'[2] son. The dog, Montmorency, who is at least affectionate. Stephen M and last, but not least, Tim Curry – smaller than I expected, dark/olive-skinned, curly-haired, with prominent eyes.

The read-through goes well. At the end Frears says the casting was exactly right, and one gets the feeling that all three of us fit Jerome's characters near enough to require no great feats of acting. Stoppard is pleased too. Rosemary Hill does not express an opinion, but is more concerned with the fact that it's going to be too long. Stoppard and Frears are clearly opposed to making major cuts at this point – so the discussion drags on in a rather desultory way. I don't think anything very worthy will ever be decided in BO 55.

Up to the bar, where I met Tim B-T and Graeme Garden (surrounded by beautiful women). They are on *Top of the Pops*, plugging their latest epic 'Black Pudding Bertha' tonight and Graeme has just had a son. They are quite envious about the *Three Men in a Boat* job.

1 An Old Vic, Royal Court actor, just beginning to make his name in television.
2 Jack Hawkins (1910-73), star of many of the classic movies of my childhood – *The Cruel Sea*, *Bridge on the River Kwai*, etc.

Thursday, June 12th, Southwold

The weather continues to be dazzling, perfect, clear hot sunshine. Up to Southwold on the 9.30 train to take my parents to see the *Holy Grail* film which starts today at Norwich. Some twenty or thirty people at the 1.40 showing. I enjoyed watching the film today more than I've ever done. It may partly have been due to the fact that I was carrying one and a half pints of Adnams, but I think it was because I was under no strain, rush or pressure, as at previous showings – premieres, etc. I was also able to crystallise and analyse my disappointments in the film – there is a patch where we really do lose touch with the audience, and that's at the end of the otherwise excellent 'Wedding' scene, through the old lady in the 'Ni' village, and the second 'Knights' which terminate in easily the most embarrassing piece of the film, when the king meets Sir Robin in the forest. But I think the parents enjoyed it, and Daddy laughed quite spontaneously a few times.

A quick trip to the cathedral, then home to Croft Cottage, where we sat in the sunshine and had a cup of tea. Daddy's chair kept tipping over and once, when he'd taken a bite of rock cake, his teeth came out firmly clamped to the rock cake.

Read Thomas Hardy's *The Trumpet-Major* as I rattled home on the 6.30 train from Darsham.

Friday, June 13th

In the afternoon I had a tetanus jab at the BBC because of the suspicious nature of the Berkshire Thames – it rather deromanticised the whole thing – then Tim, Stephen M, Stephen F and I roared up the M4 in Stephen F's very shabby Cortina, through Reading and up to Goring, where we found the thirty-foot skiff, which we will get to know rather well over the next three or four weeks. We bought some tea, and went for a trial row up the river. We fell uncannily easily into the roles. I rowed, because I like rowing and generally getting things done (being Harris), Tim, in dark reflecting glasses, languidly took the rudder, while Stephen M just generally helped.

Monday, June 16th

The first day's filming on *Three Men in a Boat*. Up at 7.00.

A brilliantly sunny morning as I drove to the BBC. It didn't stay like that and, by the time of our third or fourth shot at a boathouse at Walton, we were indoors, sheltering from the rain. But there were sufficient breaks in the showers for us to maintain a good rate of filming, despite having to get used to the boat, full of gear and Montmorency the dog. It's bad enough having to do retakes anyway, but to row yourself back for the retakes often adds insult to injury.

Stephen F comes to life and directs briskly, but not at all autocratically. We tend to cover sequences from more than one angle, and Brian Tufano, the most prestigious BBC cameraman, is painstaking over light and composition of shots.

Tom Stoppard is in attendance – very friendly – a rather languid figure in his expensive woollen jacket, loose-fitting camel-coloured slacks and Gucci bag full of scripts. He gives Tim and me a lift to one of the locations in his metallic green BMW automatic. I can't help noticing high-class jetsam in the car – an invitation from 'Mr and Mrs Kingsley Amis at home'.

I find the combination of the long hours – shooting began at 9.30 and ended at a quarter to seven – the concentration of my rusty mind on lines and performance, and the physical effort of rowing and controlling the boat, utterly exhausting.

To bed at 11.15, but woke at 3.00, and tossed and turned for an hour or so, full of depressing thoughts as to my stamina and ability to go through three weeks of this. Got up at 8.00, still feeling heavy and gloomy.

Wednesday, June 18th

Filming began at Datchet – in sunshine. Police were on hand to clear a stretch of riverside road so we could film with the houses behind. After one take they told us that one of the cars held up by the filming was the royal party on its way to Ascot!

Windsor Castle, like a huge and over-drawn backcloth for a fairy tale, lay in the sun on the left bank. We worked our way up the river, ending in a sort of surreal evening sequence in the majestic, silent serenity of Cliveden Reach. Tim, Stephen and I in our little sculling skiff, the crew on Tufano's specially designed camera boat – a simple flat-bottomed 15 feet x 6 feet rectangle with a scaffolding frame all around from which the camera hangs on a specially balanced spring (called a pantograph). It looks like a floating four-poster.

We finish filming today at about ten past eight. I drive Tim, Stephen and myself to the Swan Hotel, Streatley – our base for the rest of the film. We arrive at about 9.15. We're all rather tired and hungry after a long day.

Our first contact with the staff of this pleasantly situated riverside hotel goes something like this:

Us: 'Can we ... eat here, please?'

She (small, bespectacled, young): 'Ooh *no!*'

Us: 'Why ... er ... why not?'

She: 'It's after quarter to nine.'

Myself (seasoned to this, so valiantly co-operative): 'Oh, I see ... and there's no chance of squeezing a meal in for us?' (We do see people eating in the dining-room.)

She: 'No.'

Us: 'A sandwich ... or just a piece of cheese?'

She: 'No.'

Us: 'Is there anywhere round here ... ?'

She (oh how Jerome K Jerome would have laughed): 'There's a Chinese in Pangbourne.'

Us: 'Well ... we might try that.'

She: 'Oh, we do have a problem. We close the hotel at 11.30 and there are only two keys.'

Stephen and I – Tim adapting to the situation and choosing to sit out beside the river and sip white wine – make our way to a charming thatched-roof little pub up the road called the Bull. It's 10.15 – they close at 10.30. Here the conversation goes (after ordering a drink):

Us: 'Can we ... get anything to eat?'

She (small, fat, middle-aged – what the girl at the Swan will probably turn into): 'No.'

Us: 'Is there ... ?'

She (triumphantly indicating empty food cabinet on bar): 'Oh, no. There's nothing left now.'

We manage to order some nuts and crisps, though we are given these with heavy reluctance and much raising of eyes to heaven.

Us: 'Oh, and some pickled onions, please.'

The order arrives without pickled onions.

Us: 'Pickled onions?'

She (after brief conversation with friend): 'No, I can't give you any.'

Us (jaws going slack rather than tempers rising): 'What ... ?'

She: 'I can't give you any. I'm not allowed to.'

The combination of the Swan and the Bull was fairly deadly. This is Southern England with a vengeance. We feel like lepers, as we walk down the pretty, the fucking pretty little main street, clutching some of the crisps she was good enough to let us have.

Saturday, June 21st, Southwold

The longest day and my father's three-quarter century.

Present at the party were all our family, including Rachel, just five months. There was champagne on the lawn and then various pies, patés, cold meats, salads, strawberries and coffee, etc, inside. The house coped well with the numbers and the sunshine helped to bring the whole thing to life.

Father was not in bad form – he finds it difficult to get his words out, but he was aware of who everyone was and what was going on, and smiled and drank rather a lot of champagne and didn't get cross at all. It was really as successful as I ever dared hope.

Wednesday, June 25th, Streatley

Danny La Rue[1] has been in residence, or in evidence, at the Swan this week; he is Chairman of the hotel, a fact which must account for the occasional groups of middle-aged ladies who are to be found standing on the bridge and gaping down at it. Danny gravitated rather surely towards Tim, but, in the bar after the meal, he was clearly anxious to talk to any of us. He talked mainly about the wonderful tour he'd just finished and how he'd broken all box-office records at Scarborough, only two or three nights ago. He really exudes star and showbiz. His talk is self-boosting, he has a small entourage, including one very beautiful young man, who hover about him. I have occasionally seen his eyes flick around the bar with a sort of panic, when he has no one to talk to.

None of us have, of course, been anything less than charming to him, however. No one has so much as hinted that his hotel must be one of the most beautiful and worst-run in England.

---

1 Irish-born cabaret star. Brought the art of female impersonation out of the night-clubs and into the mainstream.

Friday, June 27th, Streatley

The weather looked like breaking this morning; grey clouds piled up, but no rain. Spent most of the morning reading James Cameron's *An Indian Summer*, basking in the near perfect balance of his intelligence, humour and sensitivity.

I read in the Mini parked by the side of a lane at Bushey Lock, on the Upper Reaches beyond Abingdon, where Stephen M and Harry Markham were doing a scene. Harry Markham was in Stephen F's highly praised *Sunset Across the Bay* and he's one of Stephen's favourite actors. He's only on the film one day, but he comes down with his wife, Edna – they're a very dear, down-to-earth Northern couple, a great anti-dote to Hampstead. I asked them about their hobby, which turns out to be walking along canals. They recently walked the Liverpool–Leeds canal.

'Oh, how lovely,' I gushed.

'Oh, bits of it are very dangerous, you know,' replies Harry very seriously.

Edna is equally serious. 'There was a gang of youths came up to us just outside Liverpool … they started fingering his windcheater …'

A pleasant lunchtime drink at the Trout at Bushey Lock – an out-of-the-way pub, with very friendly clientele. I learn a little more about Tim, who used to be rather quiet for the first few days, but has gradually opened up and become more garrulous and at times quite ebullient. He told me today that his father was a naval chaplain, who died when he was 12, and from then on he was brought up by women. There's a soft, very English quality about Tim which is quite at odds with the *Rocky Horror*/Lou Adler LP side.[1]

Tuesday, July 1st, Streatley

Stephen F doesn't really like days when there are a lot of extras. The awful depression he affects on such days, when shots take a long time to set up and then someone hasn't understood and walks slap across shot at the vital moment, is, I think, quite deep-seated.

Annie Z[2] says that Stephen totally lives the film while he's working. He's

1 Tim created the role of Frank N. Furter in *The Rocky Horror Show*.
2 Anne Zelda: actress. Stephen's girlfriend, now wife. She appears in the *Ripping Yarn* 'Murder at Moorstones Manor'.

one of life's restless pacers, she says. Some mornings he starts pacing about six o'clock.

Anyway, the first of July has a richly comic ending. 'Tucker' Leach, one of the Props boys, a cheerful stammerer, who is no intellectual giant, plays his second role of the day – as a passenger on board a steamship that nearly runs us down (again!). After complicated positions have been worked out, the shot finally gets under way. It's a good take – which actually ends on my line as the steamboat swishes past: 'I say, any chance of a tow?' No sooner have I said the line, than Tucker yells back, loud and clear and deliciously in shot, 'No way!'

Wednesday, July 2nd, Streatley

The morning's hot again, and I'm settling down to a cup of coffee and a read of the Palin Show script, before sending it off to Terry Hughes. But Stephen F finds me and, motioning vaguely to the terrace in front of the hotel, invites me to bring my coffee along and join everyone. Everyone turns out to be me and Stephen.

He tells me that, in addition to the already crowded schedule, he wants to reshoot the dead dog floating down the river sequence. It was shot in an end-of-the-week afternoon of careless abandon last Friday, and both Stephen and Brian are aware they've shot it in a dull way. An example of the difference between LE and Drama shooting. I've never, in all my experience of Python filming, both on TV and in two movies, ever been involved in a retake of a scene for purely artistic reasons.

I scribble a note off to Terry Hughes, enclosing the script.

Retake the dead dog sequence. This time it worked well – the Woolworths toy dog, which had looked rather ineffective last time, was replaced by a newly killed sheep, which gave an Oscar-winning performance.

Sunday, July 6th, Streatley

Talked to Tom Stoppard on a sunny lawn between takes. He seems to be a little preoccupied with rehearsals for *Travesties* for the US tour. Stephen M tells me that sometimes Tom's rather forthright notes to the actors have caused some of them to walk out on him. On this film he has been discreetly available – present for a few hours most days – but sometimes marooned on the wrong side of the river, as we are often rather difficult to find. He liaises with Stephen mainly and doesn't talk a great deal to us about the way things should be played. He brings his kids – his younger set of kids – out with him, and on occasions his wife, the buoyantly chatty Dr Miriam Stoppard, and at Radcote Lock the other day, he even appeared with his mother. It was rather sweet really – she sat in the limited shade of a lifebelt holder watching us sweat in the lock, with a copy of a magazine article about Tom laid open beside her.

Wednesday, July 9th, Streatley

The final day of filming. We ended, rather fittingly, with a long journey down the river in bright sunshine, from Shepperton Lock to Hampton Court. Brian T, who was in good form, kept stopping to take shots of swans, ducks, willow trees waving and other artistic items that caught his eye. As we passed Hampton Church he began murmuring about needing a shot of it, etc, and for the first time in the entire film, I thought I was aware of Stephen F curbing Brian's enthusiasm, because of lack of time. In the last two or three days word has clearly filtered through from the BBC that *Three Men in a Boat* is costing too much. Then, after we passed an island, the church reappeared with the sun behind it and framed by tall trees and Brian could control himself no longer. Stephen responded and the boats turned and stopped and the shot was taken.

Back to Hampton Court Pier and a last drink with the crew at the Mitre hotel. The last I see of Tim and Stephen Moore is on the corner of Hammersmith Broadway.

Thursday, July 10th

Wrote letters, played squash with Terry, and tried to put off the inevitable moment when I would have to re-immerse myself in the affairs of Python. I have tasted self-sufficiency for four weeks and a most agreeable taste it is.

Friday, July 11th

Our nude photo, which makes us all look rather blatantly and unsexily bare, appears as a full page spread in *Vogue*. The photo is fun, but accompanying it is the most dreadful piece of blurb about 'Monty

Python … that six-manic, smash-them, trash-them comedy commune from Britain.'

Monday, July 14th

To the BBC by 12.00 to meet Terry Hughes and so really begin the Palin Show project. Both Terry and Jimmy G have apparently liked the script. It's clearly too long, but I'm heartened and encouraged by Terry H's attitude, which is to try and do it as a 45-minute special. Jimmy G is adamant at the moment about 30 minutes.

We discuss the thorny subject of casting briefly. Terry J wants to play Tomkinson's mother, but I'm afraid that TJ in drag does have an instant link with Python and may disturb the reality which the character needs in this particular script. But major decisions are put into abeyance until we have done our rewriting.

Sunday, July 20th

Wrote to Al Levinson, the wise, likeable American I met at the Henshaws' last year. His letters still outnumber mine three to one, but I enjoy writing to him. It's being required to step back and look at yourself and your life in relation to someone 3,000 miles away, whom you have hardly met, but with whom you feel an unexplainable empathy. Ours is purely a literary relationship, a written relationship. It's different from all my other relationships. That's what makes it interesting and stimulating too, I suppose.

Tuesday, July 22nd

Terry and I worked together today on *Fegg*. It's the third successive day I've spent on new material for the book [for the upcoming American edition].

Then up to Dr Chapman's house at Southwood Lane, Highgate, for an interview with a Yugoslav journalist – for the Yugoslavs have apparently bought the *Holy Grail* film. A squat, rather scrubby-bearded man with a tape recorder was sitting on his own in what passes for Graham's sitting room. I said hello, then heard a shout of 'Get your trousers off, then', in a bad Scottish accent, from the next room. McKenna, Bernard was there, surrounded by sheaves of paper, covered in his squiggles, looking harassed, while Dr Chapman sat in his usual writing attitude – glass of gin and tonic in one hand, legs stretched out, gazing into space.

Graham looked grey – as if he had spent the last five years un-dead. Which really was nearer the truth than it seemed. Graham, having lately fallen in with Ringo Starr – for whom he and Douglas have written a TV spectacular (American) – has also drifted into the Keith Moon/Harry Nilsson orbit.[1] Now Moon is a genuine loony and drives Rolls Royces into swimming pools and leaves them there, but Nilsson, as I heard from Tim Curry, and heard again tonight from a slurred and shattered Chapman, is a man bent on self-destruction. Graham, sounding like a Sunday school child on an outing to Sodom, told me how Nilsson had had to be helped from GC's house last night utterly and totally smashed. Graham had bruises today to show for it. Nilsson drinks neat gin – a bottle in one evening – pops every pill possible, but most of the time prefers cocaine. Graham was really shocked.

We talked for an hour or so to the very affable Yugoslav, who told us that there had been many anti-Python protests in Yugoslavia, but that the show had become a rallying point.

Sunday, July 27th

I began work just after 9.00, writing up a couple of new ideas. Terry, Alison and Sally arrived about 10.00 and, whilst Helen packed and Alison and Sally took William up to Parliament Hill and Thomas watched *Thunderbirds*, Terry and I sat in the increasingly uncomfortable heat of the work-room and slogged away at *Fegg* with a ferocious concentration.

The room became hotter – outside the temperature was over 80° – and we finally emerged, like the National Union of Railwaymen after an all-day attempt to avert a strike, sweaty, crumpled but happy, at 9.30 in the evening.

We opened a bottle of champagne and celebrated wearily amongst the piles of washing, clothing, toys, cameras and books destined for Italy. For myself, it couldn't be better timing. To have worked literally to the last moment, and to be able to leave for a month in Europe, after

[1] Keith Moon, drummer of The Who. Harry Nilsson, rock musician, huge fan of Python and excess generally. Died, after a heart-attack, in 1994, aged 53.

such a mind-draining concentrated spell of work, gives me that warm, satisfied feeling of all the systems being totally and fully used.

After a three-week holiday in Italy with the Davidson family, it was time for yet another trip to New York, this one occasioned by publication of the Fegg *book in the US.*

Wednesday, September 3rd

All-out onslaught on letters, etc, before leaving for NY tomorrow. The American fan mail is sometimes quite extraordinary. Less restrained than the English. I received one quite steamy letter, full of declarations of love, meant for my eyes only, which ended with the note, 'I hope you're the one I mean', and another from what must be one of the world's least-known organisations – the Michael Palin Sub-Committee of the Python Fan Club of Apartment 4c, 825 West End Ave, NY.

Thursday, September 4th, New York

To New York again. Very smooth, easy flight from sunny Heathrow at 11.00 to sunny New York at 1.30.

By 4.00 we were at the offices of Berkeley Books at 200 Madison Avenue to meet the publishers and designers of the American *Fegg* book. Ned Chase, a 50-year-old, who looks lean and well exercised, and has a Harvard correctness to his accent and general bearing (he was at Princeton, in fact) and Steve Conlon, big, white-haired, white-bearded, looking like a slim Burl Ives and using more down-to-earth Americanisms – his speech is littered with 'son of bitches' and 'get the fuck out of its' – for the publishers. And two younger men – about our age – Mike Gross and David Kaestle, who used to work as staff designers and illustrators on the *National Lampoon*.

Certainly their work is impressive – they have designed, and Mike Gross has drawn, some of the parodies of famous American artists on the *National Lampoon* Bicentennial Calendar – which is a calendar devoted entirely to disasters of one kind or another, ranging from assassinations and political scandals to typhoons and mass murders in the 200 years since the US was started.

They are also instantly likeable – because they like *Fegg*, I suppose –

and the combination of their obvious experience and flair and their immediate sympathy with the *Fegg* character and material made us both very pleased and the meeting quite a success.

Saturday, September 6th, West Granby, Connecticut

Left the Navarro at 8.45 for a weekend in Connecticut at the invitation of Steve Conlon.

My first glimpse of New England. It is like Sussex, only with more space. No black faces up in Northern Connecticut. Houses all of wood are rather attractive, and Steve's place is magnificent. It's a large barn, across the road from a farmhouse, white and weather-boarded, in which lives Steve's brother Henry (at weekends). Steve and his neat and organised English wife, Bet, have been converting the barn for about thirty years and it's now complete. Very fine interior, all open plan except for three guest bedrooms at one end. The original wooden beams complemented with some simple old pieces of wooden furniture, a feeling of comfort, but not luxury. Immediately in front of the barn is a spacious meadow.

So a feeling of space, quietness, and inside the barn, comfortable orderliness. An utter contrast to the throbbing, noisy heartbeats of NYC.

Later in the day two other Berkeley authors arrive. Lyn and Sheila – they wrote a best-seller some years back about research into psychic phenomena in Russia.

The pace quickened and we were joined for cocktails (their word, not mine) and dinner by a local Episcopalian minister, George, who Steve rather carefully made a point of telling us earlier was doing good work with homosexuals, and two local young men, Frank, a teacher in West Hartford – again with a very New English accent – and Charles, another youngish man, with a small moustache and a lazy left eye, who was a violinist and brother-in-law of Ted Sorensen (of Kennedy clan fame). All very jolly.

TJ was in high spirits and expansive good form. I sat beside the violinist and the Episcopalian minister, feeling rather dull. The minister talked softly about his work, describing how he counsels boys who come to see him. 'I give them the names and addresses of some gay clubs, gay discos, you know, and I tell them go on ... off you go, there's nothing wrong.'

We eat an excellent chicken casserole and a grape and cream

concoction for pudding – once again served up by Bet with a sort of clean efficiency which almost detracts from one's enjoyment.

Steve is a little shirty throughout, as the water supply appears to have run out. The fault is traced to our toilet cistern, which jammed and was left running. I think he is a little cross that the smooth running of the place, which he clearly prides himself on, should be interrupted on tonight of all nights – and I get the feeling he blames it on us.

Sunday, September 7th, West Granby, Connecticut

The sun is high and hot in a clear sky. We visit a nearby store for some last minute provisions. There is a comfortable neatness about the shop – untainted as it is by any slightly exciting food. Buy the *New York Times* and the *Hartford Courant* – both with about thirteen sections and several hundred pages – then back to the barn, where we read them lying in the sun. There's a lunch out of doors, which Bet is extremely proud of – because it is so well organised. All the cold meat and cheese is symmetrical. But in fact the lunch is very congenial and everyone seems a lot more relaxed than yesterday.

A drink in the early evening with Charles and Frank, whom we met last night. They live together in a wooden house on stilts with a fine view from the top of a hill. We drink whisky sours. Frank, whom I like a great deal, gives me a book of early Maurice Sendak drawings, not usually available. He knows Sendak apparently. However cynical one may be of this clean, bland American way of life, the people are exceptionally generous to strangers.

To bring us back to reality with a bump, we watched the first of the new Monty Python series to be shown in the States. It was the 'Scott of the Antarctic', 'Fish Licence', 'Long John Silvers v. Gynaecologists' programme. Strange how many of its items have become legendary, and yet looking at them, TJ and I were amazed and a little embarrassed at how very badly shot everything was. Ian really has improved but, judging by that show, he needed to. Was this really the greatest comedy series ever? Steve slept through it.

Monday, September 8th, New York

Steve wakes us at 6.10. We leave the barn just as it's getting light – about twenty to seven.

We arrive at Grand Central Station – in dark, dingy bowels, which make Liverpool Street look like some exquisite classical drawing room – at 10.10. Spend the morning and lunchtime and afternoon working on alterations to the *Fegg* material, in our room at the Navarro.

At 6.00 an historic moment. After three trips and at least a dozen phone calls, I meet Al Levinson, my new American friend, for only the second time. He and wife Eve come to the apartment. Al, big, bronzed, an almost olive colour; his face, I notice, like the bust of the Greek emperor I saw today in the Metropolitan Museum, fine, firm features. He looks serious underneath it all, as though the troubles of the world hung heavy on him when he stopped to think. Anyway, the great relief is I really do like him – and we get on easily, without infatuation on either side.

Nancy arrived to join us, so quite an impromptu party got under way before myself, Al and Eve left to have a look at Al's new house in Gramercy Park, which is right in the heart of nineteenth-century New York. They both clearly love it. The apartment is small, but in a four-storey brownstone which stands on its own, next to a Quaker chapel of the 1860s which has a preservation order on it.

We wound up at Nancy's drinking wine till after midnight. Met Dave Hermann, DJ of WNEW's morning show – he promised to wake me in the morning. He tells the story of how he was playing the 'Fairy Story' from the Pythons' second German show on the air and managed just in time to bleep the word 'tits'. (These progressive stations still have to be careful – after all, they're spending advertisers' money.) Then a phone call came through and Dave left the record playing only to hear, as he was winding up the phone call, 'Because she's a fucking princess.'

Tuesday, September 9th, New York

Listened to DH's early-morning programme. Sure enough, at 9.45 he told his audience that somewhere in NY MP and TJ of Monty Python were waking up. He played some music for us, which was very kind and silly.

To Sardi's restaurant, where we had a truly appalling meal, but did meet Arthur Cantor, a Broadway impresario with a fine sense of the absurdity of it all.

Cantor talks straight and doesn't try to impress. He would like to know if the Pythons are interested in a stage show in New York at the

City Center Theater for three weeks starting April 11th 1976. The theatre is owned by the City of New York, it's old and has an ornate interior and a seating capacity slightly larger than Drury Lane, though it feels equally intimate – we went to see it after our meal.

I like the theatre, I like the dates, I like the fact that the seat prices would not be as high as they would be on Broadway and I like Arthur Cantor. So I'm converted to a three-week stage show – if Python still exists!

From seeing Cantor and the theatre we go to a final meeting with Gross and Kaestle to look at the page layout. Everyone chips in with ideas and Ned and Steve discuss business, copy runs, initial prints, costings, etc, quite openly. There is no hierarchical aspect to the discussion.

Then we take Steve back to the hotel. Before we leave for the airport, we finish off our wine and beer with Ed Goodgold, Nancy Lewis and Ina Lee M and Steve, her partner.

Ed brought me a couple of cigars for the trip, which I appreciated, but eventually left in the bottom of a chest of drawers, beside a half-used box of sanitary towels left by some previous resident.

Left NY on the 10.00 BA flight.

Friday, September 12th

In the afternoon TJ and I go to the BBC for a meeting with Terry Hughes.

The *Tomkinson's Schooldays* scripts arrive with the title 'Michael Palin Special' writ large across them. But the meeting with Terry H goes well. Milton Abbas School in Dorset have given us permission to film there, and even to use the boys, provided their faces are not featured. We look through *Spotlight*. Judy Parfitt looks right to both TJ and myself as the mother, and TH says she's fun to work with, so she gets a call for the mother's part. TJ is still to play the School Bully, though TH suggests Ian Ogilvy, who strikes both of us as ideally physically right.

Tuesday, September 16th

Gilliam and Maggie round for a meal this evening – TG to tell me about his *Jabberwocky* film, which he wants me to write with him. He has an overall plan for the film now, which I like the sound of very much. In addition he has the backing of Sandy Lieberson, an American, who, with the Englishman, David Puttnam, runs Good Times Enterprises, who have a record of backing and setting up better-than-average movies.

I'm undecided about whether to work on *Jabberwocky*. I like it because it sounds like a starter and I like TG's sense of excitement about it, and I am quickly infected by his enthusiasm. I'm also very confident that anything he puts his mind to will at least not be dull – but I want to see how successful *Tomkinson's Schooldays* will be and how successful *Three Men in a Boat* will be and I want to find some project of my own.

For all these reasons I hang back.

Friday, September 19th

This evening is the first of John Cleese's solo efforts – *Fawlty Towers* – which he's been working on with Connie for over a year. Angela and Veryan and Michael and Anne Henshaw came round to have dinner and watch it with us. Helen and I were reduced to tear-streaming laughter on one or two occasions, the Henshaws less so and Angela and Veryan (probably put off by the intensity of my reaction) were quite quiet throughout. John has used a very straight and conventional Light Entertainment format in design, casting, film and general subject, but his own creation, Basil Fawlty, rises above all this to heights of manic extraordinariness. It all has the Cleese hallmark of careful, thoughtful, well-planned technical excellence and there was hardly a spare line in the piece or a moment when John wasn't going utterly spare. Anne said I was clearly enjoying it more because I knew John, but it was by any standards a really hard-working, well-realised performance. Whether he can keep it up, I don't know. It could become a bore and certainly there are as yet no reserves of warmth or sympathy in the character of Fawlty to help it along.

Thursday, September 25th

I spent the lunch hour in a recording studio doing three voice-overs for Sanderson Wallpaper. I really did it because I wanted to keep my hand in and a voice-over, however dull or badly written it may be, at least requires a bit of application and a little bit of performing. It's good practice. By the same token I've accepted an offer to appear as the guest on two editions of *Just a Minute*, a Radio 4 quiz game, next week.

Down to Regent's Park for a Python meeting.

Eric was very positive and I could scarcely believe that it was the same Eric who had berated us all for turning Python into a money-obsessed, capitalist waste of time in this same room in February last year. Eric's moods should really be ignored, but it's impossible because he nearly always has a big effect on any meeting. Today it was nice, kind, helpful, constructive Eric.

John had just returned from three days in Biarritz. He was the same as ever, unable to resist a vindictive dig at T Gilliam (on the usual lines of us 'carrying the animator' for three years). This didn't find much support amongst the gathering and squashed TG more than John intended.

Terry J had had a lunch with Michael White, who felt it would be suicidal for us not to make another film this year. Anne said that most 'advice' tended this way.

Saturday, September 27th

Thomas woke me, thankfully, at 8.30, with the news that the kitchen was leaking and it *was* late. He was absolutely right. At quarter past nine I was in mid-Weetabix when the phone rang. It was Stephen Frears – the plugs in his car were wet, could I give him a lift?

So we arrived, the director and I, at Ealing Film Studios, about ten minutes late. Renewed acquaintance with Tim and Stephen (who had done some work on the soundtrack yesterday) and the familiar, darkly sparkling features of Tom S. I was very happy to see them all again.

To work on re-recording the dialogue in lip-synch, as every sound-track had the noise of the camera boat's engine in the background. I found it difficult at first to slip into the character of Harris, or indeed the whole tone and atmosphere of the film. I strained for the character and my voice must have come out sharp and shrill, as they kept telling me to relax. But after a rather gruelling morning, I began to settle into it and remembered Stephen's oft-repeated instructions on the filming to avoid giving Harris a funny voice! It's a rather daunting way to start the day, though, stuck out in the darkened studio with everyone else behind you in the control room, minutely examining your every word, every nuance, every inflexion.

Tim Curry left at lunchtime. He, poor bugger, has two performances of *Travesties* this afternoon.

Sunday, September 28th

A fine, fresh, sunny Sunday morning. Glad to be up and climbing into my car when everyone else was still enjoying Sunday lie-ins. Pick up Stephen F in Belsize Village. He was standing in the middle of the unusually quiet and traffic-free crossroads and scanning through the Sunday papers. Rave reviews throughout of *Daft as a Brush* – his latest film, which went out last Wednesday night. Actually, the rave reviews were reserved for his direction, 'coolness and sensitivity we have come to associate with him' and the performances by Jonathan Pryce and Lynn Redgrave.

Anyway, Stephen was clearly pleased as we enjoyed a sunny ride out to west London. He lives for films and the group of technicians – cameramen, make-up, sound, editors, etc – with whom he works are the best in the business, painstakingly collected by Stephen over the years. He seems to have life pared down to essentials. Clothes, cocktail parties, awards, purely prestige jobs don't interest him, and he doesn't let them occupy his time or divert his efforts. At the same time, he is a critic – of politics, of the establishment, of the status quo, of television, of films, without ever becoming doctrinaire or predictable.

We worked from 10.00 till 12.15 Monday morning with a couple of one hour breaks. I'd read all the Sunday papers about four times each by the time we finished. Tom S occasionally sprawled on the floor (with either a sweet or a cigarette in the mouth) writing new lines up to the very last minute. Tom is a writer I trust, too. Like Stephen he is devoted to his craft, and will never accept an easy way out – even the new lines are charged with a special interest, they're never just fillers.

We had an Indian meal at the Karachi restaurant across the road and Tom bought us champagne. I don't think he really expected us to accept it, but it set us up well for a final three hours of some very difficult dubbing, where often there was no guide track at all – and we had to work out from our rapid lip movements what on earth we were saying. But at last, just after 12.00, we finished the last of Tim's many voice-overs. It was about Harris being a Pole and Tim had got the giggles over it earlier on and been unable to do it.

Home and a bath about 1.30.

Tuesday, September 30th

To the TV Centre at 10.30 for a day of production meetings on *Tomkinson's Schooldays.*

After Judy Parfitt turned down the part, I asked Tom, Tim and Stephen at the weekend for 'Gwen Watford'-type ladies, and Stephen Moore said, 'Why don't you ask Gwen Watford ...?' So today this is just what we did. I spoke to her agent, who was very approachable, and then to the great lady herself, and she was interested enough to ask for a script – so we've sent one off this evening and are just keeping fingers well crossed.

Ian Ogilvy is also on, as far as I know, so it's becoming an all-star cast – apart from myself!

Finished at the Beeb about 7.00. Had a drink at the Sun in Splendour, Notting Hill on the way back with Terry J. He is a little vague and not entirely happy about what to do next. I said I was also vague – and intentionally so, enjoying, as I am at the moment, a sort of directional limbo, trying to absorb influences from all sides, without having to commit to any long-term projects. For the first time we actually talked about whether he should go and do something on his own. I said I didn't want to drag his heels as well as my own.

Friday, October 3rd

At 5.15 arrived in taxi at the BBC's Paris studio – which is not in Paris, of course, but in Lower Regent Street – for recording of *Just a Minute*. A few people from the queue came up and asked me for an autograph – and there was my face on a display board outside. Inside, the peculiarly non-festive air which the BBC (radio especially) has made its own – everything from the colour of the walls and the design of the furniture to the doorman's uniform and the coffee-serving hatch seems designed to quell any lightness of spirit you may have.

Then I met Clement Freud. He stared at me with those saucer-shaped, heavy-lidded eyes with an expression of such straightforward distaste that for a moment I thought he had just taken cyanide. The producer, John Lloyd[1] – a ray of light in the darkness that was rapidly closing in on me – hurriedly took my arm and led me aside as if to

1 He later created *Not the Nine O'Clock News.*

explain something about Clement F. It was just that he had a 'thing' about smoking – and for some inexplicable reason I had just taken one of John L's cigarettes. Still, this blew over.

A depressingly half-full house filed quietly in and at 5.45 the contestants – three regulars, Freud, K Williams, the rather forbiddingly authoritative Peter Jones,[1] myself, not exactly in my element any more – and quiz master Nicholas Parsons were introduced to friendly applause and took our places at our desks. The three regulars have been playing the game together for five years – Williams and Freud for eight – and it shows. They are smooth and polished, they know when to ad-lib, when to bend the rules a little, and when to be cross with each other. I buzzed Clement Freud when he was at full tilt and, when asked why, I apologised and said I was testing my buzzer. That's the only time I saw him smile in my direction.

The game became easier, but I never mastered the technique of microphone-hogging which they all have perfected.

Before I knew it, two shows and about an hour and a half had passed and it was all over. I signed autographs. Peter Jones was very kind to me and complimentary, Freud I never saw again and Nicholas Parsons was the only one to come round to the pub and drink with us. Us being myself, Douglas Adams (who had recommended me to his friend, the producer) and John Lloyd. They seemed to be quite pleased with me and Peter Jones, as he left, said he would see me again on the show. I gather some guests manage it (Barry Took, Katharine Whitehorn) and some don't (Barry Cryer, Willy Rushton) and at least I wasn't considered amongst the don'ts.

From the Captain's Cabin to the Work House – the studio in Old Kent Road where we are to re-record 'Lumberjack Song'.[2] The Fred Tomlinsons have been rehearsing for an hour by the time I arrive (just after 8.00), and up in the control room are Eric and George Harrison. George grasps me in a welcoming hug and Eric pours me some Soave Bolla.

Downstairs, noisy rumblings of Fred Toms. I get down there to find them in the usual hearty good spirits – no Soave Bolla in evidence down there – just huge cans of beer and cider!

1 He later became the narrator of *The Hitchhikers Guide to the Galaxy*, something I'd inexplicably turned down.
2 George loved the song so much he offered to produce it as a Christmas single. It reached No. 51, but no higher as the Pythons refused to sing it on *Top of the Pops*.

Instead of dividing the song and introduction up into different takes, we just launch in, and soon we've done three versions straight through and my voice is getting hoarse from all the added shouting at the beginning. But one of the takes seems to please everybody.

George, Olivia, Kumar,[1] Eric and I leave in George's BMW automatic for a meal. We drive, if that's the word for George's dodgem-like opportunism, to the Pontevecchio in Brompton Road.

George's a vegetarian, but he managed to demolish some whitebait quite easily, and did not pass out when I had duck. (I noticed everyone else ate veg. dishes only.)

Saturday, October 4th

At half past four drive up to collect Eric and take him out to George's house in Henley to mix the song we recorded last night. Eric philosophical about his recent separation from Lyn. He laughed rather ruefully when he told me he'd taken Carey out to the zoo this morning – 'With all the other divorcees,' as he put it. But he cheers up when we get to Henley and in through the gates of Friar Park, the magnificent, opulent and fantastical mid-Victorian Gothic pile which George bought seven years ago with the Beatle millions. George's flag flies above its mock embrasures – it's an Indian symbolic design of the sun and the moon and bears 'om' mantra.

In the gardens there are grottoes with mock stalactites and stalagmites in mock caves and there are Japanese houses and Japanese bridges and all kinds of other ways in which an enormously rich Victorian can spend money on himself. George has endorsed it all by cleaning everything up and looking after it and generally restoring the place to its former splendours. The nuns whom he bought it from had let it rather go to seed and, according to George, had painted swimming trunks on the cherubs and cemented over the nipples on some of the statues.

It is delightful just to walk around and examine the intricate details of the carving – the recurring naughty friar's head motif – even in evidence in brass on every light switch (the face is the fitting – the switch is the friar's nose). It has none of the feel of a big draughty Victorian house, but one can't escape the feeling of George somehow cut off from everyday life by the wealth that's come his way.

1 Olivia, George's wife. Kumar was his assistant.

Maybe he feels the same way, for almost the first thing we do is to walk through the grottoes, across the lawns and down to the elaborate iron gates and into the world outside. Henley, with its narrow streets and the fine church tower standing protectively over the little town, with thickly wooded Remenham Hill looming behind.

This was the town my mother was born and brought up in – in fact, she had been to Friar Park for tea when it was owned by Sir Frank Crisp, a barrister. Strange to think of the circumstances that brought me into Friar Park sixty years after she came here for tea.

Anyway, we all walked down to the local pub – where we drank Brakspear's Henley Ales and played darts.

George was clearly anxious that we should stay the night, play snooker on his Olympic size snooker table, smoke, drink, mix the record and generally enjoy ourselves. But this was my second evening devoted to the 'Lumberjack Song' and I wanted to be back with Helen, so I reluctantly resisted most of the mind-bending delights of Friar Park and stuck to a couple of glasses of white wine.

Half-way through the evening, George went out into Henley and returned with vast amounts of vegetarian food from a new Indian take-away that had just opened. We all ate too much – George dipping in with fingers only.

Home about 4.00. Helen not pleased, as she had really expected me a lot earlier – and I very indignantly tried to tell her how much hospitality I had had to refuse, to get back even by 4.00. Still, it's no time of night for an argument.

Wednesday, October 8th

Lunch with Gwen Watford, who has agreed to take the part, and Ian Ogilvy. Realise that there are several peaks of nervousness in one's first half-hour show, and one is meeting the other actors – especially when they are as exalted as Gwen W. Will they be right? What will be their attitude to the piece? Is it just a light diversion which they needn't bother with much? All anxieties dispelled on first meeting. Gwen I met in the make-up department, where she'd come for a wig fitting. She's charming and very approachable, and, like Ian Ogilvy, straightforward and down-to-earth.

Thursday, October 9th

Just as the week seemed to be settling down smoothly, 'Lumberjack Song' rears its ugly head again. Anne rings to say that Tony Stratton-Smith still prefers the Drury Lane 'Lumberjack' to the new version so laboriously conceived last weekend.

There is a definite split on the two versions of the 'Lumberjack'. Graham and Adams have been in after lunch (Anne said she wasn't quite sure how compos Graham was) and prefer the Drury Lane version. Terry J prefers Drury Lane. I really feel they are so different from each other in style as to be incomparable, and I feel I would hate the weekend's work just to go out the window. Eric has rung. He has 'flu and is not happy at all. He positively doesn't want Drury Lane.

Friday, October 17th, Dorchester–London train

Rattling back home after the week's filming on *Tomkinson*. Amazingly we are still able to have a meal on the train at 9.30 – a not unpleasant British Rail steak.

I think it has been the most solid week's work in my life. Since Monday morning I have been totally involved – in the setting-up and shooting, as well as the acting, of almost every shot. The feeling of responsibility tightens the concentration and, though the actual application is hard, it's the only way – especially as I feel TJ is waiting just behind me to take over. I don't mean that in any malicious sense, it's just that I fear his enthusiasm – it's the sort that is so deeply felt it keeps me on my toes, because I must keep thinking of ideas first.

At the moment, sitting back as the train roars towards London, I feel as happily and justifiably exhausted as I have done after any filming in a long while. Not only have I enjoyed the extent of my own involvement, I've enjoyed working with Terry Hughes. After the physical and mental strain of Ian Mac, Terry is more easy-going, open, adaptable, never rattled, never defensive – I suppose it stems from the fact that he has no one to fight. He is a blue-eyed boy at the BBC – director of *The Two Ronnies*, at present the No. 1 show in the ratings – whereas Ian was always at loggerheads with his employers. And Ian had six Pythons to cope with, Terry H only has two.

Tuesday, October 21st

Down to Ray Millichope's[1] at 10.30 to see the rushes. Terry H, Terry J and myself crowd around Ray's Steinbeck[2] at his new cutting rooms next door to the Nellie Dean pub in Carlisle Street. Euphoria gathers as we watch almost two hours' worth of rushes.

I feel very, very happy this afternoon as I drive back home. I think for the first time that *Tomkinson* is going to work in the area in which it is most distinctive – the area of quality, of atmosphere, of style.

Friday, October 24th

This morning we (i.e. the Pythons) are to meet Alan Freeman for an interview for some US radio programme he does. Freeman is one of those folk heroes of the sixties – *Pick of the Pops*, etc – who's still around and amazingly durable in the '70s. Graham tells me he's keen on motor bikes and leather and men.

I was twenty minutes late, but the first one there. Greeted with the same warm enthusiasm which gets Freeman so much work. His shirt is a little tightly stretched over a few folds of good living, and he seems a little hot in the face. He talks compulsively and shows me into the flat, furnished lushly with a great deal of ormolu and marble and rather fussily camp objects. A cigarette lighter is never a cigarette lighter … it's a gun or a sea-shell. A very likeable man – who endeared himself even more to me personally by raving about the Python credits. Said he was embarrassed that he didn't know our names, but he'd rung Python Productions for photos and they said they hadn't any.

Alan F taped quite cheerfully. He asked me if I ever regretted not playing a musical instrument and I got going on that. When he wasn't asking questions, we (Terry G, Terry J, Gra and myself) fell into a rather serious vein and talked about the problems of the world, etc. Graham said contraception and the control of the population was the world's major problem. At least he's doing his bit to limit the population.

John C, not unpredictably, was absent from all the various Python functions today, but the last of his *Fawlty Towers* series had me laughing as long and as loud as anything since *Hancock and the Vikings* – which must have been 15 or 16 years ago.

1 TV editor who worked on *The Frost Reports* and the Python TV shows.
2 The most commonly used machine for editing film in the pre-digital age.

Wednesday, October 29th

Just after 9.30 this evening, when I'm getting my Chinese take-away out of the oven, and my bottle of champagne out of the fridge, prior to watching England v. Czechoslovakia all on my own, I hear the dull thud of a blast. It could be anything, but it's a measure of the times that I am certain it was a bomb. Sure enough, on the 11.30 news there are the familiar pictures of ambulance, police cordons, etc, etc. At 9.40 a bomb went off in an Italian restaurant in Mayfair. No warning – eighteen injured. But the fact that I heard the explosion in our kitchen seemed to bring the whole horror closer to me – and genuinely set me thinking as to what I would do with myself and the family if a totally indiscriminate bombing campaign (as this recent one seems to be) continued in London.

No conclusions of course. I shall carry on shopping in the West End, parking in the West End, working in the West End, eating in the West End, as everybody else will – all helpless potential victims.

Saw Stephen Frears and Annie Zelda in the Welcome Chinese earlier. *Three Men* is ready, apart from the music. Stephen quietly, with eyes slightly mischievous, murmurs, 'The word is it's good.'

Saturday, November 1st

Studio recording day for *Tomkinson's Schooldays*. I estimate this will be getting on for the seventy-fifth half-hour I've performed in and helped to write since *Do Not Adjust Your Set* began in 1967.

I feel more and more confident as the day goes on. Strangely enough both Gwen and Ian are a little less at ease. After all, neither of them have ever done a TV show to a live audience – whereas for Terry and myself this is our world, for both of them it's an unfamiliar territory. But both play well during the recording and the audience seems to receive the show with many laughs.

I am racing around changing like a mad thing, and at the end of the one and a quarter hours recording, I think I'm the least qualified person in the entire studio to judge how it went. A feeling that I cannot get rid of is that the studio scenes received less reaction than they should have done – but everyone seems happy.

Tuesday, November 4th

Reactions to Saturday night's recordings have been so far favourable. Anne H and daughter Rachel liked it very much. Robert H enjoyed it and laughed a lot, but thought I was a bit *Whacko!*[1] I've had two long chats with Simon Albury, who liked it generally, but felt that there should have been more character detail – the School Bully especially, he felt, was one-dimensional and didn't like him at all – whereas Graham Chapman (the only Python apart from TJ at the recording) thought the Bully was very good. More basically, Simon felt that I came out of it too softly, self-effacingly and passively – if the object was to make it into a Michael Palin series.

On the phone today with TJ the difficult question of *Tomkinson* and our own working relationship came up. Tony Hendra (of *National Lampoon*) had offered him a pirate film to direct. Terry was writing back to say he couldn't do it – whereas in fact he really didn't want to do it because it would mean a lot of hard work which he didn't have time for if we were working on the series.

Well, we eventually talked it out over lunch at the Brasserie du Coin in Lamb's Conduit Street. I suppose it was a little awkward, as it always has been whenever we've had to stop and examine our relationship – which has, for ten years, grown, stretched and adjusted itself by fairly effortless natural processes.

Terry said that he didn't feel particularly frustrated or unfulfilled by the imbalance of writing and performing on *Tomkinson* and he would be quite happy if that same imbalance were to occur in a future series, but what he wanted to establish was that his own ideas and suggestions were treated with equal importance – if they weren't, and if I were 'in control', then it would not be a relationship he was satisfied with. He thought it quite reasonable if I should want to be 'in control', but then it would be a Michael Palin show and not a Jones/Palin show, and, in that case, TJ would be happy to come in and edit and work on scripts after I'd written them and do some performing if needed, but in the meantime would rather get his teeth into another project of his own.

However, I value Terry and his judgement too much to just use it for a half-day every two weeks – and I know that Terry would never be

1 A reference, I think, to the broad comedy style of Jimmy Edwards, who played the headmaster of Chiselbury School in the TV sitcom *Whack-O!* (1956–60; 1971–2). It was written by Frank Muir and Denis Norden.

happy if he didn't have the freedom to contribute and develop ideas from the start. So, though I do want to keep it the Michael Palin show, I do not want to lose Terry and so we agree that it will be an equal talents, equal involvement show.

All happy at the end of the meal – except that I can't quite see how it can be equal if I am to do the bulk of the performing.

Friday, November 7th

To Robin Powell's in the morning. Deborah cleaned my teeth out as usual with the frightful pointed, nerve-jarring steel prong, but she talks more about Python, etc, each time I go, and this time we chatted for 25 minutes and gum-gouged for only ten. She tells me Robin Powell is to be made a professor. It's all very hush-hush at the moment, but he's the first ever Professor of Periodontal Surgery. Feel quite proud to have been treated by him. Despite his gloom three or four years ago, my teeth are still not falling out.

Monday, November 10th, Southwold

Up to Southwold.

Last week Father had a fall when out walking past Bullard's Farm – and cut his head in several places. He was taken to Southwold Hospital for stitches and is being kept in there, as Dr Hopkins is worried about the state of his legs – for the fall this time was quite serious, and seemed to have no other cause than his legs giving way.

Southwold was cold and inhospitable today. In the little cottage hospital Daddy was sitting up, but his head looked in a bad way, with three quite severe lacerations and lots of minor cuts and bruises.

He seemed pleased to see me, and laughed self-deprecatingly when I mentioned his fall. But he couldn't say more than half a dozen words in the entire hour we were there. This appalling difficulty with his speech – which, as he cannot write legibly for more than half a sentence, amounts to an almost total inability to communicate – was the single most obvious indication of the deterioration of his condition since I last saw him. This Parkinson's does demean people so much. It certainly has rendered him almost helpless – and on today's standards, I can't see any likelihood of him returning to the form of his 75th birthday party.

Tuesday, November 11th

A gorgeous morning. A slight frost disappearing as the bright November sun makes the fields steam. Sharp fresh smells of the countryside.

Back to London by a quarter to twelve, time to get back home on the Broad Street line, change, grab a quick coffee and drive down to Berkeley Square to have lunch with John Cleese at Morton's. I rang John at the end of last week, as I just suddenly felt like a chat with him – warmed, as I had been, by his quite superbly funny performances in *Fawlty Towers*.

We drank a couple of whisky sours at the bar and, as so often happens to John, we're joined at the bar by a rather boring man, an architect, who was just off, as he put it, to 'Saudi'. Five years ago, if a man had said he was going to Saudi Arabia, you'd probably think he'd been in trouble with the police. Now it's where the money is – and the resourceful Brits are engaged tooth and nail in the process of bringing back the money we're paying for the Arabs' oil.

We go up to the restaurant and, despite his having just completed a very funny, widely praised series on the awful way people can be treated in hotels and restaurants, John and I are shown to the smallest table in the room, at which John has great difficulty in actually sitting. We share a bottle of Puligny Montrachet and tuck into smoked trout and eggs Benedict, looking out over Berkeley Square.

John is still not living with Connie and sounds sad about it … my God, he's the third person I've had lunch with in five days who's separated in the last year. Otherwise a good chat – both John and I feel that everyone is better off for having less involvement with Python.

He was strongly defensive when I suggested that there was a certain resentment that he had never been present on any of the film publicity trips. 'I thought people liked going,' was John's response.

There was not much feeling of latent group responsibility in much of what he said – but we nattered on quite absorbed until nearly four o'clock. I then went down to the King's Road, and bought clothes and some very fine Victorian ceramic tiles for our new sitting room shelf.

Dark nights shopping in the King's Road made me long to be warm and indoors, so I dropped in at Nigel's studio to see him and Judy. All was quiet. Nigel says the art market in England is in a deplorable state. They sit sometimes for days with no one coming round – Nigel seems to manage to make ends meet by sales in New York. American money does have its uses.

Sunday, November 16th

A wild, black November day. Rain, strong winds and grey and gloomy light. Nancy L rings in the morning. She's in London for a week.

Nancy is with Arthur Cantor, the genial Jewish impresario who is to put on our show in NY next April. He is a very unobtrusive sort of hustler and has plenty of other things to talk about besides when, where and how much? He is very pleased with himself this evening as, in a collection of 1,000 books which he bought for £550 from the estate of another impresario, 'Binkie' Beaumont, he has discovered some little masterpieces. He showed me two postcards, hand-written by George Bernard Shaw, which he had found tucked into a book. In one of the cards – to a producer or director of *Caesar and Cleopatra* – he tells the recipient not to worry unduly about the casting of Cleopatra, as the play is Caesar's anyway.

Tuesday, November 18th

In the evening I go with Nancy to the Bruce Springsteen concert at Hammersmith Odeon. This is the first show outside the US for a 26-year-old New Jersey boy who has been hailed as the new Dylan, Lennon, Van Morrison and so on. The trouble is that the enormous reputation has been chiefly created by CBS Records and there is a certain scepticism around as to the legendariness of Springsteen. So, was this the New Messiah? Was this to be one of those concerts which fathers tell their sons about in years to come?

Of course the concert didn't start until 45 minutes after the advertised time – and we kept having wretched announcements about it being your last chance to buy cigarettes and smokes before the concert began. The air inside the Odeon was so foul and heavy that this was hardly doing anyone a favour.

Nor did Springsteen start too well. A solo with piano. His croaky, straining voice sounding as though he'd just done a six-week Gumby season, the spotlights all over the place. No, definitely no magic until the full six-piece band strolled on and everyone was riveted by the white suit and matching white trilby of the tubby, middle-aged sax player, Clarence Clemons.

The band went off at such a lick that one could sense the relief. Springsteen leapt into action – twitching and leaping and throwing himself into strange spasms as he urged the band on. The sound system failed to make head or tail of Springsteen's poetry, but the band kept the evening alive – and he did three encores.

Afterwards, a party given by CBS in the balcony bar. Talked with John Walters, a very funny man. He and Peel, whom he produces, are a formidably intelligent pair – well above the general level of Radio 4.

Final word on Springsteen from Walters – 'We came expecting the Messiah, and got Billy Graham instead.'

Wednesday, November 19th

William's five today. He is very neat and tidy with his presents, quite unlike Tom. Having taken them out of their boxes, his chief delight is to put them back in again, and then collect them all together in a cupboard.

Thursday, November 20th

A Python meeting at 22 Park Square East to discuss the New York show in April and to meet A Cantor. John C on the latest form of table-booking at select Mayfair restaurants, 'Er … excuse me, are you being bombed tonight?'

We have a lot of fun deciding on silly names for our US company, or partnership, or whatever it's called. 'Evado-Tax' is the one we all wanted, but Anne really thought there may be problems, as the company is operating on the fringes of legality! So I suggested Paymortax – and so we now have an American company called Paymortax and McWhirter!

Some time spent on the title for the American show. I'd suggested 'Monty Python v. Muhammad Ali' – with 'Muhammad Ali' in enormous letters but very obviously crossed out. John C was worried in case Muhammad Ali got more out of it than we did – and also I think he was afraid that the living legend would come along and thump us on the opening night.

Tuesday, November 25th

Terry comes up after lunch and we go over to Studio 99 in Swiss Cottage to look at the cassette recordings of Python's first ABC compilation.[1] A very cool American voice – the kind we would only use as a send-up – announces, quite seriously, that 'The Wide World of Entertainment presents the Monty Python Show'. It started well, with 'The World's Most Awful Family', which works a treat after the smooth and glossy ABC packaging of the show, but then the cuts begin. The cat-in-the-wall bell push (a big laugh in the studio) is cut, the man pouring blood all over the doctors is cut after the opening lines – before the point of the sketch has even begun. In the 'Montgolfier Brothers' the words 'naughty bits' are bleeped out!!

In fact any reference to bodily function, any slightly risqué word, anything, as Douglas Adams put it, 'to do with life', was single-mindedly expunged.

The cuts which to me seemed the most remarkable were in the 'Neutron' sketch, when I played the US Bombing Commander who had personal odour problems. The character was in, but every appearance was topped and tailed to avoid all reference to his bodily hygiene. As that was the only original and Pythonesque twist to the character, he just came out as a below-average imitation of George C Scott.

Our reaction turned from disbelief and amazement to anger and outrage and eventually resolved into a very clear and simple position.

The first step as far as we're concerned is to let as many people in America as possible know that we disassociate ourselves from the ABC sale and, better still, to let as many people as possible know the reason why. It was suggested that we use our seventeen thousand lawyers to try and put together grounds for an injunction to prevent ABC putting out the second compilation (due in December). However legally unenforceable this may be, at least it's a fair try for a story – 'Python Sues ABC' would be all we'd need.

Monday, December 8th

My wretched cold is hanging on into its second week and really bringing me down. I can't even think straight, let alone smell anything. Terry J

1 ABC, one of the big three American commercial networks, had bought Python's fourth series (without John) and reorganised it into two specials. We had been tipped off that the result was not good and that we should take a look at it.

drops in later in the afternoon. We're both very pleased with the cover of *Dr Fegg's Nasty Book of Knowledge*, which arrived from the States this morning. It's funny and, what's better, it's actually quite interesting as well. There's a lot of detail in Bruce McCall's vision of the 'Great New World of Technology' which you only see after looking at it several times.

Terry and I plunge into discussion of the future. Terry is, as he says, restive at the moment – wants to unleash his straining enthusiasm in some direction, but doesn't know where to go. The Tony Hendra pirate film, *The Legend of the Nancy Hulk*, is still on offer and could tie him up for six or seven months on a major project. I read it at Southwold over the weekend and feel Terry shouldn't do it. Although very funny in some ways – the awful pirate crew are a fine invention – it seems to me to be very second-hand Python. Its costume and period flavour lend a similarity to the *Grail* which is just not backed up by the originality of the writing.

Wednesday, December 10th

To see Dr Freudenberg – as my cold had developed into a regular and implacable headache. In the waiting room, with her little baby, was Lindy, wife of Nick Mason of the Pink Floyd. She was cross – her appointment had been at 10.30, it was now after 11.30. A nice chat. They're not sending their child, Chloe (a little younger than Willy) to Gospel Oak, partly because the classes are too big. I sympathise. She grumbled a little about the legion of financial advisers, etc, which come automatically with all the loot Floyd must be making. They're not the house in Switzerland, private jet mob, though – it's state schools and Kentish Town, and they can't stand the thought of having to leave England for tax reasons. The wealthy anti-rich.

Freudenberg says I have a touch of sinusitis and bronchitis.

Arthur Cantor rang and tried to ask Helen and me out to see the new Ben Travers farce *The Bed Before Yesterday* at the Lyric. Every date he suggested was already full. 'This is getting like the Cheese Shop,' rumbled Arthur. We settled on Monday next. For some reason he has a soft spot for me, and he asked if I would write a play for him. He was very keen and said he would commission it. He sounded as though he wanted me to sign then and there, so I retreated into the Palin shell and promised I would think about it. I really wouldn't mind writing a play –

on my own. But I immediately felt guilty about Terry and cross with myself for feeling guilty and really in quite a muddle.

In the evening we drove over to Wimbledon for a party at the house of Jacqui, David Wood's[1] new wife, next to the Crooked Billet beside Wimbledon Common.

Talked with Andrew Lloyd Webber – he of *Superstar* fame – who made a fortune from a smash hit as soon as he left Oxford.[2] A rather nervous, soft-spoken chap, he said his investment in the Python film was the only thing keeping him going at the moment – after *Jeeves*.[3] He promised to send me a review in a Toronto paper in which the reviewer raved about Python and slammed the indecency in *Jesus Christ Superstar*!

As we drove back across London from this convivial houseful, we passed the police cordons around Dorset Square and, as we waited at the traffic lights, we looked across to the anonymous first-floor flat in Balcombe Street which has suddenly become the focus of national attention. In the flat are a middle-aged couple and four Irish terrorists, one of whom may be, according to the police, the organiser behind the London bombings and shootings of the past two winters.

The flat was floodlit. Groups of police, smiling, telling jokes, stood around at the barriers. There was a Thames TV van with a camera crew on top – even location caterers. It seemed quite unreal. Surely it must be night filming? Surely it must be a scripted adventure? But I suppose in that little living room in Balcombe Street, there are five people whose lives have now been totally altered. The lights changed and off we went to our cosy, non-floodlit little home.[4]

Thursday, December 11th

School concert. Tom was the Pied Piper, with words to say and music to play. He looked lovely and full of mischievous grins at the audience. Willy was a snowflake in his first ever concert.

1 Actor, and writer of many children's shows, David had appeared in *The Oxford Line*, a revue I produced and directed for the Edinburgh Festival in 1965.
2 This was *Joseph and the Amazing Technicolor Dreamcoat*. Lloyd Webber was a small investor in *Holy Grail*.
3 *By Jeeves*, a rare Lloyd Webber/Tim Rice flop.
4 The six-day siege ended, peacefully, two days later, when the IRA gunmen gave themselves up. They were charged with ten murders and twenty bombings and jailed for life. They were released in April 1999 as part of the Good Friday Agreement.

Friday, December 12th

Anne rings in the evening. Everyone apart from Eric and Graham, who hasn't been contacted, is solidly in favour of legal action – i.e. the injunction against ABC. Ina Lee M has already spent several thousand dollars of our money to take advice as to whether or not our case is strong. She assures us that we will only have to pay $15,000 *if* the case is to be fought and, if we win and they appeal, maybe $20,000 more on the appeal. So the injunction is almost on its way and I feel it *is* worthwhile carrying it through.

In the evening Jimmy Gilbert rings. He tells me that *Tomkinson* is to be shown on BBC2 on January 7th. He calls its transmission 'a first night' – a chance for him to gauge reaction. So clearly he is not yet decided on a series.

Sunday, December 14th

Things are gathering momentum. Just after 10.00, with fresh papers to read and bacon and eggs cooking, phone rings. It is T Gilliam. He wants me to go with him to the US tomorrow to be present in New York as Python representatives during the injunction action, etc, etc. We would return Wednesday.

Monday, December 15th

Very heavy frost. Collected by large Jaguar at 9.15, full of Terry Gilliam, in his big white furry Afghan coat, which he is painting himself. From 11.00 to 4.30 sit on our British Airways jumbo jet at Heathrow gazing out at the ever-thickening fog. Feel very glad that Anne talked us into going First Class – despite our guilt feelings. Attentive waiters served champagne and, when it became obvious, round about 4.00, that there would be no flights from Heathrow today, they offered to serve those of us who wanted it a meal.

The airport was silent and visibility down to about ten yards when we left. The cab journey home took well over an hour. But Helen was glad to see me back – and we enjoyed a sort of bonus evening – an evening we weren't meant to have.

Nancy was apparently waiting with newsmen in New York – all eager for the story – whilst Gilliam and I were enjoying a rare uninterrupted natter, lasting from nine till six, aboard our fogbound restaurant at Heathrow.

Tuesday, December 16th, New York

When we arrived at Heathrow at about 11.15 it was fairly obvious that the Queen Mother herself could hardly expect to get a second look at the check-in counters. The BA Intercontinental check-in area was a mass of people, becoming more solid all the time.

In eccentric British fashion, many people were trying to be more cheerful in the face of it. One cantankerous Scotsman was the only exception to all this. He carped and grumbled loudly and consistently and wagged his finger at the BA girl when he got to the counter, telling her how she couldn't expect him to travel by her airline again – which must have been the only bit of good news for her that morning.

Anne had fortunately also booked us on TWA's 2.30 flight, so we fought our way out of the crush and across to the TWA section. It was almost deserted – and not only this, but they were duplicating their flight of yesterday, and did have two seats in First Class. So, from the totally unproductive frustration of a few minutes earlier, we suddenly found ourselves within an hour taking off for New York. A day and a half late, I suppose.

We reached New York about 3.30 their time, after a long, clear run in down the length of Long Island. A huge limousine, sent by Nancy, met us at JFK, and drew us comfortably across the 49th Street Bridge and into the Big Apple. All fine, except that TWA have lost my bag.

There is a great deal of interest and sympathy for Python's case. We make short articles on the Television pages of the *New York Times* and *New York Post*. In the *Times* we learnt for the first time that Time-Life had edited the shows in collaboration with ABC – and that several of the cuts had been made by ABC, said a spokesman, because some passages were considered 'inappropriate'.

One slightly ominous note, though – Nancy says the court hearing is on Friday – and yet we have to leave Thursday night at latest.

Wednesday morning, December 17th, New York

Up at 9.30. Walk across to the Stage Delicatessen for breakfast. Eggs, bacon, coffee, bagels, cottage cheese.

Up to Nancy's office at Buddah where we meet Rik Hertzberg – good old friend from *The New Yorker*. We have a good time and give him a lot of information, including, for the first time, copies of letters, affidavits and other court material. Rick is not just a good and sympathetic friend – he also, in his *New Yorker* piece earlier this year [welcoming the Python TV series], has the immeasurable skill of being able to quote our material and still make it sound funny.

After an hour or so with Rick, we take a cab down Broadway to Sardi's for lunch with John O'Connor – another Python sympathiser and TV critic of the *New York Times*. It's interesting how much greater access we have to TV journalists and writers in New York than in London.

From Sardi's the Dynamic Duo, the Fighters for Freedom, find themselves in a rather dingy doorway next to Cartier's shop in Fifth Avenue, waiting for an elevator up to see the lawyers whom Ina has hired to represent us in our struggle against the American Broadcasting Companies, Inc.

They're led by short, blond-haired Robert Osterberg, he must be mid-thirties. A fit, tidy, rather bland sort of man with the eyes and smile, but unfortunately nothing else, of Kirk Douglas.

He begins by saying that we really ought to be in court on Friday. He says, quite rightly, that if no Pythons are prepared to be in New York to defend their own case, that case is immeasurably weakened. And so on. He's right of course, but both Terry and I have avoided confronting the awful, stomach-gripping truth that we will actually have to defend our position in a US Federal court. Now that's almost a certainty and I have to let Helen know that I won't be back for the Gospel Oak Old Folk's Party. In addition, TWA have still not found my case, so I'm unshaven and crumpled and tired as well as shit-scared.

Thursday, December 18th, New York

Feel much calmer about the whole court bit now. Rang Helen, which was the worst thing I had to get over. It was twenty past eight here and I was in bed in the Navarro, with sunny New York outside – and Helen was in her fog-bound Gospel Oak kitchen with the kids all wanting things. There really couldn't be much contact. I just had to tell her the facts – very unsatisfactory, but now she knows, I know she'll get over it and begin to make other plans and I'm sure friends will rally round. So I feel better now. I feel ready for a fight.

We breakfast at the Grand Central Café. (Good news for Grand Central Station fans – yesterday a demolition and development plan for it was finally quashed.)

A visit to the lawyers, then all of us in a deadly accusing phalanx – Ina, Osterberg plus one, Terry G and myself – make our way over to ABC TV. A slender, not unattractive thirty-five-storey dark stone and glass block … this is what we're taking on.

Up to the twenty-first floor.

We're at ABC today because they yesterday relented their earlier decision not to let us see the proposed December 26th compilation – and the lawyers regard this viewing today as a significant concession. ABC's point is that, if we find that the compilation we see at today's viewing is acceptable, then the whole case may be dropped.

We meet, for the first time, the highly plausible and eligible Bob Shanks, who is Head of Night Time and Early Morning Programming at ABC. Intelligent, charming and the man ultimately responsible for our being in New York today. With him is a member of their legal department – a lady in her late thirties, early forties with a long-suffering look in her eyes and a kindly, almost saintly face, as in a sixteenth-century religious painting.

At this stage it's smiles, handshakes, genial informality as far as we're concerned – but for Ina and Bob Osterberg detached cool politeness is the order of the day. At one point early on in the discussion, Bob appears quite irrationally strong with Shanks – and we feel the first hint of a fight … the first punch thrown and missed as Osterberg raises his voice over a point and Shanks charms quietly back, 'Let's not shout at each other … let's just talk about it in a reasonable way.'

ABC at this point present us with a list of their cuts in the three shows we are about to see. A cursory glance at the list shows that our trip to New York has not been wasted. There are thirty-two proposed cuts. Some ludicrous – 'damn' cut out twice, 'bitch' as describing a dog cut out, etc, etc.

I think that ABC were quite honestly taken aback by our reaction. I just wanted to walk out, but Osterberg advised us to see all the shows, which was obviously good sense.

Next to me on the couch as I told them that the cuts they suggested were totally unacceptable and, in our opinion, ludicrous, was a young, short-haired, conventionally handsome executive, whose eyes would not look at ours for long, and whose face was flushed with confusion. He turned out to be the head of ABC TV's Standards and Practices Department and a Vice-President of the Company.

This was the man whom ABC pay to censor their programmes – the man who had actually decided that the American public wasn't ready for 'naughty bits' – the man who had decided that Eric Idle as Brian Clough dressed as Queen Victoria was a homosexual reference and should therefore be cut. Judging by the list he had compiled one would expect him to be a sort of obsessive religious maniac. A wild eccentric who lived on top of a mountain seeking to preserve himself and his few remaining followers from the final onslaught of the people who say 'damn'.

But the deceit is that of course he was himself no more offended by these words than I am. He laughed, as they all laughed, when we talked about cutting a 'tit' here and a 'tit' there – and yet he will not permit others in his country to have the choice of laughing at those words as well. 'It's alright for us, but we've got to think about people in the South – in Baton Rouge and Iowa as well.' Then we tell him that Python has been running in Baton Rouge and Iowa for over a year on PBS, without complaint.

It all seems so pointless, in this little viewing room in a comfortable office block with a group of people playing idiotic games with each other, but then I remember the power of ABC – the ability to beam a show simultaneously into all the sets in the USA. The papers we have talked to, the radio shows we have talked to, can never hope to reach anything but a small proportion of the audience our mutilated show can reach via ABC.

Our lawyers play games – their lawyers play games. After viewing all the shows we begin sort of negotiations. This involves a worried lady lawyer for ABC asking us if we would ever consider the possibility of re-editing. Yes, we say, despite the obvious harm the 90-minute format and the commercial breaks will do, we would consider re-editing. Their ears prick up. Our re-editing would be based entirely on artistic and comedic criteria. If in the course of *our* cutting some of their censored words were lost, then fair enough.

'Are there any cuts which we propose,' she says, 'that you would agree with?' 'No,' we say, 'It's easier for us to tell you cuts on which we will *never* negotiate and you can work backwards from there.' We single eight points out of the first twelve on which we are immovable.

Much to-ing and fro-ing. The lady and the zombie reappear. Yes …

there could be some negotiation, but first can we tell them the points in the two other shows which we would be prepared to talk over. Here Osterberg starts to play the impatience game. And quite rightly. He insists, on behalf of his clients, of course, that ABC must first agree to restore all the eight cuts which we regard as non-negotiable. And here they baulk, and the lady lawyer looks more and more desperate, and the zombie walks out and leaves her to us, just as Shanks has earlier ditched him.

Osterberg orders us to put our coats on and we make our way across the heavy, soft carpet, past the clean, neat white desks, with their clean, neat white telephones, towards the elevators. The lady lawyer implores us to keep talking. 'I've been asked to settle this,' she pleads, her eyes moistening with what I would say was genuine fear – whether of us or of her superiors I don't know. Terry G and I smile sheepishly and the elevator doors close.

Over to the Stage Deli for lunch to restore our sense of proportion. Thank goodness we have each other to compare notes with. I like TG because he is very sane, very realistic, entirely down-to-earth. A couple of waitresses ask us for autographs. They'd loved the *Holy Grail*.

Back to the lawyers later. A gruelling and concentrated working-over of our testimony for two hours, followed by further rehearsals and a taste of cross-questioning.

It was decided that Nancy L should be our first witness in court, followed by myself – through whom Osterberg would bring out all the salient points of our testimony – followed by Terry G, who would weigh in with lavish doses of enthusiasm, conviction and generally play the bruised artist.

Ray, Bob Osterberg's junior, gave me some sample cross-questioning. Although I knew full well it was just a rehearsal, I couldn't help getting thoroughly riled by his techniques of incredulousness, heavy sarcasm and downright mocking misrepresentation. All – he assured me afterwards – perfectly permissible legal techniques for breaking down witnesses. All I can say is, they worked. I left the office around 11.00 feeling tired, depressed and angry. Totally evaporated was my clear-eyed crusading enthusiasm of yesterday. I realised now that it was to be a sordid struggle played on their terms, not ours.

Friday, December 19th, New York

Woke about 6.00 this morning. Felt well rested and, after a pee, turned over to go to sleep again when it hit me – with a sudden heart-thumping, palm-sweating realisation. In three and a half hours I would be reliving the horrors of the evening before – only this time in court and for real. Across the suite, in the other bedroom, TG had woken at about the same time.

I lay there and tried to accept the extraordinary day ahead philosophically. There was no alternative – we were doing the only right thing. We weren't having to lie or defend a dishonourable course of action. We just had to remember the purity of our initial indignation and it would all turn out fine – and anyway, by this evening we'd be on a plane back to London.

And yet my mind kept racing over possible fresh arguments, trying to turn and hone fine new phrases – only to suddenly discover weaknesses in my recollection. Surely lawyers didn't go through this every morning before an important case – they'd go mad.

As I was shaving – my case having been finally delivered to me by TWA in the early hours of Thursday morning – TG appeared, with a towel wrapped round him. He paced the room restlessly, looking quite idiotic in his towel and saying, 'I've got it … the *real* point is …' Then his eyes would take on a Martin Luther King-like intensity and I would hear phrases like, 'If just one. Just show me one person whose opinion of Python has suffered as a result of ABC … just one … and that is enough for me.' This was Gilliam's new line. He seemed on good form, but he and I nevertheless took a good shot of Bourbon before leaving the suite.

I try hard to keep a hold on reality, but it's difficult as TG and I and Nancy, with our entourage of lawyers, mount the steps of the vast twenty-storey tower of the US Federal Court House in Foley Square.

At first glance the courtroom was softer, warmer and far less intimidating than I expected. As plaintiffs in the case, we were allowed to sit with our lawyers at a vast and solid table in the front of the court, with the judge's box raised about four or five feet above us, and between him and us the enclosure for the clerks of the court and the court recorders. On our left the jury box, empty of course. Behind the jury box a line of tall windows brightened the court. Immediately behind us the ABC lawyers' table and then, at the back, about a dozen rows of wooden benches for spectators.

The hearing began with the entry of the judge behind a clerk of the court, who was not the old and wrinkled be-robed gent I had expected, but a young, casually dressed, Brooklyn-accented, probably Jewish, 20–25-year-old girl. She looked like the archetypal Python fan, and it's some indication of how surprisingly and pleasantly informal it all was, that I very nearly corpsed when she stood and made some odd opening ritual about 'Hear ye ... Hear ye ... Yeah verily ...' and other strange nonsense. I was reminded perversely of *The Exorcist*, in which another perfectly ordinary all-American girl is made to say strange things and speak with strange voices.

The judge, Morris Lasker, was not robed either. I wondered whether or not he had seen the Python show which went out in New York on PBS last night, which contained a sketch about a judges' beauty contest!

Nancy testified first – speaking softly and looking composed, but endearingly vulnerable. The judge was correspondingly gentle with her. He was a honey-voiced, sensible, straightforward sort of fellow, anxious it seemed to avoid long legal discussions. As he said, he had read and studied the legal side of the case – today he wanted to hear witnesses. After Nancy, there was a short break for no apparent reason, then I gave testimony.

It was quite comfortable in the witness box – there was a chair, which I hadn't expected, and I was on the same level as the judge, which helped to put me at ease. As with Nancy, he was kindly throughout my evidence and cross-examination, repeatedly overruling ABC lawyer Clarence Fried's objections. I was not grilled particularly hard by Mr Fried. He had a face like an old, wrinkled prune, and kept pursing his lips in a sort of twitch. He wasn't anywhere near as aggressive or sardonic or incredulous as I had anticipated from the cross-questioning rehearsal last night.

The most difficult bit was having to describe sketches to the court which had been cut and make them sound funny.

One of the ABC-mutilated sketches which I had to describe to the court actually involved a fictional courtroom, in which an army deserter is being tried before a judge who is constantly interrupting with highly detailed queries. At one point the judge is particularly persistent about a pair of 'special' gaiters worn by the deserter.

What made the gaiters 'special' asks the judge?

'They were given him as a token of thanks by the regiment,' replies the prosecutor.

The judge asks why.

'Because, m'lud, he made them happy. In little ways.'

'In which little ways did he make them happy?' persists the judge.

At this point a bizarre situation became truly surreal as the prosecutor in the real court interrupted me and addressed the judge, in the real court. The following exchange is from the official transcripts:

'Mr Fried: Your honor, this is very amusing and interesting, but I think it is off the track.

'The Court [Judge Lasker]: Mr Palin is trying to tell me what the original was like so he can tell me what the effect of the excision will be. Overruled. Go ahead. I am not sitting here just because I am amused, although I am amused.'

Terry Gilliam testified after me. From where I was he sounded very straight, honest and direct. A real all-American boy.

Then, despite attempts from ABC's lawyer to put it off, the really damning evidence was produced. A colour TV was wheeled in and the judge, and as many as could squeeze in around him, took their places in the jury box to watch two tapes. The first was Show 3 of the fourth series of Monty Python – as it was shown on the BBC. A good show, with the 'Court Martial', 'Gorn' and 'RAF Banter' sketches in it. It went down well. The court recorder chuckled a great deal, as did the judge and the people operating the TV recorder. Definitely a success. Then was shown the ABC version of the same show.

The ABC version contained long gaps of blank screen where the commercials would go. Three such major breaks in the course of half an hour. The effect on the audience was obvious. It was the end of a very good morning for us.

After lunch Fried began to call his witnesses. A Mr Burns of ABC's Contracts Department spoke laboriously and with infinite, finely tuned dullness about the possible loss of money caused if the show was cancelled.

Shanks was next. He turned on a bravura display of ingratiating smugness. Oh, he'd been a writer in his time, he grinned. He knew the problems ... goddammit, he wouldn't like to lose a line of his own material ... but ... (Could this be the same man who was quite prepared to authorise the excision of 22 minutes out of 90 minutes of Python material? Talk of not wanting to lose a line – we were losing one line in every four!)

Fried bored the pants off everyone with heavy-jowled witnesses from Time-Life who all looked as if they were concealing mass-murders.

But a jarring note was struck at the end of the day when a lady at ABC testified that Ina Lee Meibach had rung her on December 10th and had told her that we were not only going to sue ABC, but we were going to drag their names through the mud and squeeze every last ounce of publicity from their predicament. For the first time in the entire proceedings we suddenly felt bad. We were found to be using distasteful, though doubtless common, tactics, and I think it reflects a serious weakness on Ina's part. She is sometimes *too* tough – she takes firmness to the point of vindictiveness.

At 5.00, as it darkened out in Foley Square, the judge finally withdrew. He re-appeared a half-hour or so later and delivered an impressively fluent summing-up which began by raising our hopes at the plaintiffs' table.

He found that ABC's cuts were very major and destroyed an important element of Python's appeal. He found our material was irreparably damaged. My heart leapt. 'But,' he went on to say that he could not grant the injunction for two reasons. One was that the BBC owned the copyright of the tapes sold to ABC, so the BBC should really have been in court too. He was disturbed by the delay in our proceeding against ABC, and had to take into account the amount of damage to ABC by our proceeding against them less than one week from the transmission date. So ... ABC were off the hook. We'd tilted at windmills and lost.

'But ...' Lasker, with a fine sense of timing, had one more twist for us ... because of the nature of the damage to us, he would look very favourably on any disclaimer the Pythons would like to put in front of the show when it went out on December 26th. There he finished – and our hopes were raised again. A disclaimer could be as strong and effective as a total ban on the show. Everyone would see us blame ABC openly.

Typical of ABC's extraordinary lack of understanding was that, following this verdict, they approached Terry G and suggested we work out a jokey little disclaimer together!

Out in Foley Square about 6.15. The cold, sub-zero wind whipping around us as we search for a subway entrance. A dark-coated, pipe-smoking figure, head bent down against the wind, crosses the square towards us. It's none other than Judge Lasker. He shows we three frozen plaintiffs the subway and walks down there with us. Alas we have no tokens for the barrier. The judge scrabbles around in his pockets, but can only find two to give us. Give me the money, he suggests, and he'll go through the barrier, buy us some tokens from the kiosk on the other side and hand them through to us.

We travelled, strap-hanging, with the judge, up to Grand Central Station. The nearest he got to talking about the case was when Terry G voiced his worries that the existence and the modus vivendi of the Standards and Practices Department of ABC was never questioned, and surely should have been. Yes, said Lasker, he too was worried about the Standards and Practices Department.

He merged into the crowds at Grand Central and we made our way back to the Navarro, packed our bags and, leaving Nancy and Kay-Gee-Bee Music with the bill, stretched out in an enormous limousine which bore us from the rather pretty Christmas atmosphere of New York away out to JFK yet again.

All usual flights to London until next week being booked, we found ourselves on Air Iran's flight to Tehran via Heathrow. So new was the flight that apparently the booking clerks at JFK didn't even know it stopped at London.

Saturday, December 20th

Woke uncomfortably with the dawn. Feeling dirty, crumpled and dreadfully tired – as only those who fly the Atlantic overnight *can* feel. The plane started to drip on Terry G ... but the hostesses were cheerfully dismissive of his complaints.

I have to wait for at least an hour at Christmas-crowded Heathrow before ascertaining that my case is definitely on its way to Tehran.

Monday, December 22nd

Further news of Python's ever-increasing international status – some fine reviews for *Holy Grail* in France. 'Mieux que Mel Brooks' – that sort of thing – and the film has apparently opened at a fourth cinema in Paris.

Wednesday, December 24th, Abbotsley

The harsh realities of the world away from the cosy log fires of Church Farm impinged deadeningly and depressingly. Terry Gilliam rang to say that, after Judge Lasker had accepted, with minor alterations, our disclaimer for the front of ABC's Boxing Day Special, ABC had appealed, on Monday afternoon, to three other judges, who had overruled his decision. All that will appear are the words 'Edited for television by ABC'.[1]

So, in terms of actual tangible legal rewards for our week in New York and the $15,000 of Python money spent on the case, we were left with very little. I wait to see evidence of the non-legal rewards, in terms of press coverage, etc, etc, before totally writing off our trip, but today's news was a pretty nasty Christmas present. But at least my bag arrived, having reached Abbotsley via Tehran.

Wednesday, December 31st

Almost the last event of 1975 is also one of the most important – the showing on BBC2 of *Three Men in a Boat*. We have quite a houseful here by 7.50 when it begins. Catherine Burd is watching with Tom and Willy (who are allowed to stay up) and Jeremy and Alex [neighbours] with their children, both a long way from the sitting still and shutting up age, are here as well. So quite a crowd, and it's rather difficult to judge the piece – especially as Stephen has opted for a very gently paced, softly played treatment – which seems to be at least ten decibels quieter than any other TV shows. I keep turning the sound up and sitting nearer, but it's very difficult not to be distracted and I really don't feel I've seen it in the best circumstances when it draws to its languid conclusion at 8.55.

1 We had wanted: 'The members of Monty Python wish to dissociate themselves from this programme, which is a compilation of their shows edited by ABC without their approval.'

1976

Up at 9.00 to gather all the papers. The *Daily Telegraph* calls *Three Men* 'as near to television perfection as makes very little matter'. A rave, no less. But, as I had expected, reviews were mixed and there was a very extensive and less friendly review in *The Times* by Michael Ratcliffe. Large photo above it and ominous heading 'Playing A Very Straight Bat'. Criticism of the lack of humour was the key note – Frears accused of being unable to 'find a comic style faithful to both writers' – Jerome K Jerome and T Stoppard, I presume. A pity that the *Times* review will be the one my friends will see. The *Daily Tel* may be a blue-rinse rag politically, but they do have extremely perceptive TV critics! No other reviews.

A very cordial Python meeting at Park Square East to discuss the content of our stage show in New York. Once again proved that Python works well as a group when discussing the creation of sketches and jokes – the reason, after all, why we originally got together. Python group at its worst discussing business, contracts, hiring and firing personnel, and other areas which we are better at making fun of than taking seriously.

Today, 'Blackmail' was added to the list, John having said that, although he may be sounding rather selfish, he wanted to cut down the number of sketches he appeared in, and he felt that I was very light in number of appearances. So 'Michael Miles' out and 'Blackmail' in. Graham protested briefly, but the general consensus was that 'Cocktail Bar' should go, along with the 'Bruces' and the 'Pepperpots' in a big purge of the generally accepted weak middle of the first half. In went 'Salvation Fuzz' (entirely new to stage), 'Crunchy Frog' (ditto) – with Graham taking John's role as Inspector Praline – and an amalgamation of court sketches to replace 'Silly Elections' as a closer.

Judging by today's meeting, it really seems that Python has emerged remarkably healthily from the mire of the last two years. There's a much friendlier, looser, more open feeling amongst the members of the group now. I wonder if it will weather the month's hard work on the New York stage show, and if it will produce an equally friendly and relaxed working atmosphere for September and October, when we get together to write the third Python film.

Strong, violent, gusting gales tonight. Up to 105mph in Cambridgeshire and many people killed (twenty-four).

Saturday, January 3rd

A busy, socialising weekend. Liz Garden rang on Saturday morning to ask if they could come over and fly Sally's new kite on Parliament Hill. I warned her about me and kites – that the two should never meet – but, despite warnings, Graeme, Sally, Tom, Willy and I braved a finger-numbing wind on the lower slopes of Parliament Hill. Bill Oddie had given Sally the kite, as he is now apparently a very serious kiter – a 'Formula One' kite flyer, as Graeme calls him.

True to form, I rip part of the thin cellophane fabric before the kite's even been flown. Several desperate attempts to get it in the air – it twists, wheels, turns like a bucking stallion at a rodeo, before plunging, inevitably, into the ground. After half an hour, when we think we have at last mastered the ballistics problem, Willy treads well-intentionally on one of the struts and the kite is finally written off.

Off to Le Routier at Camden Lock for lunch.

Very different from our local Queen's Crescent Market – the stall-holders are your traditional cockneys there – here at Camden Lock the stalls are run by the New Wave of stallholders – young, middle-class, usually feminine, emphasis on the arts and crafts and inter-stall talk about recent Fassbinder movies. Also appalling tat – they will clearly sell anything – as evidenced by several copies of the 1971 AA Book.

Sunday, January 4th

A couple of reviews in the Sundays. Philip Purser very favourable in the *Sunday Telegraph* – 'the languid trio was beautifully cast' – while Peter Lennon in the *Sunday Times* gave a brief and rather churlish dismissal of the whole piece, saying that Frears allowed his actors to settle 'for a relentlessly arch air which quickly grew tedious' and the Three Men 'suffered from an inability to sound at ease delivering lines which read agreeably enough in quaint, old-fashioned essay, but needed more drastic transformation by Tom Stoppard to work as dia-logue'. So raps on the knuckles all round. Against all my better feel-ings I was goaded into a short burst of bitter anger by the *Sunday Times* review. But it passed and rational thought returned.

Took boys to swim at the Holiday Inn for an hour, then Terry with
Alison and Sally arrived bringing their Christmas presents. They gave
Tom and Willy a steamroller, a beautiful, solid, working model, complete with whistle which blows a column of steam up your nostrils if
you're not careful. Terry and I then drove out to Acton to play in a
charity football match.

A rather forlorn, rain-soaked notice tied to the railings, which read
'Big Charity Match: All Stars XI v Happy Wanderers'.

A very strange afternoon altogether. I scored an own goal (though
we won in the end). TJ scored his first goal since he was ten, there was an
apparently total absence of any paying spectators, the changing room
was minute and the beer was Watney's Red Barrel. Oh, the glamorous
life of an All Star!

Wednesday, January 7th

Very warm again. Temps over 50. Sitting up in my room as I have done,
with great pleasure, for the last three mornings. The boys went back to
school on Monday and I embarked on a vast pile of letters – mostly
from America. In two days I wrote about twenty-three replies to fan
letters (*not* the very naughty ones!) plus a four-page New Year missive to
Alfred Lord Levinson.

Today is *Tomkinson* day. To Terry J's to watch the show. Also there
are Eric, Terry Gilliam, Chuck A,[1] Nigel and Dizzy.[2] The show looks fine.
The reaction within the group of us was very, very good. Terry G ... 'Ah,
well ... you've got no problems with that.' Chuck chuckled throughout.
Eric was highly enthusiastic. Terry Hughes rang to tell me that Ronnie
Barker had called him as soon as it finished to say how much he liked it.

When we got home later my head and stomach were suffering from
excitement, relief, tacos and too much cheap Spanish wine. Kitty, our
baby-sitter, had a list of calls which she'd rather nicely headed 'People
who enjoyed *Tomkinson's Schooldays*'. Graham C rang to say how much
better it was than he remembered it. Went to bed feeling rather ill.

1 Charles Alverson, American thriller-writer friend of TG.
2 Terry's brother and sister-in-law.

Thursday, January 8th

Gradually dawns on me during the day that *Tomkinson* has been something of a success. But for all the right reasons – nearly everyone who has liked it has mentioned its quality. Fresh, different, etc, etc. A meaty and handsome review in *The Times* by Alan Coren makes my day. Met Denis Norden in a shop, and he grasped my hand and told me he hadn't laughed so much since before Christmas!

Finally, as the shadows were lengthening over Gospel Oak, Jimmy Gilbert rang to give the official BBC verdict. He wants me to go in next Monday and talk about more shows.

I'm as pleased for Terry Hughes as I am for anyone. He worked the BBC system superbly – got us everything we wanted. He was always in sympathy with the script and its intentions and had an instructive and highly accurate sense of where it worked and didn't work.

Monday, January 12th

The continuing backwash of enthusiasm for *Tomkinson's Schooldays* has helped enormously – our reception by Jimmy at lunch in his office was tinged with more than just his usual cordiality – there was an undeniable air of self-congratulation which resulted in broader smiles, firmer handshakes and a generally more relaxed feeling. Only on a couple of occasions after Python's success did I ever feel this warm glow of unstinted BBC approval and even then it seemed qualified because of our naughty, enfant terrible reputation.

Then there's the question of front money from America. Jim clearly regards himself as something of a transatlantic supersalesman, and is working hard on Time-Life (whom Gilliam and I dragged into court less than a month ago!) to buy a series based on the successful *Tomkinson*, and therefore put up front money so that the BBC can afford our expensive services.

Out of all this we won several points. In the end Jimmy agreed that Terry Hughes should direct them all, he also agreed (a momentous point of principle here) that we could, if we needed to, do entire shows *on film*. I never thought I would live to hear a BBC Head of Comedy make such an heretical suggestion. In return for all this, Terry and I will supply the BBC with thirteen *Tomkinson*-style shows by mid-summer 1978.

Thursday, January 15th

About 1.00 Terry and I drove out to Beaconsfield in Bucks to talk about ourselves to the National Film School (Brian Winston, ex-Oxford and *World in Action*, having hustled us into it quite successfully).

It has the run-down air of a half-deserted RAF camp. There are suggestions of over-grown roads and pathways – the buildings are stark, functional and presumably cheap brick and concrete constructions without any refinements. It used to be the Crown Film Unit Studios, where 'chin-up' patriotic films were made to boost the nation's morale in wartime. Ironic, really, because it wouldn't do the nation's morale a lot of good to see it now.

Terry and I are there as part of a week's seminar on comedy. Winston told us afterwards, rather glumly, that there wasn't really anyone there who wanted to, or could, make comedy films. They were all too serious. We talked for almost two hours to about twenty students. They had watched *Tomkinson's Schooldays* in the morning and discussed it in terms of social relevance, criticism of authority, etc. I think they were a little disappointed when I told them that the choice of public school for the story was made simply because its absurd rituals and closed formal world were a very good area for jokes. Even Brian Winston, who was trying hard to defuse any pretentiousness, still referred to the nailing-to-the-wall joke as the 'crucifixion' sequence.

Friday, January 16th

Anne had had quite a traumatic meeting this afternoon with Arthur Cantor (who is over in England for two weeks) and Jim Beach[1] to try and finalise the Live Show deal for New York. The outcome was that Cantor has at last backed out. Cantor is a cautious, kindly theatre producer who likes to get to know the people he's working with and is temperamentally quite unsuited to the world of big advances, limousines, $75,000-worth of publicity – mostly to be spent on 'Sold Out' kind of advertising, and general image-building, which Nancy and Ina's people have been insisting on. Ina's office lose yet more popularity points by having apparently on our behalf been thoroughly unpleasant to A Cantor – who may be a little over-cautious and vacillating, but is a decent man.

1 Our legal adviser at the time. Later manager of Queen.

So now Anne is having to fix up Allen Tinkley [another American producer] and yet another rather shoddy chapter in Python's American adventure is closed.

Saturday, January 17th

Took the boys out in the morning to a Journey Through Space exhibition at the Geological Museum in South Ken.

Afterwards Tom and Willy pressed buttons in the How the Earth Began exhibition and we watched a film of a volcanic eruption, with a truly fantastic shot of a wall of lava just slowly enveloping a country road. Even better than the Goodies.

Late afternoon, and T Gilliam comes round. He now has a typed script of his *Jabberwocky* film, which runs at two and a half hours! He has seen *Jaws!* and was impressed – he's decided to try and make the threat of the Jabberwocky as frightening as the threat of the shark.

Wednesday, January 21st

I sat and dug deeper into *Something Happened* after supper. Joseph Heller is another important and original American humorist, but *Something Happened* doesn't make you laugh like *Catch-22*. It's a bleak account of modern American materialistic man and the extraordinarily bad state of his personal relationships and his ability to communicate. The portrait of Slocum, surrounded by family and friends, is nevertheless of a man as apart from his fellow beings as Meursault in Camus' *L'Étranger*. But Heller has a good, perceptive eye, and the joy of the work comes from catching a glimpse of yourself in a mirror – a moment of recognition of yourself – and of yourself in relation to other people.

Finally, watched *The Glittering Prizes* – a 'major new drama series' as the BBC call it. Scripts by Frederic Raphael (who wrote *Darling, Nothing But the Best* etc), six 80-minute plays about a group of Cambridge students of the early '50s. I rather admired this first one – 'liked' isn't quite the word – it was cleverly, neatly written, it bore all the trademarks of the Cambridge urbanity, wit, worldliness, which Oxford never seemed to quite share – certainly *I* didn't (perhaps that's what I'm saying).

Thursday, January 22nd

Tomorrow I must be on the ball, for even more important discussions, this time about the professional future, must be raised with Terry as a result of a couple of calls from Jimmy Gilbert who has once again emphasised that he would like the *Tomkinson* series to be a Michael Palin series, written by Michael Palin and Terry Jones and starring Michael Palin.

Friday, January 23rd

Today, upstairs in Terry's work-room, I told him of Jimmy's attitude. TJ looked hurt – but there was a good, healthy fighting spirit there too. TJ feels that *Tomkinson* may well have been originally my project, but it worked as a team project and Terry is now very angry that the BBC want to break the team by institutionalising a hierarchy into our working relationship – i.e. The Michael Palin Show.

We talked ourselves round in circles. I couldn't honestly say that I was prepared for TJ to take an entirely equal part in the acting, because this would involve me in a tussle with Jimmy over something I didn't feel was in my own best interests. We break off for lunch with Jill Foster at Salami's in Fulham Road.

It certainly seems that 1976 is all-change year. After almost ten years together, Terry and I are exploring and altering our relationship and Jill Foster and Fraser and Dunlop are doing the same. In short, Jill is leaving. She felt stifled at F & D, so now she wants to set up on her own.

We think we'll stay with Jill, despite the various problems that have cropped up over our Python activities. She's a good agent for us in many ways – a good talker, not renowned as vicious or hard in the business, but always seems to deliver an efficient, worthy, if not startling, deal.

After lunch we drive down to Terry's, talking again about the series. A peripatetic day, in fact, both literally and metaphorically. We decide to meet Jimmy together, but he can't make it until Monday. So I leave about 5.00 – with Terry still reeling slightly under a blow, which he hadn't after all expected. It's a rotten situation and rotten to see someone you like and whose friendship is so valuable being given a hard time. But it's all got to be said and to be gone through.

Monday, January 26th

Another meeting about the Jones/Palin relationship. This time at the BBC. Meet TJ for a coffee first and he, as I had expected, had taken stock of the situation over the weekend and come to an optimistic conclusion. He would write the series with me and then go off and make a film for children (a project he's had his thoughts on before) whilst I was filming. He seemed very happy.

However, once in Jimmy's office, TJ took a rather less accommodating line (quite rightly for, as he said afterwards, there was no point in the meeting if he didn't try to change JG's mind with a forceful view of his own).

I didn't do a lot of talking – I let Terry say all he wanted to say and Jimmy say what he wanted to say. JG was excellent I thought. He held to his position, but was sympathetic to all Terry said so, at the end of one and a half hour's meeting we were all still friends – and Jimmy adjourned us for a week to think about it. TJ did seem to be less angry than impatient with Jimmy and we went off for a lunch at Tethers.

I'm trying to avoid an utterly basic dissection of our relationship, because I think it's a relationship that obeys no strict rules, it works without introspection – it's an extrovert relationship based on writing and often performing jokes together. It's instinctive and I don't want to damage it by over-examination. I want (for such is my half-cowardly nature!) to solve this re-adjustment crisis without tears.

Tuesday, January 27th

Spoke to Terry, mid-morning. Rather than pursuing the Children's Film Foundation, TJ has instead revived that most hardy perennial – the *Fegg* film. He has rung John Goldstone, who reckons that 'The Nastiest Film in the World' has distinct possibilities!

Wednesday, January 28th

Another gorgeous day of clear, crisp, sharp sunshine. Terry comes up to Julia Street to talk about the *Fegg* film. We have some nice ideas – Fegg is a brooding and malevolent influence who lives in a corrugated iron extension up against a Gothic castle, near to the world's prettiest village, where everyone is terribly nice to each other. But the presence of Fegg (whom we see in a sinister, opening build-up sequence letting the air out of someone's tyres) is too much for them. They advertise for a hero. Scene cuts to a Hostel for Heroes, where unemployed heroes sit around in a sort of collegey atmosphere – occasionally getting jobs.

At the end of our day on *Fegg* – and with a possible commitment to writing on *Fegg* until we go to the US – I suddenly feel a touch of panic. Helen, with her usual down-to-earth perspicacity, provoked it by her reaction to the news of the *Fegg* film. I know she's right – I am taking on too much. The *Fegg* film is going to take time and ideas away from what should really be my primary project of the next two years – the BBC series of thirteen. Helen forces me to confront the fact that I am in danger of losing what I am trying to save.

Thursday, January 29th

Very cold again, but sunny. Reading the papers, hearing the news (imperfect form of information though that is), I get the feeling that there is an air of optimism about, a general air of improvement in the state of the country, which has been so battered over the last few years.

The Balcombe Street siege has, touch wood, marked the end of a couple of years of IRA terror, but it was the way in which the siege ended – peacefully, almost sensibly – and the way in which Jenkins[1] and the government refused to restore hanging in response to the primitive blood lust emotions of probably the majority of the country – that was the most hopeful outcome of the whole affair.

I rang Terry towards the end of the morning. He, too, had been worried when faced with actually writing the *Fegg* film, together with all our other commitments. But, later in the call, as we meandered around the area of commitments and involvements, Terry asked again the very basic question – 'Sod Jimmy Gilbert, Mike … what do *you* actually want the series to be?'

The almost continuous reflections on this subject over the last couple of weeks, the gut feeling that anything less than the independence I felt on *Tomkinson*, made me feel somehow, somewhere, dissatisfied, really gave me only one possible answer … 'Yes … I think I *do* want it to be the Michael Palin Show.'

1 Roy Jenkins. Labour government's Home Secretary.

Once I said this – and I had never said it with quite such conviction before – the debate and discussion was as good as ended. Terry accepted that – reluctantly, obviously, but quite generously and with relief that we were being honest with each other. God knows how it will turn out from here on, but the crucial question has been answered. Yes, I *do* want my independence, yes I *do* want the responsibility to be ultimately mine.

Fegg, we decide to shelve for a while. A well-intentioned attempt to please everybody, a project which I am genuinely enthusiastic about, but, thank goodness, this morning realism has prevailed all round.

Friday, January 30th

January draws to a close in bitter cold. Last weekend there was some snow – which was preferable to the bitter, ear-aching, sub-zero winds which blow around London today. But it's sunny again this morning. I have a meeting at the BBC with Jimmy G and Terry Hughes. Bill Cotton flits through, shakes my hand and says how pleased he was with the reaction to *Tomkinson*. The official warmth of the BBC's approval wafts around. I fear and mistrust it. Self-doubt and official disapproval are better for you.

We talk about money. Jimmy would like £4,000 per show guaranteed front money from the US. *Tomkinson*, according to computer forecasts (the BBC have a computer!), will cost £34,000 per episode in 1977, about double the average LE sit-com episode.

Thursday, February 5th

A Grammy Award Nomination arrives in the post from LA. *Matching Tie and Handkerchief* has been nominated for Best Comedy Album of the Year. The Americans are very good at the Awards business – the Grammy nomination is impressively announced all over the envelope (postmen and friends please note). The awarding body is the extraordinarily impressive National Academy of Recording Arts and Sciences and the letter, when opened, brings tears of joy and emotion. 'We extend our sincere congratulations to you for this honor bestowed upon you by the Recording Academy's voting members who are your fellow creators and craftsmen.' I could almost hear soaring strings and stirring brass play as I read these words. It's exactly the sort of pomposity that Python's LPs attempt to deflate, but it was still a Truly Wonderful Letter to Receive.

By February 13th we have to decide how we are going ahead on the ABC case. Osterberg is keen to fight on; feels that Lasker's summing-up was 'transparent', and that his decision would be reversed by the Court of Appeals. However, O has given us no indication as to how this would be achieved and on what grounds Lasker was 'transparent'. In view of the costs involved, and the fact that no one really has the time to single-mindedly pursue the case, I reluctantly tell Anne that I feel we should pay Osterberg's $15,000 and forget it.

Wednesday, February 11th, Southwold

Arrived at Darsham at 11.30 – from the train I could see Father hunched up in the car – it's not so easy for him to come on to the platform, especially on a wet, cold morning like this.

His speech is a little better, but he has great difficulty eating. The latest refinement is for him to use his teeth as and when required. He has them beside him in a plastic container and puts them in if there is some particularly tough piece of food to cope with.

The wind increases during the day, until by night-time it's nearly gale-force. It's the kind of weather which emphasises the bleak aspect of the east coast. But it's cosy enough inside Croft Cottage – with the fire and my appearance on *Just a Minute* to listen to on a crackly radio.

This morning an IRA man, Frank Stagg, starved to death at the end of a hunger strike in Wakefield. The IRA have sworn to 'avenge' his death and made various threats about England 'paying for it' … which everyone knows they can carry out. An atrocity isn't far off, I feel.

Friday, February 13th, Southwold

Woken by Father drawing the curtains at 8.30.

Glad to stay in, as the gales roared out of grey skies all day long. Managed an hour or so's work on a whodunnit – for the *Ripping Yarns*.[1]

---

1 The name came from a suggestion by Terry's brother, Nigel, who'd spotted a book on one of Terry's shelves with a similar style of schoolboy tales.

Train back to London at 6.30. Leaving them both with a certain amount of optimism for once. Clearly, Father is at his happiest at home and the fact that a nurse now baths him once a week and he goes to Blythburgh Hospital for therapy, etc, twice a week, has lightened the load on my mother a little.

In the station buffet at Ipswich the newspaper seller has a rumour for us – a bomb at Piccadilly Circus. When I finally get back to an eerily quiet London, I hear that the bomb was at Oxford Circus and didn't go off. But it was twenty pounds-worth of TNT in the main concourse on the Underground. It could have been the bloodiest explosion yet.

Saturday, February 14th

A sunny morning. We pack the car for a weekend at Abbotsley. The sun brings people out as if it's a holiday. Thomas gets a Valentine from Holly – which he can't stop talking about – and Holly, of course, doesn't want him to know it's from her. All I get is a bill from the dentist.

Vivid impressions of South East Asia in Paul Theroux's *The Great Railway Bazaar* – a book which has stirred up so many of my travelling impulses.

Monday, February 16th

Worked all day adapting the Fegg book's 'Across the Andes by Frog' for one of the *Ripping Yarns*. Terry rang in the morning. He sounded very down – he was getting yearnings to make films, programmes, to make something – and saw the year ahead passing without achieving this.

However, he had cheered up considerably by the late afternoon and we played squash – quite hard games – and afterwards drank beer and chatted about life, art and other Hampsteadisms up at the Flask. It was nearly eight o'clock when he dropped me back home. Out to dinner with Robert H.

Bomb-scare talk with the cab driver. So far no deaths or dangerous explosions since Stagg's death, but the cabman tells me that Warren Street Underground has been cleared and that there's a road block at Notting Hill Gate. Pick up Robert and on to Odin's – which has been boarded up outside like a wartime restaurant. There is a man standing outside who checks your name on the reservation list and only one small rectangle of glass on the door has been left uncovered. I suppose the more expensive the restaurant the heavier the bomb-proofing – there was nothing at all over the extensive glass frontage of the Italian caff on the corner opposite.

Home about 12.15, feeling a bit swivel-headed – and remembering that we drank a whole bottle of champagne as well. What swells we've become in the thirteen years we've known each other. The potential was always there, I suppose – but the money never was!

Tuesday, February 17th

Afternoon visit to a showbiz, sorry, *the* showbiz throat specialist. Jill F had suggested I go and see him before taking any voice projection lessons, just to check that there was no damage to my vocal cords, etc, since previous screamings.

His surgery is in Wimpole Street, where illness and privilege combine to create a pleasantly elegant part of the world. The ceilings were high, the hallway opened out into a sort of circular covered atrium with heavily impressive, brass-handled doors leading off on all sides – like a dream where you have to choose between six identical doors. They apologised for their heating having gone off.

Mr Musgrove was at his desk in the far corner of a huge room. I noticed a leather armchair, but that's about all. He wore a reflector plate on his head, talked beautifully and, from where I was sitting, he could have been Kenneth More playing the role. He sat me down on a swivel chair beside a table full of instruments, which looked like a still life from a book of Edwardian medical studies.

Holding my tongue and nearly bringing me to the point of vomiting, he investigated my vocal cords, occasionally sterilising his mirror in a small gas flame.

But he was efficient, convincing and reassuring. No sinus problems and, he was glad to say, my vocal cords were in good shape – no trace of damage. Prescribed some nose drops for me to take only if things got really bad. He told me he'd treated Julie Andrews every day for six months when she was shooting *Sound of Music*. 'Oh, yes … we got her through,' he said. Suddenly I felt my problem was really quite insignificant – which I'm sure is the best way I should feel about it. I paid him £10 thankfully.

Thursday, February 19th

Down to Wimpole Street (for the second time in a week) for a medical examination for insurance for the City Center Show. After having my throat, eyes, balls, back, thighs, glands and penis examined (in a way which made me feel more like a racehorse being checked for doping), I took myself off to South Kensington to Willy Rushton's apartment in Old Brompton Road. It looks out over one of the busiest, most cosmopolitan, open-all-night stretches of London, just by South Ken tube. WR describes it as rather like a 'cold Tangier'.

Ian Davidson, Terry J, Willy and myself are performing 'Custard Pie'[1] at a charity show at the Old Vic on Sunday night in memory of an actor called James Mellor, whom, it transpired as we sat around the table at Willy's, none of us actually knew. Willy R does rather a lot of these good causes (shows for Angola, Chile, refugees, etc) and we fantasised on the idea of professional charity performers having a 'Chile show' that 'might run' and 'a week on Namibia in June', etc, etc.

Willy knocked back two and a half pints very swiftly and, about 9.00, we made our separate ways, to meet again at the Old Vic on Sunday. 'I'm never quite sure where the Old Vic is,' says Willy, in his famous crusty-colonel voice, which, as far as I can gather, is his actual voice. I like him. He makes you laugh, and enjoys being made to laugh himself.

Sunday, February 22nd

At the Old Vic, Albert Finney is on the stage sorting out the acts.

We run through 'Custard Pie', then hang around in the not altogether convivial atmosphere of dozens of well-known faces. Jimmy Villiers, Mike Jayston (they are familiar via the footy matches), John Le Mesurier, Julian Holloway, Barry Rutter, Glenda Jackson, Gaye Brown, George Sewell, Joss Ackland, Ron Pickup, Bernard Cribbins (lovely feller) etc, etc. Everyone being a wee bit defensive, so am quite glad when we four dilettante comedy artists, who find ourselves at the end of a bill lasting at least three hours, leave the claustrophobic clutches of the Old Vic and end up across the road in the George Inn, London's last galleried pub. Inside, on uncarpeted floors, with black beams and yellow-

---

1 A deadpan lecture about slapstick, with demonstrations, originally written by Terry J, myself and Robert Hewison for an Oxford Revue in 1963.

ing walls and benches and tables, we find the perfect place to while away a couple of hours. We drink a few pints and swap stories of old cabarets.

Back at the theatre we stand in the bar and watch the performance on closed circuit TV. It's 10.00 and they are still doing the second act – we are at the end of the third.

Willy R was now on the double scotches and philosophising about this being the ideal way to go to the theatre. Sitting in the bar watching it all on TV – perhaps all the theatres in London should be wired up so, drink in hand, you could switch over to the Wyndhams when you got bored with Ibsen at the National.

We went on eventually and did our bit. Albert Finney was drinking champagne and swaying about a little as he introduced us. We proceeded to do less than the best version of 'Custard Pie', but no one cared by then.

Tuesday, February 24th

Worked a near four-hour stint this morning on the 'Mystery at Moorstones Manor' whodunnit story. Useful reading it to the Herberts on Saturday night last, their reaction helped me to sort out a new sense of direction for the sketch – which is nearing an ending – as TJ arrives up here about 1.30.

We chat, Terry had a bad week for writing last week – he was buying cars for Nigel, etc, and lost all the afternoons. My strategy of fairly disciplined writing and trying hard not to get involved in side work has paid off with the whodunnit, which TJ liked a lot and he's taken it away now to think of an ending.

Wednesday, February 25th

Work on the 'Curse of the Claw' – a story begun by Terry and featuring the wonderfully scabrous Uncle Jack, the boy/narrator's hero who has all the diseases known to man, at the same time.

Both Terry Hughes and Jimmy G were on the phone today to firm up arrangements for the twelve *Ripping Yarns*. Python film writing is now almost certainly shifted to November/December this year, leaving September/October free to film two *Ripping Yarns*.

Then comes the problem of the day – a bulky script bound in livid purple and called *Jabberwocky*, which was dropped in by T Gilliam yesterday for me to read. He wants me to play the part of Dennis, the peasant, one of only two central figures in the script. It sounds some-thing I would like to be involved in, but will require a two-month commitment in the middle of the year.

Talking to Jill F on these matters, she tells me that she had been asked about my availability for a new Tom Stoppard play at the Open Space. Job of jobs! Delight of delights! But unfortunately it's in April and I'll be treading the boards on Broadway. Well, *near* Broadway.

Friday, February 27th

I work through until 5.00. Steady and pleasing progress on 'Across the Andes by Frog', one of three storylines which are already in sight of an ending.

The last two weeks' work have been very prolific and satisfying, with only a couple of days when I chased a red herring and got stuck up a gum tree in a cul-de-sac, and very little dull stuff. Most of the writing has been a pleasure to read the next morning, which is the best test of quality. I enjoy the writing, I enjoy my house, my family and, more than anything I enjoy the feeling of seeing each day used to the full actually to produce something. The end.

Monday, March 1st

A cloudless, blue-sky day. London sparkles, everyone and everything looks better for this dose of reviving spring sunshine. To the Aldwych Theatre for the first of my lessons with Cicely Berry – premier voice-training lady of British Theatre (so everybody says).

She concentrates on transferring my breathing from the top of the rib-cage to the stomach. Once, and she says it will take time, but once I can feel myself breathing out of my stomach, then the tensing of shoul-der and back muscles will not affect my voice production, as happens now. Read out Dylan Thomas poem and tried the new breathing techniques. I see her again on Friday.

Call from TG. He says that Sandy Lieberson, producer of *Jabberwocky*, is now going off the idea of Michael Crawford and is almost persuaded to employ me. Apparently the condition he made today is that J Cleese should be in it as well. TG rang John and offered him a couple of days' work in August. John apparently accepted without wanting to see the script.

Wednesday, March 3rd

Writing at home during the day. Terry is scribbling down in Camberwell. In the evening a meeting with Michael and Anne Henshaw re what to do with the Palin millions.

As I sit, like a spectator at a game of tennis, watching Michael and Anne lob and volley tax avoidance chat, very little of which I begin to understand, I feel that same surge of panic in my ignorance as when I was taught maths at school, and as the problem, equation, or whatever was remorselessly expounded, I found myself nodding helplessly along with the rest of the class, knowing full well I didn't know what was being talked about, but realising that if I asked I would still panic again when it was explained. I sometimes think the Inland Revenue are doing me a favour – it would be the simplest thing to let them do all the sums and take the money and pat me on the head and leave me to the rather modest way of life which is the despair of a true accountant.

Thursday, March 4th

TG rang this evening. Evidently, after some hassles with 'them' – i.e. the producers – he has finally persuaded them that I should play Dennis the Peasant in *Jabberwocky*. So, contracts permitting (and I'd do it for no money anyway), I shall be filming from July 27th to the end of September, and straightaway after that filming two *Yarns*.

Drove down to Terry J's for a couple of hours of reading new material. London splendid in the hazy sunshine.

'Across the Andes by Frog' and 'Mystery at Moorstones Manor' are virtually complete and over the last couple of days I've made some headway elaborating on TJ's very funny start to 'The Wolf of the Sea'.

A couple of bomb explosions as we're eating our supper. That makes three today, but no one hurt in any of them.

Start to read *Jabberwocky* again – realise that I get peed on twice by page fifty!

Friday, March 5th

To the Aldwych Theatre for another session with Cicely B. Cicely as usual exuding her air of comfortable friendliness. She's the kind of person you meet once and would tell everything to.

Another very satisfactory hour's session on the voice. I do think I know and can actually now put into practice the main part of her advice, which is that we should breathe up from our stomachs, which is, after all, the centre of the body, and try and forget chest and shoulders. I try Gumby at full stretch a few times. Cicely cowers away.

Tuesday, March 16th

Harold Wilson is resigning. Quite a bombshell, for there were none of the usual press leaks. But he has just 'celebrated' (as they say), his 60th birthday, which is a very statesmanlike thing to do, and Harold, of all recent Western politicians, from Kennedy and Johnson through Brandt and Nixon and Maudling and Thorpe, is still clean – so presumably he's getting out while the going's good. Still, he's been PM for nine years and was becoming as secure a British institution as the Queen or Bovril.

Terry G rings, distraught. The Neal's Yard property is in jeopardy[1] – evidently the owner, who had constantly reassured TG it was his, now says he has another buyer. TG very worried, as he has bought the film equipment and needs to set it up somewhere before April 5th – end of tax year!

In late afternoon, down to Covent Garden with TG to look at premises. It's exciting down there – a lot of well-designed shop-fronts, and well-renovated, sturdy old buildings. Art designers, film and recording studios, craft shops and ballet centres are moving into old banana warehouses and there's a good healthy feeling of an area coming to life again. Neal's Yard premises look perfect for us. I hope we don't lose them.

Monday, March 22nd

Arrived at Anne's about 10.00 for the first read-through of material for an ambitious charity show in aid of Amnesty International. As I'm parking outside Park Square East, I nearly run over Jonathan Miller – who is to produce the Amnesty show – loping towards Anne's door. His curly hair is unbrushed, his clothes are an unremarkable heap of brown, and his eyes look a little red. He greets me very cheerfully.

1 Encouraged by Terry Gilliam and Julian Doyle, I was about to become part-owner of a property at 14/15 Neal's Yard, in Covent Garden, which we hoped would become a production base for Python and individual work. André Jacquemin's sound studio, in which I already had a financial interest, would be an important part of the mix.

As we go upstairs, I catch sight of a gun mike pointing in our direction and a blinding early morning sun shining directly at us suffuses the scene with a Gala Premiere-like quality. The mike and the camera belong to the Roger Graef team, a 'specialist' documentary group, whose typical product is the long, minutely observed documentary of people at work. Evidently they are going to trace the whole process of putting on the Amnesty show. They try to work as unobtrusively as possible. They don't use any artificial light and Chas Stewart, the cameraman, usually crushes himself discreetly, if uncomfortably, into a corner of the room. Only the flick of the gun mike is impossible to ignore.

Jonathan Miller is disarming and jokey, and not at all daunting, as I think I had expected. He certainly has a very encouraging attitude to the Amnesty show. Organise it, direct it, by all means, but let's keep the feeling of a spontaneous, anything-might-happen evening.

After a half hour's discussion and coffee – when it was agreed that Peter Cook should take over Eric's role as the condemned man in the 'Court Sketch' and that Terry J should be transferred to a Cook, Bennett, Miller sketch, in lieu of Dudley Moore who is in the US – Miller left, but with a very good parting shot. He gazed out of the windows into Regent's Park and murmured nostalgically, 'I used to play in those gardens when I was three. I remember a girl of eight asked me to show her my cock … It's never happened since,' he concluded, rather sadly.

R Graef is a very bright, approachable and likeable man. He shares the view of the *Weekend World* team that news presentation is, generally speaking, dead and flat and goes on to say he feels TV as a whole fails to involve its audience. His prolonged documentaries are an attempt to involve the TV viewer, without the smooth, glossy aids of well-worked storylines, and rather by presenting real people 'warts and all'. His technique begs a lot of questions, but it's refreshing to talk to someone who feels that something *can* be achieved on TV and is not for ever shaking his head sadly and saying 'Well of course, it would be lovely to do this, but …'

After lunch Terry and I play squash. Not a bad game, considering we both had curry behind us. Terry has a theory this is why Pakistanis make such formidable squash opponents.

Tuesday, March 23rd

At 12.00, via the bank to Anne's to drop off visa forms plus ghastly photo of Helen for States. Then to Fetter Lane for an extremely civilised hour of culture with Robert. We had lunch (white wine, smoked ham, Camembert and granary bread and salad) and I looked over Chris Orr's Ruskin etchings,[1] which will be the basis of the book I'm funding. I like them very much. Quite different from what I had expected, they are full of references to Ruskin's (Chris Orr's) sexual repression and fantasies. This theme gives the etchings a clear unity, but within that there is a wealth of detail and some very successful theatrical effects in the etchings themselves.

To Liverpool Street to meet my mother off the Ipswich train. Bring her back home for a cup of coffee and a quick glimpse of her youngest granddaughter. Father is in Southwold Cottage Hospital for two weeks. He's resigned to it, but not happy about it, but Mother really does need the breaks if she's to survive.

From here I take her down to Angela's, where she's to spend the next couple of days. As I leave Angela tells me that she is really feeling awful – she's in the grip of a repetition of the depression which hit her over ten years ago. She's on pills and anti-depressants, but these seem to do nothing for her confidence, though they may overcome the symptoms for a while.

She warned me that Ma would have to hear about it all and, as she put it, I would 'have to pick up the pieces' when Ma came over to stay with us on Thursday. I walked back to the car feeling almost as Angela was – on the point of tears. I feel so helpless.

Friday, March 26th

At the Tate Gallery for the Constable exhibition. It really was packed and, not having the time or the inclination to join the line of people two or three thick slowly moving round the 300-odd works in the exhibition – like a crowd lining up to pay their last respects to a dead monarch – Granny and I weaved in and out, wherever there was a gap. Once again, with pictures like the Haywain, seeing the original makes one aware of what a gross disservice to the painter are reproductions – and especially with a popular and acceptable painter like C, whose paintings are on matchboxes, chocolate boxes and soap boxes ad nauseam. There is so much delicacy of detail in the Haywain that these reproductions miss

1 The artist Chris Orr was introduced to me by Robert, who was a big fan of both Chris Orr and John Ruskin.

totally and it's really a far better painting than its clichéd popularity led me to think.

I go and do some shopping in Long Acre and Piccadilly – a gorgeously rich blue sky, Londoners on their way home blinking in the bright sunlight, buildings picked out in sharp definition by the evening sun. I could have enjoyed London for another couple of hours, as it emptied for the weekend, but I had to get home.

To bed late again. Can't bear to think of what there is to do before we fly off to New York now – only just over a week away!

Sunday, March 28th

Spend the morning at a rehearsal for 'Poke in the Eye'.[1]

Jonathan Miller took the part of the director. Rather well, I thought. He made intelligent suggestions, managed to avoid sounding bossy, kept the work-rate going steadily, and didn't at all justify John Cleese's early grumpiness. 'I wrote a film for Video Arts yesterday about how to chair a meeting, and one of the most vital things is for the chairman to have done his homework,' said Cleese icily.

All in all a very jolly morning – when people started going through their pieces it was like an old folk's nostalgia evening. Alan Bennett did his 'Norwich' telegram piece, Eleanor Bron some witty Michael Frayn material – performed with her stunning, but sometimes quite alarming sense of realism. John Bird arrived, looking windswept and awry, as if just woken from a very long sleep, just in time to rehearse his Idi Amin speech.

By way of a complete contrast Barry Humphries swanned elegantly in, fedora at a rakish angle, smart herringbone suit on and giving off a delicately perfumed fragrance. He was off to a dinner engagement so couldn't stay long.

Roger Graef and team filmed away, drawn to Jonathan M, as far as one could tell, like moths round a flame. The more I see of them at work, the more dangerous I think it is for them to give the impression in their programmes that they are following and revealing everything important as it happens. Their own selectivity dictates the programme.

Robert H round in the evening. We finalise details about Chris Orr's Ruskin book, which is to be a Signford[2] publication. They'll print 1,500 copies and I'll put in £1,500.

1 *A Poke in the Eye with a Sharp Stick* was the title of the Amnesty extravaganza.
2 Signford was an off-the-shelf company and my first, and last, publishing enterprise.

Monday, March 29th

Lunch with Terry H at the Arlecchino in Notting Hill Gate to discuss script of 'Moorstones' and 'Andes by Frog'. Terry J also there.

Terry J talks of what a wonderful unit Python was together, how we functioned best then. I feel I'm functioning best *now* – with my hard-won independence. It's not selfishness or conceit, it's just to do with avoiding the wear and tear on the nervous system.

Shopping in the King's Road all afternoon, then dropped in to see Nigel [Greenwood] at the gallery. He was in, the gallery was empty. It was six o'clock, so it gave him an excuse to bring out the scotch. We drank and chatted for an hour. I told him about Robert and the Ruskin book. He was interested to know who was publishing, as he himself publishes books. He's just spent thousands on a Gilbert and George[1] book which the printers have heavily fucked up.

He said that, although the gallery has a very experimental attitude and is known for showing the most unconventional and outrageous works, the artists he shows don't like the gallery world ... Nigel a bit resigned, but rather rueful about this.

Wednesday, March 31st

The Amnesty bandwagon gathers momentum today – a second and final rehearsal on stage at Her Majesty's, with Roger Graef and team poking about. I notice them filming, at great length, a conversation between Cleese and Peter Cook on the stage, and it occurs to me that, as the cameraman himself is small (or average) compared to them, he's probably much happier filming tall people. I asked Graef whether I would be a better bet for tele-verité if I were six inches taller ... 'Oh, yes, undoubtedly,' he assured me. 'They can get lovely angles if you're tall – shots against the sky, or, in this case, against the spotlights.' Yesterday they'd been filming the Goodies at rehearsal and the cameraman had found Bill Oddie quite a problem.

Peter Cook – who apologised for his slightly glazed state, saying he was recovering from a long night spent with John Fortune discussing Lenny Bruce's drug problem – steadfastly refuses to learn the words of

1 Artists who called themselves 'living sculptures'. They were just beginning to make a wider name for themselves.

the Condemned Man in our 'Court Sketch'. He does ad-lib very well, but it gives Terry J a few hairy moments.

At about 12.30, more press photos outside. For some reason a *Daily Mirror* photographer issues us all with pickaxes – no one knows why until we see the photo in the *Mirror* on April 1st with the caption 'Pick of the Jokers'. No wonder the *Mirror* are losing their circulation battle.

Thursday, April 1st

At the theatre the last of the bare-breasted *Ipi-Tombi* dancers[1] are leaving (in sensible Jaeger sweaters and two-piece suits!). Neil's band Fatso are heaving in their equipment. Outside in King Chas II Street the Manor Mobile Recording Studios are parked with cables and wires running into the stage door.

People milling around. We're all in one dressing room – Cook, Bird, Jones, Gilliam, Cleese, (not Bron), Bennett – all of us plus Roger Graef's camera and mike, which searches around picking up snatches of conversation here and there. Brief 'Lumberjack Song' rehearsal. A book is opened at P Cook's instigation on the length of the show.

Curtain up at 11.35. Jonathan and I walk out. Me sweeping the stage, him directing me. Then into 'Pet Shop' and we're away. First half runs till 1.00. JM does some ruthless cutting of the second half. Eleanor and Johnny Lynn[2] fed up their bits have been excised, but so has 'Crunchy Frog'.

Roar of recognition and applause (still!) on things like 'Argument', 'Lumberjack' and 'Pet Shop'. End with making a balls-up of 'Lumberjack Song'. I start too early, try again – too flat – try again and we get through it.

Many curtain calls at the end, though – they really enjoyed it. It's 2.15 and Roger Graef is filming 'after the show' atmos. Feel tired, depressed, just want a scotch.

Saturday, April 3rd

Probably the best night of all tonight, though 'Argument' is cut for time and Graham is boisterously drunk. Alan Bennett feigns mock-horror in

---

1 *Ipi Tombi*, a South African musical about a boy looking for work in the mines of Johannesburg. It was said to be the first musical performed by nude actors in London.
2 Jonathan Lynn, film director. Creator and co-author of *Yes Minister*. Cambridge contemporary of Eric Idle, whom he later directed in *Nuns on the Run*.

the dressing room as Graham, at his most baroque, is fondling Terry J as he changes. 'Oh dear,' says Alan to Jonathan, shaking his head with a worried frown, 'We *never* used to do that sort of thing. We never used to touch each other.'

Graham and Peter make a strange pair – both with inflated eyes and a sort of boozy calm which can and does easily flare up. Graham's bête noire tonight, and not for the first time, is Bill Oddie. Tonight is the only night the Goodies appear. They are in a different world from everyone else in the show, with their 'Funky Gibbon' pop numbers, complete with dance movements – a rather gluey, trad. middle-of-the-road *Top of the Pops* appearance.

John Bird has useful suggestion for 'Court Sketch', which I worked on hard tonight. He says I'm doing my Prosecutor in the same way as Cleese (i.e. starting with outrage and working up from there) and I should play it differently. Good thinking.

We may have made £15,000 or £16,000 for Amnesty from the three nights.

Sunday, April 4th

A winding-down day. No need to prepare for America until tomorrow. So just enjoy, for once, the laziness of Sunday. Up at 9.15 – no adverse effects from Amnesty show – brain damage, throat damage, hangover, etc. Feel in good shape. Buy croissants and papers up at South End Green.

Spend a couple of hours in the evening working my way through the entire American show, trying to look carefully at characters, possible rewrites for US audiences, dangerously difficult English regional accents, etc, etc. I feel it's very important to sit quietly and work out one's own problems before we reach New York. After tonight's session, I feel I know the show much better and, if we suddenly had to put it on tomorrow, we could.

Tuesday, April 6th, New York

Sunshine in New York and a freshness in the air – a perfect spring after-noon. First sight of our home for the next four weeks, our very own brownstone in East 49th Street between Second and Third Avenues.[1] No.

1 I shared the house with Terry J – and, later, our families.

242, once home (still sometimes the home, I presume) of a writer, Garson Kanin,[1] and his actress wife Ruth Gordon. A feeling of euphoria swept over me as I explored its four floors – none of which had a room, a picture, a piece of furniture, an ornament, an element of any kind which wasn't pleasing without being pretentious. There were no disappointments – no dingy back rooms or peeling wallpapers or Formica partitions – and, at the same time, no forbidding luxuries. Though it's clearly the home of wealthy, or once-wealthy collectors and high-livers, it has a comfortable, warm friendliness about it.

As if the house itself (complete with library) wasn't a joy in itself, it backs on to a Spanish-style pattern of gardens, known as Turtle Bay Gardens. Courtyards with trees and flowering shrubs and daffodils and a fountain – again, like the house, cosy, comfortable, peaceful in the heart of a city which is unceasingly noisy.

I bounded around the house, probably boring TJ stiff with constant and repetitious enthusiasm.

Wednesday, April 7th, New York

Woke about 4.00, feeling distinctly unsleepy.

The incessant hum of New York begins to build up to what is, by Oak Village standards, an early-morning roar. It's almost like a magnet, drawing you up and out, defying you to stay in your bed, defying you not to get involved.

Later in the morning a huge black limousine swishes up outside and drives Terry J and myself plus Carol and Terry G to the helipad on the East River, whence we are to be airlifted over the steel mills and scrap yards of the Garden State. In about 40 minutes Philadelphia can be glimpsed on the horizon straight ahead – a cluster of tower blocks and skyscrapers rising skywards like a petrified explosion.

We land on the roof of a bank, and are whisked downstairs and across the road to the Westinghouse TV Studios where the Mike Douglas Show is recorded. We're told it's the biggest regular single TV audience in the world – 40 million watch each show.

He showed two good clips from the TV Pythons and the Black Knight fight in its entirety from the film. The Black Knight fight

2 Garson Kanin (1912–99), New York-based actor, writer, director and author of very readable Hollywood novel *Moviola*.

contrasted nicely with the clean teeth and the 'He-Tan' make-up of all the guests. There was Ron Vereen, who didn't need He-Tan as he was black, but wore a very well-tailored Savile Row suit and kept smiling. And there was Gabriel Kaplan, a TV comic who kept smiling and another TV actor called David Soul, who was very blond and slightly embarrassed when Terry J sat on his knee after we'd all been introduced. But I did get to meet one of the folk-heroes of my youth – in fact I sat next to him and smiled along with him for all the forty million viewers to see – Neil Sedaka, writer and singer of great hits of my teenage years, made-up lavishly, like a badly restored painting. 'You guys are just crazy,' he cooed.

Thursday, April 8th, New York

This time I must have woken even earlier – 3.30 or so. I tend to wake up with that momentary flash of terror, as if something really nasty is going to happen today. I chase the feeling away quickly enough, but I suppose it will continue to be there until the show has opened, settled into a routine and the pressure on us to be brilliant and successful is relaxed.

About 8.00 get up, do a half hour of voice exercises, soak in the bath and read a little Pirsig,[1] which concentrates the mind wonderfully. Coffee for breakfast downstairs, then a 25 minute walk across town to our rehearsal room near Broadway. Big, functional, mirrored rehearsal room.

Bad news of the day is that Eric has been ill in bed since yesterday and may have a mono-something or other – a liver problem – and be bad enough for us at least to discuss an alternative show if he couldn't make it.

The rehearsal is quite gruelling and, around 1.00, a rather aged and slow camera crew arrive with a pleasant, dumpy compere to film us rehearsing for use on a news/current affairs show later this evening. They are certainly no Roger Graefs, and the result is an extra hour of rehearsal, until after 2.00. Everyone is a little short-tempered and, when the interviewer finally interviews each one of us and says he wants us to be as loony and silly as we want, the numbing feeling of being rats in a cage comes over me again. We manage some facetiousness and paltry slapstick.

1 *Zen and the Art of Motorcycle Maintenance* by Robert Pirsig.

Terry and I have an evening appointment with the singular Mr Conlon, our publisher. He meets us in the lobby of the Yale Club, on Park and Vanderbilt. Classical columns, and old group photographs. We are both given ties to wear and copies of *Dr Fegg's Nasty Book of Knowledge* – our first sight of the completed new American version of *Fegg*. Both of us are very pleased with the look of it. Steve is full of disparaging banter. It's cost them far more than they'll ever get back, he says. The recent batch of alterations finally broke the chances of economic success and anyway the book is stuck at the printers in Wisconsin because of stroppy truckers. 'Goddamn truckers rule this goddamn country,' he grunts sourly, then breaks into a broad grin and introduces us eagerly to a man called Marvin Goldwater, who is president of 'Beards of America' and cousin of Barry, the Vietnam Hawk himself.

Saturday, April 10th, New York

Beginning, slowly, to relax into New York pattern of life.

A lunch in our garden in the sun with Neil and Yvonne, Miles and Luke[1] and Al Levinson – looking tanned (from Jamaica), curly-haired and broad-shouldered. As he quotes someone in one of his poems as saying on first meeting him: 'I cannot imagine you indoors'. Al brought, apart from jokes and good company, a bit of New York intellectual class and a bottle of scotch for the house.

At 2.00 the others (bar Eric) begin to arrive and we have a very good three hour rehearsal upstairs at 242. Al remarked on how well we mixed and how there was no apparent leader.

Nancy arrived and she and I went round to Stephen Sondheim's house, next door but one. SS's housekeeper, Louis, apparently organises cleaners, etc, for 242. The Sondheim house is decorated in a more modern and much more opulent style than 242 – yet with carefully restrained taste. Full of remarkable surprises, too. One room full of antique nineteenth and twentieth century games – early skittle alleys, very old pinball machines.

Louis – Spanish, I should think, small, chunky, camp, with a ready smile and friendly open manner. Very excited to meet a Python. He shows me a copy of *New Yorker* for the week, which contains a long article by Hertzberg about the court case in December. A long and very

1 Yvonne Innes, Neil's wife. Their boys, Miles and Luke, and ours had become firm friends.

accurate article with quotes from Gilliam and myself – 'Michael Palin, charming and boyish'!

On the way downstairs I meet the distinguished Mr Sondheim. He shakes hands briefly, distractedly, as he flits from one room into another with a grand piano in it.

Tuesday, April 13th, New York

Lunch at Ina's office, where a Python business meeting has been called to discuss offers of a TV special to be made of the show. Terry J is, as usual, the chief originator of doubt about the project. He wants a Roger Graef-style film of the stage show, whereas Ina thinks we can only sell a TV special of the show, to be made after the end of the run at the Ed Sullivan Theater. TJ and TG against, John keen to earn the extra £3,000 we're promised for doing it. I urge that we examine more carefully what is involved in moving the show to another theatre and preparing it for TV. It's all being sold to us as a two day extension – I think we'll be here an extra week!

Really I couldn't care less. Here we are all being encouraged to be very greedy and complicate our lives further, when we have a theatre opening down the road in a day and a half and we haven't even been on the stage.

Two incidents at the end of this unsatisfactory meeting. John, who has been lying on the floor to 'relax his shoulders', gets up and, as he does so, dislodges a huge picture on the wall, which crashes down on his foot, eliciting Fawlty-like shrieks of pain and explosive anger. I think he really did shake his fist at it. Then we find he actually has sliced a bit of flesh off his heel and he is sat down and a doctor called. It's his 'Silly Walks' foot too.

Wednesday, April 14th, New York

One of those totally gruelling days that only happen in the theatre and, if they didn't have to happen, the theatre would invent them.

Breakfast of fresh orange juice, grapefruit and scrambled eggs and bacon at Francine's – a coffee shop across the street from the stage door. Eric came in – he's all right.

10.00 into the theatre, past the small knot of girls who seem to have already taken up permanent residence there. An a.m. technical stagger-through, topping and tailing.

In the afternoon, a dress rehearsal. Our first and only, despite Hazel's usual protestations. I seem to have the most changes, seventeen or eighteen. Gloria, my dresser, a Patricia Neal look-alike, looks worried, but I'm told she's 100% reliable. One thing that irritates me about the afternoon run, which is so important to us, is that we have not been warned – or I have not been warned – that the press has been allowed in.

I felt even more cross by the little production chat we had at 6.00. No one smiled. Anne frowned, Allen Tinkley [our producer] frowned, they all seemed to be deeply gloomy and I just wanted to get away from them all and do the show.

At 8.00, almost punctually, the curtain rose to prolonged applause and cheers.

The whole show went predictably well, with very few problems and the usual reaction of ecstatic recognition of sketches. The only trouble spot was the 'Court Sketch', which was running 15 minutes and failed to work at any stage and 'The Death of Mary Queen of Scots' which was too long.

Afterwards I felt hugely relieved. My voice had survived four run-throughs in two days, which it would never have done before Cicely Berry, and the reaction to the show was as good as it had ever been. I think we're in for an enjoyable run.

Charisma gave us an after-show party at Orsons. That's where the voices really become strained – not during the shows! Tomorrow the family arrives.

Thursday, April 15th, New York

A complete change in the weather today. The temperature has hurtled up into the 70s and is heading for the 80s and the cool crispness that has made New York so acceptable this past week has been replaced by a clammy balminess.

A limousine picks us up at the Navarro and takes TJ and me out to Kennedy Airport to meet the families. Small blond heads are glimpsed through the customs shed door at around 1.00 and soon we're all packed in the limousine heading into NY over the Triborough Bridge.

A couple of hours settling in at 242. The house is not a perfect house for kids, and I'm suddenly aware of the enormous numbers of stairs. Terry and I get very hot and bothered moving the two enormous cots we've rented for Rachel and Sally. We keep knocking Noël Coward's painting off the wall as we struggle to get them up two or three flights.

In late afternoon TJ and I have to go to a reception being given by the BBC. A couple of gin and tonics, and the good news that we have a rave review from Clive Barnes of the *NY Times*. The review, out tomorrow, was circulating the party, as was its author – small, owl-like doyen of NY theatre critics – Clive B himself. I was introduced to him by Nancy. He said how much he'd enjoyed it, I went over some of the things that had gone wrong – e.g. the till not working in 'Blackmail' – he said that sort of thing made the show even more fun, and excused himself, but he had to dash off and see a play in New Haven.

After tonight's show another party – this time quite a cheery affair thrown by Arista in the New York Experience – an exhibition in the bowels of the Rockefeller Center.

At the party – Clive Davis, of course, with photographers in careful attendance. Talking with Clive is like going into one of those photo booths on stations. The lights start popping and, before you know it, 600 pictures of you and Clive happy have been taken. But Clive doesn't embrace you for no reason – throughout the session he's working on me to agree to extending our visit by taking the show on to LA until the end of May. It'll sell so many records if we do go to the West Coast.

Meet John Cale, another complete Python fan. A breathless PR lady rushes up and asks me to come and have my photo taken with Leonard Bernstein. This means being pulled through the crowds of ordinary plebs and being held in position, like a greyhound in a stall, whilst Lenny finishes talking to someone else. Then, after a while, Lenny turns, shakes my hand. He's smaller than I expected; short and dynamic. The flashbulbs go crazy. Lenny introduces me to Adolph Green, another songwriter, who is nice and quiet and amiable. As I talk to Lenny I'm actually being pulled to one side by this wretched PR lady so that I don't spoil the shot by obscuring his face from the cameras. He goes on about how he and his kids adore the show. Later he asks John and Eric to do bits of sketches and Eric replies by demanding that Bernstein sing a bit of Beethoven.

Clearly the little fellow loves the publicity and plays up to it – sending it up rotten, but playing along nevertheless, and, always behind and around, the acolytes, the standers and watchers.

It's the NY treatment, and it goes on till two or three – I forget which – when the waiting limousine whisks us back, exhausted, to 242.

Friday, April 16th, New York

A night to remember. For its sheer awfulness. The children up and about even before dawn, myself trying desperately to catch up on much-needed sleep and poor Helen, up and down calming or quieting the kids, then back to a bed which she found terribly uncomfortable. I had been aware that it was a hard bed, but had put my lack of sleep down to nervous energy rather than discomfort. Now Helen's misery made me feel just how hard the bed is. I can't sleep, she can't sleep, the children can't sleep.

I ring home, to be congratulated by my mother on our tenth wedding anniversary, which I'd totally forgotten.

Try to buy a mattress for the bed – very difficult on Good Friday. Finally track down a foam rubber store and, with the help of a huge Cadillac limousine, provided by Nancy, I'm able to buy and bring back a 6' x 6'6" piece of foam rubber before the shop closes at 2.00. Many strange looks as the impressive limousine purrs uptown with a huge ball of foam rubber taking up the entire back seat.

In the afternoon everything improves. The new mattress is a winner (the best $43-worth I've ever spent). The evening show receives the best reaction yet – a truly thunderous ovation.

Saturday, April 17th, New York

Two shows tonight: 6.00 and 9.30.

At the theatre Neil tells me that their flat has been burgled. He's now about the fourth or fifth of the Python group to have lost money or had it stolen since we arrived in NY. Charles K,[1] Mollie[2] and Carol have all had money taken and, in a strangely un-detailed episode, I gather that John C was rolled by a couple of hookers!

At the first show someone is letting off firecrackers very irritatingly. It comes to a head in 'Argument', in which a crack completely obscures a line and Graham leaps in, doing his favourite bit, shouting – or rather, yelling – at hecklers. As he's just done the Man Who Gives Abuse, it all fits in very neatly. The offender is seen to be removed forcibly from the

1 Charles Knode, tall, droll, costume designer friend of Hazel's. After the flying saucer sequence in *Life of Brian* he utters the immortal words 'You jammy bastard!'
2 Mollie Kirkland, stage manager.

theatre by Jim Beach. G's volley of abuse follows him right up the aisle. The sketch goes swimmingly after that.

Sunday, April 18th, New York

Well here we are, about to play two shows at the end of one of our hardest weeks ever, and the temperature hits 96° – the highest April temperature recorded in New York.

Crowds outside stage door now number forty or fifty. Much screaming and autograph signing. Nothing like this in London. It's quite nice for a while. Am given two beautiful Gumbys – one made in plaster, and another elaborately and painstakingly embroidered – plus flowers, etc. TJ is given a flower for every performance by one fan.

Tuesday, April 20th, New York

An incipient sore throat. It worsened, perversely, on the day off, probably as a result of heat and dust and tiredness. Today's schedule gives it no chance.

At 10.10 we all leave the house to go to a Warner Books 'Literary Reception' at the Bronx Zoo. A good chance to mix business and pleasure. Due to a mix-up with the limousines, we do not arrive at our destination for an hour and 20 minutes. It's free day at the zoo and the place is packed. Our limo noses its way through the crowds to the back of the reptile house. Unbeknown to us, Warner Books have laid on a stunt. We are to present a python to the zoo, and this involves us in having to hold the thing whilst press and TV take their photos.

An unpleasant little episode. Eric refuses to join in. The press and photographers are singularly objectionable and the python is getting very hot and disturbed. It's about eighteen feet long and, after a while, its huge body begins to writhe slowly in discomfort. The idiotic pictures go on and on … 'Would you stand here by its face, please?' 'Come on, someone tell a joke …' 'You're Pythons – do something funny for me.'

We have to hold up a copy of our book by the python's head. All of us, including the snake, are getting hotter and crosser. Finally I can't take any more of these asinine remarks from the cameramen and I walk away, muttering angrily. Most unpleasant.

At the show tonight George Harrison, looking tired and ill and with short hair, fulfils what he calls a lifetime's ambition and comes on as one of the Mountie chorus in the 'Lumberjack Song'. He's very modest about it, wears his hat pulled well down and refuses to appear in the curtain call. He's now off on holiday to the Virgin Islands. He needs it.

Thursday, April 22nd, New York

Suddenly we're half-way through.

After the show, who should come round but Ruth Gordon and Garson Kanin, owners of 242. My heart missed a couple of beats as it was only today that Sally Jones[1] had painted a mural over one of their walls. But they were a charming, disarming pair. She, who must be 80, full of life – a real sparkle in her eyes. Did she enjoy doing *Where's Poppa?* (one of my favourite comedies), I asked cautiously. No, hated it, she replied, quickly and convincingly – then, with a broad grin, accepted the compliment and eulogised over the film with me.

They had both loved the show and Kanin commented on how surprised he'd been by the mixture of people in the audience – young, middle-aged, old, smart Broadway pros, scruffy college kids and boys and girls with their parents. 'Just one thing,' said Ruth G, as they left, 'When you write another Python movie, make sure there's a part for me in it.' I will, too.

Friday, April 23rd, New York

Up at 10.30 after good sleep. Breakfast at coffee shop. Oh, the fresh orange juice! Nancy rings about 11.00. Familiar tale – could I go to an important ABC radio interview with Gilliam this afternoon? Eric won't, John has a 'prior commitment'. Either I refuse and Nancy breaks down – she sounds very weak, having been up all night on the LP – or I accept the emotional blackmail. I feel good this morning – New York's sunny. A perfect day. Yes, I'll do it.

On the way out my one and only encounter with our legendary neighbour – Kate Hepburn. She's at the wheel of an unpretentious green car, she wears a headscarf which carefully covers most of her face. Low, gravelly voice offers Tom and Willy the use of her fountain to paddle in.

---

1 Terry's daughter. She was three at the time, and is still an artist!

I introduce the boys. 'Oh, *I* know Tom and Willy, I've seen them out in the garden.'

From ABC and the crowds in sunny Sixth Avenue, I meet Helen and the boys and we take a cab down to Battery Park and out to the Statue of Liberty. A great success. The weather sunny and clear. Fine views of Manhattan skyline and climbing inside Liberty's 'skirt' appealed to the boys' imagination. 'We'll soon be at the underpants,' says Willy – as the three of us toil towards the crown.

Sunday, April 25th, New York

The boys come to see the matinee this afternoon. Favourite moment – Gilliam's exploding stomach!

During the second show a two-foot-long prick is thrown on stage. Eric – 'One of these little American penises.'

Wednesday, April 28th, New York

The boys, dressed in their new Spiderman outfits (bought yesterday), escorted me across Second Avenue to the coffee shop. At 11.00 all the Pythons, bar Terry Gilliam who is giving a court deposition, arrive at 242 for the first meeting/discussion about the next Python movie. It's a pleasant day. Sunny and warm. Resist temptation to work out in the gardens and use Ruth and Garson's living room, where, beneath the Grandma Moses hanging above the fireplace, we have the first positive thoughts about a new movie.

Are we or are we not going to do a life of Christ? All feel that we cannot just take the Bible story and parody or Pythonise every well-known event. We have to have a more subtle approach and, in a sense, a more serious approach. We have to be sure of our own attitudes towards Christ, the Scriptures, beliefs in general, and not just skate through being silly.

John provides a key thought with a suggested title – 'The Gospel According to St Brian' – and from that stem many improvised ideas about this character who was contemporary with Jesus – a sort of stock Python bank clerk, or tax official, who records everything, but is always too late – things have always happened when he eventually comes on the scene. He's a bit of a fixer too and typical of St Brian is the scene where he's on the beach, arranging cheap rentals for a fishing boat, whilst, in the back of shot, behind him, Christ walks across frame on the water. St Brian turns, but it's too late.

So at the meeting, which breaks up around 1.00, we seem to have quite unanimously cheerfully agreed to do a film, and a Bible story film, and have had enough initial ideas to fill all of us with a sort of enthusiasm which has been missing in Python for at least a couple of years.

Tonight Harry Nilsson joins me on stage for the 'Lumberjack Song'. He is coked to the eyeballs and full of booze too, but grins benignly and seems to be enjoying himself, when, at the last curtain call, I see him suddenly lurch forward towards the edge of the stage, presumably to fraternise with the cheering audience. As he goes forward, the curtain starts to fall and, before I can pull him back, Harry keels over into the front row and lies helplessly astride the wooden edge of the orchestra pit. The curtain descends, leaving me with this bizarre vision of a drunken Mountie lying on top of the audience!

Thursday, April 29th, New York

Nancy rings at 10.30. A CBS film crew want an interview, walking in the park or something, this lunchtime. Should help to sell a few seats for the weekend. It's important, of course.

Today Helen and the kids are going back home and here am I, with pathetic lack of resistance, sucked into the publicity machine.

A less productive film meeting at 242 this morning, although we take the Bible story into wider areas, Rome perhaps or even the present day. A silly World War I opening is suggested, which starts with a congregation of English soldiers singing in some chapel. A moving scene. Except in one row at the back there are four Germans singing. Nobody likes to look at them directly, but heads begin to turn.

When I get home, Helen is in the throes of packing.

Took a cab across town and picked up the boys from Yvonne. They'd been up the Empire State Building and had more pressies in their hot little hands. Back to 242 with them. Give Helen a goodbye peck, grab my thermos of tea, which I've been taking into the theatre for the vocal cords. So off I go, clutching my thermos like a miner going off t' pit.

Sunday, May 2nd, New York

Woke with the nightmarish realisation that I had no voice at all. I croak, ooh and aah and try a few of the exercises, but realise with a flush of horror that my voice has disappeared – more suddenly and severely than I ever remember. My reactions – it's about 11.00 and I've slept a good nine hours – vary from urgent panic to reluctant acceptance and then to cautious optimism. I have often heard of doctors who deal with this sort of vocal paralysis with one squirt or one jab. So, I try to ring Nancy. She's not there. So I try to ring doctors myself. This isn't much fun as I have to croak gutturally into the phone and it's difficult to make them hear. Dr Lustgarten, the Park Avenue specialist, is away. His partner, Dr Briggs, will ring me back. Dr Briggs doesn't ring me back. I have a bath.

My predicament seems like a particularly vicious stroke of fate. Only two shows to go, and, instead of recovering and consolidating during the night and day (as it has done throughout the run), the voice has perversely decided to vanish today, leaving me the last two shows – the two fun shows, when everyone will be happy and jolly and enjoying themselves – as millstones.

I try a contact of Dr Lustgarten's. He's also away, but a Dr Ryan rings me back. Dr Ryan has not got the expected message of hope – all he can suggest is that I buy 'Afrin' nasal decongestant and try and squirt it on my vocal cords. This doesn't sound like the miracle cure I've heard so much about, but I'll give it a try.

Out around midday. It's a warm, sunny Sunday morning. Walk along Second Avenue to try and find a pharmacy with the miracle 'Afrin'.

Police everywhere. A buzzing feeling of something being about to happen takes my mind off my own predicament. Turns out there's to be an enormous 'Free Soviet Jewry' march on the United Nations, only about half a mile away from our house. Find 'Afrin'; head home as the police take up their positions in serried ranks along Second Avenue.

Absolutely no effect. Depression and gloom close in again. Buy a huge copy of the *New York Times*; and decide to sit out in Turtle Bay Gardens in the sun with a beer and hope that rest will somehow save the remnants of the voice.

It's 2.00 and time to go to the theatre. Once there, I decide to try everything and see. Funnily enough, Gumby is the easiest. The grunting can be easily brought up from the depths of the stomach in the proper way – it's things like upper-register incredulity and emphasis in 'Travel Agent Sketch', for instance, which prove most difficult.

At half-time in the first show Dr Briggs arrives. Smooth, receding hair neatly brushed back with a precision only doctors seem to achieve. He has his daughter with him and seems more anxious to get my autograph than to treat the voice. He whizzes me upstairs, whilst they hold the curtain, and gives me a Cortisone jab in the arm and sprays my throat with Novocaine. The spray is re-applied midway in the second half. My voice is now a rather sinister manufactured thing, like Frankenstein's monster. At the end of the first show I'm supposed to rest it, but instead there's a birthday party organised for me by Loretta and Laura, two fans who've been outside for every single show. They've made me a cake, given me a present of two T-shirts and other presents for the kids and even bought me a bottle of Great Western New York State Champagne. Everyone sings 'Happy Birthday' to me in a hoarse whisper.

Clearly Dr Briggs' much-vaunted Cortisone treatment hasn't worked by the second house, despite his confidence – 'I got Robert Eddison on to play Lear and his voice was far worse.' I suppose there are better people than Dr Briggs, but I was paying the penalty of losing my voice in New York on a Sunday. No one was there. Before the 7.30 show another doctor, this time with halitosis, appeared, and, before he looked down my throat, asked me who was going to pay him the $40. Then he treated me utterly ineffectually and went away.

Neil, meanwhile, kept offering me large swigs of scotch as 'the only cure'. He was right. I drank enough not to care, and managed to survive the last show. As the audience knew my voice had gone, they were very sympathetic and we made some capital out of it. But there is still something terrifying about going on stage in front of 2,000 people and not knowing if you will be able to speak.

Monday, May 3rd, New York

A record-signing had been laid on at Sam Goody's Store from 12.00–2.00. A limousine with all the others in was supposed to pick us up at 12.00. It didn't arrive. It was getting rather cold suddenly and we were all in summer gear, feeling like Indians in Aberdeen, pathetically trying to ring Nancy. No luck.

At 12.10 we set off for the record-signing – and then realise we don't know where the store is, so we stop and ask a pretzel seller. All at once we're there. Through the traffic, on the opposite side of the road, a queue half a block long. And they're waiting for us. With an increased confidence in our stride we cross the road. A few screams and shouts and we're into the store. The entire basement is full of Python records. The album *Live at City Center* has been marketed in only ten days since the master was cut. There they are. Racks of them. And it's playing in the store as well.

8.30: Limousine arrives, pack the cases and the best journey of all begins – out to Kennedy, with Alan Price's 'O Lucky Man' score playing on the cassette, with a kind of appropriateness. I had seen the hard side of New York today, the constant pressure to say something, to stand up in case people don't recognise you. That's the trouble with the city, that's why it's unrelaxing – because of the fear that if you sit down and relax for half an hour everyone will forget who you are.

Monday, May 10th

Last twelve months have been the driest since records began in 1727. Drought conditions near in some parts of the country. Cathy Gib took it all very seriously and was going around putting bricks in the cisterns.

TG and Maggie come round in the evening – talk of *Jabberwocky*. It may now be largely shot in Chepstow and Pembroke Castles and far less in Shepperton Studios than originally expected. I approve. Arthur Lowe wants to be in it, but Iain Cuthbertson has said no.

Monday, May 17th

Began a *Ripping Yarn* script about a Northern family, but was only able to work on it for about an hour, then a series of prolonged phone calls.

With Helen to the Academy, where we saw *Spirit of the Beehive*, a beautifully photographed, unpretentious, unspectacular, gentle Spanish film by Victor Erice. Delightful and satisfying. And afterwards Piero kept his restaurant upstairs specially open for the two of us (even the guitarist came back and played for ten minutes!) – superb meal. Piero has achieved a consistent excellence at the Pavilion, which has never let us down.[1]

1 Despite Piero's death and the disappearance from Oxford Street of the Academy Cinema, the Pavilion, now run by his friend Vasco and his son, remains our family's favourite. It has moved to Poland Street.

Wednesday, May 19th

The weather's cooled down perceptibly. Writing easier and actually I make a good start on a First World War *Ripping Yarn* set in a prison camp.

Down to 14 Neal's Yard, which is, since last Monday, the leasehold property of Messrs Palin, Doyle and Gilliam. We discuss how the buildings will be used. André and the studio are settled and it's looking good. He could have builders in on Monday.

Home around 8.00. Watched Liverpool win UEFA Cup Final at Bruges.

Thursday, May 20th, Sheffield

Caught 13.05 from King's Cross for the opening night of *Their Finest Hours*.[1] Arrive at the Crucible about 7.15. Jill Foster is there and we meet Norman Yardley and his wife as well. Yardley, a childhood cricketing hero,[2] is gentle and genial and his wife, a bright attractive lady, is nice to us as well.

As soon as *Underwood* starts I know we'll be alright – the audience warm instantly to the situation, the cast play it impeccably, the pace sustains and so do the laughs, coming with a volume and consistency which I just didn't expect. The whole of *Underwood* works like a gem, including the ending, when an entire cricket team walks through and the mother rises up to the strains of the 'Hallelujah Chorus'. Came out feeling almost tearful with emotion and gratitude to David Leland and the cast.

Buchanan was slower, but the effect of the boxed-in cast worked superbly. Clarity a problem, but much, much better performance from Philip Jackson as the Italian – he was splendid – and Julian Hough hardly missed a laugh as the Frenchman. Again the audience reaction sustained well, apart from a morose, fidgety lady, who finally left halfway through *Buchanan* and was, I heard later, the *Guardian* critic!

---

1 Our one-act plays. *Underwood's Finest Hour* is set in a labour room with a mother straining to give birth and a doctor straining to listen to a particularly exciting Test Match. *Buchanan's Finest Hour* is about a marketing idea gone awry. The cast, including the Pope, are trapped inside a packing crate throughout.
2 Norman Yardley, Yorkshire and England Captain. Cricketer of the Year 1948.

Friday, May 21st, Sheffield

Woke up in the small hours with a dream of awful reviews. Terry had had exactly the same dream!

At 7.30 a knock on the door – a cup of tea, *The Times* and the *Morning Telegraph*. Nothing in *The Times*, but I hardly expected it – but Paul Allen in the *Morning Telegraph* gives us a useful and quite charitable review. He was impressed with the experiment with the boxes, and also said there were 'breathtakingly funny moments'. Read it again while shaving. Fourteen years since I last searched the Sheffield papers for the theatre reviews![1]

Outside my window it's a bright, sunny morning. Directly below me the forlorn and deserted platforms of Victoria Station, once the starting place for Sheffield's own prestige express – the Master Cutler. Now it's boarded up and even the track has been taken out on Platform One. Allow 30 seconds for bout of railway nostalgia.

Downstairs to meet Jill and very crumpled Terry – I tell him to go back to his room and get up again. Despite a lot of discussion on how much better it is to go back to London early and not lose another *Ripping Yarn* writing day, TJ remains unhappy about not talking to the cast – even though David isn't planning to meet them until this afternoon. Even after we've left Sheffield on the 8.30, ordered breakfast and settled down, Terry is still itchy with indecision and at Chesterfield, our first stop, he suddenly grabs his bag and, with a muttered 'I'm going back', he disappears off the train.

The bemused restaurant attendant has just cleared away Terry's breakfast things when he reappears. 'It's 55 minutes until the next train back,' he says resignedly, and sits down and comes back to London.

A bad review in *The Guardian*, coldly and heavily giving away the plot and all the surprises (such as they are) of *Buchanan* and saying that if *Their Finest Hours* could have been *Their Finest Minutes* it would have got a few more laughs.

Strangely enough, no sooner am I back in London and at my desk than Bob Scott rang from the Exchange Theatre, Manchester, to ask me to do an 'evening' up there later in the year. He knew the *Guardian*

1 During my 'gap' year in 1962, I joined a local amateur dramatic society – the Brightside and Carbrook Co-Operative Players. Won Best Perf. (Gentleman) at Co-Op (N.E. Section) Drama Festival in Leeds in 1962.

reviewer and confirmed she was a sad lady, who even found Strindberg light.

Good news from David Leland later in the day, telling us the Crucible want to extend its run beyond June 5th.

T Gilliam drops in to say John Bird has plumped for the part of Reek in *Jabberwocky*, and Harry H Corbett for the Squire. Both pleased me – they sound very right. John C has now definitely backed out, but apparently rang Terry G and was very contrite and even offered to come and talk about the script with him.

Finally got down to reading some more of Al Levinson's long, unpublished novel, *Millwork*. Like most books it repays a longer session rather than three pages at a time before falling asleep. Am getting quite involved.

Saturday, May 22nd

Lunch down at Dulwich. Angela looking well and tanned. She plays tennis very regularly now (to keep her from sitting in the house brooding, she says). Much more positive, or certainly less negative, than when I last saw her. Veryan is away walking the Ridgeway.

Jeremy hovers, trying, whenever he can, to get in a plea for his latest passion – owning a moped. He's not allowed to ride one for a couple of months, but apparently most of his friends at Alleyn's School have them. He shows me his electric guitar. Looks fine, but he's trying to play the Led Zeppelin songbook, before he's learnt basic rock 'n' roll. I can understand how his few oft-repeated heavy rock chords can send Angela batty.

I feel sorry for Angela, suddenly confronted with Jeremy's emerging independence. Just how long should he stay out at the pub listening to Meal Ticket tonight? Either she's cautious or she's taking a risk. No solution. I suppose we've got it coming.

A pleasant wander around Crystal Palace Park with the kids. Lots to see and do. The prehistoric monsters on the islands are still one of the sights of London; there's a little zoo where goats and sheep wander around 'mingling' with the crowds. Rachel loved them – and wandered around in primal innocence tapping rams on their bottoms and laughing.

Sunday, May 23rd

Sunny and dry again. After morning's swim at Holiday Inn and completion of a letter to Al L, we drive over to the Davidsons' for lunch.

Ian tells a good Barry Humphries tale[1] – apparently Barry was in full swing as Edna in his show at the Apollo, when a man in the front row, ever so discreetly, ever so carefully, left for a pee. But he couldn't really escape Edna's eye and Edna remarked on his absence and talked to his wife for a while about his waterworks. Having found out the man's name, Edna and the audience plotted a little surprise for him. So when he duly reappeared from the gents and made for his seat, once again stealthily and soundlessly, without disturbing a soul, Edna gave a cue and, as he was half-way down the gangway, the entire theatre chanted 'Hello Colin!'

Wednesday, May 26th

Drive down to Terry's in late morning for a combined session on *Ripping Yarns*. Don't really get down to work until after lunch. TJ has made a very funny start on an episode centring round a vicar and an adoring women's club who all want to marry him. Nicely written nineteenth century polite language. We chat about it and decide it could make a half hour of the *Tenant of Wildfell Hall, Wuthering Heights*, Brontë/Austen/Eliot style. Lots of repression and social restrictions and smouldering passions and breaking hearts.

I read 'Escape from Stalag Luft 112B', which I've been working on these past seven days. Despite one or two blockages, it wrote itself fairly easily and Terry was very pleased. He thinks it's nearly half an hour already. Within a few minutes of talking about it Terry came out with a very clear and funny ending, so I don't think we were over-optimistic in thinking that we have another *Ripping Yarn* as good as finished and a strong idea for a fifth script. I took the vicar and left TJ with the escape.

Tuesday, June 1st

I find myself at the door of the Hampstead Theatre Club. This highly respected little theatre still has the air of a gypsy caravan in a bombed site.

---

1 Ian collaborated on material for Barry Humphries' stage show.

Meet David Aukin at the door of the caravan. He looks thinner, otherwise the same as when he and Rudman were carrying off the glittering prizes on the Oxford stage in '62/'63. Mike Rudman joins us. He has that slight edge of American forthrightness, or aggression, or perhaps directness, which always makes me a little uncomfortable. I reach quickly for my English defence – and make a few jokes.

My task is to deliver the scripts of *Finest Hours* to him, in the hope that he will be able to go and see the plays and maybe bring them back to the Theatre Club. For some reason I am still a little uneasy as I push them – for I feel that they're lightweight.

Off about 7.00 to drive down to Whitechapel Galleries, where Chris Orr is having his first complete exhibition and his first exhibition in London.

After a few attempts, find the Whitechapel Galleries – they're well off the beaten artistic track, in the Jewish East End a few doors down from Blooms Deli, which makes me agreeably nostalgic for New York, and facing out over the bewildering, traffic-filled wilderness of the new, improved, enlarged Aldgate roundabout for cars and not people.

Chris Orr is very helpful and shows me round his stuff. Find a mutual admiration for the work of Pont, the 1930s cartoonist, whose gentle, satirical studies like 'The British Character' come to mind when you look at some of Chris's finely drawn pictures.

Robert shows me the 'rushes' of the first Signford production *Chris Orr's John Ruskin,* which is out in a couple of weeks, but later he tells me of a much more interesting proposition involving buying a fifteenth-century barn, owned by New College, Oxford. It could, R thinks, be bought for a song, and both Helen and I liked the adventure of working (Harold and Vita-like!) on an old, historic hulk and literally shaping the interior ourselves.

Wednesday, June 2nd

Have to buy the *Mirror* today as the first page trails a picture of John and Connie and the heading 'When Love Turns Sour at Fawlty Towers'. Inside, disappointingly accurate account of J and C's new living arrangements, whereby they share the house, but not the bed.

The boiled egg is scarcely dry upon my lips, when a man from the *Evening News* rings asking for JC's phone number. I decline to give it as politely as possible – but nearly spill the beans about the time John ... later, later.

Wednesday, June 9th

Terry rings. Mike Rudman of the Hampstead Theatre Club has read *Their Finest Hours*. He loved *Underwood* and disliked *Buchanan*. *Underwood* he wants to bring down and put on, and tentatively asked if we would be prepared to accept a commission to write another one to go with it! Back to square one.

Dave Yallop, friend of Graham's, and one of the few men I've seen tell Frost to shut up and sit down (when Dave was floor managing *Frost on Sunday*), wants to write a documentary about Python's court experiences in the US. Dave has good credentials – he wrote a respected and hard-hitting documentary on the Craig-Bentley case, and he's approaching the US case from the anti-censorship angle, which could and should be aired. It appears that Rik Hertzberg's prestigious *New Yorker* piece has started a few balls rolling since it was reprinted in the *Sunday Times*.

G Chapman, whom I also spoke to, is well set in his new career of film producer (on *The Odd Job*). Only yesterday he'd tried to get hold of Jack Lemmon, through his agent, a Mr De Witt – only to be told by a secretary that he couldn't speak to Mr De Witt, as he'd just died!

Thursday, June 10th

Work on a possible new *Ripping Yarn* – 'The Wreck of the Harvey Goldsmith', just because I like the title.

Squash with Richard[1] in the afternoon and Ian and Anthea D and Michael and Anne Henshaw to supper. We watch Monty Python Series Four repeats. It's 'Golden Age of Ballooning', a very rich show and I still can't quite figure out people's disappointed reaction to it when it first went out. Interesting to note in *Stage* today that after its second programme, Python was rated by Jictar[2] No. 2= in the London area and 5 in the south (both times above *Porridge*). In the rest of the country, nowhere.

---

1 Richard Guedalla, a neighbour.
2 Joint Industry Committee for Television Advertising Research.

Sunday, June 13th

Finish the day, and Al Levinson's *Millwork*, sitting outside my room in the gathering dusk with a glass of scotch. I liked the novel in the end, after a sticky start. It's warm and friendly and sympathetic and generally full of Al's humanity. Must write my review to him tomorrow.

Tuesday, June 15th

At five o'clock this evening to Neal's Yard. Four or five builders working in André's studio; they glower at me rather resentfully as I wander in, looking as if I owned the place, which of course I do. Terry Gilliam has summonsed me to my first piece of work on *Jabberwocky* – to do a scene with an American girl, Deborah Fallender, whom TG wants to screen test as the Princess.[1]

Upstairs, in Terry's part of 14/15 Neal's Yard, Julian has set up the camera. Terry Bedford, his small frame bulging a little in places, indicating incipient symptoms of the good life, which he must be enjoying as a highly paid member of the world of commercials, has already stuck a pair of tights over the lens to achieve his award-winning soft-lighting effect.

Deborah is very nervous, but quite sweet, and with a good sense of humour. We do the scene two or three times – unfortunately it reminds me so forcibly of the Castle Anthrax scene that I can't tell how good or bad it is.

To meal at the Siciliano with the Walmsleys and Simon A. Jane W very fed up that 'Kojak' – Telly Savalas – has today won a libel suit of £34,000 damages at the Old Bailey. He sent each member of the jury a signed photo of himself with 'Thank You' written on. Now, as taxi drivers say, there must be a sketch there. Jane W has interviewed the said Savalas, didn't like his pushy arrogance one bit, and finds it easy to believe the libel.

Thursday, June 17th

At 11.30 have to drive over to the Beeb to meet Fred Knapman, senior designer at the BBC, who's going to show me a possible Peruvian village set for 'Across the Andes by Frog', out at Pinewood.

1 She got the job.

The set, on a back lot, is in quite a run-down state (T Hughes tells me it was made for Dirk Bogarde's *Singer Not the Song*), but for that reason rather good for our purposes.

They are preparing for a new James Bond film at Pinewood – starting shooting in August – and a 300-foot-long, 40-foot-high steel-frame building is being erected there for one set-up! I feel very cheap, grubbing around the decaying back lot!

Down to Regent's Park for a Python Annual General Meeting. We have three companies – Python Productions Ltd, Python (Monty) Pictures Ltd and Kay-Gee-Bee Music Ltd. We manage to go through the official convening and closing procedure of all three companies in four minutes!

Terry J models the Python T-shirt, which is approved, with a few design alterations.

Finally we agree to spend £30,000 on acquiring full rights from Bavaria TV to the two German specials.

Taxi back with Dr Chapman, who has had a very tiring week film producing – and finds the whole thing much harder than he expected. Apparently Peter Sellers is very anxious to do the odd job – and is muscling in through his agent – whereas Graham wants Peter O'Toole in it, but O'Toole is less 'bankable' than Sellers.

Monday, June 21st, Southwold

My father's 76th birthday. I decide to go up to Southwold for the day, which is a pleasant way of giving him a present and marking the occasion, even though I suppose I should be writing away in London.

He's watching the Test Match on TV when I arrive at Croft Cottage. I take him cards from us all and a collection of reminiscences from a BBC Radio series about the British in India from 1900 on, which I hope will find an echo amongst his own memories of India, which seem to become more vivid the older he gets.

A bottle of champagne for lunch and a little stroll outside on the lawn, where a year ago we were drinking and eating with quite a crowd as we celebrated his 75th. Today just me and Mother, but he has had a letter from Angela and Aunt K [his sister].

Head down over lunch – he must concentrate all his energies on getting the food into his mouth, and cannot talk. Even after lunch, when there is discussion as to what to do in the afternoon, he cannot manage to make the word, so he writes down 'Rhododendrons'.

I take him for a drive to see the rhododendrons, which flank the road near Henham in lush profusion at this time of year. Sadly they've been heavily trimmed back and there's little to see, but he's enjoyed the ride in the car and didn't seem to want to do anything more ambitious.

Read Pirsig's *Zen and the Art* on the train back and found the simplicity and effectiveness of some of his words of wisdom revelatory. A sort of enlightened calm had taken hold of me by the time I got home. I really was reacting to things in a quite different way. Books affect me a little like that anyway, but this more so than any I have read.

Though on this tranquil summer's evening his theory of quality as reality may induce fine thoughts and comfort, it's going to be difficult when the radios start playing on the building sites and the ads blare out of my car radio and the phone starts ringing.

Wednesday, June 23rd

Drive into London to watch a two-hour showing of the Amnesty documentary shot by Roger Graef at the end of April. Jonathan Miller and I are about the only participants there.

It's a fascinating start – all the little glimpses of rehearsals in progress. The Goodies stand out like a sore thumb when rehearsing 'Funky Gibbon', but come out as nice, human chaps when they sit around talking, and Alan Bennett's asides and revelations on his Fringe colleagues are sweetly, disarmingly, catty. Talking to TJ about Python, he ends up rather sadly, 'Well, if you ever want another member for the group ...'

Am struck by how relaxed and worldly-wise the *Beyond the Fringe* team are. Beside them, not that the film makes comparisons, the Pythons seem jolly but sort of more businesslike, less rambling and discursive. Maybe in ten years' time we'll have aged and mellowed in the same rather comforting way.

Thursday, June 24th

I enjoy a rare day with no need to go out – not even a game of squash. And I find myself with time on my hands. I read Sylvia Plath's *Letters* at lunch and outside in the evening. Rather brittle, full of sudden ups and sudden downs. Plathitudes. Life/Man/Work is one day marvellous, brilliantly handsome, ecstatic, unbearably wonderful, and the next depressing, frightful – a great monster of awfulness. She expresses herself so articulately, but her underlying wide-eyed attitudes are the same as any awkward teenager's.

A hot evening – doors and windows open all over Gospel Oak.

Thursday, July 1st

So far an excellent week for writing. On Tuesday I worked an almost unbroken seven-and-a-half-hour-stint typing, correcting, revising, sharpening and generally putting together the northern tale ('The Testing of Eric Olthwaite').

Talk to Gilliam at Neal's Yard late Tuesday, where I'm having a fitting for the Dennis costume. He's slightly worried, and so am I, that various actors are very keen to get in ideas of their own – which don't exactly fit in with the spirit of the movie. Harry H Corbett wants his codpiece to be gradually enlarged throughout the film. Max Wall suggests putting small rubber balls in the end of the fingers of his gloves, so when he takes them off they bounce.

Down to Terry's, revelling in the Mini sunroof, where we work on with 'Curse of the Claw'.

The writing seems to come easily and the plot and story falls into place so well that by 4.00 we have completed a sixth Ripping Yarn! The third since we began writing again after New York – so that's three half-hours in five weeks.

So I left TJ at 4.30; we don't in fact need to write any more scripts until next year – and July will see us, for the first time, largely going our separate ways. And yet during this last spell of writing I've felt closer to TJ than at any time since before the Grail. I feel happy that the demarcation problems following on from Tomkinson have not, in any way, appeared to lessen our writing strength, or weaken our writing relationship. We've adjusted (or is it just me?) to our new work relationship and actually improved our personal relationship (or is it just me?).

From TJ's to Anne's. Whilst I'm there a phone call to say that the appeal judges in the US have just laid down a twenty-page judgement on the Python v ABC case, which is unequivocally favourable to Python. This sounds better news than we ever hoped for.

Saturday, July 3rd

Woke this morning determined to drink only moderately today. Failed hopelessly. No sooner had last night's mixture of lager and cider seeped through my system than it was being quietly worked on by some very more-ish sangria at the Denselows.[1] Helen and I and Rachel were round there for a lunch party, which turned into a very late barbecue.

An interesting split of guests between a large group of peaceful, rather bucolic folk, who turned out to live in a commune in Haverstock Hill. They sat indoors most of the time, whilst out in the blazing heat – near the drinks – were Robin's media friends from *Panorama*, Bush House, *The Guardian*, etc.

The communites were amicable, but tended to talk about 'cosmic awareness' and 'waves of communication responses'. I find unless you know a little of their terms of reference, it's hard to climb aboard their thoughts. But a man called Ian, who was a sort of translator-figure for them, was very chatty and asked us along any time. He said he was in charge of security.

Tuesday, July 6th

Off to some bookshops and then over to Professor Dr Powell for what turns out to be quite a tough piece of surgery on my back left lower teeth, which have been giving me trouble over the last two months. Powell digs deep and furiously. It's the first surgery since 1972 and he certainly is thorough over it. It's stitched and I experience with a stirring of nostalgia the taste of the dressing over my gums.

I drive from Powell's over to Shepherd's Bush. Join about fifty others in the tiny Bush Theatre to see *Blood Sports* by David Edgar.

I only stay for the first hour – but saw an actor, Simon Callow, who I think would be excellent for RSM in 'Across the Andes' – because I know the injections are about to wear off and the tooth (or what's left of it) will start hurting. 'Bone just melts away in your mouth,' was one of the encouraging things Powell had said as he levered and drilled and scraped away at my jaw.

Well, it did begin to hurt. Hardly slept at all. I listened to two sides of

1 Robin Denselow, *Guardian* music journalist, BBC documentary maker and reporter. Lived a few doors down from us with his first wife Bambi.

'John is, on a good night, one of the world's greatest corpsers.' And I am not far behind. 'Silly Walks' at Drury Lane, 1975.

Passport photo, 1975: big collars and mad, staring eyes. Why did anyone allow me in their country?

On Central Park South, first New York publicity trip, March 1975. I am reading from the guidebook, which always used to annoy Graham.

Terry, Ma, Jeremy
Herbert, Al and me,
Camberwell.

Helen, Rachel, Will
and Tom with friends
Diana and Sean
Duncan on their boat,
Pilcomayo, on the
River Dee, 1975.

Fans in America, 1975.
Graham lights up
behind me.

Python publicity
photo with Neil Innes
selflessly standing in
for Terry Jones.

Summer of '75,
Three Men in a Boat.
Stephen Moore,
me, Tim Curry and
Montmorency the dog.

Prelude to disaster. The
photograph sequence
(followed by the boat
getting trapped in the
lock gate). *Three Men
in a Boat,* June 1975.

With Ma and sister Angela at Dulwich.

Next generation. Miles Innes and Tom Palin became good friends during *Live at City Center*, New York, 1976.

Rachel, Helen and the back garden, Gospel Oak, London, 1976.

'Peter Cook, who apologised for his slightly glazed state saying he was recovering from a long night . . . discussing Lenny Bruce's drug problem – steadfastly refuses to learn the words of the Condemned Man in our "Court Sketch". Amnesty show at Her Majesty's. (March 31st, 1976)

My vocal nemesis, 'Gumby Flower Arranging' at full blast. City Center, New York, 1976.

'You're Pythons. Do something funny for me.' An unpleasant little episode at the Bronx Zoo, New York. (April 20th, 1976)

Photos by Bill Meng, NYZS

. . . Monty Python's Flying Circus at the Zoo. On an awfully sunny Tuesday in April, six, er . . . rather five British Pythons—Terry Jones, Michael Palin, Graham Chapman, Terry Gilliam, and Neil Innis—presented a python (named Monty, of course) to General Director William G. Conway and the Reptile House keepers. (Another member of the Python group, Eric Idle, is afraid of snakes and would not take part in the official presentation. Phoo!)
The snake—a real Burmese python about fourteen feet long—was donated to the Bronx Zoo by Warner Books to commemorate the 100,000th sale of Monty Python's Big Red Book (which is really blue and very silly).

'Really quite enjoy flashing a naughty part of the body in a public place – and getting paid rather than arrested for it.' *Jabberwocky* filming at Chepstow Castle. (September 16th, 1976)

'I like my gear. At least it's going to be a deal more comfortable than the armour of *Holy Grail*.' As Dennis Cooper in *Jabberwocky*. (July 14th, 1976)

Helen and our friend
Ranji, Amsterdam, 1971.

Perks of being a
director of Shepperton
studios; submarine
cannon from the film
*The Land That Time
Forgot* is saved from
the rubbish tip and
ends up in my back
garden, 1978.

a Lenny Bruce LP. I sat outside in the garden with a glass of Laphroaig at
3.00. I read the local paper cover to cover at 4 a.m. I was up at my desk at
6.00 – and finally fell into a deep sleep at around 6.30 in the morning.

Friday, July 9th

Anne brings me a copy of the Federal Court of Appeals Judgement in
the Python v ABC case. The Judgement was dated June 30th 1976 and is
very strongly favourable to Python – they recommend that the injunction should be upheld. So Terry's and my trip, in that cold and bleak
December (which seems light years away now) was worthwhile after all.

The Judgement indicates that, in the judges' opinion, Python would
have a substantial chance of a favourable verdict in the courts and
damages and all else that could follow.

I personally am against a big damages award – it may be the way
lawyers play it, but I think that the popular image of Python winning $1
million would erase in people's minds some of the reasons why we won
it. But I think we should have a strong bargaining counter in any
attempt to recover our costs. We shall see.

Monday, July 12th

Hard look at *Jabberwocky* script this morning. It's all held together by a
manic intensity of vision and atmosphere, and if this intensity can be
sustained in the characterisations as well, the film will be, well, certainly
not dull. The writing in certain individual scenes is sometimes flat,
sometimes conventional and occasionally gives the impression of being
rushed – but I think a careful look at the script before each day's shooting will tighten up dialogue, which, by comparison to some of the *Holy
Grail* scenes – the death cart, the philosophical peasants – is sparse in
comic impact.

But the shape of the film is good, and it's just up to Terry G to try
and achieve the Herculean task of recapturing his animation style in a
live action movie – and for £400,000.

Wednesday, July 14th

Posted off the *Esquire* article about Python's New York adventures to Lee
Eisenberg, plus long missive to Eric in France.

At ten down to Fitzroy Square for a read-through with some of the *Jabberwocky* principals. Max Wall and John Le Mesurier speak softly together in one corner. Old Acting Hands, both of whom have been through long spells of rejection and have come out wise, kindly, but above all unhurried. Then there are the Actors – Derek Francis, the Bishop, Peter Cellier as the Leading Merchant – working actors, not stars, not personalities, their personalities are their parts and they click into theatrical speech and gesture from the first read-through.

My friend for the morning is John Bird, amiable and sharp as ever. He's playing the Herald, and is not particularly happy with it. 'I do hate shouting,' he mutters sadly.

He and I are joined after half an hour by John Gorman, so there are now three of us in the Brash Young Men of Revue corner. Gorman's down from his Old Bakery in Suffolk. Slightly subdued – which means quite over the top by anyone else's standards. Covered in strange badges – including one for 'The Womble Bashers', which I like.

John Le Mes is marvellous, his pained double-takes are a joy to watch. Max has difficulty finding his lines, but as they mainly consist of 'Er … Oh …' it doesn't really matter. The Actors Act and John G and Bird make people laugh.

At lunchtime costume fitting session. I like my gear. At least it's going to be a deal more comfortable than the armour of *Holy Grail*.

A drink with Terry G, Max W and Bird. Max tells long, rambling, discursive tales – very funny if you've got an afternoon to spare. He drinks pints of Guinness in the pub at Seven Dials – but he drinks them slowly. He's also deaf in one ear and most of what Bird says in his low murmur (which is almost incomprehensible anyway) is totally lost on Max. But always those kind, wise, soft eyes and slow smile.

Back home via Dodo in Westbourne Grove, where I buy Graham and David a huge basket of plastic fruit for their tenth anniversary party tonight.

Off to the theatre at eight to see *Funny Peculiar* by Mike Stott. Only ten years ago you couldn't carry a plank across the stage without the Lord Chamberlain's permission – and now here's a comfortable, rather staid, London theatre audience, watching two women quite explicitly sucking off a man as he lies in his hospital bed. Funny and liberating, but deeply shocking to a man used to writing for television!

Off up to G Chapman's party. Sangria, champagne and good nosh. The house was cleaner and tidier than I'd ever seen it. The gathering was smallish and quite organised – the garden floodlit by Strand Electrics. Graham, on very good behaviour, wandered through in white suit looking like a benevolent tropical planter at a festivity for his employees. Peter Cook was soberish too.

Alison (still great with child) and Terry, Neil and Yvonne, Barry Cryer, Jo Kendall,[1] David Yallop are all there. But we're all getting older and staider, I thought, until Graham, Bernard McK and Dave Yallop gave their rendition of 'Without You' to a bemused audience. They stand in Gumby-like rigidity and yell the chorus to this lovely song at a hideous, horrendously loud pitch – and with trousers down for the second chorus.

Back home around 1.15.

Friday, July 16th

After lunch walked round balmy, humid London – to the studio, to the *Jabberwocky* office. To Great Titchfield Street to meet Warren Mitchell and read through my part with him. A tough little guy – close cropped hair, a tight, intense way of talking … but busy and extrovert in his command of a conversation.

Talk for a while about how bad actors are at dealing with praise. Warren said he approached Paul Scofield once and told him how marvellous he'd been in something, and, as Warren described it, 'the poor guy didn't know where to put himself'.

A bit of a read through. Warren tries his funny teeth he's brought along. Eventually fall to chortling over *Till Death*. Warren says he was third choice for Alf Garnett. First choice was Leo McKern! Problems of success of *Till Death* – who created Alf Garnett? Was it [writer] Johnny Speight or Warren? Clearly they both think they own more of Alf than the other thinks they deserve. God, if Python split over who created what, it could be the court case of the century!

'Silly old moo' – the famous phrase, Warren says, wasn't scripted. It came out during a rehearsal when he forgot the line 'Silly old mare'.

---

1 A Cambridge contemporary of John and Graham, Jo was in the cast of *Cambridge Circus* with them and later in *At Last the 1948 Show*.

Monday, July 19th

To Southwold for last visit before *Jabberwocky/Ripping Yarns* filming begins. Notice today how frail Ma is becoming, at the same time as Dad's muscular mobility is worsening.

There are no solutions to the problem which can give anyone any pleasure. The wretched twin attacks of Parkinson's and hardening of the arteries are destroying Father physically and the permanent hospitalisation which looms, now I would think, within the year, will destroy him mentally.

It rains hard as the train pulls into Liverpool Street at nine. Clatter home on the Broad Street Line. Comforting melancholy.

Wednesday, July 21st

Rehearsals with Harry H Corbett (a good actor, but oddly unsure of himself – he wears a suit and he mumbles rather self-deprecatingly that he feels it's important to look smart on the first day of a job! And I think he meant it.). But we get on well, and the scenes together will be funny. The same with Paul Curran, who plays my father. A Scot, friend of Jimmy Gilbert and Ian MacNaughton, from the seemingly inexhaustible supply of actors spewed out by Glasgow Citizens' Theatre.

Take Tom swimming after game of squash with Richard. In the evening Simon A rings and asks me to go and see *Hester Street* (written and directed by Joan Micklin Silver) with him. A delightful film – unpretentious and wholly successful. 10/10.

Back from this sensitive, sensible look at early Jewish immigrants struggling to settle in New York in 1896 to a phone call from Michael Henshaw to tell me that a meeting of lawyers and accountants representing all the Pythons have decided (not even recommended) that the next Python film should be written abroad. Oh ... and that they had projected its profit at £1 million.

Talk into Thursday with Simon A over the question of lifestyles and the way money isolates you from people. Simon quotes the case of a house in Mill Hill which he went to at the weekend, where there is opulence on a scale which stunned even Simon. It's the home of a man who just does deals. He benefits no one but himself, is surrounded by non-friends and basks unhappily in wealth that could rehouse half Camden's waiting list in a week.

Contrast with Clive Hollick, Simon's City friend[1] – head of Vavasseur and Shepperton Studios, etc, and a committed socialist who feels the City is hopelessly corrupt, but is trying to change it from within. He won't take any more than his £15,000 salary and refuses all expense account perks. A man to watch.

Monday, July 26th

Letter from *Esquire* (Lee Eisenberg) to say they like the article,[2] will print it almost uncut and have offered me $1,500 payment! Which, given the present dilapidated state of sterling, is nearly £800.

Jill rings, hardly able to contain her excitement. They want me for two days, to advertise Mattessons' sausages, and will pay £10,000 and may go higher! Jill is obviously keen for me to accept (it will mean £1,000 to her, after all), but I can't – and in a sense the enormity of the money offered (almost double my entire writing fee for thirteen *Ripping Yarns*!) makes my refusal easier. Jill clearly thinks I'm bonkers, but we decide to elbow any further commercial offers – and there have been a spate of them in the last few months – until March next year.

Filming on *Jabberwocky* began this morning at Shepperton, but I'm not required until Wednesday and have no words until Friday.

Wednesday, July 28th

A leisurely start to *Jabberwocky*. I'm not called until 10.30. No cars available on this picture, so I drive over to Shepperton myself to see how long it takes. Miss the turning off the M3 and career on for a further twelve miles before I can turn and roar back again. At the gates of Shepperton a uniformed gateman has no idea where *Jabberwocky* is being shot and directs me to a back lot where there is nobody to be seen. So my carefully nurtured calm is ruffled a little.

Eventually sniff out the studio where they're filming the crumbling court of King Bruno. The entire set is thick with dust and debris. The normally searingly bright studio lights are veiled with black drapes, giving the set a dim, sepulchral, twilight appearance. Pigeons cluck at

1 Clive, later Lord Hollick, and Simon Albury were friends from Nottingham University.
2 About Python in New York.

the top of the throne, rubble is dropped during the takes, whenever John Bird as the Herald bangs his staff.

In the middle of this murk, little figures, dwarfed by the height of the set, move around. Two cameras are in use. TG looks thin, but excited. He directs softly, padding around the camera, letting the First Assistant do all the shouting. They're a half-day behind already and the producers are looking around with fixed grins. Terry agrees it's like the first week of the *Grail* – an immediate artistic/economic gap.

Max looks wonderful as a little, wizened king. He's taken his teeth out and hasn't shaved. He is the personification of death warmed up. John Le Mes in his severe black skull cap looks more sinister than I've ever seen him. It's a magnificent fusion of imaginative costumes (Hazel and Charles), imaginative sets (Roy Smith), and imaginative make-up (Maggie).

Terry says that Milly Burns and Bill Harman have done a jackdaw job all over Shepperton, pinching bits of other sets. They've just finished a German co-production of Mozart's *Figaro*, from which quite a few props/sets will recur in *Jabberwocky*!

I wait until 3.30 to play a short and rough scene with Bernard Bresslaw and Bryan Pringle. TG says it looked terrifying. We do an impromptu fight – none of us knowing quite what's going on – but there's a rush to get Bernard B off to Bournemouth, where he's doing a summer show on the pier.

Friday, July 30th

Up at seven. The first taste of the real joys of filming. As Eric puts it in his letter from France which arrived today … 'Up early to be carried around by talkative drivers to wrong locations in time to get into the wrong costume and be ready to wait for five or six hours for a couple of seconds' appearance on celluloid.'

It's not as much fun as that yet.

On set by 8.30, rehearsing a long scene in the Queen's Haemorrhoids with Bernard Bresslaw and Harry H Corbett, both of whom get to fling my (only eleven stone two by our scales this morning) body around. Bernard is kind, friendly, soft and cheerful as ever and I learn to my amazement that he's breaking at ten to go to his brother's funeral.

Harry and I are quite soon into the turkey-eating scene and Terry G says that this is the fastest they've worked all week. Yesterday had been particularly frustrating. He had spent 45 minutes with Peter Cellier, who plays the Merchant, trying to overcome his reluctance to pick his nose on screen.

A long day. One hour's lunch break – I eat with Harry H in the grim canteen. (Like much of Shepperton Studio Centre, it bears all the tacky indications of an enterprise on its last legs, which was being dismantled by the broker's men as a reprieve came through.)

Harry doesn't enjoy film acting. He finds the dehumanisation of the actor on a film set troubles him. I noticed today that even an actor of his experience seems to harden and tense up on the take – losing a little of the fun he's had on rehearsal.

On set from 8.30 until a quarter to seven in the evening – then gratefully and happily into a hot bath to clean off the sweat and grime of the day's work. This kind of manual acting takes it out of you.

Monday, August 2nd

Out on the *Oliver* lot[1] for most of the day, doing stunt work rather than acting. Much lying face-down in the dirt (peat and hay mixture) with Bernard Bresslaw, who is in fine form.

Encouraging viewing of Friday's rushes. The painstakingly lit sequences are not as good as the hastily grabbed, hand-held shots of me trying to distract Bernard's attention in the pub. This sequence was fresh, fast and – to prove the point – got consistent laughs at rushes.

I learn from the rushes that I must keep my performance up – the naturalistic way of playing (Frears' influence here) is not sufficient – a touch of silliness is required.

Tuesday, August 3rd

Cope with letters in the morning, phone calls, and eventually at lunchtime sign *Jabberwocky* contract (£6,000 due by end of filming, £1,500 deferred and 2½% of producer's gross). A motorcycle messenger in big boots and a rubber suit witnesses this impressive document.

Robert's for a glass of BBC Chablis at 6.30. He's been chairing a discussion programme for the Beeb Foreign Service on philosophy – Stuart

1 The set had been built in the mid-sixties for the hugely successful musical, *Oliver* by Lionel Bart. Directed by Carol Reed (*The Third Man*).

Hampshire and Ben Whitaker amongst the participants. Robert jokes about it, but I'm quite impressed. We walk from Robert's, through the Dickensian back alleys north of Fleet Street, skirting round the Inns of Court and across Waterloo Bridge to the concrete cultural wilderness of the South Bank.

At the National Theatre (the first time I've been inside it) I long for that hustle and bustle you get in St Martin's Lane and Shaftesbury Avenue. Here the audience is entirely made up of respectable bourgeois folk like ourselves. No coach tours here, no stout elderly ladies out for a giggle or a treat. Just a flood of serious, trendy, culturally aware, white wine bibbers like myself.

It's comfortable inside the Lyttelton Theatre, and the sight lines and acoustics require no effort or strain as in many other London theatres. The play *Weapons of Happiness* by Howard Brenton is not, as they say, 'my cup of tea'. It belongs to the belligerent, strident, didactic school of theatre, in which dialogue is sacrificed to monologues, characters depressingly clichéd, angry cockney workers, champagne drinking employers, etc. Occasionally some pleasing and quite moving writing, but as a whole I disliked it, as I felt most of the audience did.

We eat at the Neal Street Restaurant. David Hockney posters on the wall and David Hockney himself at a table.

Walk back to Fetter Lane discussing possibilities for a new Orr/Hewison/Signford book – a catalogue of 'All The Things You Ever Wanted'. Busy, by the light of the *Daily Mirror* building, discussing and enthusing over who would contribute to it, when we discover it's a quarter to two.

Thursday, August 5th

Cast of many at Shepperton today for the flagellants' procession. Graham Crowden is the leader of the fanatics. He's a splendid figure, but has trouble remembering his many and strange words. Hugely impressive takes of him and his crowd of grotty followers streaming up the mediaeval streets keep ending with Graham, white beard flowing and hand up-raised like Ivan the Terrible, coming to a sort of paralysed halt with a heartfelt 'Oh, fuck!'

Lunch with Christopher Logue. A nice, gentle chap, he's playing a flagellant with heart-warming enthusiasm and enjoyment. I ask him about the *Private Eye*/Goldsmith case soon to come into court. He says

Goldsmith is a nasty piece of work, but there is one, though only one, untruth in all *Private Eye*'s allegations – when he was said to have attended a meeting he didn't in fact attend.

Michael White is down today. Michael looks around at TG's carefully chosen extras and declares that this must be the ugliest film ever made.

It's a long day and the shocking canteen food doesn't raise any spirits. The chicken at supper tastes, as Crowden puts it, as though it had done panto for two years at Ashton-under-Lyne.

We night shoot until 12.30 a.m. (the extra half-hour will cost thousands as the unions can claim for an entire extra day) catapulting a blazing fanatic over the walls of the castle. The effect works superbly and everyone trails back to the dressing rooms.

Home and to bed by two. A nineteen-hour day, I reckon.

Friday, August 6th

Only the jolly, down-to-earth good humour of Bryan Pringle and the unquenchable cheerfulness of Bernard Bresslaw make this long day of waiting bearable. Finally, having been on set since eleven, am used at five for a 30-second take. It's the getting dirty and the cleaning up – a process lasting an hour at least – which is the most wearing and when I get home at 8.30 I'm in the mood for a good meal and a chat.

Ring Simon Albury and we go to Au Bois St Jean. Simon very interested in Shepperton – my remarks about food, etc, have led, I'm told, to speedy action from Mr Hollick! SA says he may be asked to run the place (i.e. Shepperton), but says it's all very vague.

Saturday, August 7th

The alarm shrills into my hangover at seven. God – only five hours' sleep behind me and I have to curse my enthusiasm in arranging a horse-riding lesson at Luton at nine this morning!

In my still-hungover state, I'm fairly relaxed and once I've got used to the size of the horse and the unexpectedly long distance from the ground, I get on well. The horse is used to it – it was under Glenda Jackson on *Elizabeth R*! Also ride a mule and a donkey, which cleverly made straight for a metal-roofed cow shed and nearly scalped me.

Tuesday, August 10th

Rushes at lunchtime today were very encouraging. Yesterday we had shot the Knight and Dennis departing the city and Dennis arriving back. For once everybody seemed pleased.

The donkey behaved marvellously this morning and manoeuvred the cheering crowds with great confidence. Better than yesterday when I had to sit on boxes and rock gently, to give the impression I was on a donkey.

Max Wall, as the King, looks quite marvellous and he and John Le Mes have developed this sad, forgetful, melancholic, vaguely homosexual double-act which suits the crumbling kingdom perfectly.

Max has a wonderful drawing power. He sits there, curled up like a caterpillar in his vast robes, never complaining about any discomfort, and people are attracted to him like a magnet – especially a willowy young lady photographer from *Celebrity* magazine, who sits beside him adoringly. Max enjoys this. His conversation is slow, measured, nostalgic, gentle and wise.

Wednesday, August 11th

In to Shepperton by two. It's the scene with the Princess and me driving away after we've been married. The Princess makes my nose run every time she kisses me. Gilliam instructs 'No French kissing … I don't want to see any tongue work there.'

Drive into Soho to see Herzog's *The Enigma of Kaspar Hauser* – a beautiful, careful, memorable little movie. The subject of the 'noble savage' suddenly faced with the world seems to lend itself to film – Truffaut's *L'Enfant Sauvage* was another excellent and intelligent movie on this theme.

Ate a curry at the Gaylord to try and chase away my cold.

Sunday, August 15th

Terry Gilliam and the script appear to be losing the battle for survival at the expense of Terry Bedford and the technicians, who have, fairly ruthlessly, dictated the pace of the shooting so far. Every day now, as the confidence of the camera and lighting department grows, the shooting schedule falls further and further behind.

Rumour has it that the Rolling Stones are rehearsing here this week – across on Stage A. Will wait to hear more. Last week I got a letter from an hotel on the Cap D'Antibes, written by Ronnie Wood (whom Eric has been gallivanting around with this summer) saying that Eric was too busy to write, but he'd asked Mr Wood to write and tell me that if my letters didn't become more interesting he'd have to write to one of the Goodies.

Thursday, August 19th

The day drags on – the unions are asked to work until eight. Much muttering and sounding. They seem to agree, but no one can have asked the electricians, who, at seven, pull the plugs out and that's it for the day.

Home to see the last hour of *Sunset Across the Bay* – Frears/Bennett/Tufano teleplay. Wish I'd seen the lot. Terrific playing from Harry Markham.

How I would love to work on something with Alan Bennett – I really admire and enjoy his writing and performing. It's spare and honest. His world and his characters unglamorous, but delicately drawn and wonderfully believable. He portrays lack of confidence with confident assurance. A craftsman too – he works with care and deliberation on the simplest of lines and his scripts are like softer and gentler Pinter – with the same good ear that Pinter has for human small talk.

Friday, August 20th

Eric rings and comes round for lunch – or with lunch, I should say. Bearded, tanned, in a white cotton boiler suit and a gorgeous perfume. Helen is rather rude about Eric's smell and says it stinks the kitchen out. Eric is very patient with her! We open a bottle of Jules Laurier sparkling blanc de blancs and eat up kipper pâté, cold beef and salads which Eric has brought from Au Bois St Jean. Spend afternoon chatting outside.

Eric tells me about his summer with the Rolling Stones, or Ronnie Wood, mainly. He likes Ronnie – he's good company and a laugh – but is more guarded about Jagger (very sharp business mind) and Keith (pleasant, but so doped-up Eric reckons he has only a year to live).

Eric is going over to New York in early October to appear on and co-host *Saturday Night Live* – the Chevy Chase late-night programme that's swept the US and which Pythons have, as a group, quite regularly turned down.

As Helen says, Eric 'doesn't lack confidence', but I feel that he's still lacking something. He is very anxious to get back to Python writing and performing, as if he feels that the fast France/New York world which he's recently joined and in which friendship tends to be based on how many LPs you've had in the charts, does not offer the feet-on-the-ground atmosphere of the Python group.

But, as always, EI is entertaining and amusing and it's a lovely way to lose an afternoon off!

Saturday, August 21st

In the evening Helen's cooking again, this time for Terry G and Maggie. They arrive – TG looking unusually gaunt and unshaven, pale-faced and completely without his little bulging stomach. He has some quite impressive news. Apparently Terry Bedford is no longer on the picture.

Yesterday, while I had been pleasantly reminiscing in the sunshine with Eric and sparkling white, Gilliam and Terry B had almost come to blows on the set, after a morning when only two shots had been done. A shouting match had developed and, whilst Max Wall sat patiently in a pool of water (for it was the scene in which John Le Mes wakes him up by throwing a pail of water over him), Terry B had walked off.

The producers rallied (Goldstone being especially calm and level-headed, according to TG) and began the search for an alternative cameraman. Sandy rang Nic Roeg, who was quite prepared to do it himself, but couldn't, so suggested young whizz-kid Tony Richmond. Richmond couldn't take over for a week, but suggested John Wilcox. John Wilcox, a veteran of 60, was checked out and found to have the highest recommendations.

So tonight we have a new cameraman. To me it seems indecently sudden, but on this film, as it is totally his brainchild, TG must be the boss. He's a thick-skinned fellow and very harsh words must have been spoken to wound him like this.

We talked a little about Python and the next movie. TG said he reckoned the film was TJ's to direct – he'd far rather be directing another film of his own. He has an idea for using the Port Talbot industrial complex as the basis for a science fiction film which, as he says, he'll 'write with *anyone*'.

Monday, August 23rd

Terry Bedford is still the cameraman. Julian [Doyle, editor] tells me that he rang around on Sunday and placated everyone and told them that the good of the film was the co-operation of all the elements in it. Julian persuaded Terry B to ring Gilliam – because he knew Gilliam wouldn't ring Terry B.

It's hot, hot, hot still. The Prime Minister's having an emergency Cabinet meeting about the drought.

Tuesday, August 24th

Chasing up and down corridors. A bit of sub-Errol Flynn work. Anti-swashbuckling. To be actually living these childhood dreams and fantasies – and getting paid handsomely for them – I have to pinch myself mentally to be sure it's happening. Fifteen years ago Graham [Stuart-Harris] and I were lapping up all the films, good or bad, that hit Sheffield, and now here I am making the bloody things.

Eric (complete with specially printed T-shirt 'Jabberwocky – The New Python Movie') and Susie the wet-lipped Aussie model, came to see us on set. Eric brought me a signed advance copy of the book which he says has already had massive re-orders, The Rutland Dirty Weekend Book (containing three pages by M Palin!), to be released next month. It's a lavish production job – a combination of the Goodies and Python book designs over the last four years, but fused and improved.

I feel that it pre-empts more Python books – a particular area of comic book design has been capped by the Rutland book – and if the Python 'periodical' which is being heavily sold to us by Eric, is to be the work of these same designers, I fear it will look unoriginal – and that Python, far from creating a bandwagon, will appear to be climbing on one.

Sit in the sun and read more of The Final Days,[1] chase up a few more corridors.

---

1 Woodward and Bernstein's book on Nixon. Famous for Deep Throat's disclosures about the Watergate break-in.

Thursday, August 26th

At the location by eight and on my donkey to take advantage of early-morning shafts of sunlight through the pine trees.

After about 10.30, the sandy hollow, a dry dust bowl at the bottom of it and ringed picturesquely by pine trees, becomes like some gladiatorial arena. The school kids and the various hangers-on of the film unit – press, producers' friends, etc – sit up in the shade of the trees, looking down on the little group around the camera who work away, exposed in the sandy arena to the increasingly hot sun. Every now and then actors troop back after their takes to rest in the shade, or a clapper boy or production assistant walks down with cold drinks.

Warren Mitchell loses his temper briefly, but ill-advisedly, with John, one of the hard-working props boys, who accidentally treads on Warren's hand. A ripple of tension. Warren is a hard worker and an extrovert. He leads a full and busy life and talks about it a great deal.

But it's a long, hot day and we're still shooting at seven in the evening, when I lose my temper during a shot in which I have to run away from camera carrying a large, unwieldy pack. I do all that's required, but behind me I can hear someone yelling and shrieking. I can't think what I'm doing wrong and I can't hear what it is they're shouting. Finally turn and stop and bitterly throw my pack down. The crew are grinning back there in the distance, but I still don't know what the hell I was being shouted at for. It turned out it was only TG doing some off-camera atmosphere noises. He did that this morning, when he was trying to help my reactions by giving me an off-camera impression of raping and pillaging. The result was so extraordinary I just broke up.

Home about 8.30. Wash away the day's grot. Then Helen, in keeping with the drought spirit that has gripped the land, waters the flowers with my bathwater.

Long phone call home to find out the latest on Father, who yesterday fell quite severely. The doctor says it's time for him to go into hospital permanently, but a geriatric specialist visited him today and pronounced him much fitter than he'd expected. The specialist says my ma should not do so much for him – and should let him spend all day dressing if he needs to. Mother needed calming down after this theoretically very humane, but practically rather callous verdict.

Friday, August 27th

Feel confident and eager to work on these opening scenes. Presence of Paul Curran, who's playing my father, increases this spirit of enjoyment. We complete our early part of the scene quickly, then Warren appears and we work on the main body of the scene. It goes well and feels lively. Warren says he enjoys working with Paul and myself – I think because we adapt to his rather naturalistic way of playing. He says he throws some actors who complain that their sense of 'timing' – W makes it sound like a dirty word – goes if there is any improvisation at all.

But the irrepressible Mitchell ego, which has been bristling over the last couple of days, suddenly and quite abruptly bursts out. A BBC *Film '76* camera crew hover and start to film us rehearsing.

Warren: 'Who are these people?'

Mumbled lack of response from everyone.

Warren, louder: 'No, come on, who *are* these people? What are they doing?'

By now he's got the embarrassed attention of most of the unit. He refuses to be filmed rehearsing. He, quite reasonably, if rather loudly, points out that no one asked him if he would mind. Barry Norman[1] is seen scowling in the background and after a hurried discussion they very huffily leave.

Wednesday, September 1st

An incident at Shepperton. I'm being made-up when I hear raised voices in the corridor outside. One of the extras, a short, stocky, barrel-chested man with a nose spread all over his face, is shouting loudly and angrily at Maggie Gilliam. But the shouting is of a particularly vicious, abusive and violent kind. He sounds more than just angry, he sounds dangerous. I intervened and he turns on me. I could see his eyes blazing – he shouted at me to keep out of it. Who did I think I was? Sir fucking Galahad? (Wrong film, but nearly …)

He was shaking with a barely repressed threat of physical violence, so I found Peter, the second assistant director, and told him to get the man out. He'd reduced Maggie to tears (not an easy task) and I said that I

1 TV presenter and journalist. Originally asked to front *Film '73* for a few weeks, he made it his own private domain until *Film '98*.

would refuse to go on the set with him. Peter went upstairs and later the extra left.

It turned out that he was no ordinary extra, but a mate of Peter's who had been Frank Sinatra's bodyguard and was no more or less than an East End villain. It's terrifying the feeling of violence which one man can give off and all because he thought Maggie might clip his moustache! The incident left everyone involved rather shaky.

Work late again. I'm in the coracle at half past six. Then goodbye to Shepperton – this tatty, crumbling world which I've grown rather fond of. I'm pulled across the lake for the last time – across the same waters Huston used in *The African Queen*, and the same waters George Sanders must have got to know in *Sanders of the River*. (Did they have to keep stopping for planes landing at London Airport in those days?)

Tomorrow Wales.

Tuesday, September 7th, Pembroke

Bright and sunny as we film in the castle. Harry H and I have two or three scenes together.

Max Wall arrives tonight. We all eat together. Harry H expresses his admiration for Laurence Olivier – Max his for Enoch Powell.

Wednesday, September 8th, Old King's Arms Hotel, Pembroke

Work until twelve – chasing turnips round the keep – then I'm finished for a while as they start to shoot the joust.

Later in the afternoon a long, rambling chat with Max. I warm to him and the strange Joan Lee, daughter of Stan Lee of Marvel Comics fame, who drapes herself around him. Max listens courteously, talks effortlessly, humorously and intelligently – but he wanders occasionally into obscene asides, or stops and marvels at a word he's said, or suddenly laughs. He's such an original – conversations with him are like setting out on a voyage without a map. I think he sat all afternoon in the bar with his Guinness and Joan.

Thursday, September 9th, Pembroke

Breakfast with Dave Prowse. His enormous shoulders look as though he has full armour on under his shirt. He's back to London after this to go back to his lucrative body-building salons at the Dorchester, etc. A nice, amiable, soft, but deep-spoken giant. A man who used to be almost a cripple – he grew so fast – but overcame it spectacularly to become one of the leading body-builders/muscle-toners, etc. He took two stone off Edward Heath and says he gets a lot of politicians at his gym. Dave is to be the figurehead of an £800,000 campaign to teach kids the Green Cross Code [and later became Darth Vader in *Star Wars*].

Write p.c.s in the room. Terry Hughes phones with a lovely, heart-lifting piece of news. Iain Cuthbertson wants to play the Scottish doctor in 'Murder at Moorstones'. This is marvellous. It was a complete stab in the dark – all I wanted was an Iain C type, and never expected that an actor with a TV series of his own [*Sutherland's Law*, 1973–76] would be at all interested in this small and rather silly role. But he's read the script, loves it, and is very pleased that the piece is to be staffed by actors rather than just comics.

No chance of Simon Callow for RSM in 'Andes' – he wanted to, but is totally committed to Joint Stock Theatre Co. But Terry, now in his second week as Assistant Head of LE Variety at the Beeb, is confident of Isabel Dean as the mother in 'Moorstones' (I don't know her, but every-one says she's great), Frank Middlemass as the father, and Bob Hoskins for the RSM in 'Andes'.

After lunch up to the castle. The fierce cold wind is lessening, but everyone looks huddled and besieged. The tents won't stay up. The horses are more frightened than ever. The peat that's been spread around the lists is blowing in people's eyes. The good extras of Pembroke, on their pathetic £5 a day, are working hard and remarkably cheerfully. But I hear that their lunch was actually cut down today, pre-sumably to save money, which is scandalous and, as Elaine[1] pointed out, unpleasantly ironic in a film which had more than a bit to say about the oppression of the peasants!

There is much discontent amongst the crew – meetings in small groups are constantly being held – and it centres over daily food allowances, which most of the crew feel at £3.50 are mean and unrealis-tic. Sandy, who looks hunted as anybody approaches, but at least is always available, has made a £4 offer. This has been refused.

I don't know where they go from here, but as long as people know

1 Elaine Carew, worked closely with Maggie Weston on make-up for Python and Gilliam films.

that Sandy is getting 15% of the film, and as long as the rushes continue to be as encouraging as they are, the producers are in a losing position. If the film looked bad, and Sandy was manifestly broke, it could be different – but the hard-worked crew are not in a mood to be charitable.

Friday, September 10th, Pembroke

Waiting again. Breakfast with Max at half past nine. Read *The Guardian*, which has only been printed in London once this week. Realise how poor a substitute is the dry, in content, style and format, old *Times*. Can't bring myself to buy the *Telegraph* instead – with its right-wing scare stories – especially as it's a lot better in amount of news, presentation and general interest than *The Times* and I might begin to like it.

Rushes of the knights playing hide and seek are very funny. Terry, as usual now, seems more inclined to bemoan than praise what's going on. The processes of dealing with the people involved in keeping the film going, with all their different egos and personal ambitions, Terry cannot deal with; people get him down daily.

But all this doesn't matter too much, because Terry's greatest contribution – his visual sense – is working well. He still niggles a little at the praise that Simon and Terry B get for shots – which praise, he says, is as much for Hazel's costumes, Maggie's make-up, Milly's designs and hell! says Terry, I choose the shot.

Saturday, September 11th, Pembroke

More familiar British weather is returning. Though it dawned blue and cloudless, stormy wind and rain spread throughout the day, buffeting the castle yet again. Tents blew down, the crowd huddled into any available Norman-arched doorway in the castle walls between shots. With cameras wrapped in polythene bags and in between vicious cold squalls of rain that turned umbrellas inside out, the joust scene gradually progressed.

It was 7.30 in the evening when Bill Weston's last and most spectacular stunt ended the miserable day and ended our filming in Pembrokeshire. He was pulled backwards off his horse by Derek Bottell – the 'jerk-off' specialist!

The crowd, who had stoically defied the weather – and were really in

a state of high excitement which had carried them through it all –
swarmed off through the Barbican gateway and across the road to the
pub. Here Terry Gilliam bought them drinks for two hours – and later
that evening he appeared at the Old King's Arms, shaven for the first
time in a week, and rosy-cheeked, his eyes tired, but glazed, in a very
happy, silly mood.

In the bar until late. I think Max has finally tired of the attentions of his
chief acolyte – he muttered something uncharacteristically uncharitable
about her being the sort of person who might turn him homosexual!

Sunday, September 12th, Chepstow

Wake at nine, surprisingly clear-headed. It's a grey day. Winter's in the
air suddenly. Buy papers, breakfast, pay fond farewells to the Old King's
Arms, Pembroke. A nice town, a marvellous hotel. Up at the castle the
last windswept remains of the pavilion and lists are being packed.

Go for a three-hour walk by the sea, along Stackpole Quay to
Freshwater Bay East Coast Path. A few hours of solitariness, a rather
vital release from the gregariousness of filming. A quick look at Castle
Carew – a splendid Gothic ruin, full of different architectural styles,
deserted great halls and ivy-covered walls, with crows nesting.

Depressing arrival at the Two Rivers Hotel, Chepstow. It almost certainly had to be an anti-climax after the Old King's Arms, but I did not
expect the belligerent sullenness of the receptionist, nor the total tacki-
ness of all the decoration. A 'Fresh-Aire' machine in the corridor near
my room gurgles dyspeptically and discharges a foul and sickly sweet-
smelling gas up the passage.

The evening cheers up with the arrival of Neil I. At the Two Fingers
Hotel (as we've decided to rechristen it), we end up round a table in the
restaurant with Max, Joan Lee, Johnny Cole the props man and wife,
making up limericks.

Thursday, September 16th, Chepstow Castle

A moment of quite stimulating liberation when I am required to drop
my trousers in a shot and reveal my un-knickered bum to all and
sundry. As we're outside the main gates to the castle, quite a little crowd
has gathered to watch the filming – about fifty or sixty in addition to the
fifty extras in the scene.

Realise I feel less embarrassed than they do, and really quite enjoy the experience of flashing a naughty part of the body in a public place – and getting paid, rather than arrested for it. Can see the exhilaration of 'streaking' – a sort of heady feeling of freedom comes over me as I point my bum for the third time at a twin-set and pearl-bedecked lady standing not ten yards away!

Saturday, September 18th, Chepstow Castle

Yesterday was the last day of principal photography – contracts for most of the crew ended at 5.30 on Friday evening. But everyone is aware of how incomplete the film is – it's more than days, it's at least two weeks away from completion. So today work goes on, but without Terry Bedford, Jenny, Simon, Mick the Loader and other familiar faces.

I miss them, though I know Terry G and Julian don't. They've been longing for this day. Longing to be rid of 'The Circus' as they call them.

Roger Pratt[1] is still there – doughty, reliable, straight and reassuring (not a 'Circus' man, I'm told). Julian and Terry G do most everything else, leaping around with the unbounded delight of those from whom a great weight has been lifted.

Terry operates like he so much wanted to do. Julian can organise in his direct and unsophisticated way, which never worked with a full crew.

I feel at last drained and physically exhausted. I want to go home. Just for a couple of days, that's all I need. Away from dirt, discomfort, cameras and castles. I want to stop being stared at for a day or two.

I begin to harbour murderous thoughts towards the vacuous tourists who cling to the unit like leeches, ordering their spotty, whiny little kids to stand beside me and have their photo taken. 'Could you sign these for two little girls who are friends of the lady who works Thursdays only in the shop next to the one I work in?' 'When are you doing more Pythons?' 'What is this?' 'Who are you?' It's all becoming a big nightmare from which I want to wake up and scream 'Fuck off!' from the battlements of Chepstow Castle.

At a quarter to six I run up the stairs as Gilliam films me, for the last time. It's over. Throw my potato the length of the Outer Bailey – and by 6.30 I'm heading for London in my Mini, with a huge and generous

---

1 Focus puller. Worked as lighting cameraman with Terry Gilliam (*Brazil*, *The Fisher King*, *Twelve Monkeys*) and has since shot two of the Harry Potter films.

sunset behind me – a final farewell from Wales, for which, despite today, I shall only have the happiest of memories.

Home around 8.30 (praise the M4). Willie, naked, runs down the stairs to open the door for me. Cuddles all round. Even Rachel hasn't gone to sleep and she welcomes me with a soft, broad grin which warms me no end.

Tuesday, September 21st

All day at the BBC working on pre-production for *Ripping Yarns*.

Casting continues to provide surprises. Denholm Elliott has agreed to play Gregory in 'Andes'. Terry H keeps telling me not to underestimate the scripts when I show stunned incredulity at the involvement of an actor of D Elliott's legendarity.

Wednesday, September 22nd

Pouring rain (still rare enough to be remarkable) as I drive out to Shepperton, after a BBC wig and costume fitting, to see the final Welsh rushes and an assembly of the film so far.

The opening castle stuff works surprisingly badly – even Max doesn't come across as positively as he should – and the chiaroscuro lighting effects, and some quite wretched minor performances, make the whole thing irritatingly difficult to follow. Moment of depression – it's misfired. But it perks up and lightens and brightens and, by the end (when the editor has skilfully put on some wedding music), the film, despite its 'Scene Missing' caption cards and its lack of effects, has grabbed people enough to elicit spontaneous applause. John G and Sandy are very happy. Happier than I ever saw producers on the *Grail*.

I'm happy too. Deep down, and confiding this only to the diary, I'm pretty pleased with myself – like I never was on *Grail*. There are only a few moments where I let my performance slip. I was trying hard on *Jabberwocky* to make up for what I felt were unrelaxed performances on the *Grail*. God, it's been a long time since I've really enjoyed my performance.

Friday, September 24th, Southwold

Up to Southwold – left London in pouring rain.

Saw Father in hospital. Sitting hunched, huddled and silent with three others. He's draped in a cellophane sheet under his dressing gown like a chicken in a supermarket. He seems pleased to see me and gets a few words out in the 45 minutes we're there – something about having a picture of myself (walking) in my old school tie. The sooner he gets out of Southwold and to Blythburgh, where he will be made to walk and work a lot more, the better.

At present he's not steady enough to be at home – so sits in this strange silent world, of grunts and occasional indecipherable ramblings from the other patients – one of whom, Percy, tries to push himself out of his chair and, as he does so, pees all over the floor. Silence. No nurses rushing to him, he cheerfully sits down again.

Monday, September 27th

This morning back at familiar Shepperton. A short scene with Harry H (full of doubts again, but I've grown very fond of this strange, self-critical, introspective extrovert). Then a strange and uncomfortable series of shots of me being flung around on the end of Bernard Bresslaw's legs and picked up and hurled out of the Queen's Haemorrhoids – a harness of quite unbelievable awkwardness for this shot – and finally into the rain-soaked woods in the back lot for a scene of wood-gathering, when I'm surprised by Terry Gilliam (playing Patsy from the *Holy Grail* again). Much crouching and being savagely attacked.

Terry is very sick today and keeps having to retreat to the bushes to throw up. But he battles bravely on. How he will shape up to the week, I don't know. It's going to be hard and they're already behind. I must finish Sunday – I start *Ripping Yarns* on Monday – but it'll be a hell of a push.

Tuesday, September 28th

No Jabberwocking for me today, but my last day off, apart from Sundays, until late October. Letters, visit Anne Henshaw. She has her head down in the labyrinthine affairs of Python as usual. She reports that the sooner we start writing the Python film the better for some in the group – she says Graham especially seems to be at a loose end and drinking more, with several of his projects, TV series and his film of Bernard McKenna's script, having collapsed.

Shopping in the King's Road – have to give brief run-down on Python plans in almost every shop – the assistants all seem to recognise me and want to talk.

To BBC to meet Don Henderson – T Hughes' selection for the RSM in 'Across the Andes'. I'm in trepidation for this is a major role and I don't even know the guy.

Fears allayed – he looks good – with a rather fierce, red face and a good sense of humour. He's easy company and seems to understand the role well. Still no Dora – as Michele Dotrice turned down the role (the first artist to turn down a *Ripping Yarns* role this time around!).

Out to dinner in the evening with Robin S-H and Barbara.[1] By a strange stroke of coincidence a Peruvian is present. I tell him about 'Across the Andes by Frog' – and to my amazement he tells me that the biggest frogs in the world live in Lake Titicaca, Peru, and that the frog is a common motif in old Peruvian carvings!

Thursday, September 30th

At Shepperton – on waste ground behind the *Oliver* set – our little unit struggles through the day. Terry G is even more terrier-like than usual – leaping around with the camera, building sets and taking time off only to curse some particular piece of inefficiency.

I just grin and bear it. Much walking with banner and pack after a morning spent under the belly of a horse being prodded by bandits.

Away on H Stage they are on the first day of shooting *Julia*.[2] There are 300 extras in beautiful '20s costumes and a huge ocean liner set to go with it. Meanwhile, on the rubbish tip, *Jabberwocky* works on!

Monday, October 4th

Slept well, and was at Pinewood for the first day of 'Across the Andes' shoot, feeling quite fresh. In the village our cameraman Peter Hall was directing a lighting rig the size and scale of which made *Jabberwocky* look like home movies, a track was being laid, flags being nailed up, statues erected. A feature film atmosphere of bustle and preparation.

---

1 Robin, younger brother of my childhood friend Graham Stuart-Harris. A doctor. Married Barbara, a New Zealander.
2 Fred Zinnemann's film about Lillian Hellman, starring Vanessa Redgrave.

Terry H and I stood in the square – me in my Snetterton shorts and helmet – and surveyed it. Terry must have read my thoughts. 'D'you ever feel responsible for all this?' he asked with a half-smile.

Denholm seemed to relish his part as the seedy Vice-Consul. An actor of enormous experience – he was one of my childhood heroes in *The Cruel Sea* – and greatly respected and in constant demand. But here he was doing his first part after three months off in Spain, and he'd chosen to do a *Ripping Yarn* because he loved the script and because, as he explained in his effortlessly classic English upper-class accent, it was nice to do some comedy. He'd been offered some life of Marx thing, he told me with an unhappy frown, and was soon off to do 'some bloody Brecht' for the BBC, which didn't seem to make him much happier either.[1]

Friday, October 8th

Before night filming, Jimmy Gilbert drops in to see Terry H and me. He's read 'The Testing of Eric O' and is very enthusiastic. According to TH, Jimmy is treating the *Ripping Yarns* as one of his major projects – which is exhilarating and frightening at the same time. Each episode is costing twice as much as each episode of Python. All the more reason why they *must* work so well. There can be no excuses.

A long, but mercifully warm and dry night at Pinewood. We get through a great deal, but Don Henderson and I are still quelling a frog riot at three in the morning. Home by five.

Monday, October 11th, King's House Hotel, Glencoe

Marvellous journey from London, ending up on the West Highland Line – pulling past Loch Lomond and into ever higher remoteness. It's very wet. Streams are pouring off the slopes like water off the back of a newly emerged whale.

Our little band – some fifteen strong – disembarks from the Euston sleeper at Bridge of Orchy Station – so small that it takes one or two tries before the driver can get our carriage parallel with the platform.

To the King's House Hotel – haunt of previous Python filmings.

---

1 Denholm caused consternation by enquiring, very politely, if it might not be too much trouble to make his call a little later in future. 'Only I do like a fuck in the morning.'

Misty cloud swirls across the tops of the mountains. Have learnt from past experience that it's no good belting all over the Highlands for just the right mountain. Some of the best are right by the hotel and, because of the enormous benefits of being near our base, we decide to locate Snetterton's camp about 300 yards from the hotel with the dark, stony, fierce pyramid of Buachaille Etive Mor as our El Misti.

Monday, October 18th

Lunch with Clive Hollick (and Simon A) at his invitation. Clive, whose group, Mills and Allen, own Shepperton Studios, wants me to join the board of Shepperton as a non-executive adviser – representing the users of Shepperton from the artistic side.

He has plans to brighten Shepperton's image and make it into the most exciting studio to work in in London. Pin-tables and neon lights announcing who's in today, may be going a bit far – but a bit of showmanship will not be a bad thing for the film industry, which needs any boost of confidence it can get. As I prefer Shepperton to the more oppressive, institutionalised atmosphere of Pinewood, I feel quite amenable.

Monday, October 25th

Woke – in advance of the alarm – at about seven. A dull, heavy, uninspired feeling. One thing I know for sure – I don't want to work today, or for a long time. But I have two weeks of filming ahead, in which another *Ripping Yarn*, 'Murder at Moorstones Manor', is to be put down. The script has been acclaimed and yet I feel as if it's the first day of a winter term at school.

A great deal of dialogue to do today, which took me a couple of hours of concentration to get under my belt last night. It takes me a little over 45 minutes of not difficult driving out along the A40 to get to Harefield Grove, a once-stately home near Rickmansworth.

Isabel Dean, who plays the key figure of the mother, is gloomy following the West End opening of *Dear Daddy*.[1] She looks perfect for the part, but seems a little strained and tired and has trouble with her words.

1 Written by Denis Cannan, it ran eight months at the Ambassadors. Isabel left the cast before the end of the run.

Friday, October 29th

Out to Harefield again. I enjoy these early morning drives now – I happily let Capital Radio, with its inane links and good music, flow over me. It's a relaxing 45 minutes. There's now much to look forward to – the week has steadily improved. I seem to have survived a peak of tiredness, which was at its worst on Tuesday morning, but has since receded.

Terry H shows no signs of anything other than totally enjoying himself. Isabel worries on, but could be giving a perfect performance – I'm just not sure until we see it. She's a much more jolly, funny person than her somewhat anxious exterior might indicate – and is gratifyingly happy to be doing this during the day alongside *Dear Daddy* in the West End – the play and cast of which she can't stand.

Wednesday, November 3rd

Evening meal in Chelsea with Iradj B[1] and Frank and Franny Reiss.[2] Iradj has been selected (by the Shah himself) to start a publishing industry in Iran. No books are made or printed there as yet, so Iradj (and Time-Life whom he works for) would be starting literally from scratch.

I would think it a dangerous job – how much freedom will he have to publish what he wants? But Iradj is a pragmatist, he'll end up on his feet. One of his problems is an illiteracy rate of 50%, but he maintains there's a functional illiteracy rate of 75% (people who can read nothing more than simple signs, instructions, etc).

He hadn't changed from the slightly patronising, but totally engaging, aristocratic Persian layabout he was when I shared a room with him in Germany for ten weeks in the summer of '63. I feel Iradj is one of those people who is now as old as he will ever get. Also one of those people who will keep recurring at odd intervals and in odd places throughout one's life.

---

1 Iradj Bagherzade inveigled me into an unsuccessful attempt to sell encyclopaedias to American servicemen in Germany during my first summer at Oxford. I sold four sets in ten weeks, one to a family who defected to the Soviet Union.
2 Friends from Oxford days.

Monday, November 8th

Half a year and a few days after we last played *Python Live at City Center* in New York, the Pythons reassemble at 22 Park Square East for the first day of a two-month writing period on our new film. A fine, sunny day, a good day to take resolutions and make plans.

John suggests straightaway that at some point during this writing period we all go abroad to the sun for a week or ten days (to 'really break the back of the film'). This is shelved. As Terry J says, 'Let's all see if we like each other at the end of the day.' But we make plans for the next year – writing until Christmas, rewriting throughout March and filming delayed until September/October 1977. There follows some good chat and exchange of ideas about the story and how to treat it. JC now thinks the film should be called 'Monty Python's Life of Christ'.

At lunchtime, TG leaves to complete filming of the *Jabberwocky* monster in Pembroke. We all go off to Auntie's restaurant. A bottle of champagne (that's all) among us to celebrate the reunion. They all want to know about *Jabberwocky*. The worse news the better, I sense! John's passed his driving test and now has a car of his own – 'A very *old* Rolls-Royce,' he tells me, unable to stifle a trace of embarrassment.

Wednesday, November 10th

Writing with Terry – some hopeful starts, but nothing great as yet, the most promising being a piece Terry has begun about the Three Wise Men, confused over which star they're following and being constantly mistaken for the wrong sort of astrologers and having to tell people about their star sign. In the classic Python mould of the humour of frustration; irritation at constantly being diverted by trivia.

Friday, November 12th

Python meeting at Park Square East at ten. All there except TG. Anne sits in (having asked if we didn't mind). All rather institutional. It falls to Palin to start the ball rolling and read the first new, all-Python material since we wrote the *Holy Grail*.

Enough good material from everybody to suggest things haven't changed. In fact, in John and Graham's case, I think they've improved.

They wrote the stoning section and an ex-leper and psychopath section – both of which were back on their best form. Very funny.

Anne supplies lunch – prawns and smoked salmon and no booze, except for GC who seems to find a G and T from somewhere. He is on fine form and really elated by his writing week with John. By contrast, I feel our week has not produced strong material. I'm suffering from slight, post-filming loss of energy. Terry J is too preoccupied with domestic and philanthropic problems.

Sunday, November 14th

Today I am going with TJ to the BBC to see a rough cut of 'Across the Andes'.

It didn't strike me as as funny as it should be, but he liked a lot of the shooting and the acting. Terry J's main worry was my part. I think I'm not at my best with sub-Cleesian public school aggressives – and Snetterton is a middle-man figure, not extraordinary in himself. TJ feels that the prominence of Snetterton should be built up more – putting him squarely and confidently as the centrepiece of the film. Then at least he would become less of an irritating attempt at someone being irritating.

Wednesday, November 17th

Film writing with Terry. He's still not producing much – what with helping his brother Nigel move, etc – but today we have a good read-through and work on with the Three Wise Men. Squash together at five. Two games all.

Drive over to Kingston for dinner with Nigel Pegram and April O.[1]

Nigel as dapperly charming as ever; someone it's very difficult not to like. April was telling me quite extraordinarily Pythonesque stories of her neighbours. She has a woman who came in and asked April if she would go and sniff her house! She meant it literally too – she was worried about some smell in the house and people were coming round. Also of a neighbour who knows King Olaf of Norway, who is apparently

---

1 Nigel was one of the cast of the Oxford Revue at the Edinburgh Festival in 1964, with Terry Jones, Annabel Leventon, Doug Fisher and myself. He married the actress April Olrich.

a compulsive farter. This is well known and hosts are now prepared for it and cover up for him in all kinds of ingenious ways.

Thursday, November 18th

A writing meeting of all the team this afternoon. John and Graham had written little and were not as pleased with themselves as before. Eric had done more thinking than writing – whereas Palin and Jones had produced a mighty wodge of at least 25 minutes of material. So reading was not made easier by the fact that there was a total imbalance of contributors. Fortunately Terry Gilliam had taken time off from editing at Shepperton to be at the meeting and his generous and noisy laughter helped a great deal and, by the end, we'd acquitted ourselves quite respectably.

The sketches, or fragments, which work least well at the moment are those which deal *directly* with the events or characters described in the Gospels. I wrote a sketch about Lazarus going to the doctors with 'post-death depression', which, as I read it, sounded as pat and neat and predictable as a bad university revue sketch. The same fate befell John and G's sketch about Joseph trying to tell his mates how his son Jesus was conceived. The way the material is developing it looks as though the peripheral world is the most rewarding, with Jesus unseen and largely unheard, though occasionally in the background.

John and Graham are troubled by the lack of a storyline. At the moment, after only about seven or eight days' writing, I feel it's the least of our worries and that we should carry on writing and stockpiling funny material to be fitted into a storyline later. 'But we only have another thirty-two and a half days' writing, little plum,' says John, consulting his diary.

Friday, November 19th

In the same week as I describe in *Melody Maker* the pain and joys of filming *Jabberwocky* on a rubbish tip at Shepperton, I find myself filming *Jabberwocky* on a rubbish tip at … Shepperton.

Nearly four months after my first shot, I'm being made up as Dennis again, with the blood, the dirt and the fringe – only this time we can't afford a make-up girl on set, so I have to go up to South Hill Park to see Maggie, who makes me up before breakfast.

At Shepperton we find a haggard and unshaven cameraman – played by Julian Doyle. The three of us make our way to the rubbish tip. Julian, by this time, has found some ends of film to use up. We retrieve a chair from the tip, which Terry G stands on. I climb under my shield and drag myself across the dirt patch while Julian squirts smoke around us. A lonely, surreal little scene, which *Film '76* should have captured.

Sunday, November 21st

A new thing in Hampstead trendiness, a croissant delivery service. A long-haired young man with brightly-painted Citroen Dyane out in Oak Village at nine o'clock, distributing croissants to the discerning – like a sort of super-sophisticated Meals on Wheels.

Take Tom and Willy swimming at midday, then over to Carlton Hill, St John's Wood, where I've been summoned to meet Ronnie Wood – once of the Faces, now of the Stones and, perhaps, apart from Paul Simon, the closest and most genuine of Eric's friends in the pop aristocracy.

Whilst Tom and Willy play records on the juke-box in Eric's kitchen and generally complain about being there at all, I explore the house. Rather like a seaside farce, there's a lady called Charlotte in the sauna, and on the top floor, next to Eric's work-room, with its 'Bible' commentaries on the desk, an Australian girl called Shirley is staying.

'Woody' arrives in a chauffeur-driven Mercedes, neatly dressed, dark-haired and with such a tan it looks like make-up, but of course it isn't, he lives in Malibu. I thank him for his letters and assorted scribbles during the summer. Eric opens a bottle of Dom Perignon (a gift from Dark Horse Records for writing and directing a couple of promo films for George's album *33 ⅓* in the summer) then we walk in the crisp November sunshine round to the Clifton Arms. It's full of people and smoke and Woody solicitously finds a kids' room at the back. He's a nice, unaffected, friendly man – very warm.

He describes Stones business meetings – they have even more than Python – with Keith Richards, who sounds *very* eccentric, lying prostrate and apparently dead for much of the meeting, apart from the occasional devastating one-liner. Charlie Watts remains very silent until suddenly, out of the blue, coming up with an idea about plastic record covers.

His position as a relatively new member of the Stones is considered differently by the Stones and their 'businessmen'. As he puts it, the band are all very democratic, split everything equally, 'but as soon as the businessmen come in it all changes'.

In the early evening Al Levinson comes round, in a mellow haze of cigar smoke. It seems that my favourable comments on *Millwork* really encouraged him and he's now writing fast and furiously on a new 'Fish'[1] novel, 'Fish Full Circle'.

Wednesday, November 24th

A good, workmanlike Python meeting. John and G have a good idea for a *Brian* storyline and their two new pieces, though short, are not just on the point, but very funny – writing 'Go Home Romans' on the wall is going to be a little classic. I wish I'd thought of such a neat idea.

From 22 Park Square East we all (except Gilliam) pile into John's Rolls and purr down to Audley St, Mayfair, for a viewing of selected Biblical epics, which we feel we ought to see. We nearly run over Elton John in North Audley Street and muse on what a strange headline it would make – 'Elton Run Over by Pythons'.

The viewing theatre at Hemdale is very comfortable, which is just as well as the films – *Barabbas, King of Kings, The Greatest Story Ever Told* and *Ben Hur* (we see bits of each) – are extremely heavy and turgid. Best performances and best writing always centre on the baddies – Herod, Pilate, etc – and the nearer you get to Jesus the more oppressive becomes the cloying tone of reverence. Everyone talks slower and slower and Jesus generally comes out of it all as the world's dullest man, with about as much charisma as a bollard.

We had a few good ideas during the viewing (midst much silly giggling and laughter). I suggested we should have four Wise Men – the fourth one being continually shut up by the others, who always refer to themselves as the Three Wise Men. '*Four*'. 'Ssh!'

Tuesday, November 30th, Southwold

Depressing visit to the hospital in Southwold. Daddy looking thinner than before. His staring, largely immovable eyes register my appearance briefly, but cannot manage much more. His speech in fits and starts.

---

1 As Updike had his Rabbit, Al had his Fish – Leo Fish, his alter ego and central character of all his novels.

Sometimes he doesn't make sense at all. Much talk of ties and headmasters.

Look out towards the church, the beautiful Southwold Church he loved so much and the grey November afternoon closing around it. A pretty melancholy realisation that my father will never be at home again.

It was ten years ago to the day that they moved to Southwold from Sheffield. Then he was full of hope and excitement and relief that a drab and unhappy salaried life was past, and he was back where he always wanted to be, amongst old churches, choirs and organ music.

Thursday, December 2nd, Oxford

Arrive at Oxford to speak in a debate only to find there is a strike of hotel workers at the Randolph so, rather than cross the picket lines, I make for the nearest hostelry in Broad Street and sort out the seven or so foolscap pages of my speech into some order, over a pint of Burton Ale.

The debate starts at 8.15 with the usual nonsense about elections and re-elections, spiced up a bit this year by the hawk-nosed grace of Benazir Bhutto – daughter of Pakistan's Premier and next year's President. She looks incongruous amongst the Tory rowdies who make up the Union establishment and bay most unpleasantly at some poor man who stands up to protest against 'the scandal and malpractice within this Union'. I long to hear what the scandal is, but the hounds of reaction stalk him out of the hall. I feel embarrassed being in my DJ up at the front with these idiots.

About ten, I'm eventually called upon to speak. A warm and rather surprising round of applause. The speech goes well. Some good laughs and for some reason, after a bad joke half-way through, I pour the water glass provided over my head. Even bigger laughs, but it makes the ink on my script run and the pages stick together and the last part of the speech is less successful.

The whole thing ends, much to my relief, about 11.30. Talk to three or four undergraduates who are trying to set up a magazine called 'Passing Wind' in Oxford next year. They all seem rather earnest and sit me down in a big armchair and treat me far too like a guru. I hope they aren't short on humour. One of their interview questions was (quite seriously) whether there was any relationship between Neil Innes and Eric Idle.

Monday, December 6th

Clive Hollick rings in the evening to say that Shepperton Studios *did* make a profit last year (£40,000) and have clinched the *Superman* deal. They want the stages for fifty-two weeks next year. Marlon Brando and Gene Hackman will be there, so it seems a good time to accept their offer of a directorship.

Wednesday, December 8th

A Python writing meeting in the afternoon. Quite substantial chunks of material from everyone, including a neat and funny bit by Eric with a magnificent creation – a Jewish Hitler called Otto the Nazarene, who wants more Lebensraum for the Jews.

Is it paranoia, or did I detect a sort of wariness of Palin/Jones material? Our stuff was received well, but both John and Eric unable to accept anything without qualifying their approval – and there also seemed to be a marked resistance to reading all our material.

I think this is partly the fault of late meetings. Two-thirty is not the time when everyone is freshest, and by 4.30 Graham was probably right when he said he felt we were 'sated'. But I don't approve at all of stifling Python at source. We always used to give everything anyone wanted to read a hearing, then throw it away.

Thursday, December 9th

Willy's school concert. Willy plays a tree – one of the leading trees, I hasten to add. Quite a difference from the frightened little snowflake a year ago, who could hardly leave go of his teacher's hand. This time he sang lustily. I noticed he was quite tall – and towered over Bonnie Oddie, who was next to him.

Sunday, December 12th

Round at Eric's in Carlton Hill by 2.30 to say hello/goodbye at his party. Oysters and black velvet in the kitchen, plus strangely and brightly attired young folk and reassuringly stocky, functional frame of Derek Birdsall.[1]

1 Designer of the first Python book.

Everyone seems to have seen the clip of me and Terry G on *Film '76*, which shows that these casual little interviews are worth doing well.

On one end of the talent-packed sofa is Jagger. He's smiling in a rather far-off way, but much chattier than when I last met him. He's 33 as well – like George and Eric. We talk of old record albums. I really never listen to the LPs we've made, I say, and I don't know what's on them. Mick agrees. He apparently never can stand listening to an album after he's been through the grind of making it.

Brief chat with EI, who seems concerned that Terry J should not have too much control of the next Python movie. He does blow hot and cold. It was only a few months ago that Eric wanted TJ to direct his TV series! But now he feels that TJ's problem is that he doesn't appreciate compromise.

Our chat was inconclusive, but I can see that the direction of the film will be a difficult issue looming up.

Tuesday, December 14th

Last night T Gilliam rang to tell me that my impending appointment at Shepperton is causing quite a stir. TG was talking yesterday with Graham Ford, the general manager, who said that more has got done in the last two weeks than in the last two years. The reason is that the three other directors are quite rattled at the thought of someone who knows the remotest thing about films being appointed to the board. TG says I might save the British Film Industry after all!

To 22 Park Square East for an all-day Python session.

Quite a successful meeting. John reckons we have about 40 per cent good material – good meaning strong. I think I'd put it a little higher, though not much. Today we decide on a public school opening – details of which are improvised at the meeting – and also the rough pattern of Brian's life – a bastard with a Roman father, toys with joining various Messiahs, is disillusioned, joins, or dabbles, with the resistance, is caught, escapes from the Romans, disguises himself as a prophet and gains a large and devoted following which he also tries to escape from. John and Graham seem to be keen on using my 'Martyrdom of St Brian' (the soft and luxurious martyrdom) as an ending … but it's on endings we're weakest.

Thursday, December 16th

Almost a year since we went over to defend our reputation in the US Federal Court, we have heard the terms on which ABC are prepared to settle the case, following the successful hearing of our appeal in June. ABC are prepared to pay our legal costs up to $35,000 and are undertaking not to edit any shows without our co-operation and approval. We have established that, should we refuse to edit, the shows cannot go out. From the BBC and Time-Life we have won deadlines within the next five years when the ownership of all the tapes will revert to us.

This was neat justice. The BBC had allowed ABC to make cuts without bothering to consult the Pythons because they didn't consider the American market anywhere near as important as the UK market. So, after US Federal Court judges had deemed this breach of copyright, the BBC were prepared to give us back the rights to all our tapes, so long as they hung on to those for UK TV.

Not only did they still fail to appreciate the growing strength of Python in America, they also failed to predict the burgeoning growth of video and other ancillary rights. Thanks to the BBC's dumbness, sorry, generosity, we were able to negotiate all these valuable rights for ourselves, and the licence payers missed out on quite a few bob.

Sunday, December 19th

In the evening to TV Centre for the BBC Light Entertainment party. Helen looking very impressive in a flowing, sort of crêpey black dress with a halter neck and embroidered borders which we'd bought together up Hampstead. Me, almost conforming to the intolerable black-tie stuffiness, but in the end the size of my black bow tie – acquired hastily in St John's Wood for the debate in Oxford – brought such instant laughter from Helen that I was forced to abandon it in favour of an ordinary dark blue tie and black velvet suit.

Everything in full swing when we arrived, but as I hadn't been there since the 1973 LE party, we went in the wrong entrance and found ourselves in a small ante-room, empty save for Jimmy Savile, crouched over a large plate of food. A cheery exchange and we walk through to find a throng of people we once saw so much. Tim Brooke-Taylor and I commiserate over our eternal branding together in John's mind as 'nice' people. Bill Oddie, small, dark and glowering. 'I don't know why I come here,' he says. Yet he always does.

Tuesday, December 21st

Another very dark day – it's been like this now for a week. Real Day of Judgement conditions. To Park Square East for a final Python reading meeting.

High standard from John and Graham, Eric average and Terry's and my first offering frankly bad. A poor rewrite of a poorly written original is never going to stand much chance before this audience – and it bombs embarrassingly.

A second very encouraging piece from John and Graham – about the crowd outside Brian's home being talked to sharply by Brian's mother.

My personal gloom finally lifted by the reading of our piece about Brian and Ben in the prison and the Centurion who can't pronounce his 'r's. This five- or six-minute piece, read right at the end of the meeting, with both GC and JC poised to leave, really brings the house down. It could be pre-breaking-up hysteria, but it's a good note to end this six-week writing stint.

John Goldstone rings to say the censor has seen *Jabberwocky* and, subject to the removal of one 'bugger', given it an 'A' certificate.

Wednesday, December 22nd

To the Coronet Viewing Theatre in Wardour Street to see the two Python German TV shows in order that we may finally decide whether to buy them for Python Productions or not.

The first German show, in German, is, apart from 'Silly Olympics' and 'Little Red Riding Hood' and one or two bits of animation, fairly difficult to follow and looks a little rough, whereas the second looks smooth, polished and expensive. John is anti buying them and Eric very pro.

In the end I side with Eric. The money we use to buy the shows would otherwise be taxed very heavily and I feel that it is a good principle for us to buy the world rights to our work wherever they become available. John keeps saying 'My mother's in London', but he agrees before leaving to the purchase of the shows (cost around £42,000, largely owing to the strength of the Mark and weakness of the pound). Eric agrees to undertake their re-editing.

So Python finally breaks up for Christmas and for me a huge pile of work, stretching unbroken from October '75, which I once thought insurmountable, is over. Six weeks of comparative freedom from schedules stretch ahead.

Soho is packed with pre-Christmas shoppers and *King Kong* posters are going up outside the Casino in preparation for the biggest ever simultaneous world-wide opening, as I walk back to my car.[1]

Thursday, December 23rd

To Southwold on the 9.30 from Liverpool Street.

Ma and I drive over to Blythburgh Hospital to which Father has recently been moved.

Surprised at the number of people packed into the ward – twenty-two I later discovered – but as he is wheeled by a cheerful Pakistani nurse – a young man with a ready smile and an apparently total resistance to the rather depressing conditions around him – I notice how small he appears, almost shrivelled in his chair. He reacts to seeing me, with a half-smile of pleasure, but after five minutes of talking his eyes wander and he appears to switch off.

Whilst we were having lunch at Croft Cottage, we heard, via various phone calls, that Aunt Katherine[2] had died of a heart attack in the night. This was totally unexpected. Aunt K was always the most vigorous and vital life force – loving her work, although she always seemed to have too much – whereas Uncle Hilary, her husband, has been very ill, with an apparently uncurable long-term depression, and has been suicidal over the past month.

Still, we had to tell Father about the death of his only sibling. I wondered how he'd react. For a moment it looked as though he would completely break down. His mouth hung open and seemed about to form a word, but couldn't. His brow contracted, his eyes took on a stare of what looked like disbelief and began to fill with water. It's difficult to tell the extent of his feelings behind the mask of Parkinsons. Was it utter desolation for a moment, or what … ?

1 This version, directed by John Guillermin, starred Jeff Bridges and Jessica Lange.
2 Katherine Greenwood, née Palin, my father's younger sister.

A few minutes later, unable to get anything more than three or four rushed words out of him, we left. The cheerful Pakistani seemed very ready to talk to us about him and I also briefly met the physiotherapist who says he can only just stand up and cannot walk at all yet. Is this the result of being stuck in hospital for the last three months? Could we have done more to keep him mobile?

All imponderables. On the debit side of Blythburgh are the feeling of crowding, the TV room full of stale smoke because no one can replace the air extractor, and the constant presence of old men coughing – great chest-ripping, rheumy roars rattling their ribs, a truly awful sound. On the credit side, the enthusiasm and spirit of the staff, which counts for a lot. It's busy, too – Christmas trees, trolleys with various goodies on are wheeled through the wards by middle-class, middle-aged social workers with tweedy skirts.

On the whole I feel the credits outweigh the debits, but there's no escaping the wretchedness of his condition.

Saturday, December 25th

The weather's good – cold enough for fires and other housebound comforts, but bright and sunny too. And silence over Gospel Oak – only the sound of a dog barking – the rush and bustle of London is off the streets and indoors.

After breakfast helped prepare tables and things. Helen had polished all the family silver, which glistened on the white tablecloth in spectacular fashion.

The only really new departure from the traditional family Christmas was taking Tom, Willy and Catherine to the Holiday Inn for a pre-lunch swim. We were about the only people there. Great spirit of Christmas – the attendants threw each other in fully clothed whilst Tom and Willy and Cath watched open-mouthed.

All went well, despite Mary and Ed forgetting the Christmas pud and Ed uncharacteristically dropping it on the floor when he went back for it.

Everyone went home about eleven. I think I've learnt to handle these family Christmases a bit better. I feel tired, but not heavy, fat or blotto with it. Sit and appreciate the tiredness over a film in the excellent BBC 'Christmas with Cagney' selection. I find Cagney quite mesmeric.

Thursday, December 30th

Trying to write a *Jabberwocky* trailer whilst Rachel sits on one knee playing with the telephone – 'Hello Granny,' ad nauseam. In the middle of all this, the Health Visitor arrives – an unexpected bonus, as she looks after Rachel for a quarter of an hour, whilst seeing if she can walk and talk properly.

Drive out to Shepperton to meet Graham Ford, general manager of the studios. I had arranged to meet him on my own initiative, just to get a little background on how Shepperton works from the man on the shop floor, as it were, rather than the directors, of whom I am now officially one.

Ford is young (around my age), thinning hair, waistcoat stretched over an incipient paunch, looks like the young manager of a prosperous record store. Smart office – the only part of the Shepperton complex that looks at all dynamic.

Over lunch he elaborates on the rumour I've heard that he doesn't get on with Clive [Hollick]. In fact, he likes Clive personally, but makes the very good point that Clive is a director of several companies, not just Shepperton, and Ford feels that Shepperton is just a name on a list. Though from my talks with Clive I feel he is in sympathy with Ford's desire to brighten up Shepperton, I quite appreciate that his decisions take a long time to come through.

I come away feeling that, as a director without sixteen other directorships, I could be the one who cares most and most directly about Shepperton. We agree to meet and chat regularly.

1977

1977 began with a new departure for the Palin family, a winter sun holiday. We spent two weeks on the West Indian island of Tobago. Helen learnt to stay up on one water-ski and the children loved being by the beach, but according to my entry of January 15th I had mixed feelings about it.

'Seldom have I enjoyed a holiday as much and wanted to get home as much,' I wrote. 'I have a feeling my brain could atrophy in this alluringly beautiful part of the Caribbean.' Once home, and back in my hair shirt, I worked on an article about the holiday for Lee Eisenberg of Esquire, and took it personally to him in New York, only to find he'd resigned from the magazine.

Meanwhile my father's condition had deteriorated and he was now permanently in bed at Blythburgh Hospital, just outside Southwold. His previous accommodation, St Audry's at Bury St Edmunds, had been built as a lunatic asylum, this one as a workhouse.

Monday, January 31st, Southwold

Even the old workhouse at Blythburgh looks like a French chateau in the crisp sunny beauty of this winter's afternoon. Father is lying in bed, with the iron side up, like a cot, his glasses off, his face so thin, his eyes shut and mouth open. He looks more like a corpse.

For a while he seems bewildered, his eyes stare, as he's probably just woken up. Then he sees us and his look softens a bit. Colour returns to his face, and he manages to get more words out than usual, though hardly any complete sentences, so you don't really know what he's saying.

Much entertainment from the rest of the ward, though. One rugged-looking old man with large, piercing eyes, beckoned urgently towards us. When Ma went over to speak to him, he fixed her with a very serious gaze and asked her if she was wanted by the police.

At the next door bed, from behind the curtains, meanwhile, repeated BBC radio acting cries of 'Gawd! Oh my gawd! Oh gawd! Gawd! Gawd! Oh bloody gawd!' I was told that this stream of half-hearted, and yet strangely heart-felt cries is a common sound in the ward.

When I first came here to see Dad, it was an unfamiliar world, from which I rather shrank back. The sight and sound of twenty old men in one room takes a little getting used to. Now I feel much easier and happier there. The nurses are not only dedicated, but, I think, cheerful and sensible.

Back to Croft Cottage for local fish (delicious) and a bottle of Alsace and a game of Scrabble and to bed with Doctorow's *Ragtime*. In the company of Houdini, Evelyn Nesbit and Commander Peary of the US Navy, January dwindled.

Tuesday, February 1st, Southwold

After lunch, drove over to Blythburgh to see Dad. He was in his chair today, dressed and looking much improved. His lack of speech is still the greatest drawback, but he responded with pleasure to seeing us. He seems to drift off, though – as if his concentration easily goes, and he sometimes stares fixedly at some point, as if seeing something we haven't. His fingers pick at surfaces and edges – whether it's the corner of the sheet on his bed, or the wooden rim of his table.

But he'd fed himself lunch, and they were pleased. I hope he has more days like today – and that he doesn't linger and waste away to his death.

Wednesday, February 2nd

Am going to try to keep to a routine of an hour's work before breakfast. Managed to wake up at ten to eight today, so did 40 minutes. Worked on Shepperton business.

John Goldstone rings and, in his dangerously persuasive way, makes me agree to meet Don Rugoff, American distributor, for a chat about advertising slogans for *Jabberwocky*. So I find myself at the Connaught Hotel at ten to six, heavily wrapped up, blowing my nose every four minutes and reading the *Evening Standard*. Don doesn't arrive until about 6.15. He seems more like a gargoyle every time I see him. With him is his glamorous assistant, Susan, who doesn't seem entirely at ease, but then who would be, having to accompany Don all day.

Up to Don's room, or rooms. (I like the Connaught. It's small, intimate and Edwardian – much less dauntingly impressive than I expected.) We drink flat Perrier and Don reels out a list of slogans he's thought of. It's back to square one – and I feel depressed and trapped having to re-explain basic principles about avoiding the comparison with *Holy Grail*, etc, etc.

But Don has a technique, unsophisticated though it may be, of acquiring co-operation and, as the evening rolls on, we begin to warm to the spirit of the whole silly operation, and run up quite a list of ad-lines. I really liked Don's 'At last! A film for the squeamish!'

Before I leave, just after eight, he's not only wheedled a whole new crop of ad-lines from me, but also several trailer ideas. Don cleverly flatters me – 'Oh, wonderful, that's wonderful' – thanks me profusely and effusively and shuffles me out into the passage.

Home, very hungry, by nine. It's been like a session with a mad psychiatrist.

Thursday, February 3rd

Arrive BBC about a quarter to two. Terry Hughes and I lunch in the canteen. I am to meet Jimmy G at 2.30 to discuss the situation. I just learned yesterday from TH – that the BBC will not release him for the filming of the next three *Ripping Yarns*.

I had an inkling when he was made Assistant Head of LE Variety last year that this would come. TH has repeatedly said he regarded these shows as the most important and satisfying things he's done. But he seems to have yielded to the blandishments of high office and, as Bill Cotton sounds to be about to leave Light Entertainment for higher things, I understand their cultivation of the Golden Boy.[1] He will remain executive producer, however, and Jim Franklin will direct. Luckily I like Jim and find him unassuming, efficient and very down to earth. But I slightly resent the fact that I wasn't consulted at all, until a fait accompli had been prepared.

Jimmy Gilbert tells me the BBC wiped the tapes of the first two Python series! But he is trying to find film copies from all over the world to get together the three early Pythons they're planning to show in April/May.[2]

---

1 Terry was duly promoted to Head of Variety at the BBC, and no longer allowed to direct individual shows. Two years later he was seduced away to America by EMI, where, among other things, the golden boy made a name for himself directing *The Golden Girls*.
2 I'm not sure of the provenance of this scare story, but Terry Jones remembers being alerted by a BBC editor, Howard Dell, that plans were afoot to wipe the series in the early '70s. Terry J had them recorded onto Philips VCR tapes and stored them at his house. For a long time, he thought the only copies of Python TV shows were in his cellar!

Tuesday, February 8th

Finished, at last, a six-month-old pile of fan letters. Mostly from Japan, beautifully written, generally on very delicate paper, and nearly always beginning 'I am a schoolgirl of 14', as if to add a frisson of danger for the reader. The language is fine too. Python is translated as 'Gay Boys' Dragon Show' on Japanese TV, and one of the letters eulogises 'Upper Class Twit of the Year', but calls it, splendidly 'The Aristocratic Deciding Foolish No. 1 Guy'. American letters, too, but coarser and more violent generally, shouting at me off the page.

In the evening Helen makes a delicious, non-meaty repast for David and Stephanie Leland, who bring Chloe with them to sleep here.

David is in the process of leaving his agent. As he says, you 'fire' solicitors, and you 'change' accountants and you 'leave' wives and agents. That's what makes it difficult.

He wants to do a season of three or four new plays in repertory at the Crucible next autumn. He wants to remove the 'new play' from its neat little slot amongst all the trad classical revivals and generally show that the theatre and that playwrights are very much alive and modern in their outlook and topics.

I suggest that the only way really to ensure that a provincial theatre receives the credit and attention it deserves for pioneering new plays is to have a clause in the contract which says the play cannot be shown in London for a period of, say, eighteen months from its out of town opening. Then get Tom Stoppard, or some other London darling, to write a masterpiece, and for eighteen months the provincial theatres might be full of coachloads from Hampstead and Kensington.

Sunday, February 13th

Our croissants, duly delivered, slipped down a treat and, after breakfast and a quick check to see that Sheffield United had resumed their slide down the Second Division, I took all three children to the Holiday Inn for a swim.

Rachel 'helps' us all get dressed. She likes these sort of activities and supervises most efficiently – wandering up with various pieces of clothing which, if you are not exactly ready, she will drop in a puddle on the floor.

Monday, February 14th

It's another splendid morning and I go down to Camberwell on the bus. It's good to be able to pace one's life, so that if I want to take an extra 30 minutes to get to Terry's by bus I can. The walk at the other end is a slog, but on a day like this it's all justified by the feeling of busy, buzzing London life all around. Faces in the sunshine. The river sparkling as we ride over Westminster Bridge.

Terry suggests a beer for lunch and we have a couple of pints at a rather unpleasantly refurbished Young's pub beside Peckham Common. Sitting next to us are a very odd middle-aged couple, a little tipsy. They have two Pekinese dogs which they treat with affected bantering politeness. The woman licked pieces of chocolate before giving them to the dog and the man accused Terry of coming from Wrexham.

Wednesday, February 16th

To the BBC. Meet Jim Franklin and his PA Eddie Stuart. Jim Franklin, straight, direct, likeable, a special effects boffin, who lovingly describes how he yesterday shot John Cleese being run over by a bus with a flowerpot on his head for a Diana Rigg show.

We talk over attitudes to the shows. Should we have an audience on? Jimmy Gilbert pops his head round the door to say he wants to show it to an audience. When we ask why, he says 'Because it's funny.'

'Well, then it doesn't need an audience to tell people that,' I counter.

'I've heard that before,' says Jimmy.

I wouldn't worry, but he has an infuriating habit of being right.

Thursday, February 17th

Down to Camberwell on the bus again. An hour and a quarter door to door. Normal car journey: 35 minutes. Read *Memoirs of George Sherston* – a world away from Walworth Road in the drizzle. But then not as far away as one might think, for Sassoon is always detaching himself from the stereotyped county hunting image. He's interested in people, really. And there's a lot of them in the Walworth Road today.

A solid work day at Terry's. By the time I left at five, 'Eric Olthwaite' felt in much tighter shape.

In to London to the studio, passing through Covent Garden on the way. Studios, galleries and smart new restaurants are sprouting daily now. The rush is on to be in the new trendy quarter of London, now that threats of large-scale demolition and 'development' seem to have receded. Once again feel that going in with Terry G on Neal's Yard was one of the best things that could have happened to a lad with £70,000 to spend.

Drop in at Penhaligon's to buy some of their aftershaves, which brighten up my mornings immeasurably. Talk with Sheila Pickles,[1] who I think at first thought I was something the cat had brought in. I had on my Kickers with holes in, my jeans with holes in and my Fiorucci anorak with the hood up. And her shop is very smart.

Sheila promised to publicise my studio to her well-connected film friends. Zeffirelli apparently is working on the *Life of Christ* at such a slow rate that Python could still pip him to the post. He has to make it in different lengths for different countries. Six one-hour episodes for Italy, three two-hour episodes for the US, two three-hour episodes for the UK. It's a bit like ordering meat.

Saturday, February 19th, Abbotsley

After a bath, in which I read a fascinating chapter from *Plain Tales from the Raj* – a book of reminiscences about the British in India [by Charles Allen] – and concluded that we must write a colonial *Ripping Yarn* next year, walked to Highgate West Hill and caught a 214 bus to King's Cross and then the 9.30 Cambridge train and reached St Neots at a quarter to eleven.

On the journey read a synopsis sent to me in the post today by Christopher Matthew's agent with a letter beginning 'Over lunch with John Cleese, Christopher Matthew said how very much he would like to turn his *Sunday Times* column – "Diary of a Somebody" – into a television series. John's instant reaction was that you were absolutely the right person for it.'

Actually I like the columns – a modern *Diary of a Nobody*. They're very well written and he can turn a humorous phrase, but, even if I did have time, I reflected, as the train chattered through the industrial estates of Stevenage and Biggleswade, that I didn't really want to do

---

1 I had met Sheila through mutual friends – Ian and Anthea Davidson. She started the Penhaligon's perfume business.

comedy all my life. A commitment to this would be a commitment to light, rather parochial comedy for another two or three years, and then I'll be nearly 40 and too old for the Robert de Niro roles I subconsciously yearn for.

Monday, February 21st

Woke feeling gratefully fresh, after a long, deep sleep. Another day of fairly continuous rain showers. Terry came up here to write.

At two we went up to Hampstead for a pizza and saw the Goodies, Tim, Graham and Bill, all in almost identical blue anoraks walking up Flask Walk ahead of us. Enjoyed ourselves immensely, shouting loud and coarsely after them – 'Goodies!' 'Eric Cleese!' 'Do us your silly walk!' 'Where's your bicycle?' and watching them deliberately not turn around or quicken their pace in the face of this volley. Even at the top of the hill, when we were almost beside them, they only looked round very furtively and then away again. Finally Bill did an enormous double-take.

Friday, February 25th

More writing on 'The Curse of the Claw'. Helen leaves for Amsterdam at a quarter to four [to visit her friend Ranji]. The kids are all very good, though boisterous (Tom has his friend Jud for tea). But I get them all out of the way by 8.15.

Monday, February 28th

The weekend with the children was very successful, but rushed, of course. To the Columbia Theatre for the children's 'trial' preview of *Jabberwocky*. I took Tom and Willy, Nicky[1] and Catherine Burd.[2]

It still strikes me as a very good film overall, but the high spots – jousts, monster and black knight fights – are so good that I couldn't help noticing points where the flow of the film – the headlong, extrovert flow – gets snagged up in little scenes which don't have the vitality of the rest. But the children enjoyed it. For Thomas it was the best film he'd ever seen, much better than *At the Earth's Core* or *Island at the Top of the World*!

1 Nick Gordon, a friend of William's, and now a director of commercials and pop videos.
2 Helen's niece.

Saw Terry G afterwards. He'd been at the back, taking, as they say in the States, an 'overview'. He had just returned from a crash course in US film distribution. Apparently, after a week of showings and discussions and soundings, Rugoff's now convinced *Jabberwocky* could be a big one, and is talking of ordering 1,000 prints.

Terry said the energy of this apparently sloth-like man is incredible. They never finished a meal and, when Terry suggested that the reactions to the film were so far all from sophisticated New York audiences, Don Rugoff nearly flew him off to Austin Texas on the spot. But Terry and John looked very happy, both with the States and with the enthusiastic reaction from the kids today.

To Mary and Edward's for a very pleasant, effortless Sunday lunch, then Willy is off to another party. The Willy phenomenon has to be seen to be believed. No sooner had the door opened at the house of the party than William was grabbed by two or three girls, and soon a whole crowd of them had gathered around him chanting 'It's William! It's William!' and he was borne away into the party by the adoring mob.

Friday, March 4th

Python reassembles. The meeting is at 2 Park Square West, the first time we have met in the Henshaws' sumptuous and very well-appointed new house [on the opposite side of Regent's Park from their previous one]. It gleams and glistens and the front door is being painted as I arrive.

Eric is there (as usual) already, John arrives shortly after me, then Terry J, and we have to wait for an hour before Graham joins us. We've put a rather hard wooden chair out for him with the words 'Latecomer's Chair' written on it, and 'Dr Chapman' written across the back.

But the general tone of the meeting was of optimistic good humour, stretched almost to the point of hysteria. It was almost impossible *not* to get a laugh. We talked for two to three hours about the script and very silly ideas like a stuffed Pontius Pilate came up. I was in tears on several occasions.

Eric suggests we do our next Python stage show on ice, but don't learn how to skate.

Towards the end of the meeting, Eric asks me if I would be interested in writing for a George Harrison TV special in the States. I say no on grounds of time. Eric, too, doesn't think he can do it as he appears to have lined up an £800,000-budget film for NBC on the Rutles (Eric's and Neil's pop group parallel of the Beatles). Clearly he commands enormous respect from NBC, who are letting him direct the thing as well.

Sunday, March 6th

Read Hunter Davies' article on JC over my croissants. Not a bad article, some nice observations, but Python gets short shrift, and Graham even shorter. Connie, on the other hand, is effusively praised, and I get pulled in too – 'She's enormously fertile with funny ideas. Only Michael Palin compares with her for funny ideas.' An unexpected acknowledgement which was nice of him and quite makes my Sunday.

I thought his mother came off best out of the article. She had some very humorous quotes, if unintentionally so. 'I know John goes on about us never allowing him a bike. But he didn't need one. The school was opposite our house anyway.'

Swimming with Tom and Willy at Holiday Inn. Willy to a party. Another girl, another Valentino entrance. William starts being silly/funny before he arrives. He does it, he says, to cheer them all up.

Helen and I and Rachel cap a very Londony weekend by walking up and around the roads of Parliament Hill neighbourhood, with half an eye for houses.

Decide when we get home that we're very lucky to be in a house with such character. The late-Victorianness of North Mansfield Road, Parliament Hill, even when restored and cleaned, leaves a depressingly claustrophobic feeling. I was very glad to be back in our mid-Victorian shoe box.

To dinner with Peter Luff and Carolyn.[1] Peter had been with Tom Stoppard to visit Amnesty cases in Russia. He gave me a lovely box full of about twenty boxes of matches, all with rather nice Pushkin drawings on them. Each box had been thoroughly searched by the Russians before they left the country.

Parts of Moscow and most of Leningrad are very beautiful, he said, but Russian official behaviour sounds pretty wretched. Notebooks confiscated. Tom Stoppard had apparently yelled at them as they took his notebook away 'If you publish that, I'll sue!' It was returned, copied presumably.

1 Peter was behind the Amnesty charity show in 1976.

Peter doesn't think the Soviet Union will ever work – there are too many forces of nationalism, etc, within it. At present he says there is a repressive regime, reacting to the liberalisation under Khrushchev with surprising force.

An interesting evening.

Monday, March 7th

Down to 2 Park Square West. We're all there, TG included, for chats about 'Life of Christ'. John a little embarrassed when Terry J comes in asking 'Who were the two, then?' – referring to John's rather bald statement in the *Sunday Times* article that towards the end of Python there were 'two people' he couldn't get on with. But he skated over all that successfully and avoided having to say.

A good ideas session. We talked until four. Cleaned up the ending a good deal. The Centurion who can't pwonounce his 'r's has become quite a leading figure now – in fact he's probably Pontius Pilate.

At lunch we all split for an hour. Anne had made sandwiches. I felt bad at ignoring them, so Eric and I packed a bag of sandwiches and Perrier water and walked into Regent's Park, sat and ate our lunch in the rose garden. Rather sweet.

Eric tells me he's becoming vegetarian. Presumably under the influence of George H.

Tuesday, March 8th

To Buchanan House, Holborn, to meet the Shepperton Studios Board. First of all we had lunch – pâté, beef, cheese and no wine – and I met fellow director Charles Gregson, ebullient, talking in that enthusiastic upper-class rush. His hair was longer and he was much younger than I expected. Rather schoolboyish in fact. He's the Managing Director. Burrows is the Financial Director, older, quieter, rather neat and shy. Fawcett, the Company Secretary, is the only man from Mars. He talks in a delicious, rich, aristocratic rumble, which he uses tantalisingly rarely. He wears a perfectly tailored pin-striped suit and an elegant pastel shirt with white collar. Have a feeling he is either less or more intelligent than he appears. Probably less.

Clive [Hollick] displays the sort of sharpness, easy intelligence and businesslike charm which must have put him where he is. He handles the Chairman's job as if he'd been used to running things all his life – but at the same time creates a good, participatory working atmosphere.

The board meeting begins with financial reports. Then our debtors are discussed – *Lisztomania*, Ken Russell's last great folly, a monumental flop, is top of the list.

Brando is expected on March 21st. Discussion as to what we should lay on for him. Charles Gregson suggests, rather pathetically, putting flowers in his room. I suggest a couple of bottles of champagne might be more realistic.

The only real excitement of the meeting is discussion of the highly confidential Ramport negotiations. Ramport are the production company of The Who, who already have an almost permanent base in one of the Shepperton studios. They want a 999-year lease on an area of property within the Shepperton complex, including the old house, the lawn in front, some office buildings and J and K Studios (both small).

The asking price is nearly half a million pounds, which would, at a stroke, clear Shepperton's debt, pay for major improvements to the heating system and generally set the place up on a very sound financial basis. Against it are the usual arguments over losing any part of a film studio. Allegations of asset-stripping will be revived.

Thursday, March 10th

March has been delightful so far. Helen drops me in Regent's Park and I walk across this beautiful expanse, flanked on one side by Nash terraces and the other by the copper dome of the new mosque.

Eric very positive and clearly the one who's done the most work on our two 'separate' days since Monday. He has worked out a putative running order which is a good basis for discussion. By twelve we are all there, including Gilliam, who has been at the final dub for *Jabberwocky*.

High point of the day is writing an extremely sick piece for use at charity shows (which we are all rather tired of being involved in). A speech about the 'so-called handicapped' who get so much attention anyway, and why should not the carrot of financial reward be dangled before those who are, by no fault of their own, normal, etc, etc. I don't know who'll be brave/foolhardy enough to do it. At the Albert Hall.

We decide to send a very lushly packed gift box of sexual aids for

Ina's wedding present and a golden foot for Robert Osterberg[1] is to be inscribed 'To Our Dear Friend Roy Ostrichberger, From Monty Python – In Lieu of Fee'. I'm against 'In Lieu of Fee', but was out-voted.

Friday, March 11th

Decide not to send a gift pack of sexual aids to Ina for her wedding present. Still, it was funny at the time.

Down to Gerry Donovan, my first London National Health dentist. Half of the bridge Gerry put in has just come adrift.

Home by public transport. It takes me an hour, including a 20-minute wait at a bus stop for buses advertised as every six to eight minutes. As I wait I become aware of how important time has become to me now. To stand at a bus stop for 20 minutes staring into space seems a crime.

It does rather throw my working day, but I manage to write some more of the 'Twibune'. Helen suggests he should have a friend, so I write in Biggus Dickus, who thpeakth with a lithp.

Wednesday, March 16th

In the post, an invitation to the preview/premiere of *Jabberwocky*. I notice they've spelt my name wrong on the film credits – '*Michel* (sic) Palin'.

Slowly begin to overcome some indefinable resistance to writing any new material for the 'Bible' story, and by mid-afternoon I'm beginning to gather momentum. Complete a new 'Headmaster' piece for the opening, then literally race along with an ending montage, pre-crucifixion. The ideas suddenly seem to be released.

I work, with no interruption, until nearly six. Outside it's pouring. Feel very pleased with the day's work. I suppose I needed a day on my own at my own pace.

Completed my will. Put the envelope in the post, but cannot kill myself yet, as it was only a draft will.

---

1 Ina and Robert were the driving forces behind Python's action against ABC.

Thursday, March 17th

Across sunny London to the Columbia Theatre, where the *Jabberwocky* magazine-writers' preview is just finishing.

I am warned that there are men from the *Sunday Mirror* here, who have not bothered to see the film. They stand, like Tweedledum and Tweedledee, grinning ingratiatingly and nosing out any sensation there is to be had like pigs searching for truffles. I find myself talking to one of them, in the event of Columbia-Warner bringing no one else for me to talk to, about Python and then about the new Python film. The notebook suddenly slides out and I realise that he is onto a 'story' – a 'Python to send up Bible story' story. So I remember why I'm here and move away from that one.

Peter Noble waddles by, fondling my arm like an overfed but harmless Roman patrician and lining me up for a snap of him talking to me, for his newspaper, *Screen International*. Then he waddles off.

Max W is there. Seemingly unchanged by his bad reviews for Malvolio at Greenwich and as endearingly chatty and jokey as ever. The world could be ending outside, but Max would keep up his gentle monologue. He has never, as long as I've ever been with him, showed any trace of alarm, or sudden reaction of any kind. He paces himself beautifully and I found talking to him was like finding the eye in the centre of the hurricane.

I found amongst the gathering a qualified enthusiasm. Words like 'smash hit' and 'success' were not on everybody's lips.

Friday, March 18th

Difficult, but finally constructive Python meeting at 2 Park Square West. We assembled at 10.15, but Eric looked unwell, and John did not arrive until ten to eleven.

So neither of those two seemed in the best of moods, and Terry's suggestion that the 'Healed Loony' sketch should open the main bulk of the film (after the 'Nativity') was very sulkily received by John and Eric. The rest of us, including Graham, all remembered liking it and still liked it, but John claims he didn't and Eric doesn't think it's funny enough to start a film with.[1] Terry looks terribly hurt and deflated and

---

1 It never did get into the film, but is reproduced in the *Life of Brian* book, along with the 'Headmaster' and other plucky failures.

says things like it was putting this sketch first that suddenly restored his enthusiasm for the film. But Terry's enthusiasm can work two ways, and it was clearly only hardening John and Eric's attitude today.

Well, fortunately for the meeting, the script and all concerned, we soon got out of this area and began to make some rapid progress with the end, which is now to culminate in a huge crucifixion musical number.

It's interesting to know how people would react. We have de-Jesused the crucifixion, by keeping him out of it (although there were lovely fantasies of him saying to others in the crucifixion procession, 'Oh, do come on, take it seriously'). Instead we have about 150 assorted crooks being led out for crucifixion – which was, after all, a common enough event at that time. But the crucifixion has become such a symbol that it must be one of the areas most sensitive to the taint of historical truth.

Monday, March 21st

Phone call from John Goldstone – the IBA [Independent Broadcasting Authority], or powers that be, have heard our *Jabberwocky* radio commercials and will not let us say 'warm, brown heaps', mention the Queen, name roads (e.g. M40, A4), say 'here is a flash', dub on screams or sirens, and we can't say the word 'motions' in an ad in which a little boy is saying that he was on his way to school 'when a huge, fire-breathing monster ate the entire school buildings, including the toilet. The headmaster says the buildings may reappear in his motions, but until then we've got the day off.' To think that someone is drawing a salary for preventing people hearing the word 'motions'.

Wednesday, March 23rd

Do not wake until eight, despite reasonably early night. The hour before breakfast doesn't seem to be falling naturally into my schedule. Both body and mind, but in that order, seem to be rebelling. But I just don't feel I can do all the work that I've let myself in for at the moment without that extra hour.

The Python meeting is very constructive. Eric, who hadn't written much apart from a song, which wasn't that special, was nevertheless on good analytical form, putting his finger time and time again on what was right and wrong with the more sizeable contributions from John C and Graham, and Terry and myself. But we had supplied some good ideas, especially for the end, and the morale of the meeting was high.

We decided that John Goldstone should produce it, and the shooting dates would be January/February/March 1978, abroad. Cleese is anxious to take a tax year out of England and does not want to work here after April 6th 1978. He'll be doing this plus a series of seven *Fawlty Towers* before then. We have given ourselves a three-week writing session in July and a final session in October. We didn't discuss director – I feel that Terry J will do it, unless anyone feels strongly enough against.

Terry J suggests a press ban on discussion of the film. We agree to keep it a secret. John and Eric particularly vociferous about press on set. They just get in the way and do no good. Eric very positive on no deals with censors or producers over language or taste. We and we alone must decide what the final form of the film is to be.

With a great show of solidarity, we adjourned to Odin's restaurant for lunch. The only other diner anywhere near our noisy table was Harold Pinter, dining alone and darkly debonair in a corner, shaking me for an instant with immediate recall of him sitting in a restaurant in *The Servant*. Rather comforting to sit beside Harold Pinter after a long writing session.

Back home. Unsatisfactory attempt to take Tom, Willy, Jake and Rachel swimming. Pool closed. Marine Ices (our second choice) closed. Ended up at 32 Flavours in Hampstead though even there sixteen flavours were off!

Heard from John Goldstone that after Sandy Lieberson had personally canvassed the Managing Director of Capital Radio, he had withdrawn a number of objections to our commercials, but we were still not allowed to call a commercial a commercial, we can't mention 'motions', and 'large, warm, brown heaps' can only be 'large heaps'.

Sunday, March 27th

We drove up to Abbotsley yesterday morning.

Today it rained incessantly, though never very heavily. But icy-cold north winds kept us indoors for most of the time.

In the early evening the steady rain gave way to showers – some of hail and snow – and dramatic skies – huge, black clouds against white, sun-filled patches. Took William out up the road and he learnt to ride his bike. A snowstorm swirled around us as we came back – Willy's cycling career heralded with a virtuoso display of weather.

Back to London by nine.

By this time next week I will at least have *Jabberwocky* opening behind me, and we'll have finished the first real draft of the *Life of Brian*, as Eric suggested calling it on Friday.

Monday, March 28th

At 7.30 took seats in the Columbia [for the *Jabberwocky* premiere] (in a row with Terry J and Al and Terry G and Maggie). The theatre was full – caught sight of Ian Ogilvy, Ned Sherrin and other premiere luminaries. Unfortunately there seemed to be no representatives of yer average viewing public, and their absence was all too apparent as the film got under way.

It was hard work, sitting there watching yourself on screen messing around in the Middle Ages, and experiencing the almost tangible sensation of mild audience enthusiasm. Laughs – real laughs – seemed to come reluctantly, but when they did I breathed easily before going back into a sort of dry-mouthed muscular strait-jacket which tightens whenever I'm watching myself.

Eventually the quest and the undeniably effective monster fight won them over – and the applause at the end was not just sycophantic – but it was a tough viewing. I could hardly believe it was the same film I'd seen with the children two weeks before. Then there was a real sense of excitement and enjoyment and involvement. Tonight I felt that no one quite knew how to react.

One or two handshakes. We were all promptly cleared out of the foyers by a zealous theatre attendant and Helen and I gave Neil Innes and Yvonne – our good friends of these occasions – a lift down to the London Dungeon where the *Jabberwocky* is now permanently on display.

Wine and much chatter in the cold and semi-darkness. There seemed to be equivocal feelings about the movie itself. Some unreservedly loving it, others, like Eric Idle, now hardening into strong opposition to it. (Graham Chapman left half-way through! John C rang at the last minute to say he couldn't make it!)

One strange looming man shook my hand warmly and advised me that I was 'about to make the quantum leap. Men in America will see this and within two years you'll be an international star.'

Tuesday, March 29th

Woke early – about sevenish – heart thumping like a tugboat engine, head aching. The sort of feeling which resolves me never to touch alcohol again.

To Park Square West for a Python writing meeting. A very good session. Our rather hastily written and assembled ending up to the crucifixion reduces people to crawling the floor with laughter. Simple expedients like funny voices finally triumphing over careful intellectual comment.

So all immensely cheered. The film now has an ending – which is something the *Grail* never had – and we seem to have successfully tackled the difficult area of the crucifixion – by treating it all with historical unemotionalism.

In the evening revel in the beauty of Ken Loach's *Price of Coal*. Script, camerawork, direction, acting – everything combines to warm and comfort with its rightness and honesty. No artifice evident – a straightforward, highly competent piece of filmmaking. The best view of Yorkshire since *Kes*. It made me feel homesick – and said in fewer, funnier words than any polemical film, that working class life isn't just noble or fine or any of those overblown words used by the non-working class – it's a good life. Very funny, and it had all the production qualities I would like to achieve in *Ripping Yarns*.

Wednesday, March 30th

Morning writing session on Python. Though we work far fewer hours together now, the sessions are becoming more efficient.

Problems once so complex are being solved with a natural ease and unanimity which seemed impossible a year ago. Terry J will almost certainly direct. Gilliam may be in control of design. There is no room as yet for animation.

Thursday, March 31st

My bottom thrusts itself at me from *The Guardian* accompanied by a review from Derek Malcolm which begins 'I like *Jabberwocky*'. He goes on at some length and it is a very complimentary, but not uncritical review. An enormous encouragement.

Time Out dismisses the film as a straining attempt to make people laugh, which doesn't ultimately succeed. It seems to me there are two sorts of critics – one lot would prefer to like the things they review, the others prefer to dislike the things they review.

Friday, April 1st

All Fools' Day. Begins badly. Mercifully brief, but poor reviews of *Jabberwocky* in *The Times* and the *Telegraph* and the *Mirror*, which calls it tedious. Doldrums for a while.

At two drive over to Notting Hill Gate to J Cleese's rather sweet little cottage at the back of the Notting Hill Gaumont.

Much appreciation of a very good *Guardian* April Fool – a seven-page report on a totally fictitious island in the Indian Ocean called San Seriffe. Very well done – complete with photos and adverts and always just on the right side of probability. Eric suggests we send them one of our golden feet (originally made as a present for our US lawyer, Bob Osterberg). Anne is contacted and we send the foot to *The Guardian* 'for services to San Seriffe' on paper headed 'Python Productions Ltd, Evado Tax House, San Seriffe'.

(It's not the first time this week that Python has been moved to feats of appreciation by the newspapers. A *Guardian* report on Monday that *Gay News* are short of £12,000 funds to help them fight the blasphemous libel case brought against them by M Whitehouse for publishing a poem which suggested that Christ received some sexual favours while on the cross, moved us to send £500 as a Python contribution to the mag.)

Sunday, April 3rd

For about the fourth day running I have to buy every morning newspaper as *Jabberwocky* breaks over London. After Friday's setbacks, I'm prepared for everything or anything.

Relief comes in grand style. Alan Brien leads his *Sunday Times* 'Cinema' column with a long, funny, appreciative review, and we get the photo too. Marvellous – the best review so far. We also get the photo in *The Observer*, which turns in a long *Time Out*-ish review, quoting many of the funnier ideas of the film, calling me well-cast, but wasted, and lauding Max Wall, but ending by calling the film 'forgettable', which seems an odd adjective to use at the end of a long and detailed review.

But the *Sunday Telegraph* is unequivocally favourable, as are the *Sunday Express* and the *News of the World* ('loveable lunacy'!). So I settle down to my croissants reassured and revived.

Monday, April 4th

Spend the morning mugging up on latest financial reports, etc, etc, in preparation for a board meeting. Drove out to Shepperton – approved of the big new sign outside. Air of great activity about the place. Passed Brando's caravan and drove on round to Graham Ford's office.

Cheerful chat about *Jabberwocky*. Both Graham and his wife/secretary very enthusiastic but, as no one had turned up after 20 minutes, I ventured to ask how things were with *Superman*. Then Ford quite casually dropped his bombshell. *Superman* is leaving Shepperton in a couple of months to complete at Pinewood. Ford blathers chirpily about some financial deal which *Superman*'s producers must have made with Pinewood and quite steadfastly refuses to get angry, anxious or even excited about the whole matter.

With this shadow hanging over us, we walk over to the restaurant. At a table are Richard Donner, tall, bespectacled, with a greying mop-head of hair and an intelligent face – director of *Superman* (and *The Omen*) – Ilya and Alex Salkind, the producers. At another table is a quiet, regular-faced young man with a college boy look and a battered old sweater with a huge hole in it. This is Superman (Christopher Reeve). A man keeps looking over towards us rather nervously – as well he might. He's the English producer, who got the production into Shepperton.

Clive H and Chas Gregson arrive, with them is Clancy Sigal, an American writer now working in England, who's come to do an article on Shepperton and *Superman*. Oh the ironies of the day!

Clive has been to see the Salkinds, and his account of the meeting tends to Ford's theory that the Salkinds have done some deal with Pinewood (which is empty, and yet fully union staffed). *Superman* has moved studios already – from Cinecitta, Bray and now Shepperton – it is running behind schedule and Pinewood is owned by Rank, who also own one of the two main distribution networks in the UK.

Salkind says Shepperton has no major shortcomings itself. The inefficiencies here, he said to Clive, were like a splinter in the toe – a source of irritation, not enough to stop you walking. He (Salkind) doesn't seem angry at Shepperton, or want to make any big publicity point about moving. Clive reckons £190,000 is owed to us by *Superman*. Brando and Hackman *have* to be filmed here, because of their limited availability, so we appear at the moment to be in quite a strong position.

Wednesday, April 6th

Five past twelve – settling in bed with Siegfried Sassoon and the Somme Offensive, when the phone rings. It's John Goldstone. Rugoff wants to open *Jabberwocky* at Cinema One in New York on Friday, April 15th – a week earlier than he had planned. I tell him that I can't really go until Wednesday of next week – Easter, with trips to Abbotsley and Southwold, being almost upon us, and a day looking at locations on Salisbury Plain planned for next Tuesday. John will transmit this news to Rugoff.

Back to the Somme.

Tuesday, April 12th

Wig fitting with Jean Speak at ten. Then along to Jim F's office. The buyer, John Stevens, is there, with a catalogue of cars for the 'Olthwaite' episode. We have blithely written in police cars for a chase (dated 1934), but find that they didn't have police cars until 1938. This does seem to have given robbers an unfair advantage, but Jim says robbers couldn't afford cars either.

Drive down to Salisbury Plain to look at the locations they've chosen for 'Escape from Stalag Luft 112B'.

Spend an afternoon in huts, built during the First War, which are still used during training exercises. They are Spartan and the attempts to brighten them up are very tacky, and only emphasise the gloomy temporariness of the camps themselves, which cling unconvincingly to the Plain in the teeth of vicious winds. It's so remote and exposed up there that one could almost be in Labrador rather than one and a half hour's drive from London.

Drive back along the M4, arriving at the Centre about 7.30. Taxi home, where I arrive, feeling well and truly flattened, to a volley of phone calls and phone messages which have accumulated over the weekend and in anticipation of my departure for New York tomorrow.

A little clump of unkind press cuttings about *Jabberwocky* don't raise my spirits. John Goldstone sounds cheerful over the phone. After a poor weekend, *Jabberwocky* attendances are up again, and it's doing remarkable business in Bromley!

Wednesday, April 13th, New York

The *New York Times* has a total Python-style ad. 'Michael Palin and Terry Gilliam will be giving away 1,000 potatoes at Cinema One on Friday.' The motif for the ad is a cowering Dennis figure with a sword and Don is using, to my distress, slogans such as 'Makes King Kong Look Like an Ape', which came up at the Connaught meeting in February and was, I had hoped, firmly rejected.

Terry G has a bagful of books of illustrations by Doré and others, and he is going to redesign the poster yet again.

Biggest problem of the day is the rating. After viewing the film the authorities have given it an R (Restricted) rating – which means anyone under 18 has to be accompanied. Python was PG – a wider certificate and the one we really want. They say that we can have a PG if we trim the shots of the steaming three-quarters-eaten bodies of the two Terrys and cut the shot of Dennis being peed on as he wakes up.

Terry refuses to make the cuts.

Friday, April 15th, New York

The afternoon audiences have been depressing, but the 700-seat cinema builds up to over half full for the evening shows.

At ten o'clock the next morning's papers arrive. Don and his producers pounce eagerly on the *New York Times*, searching for the word of Vincent Canby. Exactly the same feeling as on the *Grail* opening in this same cinema two years ago.

Except that the review is better. It's longer than the *Grail*, it's headlined '*Jabberwocky*: Monster With Heart', it's the top film previewed, and there's a photo too. The review is a joy, better than anything so far in the UK or US. Vincent clearly loves *Jabberwocky* and went to some lengths to say so. Not a harsh word or a qualification – 24-carat gold praise.

Don and the executives of Cinema-5 (who suddenly materialise from the foyer) are overjoyed and read and re-read the paper like men who've just won the Pools. So it is a good picture after all, they seem to be saying.

Saturday, April 16th, New York

To breakfast with Terry. Bought *New York Post*, which slams the film most violently. '*Jabberwocky*: Read Meaningless' is the headline – and the reviewer hates the film as violently as Canby likes it. His only non-violent comment is that I was 'amusing but misused', the rest is hatred.

Terry G, I'm glad to say, laughs, and indeed the intensity of the man's dislike would make grand reading next to Canby's panegyric. If they're both talking about the same film, it would make me curious to see it!

Back to my room for an interview with college kids from Princeton for a syndicated radio programme called *Focus on Youth*. A grim, two-hour ordeal by pretension.

After a quick shopping spree in FAO Schwarz (a magic set for Willy, a bowling game for Tom and a wooden scooter and painted bricks for Rachel), and a hasty snack at the Plaza, we are just in time for the end of the first Saturday performance at the cinema.

Not a bad crowd, but they certainly don't fill the place. A one-legged man approached me as I was about to cross Fifth Avenue. 'Hi Mike,' he shouts, 'How's this for a silly walk!'

Sunday, April 17th

Arrive at Heathrow at a quarter to eleven at night.

Make for the taxis and home at last. No taxis – just another long queue. Resign myself to a late arrival home and decide to take the airport bus. But this only goes to Victoria, and can't leave until it's absolutely full. We are forced to wait for nearly half an hour.

The bus rattles down to Victoria. It's all rather embarrassing and dis-heartening to realise that for most of the passengers (American tourists) this is their first impression of England. Even more disheartening is to be dumped at the Victoria terminal, which has no facilities and, today, no taxis.

Wander up Buckingham Palace Road with the handle of my FAO Schwarz bag now cutting into my fingers. At last find a cab, but he refuses to take me to Hampstead, saying it's too far away.

Almost going spare, I suddenly glimpse an N90 bus with the magic words 'Camden Town' on its destination board, stopped at some traffic lights. I race towards it, and leap on with the same feelings of gratitude and relief that someone lost in the desert would show towards a water hole.

But the conductor, a crusty, near-retirement veteran, was clearly not going to have weary travellers thankfully boarding his bus at half past midnight.

'Where are you going?' he demands.

'I'll go anywhere you're going,' I reply, still full of happy relief and not yet aware that the man has no sense of humour. This doesn't go down at all well.

'You tell me where you're going and I'll tell you where I'm going,' he snaps.

We settle on Camden Town.

The bus trundles on through Pimlico. My breath is coming back and I'm beginning to recover from the last two hours, when an unfriendly voice cuts through my grateful reverie.

'You'll have to move that, you know.'

It's the conductor indicating my FAO Schwarz bag, once the pride of Fifth Avenue, now the target for abuse on the N90. 'Yes, alright … I will move it, but just for a moment let me get my breath back.'

This perfectly reasonable request makes his face twitch and his eyes dart angrily from side to side, but what finally makes this kind and long-suffering man explode is when I ask him to 'Cool down'. He moves quickly into a fury, tapping his badge and screaming that this is his bus and no one is going to ask him to cool down.

Well, I reckon if it's this bad at this stage of the journey, by the time we reach Camden Town one of us will have died of a heart attack, so I pick my cases up and get off.

Once I'm off the bus and waiting for the lights to change, he changes his tune completely. 'I was only doing it for your own good,' he cries. And 'You'll never get another one, you know.'

As the N90 finally disappears, leaving me laden down in a dimly lit, anonymous Pimlico Street, at a quarter to one in the morning, shouting 'Keep Smiling!' at the top of my voice, I find it rather pleasing to think that 24 hours ago I was the star of a New York film premiere.

Eventually find a cab who has no moral, ethnic, financial or personal reasons for not taking me to Oak Village, and I finally arrive home at 1.30, it having taken me nearly half the time to get from Heathrow to Oak Village as it took me to get from New York to London.

Thursday, April 21st

Wig-fitted by an excited Scotsman at Wig Specialities, who greeted me with a little clap of the hands, 'I've seen your bottom simply everywhere.' (I suppose *Jabberwocky* has made modesty in my case rather superfluous.)

A tall, gangly lady, with attractive bony knees rather like Helen's, was also being wig-fitted. It turned out she was Fiona Richmond, star of most of Paul Raymond's sex shows – like *Pyjama Tops* and *Let's Get Laid*. The little Scotsman couldn't control himself after she'd gone. 'Well I never,' he said. 'Two of the country's top sex symbols in here together!'

I've taken the rest of today off to escort my Ma to *Jabberwocky*. She arrives at Liverpool Street on the 11.30.

To Old Compton Street for tea at Patisserie Valerie, then to the 5.40 showing of *Jabberwocky* at the Columbia. It's only about 150 souls full, but the audience does seem to enjoy it and only three people (young, rather attractive girls) walk out. I try to hide myself in my coat, but am spotted by the usherettes, who are frightfully excited, and rush up, saying very nice things about me.

My mother seemed to enjoy it a lot, and I felt that same feeling of enjoyment which I had when I first saw it put together. There are faults, but at least Terry has made a film which, for most of its length, involves, amuses and entertains an audience – with striking and original images and a brilliantly effective evocation of the crumbling mediaeval world. The modern allusions seem to be the ones which sit most uneasily within it. But I felt again what a good piece of work it is.

Saturday, April 23rd

Woken at 7.15 by Tom telling me the phone was ringing. It's Granny. Father is not expected to live much beyond lunchtime. She is just off to the hospital. I promise to get up there as soon as I can. Feel dreadfully bleary and tired. Tell the children. Willy says, quite seriously, that he hopes Rachel (who's got a slight cold) won't be dead by lunchtime too.

Ring Angela. By a quarter to nine Veryan has brought her round and I have woken up sufficiently to drive us both up to Blythburgh. It's a sunny day, which helps to keep the gloom from settling too heavily. Angela natters on compulsively about her job – her social welfare work in Croydon sounds far more harrowing than anything we are experiencing today.

Arrive at Blythburgh Hospital just after eleven. As we walk from the car, neither of us, or certainly I myself, have any real idea of what to expect. I have never been near anyone dying before.

Daddy is breathing heavily and noisily on his back in bed, eyes almost closed, one half-open, glazed and unseeing. His skin is pale and parchment-like and drawn tight over the bones of his face. Mother sits at the bedside, hardly racked with grief. Indeed she greets us very matter of factly, as if we'd just arrived at a coffee morning.

A marvellously sane and intelligent middle-aged lady doctor takes us into her room after examining him and tells us that he has pneumonia on the top of one of his lungs and is not likely to survive. She has brought us in here, she says, because, although he is unconscious to all intents and purposes, one never can be sure about the sense of hearing. This worries me a little, as I had, when I arrived, rather loudly queried whether it was terminal.

The doctor, grasping my mother's hand in a firm, comforting, but unsentimental clasp of reassurance, cannot give us any real estimate of how long Dad will live. His unconsciousness means that the heart has the minimum of work to do and he could survive for anything from an hour to two or three days. She suggests, very tactfully, that there is little to be gained from us all clustering around the body waiting for him to die, so on her advice I take Ma (who has been at his bedside for five hours) back to Reydon, where we do a bit of shopping and have some lunch.

We return to the hospital just after two. His condition is the same. I wait beside the bed, and after a while find myself becoming quite accustomed to the rattling gurgle of deeply drawn breaths which had so unnerved me when I first saw him.

As we really don't know how long he will survive, it's decided that I shall go back to London and Angela will stay with Mother, at least until Monday. Tomorrow I have to travel to Durham and on Monday morning the first of the last three *Ripping Yarns* begins filming.

On the way back I stop at the hospital. Father has been moved up to one end of the ward. He's breathing as heavily and noisily as before. The nurses still wash him and turn him regularly. He lies in a clean and comfortable bed. In the background the news and the football results. What a ritual *Sports Report* always used to be on a Saturday. At about 6.25 I leave.

I'm 33 and he's 77 when I last see him, an emaciated, gravel-breathed shadow of the father I knew.

Say goodbye to the nurses, knowing I won't see them again. One of them says he'd really grown to like my dad, which is nice, because it didn't happen that way often during his life.

Into the car and down the A12 to London. Beyond Ipswich, a colossal rainstorm. I must have been passing Colchester when Father died – at 7.25. Mother and Angela were almost at Blythburgh, slowed down by the heavy rain. He was dead by the time they got there.

Sunday, April 24th, Durham

Preparations for departure. Packing cases, writing last-minute letters, regretting lack of time and feeling of unpreparedness for the weeks to come.

Swimming – always good for calming the troubled breast, then a roast beef lunch, and am driven down to catch the three o'clock train at King's Cross.

Settle into the seat, armed with unlearnt script and the Sunday papers, and it's only as we pull out of King's Cross and are rumbling through Hertfordshire that the pressure of events in the last few days hits me with a wave of depression. Fortunately I only feel such depression very rarely, but it intensifies as the train nears familiar stations like Sandy and familiar views like the fields beyond St Neots. I miss home and family. I feel unutterably sad that I am going away to the grey north having seen so little of them for the last two weeks. I feel, too, the sadness at my father's death which eluded me yesterday.

It's a feeling of loneliness. A feeling that I am speeding away from the familiar world, which for some reason I need at the moment, to an unfamiliar world of new faces, new people, new work. And the skies turn greyer too. Increasing the melancholy.

Fortunately this despondency does not last even the length of the journey and I'm a little more phlegmatic about things as the train edges round the curving viaduct with the splendid mass of Durham Cathedral looming across the River Wear.

To the County Hotel – an old, probably Georgian building, which has been expanded, in the process becoming rather airport loungefied. Met by Eddie S, Liz.[1] Aware of the slight awkwardness with which they bring up the subject of Father's death. No mention of death, just 'Sorry about your news'. They're kind people, though, very straightforward.

1 Eddie Stuart and Liz Cranston – members of the production team.

Decide not to eat that night, still feeling metabolically maladjusted. A few drinks in the hotel bar with a smattering of wardrobe and props boys. Put on as cheerful a face as possible.

Friday, April 29th, Durham

Tonight Jim [Franklin, the director] has laid a car on for me to return to London, for tomorrow is Father's funeral, and we film again on Sunday.[1] Say my goodbyes to all, including Ken Colley, who, I'm pleased to say, has turned out to be a stroke of genius choice for the part of the Robber. He's not only a very good, no-nonsense actor, he's also very good company.

Saturday, April 30th, Southwold

We troop off to the church, taking Mrs Pratt[2] with us, in time for the service at two. Father had been cremated at Gorleston during the week, and so it's more of a memorial service than a cremation. There is a representative of the Funeral Directors – heavy dark coat matching his eyebrows, despite the warm afternoon. Then there is the vicar, muted, grave and cold.

Quite a small congregation – thirty or forty at most. Father's ashes are in a small wooden box at the end of the aisle. I am quite severely nervous for the first part of the service – 'The Lord's My Shepherd' – as I am to read the lesson, a heavy piece of Revelations. But that goes well, as does the service, and even the vicar's little address (about my father being a man of patience, bearing with extreme tolerance and fortitude the slings and arrows. I suppose in a sense he was patient – for a man carrying a severe stammer for much of his life. I just remember so many moments of *im*patience and *in*tolerance).

At the end we process out behind the box of ashes and into the churchyard. The solemnity and dignity of the occasion is somehow less easy to maintain the further we process from the organ and the hymn singers, and I find that we are wending our way in a direct line towards the Southwold Cottage Hospital where I have an awful feeling that Father's spirit was finally broken last autumn.

His ashes are lowered in – 'Dust to dust', etc, etc – and the ceremony is over. Shake the vicar's hand and receive in exchange a bland smile.

1 On 'The Test of Eric Olthwaite'.
2 Lily Pratt, my mother's neighbour.

Still, Father would have loved the church today, filled with sunlight, the mediaeval pews and the fine old screen which has witnessed funeral services for 500 years.

Back to Croft Cottage for tea. No tears, except from Camilla, a little, and Angela, a sniffle. Mother quite composed about the whole thing. Tea turns into a jolly family reunion in the best tradition of funeral teas, and we leave for London at about five.

Thursday, May 5th, Tow Law and Durham

Birthday on location again. Thirty-four, and I feel it.

Out in the bus to Tow Law. This is an exposed and underprivileged sort of town. A long line of small houses and not much more. No green, no parks, no opulent houses or even well-off areas – just the skeleton of a town custom-built for mining, in the days when there was something to mine. A cold wind whips through the grid-frame streets and all in all it's a depressing place to spend a birthday.

I organise free drinks at lunchtime for the crew and all at the Tow Law Hotel. A blind pianist plays 'Happy Birthday', with lush holiday camp trills thrown in, on an organ. I am presented with a shovel, signed by all the crew, which is very touching. I'm also given a birthday cake with one candle. But it's a celebration only just on this side of tragic. The place, the town, the hotel are all grim.

Friday, May 6th, Durham

We were supposed to return home yesterday, but the bad weather on Tuesday put us a day behind.

Somewhere away to our north-east, ten or fifteen miles, President Carter is pressing the flesh in Newcastle. The Tories have swept Labour under the carpet in the local government elections – Wearside and Durham County are amongst a tiny handful of councils where Labour has held on. I fear for Helen's Ma, so vociferous is the reaction against the government, Labour and their sympathisers.

At the very moment that Peter has set up a skyline shot with a colliery wheel in the background, Eddie Stuart appears over the hill with a man in a suit and helmet who looks very unhappy. This turns out to be the colliery manager, who is concerned, as it turns out, about the image of the National Coal Board.

With much palaver and banging of helmets and raising of spectacles, the manager pronounces that we can film on, provided we go easy on shots of the slag heaps.

We then move on to a windswept line of stone-built houses with a rather dark and moody back alley running alongside them. A lady berates us for filming the alley, calling it a disgrace, and bemoaning the fact that her husband's wheelchair gets stuck along it in bad weather. At another house, a family who've just returned from two weeks' holiday in Spain. It seems the days when you could point to a street and sum up its character straightaway are gone.

Saturday, May 14th, Abbotsley

Drove up to Abbotsley for two-day break from city and work. Long bicycle ride with Tom and Willy – the older they get the more we can do together. We cycled all the way to Waresley, where we met a dog which followed us all the way back. In the end Helen and I had to drive it back in the car. Tom collected a hoard of spent cartridges from roadside shoots along the Tetworth Hall Estate. Very happy day and fine May sunset.

Sunday, May 15th, Abbotsley

Worked hard in the morning, mowing and clearing the grass and weeds which have grown in lush profusion this year after the wettest winter for 100 years.

Roast beef lunch. Helen's Ma, who lost her seat in the council elections of May 5th, is just beginning to feel the effects. She will no longer be on the Education Committee – the Conservatives are going to run it under their own tight political control, and her work will be cut down enormously. For someone who worked so hard and so thoroughly for the local people it's a tragedy that national politics should retire her prematurely. But the Tories were returned up and down the land regardless of their quality. At Eynesbury, near St Neots, a man got in who couldn't even pronounce the name of the town.

She has a mound of letters from all sorts of people, from Lord Hemingford to the Headmaster of Kimbolton and the Cambridge Borough Architect, to say how much she will be missed.

To London this evening – I must prepare for another *Ripping Yarn* tomorrow. Long learning session.

Friday, May 20th

A mixed week of filming [on 'Escape from Stalag 112B'] draws to a close in perfect sunny weather. We are on schedule and generally all has gone well. But mid-week I had some worries about performances. Roy Kinnear,[1] on his first day, seemed a little too stock – relying too much on the well-loved Kinnearish fat-man grimaces, than on his natural skill as an actor. But he began to improve and enjoy the part in a more original way as the week went on.

Marvellous props, such as the glider made out of toilet rolls.

The First World War cricket match created a totally believable atmosphere out there with the German watchtowers and the barbed wire surrounding the pitch. The more or less continuous thudding of guns in the distance (for we are in the middle of a tank-training area) helps too and puts me in mind of Sassoon's descriptions of being behind the lines in France during the First War.

Monday, May 23rd

Helen rang me in Salisbury. We are going ahead with plans to purchase No. 2, the house next door but one. Helen got frightened by the sound of prospective buyers just the other side of our wall, and she, Edward[2] and others, seem to feel it's a good thing to buy the property and enlarge our garden – give the kids a plentiful playroom, a permanent spare room etc.

Friday, May 27th

I have been filming, I suppose, daily for the past five weeks and maybe a cumulative tiredness is creeping up on me, but Wednesday and Thursday this week were days I had to drag myself through, force myself, like a runner at the end of a long race, to keep up the enthusiasm, the involvement and the energy that these films *must* have, when my body and mind are about to stage a mutiny.

---

1 Kinnear made his name on the satire show *That Was The Week That Was* (1962). Constantly in demand as a character actor, he died from a fall from his horse whilst filming *The Return of the Musketeers* in 1988.
2 Edward Burd, my brother-in-law, was an architect.

Saturday, May 28th

The hot weather continues. After breakfast, go round to see Mr and Mrs Pym, whose house we are hoping to buy. (Helen has been working hard on it all week and yesterday we made our offer, but I wanted to check with them.) 'Oh, yes,' says Mrs Pym, dismissing the subject as though it had all been settled and bustling me out into the back garden to ask how much we would give her for her rotary clothes drier. 'It cost £8, and he made a stand for it,' she reassures me, pointing at a concrete lump into which it has been sunk. Anyway, she seems far more interested in getting rid of the rotary drier, so I agree to buy it for £18,754 – with the house thrown in.

The Pyms have been there twenty-five years. They're a quiet, self-contained, working class couple. He's a dustman. She has that Welsh darting quickness and busyness.

Good news, or nice news – *Jabberwocky* has been selected as the British entry for the Berlin Film Festival, so it's brush up on the German and off to Berlin for TG and me at the beginning of July. It's still being held in at Cinema One in New York. Don Rugoff is forever devising new campaigns, hoping that kids will flock in during the long school holidays and save the picture.

Monday, May 30th

To the BBC at ten o'clock for a sort of review of the situation so far with Jim F. I think they are running into heavy production problems with 'The Curse of the Claw', one of which is casting the very difficult Chief Petty Officer part. Gwen Taylor, whom Eric recommended to me as being 'a female Michael Palin', now can't do it (because of the new dates), nor can Penny Wilton, our second choice.

Tuesday, May 31st

We talk to and read through with four girls from four until about half past five. Eventually select Judy Loe.[1] She's a straightforward, jolly, easy-going lady and straightaway understood and appreciated the part.

Up to Terry Hughes' office for a glass of wine – Jimmy Gilbert, now

1 Married to Richard Beckinsale. Mother of Kate.

Head of Light Entertainment, and Bill Cotton, new Controller of BBC1, there. Very matey and jolly and we talk about my house-buying as if we were old friends at the pub. Continually amazed at the change in their attitude (or is it the change in mine?) since Python!

But they have shown great confidence in the *Ripping Yarns*. I hope they will be as good as everyone thinks they're going to be.

Friday, June 3rd

A hot day. Into Soho to see what Ray [Millichope, the editor] has done to the still unsatisfactory 'Moorstones' and 'Andes'.

Difficult to work up in Wardour Street as groups of chanting, singing, shouting Scottish football fans are roaming the West End, waiting for the pubs to open. As I drive from Soho down through St Martin's Lane and Trafalgar Square (where one of them is later killed jumping into a fountain), I see the Scots everywhere. In high spirits – the weather, the booze and the anticipation of rubbing England's nose in the turf – they have taken over Trafalgar Square from the American tourists and they have easily upstaged the colourless pink and washed-out turquoise of the Jubilee decorations.

Lunch with Jill Foster in the King's Road. The subject of Graham C comes up. I mention how cowardly I am about confronting him with direct criticism of his wasteful lifestyle. Jill says she took him out to lunch the other day and told him he was a boozy old wastrel who was destroying himself and his chances of work. GC took a gin and tonic off her and agreed.

In the early evening, swimming with the kids at the Holiday Inn, where there are three or four men of ruddy body and glazed eye hurling themselves at the water with vicious smacks. It turns out – yes – they're Scottish football supporters. I sign an autograph for them. They can't believe that at the hotel in one day they've seen Kevin Keegan, John Conteh and now a real live Monty Python.

Tuesday, June 7th, Jubilee Day, Abbotsley

Rather grey to start with, but the rain held off. Church Farm decked out with streams of coloured flags. In the afternoon went to Abbotsley Village Sports in the field at the back of the Eight Bells pub. Helen and I came second in the wheelbarrow race and I entered for the obstacle race

– two heats – and though I came third overall, I was nearly dead after crawling under nets, etc.

Later in the evening, as it got dark, we returned to the sports field for the village firework display, having just watched the royal bonfire being lit at Windsor Castle – a dramatic sight – huge flames and great surging crowds of people. Abbotsley firework display upstaged by more expensive pyrotechnics which burst in the air above St Neots, a few miles away.

Wednesday, June 8th

Pleasant drive up into Lincolnshire.[1] Sun is out when I arrive in Rippingale, a small village between Bourne and Sleaford, lying in unexpectedly attractive country – more wooded and gently hilly than the bleak, flat Fenland just to the east. The villages are full of fine stone houses, like the Cotswolds.

The house itself is a stone-built Georgian rectory, of simple, unadorned design, with additions in red brick. It is in quite a poor state indoors and Uncle Jack's[2] bedroom needs absolutely nothing doing to it – the walls are damp, mildewed and peeling – just perfect.

Drive into Peterborough – about half an hour down the A15. An extraordinary city. A fine and impressive cathedral and all around it lines of insubstantial brick terraces, reaching right into the city centre. There is hardly anyone about – even at 5.30. Then I realise, of course, Peterborough – or Greater Peterborough as it now calls itself – has expanded along the American pattern – from the suburbs outwards. No-one really needs the centre of Peterborough any more.

Saturday, June 11th

After a great deal of heart-searching over the last few weeks, I finally sat down to write to Hamish MacInnes,[3] and excuse myself from his Yeti expedition.

1 For 'Curse of the Claw' filming.
2 Uncle Jack was a character who had all the world's diseases, at the same time.
3 An experienced climber who lived in Glencoe and who had helped us on *Monty Python and the Holy Grail* by throwing dummy bodies into the Gorge of Eternal Peril. Unfortunately he was head of Mountain Rescue at the time.

In recent weeks I had received the latest newsletters on the expedition from Hamish, which contained a rather worrying mixture of uncertainty over finance and jolly, harrowing asides like 'We will have to move fast to get out of this valley, where some years ago a Tibetan expedition were trapped and actually ate their boots before being discovered … dead.'

Despite the obvious pleasures of a trip to unknown lands in the company of top climbing folk like Hamish and Joe Brown, I have been so infrequently at home over the last year, what with *Jabberwocky* (ten weeks) and *Ripping Yarns* (seven weeks) and a week and a half in New York, that I feel I can't commit myself to two months in the Himalayas only a month or so before we plan to shoot *Life of Brian* in North Africa. But it goes against instincts I've had since early childhood to opt out of an expedition to an almost unknown part of the world.

Saturday, June 18th

Playing charity football this afternoon at Wembley Stadium. Cavernous rooms and passageways round the back.

Finally discovered our dressing room. Teddy Warrick[1] there, small and beaming, and most of the Radio One side with him – Peel, Gambaccini, Kid Jensen and Paul Burnett. Quiet, rather subdued atmosphere. Ed Stewart arrives and starts to organise everyone in a very loud voice.

On our side only Paul Nicholas here at the moment. Another quiet lad – I like him. Alan Price arrives, then Graham Chapman and John Tomiczek. John will play in goal for us and I suggest Graham, in his strange Trilby hat, should be team psychiatrist. A sort of cheer goes up as Tommy Steele arrives, bubbling, flashing a lovely white Cockney grin of the type usually described as 'infectious'. He is tacitly assumed to be senior 'celebrity', and takes over captaincy of our side.

We are given free bags and kit by some sports company, which is a nice bonus. The CID appear in the dressing room – apparently to offer us some sort of protection – and say they will guard the dressing room until we get back – if we get back. We sign programmes for them.

Gambaccini claims he didn't sleep at all last night. He can't cope with

---

1 Enormously experienced and much-liked Radio 1 producer. In 1965 he got me some work as a DJ on a programme called *Playtime*.

it all, he says. 'Three times I've played football, and already I'm at Wembley!'

Alan Price finishes a last cigarette and stubs it beneath his boot as we move off up the tunnel. The noise grows, heads turn – heads of officials, policemen, commissionaires – the flotsam and jetsam of officialdom who are allowed to hang around at the very cervix of Wembley. Ahead is the pitch, above us a net to protect players from missiles.

And suddenly we're walking out. I want to freeze the moment, savour it like the finest wine. All I'm aware of is empty terraces.

There are, in fact, 55,000 people here for the Schoolboy International which follows our game – but at Wembley that still leaves bald patches – bald patches mirrored in the sacred turf itself, ripped up by the Scottish fans a couple of weeks ago and still not all replaced.

As we kick around they announce our names, and cheers rise. Biggest for Ed Stewart (good at projecting his personality), softest for John Peel (the brightest of the lot of them).

The game (the width, not the length of the pitch) is a kick and run affair – with Tommy Steele vainly trying to organise a team of six people, all of whom want only one thing, to score at Wembley. Ed Stewart plays a miraculous blinder in goal for Radio One, and it's even scores at half-time.

In the second half I hit the crossbar and completely miss another, and John Peel scores the winner for Radio One. As Teddy Warrick put it, the best team lost, which is, along with a car sticker for Wembley Stadium Main Car Park, a free kit-bag and a No. 4 blue shirt, my only consolation.

Friday, July 1st, Berlin

Meet up at London Airport with Sir John Terry of the NFFC[1] – big and benign, like Father Christmas – John Goldstone, grinning bearishly through a beard which threatens to overrun his face, and Terry Gilliam.

I find myself sat next to a short-haired, fortyish Englishman, who talks compulsively. It turns out he's with the British Forces in Berlin, and is scared stiff of flying. He has his air-sickness bag ready, grasps the edge of the seat with hands continually clenching and unclenching. He's a crack shot and trains people in rifle use.

1 National Film Finance Corporation.

Meet Michael White in the lobby of the Kempinski Hotel. He's in a crumpled white suit and has just flown in from Paris after an all-night party given by Yves St Laurent.

The bad news of the day is that *Jabberwocky* is now *out* of competition as we have been naughty and broken the rules by opening the film in Paris before the festival. It takes some of the edge off our jaunt to know that, however well received, we can't win any Golden Bears. 'Just as well,' says Goldstone, not very convincingly. 'These sort of awards can put audiences off, you know.'

Saturday, July 2nd, Berlin

In the afternoon, after a typical German lunch, served by a large, perspiring waiter, M White hires a BMW and we all squash in and go across to East Berlin. What a change from 1972.[1] The Alexanderplatz looks cleaner, brighter, more colourful than before. The bombed and shot-up churches are being restored. Altogether a much more Western look to the place. But the coffee is terrible and the cakes are hard and it still takes half an hour to cross through the wall.

Find a wonderfully seedy hotel just beside the wall at Brandenburg Gate, Hotel Adlon. It used to be right next to Hitler's bunker, which Whitey tells me the East Germans are excavating. Tea at the Orangerie in the Charlottenburg.

Alan Brien[2] sees me reading Nabokov's *Despair* and tells me that he is mentioned in *Ada* after conducting some correspondence with Nabokov about skin disease. (Nabokov, one of my literary heroes, died last week.)

In the Kempinski, like in some grotesque dream, tarted-up, over-beautified fat ladies and heavily-sweating men gather for the Film Festival Ball, which seems to be remarkable for having nobody recognisable present.

We Brits can't get in anyway, but stay on the outside, make guerrilla raids on the rather good food and buy ourselves a couple of bottles of sparkling. M White observes that this is why Hollywood stars never leave Hollywood.

1 My only previous visit to Berlin, with Robert Hewison.
2 Author, journalist, and, at the time, film critic of the *Sunday Times*.

Sunday, July 3rd, Berlin

Kill time until three o'clock, and the first showing of *Jabberwocky*. A half-full house. Perhaps a little more. Good laughs. At the end Gilliam and I have to come through the curtains and make a brief appearance. Applause. It's not too embarrassing. The worst is yet to come.

We are shown into a back room of the Cinema Am Zoo, where two long tables are pushed together and rigged with chunky, old-fashioned mikes. A few scruffy-looking people with notepads sit around.

Wolf Donner, the organiser of the festival, is a pleasant, open-faced man with a firm, friendly handshake, who says he enjoyed the film. Questions are vague or just downright dull. Someone persistently asked us for details of the jokes we *rejected* from the film. A Turkish journalist wants to know what the monster represents in British politics today. He seems very happy when I suggest it is the rise of fascism.

John Terry gives a short, obviously well-prepared speech about *Jabberwocky* being a British film, part-financed by the British government. But there are long silences, probably because the whole electronic system of mikes and simultaneous translation may be OK for the United Nations, but is utterly dampening in a roomful of twenty people. The whole miserable charade lasts about three-quarters of an hour.

Monday, July 4th

In keeping with our way of meeting all the interesting film people on the last day of the festival, we find ourselves in a car with Barbara Stone, an American who now lives in London and with her husband runs a small film distribution network and a cinema – the Gate at Notting Hill. They are one of several new distributors who are doing very well in London, feeding quality (mainly foreign) films to the eager London sophisticates (or just, let's face it, people who enjoy a good intelligent movie). They're making money now, and are directly able to help directors (such as Derek Jarman, who made *Sebastiane*). A good sign – nice to meet someone who is optimistic about the cinema in Britain. A Londonophile too – she says they couldn't start and run a similar cinema in the States.

In the evening, despite terminal drowsiness, I have to read the Python film script, which I haven't touched for three months, and have intelligent comments on it ready for our meeting tomorrow.

Tuesday, July 5th

Eric is the first person I see. He was in hospital a week ago, being fed intravenously and with pipes through the nose to drain his stomach. Apparently there was a complication after his appendix removal, and he was back in the highly expensive Wellington Hospital for Arabs (as Graham said, when he visited him, Eric appeared to be 'the only Caucasian in the place'). So Eric is thin as a stick, long-haired and bearded. He thanks me for the pile of books I sent him. I apologised for not having had time to visit him, but I sent him an Intellectuals Get-U-Well Reading Pack, which included a potted biography of Debbie Reynolds.

According to Terry's report (he and TG went location-hunting in mid-June), Tunisia sounds the easiest of the Mediterranean countries to film in. They are well organised, there are good sites and comfortable hotels and the film entrepreneur is the nephew of the President – so no problems stopping the traffic!

But Terry J is not entirely happy with Tunisia – he is worried that we will merely be duplicating all the locations Zeffirelli used, and that it doesn't really look like the Holy Land. John Cleese had had a letter from Israeli Films, trying to persuade us to film there. Terry J wants to look at Jordan. Gilliam says the best hilly city streets are not in Tunisia but in Fez in Morocco, so no solutions are obvious.

A lunch break. John, Terry G and I go and lie in Regent's Park in the sunshine, whilst Terry J has to organise one of his many philanthropic projects (*Vole*, Kington Brewery, etc)[1] with Anne. John gets on to a well-worn theme – money. He makes no bones about it, says he, this film must make him a great deal of money. Apparently nothing else does apart from commercials. Coming from a man whom I saw having difficulty parking his Rolls-Royce this morning, that does sound a little unsad, but it's a jolly chat and indicative of a generally more relaxed, easy feeling amongst us.

This evening, a civilised and funny and enjoyable evening with Simon Albury and Derek Taylor[2] and wife. We go to Langan's Brasserie,

1 *The Vole* was an environmental magazine edited by Richard Boston. The Penrhos Brewery, near Kington, Herefordshire, was a real ale venture run by Martin Griffiths. Terry was fairy godfather to both.
2 Derek Taylor, a journalist from Hoylake in the Wirral who became the Beatles' press officer. He had a terrific, very English sense of humour and wrote memoirs such as *As Time Goes By* and *Fifty Years Adrift*.

passing on our way the Berkeley Square Jubilee Party – £25 entrance tickets, of course. Packed densely inside the railings, men with no chins mingled with ladies with large teeth. Protruding jaws spread wide into baying laughs and huge noses assailed with the bouquet of champagne. All in all it looked like a gigantic zoo exhibit – 'The Upper Classes – British – circa 1970s'.

But Langan's is, of course, posh and moneyed and quite obviously aimed at those with enough money to pay for style rather than essentials. Derek is the ideal company to enjoy such a place with. He's sensible and sensitive and articulate and enjoys laughing a lot. They have legions of children – one of whom is into punk rock at the moment.

Sadly, Derek is away to Los Angeles to live for a few years – accepting promotion to Vice-President of Warner Brothers Records. I hope he doesn't stay away for long – England needs people like him. His wife Joan is jolly and down to earth and they both know a lot of famous people (via the Beatles) and yet can enjoy jokes about people knowing famous people. They know what's bullshit and what isn't. A rare quality in the frenetic music biz.

Sunday, July 10th

Al and Eve Levinson are in London at the moment. I saw them last week, when Al proudly thrust his latest Fish novel/autobiography upon me. It's longer than *Millwork* (my favourite) or *Shipping Out* (naval larks) and has an awful pun for a title – *Rue Britannia.*

Through Eve I have made the acquaintance of Arnold Wesker.[1] I took Eve up to Wesker's in Highgate (within spitting distance of G Chapman's). Eve persuaded me to go in and say hello, and Arnold's wife got very excited and said that their daughters had been dying to meet me. In the sitting room were gathered lots of young teenage kids – mostly Weskers – and a brace of Americans, including a professor from the University of Wisconsin who is doing a paper on Arnold. Arnold stands, stockily built, but in good trim, shirt open three or four buttons revealing hirsute chest, an easy manner, but on his toes like a boxer.

Then the boyfriend of the daughter, who is an enormous fan, arrived and she introduced him to the professors, playwrights and unpublished

1 Playwright, best known for *Chicken Soup with Barley, The Kitchen* and *Chips with Everything.*

novelists' wives, but missed me out. She made up for it by saying she was leaving me to last – which she did – and with a flourish said – 'and *this* … is Terry Gilliam!'

Wednesday, July 13th

Wake heavy-headed after late night with the author of *Rue Britannia* and his wife. They dropped in last night from the theatre and much vodka (Eve) and brandy (Al) was drunk and Helen and I struggled to stay awake and reconcile our gentle domestic mood of approaching somnolence with Al and Eve's holidaymakers' energy.

I seem to remember a lot of laughter – and Eve looking very sour as I played Elgar. 'What *is* this … ?' she demanded in tones which only a true Brooklyner could affect. I changed it for reggae and Al and Eve danced to Bob Marley.

Some last-minute script work on *Brian*, then drive down to Park Square West for a group meeting. The changes and rewrites to the script are amicably accepted, but we have to agree today on some casting for Friday's read-through. This casting, whilst it need not be binding for the film, could, as Eric put it, 'stick', so we have to make fairly far-reaching decisions between 12.45 and 1.30, when John has to leave.

Eric tells John (Graham being out of the room) that he, the two Terrys and myself, are of the opinion that John would be wasted as Brian and that Graham might be the best for it – he's Roman-looking, which helps, and was quite good as the central figure in *Grail* – Graham looks good and is watchable.

John erupted at this – far more vehemently than I would have expected. Casting a quick eye at the door in case GC should reappear, he hissed agitatedly that it would be a disaster – take it from John, he'd been working with him recently and he (GC) couldn't even find his place in the script.

Then Graham reappeared and, despite John's outburst, it was suggested to him that he play Brian. Graham mumbled woollily and we went on to cast the rest – as John had to go. I was given Pilate, Ben, the Ex-Leper and the follower Francis, as well as Nisus Wettus – the centurion in charge of the crucifixion. Feel liberated from Dennis/*Ripping Yarn* juve leads at last, and into some genuinely absurd parts.

Dash off to Willy's school concert at two. Willy, looking rather bewildered, is third child along in the Monster – the Marvellous Monster from Mars. He was very proud to be chosen for the Monster – they took six children from the whole of the infants – noted for their 'patience', Willy said. Patience was also a necessity for the audience.

In the evening to Anne and Michael Henshaw – socialising this time. In the same room where eight hours before we had been casting *Life of Brian* were now assembled myself and Helen, Anne and Michael, Al and Eve and a very bouncy director called Richard Loncraine (who is, apart from Python, Anne H's only other client). Immediately friendly and jokey, he's the sort of person you feel after ten minutes you've known for years. Or else, I suppose, he drives you mad.

Friday, July 15th

Drive over to Primrose Hill for *Life of Brian* recorded script read-through at Sound Developments. A pleasantly warm July morning. Tuck the Mini into a parking space as Cleese's Rolls glides by.

Talk to John on the way in. I had misjudged exactly how much he *wanted* to play the rather dull central role of Brian. John wants to do a lead, he told me. He wants to have a go at being a Dennis, because he says it gives him more chance to work closely with the director, to be bound up in the making of the film much more intimately than he was on the *Holy Grail*.

The recording starts well – the studio is spacious and cool and the engineer unfussy. Al Levinson is there to read the voice of Christ! We make Al religious adviser to the film. When asked what advice he's given, Al will say he told us not to do it.

But as the day wears on it's clear that Graham is once again being his own worst enemy. He arrived at ten quite 'relaxed', and has drunk gin throughout the morning. Everyone else is on the ball, but Graham can never find where we are in the script, and we keep constantly having to stop, re-take and wait for him. Occasional glimpses of how well he could do Brian, but on the whole his performance bears out every point John ever made.

Saturday, July 16th

Launch day for Penrhos Brewery. At Hereford Station by one. A minibus drives us to Penrhos Court, where a wonderfully laid out array of cold pies, tarts, a cooked ham and salads various is prepared in the restaurant.

The beer is tasted and found to be good. Jones' First Ale it's called – and at a specific gravity of 1050 it's about as devastating as Abbot Ale. But the weather has decided to be kind to us and the collection of buildings that is Penrhos Court – basically a fine, but rundown sixteenth-century manor house with outbuildings housing the brewery, restaurant and Martin Griffiths' office and living accommodation – look well in the sunshine and provide a very amenable background to the serious beer-drinking.

After lunch and beer we are organised into a game of rounders in a nearby field, which affords a most beautiful view of rolling Border country – gentle hills, wooded and cultivated, with the town of Kington nestling amongst them and providing that ideal blend of nature and man which makes poets cream their notebooks.

A jolly game – or games – of rounders. Most people play, but Richard Boston reclines on bales of straw and watches and Mike Oldfield, who lives nearby, spends the afternoon taking photographs of his girlfriend. She has dark hair in ringlets and both his behaviour and his preoccupation with her seem a little narcissistic to a jolly rounders-playing fellow like me. I suffer heavy flatulence as a result of Terry's ale.

In the evening a gorgeous sunset completes the idyllic picture of hills, fields and woods in this Rupert Land.

Monday, July 18th

To Sound Developments at nine to listen, with the rest of the Pythons (bar Eric), to the tape.

We decide to simplify the central section with the raid on Pilate's palace, and cut down on the number of characters – amalgamating a lot of them – and also to shorten the end sequences. General feeling that the first third of the picture is fine.

We split up – Graham and I to write together on the middle section, because John wants to work on the end with either Terry or myself. Given GC's behaviour on Friday at the reading, I don't particularly relish a day's writing with him. I would really rather work on my own.

By chance Barry Cryer rings during supper this evening. He is disenchanted with the Chapman situation, and says he doesn't feel at home or comfortable in the house at Southwood Lane any more. Sad, for Barry was a very loyal and sensible friend of Graham's.

Tuesday, July 19th

To Graham's at eleven. A very good day's work. We complete the re-think of the whole central section and work well together on new scenes and new dialogue during our five hours writing together. The Doctor has about six gin and tonics, and when I leave at four he seems on the verge of incapability – evenings can't be much fun.

But until four we find a very easy-going, productive way of working – mainly because we have something to work on, and I am quite disci-plined about what we have to do. Occasionally the phone rings and Graham becomes a producer. He seems to find this a nerve-racking business. He puts the phone down, tells me they've got another £750,000, and then has to have a large gin and tonic to calm himself down.

Friday, July 22nd

Meet Geoffrey Strachan and the marketing man at Methuen to discuss ideas for promoting the new book of the *Holy Grail*.

We meet at Odin's. I suggest we should publish our own top ten list of bestsellers in every ad, and make up specious names like 'The Shell Guide to Dead Animals on the Motorway', or else we should do a series of direct appeals to the buying public, of an abject and grovelling tone, mentioning wives, families to support ... 'living in the manner to which we've become accustomed', etc, etc.

Geoffrey seems highly pleased and we part and walk over to Park Square West for a final Python meeting. Because we only have a little over an hour to make decisions, we work well and extraordinarily pro-ductively. No writing again until January – when we shall spend two or three weeks writing and rehearsing. The West Indies is mentioned, Eric favours Barbados.

Tuesday, July 26th

On a hot afternoon go all the way to Sun Alliance in Chancery Lane, only to be told that they wouldn't insure my new house because of my profession. 'Actors ... and writers ... well, you know.'

I didn't know, nor did I try to find out, but I couldn't help feeling something of a reject from society as I walked out again into Chancery

Lane. But my solicitor cheerfully informs me that several big companies, including Eagle Star, won't touch actors. The happy and slightly absurd ending to this story is that I finally find a willing insurer in the National Farmers' Union at Huntingdon.

Friday, July 29th

Today we dub 'Stalag Luft 112B' at the Centre. There are twenty-two music cues, however, so it's not easy.

The Goodies are in the bar at lunchtime. Tim has been in Australia (Perth) for two months doing a long part in a stage play, just to see, as he put it, 'if I could make people laugh again'.

The talk is of the two scripts for the new Goodies series which the BBC have rejected. One, Jim told me, was the first the BBC had rejected, and it was because it wasn't funny. Bill, on the other hand, said it was about punk rock and the BBC couldn't stomach it. Jimmy Gilbert came under attack for his pusillanimity – and apparently Tim had been the most aggressive of the lot with him. Times change. John C used to describe Tim as the only man who could get Hitler and Churchill to come to tea together.

Monday, August 22nd

Jill Foster rang to say that Python had been approached to appear in the Royal Variety Performance this year. She said that when the gnarled old showbiz pro who puts the show together rang her, he had been rendered practically speechless by the fact that she said she'd ask us and see, but there wasn't a great chance we'd do it.[1]

Mother very excited when I told her. I saw Tim Brooke-T and Bill at the Holiday Inn. The Goodies haven't been asked, Tim admitted. I told him to wait a week! Tim did it once with Marty Feldman, and he strongly advised me against it. The audience was made up of the rich and ruthless of British showbiz – the sort of men who, as Tim put it, 'make chorus girls cry'.

---

1 She was right.

Thursday, August 25th

A phone call from Tariq Ali, of all people, who wants me to write an appreciation of Groucho Marx, who died this week aged 86, for *Socialist Challenge*. Decline on the grounds that I don't know enough about him, and suggest Ian Davidson. But Tariq doesn't sound very interested – they're really only after big names, these socialists.

Saturday, August 27th

A fine morning for Clive Hollick's wedding party at Shepperton. We all drive over there in our Saturday best. The Old House is a perfect location. Tables have been set out on the verandah and the rich green lawn (well watered this year) stretches away, dominated by the great cedar tree. A band from Ronnie Scott's plays, there's sparkling wine and a buffet. Croquet and cricket on the lawn.

Don't know many people, but Simon A is best man, resplendent in white suit and hat, dark blue shirt, blue tie and shoes. Looking like the Young Burl Ives. A best woman there as well, as it is a very egalitarian occasion. Simon tells some of Ronnie Scott's old jokes, but they are rather borne away on the wind.

The Old House really is a remarkable relic of the days when film moguls built themselves headquarters which were as extravagantly theatrical as the films they made. As I wandered through it, marvelling at the richness of art nouveau plasterwork and fine stained glass windows, I felt a definite twinge of remorse that I was one of the four people who confirmed the decision to lease it off for 999 years to Ramport Ltd. Still, I rationalised through my glass of Veuve de Vernay, they will have much more money to look after it than we will.

Sunday, August 28th

Down to Dean Street in Soho for my postponed day on Eric's *Rutles* film *All You Need is Cash*. They're not ready, so I wander into Soho Square, which is a peaceful refuge and very quiet today without cars or bustle. A few tramps sitting or lying on the benches.

We end up shooting in Golden Square, near Piccadilly. I'm playing the part of Eric Manchester (Derek Taylor), who is being interviewed and giving confident denials about the 'petty pilfering' at Rutle Corps –

whilst behind him the entire building is being emptied. George Harrison – complete with grey wig – interviews me. Later Ronnie Wood turns up to be a Hell's Angel.

It all seems very pleasantly disorganised. The cameraman/director Gary is American. He shoots everything hand-held. It's a totally different world from the careful, painstaking preparations of Hall and Franklin on *Ripping Yarns*.

A lunchtime drink in a quiet, uncluttered pub in Poland Street with Neil I, Eric, Ronnie Wood and George H. But only minutes after saying how nice it is to be in Soho on a Sunday, we're kicked out as it's two and drinking-up time. England, oh England, you perverse and silly land.

Back home for a wash and then out to Richmond at the invitation of Ron Wood. He lives in one of the prime sites in all London. On top of Richmond Hill, with a view over the Thames as it curves round and away into the trees.

Ron is living with wife Chrissie and Jess, their son, in the cottage down the hill from the main house. It's a pretty little cottage, not too vast, and makes a change from the usual cavernous rooms and feeling of aimless spaciousness which pop stars with lots of money usually seem to live in.

He plays a tape of their most recent concert – at a small club in Tokyo, the same club where Margaret Trudeau's[1] friendship with the Stones was first noticed by the press. They played the club unannounced – everyone had come to hear a popular local band.

Anyway, after watching the sun swell and turn from yellow through orange to crimson before sinking triumphantly below the western horizon, we walked down to the cottage and drank wine and Chrissie Wood showed me round the big house and we looked out at a truly stunning view – the Thames in its valley under a full moon. The river was silver, the trees that crowded protectively to its banks were opaque, mysterious. London in 1977, and yet that view cannot have changed for hundreds of years.

On a less romantic note, she showed me the splintered door frame which was nearly ripped from the wall when fifteen policemen burst in to search her bedroom for drugs.

---

1 Wife of Pierre Trudeau, Prime Minister of Canada 1968–79. She memorably said 'I want to be more than a rose in my husband's lapel.'

Monday, August 29th

Watch repeat of *Three Men in a Boat*. It's a beautifully and confidently created world. As Eric said when he rang me later, 'Everything else seems like television.' But I felt that it was a little too meditative, a little distanced, at times – if Frears had gone just a bit closer to the characters he might have given some substance to their strange friendship. Impressive, though.

Friday, September 2nd

A Python meeting at eleven to discuss what needs to be rewritten, if anything, on the *Brian* film script. Because the retyped version only became available yesterday, no one's had much chance to read it, so we fall to talking of dates, budgets, etc.

John and Eric have very little use, at the moment, for England. John says he's made a resolution to stay away from England during January, February and March because the weather's so awful. Eric, having nearly completed the Rutles, will be relaxing and recuperating for several months in the Caribbean.

Tunisia is decided upon for all the filming, so we set aside ten weeks – starting on April 10th (the nearest date after the end of this financial year). John wants to take a masseur, and thinks the whole unit could avail themselves of his services. Eric wants to have a chef specially for ourselves. John suggests only a five-day week (which I heartily agree with). Eric wants First Class travel everywhere, and so on.

Terry G is in France (just as well, for he would be unable to watch this spectacle without making a bit of noise!) and Terry J is very quiet.

I put my foot down over writing abroad in January *and* March as preparation for the film. My life is here in London, with my family. I love travel, but I love them more. However we agree to meet and write and read and rehearse in the West Indies in January. Even writing this shocks me with its self-indulgence. Is this really the best way to spend our money?

We part on good terms – the great thing about arguments over style is that they never really scratch the surface of our personal relations. We all know we need each other and we all agree to differ. But at least we vetoed a special chef for the actors – on the grounds that there should be good food for everybody.

So Python winds down until January 1978 in the West Indies. 'See you next term,' shouts Eric, as I disappear into the rain.

Monday, September 5th

To the BBC to look at 'Moorstones' and 'Andes', which are being previewed prior to tonight's showing to an audience.

Horrified to find – not one minute into 'Andes' – that between them Hughes and Millichope have failed to leave sufficient background for the opening titles. Some ten seconds are missing. I really can't believe that, after nearly a year, these shows are still not complete.

Fortunately Alan Bell, a PA who is in nominal charge of this evening's audience recording, and Jim Franklin, who fortuitously pops in to see the preview, tackle the situation very coolly and we resign ourselves to some hasty editing before this evening.

To the Television Theatre in Shepherd's Bush to check on the night's recording. The audience watch the show on an Eidophor screen in black and white and on monitors above their heads in colour. Terry and I do a silly warm up and we kick off with 'Across the Andes by Frog'. Not a great deal of laughter and, when it does come, it grates horribly against the laid-back atmosphere of the piece.

At the end, when I ask the audience how many would rather see these shows with the help of recorded laughter, or without, the withouts are in a three to one majority.

Tuesday, September 6th

Much telephonic activity over the shows. Go to the BBC at lunchtime to watch a playback, which just confirms my feelings last night. 'Andes' is clearly wrong with an audience. As Anne Henshaw said, it's a very personal sort of show – one doesn't want other people's interpretations imposed.

Wednesday, September 7th, Southwold

Drinking fourth coffee of the morning, on arrival at Southwold, when the phone rings. It's Jimmy Gilbert. He's seen the playback of 'Moorstones' and thinks that the audience reaction is so good that it would be a waste not to use it. Quotes Aubrey Singer, the head of BBC2, who has told Jimmy that they have had a 100% failure rate on BBC2 on comedy shows with no laughter.

Mother seems well. She worries more as she gets older, but seems to have many more regular friends than when Dad was alive. Her chief worry is whether to move into the centre of Southwold or not and the feeling of isolation out at Reydon.

Monday, September 12th

It gave me real pleasure to visit Neal's Yard today. The sun was shining, there was a crisp and clear September freshness in the air. The builders were at work completing the restaurant on one side of the Neal's Yard triangle, and the wholefood store was busy sorting sacks of brown rice on the other. A bustle of activity, of which Redwood is a part.

Next door to Redwood is ALS – Associated London Scripts – a rather chic reception area leading to agents for Denis Norden and many others. And at almost the apex of the triangle, the rich mix is completed by White's the Armourers!

André [Jacquemin] and I listened to his compilation so far of the new Python album material. It sounds rather good – tightly packed Python gems. After discussion of the contents, I leave André to finish putting it all together – he'll drop a cassette in to me at home and we can edit further after that.

Up to sunny Belsize Park for a very hard game of squash with Terry, followed by a trip to the Flask.

Al Alvarez is in the Flask. Terry offers the literary lion the first edition of *The Vole*. Alvarez' eyes don't exactly light up. 'Oh yes … it's Richard Boston's thing, isn't it?' Terry, glad at least of some positive reaction, affirms. '… He's such a tit, isn't he?' muses the poetry critic of *The Observer* as he flicks through.

Alvarez seems very cynical about the readership – 'city countrymen' he calls them, uncharitably. But I know what he means, in a way.

Tuesday, September 13th, San Sebastian

To San Sebastian today for the 25th SS Film Festival – in which *Jabberwocky* rears its beautifully shot head in the 'New Creators' section. ('New Creators' sounds like some awful Biblical quiz game in which contestants have seven days to … etc, etc.)

Wednesday, September 14th, San Sebastian

As I soaked in my bath this morning, reading with admiration Kingsley Amis' *Ending Up*, I had a flash of inspiration. For my next project I would try and write a novel. A book. On my own. Cheered with relief and excitement at this simple solution.

After a breakfast of eggs, bacon, croissant and coffee, Terry, Hilary[1] and I drove to the eastern part of town, where we eventually found the Savoy Cinema, in an unremarkable street of shops and houses and garages. I really couldn't imagine *who* would come out to see a film here at what is, for the Spanish, almost crack of dawn. But amazingly some forty or fifty Spaniards – definitely *non*-press and non-film people, some of them students, some looking like lorry drivers – arrive in this improbable street at breakfast time to watch *Jabberwocky*.

At least they're rewarded with a very good print, but there are no subtitles. It must be totally mystifying to them.

We went into a coffee bar next to the cinema. Met a young, curly-haired English producer, who was showing a rather remarkable film (after ours) at the Savoy at twelve. It was a documentary account of how a small village-full of Portuguese peasants coped with an almost overnight transition from being vassals of a feudal baron to free men, during the liberation period of the early 1970s.

Tremendous feeling of history in the making. What power to the people means. A fascinating document, with an almost Pythonic, but true, scene, where an old worker has to be persuaded to give his spade to the cooperative. He clearly doesn't understand the principle. 'If I give you my spade,' he says grimly, tightening his grip on it, 'you'll want everything else – my clothes – I'll be naked …' The peasant organiser has to explain there and then the principles of socialism at their most basic.

Terry G and I and Peter Willetts, the director, sat and watched it for over two hours. I'd hardly noticed that I'd spent over five hours in the Savoy, San Sebastian, and it was only lunchtime.

Willetts doesn't see much chance of the big companies buying his film and I can see why not. It's like Al Levinson's books – honest, straight and with plenty of detail and interest, but very little commercial angle, very little to hit an audience with and make a reader/viewer see this film as opposed to 101 others.

1 Hilary Sandison, responsible for overseas sales of *Jabberwocky*.

Friday, September 16th

I am still resolved to begin the novel. Today I 'firmed up' my decision by ringing Jill F and asking her to keep me up to the mark.

I reckon I will allow myself three months – up till Christmas Day – to finish the work, and by that time there should be enough to tell me whether I can do it or not. Jill reckons I should aim to complete roughly 60,000 words by the end of November – just over two months – and leave December for edits or rewrites.

Monday, September 19th

A bad week for starting novels. Typewriter isn't working properly and meetings every day for the next three days.

Today is the Shepperton board meeting. Drive down there for one o'clock. Remember that rather sickening day half a year ago when I stood, as now, in the outer room of Graham Ford's office, only to hear that *Superman* had decided to go, and there was nothing else around.

Today it was different. A picture, *Dominique*,[1] is starting a six-week shoot at the studio today and, even as I was staring at a *Jabberwocky* publicity photo of my bum pinned on the board with the words 'One of our directors at work' written in underneath, the door to Ford's office opened and three men appeared. We all shook hands and nodded and with great relief I noted that they were bringing a picture in rather than taking it out. They were the advance guard for the new Pink Panther movie.

A third picture, *Force 10 from Navarone*, is almost certainly coming in to use H Stage (as *Star Wars* did), which, since its condemnation and sale to the council, is suddenly in demand [largely for its hangar-like size].

The bad news is still from *Superman*. Some £30,000 is owed altogether, which is not so serious. What *is* serious is a £150,000 deferment which, if they don't pay, could hit us rather hard. They are being chased.

We look around the newly painted and refurbished dressing rooms and the editing room block. All look satisfactory. Good colour schemes and the rooms are inexpensively smart. But the big new heating programme (being financed by the Ramport deal) is not yet completed and today heating is off in much of the site.

1 Thriller, directed by Michael Anderson, starring Cliff Robertson and Jean Simmons.

But generally speaking an optimistic day and, walking down to the river at the end of the afternoon and looking out over the brackish pond where the Fishfinger family in *Jabberwocky* had their home, I couldn't help feeling a deep, sentimental regard for Shepperton – not the sort of feelings one usually associates with a business – more like an old school or college!

Wednesday, September 21st

Today is Redwood/Signford day. Down to the studio for one o'clock and lunch with André, Bob Salmon,[1] Anne Henshaw (who Gilliam told me on Monday had split up with Michael, though I've heard no more) and Grace Henderson. A Kiplingesque name for a Kiplingesque lady, an oriental auditor, who effortlessly bandies international financial chit-chat with a beautiful eastern smile and an intimate knowledge of the English tax system.

We eat at Mon Plaisir in Monmouth Street, an unpretentious, small, cheerful, good quality French restaurant only yards from the studio.

Waiter in mid-service recognises me from 'le moyen age' – *Jabberwocky*. He says 'Many people in Paris like what you do.' I return the compliment.

See Terry G in the evening. He is very enthusiastic about the cover design (the self-forming box) for the new 'Best Of' album, which TG wants to call *Monty Python's Instant Record Collection*. He wants material for the cover – blurb of any kind and lots of false titles for LPs, so the novel is put off for another day.

Friday, September 23rd

Squash with Terry Jones at five. Beaten again, I'm afraid. Then up to the Flask for a drink. Tell Terry J that I shall be writing the novel (hereinafter called 'the work') until Christmas. He doesn't sound disappointed. Says that it will suit him, as he has further work to do on Chaucer, now his book has found a publisher. He's just finished a translation of 'The Prologue', which TJ says he's more excited about than the book.

Off to Abbotsley tomorrow for a quick burst of countryside, then back to London and the novel on Monday. A strange feeling – not

1 André's accountant, with a share, like me, in Redwood Studios, André's company.

knowing quite what will come out. I keep wanting to start – waking up in bed and composing cracking first six lines, then controlling myself.

Will I be able to keep the diary up? Will I choke on a surfeit of writing? Will the malfunctioning, non-reversing ribbon on my type-writer cut short a promising career? Watch these spaces ...

Monday, September 26th

After writing a few letters between eight and breakfast time, I started on the work at 9.30.

The omens were good. The sun was shining, God was in his heaven and all was well. Slogged through ten lines – without an idea in my head, but used an opening I had thought of a week ago. A man wakes up in a strange room, a strange bed, almost in limbo, and has to reconstruct his life from there.

Over to Shepherd's Bush for the showing of three *Ripping Yarns* to an audience. John Jarvis in a panic in his editing rooms because tomorrow's showprint of 'Olthwaite' has arrived scratched in one place. He's spent the afternoon re-dubbing 'Claw' because he felt the early lightning flashes weren't right. Such dedication.

A full house – over 300 people tonight – and a good and warm and responsive audience. I suppose that the *Radio Times* publicity and the start of the series last week has helped. All three films go well – I watch them much more easily than the last two – but 'Curse of the Claw' goes best of all and seems by all accounts a winner.

Tuesday, September 27th

As I was leaving home, a black Rover drove slowly up Oak Village. Inside was the Lord President of the Council of Great Britain – Michael Foot – and a doubtless well-meaning, but obviously harassed lady driver who was lost.[1] Foot had put down his *Guardian* and was looking around in some bewilderment. Their progress up Elaine Grove was brought to a smart halt by our neighbour Philip Clough doing a three-point turn in front of them.

Late as I was, I had to run back in and tell Helen there was a Cabinet Minister stuck in our street.

---

1 Not far from home. Foot lived only half a mile away up in Hampstead.

At the Beeb, watched 'Olthwaite' with Terry J, who arrived hotfoot and with a hangover. The laughter/no laughter debate began again as we were dubbing, but I tend now very strongly towards using it, so does Jimmy G. We compromised by dubbing it carefully – no words were lost, any titters or coughs were expunged and we only used it lavishly in scenes where it came lavishly.

There is an extraordinary feeling of optimism in the Beeb over the *Ripping Yarns* – despite the fact that no new ones have gone out. The top brass simply love them, and silvery-haired Mr Scott the Controller[1] came up and shook my hand and said how much he'd enjoyed 'Tomkinson' the second time.

Back home. Watch 'Olthwaite' with Robert H, Helen and the boys. All enjoy it unreservedly. I must say I felt chuffed as I watched it. It's so rich – almost too rich for telly – you have to concentrate on it hard or you miss lines, characters, beautiful shots. Whatever the press say, I feel that of all the things I've ever done, I find 'Olthwaite' and 'Claw' the most satisfying.

Friday, September 30th

At Darsham by 11.30. Am cutting back a profuse cotoneaster hedge when an 1100 eases its way into the drive before the garage, bearing Joyce Ashmore, a cousin of my father's, and holder of many of the family records.

A very capable lady with a brisk and confident well-bred manner. She has a rather heavy jaw, but seems exceedingly well and lively. She is down to earth and unsentimental about the family, but interested in and interesting about stories of the Palins.

Discover for the first time the full story of my great-grandfather, Edward Palin, who married Brita Gallagher. Evidently Brita was an orphan of the Irish potato famine of the 1840s, sent on what were called 'coffin ships' to America by some philanthropic organisation rather like those who nowadays bring war babies out of Vietnam. Brita arrived in America with only a label on her dress with her name on.

She was lucky enough to be looked after by a rich American spinster – Caroline Watson. She brought her up to be a well-dressed, well-educated young lady and in 1861 Brita and Miss Watson went to Europe.

---

1 Robin Scott, then Controller, BBC2.

Whilst at an hotel in Switzerland they met an English don from Oxford (Edward Palin), who was climbing in the Alps. Edward Palin describes their meeting rather touchingly in a diary he kept of his stay in Switzerland. Unfortunately Brita (or Beda, as he calls her), was only 19 and he 36 … 'otherwise I don't know what might have been'.

But he must have seen her again, for in 1867 they were married in Paris. Edward P had to give up a Fellowship at St John's, Oxford (dons weren't allowed to marry then). The college, who obviously regarded him highly, found him a living at Linton in Gloucestershire, where he spent the rest of his life with Brita, and their seven children, the eldest of whom was my grandfather.

But what rankled with Joyce Ashmore (granddaughter of Edward Palin) is that, when Caroline Watson was on the point of death at Linton, some years later, and wanted to change her will in favour of the Palins, my great-grandfather would not let the necessary lawyers make the change as he didn't want Miss Watson's last hours sullied by their attentions. So … the Palins missed being very rich!

Friday, October 7th

End of second week's writing. Seven thousand words for the week – 1,000 short of target. Have given them to Helen to read, and she has a useful and helpful reaction.

She liked the first character, Avery, who begins the novel waking in a strange bed, but found the introduction of the second Avery brother was a disappointment, just as the first one was becoming interesting. The third brother – the radio interviewer – she just didn't like.

Good advice, but goodbye 5,000 words.

Wednesday, October 12th

A letter from Al Lev to tell me in desperation of Eve's latest and most serious suicide attempt. He only just saved her. She'd locked the door and taken pills.

At work at 9.30, but spend first half of the morning writing a letter to Eve – a much tougher proposition than the novel. But start by twelve, having responded to Al's obvious plea for help.

Various phone calls during the day bring messages of good cheer. Terry Hughes rings to apprise me of 'near-ecstatic' reaction to

'Moorstones' at the Heads of Department meeting this morning. Terry Gilliam reports a fantastic reaction to *Jabberwocky* at the Cairo Film Festival. An audience of 800 gave the film a standing ovation! Once again the virtues of not understanding the story become apparent!

The Guardian didn't like 'Moorstones', but a review in the *Daily Mail* calls the series 'intelligent at the core'.

Monday, October 17th

Dr Chapman on the phone for the first time in many weeks. To say how worried he is about the content of the 'Instant Record Collection'. I grit my teeth, for it is a little late in the day for fellow Pythons to start showing interest in a record they all seemed fairly apathetic towards two months ago. I was left to put it together, and it was mastered last week.

But, as I haven't seen the Doctor for a while, I'm quite happy to go round and talk over the record with him, as requested, later this afternoon.

Graham, gin and tonic in hand, looks well scrubbed and far more normal than usual. His hair is brushed, not forward, but to the side, such as I haven't seen all the time I've known him.

GC definitely gives the impression of someone anxious to convey seriousness of purpose. The very summons itself is for business – but that crumples quickly and I am able quite easily to talk him out of most of his peripheral worries. GC just seems pleased to have a fellow Python to chat to.

His film, *The Odd Job*, has still got money problems, and the revised shoot is now February/March 1978. If GC is also going to play Brian in April/June '78, he is cutting it a bit fine. I think the prospect of this mammoth thespian effort is what is behind this latest attempt of his to find a level of non-drunken respectability and to restore a little of his natural seriousness to his affairs. I hope upon hope he succeeds, for I am fond of him – and the old Chapman warmth came through today despite his underlying anxieties.

As I left he told me that he was thinking of taking the whole of December off, to go away somewhere and prepare – maybe on his own. Just walking round the Highlands on his own. Brave words. But Keith Moon was coming round in a half-hour, and I notice that Graham now helps himself to gin from a bar-style dispenser – so I don't think all that much has changed.

Friday, October 21st

Four thousand words this week. I'm as bad as Leyland Cars in the constant failure to reach my production target.

Jim F tells me that Spear and Jackson[1] are suing the BBC for libel in the 'Eric Olthwaite' Yarn!! What's more, it sounds as though the cowardly Beeb are settling out of court.

Monday, October 24th

A letter from Eve Levinson. Evidently my spontaneous response to the news of her suicide attempt had contained the right things – and she touchingly said that I had said things that other, closer friends of hers found themselves 'unable to say'. I'm glad the strength of my feelings worked, expressed as rudely as they were.

Arrived at Shepperton at 9.25 for a 9.30 Annual General Meeting in the wonderful, mirror-panelled boardroom of the Old House.

I was re-elected, Clive signed various bits of paper, and we talked for a while about Shepperton and memories of the men associated with the place – especially, of course, Alexander Korda. This is the 43rd Annual General Meeting, so the place must have been going since at least 1933.

Much talk over catering. At last this has become the main problem we have to face, and Paul Olliver, the tubby troubleshooter from Vavasseur, who has been given the job of investigating the frightfulness of the catering arrangements, has now expressed a wish to run them himself!

Paul Olliver and I are booked to visit Pinewood for lunch and a look around, as I have often felt that we should know more about the opposition.

We are not offered lunch – it now being 1.30 – and are taken round by a late-middle-aged gent, who personifies all that is wrong with Pinewood. He's getting on, is rather shabby, and yet talks to us from Olympian heights about Pinewood being the greatest studio in the world, blah, blah, blah.

Pinewood seems to have set its face into the past, favouring the

---

1 A Sheffield firm which made, among other things, shovels. My reference to Eric Olthwaite's 'Spear and Jackson No. 3 with a reinforced brass handle' was meant fondly, but clearly not taken that way by the manufacturer.

traditional and the conventional. It remains Britain's biggest studio, but not its brightest. Shepperton, with its mix of commercials, pop group influence and movies, feels much more fresh, alive and relevant to the '70s.

Tuesday, October 25th

Mostly business, and have no time to write any of the novel. Instead, spend an hour reading what I have so far. It's patchy. Some sections I am pleased with, but at the moment it's like an inconsistent car engine – good in some gears, jerky in others and not, as yet, getting me anywhere.

Up to Elstree by 12.30 for the second visit to our Shepperton competitors in two days. John Skinner, our contact, is much less concerned than the Pinewood mogul with trying to pretend that everything in the garden is lovely. A realist, not a bullshitter.

Elstree, of all the major studios, was the one which committed itself most of all to TV series in the '50s and '60s. Now the only TV series made in this four-wall studio is *The Saint*, and at the moment it's empty of movies – though waiting for the prestigious new Stanley Kubrick – *The Shining* – to come in.

It's part of the magical nature of film studios that you should have such wonderful incongruities, like the front of the hotel which will be used for *The Shining*, rearing up sixty feet or so, but only a couple of hundred yards from Elstree High Street. *Moby Dick* was filmed 200 yards from the Elstree branch of Woolworths!

Drive back in the sunshine past the huge bulk of the old MGM Borehamwood Studios – chief victim of the '70s slump, now a cold-storage firm.

Wednesday, October 26th

Terry J rang about 'Curse of the Claw', last of the series. Good reactions from him and those who saw it with him. But I had to tell him that I wasn't feeling too excited about the general reaction. I think Clive James was not far wrong when he said the series 'half worked'. In defence, I'd say that it was a pioneer in many ways, and suffered from being formularised or categorised. It was a series, and yet not a series, comedy and yet not comedy.

TJ thinks that it was difficult for people to get their teeth into – there was no continuity to each show apart from opening titles and my own presence, in many different disguises. TJ also felt that I had wasted myself by playing too many dull, central roles.

Sunday, October 30th

I leave home with T Gilliam, Maggie and Amy [TG's daughter] to go down to lunch at Terry Jones' before going on to play charity football at Dulwich Hamlet. At lunch Allen Tinkley and wife Diana – who had put on Python in New York. Allen is interested in the new Python movie and has money available from Blake Edwards – whose wife Julie Andrews is, believe it or not a Python freak (she wanted us to co-star with her at the Palladium earlier this year!).

Our team is quite impressive. Peter Purves, of *Blue Peter*, is in goal and myself, Terry J, Terry G, John Cleese and Graham Chapman – who, as a new variation to his silly behaviour, actually got changed this time, but was substituted as soon as he came out, being carried off on a stretcher before the ball was kicked.

Home by seven. In my work-room this evening must reluctantly write '0' against words target for this last week.

Tuesday, November 1st

Nearly 2,000 words on the typewriter. At ten to four we have a three-hour power-cut. Willy brings me up a candle and I carry on writing in very Dickensian spirit. The children all love the blackout and there are groans of disappointment when the lights come on again.

Saturday, November 12th, Oxford

A letter from Eve Levinson. She's home and much on the mend, but now a cloud approaches. Some of the admin of her school are trying to take her job away – presumably people who try and kill themselves are unreliable. This sounds hard – but Eve does discuss the possibilities of life without the job. I think she only teaches now for the money.

Helen's mother rings to say that in last night's wild winds one of the trees in the garden was uprooted. H decides to take the children up to Abbotsley for the day to see the devastation and help her mother clear up. I stay here to prepare a chat for Brasenose tonight.

I leave for Oxford at four, having read my novel and done one hour's prep on the talk. A very wild sky – some sunshine and blue patches, blotted out by a huge jet-black cloud. Rain, high wind. But it passes over me and by the time I reach Oxford it's damp, cold and blustery, but the force of the storm has lessened.

To BNC[1] at seven. Am met by at least six rather nervous members of the 'Events Committee' in the lodge. Am taken to a room in the Principal's lodgings for sherry, and meet four other members of the committee – two women, for Brasenose is now co-ed. Sherry is drunk, but the undergraduates don't talk amongst themselves – they sit, awkwardly, and wait for me to speak.

It is a peculiar feeling to know that you are an impressive, important, well-known figure – when inside you are probably as nervous as all the faces turned towards you. A funny little unnecessary barrier exists now – which wouldn't be there if I hadn't done Python. I try to muck in and defuse the reverence as quickly as possible. Only then will I feel less of a fraud.

The JCR at Brasenose is absolutely packed, which is rather flattering. They say they've never seen as many people. Try to think back to the very few occasions in my own time when I went to hear a visiting celebrity. I remember the Union bursting at the seams for James Baldwin, but that's about all. They are literally all around me – and it makes for a good atmosphere.

In fact the whole talk works like good cabaret. They're warm and generous with laughter (especially when I read 'Fegg' extracts and mention the Goodies) and I must confess that all my latent theatricality was released and I milked them rotten. Talked and answered questions for nearly two hours – until it got too hot – then signed autographs and was treated to drinks down in the Buttery.

Sunday, November 13th

Today, helped no doubt by the hard, bright freshness of a cool, sunny November morning, I have a feeling of completeness. The world makes sense this Sunday morning. Even the weather seems to be resting, peaceful and mellowed after the angry squalls of the last two days.

There's a smell of beef and Yorkshire pudding and from where I

1 Brasenose College, my alma mater 1962–5.

write I can see the chimney letting out wisps of smoke from the fire in the sitting room.

Yesterday I read through the novel so far and was greatly heartened. I saw much that worked and I also saw clearly what didn't work. I can see the way ahead and I can't wait to get going again tomorrow.

I just feel very happy and very content at this moment. Nothing is expected of me today except to be here at home. I am perfectly well aware that around the borders of my life are problems, difficulties, painful decisions, even human tragedies demanding my involvement. I know I cannot live in a continual vacuum of happiness – but a day like today restores energies, tops up batteries, rebuilds whatever faith one has.

Today there is nothing more I want than what I have.

Monday, November 14th

T Gilliam rang with the offer of a ticket to Bertolucci's *1900*. It's an all-day job, lasting over four hours with lunch in between.

In the foyer of the NFT I see a sprinkling of critics, including Dilys Powell and John Coleman of the *New Statesman*, who gives me a cheery greeting. In the gents someone of familiar face introduces himself – it's Jonathan Pryce, whom I last met in a playground in North Kensington, where he was filming for Stephen Frears. A nice, rather gentle man, about our age. All three of us (he and I and TG) walk over to the Old Vic for lunch.

Down in the basement they have a thriving little serve-yourself restaurant with lovingly home-made pies, treacle tarts, salads and a fine selection of white wines. A mixture of folk, too – at one table a clutch of Britain's top actors – Dorothy Tutin, Derek Jacobi, Alec McCowen, all presumably rehearsing at the National – at the end of our table a couple of businessmen.

Back to the NFT for Part II of *1900*, which lasts from 2.30 until just after 4.30. As always with Bertolucci, the images in the film are clear, cool, sharp and confident – the pictures absolutely breathtakingly beautiful. But that aside, and taking into account some perfectly shot, written and acted moments, I found the whole one big soap opera – complete with unremittingly villainous villains and unremittingly decent good guys (the peasants).

I felt it was a commercial film – despite its four-hour length. Why else import Burt Lancaster, Sterling Hayden and Robert De Niro into an otherwise convincing north Italian village, filled with real Italian peasants, and dub on a soundtrack that turns it into *Peyton Place*?

Tuesday, November 15th

Up at eight. Work on Shepperton papers in preparation for a meeting with Clive at lunch. Long chat with Graham Ford on the phone – all well, except when I mention my idea of asking Barry Norman's *Film '77* bunch if they want to do 'A Day in the Life of a British Studio' (i.e. Shepperton).

Ford doesn't like Barry Norman, for the same reasons, I think, that Peter Noble doesn't – they find him too critical of the industry. I think this is his greatest quality – and a vital antidote to the 'everything in the garden's lovely' attitude of Noble. But he conceded that it is a good idea, but maybe next March when we're all smart and the new signs are up.

He completely missed my point that when we need them is now – so that we don't have to pull any wool over anyone's eyes. We have a full and thriving studio, which is good, but we also have the problems of a studio trying to heave itself out of a depression which was, four years ago, almost fatal. This is the first time I've felt seriously at odds with the competent G Ford. I was disappointed at his lack of imagination.

Wednesday, November 16th

The weather has settled down, after the frantic activity of the last week it's raw, cold and dry. The gales seem to have blown themselves out.

There's been a flurry of activity this week from Jimmy, Jim Franklin and others to try and 'firm up' *Ripping Yarns* or 'Palins', as Jimmy insists on calling them and, after their offers today, the nearest thing I have to a future now looks like stretching until the end of 1979 at least.

Friday, November 18th

My hopes of going into writing retreat at Charney Manor – beautiful house, Quaker-run, therefore lots of peace – are dashed. It's full.[1] After much phoning, end up at the Bell Inn, Charlbury.

---

1 With everything else to do, I'd fallen so far behind with the novel, that escaping London seemed the only way to finish it.

A two-hour Shepperton board meeting. I suggest that *Film '77* be approached. Clive *very* enthusiastic and the board authorises me to get in touch.

Saturday, November 19th

Fine, fresh, very cold day for William's seventh birthday. Tremendously excited (both Willy and Tom). William is up from a quarter to seven until midday before he even realises he's only got pyjamas on.

At two I drive up to Hampstead to open the Red Cross Bazaar (in lieu of Terry J, who's in Tunisia). A crowd (small) of mostly old ladies, who wouldn't know me from Adam, huddle against the cold, outside the locked door. 'Let us in,' they beseech me. But the Red Cross won't open their doors until two, so the queue shivers. It's all rather pitiful.

I give a short opening exhortation, then everyone gets stuck in at the bargains. At a quarter to three I run an auction, and by three I'm out – profusely thanked and presented with a gun (toy) to take to William for his birthday. I can hardly say 'a gift from the Red Cross' as I give him this device for blowing people's heads off.

Willy's birthday party is more an exercise in crowd control – nine highly excited nippers, apart from Willy, storm the house and hold us besieged for two hours. William very cleverly avoids most of the shindig – and tucks himself away upstairs to lay out his pressies.

As quickly as they have come, they're gone. The hurricane has passed through and Helen and I slowly pick up the pieces.

Sunday, November 20th

Chop wood for the fire and clear up in preparation for lunch party. Ron Devillier, of Dallas, Texas, the man who finally got Monty Python onto American TV, is in town, got in touch, and I've invited him for lunch with Mary, Ed and Catherine.

Ron is now the buyer for the entire PBS network and is based in Washington. Big, bearlike, bearded, with a wide, generous, easily smiling face, Ron is immensely and immediately likeable. Though he does wield power and influence, he still comes across as an almost boyish enthusiast.

Over lunch he tells the true story of Python in the US. In 1972 Ron was in New York. 'It was raining, and I had nothing to do,' was how he started the tale. So Ron rang Wyn Godley of Time-Life Sales and asked if there was anything at all left for Ron to view. Wyn looked at his lists and said there was a BBC comedy show called Monty Python, but everyone who'd seen it had rejected it. Ron was a little intrigued, and it was a filthy day, so he went over to see it.

It was Monty Python's 'Montreux' episode. Ron liked it. Took a copy back to Dallas, looked again and rang Wyn back to ask if there were any more. Wyn returned to the files and found that there were thirteen tapes available. 'Send 'em all,' asked Ron, at which Time-Life nearly fell off their seats. But thirteen tapes were duly despatched to Ron's station in Dallas.

One day, coming in to the office at six, Ron sat down and viewed all the tapes, finishing at seven that evening. Ron fell in love with them. His only problem then, he said, was to avoid racing to the phone or in 'any way letting Time-Life know that I thought they were the greatest things I'd ever seen'.

In the end he controlled his enthusiasm, but still found Time-Life asking $500 each for the right to two showings of each programme. Ron, alone, consulting nobody, wrote out the $6,500 cheque one evening. That was his act of faith – for $6,500 is a great deal to a small station.

But the fairytale ending is that the shows were such an immediate success in Dallas that, on the first night an uncut Python show was aired in the US,. Ron received more pledges of money to the station than the $6,500 he'd paid for the entire series.

New York got wind of this success and for once the smart East Coast found itself having to follow Texas, but NY paid $2,000 per show. The rest, as they say, is history. One hundred and forty-two stations since bought Python, and Ron is in no doubt that it revolutionised American TV thinking.

Last week Ron saw three of the *Ripping Yarns* ('Olthwaite', 'Tomkinson' and 'Stalag') and says he is quite sure they will go in the States. After our Sunday lunch we walk up Parliament Hill and down to Highgate Ponds and Ron asks how the *Ripping Yarns* are financed and whether or not there is any way in which PBS can invest in them at this stage.

Usually these negotiations are conducted through dozens of inter-mediaries – Time-Life, BBC Enterprises, etc – and this is why it's such a breakthrough to talk directly to Ron – the buyer – and it must be the first time such a deal has been discussed directly between American finance and the creator of the programmes. So who knows, it may turn out to have been a very profitable walk on the Heath!

Monday, November 21st, Charlbury

Arrive at 3.15. The hotel is unpretentious. My room is spacious, with a low ceiling and two exposed beams – original, I expect, and that means 1700, when the Bell was built. The wallpaper is bright and tasteful – of the pastoral variety. There are two brass bedsteads and a fine bay over-looking the main street. The table is of the right height and reasonably solid, so I set my typewriter up in the bay. By the time I'm ready to write, it's getting dark. A quarter to four, the worst time to begin. It's hard to concentrate, to shut out all the new sensations of this place, but I persevere, hoping I'm not disturbing anyone with my tapping, and by half past six have added 1,000 words to the morning's total.

Take a walk around Charlbury – deserted and bitterly cold. My ears ache in the wind. Glad to get back to the warm, cosy hotel. Ring home. Have a Glenmorangie in the bar and a good meal of haddock in a pastie and pheasant and cheese.

The ambience of the hotel is restful, pleasant and unhurried.

Asleep by 11.30.

Tuesday, November 22nd, Charlbury

Up a little after eight o'clock. A thoroughly refreshing eight hour kip behind me. Pull back the heavy salmon-pink curtains in my little bay and am confronted with clear blue skies and a sun shining brightly on the grey stone cottages across the street.

Bath and breakfast (the breakfast menu is dangerously appetising, and bigger than the dinner menu in the evening). Choose smoked haddock and half a grapefruit. Then a short walk down by the church and back to the Bell to begin work.

Start slowly – still the unfamiliar distractions, which I hope I will get used to – cleaning ladies talking noisily just outside the door, the bus which stops almost outside my window – the everyday life of Charlbury. But I don't think I would have found a place with much *less* everyday life, and the hotel grows more congenial every extra hour I spend here. Coffee is brought to me, unbidden, at eleven.

I drive into Burford for an hour's lunch break. Go to a quiet

Wadworths pub, where I am recognised and get a free half of bitter in exchange for some signatures.

Back to the Bell. Put my typewriter down, as it were, at 6.30. A thoroughly satisfactory eight-hour writing day. Four thousand words completed (half a normal week's target in one day). Greatly enthused, I take a walk in the bleak and chilly darkness down to the bridge to look at the Evenlode.

Thursday, November 24th, Charlbury

Discovery, at lunchtime, of the thatched village of Great Tew, tucked away in the steep fold of a valley, about ten miles north of here. Complete with tiny, mullioned-windowed village pub, the Falkland Arms. A front room, with a roaring fire. A crusty old gent, a real relic of the past, held forth, and in the middle of all this – as if I hadn't had a surfeit of images of traditional English life – it began to snow.

An icy cold afternoon, though, which made my warm bay window vantage point in the Bell all the more attractive. It must have soothed my mind into a productive state, for today I became deeply absorbed in a confrontation of Avery with Annie and Sarah – really absorbed – and I finished just before seven with 5,000 words done – 15,000 since I have been at the hotel.

Friday, November 25th, Charlbury

I lunched in the bar of the Bell for the first time – an agreeable stone-flagged floor, beams and a big open fireplace. It pleased me to think that nearly a third (for that is the extent of my achievement this week) of the book was written directly above this room.

Wednesday, November 30th

Just after three o'clock, the novel comes quietly to a halt. It's finished and quite acceptably so.

I christen the book 'A Bit of a Break', but I don't know if that will stick.

Thursday, December 1st

Began reading the novel through a little before ten and finished at a quarter to seven in the evening. I reckon about eight hours' solid reading. I made notes – generally about passages which were too dense, complicated or repetitive. What the book needs, basically, is clarification. The beginning is quite jolly, the middle is soggy and tends to lose its way, and the end moves fast to quite a neat conclusion.

Friday, December 2nd

Finished the novel just in time, for this morning we have the first meeting of the Pythons to begin the lead-up to the movie which starts, all being well, in April.

John Goldstone addresses us first. John, now firmly established as producer of the next movie, wishes us to help him out in raising the loot. So far the four million dollars has not been forthcoming. John virtually rules out private investors, and Michael White says there is no way he can lay his hands on the money we require – about eight times as much as we were asking for on the *Holy Grail*. So we are looking for a friendly American major to finance the film and take distribution, etc, etc.

John G says Warner's have all read it and loved it (which I can't believe), but a bit of Python flag waving would not go amiss. To this end he suggests an interview with *Variety*, *Hollywood Reporter* and other magazines which land softly on air-conditioned office desks in Burbank.

Eric is appalled by the idea. (I'll grant Eric that – his attitude to the press is one of the few that has remained consistent over the last five years!) He suggests putting an ad in *Variety* aimed at showing American producers what an extraordinary world-wide force Python is. John suggests a byline – 'You were late for World War One, late for World War Two … Don't be late for …'

The next leading question is where we should rewrite in January. For Eric and John, writing in England is out of the question. John likes to edge all his comments with a geriatric appeal – 'I don't know about you others, but I'm nearly 40 and I need more … (money, sunshine, sleep, reading, etc, etc)'.

Eric suggests Barbados – which sounds lovely – but both the Terrys look miserable. Graham, as usual, says nothing. I question whether we would actually do any work in Barbados. It's a long way to go to do a little. This consideration doesn't seem to weigh heavily on John or Eric, nor does Terry's appeal for more time at home – 'Bring the family,' orders Eric, and Terry rather meekly accepts. It was decided in JC and EI's favour, as you might expect.

We then went on to order a bollocking for Methuen for their pusillanimous handling of *Monty Python and the Holy Grail* (book), but the cover of the *Instant Record Collection* was greatly approved of. Thank you, Terry Gilliam (though I don't think anyone got around to saying that).

The *Penguin Dictionary of Modern Quotations* have been on to us – they would like to include some Python lines in their new edition. This iconolatry is greeted with such suggestions as 'That is my theory and what it is too', 'What's ten quid to the bloody Midland Bank', and 'His hobbies are strangling animals, golf and masturbating'.

Wednesday, December 7th, Sheffield

To Gospel Oak School at 2.30 for William's Christmas Concert. This year he's a Roman centurion. Less lively and spontaneous than shows in the past – the heavy hand of religion?

To St Pancras and the Sheffield train. Meet up with Terry J – we're off to spend an evening at the Crucible Studio, where David Leland's Season of New Plays is in its last week. Sit on the spindly plastic seats in the buffet car, which would appear to be deliberately designed to stop people idling their time away in the buffet for reasons of comfort. But, warming ourselves with scotches, TJ and I manage to last the whole two and a half hour journey on these nasty little things.

Chat about Python. TJ is fond of pointing out that we have all become harder, tougher individuals as a result of Python – though I think he regrets the loss of the team spirit. He thinks he's softened. He no longer holds views – or perhaps he no longer propagates views – with the same intensity. He's determined to play the film easily.

See two plays. The second, an Irish play called *Says I, Says He*, by one Ron Hutchinson, excellently performed. I am very receptive to a bit of the Irish – the prose is full, flowery and flowing and the language constantly rich. Makes English seem very dry. It's about gunmen in the end, of course. The wastefulness of the Irish is utterly depressing. At least they go down talking well.

After the plays, a kebab and retsina and several jugs of red wine with David and a director from the Royal Court called Stuart Burge, and a lady from a theatre in Amsterdam which specialises in putting on new foreign plays. NB – where is somewhere like that in London?

Thursday, December 8th

Back to London on the Master Cutler – 7.20 from the Midland station. Meet Stuart Burge and friend and join them at breakfast.

He is late fifties, of the old establishment who were once angry young men. Tells a good story of how he brought over a young Greenwich Village folk singer for a BBC TV play many years ago. The guy was obviously high when it came to the read-through at some North Acton boys' club – though at that time people didn't really understand non-alcoholic highs. Anyway, the folk singer was Bob Dylan and he sang 'Blowing in the Wind' in this BBC play, for probably the first time ever outside of the Village. The BBC have since destroyed this momentous tape.

This evening to Gospel Oak again for Tom's concert. A very loose adaptation of 'Cinderella', complete with skateboard sequence. Tom amazed me with the supreme confidence of his performances – whether in the chorus singing 'Consider Yourself' with real enjoyment and wholehearted participation, or giving a very passable impression of Elvis in a pop group, or his tour de force – a rather arch version of 'You Are My Sunshine' – he was certainly not the retiring Tom I expected to see.

Afterwards so many people came up – sharing my astonishment, but saying how good he was – that I felt very proud, and happy for Tom, too. He likes acting, he says now. If he ever does tread the boards, I think his career will date from December 8th 1977!

Friday, December 9th

Sunny, but still very cold. The novel lies at one end of the desk, untouched. A piece of good news – Redwood has won two awards at the *Campaign Magazine* Radio Commercials do last night. Only Molinaire, among London studios, took more awards. André deservedly chuffed. It sets a very effective seal on a first year's operation that's not even finished yet.

Thursday, December 15th

Drive down to Clerkenwell Green to talk with Chris Orr over future Orr/Signford plans. Clerkenwell Green is a rather attractive little backwater, as is much of the area around St Bart's Hospital and Smithfield Market – many old buildings remain and comprehensive redevelopment further east and north and the office block building boom which transformed the Liverpool Street area, have left the Green relatively untouched. In one of these graceful old terraced houses Chris Orr has his lithographic printing press – he does his engraving work down at Wapping.

One thing I'm beginning to learn from Chris is the complicated technical side of his work. The materials he works with – inks, plates, acids, zinc and special Bavarian stone tablets for the lithographic reproduction – are complex and make the process of a Chris Orr picture as involving as the picture itself.

Before I left I tried to hint that the Chris Orr I liked should be brought clear of the self-appreciative, incestuous world of the art galleries, and tried against stiffer opposition in the bookshops. Also mentioned my feeling that he should consider an animated film sometime. But although he thoroughly agreed, I felt as I said goodbye and walked down the short flight of steps into Clerkenwell Close and along towards the Wren church next door, that I was saying goodbye to Moley – someone who didn't really want the big wide world to disturb him. And I felt sympathetic towards him and worried that I had been talking like a Light Entertainment department.

We all assemble at Eric's house in Carlton Hill to look at tapes of various ladies we're considering for the Judith part.

The Judy Loe extract – the cabin scene from 'Curse of the Claw' – goes down well, John falling about especially loudly, which was gratifying. Gilda Radner from *Saturday Night Live* is seen, but an American Jewish Judith doesn't seem to attract a great deal of support. Penny Wilton's *Norman Conquests* performance goes down well, but Kika Markham is given short shrift by the Cambridge lads, who rule out her Workers Revolutionary Party involvement as being too frightful to work with.[1]

The final list is Judy Loe, Penelope Wilton, Maureen Lipman, Diana

---

1 Recently founded Trotskyite group led by Gerry Healey. Corin and Vanessa Redgrave were loyal supporters and attracted other actors to the cause. Kika later married Corin Redgrave.

Quick and Gwen Taylor – and we decide to arrange a read-through with them all as soon as possible.

Saw a glimpse of *All You Need is Cash*. It was impressive – well paced and well shot and with some very funny performances by such as Neil Innes. John needed persuading that Neil could act. The rest of us are unanimously pro-Neil for the film, but there are quite strong differences of opinion as to who and how many we need for the supporting repertory cast in Tunisia. Good company is considered by all to be a major requirement, and some of the names bandied are Roger McGough, Ken Colley and Terry Bayler (from *All You Need is Cash*).

All in all the group seems very charitable and well disposed this afternoon – except to WRP members. We break around five. Eric to return to Barbados, where we shall join him on January 7th.

Friday, December 16th

The days become slighter and slighter as Christmas nears. The cold weather has been replaced by mild, grey, greasy weather, which makes the city feel like a used handkerchief. I finally complete the prolonged job of editing the newly typed *Yarns* and take them in to Geoffrey [Strachan].

Then back up to Hampstead for a squash game with TJ. On the way up to the Flask for a drink afterwards I buy the *Melody Maker*, which contains something of a landmark in Python history – the most comprehensive, overt piece of mud-slinging yet seen in public from one of the group.

Under the heading 'Siphon the Python' is a rambling tirade from a 'tired and emotional' G Chapman. Wild, angry and drunk, Graham at last says what he feels about the *Ripping Yarns* and the various Pythons. I think it's a sad comment on our collective relationship when we can tell the papers things we haven't dared tell each other. I must admit, though, I laughed greatly when I read it – at GC's drunken audacity, which makes for brighter reading matter than most of our interviews, and just goes to show what weird and wonderful rubbish sells papers.

Gilliam, needless to say, was on the phone within hours of publication of the interview. He was jolly, but not pleased.

Oh, well, GC once again spices our life up – it's a pity he had to spice it up with such misanthropic stuff.

Saturday, December 17th

Christmas starts here – well, this weekend, anyway – with two traditional entertainments: the Robert Hewison Saturday mulled-wine party (or how many guests can he fit into 82 Fetter Lane this year?) and the BBC LE party, with its history of tortured heart-searchings as to whether to go or not to go.

Robert's do is pleasant. Chat with his editor at Weidenfeld[1] – a young, attractive lady to whom I am ridiculously coy about my novel. I should either not mention it at all, or be prepared to brag a little about it.

Simon arrives back with the boys, whom he has just taken, as a Christmas present, to see the Circus World Championships at Clapham Common. Then T Gilliam arrives – the irritation of Chapman's insults mollified a little by reported good business and reviews for *Jabberwocky* in West Germany this last week, a place in Alexander Walker's best films of the year round-up, and an award from *Films and Filming* for being the Best British Film of 1977.

Sunday, December 18th

To the BBC party in the evening.

The usual lot. Val Doonican and Eric Sykes seem to be still fans – Doonican is especially enthusiastic and towards the end of the evening even Eric Morecambe grasps my hand warmly – 'Great fan,' he says … 'Great fan.'

Talk to Richard Beckinsale and Judy Loe, who, with me, Ian Davidson and the Goodies, seem to represent the 'younger generation' in a sea of old and well-established faces.

Aubrey Singer, recently transferred to Head of BBC Radio, warns me against a precipitous sale to PBS in the States – 'The big networks *do* pay a great deal more,' he cautioned. Does he know nothing of Python's struggle against the eunuchs?

---

1 Robert's book *Under Siege, Literary Life in London* 1939–1945 had been published earlier in the year. Harold Pinter called it 'a vivid, highly readable, important book'.

Tuesday, December 20th

To BAFTA's luxurious preview theatre in Piccadilly at 10.30 for a screening of the latest Mark Shivas/Richard Broke TV film, an adaptation by John Prebble of *The Three Hostages* by John Buchan.

Whereas Scott Fitzgerald's adult view of the 1920s survives, Buchan's eternal school prefects don't. The sheer mechanics of this dastardly plot, with Hannay being constantly hypnotised and men in turbans flashing orientally sinister looks, make it very, very hard for an audience to take seriously. Afterwards Shivas, looking moderately happy, did confess that there were 'a few more laughs than I'd expected'.

Ended up drinking with Malcolm McDowell. We talked about the state of British films. McDowell dislikes the Lew Grade blockbusters that are taking over the industry and feels that there aren't any films any more which are trying to say anything. He uses Lindsay Anderson's *O Lucky Man!* as an example of a film which tried to criticise and stir up a few passions, but which was crucified by the critics. A serious chap. I like his restlessness, though. He is well-established, but anti-establishment. A useful combination.

To John Goldstone's party in D'Arblay Street. There meet Graham, whom I roundly and cheerfully take to task over the *Melody Maker* article. GC retreats in disarray, blaming the press for quoting 'only the bad bits'.

Sandy Lieberson is there – he tells me he's nominated me for the Best Newcomer Award at BAFTA!

Wednesday, December 21st

Took Thomas, William and Holly over to Shepperton. We watched them building and rigging *Force 10 from Navarone*. Twenty-two years after my heart swelled to the 'Dambusters' March', they're still building Lancaster bombers at Shepperton!

The sun came out as we wandered through the crumbling *Oliver* set and nosed around on the back lot, where odd pieces of filmic flotsam and jetsam lay about – giant rubber mushrooms and a ten-foot-high birthday cake complete with icing.

Read through the film script this evening in preparation for the Judith auditions. Embarrassed at how slight a part it is.

Thursday, December 22nd

The auditions were pleasant, easy and pre-Christmassy. Maureen Lipman, surprisingly, seemed to find it hard to become a character, but she's nice and fun and probably would, with work, have been right. Then Diana Quick, exuding confidence, swept the place with a devastatingly assertive, aggressive reading of Judith, which confirmed Terry J's suspicion that Diana, just being Diana, was the sort of character Judith should be. Judy Loe was not as forceful, and a little pantomimey.

As John C put it afterwards, he rated both Judy and Maureen as lovely, easy, friendly people whom we'd obviously have no trouble in fitting in with, and vice versa, but Diana Quick clearly gave Judith a new dimension of aggression and single-mindedness, which brought the limpid part to life. So Quick will be asked to do Judith. If she does it, she and I will be renewing a working relationship that started at the Oxford Revue of '65.

Thursday, December 29th

Despite the long holiday period, dubbed 'The Twelve Days Off Christmas' in the *Evening Standard* of a couple of days ago, I'm at work today, quite gratefully, going through the text of the *Ripping Yarns* with Geoffrey down at Methuen.

Home and Helen says to me, rather gravely, 'Well ... Graham Chapman ...' My first instinct is to ask if he's dead, but he's not, of course, although he is in hospital, having collapsed at home after four days off the bottle altogether. He rings me later, and sounds small, weak and very old. He confirmed the story that he had been trying to give up – had three days of withdrawal symptoms, seemed to be coping when suddenly today he collapsed. He added that it was remorse for the nasty things he's been quoted as saying in newspaper reviews recently about all the rest of us – but particularly about John C in yesterday's *Daily Mirror* – that shocked him into giving up.

'... I tell you one thing, Mikey, I'm never going to drink strong drink again' (and he sounded as if he meant it).

Saturday, December 31st

Late morning start on a trip with Helen, Rachel and all to the Science Museum, where there is a space exhibition. A chance to see the actual

Apollo 10 capsule – its base charred and huge chunks burnt out of it during re-entry.

How long ago all the space missions seem now. The special thermal clothing and the poo-poo disposal bags worn by the astronauts don't look a lot different from Elizabeth I's underwear in their solemn display cases.

As the days go by I grow more and more proud of myself in actually completing the novel – as well as three TV films and a Python film script this past year. But the pressure has been there. I feel it now in bursts of tension when I find it very, very hard to relax. It's not so much the work itself, but the fact that, as each year goes by, I find myself becoming a more powerful figure – a lot more people depend on me than just the wife and kids.

1978

Sunday, January 1st

John rings. He's been away in the country for the weekend. Has just returned to find a message that Graham has had a nervous breakdown. John admits that at first he saw it as just another Chapman wheeze to avoid the stick which would inevitably fly in Barbados over his newspaper interviews. Not far off the truth, John.

Tuesday, January 3rd

In the afternoon I took Willy to see the latest James Bond movie – *The Spy Who Loved Me*. I thought it most unpleasant. No attempt was made in the imbecile script to create any characters, it was wooden puppets saying wooden lines. The action sequences, of course, were brilliant, but then we all know Britain leads the world in aimless explosions. Otherwise I think it's the sort of mindless garbage Britain has no reason to be proud of. The American-inspired and scripted *Star Wars* was a far, far better adventure.

But I enjoyed being out with William. He's good fun. They all are. And they are at the stage when they respond with an infectious over-enthusiasm to everything new. Willy is absolutely *dying* to go to America. He says he wants to live there now.

Dropped in to see Graham in Southwood Lane. He came out of hospital yesterday and is not supposed to drink ever again. He looked sallow and tense. It's going to be a great struggle for him. Barry Cryer was there too. We sat and sipped tea and Barry and I joked rather forcibly. It seemed the only thing to do at the time.

If the next few entries sound a little different in tone – a little forced, a little self-conscious – it's probably because they were deliberately written for publication. As a way of garnering material for the book of the Life of Brian, *it was agreed that all of us would keep a daily diary of our time in Barbados. The six different accounts of the same working holiday would then be interestingly compared and contrasted. In the end, however, only Terry Jones and myself (both diarists already) played the game.*

Saturday, January 7th, Barbados

On the flight out, a sensational game of Scrabble with Dr Chapman.

Graham, after some deliberation, led off with the word 'fep'. I didn't challenge it immediately, thinking either that it was possibly the prelude to a longer word – feppicle, fepid, fepidicular – or perhaps a medical term which it would betray appalling ignorance to challenge. But it was Graham who looked most puzzled by it and after a while replaced the 'p' with a 'w'.

The game then surged on by 'ys' and 'ands' until Graham selflessly dropped his letters. All were retrieved, apart from the 'z', which is wedged for eternity between the seats of the upstairs lounge of a jumbo jet. Stewards and stewardesses with torches and screwdrivers tried to help out, and to anyone who came up the stairs for a quiet read and saw a large group of people clustered on the floor around a seat which had been entirely removed from its base, we smiled and assured them we were just playing Scrabble.

We reached Barbados an hour before sunset – a little after half past five their time. Drove along lanes with sugar cane plantations on either side and neat, white signposts with names on long arms.

Our way wound up the west coast of the island and from Bridgetown north it was a dense collection of hotels, shops, clubs, some discreetly set away behind shrubberies and palm groves.

Down one such turning is Heron Bay, built by Sir Ronald Tree. Our first sight of our home for the next two weeks is a sensational surprise. Its scale is breathtaking – wrought iron gates, marble floors, piano nobiles – the full Palladian bit. All built in 1947.

Through the hall, a table is set for dinner beneath an enormous hanging lantern. Mighty columns thirty feet high rise above us and balustraded staircases lead up to the piano nobile. On either side of the main house run two colonnades, off which are our bedrooms. All furnished and decorated tastefully and individually. In the centre of the courtyard are three huge spreading trees which cover the whole area in lush greenery.

John spreads himself across a huge, soft, cushion-filled sofa and declares 'This is what my whole life has been leading up to.'

We are greeted by servants, one an old, leathery-faced Barbadian who is introduced to us as 'Brown', but the two Terrys prefer to call him 'Mr' Brown, which is probably a terrible insult.

Churchill has stayed here and there's a photo of Eden and signed photos of impressive looking men in medals and uniforms. Perhaps a Richard Avedon photo of the five nude Pythons would look a little out of place among such company.

Whilst John, Eric, Terry J and myself are lying disbelievingly amongst fine things and wondering whether to set up a preparatory school here (John wants to be maths master), Terry Gilliam (whom we have designated as sports master) is eating the local apples. They're very small, they fall with sharp little whacks from the spreading trees in the courtyard, and they are, we've just been warned, poisonous.

Whether Terry will snuff it before the night's out, we're not sure, but arrangements have been made for the redistribution of his fees for the film, and anyway it's probably God's way of punishing him for having forgotten to bring his script.

Terry J and I bathe. It's very dark and there are warnings of sea urchins. Terry is very worried about the sea and thinks big fish will eat him or perhaps even a lot of little ones will gang up.

He's brought *Wild Wales* with him to read. It's difficult to believe in Llangollen and Aberdovey when you're in a place like this.

Dinner is held up for a few minutes as we await the arrival of the guests for the evening, Mr Jagger and friend and his friend Mr Rudge and his wife. When they arrive we descend elegantly to the table – also designed to match the local limestone material from which the house is built. I don't think I've ever had my dinner off a table made entirely of limestone.

A jolly evening developed – the epically proportioned piano nobile (you couldn't really call it a sitting room) was soon filled with a rather rude game of charades. Mick's graphic mime of the Sex Pistols will stay in the memory particularly.

I think dawn would have been breaking in England when we finally separated to our various tasteful bedrooms.

And Gilliam was still not dead.

Sunday, January 8th, Barbados

The sea and the beach are so clean here – and at half past seven everything shines with a sparkling brightness as if it was the first day after the Creation. I walk up the beach. Meet a man who has a four-month-old pet sea turtle which he keeps in a basin and feeds on pilchards. I think he said pilchards, but I may be doing a Graham on this one. (I told Graham that we had ended up the evening at the Pink Cottage. '*Pig* Cottage?' he asked incredulously.)

I swam – the water was clear and clean. Cleese was the only other one who was up. He'd swum at 9.15, and was now sitting at the massive stone table, looking like Christ at the Last Supper before the rest of the guests arrived.

I tried water-skiing for the first time. No one was watching here so I decided to try it. It was third time lucky – on the third start I pulled up cleanly and stayed up and was very pleased with myself.

Graham is stoutly and very worthily maintaining his non-drinking, helped by a pill called Heminevrin. Talking with Eric and Graham in the front row of the stalls at sunset – when the sky and the bay go through so many rich colour changes in half an hour – Graham suddenly asks me the date. When I tell him it's the 8th he murmurs with ruminative interest … 'Mm … It's my birthday.' So we toast GC's 37 years in fruit juice.

Monday, January 9th, Barbados

'Had egg for breakfast' takes on a new significance here. I've rarely had an egg for breakfast beneath soaring columns and beside balustraded stone staircases, and the fact that this is a fifty-yard sprint from the clear blue waters of the Caribbean only adds to the unbelievability. Mind you, the Squirrel marmalade tastes as alarming as it sounds.

We fairly roar through the script and there's a very productive feeling that at this stage anything is worthy of discussion. We are not under pressure, everyone is warm, comfortable, happy, looking forward to a swim and sunbathe, and therefore amazingly tolerant of any ideas, however devious, deadly or heretical. The script is being turned upside down and inside out.

More work in the afternoon, but we break after one and a half hours to take in the sunset. I go for another water-ski – this time with TG, who is quite impressive, considering he hasn't done it for ten years (water-skiing, I mean).

I think I could cross my heart and say that we did work hard today, with Anthony Eden surveying us urbanely from his signed photograph.

Tuesday, January 17th, Barbados

Tonight the first clouds of discontent appeared on the otherwise clear horizons of a perfect ten days.

Towards the end of last week we began to summarise what we had achieved and this meant going back over well-trodden ground. Ideas, lines and jokes lost their originality and spontaneity and false trails were too laboriously followed. The lightness of touch was lost and the work became harder. But we kept at it successfully, and over the weekend reached the stage where we were to split into separate writing units and begin to actually rewrite along the lines of the five days' discussion.

This morning we had a read-through of everyone's rewrites. Terry and I may have had the easiest part of the script, but our work was mostly accepted and approved. John and Graham had worked on the second section, which was stretched out painfully in certain areas – Eric reckoned 25% of it was superfluous. John took this well. He has remarked in several beachside chats last week on how unselfish we all are with our material.

Keith Moon, who arrived here last night – with a formidable effect – hove to, walking up the beach from the Colony Club and bearing a bottle of champagne. He generously splashed this around and we all got very sandy and talked of Shepperton and Malibu. Keith is planning to have a suite built for himself in the Old House at Shepperton. He has positive ideas about the place – including a cricket pitch on the lawn. 'And football for the roadies,' he adds.

He's lived out of England for three years and has saved a large chunk of tax-free money as a result. He bought a house in Malibu Beach, for $325,000, and since then a law has been passed banning sale of any more building land in this sought-after piece of California. All of which is great for Moonie, who is hoping to get one million for his house. It's next door to Steve McQueen and Herb Alpert. Judging from Keith's stories Mr McQueen at least will be glad to get rid of him – Keith woke the McQueen household up at four a.m. on his last birthday, trying to score coke from McQueen junior and barking at their dog.

After this jolly beach banter Terry and I set to work rewriting some of this morning's rewrites. JC and Graham were doing the same, but when I went out into the garden where they were working there was no sign of Graham – just a very aggravated JC, who muttered angrily that he had to spend three-quarters of the time explaining the plot to Graham and that he was absolutely no help at all.

Graham has just knocked on my door, as I write this, to say that Des O'Connor is coming to dinner. We have decided to try and invite someone every evening. We have scoured the island for Harry Secombe, only to hear that he's left. Marty Feldman cannot be traced, though he's supposed to be here, as is Michael Caine. Maybe Des can throw some light on this tonight.

Des excels at charades and Keith and Graham do a very good double act and it's after one before I'm off towards bed.

And even then, a rather maudlin Keith M appears in my room and I offer him some Glenlivet and he talks morosely and not immodestly about his 'talent' and how important the *Odd Job* film[1] is, as if wanting some reassurance. He's been a hit with all of us – less destructive, more gently jolly and humorous than I'd anticipated.

He takes himself and his wondrous Turnbull and Asser gold-trimmed dressing gown off along the beach to the Colony Club. It's nearly two o'clock.

Wednesday, January 18th, Barbados

Terry J is the only other one who takes any pre-breakfast exercise. He ran with me one day, but now only swims. We compare notes about the sea-lice content of the Caribbean. These invisible creatures are felt, usually in the mornings, as very minor electric shocks along the arms and legs.

I've been reading a little about the instigator of this 1947 classical gem – Sir Ronald Tree. Mr Tull[2] obviously admired and respected Tree a great deal. He has lent me his own, well-thumbed copy of Tree's book *When the Moon is High*.

Tree bought Ditchley Park, a 1720 Gibbs house near Charlbury in Oxfordshire (there's a neat tie-up with eight weeks ago). In the early years of the war, Churchill's house at Chequers was considered to be at risk from enemy bombing on well-lit, cloudless nights. On these occasions Churchill asked if he could spend his weekends at Ditchley Park. 'When the moon was high.'

1 Written by Graham Chapman, it was to be made later in the year. He wanted Moon to star in it.
2 Who looks after the house with Brown.

Tree's finest work, apart from hosting Winston, Eden, General Sikorski and others, was to exert as much pressure as he could to bring America into the war. He tells in his book of meeting leading American businessmen who, in 1941, were predicting a defeat for England – and the Chairman of Sears Roebuck at the time told him it would be a good thing anyway, Britain had become degenerate and Europe badly needed German leadership.

The servants here were very fond of Sir Ronald, and I think his death two years ago has left a vacuum which has not been filled. There is no one of his stature for them to serve loyally and I think that the Pythons, sauntering around in *Muppet Show* T-shirts and torn off denim shorts, are really no substitute for the elegance of the Trees.

Graham seems to me to be the one who would fit best into that world. He always looks a little smarter than the rest of us, and his pipe adds a definite air of distinction. He's also a fully qualified eccentric, and I think in twenty or thirty years he will be a well-matured loony, in the best traditions of the English privileged classes. During this afternoon's session he fills up the teapot with hot coffee.

Apart from a break for lunch today we work assembling the script from 9.45 until 1.00 and 3.30 until 7.30.

And suddenly it's there and ready.

There is now casting, reading-through and minor line rewrites left. John suggests a light day tomorrow, and nobody really argues. We're all feeling rather pleased with ourselves.

Celebrity note: the Michael Caine/Marty Feldman rumours have taken a bizarre twist. It appears that neither Marty nor Michael Caine are on the island, but Marti Caine[1] is.

Thursday, January 19th, Barbados

At breakfast today, TJ, John and I compare notes of books we're reading. It turns out that all of us are reading books which irritate us. John is reading *Twelfth Night* and it's driving him potty.

His indignation over Shakespeare is intense – even at this time of the morning. He claims that Shakespeare's jokes wouldn't even get on a BBC

---

1 Sheffield-born comedienne (1945–95) with her own show on BBC. She had plastic surgery to make her nose smaller. 'The old one kept knocking people off bicycles,' Mark Lewisohn's *Guide to TV Comedy* quotes her as saying.

radio show these days. Terry J, no great supporter of Shakespeare, demurred here, feeling that this was just too harsh a judgement on anybody (apart from BBC Radio, presumably). But John will not be moved from his growing conviction that much of Shakespeare is second-rate and panto, and he wanders off in his *Muppet* T-shirt shouting 'Zounds!' and 'Forsooth!', much to the amazement of the local labour force who appear in the morning to rake the grass.

Terry J is reading *Watership Down*, which he doesn't look to be much enjoying. He says he doesn't think he'd like Richard Adams and finds it all very old-school, reds under the bed and unsatisfactory politically.[1]

Time passes strangely here. I feel as though these days have been weeks. There's an all-embracing benevolence in the climate which means that at any time of day or night there is the same balmy, soft warmth. It's difficult to punctuate time. And unnecessary, I suppose.

Friday, January 20th, Barbados

Why do things always happen to Graham? Today at breakfast he was spreading soft butter on a little piece of toast, and yet broke his knife. Extraordinary.

Casting completed this morning. Most of the main parts re-affirmed. Brian is Graham (unchallenged), Terry J Mandy (John being the only other one in the running, but it was felt that a motherly rat-bag was needed, and TJ's women are more motherly than JC's long, thin, strange ones), Eric Otto, me Pilate, and so on.

TJ feels that the Pythons should play as many parts as possible. John C feels we should be able to afford to take really good actors to play supporting parts, but the general consensus is that our rep company should avoid actors, and be composed of people who can act but will, more importantly, be good companions over ten weeks in Tunisia. John C suggests Ian Davidson (carried nem con) and Neil and Bernard McKenna go on to the list.

Today is our first cloudy day, which means that there are only eight hours' sunshine, instead of ten. There are rumours of apocalyptic storms and floods and snow in England, and Margate Pier has been washed away.

A bad afternoon for morale. Can only keep up on one ski for about

[1] I think I was battling with *Daniel Martin* by John Fowles.

100 yards, whereas TJ, who began water-skiing a day after me, is now almost better on one than two.

Saturday, January 21st, Barbados

Paradise was soured a little by some strange texture to the orange juice. Graham later described it as 'Brown's revenge', which I'm sure is not entirely unlikely. Brown can be very smiley and jokey and his face like an old Brazil nut can crack very easily into a grin, but at the same time he can put over the impression of glowering resentment as well as anyone I know. I think he likes us, but is disappointed in our style.

We are about as well dressed as shipwrecked mariners. We have tolerated a situation where Brown and Tull are the only ones who dress for dinner. In addition, we are guilty, I fear, of being too apologetic, too accessible, too informal.

I have noticed a misogynistic streak in Brown, too. Tania[1] tells me today that every time he brings round the salad bowl he bangs her on the side of the head, ever so slightly, but quite deliberately.

The sunset was ten out of ten today – as if laying on some special final perfect treat for us to remember the island by. Eric, in his long Messianic white robe, strummed his guitar beside a beach fire, with a full moon shining over the Caribbean.

Tuesday, January 24th

More sombre weather. Set about organising our *Ripping Yarn* book-cover photo-call for tomorrow. Milton Abbas School have finally indicated their disapproval of 'Tomkinson' and will not let us film there again, so it has to be Hampstead Heath.

Thursday, January 26th

The rain is back. Find myself unable to settle to very much. Post-Barbadian lethargy. Feel sleepy and incapable of dynamic thought or action.

---

1 Tania Kosevich became Mrs Idle in 1981.

Monday, January 30th

Gather at 12.30 at 2 Park Square West. Summonsed by John Goldstone, who has news for us. Only three Pythons – myself, GC and TJ – left in the country.

John G settles us down and goes into quite a performance. Refuses to let on whether it's good news or bad. After a lot of long looks and glum expressions, he produces papers which he hands to all of us. Set out in the type-written sheets are the terms of an anonymous offer which looks to provide us with what we were asking for: £1,240,000, which covers our budgeted below the line costs, and £512,000 (less than the £600,000 we asked for) for above the line. Artistic controls are not required and the terms of finance are 50% of the profit.

So far so good. John, warming to his theme, gives an impish smile and is very coy about revealing who it's from. 'The National Front?' I asked him. John grins and produces another piece of paper headed with the dread name EMI. So EMI are back. EMI, who turned down the *Holy Grail* – then later picked it up for distribution and produced a pusillanimous campaign which rejected nearly all our ideas.

Now, three years later, we have a memo which reads 'The board have already said it would be scandalous if EMI did not support its own major talent [i.e. Python] and let it go to an American major.' Ho! Ho!

For the volte face we have to thank the new brooms of Michael Deeley and Barry Spikings, who used to run British Lion, and have now been brought in to zip up EMI's film production. They already have a De Niro film – *The Deer-hunter* – and a Kristofferson picture – *Convoy* – in production. All this happened in the last week.

JG is very happy and recommends acceptance. It certainly brightens the drab day. And makes the new film a reality suddenly.

In the evening Nancy L rang. *Saturday Night Live*[1] definitely want me to be a guest host sometime during the next full year's schedule.

Tuesday, January 31st

January washes itself away. Brighten a drab day with lunch at Bianchi's in Frith Street with Julia Nash, an editor at Heinemann. We talk over Al's

1 This 90-minute, topical, comedy-variety series began in October 1975. It became an American institution and was recently renewed by NBC until 2012.

Rue Britannia, which she read. Although she didn't feel it had enough story development to make it a commercial proposition, she said it was good to read a manuscript by someone who could write. Nine out of ten unsolicited manuscripts are frightful, she says – and she's not a tough or vindictive lady.

But sadly I agree with her assessment of Al's commercial potential. His writing is solid, dependable, honest, sometimes poetic, but his sense of story and incident and development of plot is very low-key. As Julia said, she became involved in the set-ups, then nothing happened.

Afterwards across Compton Street to Bifulco, to buy sausages for supper tonight. Then to see Gerry Donovan in Harley Street.

Gerry has been in touch with Kieser.[1] He is proposing to take out three of the more precarious teeth on my upper jaw and replace them with an acrylic denture plate. Dentures are essentially jokey – and I view the prospect of them with mixed feelings. Actually, I think I might quite enjoy the notoriety they will bring to my mouth. And of course I'll be all ready for playing prisoners and old men in the new Python film.

Wednesday, February 1st

Just as I am recovering a little after last week's lethargy, comes a considerable blow to the pride. Last week, whilst rooting out my piles of letters and scripts in an effort to clear the desk, I came across 'Arrochense Los Cinturones', the article I wrote after Tobago, and which foundered in New York a year ago when Lee Eisenberg left *Esquire*. It didn't look bad in parts, a little long, so I trimmed, chopped, and with a swallowing of pride and an apologetic covering letter sent it off to nice Mr Alan Coren, editor at *Punch*.

Today it arrived back rejected, politely but firmly. 'Sending back a Michael Palin piece could well be the sort of action that would cause posterity to desecrate my grave.' But his reasons for rejection were very sound, absolutely correct and put me well in my place.

But I determined that in order to salvage my pride, I would write another article and send it off by return. It was to be about a man whose articles are constantly rejected.

Simon Albury came round and read both the new piece and Tobago,

---

1 Bernard Kieser, a South African, had taken over the unenviable task of looking after my mouth after Robin Powell's return to Australia.

and, good friend that he is, gave them considerable thought, and finally confirmed my own suspicions that both misfired. His comments made me aware that I had fallen into the 'Humorous Article' trap. It's not me, he said, it's not the way I talk or the way I express myself – it's an affected style. I feel a little better after our long chat and resolve not to waste any more time on the matter tomorrow.

Friday, February 3rd

Sit up in my room full of the joys of life and write a long letter to Al L, detailing my slow recovery from West Indian culture lag. I'm thirsty again for books, films, magazines, the lot, and am currently reading Harold Nicolson's 1945-62 letters in a curious tandem with John Dean's *Blind Ambition*.[1] Two very different descriptions of the same subject – power. It does strange things to people. You can't carry a comparison between Winston Churchill and Gordon Liddy too far, but the fact you can start at all is food for thought. I mean, both did very odd things in the name of power and both were rather aggressive, pugnacious men, concerned with the problems of leadership.

Interesting Nicolson observation that the Tory Party really were embarrassed by Winston's presence after the defeat in '45. The problems of living with a living legend!

A lovely morning to myself, followed by a meeting in the Nag's Head, Hampstead, with Gwen Taylor – who seems to be on for our leading rep lady in Tunisia. [We were still searching for someone to play Brian's girl-friend, Judith.] Unassuming, straightforward and likeable – a good addition to the cast.

Drive from Hampstead out to Shepperton for a special viewing of *Dominique*, which has been laid on for the Shepperton staff, wives and families.

At the end Charles Gregson says, with his effervescent cheeriness, 'Not bad for one million two.' I thought it was very bad for that.

Monday, February 6th

Must begin work today on this year's *Yarns* – as much as possible to be written in the two months before we leave for Tunisia.

---

1 Insider's account of the Watergate scandal, by Nixon's White House lawyer.

The great imponderable is TJ's time. He valiantly underestimates the extent of his directing involvement on the new film – he was going to run the shot-list off in a couple of days, it'll now take a couple of weeks. So I am preparing for the worst – which is to write the stories myself and rely on Terry for heavy checking. That way it won't be a brake on the work and it will be a great bonus if he can find a clear week away from the film.

Having decided this, also decided to try and continue my last year's effort to work before breakfast.

To be honest there was little enthusiasm for the work. In the back of my mind lies a distinct reluctance to work on more films for the BBC. Is my reluctance something to do with the bland reaction to the *Yarns*? Is it that the *Yarns* form looks dull compared to the new film, which will take up much of the year?

It's all those things, plus an unresolved yearning to do something a little more serious – or a new direction at least. It could be the novel … it could be a film. The more involved I become with the film world (via Shepperton) the more tempted I am by its freedom. I don't want to get stifled by BBC thinking.

Well, all this jumble of vague hopes and dissatisfactions was holding back my progress this morning. I wrote, but wrote mechanically – the sheer joie-de-vivre of embarking on a new series was sadly lacking. I wish I knew what I really wanted to do.

Tuesday, February 7th

Down to Soho to meet David Dodd[1] at the Falcon pub on the corner of Lisle and Wardour Streets. David says he knew of it before – his father, who was Inspector of Police eventually, was in the 1930s a London copper in the days when Soho really lived up to its naughty image. Vice rings abounded and the Falcon was a meeting place for pimps and peddlers. Mr Dodd, Constable Dodd, used to sit in the corner behind his *Sporting Chronicle* and smoke a pipe and clock his suspects as they came in.

David claims he only knows one man in Guyana who is faithful to his wife. Everybody else, from the PM downwards, is balling on the side. Only the men, it seems; the women marry and stay at home – their side

1 A friend from Oxford who was working at the time at Georgetown University in Guyana.

of the marital contract honoured – but the men are at it like rabbits, all over the Caribbean.

David said he had given words of caution to Judith Hart, the Minister for Overseas Development, who had recently been in Guyana and had addressed a meeting of Guyanese with statesmanlike words about nurturing democracy, guarding the fragile plant which is growing here, etc, etc. David said all this meant nothing – but the £10 million aid cheque she was in Guyana to sign did.

Hearing David I can't help but feel that ideals wither and die in the Tropics. Our culture, our western culture, especially the Protestant form, becomes irrelevant in the heat.

Thursday, February 9th

Gerry Donovan pulls out three of my upper teeth.[1] All very neat and quick (G Donovan goes up in my estimation for turning out to be a fan of *Stay Hungry*[2] – my favourite movie of 1977).

Saturday, February 11th

Take Tom, Willy and Louise Guedalla to see Chinese New Year decorations and we eat an excellent meal at the Dumpling Inn in Soho. Louise tells me that, according to her mother, 'some of the nastiest people in the world live in Soho'. I must say, such was the ignorance about the place when I was young, that my parents would probably see me as little more than a child pornographer for taking three children to Saturday lunch in Gerrard Street. Now, of course, it's full of very well-turned-out Chinese entrepreneurs and sleek Euro-tourists.

Tuesday, February 14th

Write a lyric for the Shirley Bassey-style *Brian* song which I want André and Dave to have a go at – just to see whether it works. They have a choir at their disposal for a session, and actually asked me if I had anything I wanted them to do. Should be interesting.

1 Gerry, an Australian, had been recommended to me by Eric Idle's mother-in-law, Madge Ryan. Apart from installing false teeth, he also wrote the B-side of Eartha Kitt's 'An Englishman Needs Time'.
2 Bob Rafelson film starring Jeff Bridges and Sally Field.

Worlds collide, restoration
drama meets John Belushi,
Saturday Night Live, April
8th, 1978.

'The Chilites dance
routine does not
please Lorne and is
cut just before dress
rehearsal. "You'll
thank me in years to
come," says Lorne. I'm
thanking him now.'
Garrett Morris (left),
Bill Murray, myself
and Dan Aykroyd.
(April 8th, 1978)

'An awful, monumentally awful moment.' Dancing with live cats down my trousers, *Saturday Night Live*, New York. (April 8th, 1978)

Eric and Carey,
me and Rachel, *Life
of Brian*, Tunisia, 1978.

Holidays at Roques.
Helen and me, Tom,
Anthea, Ian Davidson
and Edward Burd.

'Tom decided he would
like to appear in the
afternoon's filming . . .
It was one of the less
comfortable scenes but
graced by the presence
of the visiting George
Harrison. So at least he
can say he was in a
scene with Pythons and
Beatles.'
(*The Life of Brian*,
October 22nd, 1978)

Happy family. The
Coach House, Sag
Harbor, NY, 1979.

'1979 comes in cold.
Very cold.' On the
pond at Abbotsley.

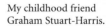

My childhood friend
Graham Stuart-Harris.

'I have to open a fete at
William Ellis School
. . . I smile and sparkle
and fail to hit anything
with seven balls.'
(May 19th, 1979)

Mary and Edward
Burd, Roques.

Saturday Night Live.
Lorne Michaels
hypnotises me before
the show.

'Mikoto comes to cook us a Japanese meal. The preparation is a painstaking and delicate business – as indeed is communication with Mikoto.'
(June 12th, 1979)

Al Levinson, my American friend, with Rachel, Sag Harbor, NY, July, 1979.

'They gave us grapefruit segments, beef in a brown and unexciting sauce ... and a trifle which looked like the remains of an unsuccessful heart-swap operation.' With Donald Carroll (left), Jilly Cooper, Steve Race and Katharine Whitehorn at a *Yorkshire Post* literary lunch.
(October 25th, 1979)

Gospel Oak, 1979,
with Will, Rachel
and Tom.

Yield to Willy's insistence and take all three kids round Madame Tussaud's. A really basic misconception about Tussaud's is that you will see famous people looking utterly life-like. Well, the figures, with their waxy pallor and their disturbingly piercing glass eyes look uncannily death-like. Many of them – Prince Charles and Paul McCartney to name a couple – are grotesquely bad, and I'm surprised the royal family haven't been down there to kick a few heads.

Wednesday, February 15th

Spent half the morning on a play idea. It's very neat – a day in the life of a BBC film unit, but also a day in the life of the beautiful mediaeval church where they are filming. Lots of possibilities for characters – from the Greek chorus of sparks through to the murky romantic involvements of PAs and make-up artists, to the power struggles of the director and cameraman, and with the infinite possibilities of the arrival of the Orson Welles figure who is to present the programme. He stirs up and rearranges all the internal relationships and is the deus ex machina who tips the whole thing into a climax of literally Gothic horror, as he orders parts of the church removed and sawn down – better to accommodate the cameras. Anyway, I made a start this morning.

TJ arrived midday for a session on the *Yarns*. Needless to say it was Python film business which dominated.

We spent a couple of hours on a rewrite for the second Pilate and Brian scene, which benefited, I think, but I'm always wary of duty rewrites – alterations resulting from irritation with other alterations. I tend to think that a lot of final details are best sorted out when we rehearse together.

Sunday, February 19th, Brighton

Have to be in Brighton this evening for a banquet at the Old Ship Hotel laid on by BBC Enterprises in order to launch a week's selling of their progs – *Ripping Yarns* being one they are specially anxious to push (presumably because they cost so much).

Read in an old copy of *The Times*, on which I was cleaning my shoes, that there are 450 bookshops in the whole of the United Kingdom – whilst, in Europe, Berlin alone has 263 bookshops and Munich 244.

Train down from Victoria. A dirty Sunday train – quite an

embarrassment as I hear guttural continental voices in the compartment next door.

A tiny, mean, British measure of scotch in the 'Regency Room', which confirms my suspicions that this hotel may once have seen stylish days, but has now fallen on plastic times. Meet a cheerful Finn and a very anglicised Dane, who wants me to go to Copenhagen in October and talk about *Ripping Yarns* (he seems decided to buy them, which is nice).

Then we're all ushered into a long room, overlooked by a balcony on which Paganini was supposed to have played in 1831. An average meal, but a jolly table with a well-preserved Swedish lady with a Mai Zetterling mixture of brains, looks and years, and my kind Danish friend. Frightfully uninspired speeches. Alan Bates, Billie Whitelaw and myself and others have to stand and be acknowledged.

After the meal, Terry Nation (creator of Daleks and presently writer of *Blake's 7*) seeks me out and lavishes praise on the *Yarns* – but especially on 'Olthwaite', which he can hardly stop talking about. He brushes aside my return of the compliment and raves on. Fall in with two very jokey Irishmen from RTE, one of whom has a twitch which causes his right hand to shoot out towards the bar after every third sentence.

Monday, February 20th

All is calm and quiet here. The two Terrys, Goldstone and others are in Tunisia on a week's recce. The boys, and Rachel, have gone back to school after half-term. It's very cold outside. I have no games of squash planned and no meetings. An ideal set of conditions for writing. And yet, once again, it does not come.

I realise that I am severely short of motivation. Apart from the odd manic enthusiasts – like Terry Nation and Mel Calman[1] – most of the rest of my friends have found the *Yarns* flawed in some way or other. Whatever the reason, the *Yarns* have, I feel, been un-rated rather than underrated. I know the BAFTA nominations are now complete, and I have heard nothing from anyone in the know – which gives me the sinking feeling that the *Yarns*, quite aside from being wiped off the board by the Muppets, may not even be nominated.

To cheer myself up I go down to Thumb Gallery for a private view.

---

1 Cartoonist and good friend. Never have I laughed so much with someone so morose. He died in 1994.

Robert H and Chris Orr are there. Robert is as up as I am down. He's doing a Ruskin film with Les Megahey (ex-Oxon) for *Omnibus*.

A girl comes up and asks me if I'm Kenny Everett. When I tell her I'm Michael Palin she says 'Oh, yes, I *meant* to say that.' Such is fame.

Wednesday, February 22nd

Spend most of the afternoon in the Owl Bookshop, Kentish Town, rather frustratingly trying to spend a book token. The trouble is I want to read everything. Come out with several books for the kids – including T H White's *The Sword in the Stone* and a 'Biggles' comic book for Tom. For myself, three novels by 'Britain's most underrated twentieth century novelist' – Henry Green – plus Kingsley Amis' latest, *The Alteration*. My reading veering towards novels once again, having completed the sorry, but compelling, story of John Dean.

Discovered the joys of T H White whilst reading to Willy tonight. Such richness – such a delightful and intelligent and satisfying mixture of humour, excitement and interest. Smashing.

Thursday, February 23rd, Southwold

Yarns stop for two more days, as I take a 48-hour trip to Southwold.

On the train a silvery-haired and dapper gent opposite introduces himself to me. His name's Whinfrey and I've met him several times at *Punch* lunches. He's the business manager of *Punch*. Will I be writing an article for them again soon? I say I have and it was rejected. He laughs uncertainly and goes on as if I hadn't said anything.

Walk with sprightly Ma along the front. The sea in heavy swell and the familiar Promenade littered with the remains of beach huts wrecked in the January storms. The 'Bide-A-Wees' and 'Little Huts' and 'Rocamars' twisted and smashed.

Saturday, February 25th

Work days slip away. Another week has gone by – and only one day's work on the *Yarn*. Still, I'm very happy and beginning to feel a cautious return of the writing urge.

Tom, Willy and I lunch at Nontas Greek in Camden Town, the idea being to try them on a lot of different countries' cooking. Willy wants to go and eat Turkish because he's heard that you can burp after the meal.

Sunday, February 26th

André J brings round the tape of the Shirley Bassey-type *Brian* song that they've put together. It sounds stupendous. Massive brass backing and a great female voice. All done by three people and a lot of mixing.

Back home, ring Graham to wish him well for the start of *Odd Job* filming – at Shepperton tomorrow. His new director, Peter Medak, seems to have won the casting battles hands down. Keith Moon is out and not because he was too busy with The Who – this was the official reason given to the press because Medak and others didn't want him. Replaced by David Jason. GC has brought Diana Quick in to play his wife. She signed up only last Friday. I wished GC well, and told him to make sure he was still in it!

Monday, February 27th

To Gerry Donovan's for a first glimpse of my false teeth. Try not to read too much psychological significance into this, but I never imagined I would be wearing false teeth at the age of 34. This is ridiculous, of course, for I've had bridges fitted for two years, but false teeth to me are things you take in and out and leave in a bowl of water beside the bed at night – they are like mothers-in-law and big tits, a traditional joke area. Now I have them – a little pink band to go across the roof of my mouth, a little dental chum to lie beside me at night. I feel a little – uncool, man.

To Anne's for a meeting. Played the Bassey *Brian*. Good reaction, especially from JC. All full of admiration for André's arrangement, though not for my lyric particularly. I agree.

Tuesday, February 28th

J Cleese has asked Helen and me out to dinner this evening. We called round at his still-scaffolded Ladbroke Road house, recently acquired from Bryan Ferry, the singer and generally chic society figure. Huge rooms, and lots of them, and only John there, wandering through it, rather lost.

We eat at a rather tasteful little restaurant – a bit elaborately frilly and soft-furnished – called Pomme D'Amour in Bayswater Road. Pleasant, easy chat with just the three of us – about books, Alexander Technique (JC's been at it for three years) and JC's desire to do a *That Was The Week That Was*-style show – mainly I think because he feels that the people who need the boot in now are not the old hags of the Macmillan right-wing establishment, but the new and humourless tyrants of the left.

Wednesday, March 1st

Am finishing typing a *Telegraph* 'Opinion' piece, when a grave S Albury enters the writing sanctum. He's been talking to Barry Spikings, who's been talking to Lord Delfont, who has stopped the EMI/Python deal because he was so outraged by the script.

My immediate reaction is a surge of relief, spreading to all parts of the body. Breathing space to write the *Yarns*, confirmation of fears that I had pushed back into my subconscious that EMI would 'find us out' at some stage and get cold feet. But I'll believe it when I hear it and am not going to race to the telephone.

Instead I pour myself a glass of wine and go off with Simon and [his wife] Phillida to see *Smile Orange* – a sort of black *Fawlty Towers* with a hint of *MASH* and with as much humour and far more endearing characters than either of them.

Thursday, March 2nd

It's pouring solidly at 9.30 and Helen and I are eating rather cosily and discursively in the kitchen, when John Goldstone calls. The facts are correct. Michael Carreras[1] showed the script to Delfont, who vetoed it. Spikings, however, has undertaken to provide us with £50,000 to keep our production team together whilst we find new backing.

Friday, March 3rd

Evidently none of the Pythons is distraught over the collapse of the EMI offer. Terry J greatly relieved that Python still has its powers of aggravation. EMI are the black-tie gala luncheon, awards dinners establishment

1 Film producer, specialising in Hammer horror films, and at the time working for EMI.

– the Grades and the Delfonts of this world – and no territory is less familiar or acceptable to us than this chummy world of showbiz conformists.

This morning's newspapers, by coincidence, show that EMI's half-yearly profits have slumped and yesterday £19 million were wiped off the value of their shares.

Just before lunch my ragged morning is brightened by a phone call from Terry Hughes, who informs me, joyfully, that *Ripping Yarns* has not been forgotten. It's won the Press Guild Critics' Award for Best Comedy Series of the Year. This boost, coming together with the news of the dates of repeats and with the extension of writing caused by the postponement of Python, revives the *Yarns*, which a week ago I felt were in danger of foundering under my lack of enthusiasm. Now, with such a confirmation of appreciation, shall begin an assault on them with renewed spirit.

Monday, March 6th

In to work-room by 7.20. After breakfast JC rings with comments on the rewritten *Brian* ending. Generally he finds it an acceptable and much improved replacement, but there are one or two points – like the stammering Gaoler – which he has always disliked, and when he turns the full beam of his intellectual logical judgement upon what strikes us as spontaneously funny, it does wither the material. I predict a stubborn confrontation on that scene. But all else constructive.

I now favour a clear decision to avoid the summer and begin *Brian* in autumn, but there are difficulties – costumes are hired, sets in Tunisia are apparently not available in the autumn, etc, etc. Meanwhile, wigs are measured, scripts are rewritten and costumes continue being sewn.

Wednesday, March 8th

Gilliam rings for half an hour, proposing a new course of action on the movie – i.e. to cut our budget to a reasonable size by abandoning plans to film in Tunisia, using Britain and finding unusual locations and using a stylised design treatment. The talk turns to castles and salt mines in Wales. 'Jesus of Shepperton', I call this plan.

Thursday, March 9th

Nancy rings in the evening. Evidently it's the first day of spring in New York and she's in very high spirits. Once again she puts a little pressure on to get me to do *Saturday Night Live*. Once again I resist, but then Helen shouts from the kitchen that we need the money. On reflection I certainly could do with a break. Promise to ring Nancy after next week's movie decisions.

The Delfont story is out. A restrained piece in the *Evening Standard* which could help us.

Friday, March 10th

Eric rings – normal waking hours for him, late for me – at half-past eleven. Mainly to let me know how well *Rutles* is going to do in the States. He urges me to get over there and, via *Saturday Night Live*, try and emulate this success. 'Stop piddling around with the BBC, Mike ... get over there ... it's the next step,' and this sort of talk.

The trouble is that I know that the American 'success', in our line of work almost certainly involves a constant compromise with quality and with personal, individual control. If we accept their terms from the start, we will never produce something which, like Python, was truly our own.

Still, I must admit Eric plays the American game well. He has flair, intelligence, skill and style – and is shamelessly good at using them. But I fear he is in danger of becoming the victim of his own image – of believing that the shimmering reflection is the reality.

Sunday, March 12th

In the evening drinks with our next-door neighbours, who are leaving to work in Brunei for ten years. He's a lawyer, middle-aged and, having missed great attainment, is left with something of a chip on the shoulder – elegantly carried, though. I think Brunei will suit him. He says it is almost fanatically Anglophile – which will make a change from Kentish Town.

Monday, March 13th

At 9.30 Python, less Graham, assembles to contemplate the wreckage of the EMI deal. Surprisingly little vindictive comment or post-mortem gloom – though we all feel that EMI should be pressed as hard as is legally possible to provide some recompense for pulling out of a deal after hands were shaken and firm commitments given verbally and literally.

Meanwhile all potential money sources are to be tapped – and Eric suggests that he and J Goldstone go to New York together and try to rifle the pockets of heavily solvent record companies. Anne is to investigate the legal and commercial likelihood of raising the money by shares from the public (fans, etc). Meanwhile Python (Monty) Pictures is left with a near £70,000 bill to pay for work on *Brian* so far. It looks as though all our income through Python will have to stay there for at least six months. Times look hard again.

Tuesday, March 14th

Nancy had rung several times to try and force me into a decision on *Saturday Night Live*. Finally I agreed to host the April 8th show. Nancy sounded overjoyed.

At half past ten drove round to Eric's to watch a couple of *Saturday Night* tapes and talk to him about his experiences of the show. He didn't make a great deal of sense. 'They love Python, be yourself. Enjoy being King of New York for a week.'

Wednesday, March 15th

Lay in bed around eight and decided that if this was to be a fragmented 'sorting-out' week, I should try and clear the decks of tasks and duties which lie in the back of my mind – such as visiting Shepperton.

The place is overflowing with work. Portakabins are being hired to accommodate everyone – it looks like a Yukon town at the height of the gold rush. *Odd Job* and *Pink Panther* are shooting. *Alien*, needing three stages, is building. *Thief of Baghdad* is in pre-production too.

Chat to Ford for a while, then walk over to the canteen. It causes me great personal distress that in my year on the board of directors I've been unable to make any discernible improvement in the catering at the studio. It sounds a small point, but the service and the surroundings are appalling by any standards, and this can only reflect badly on Shepperton's reputation. I have pushed and pushed for some improvements, but, although everybody agrees the situation is grim, nothing seems to get done.

The catering manager reigns supreme, reaping the benefits of this Shepperton boom which he did nothing to create. When I finally reached the dining room I found I had walked into a hornet's nest. I was greeted with shouts, not altogether of a friendly nature, from a long table consisting of Graham Chapman, David Jason, Bernard McKenna, Diana Quick and a very doleful looking man who was introduced to me as the *Odd Job* publicity man. They had been waiting for half an hour for their food to arrive, and had to be back in the studio, on the floor, in another 20 minutes. I felt rather like Lee J Cobb confronting the mob in *On the Waterfront*. They were right and all I represented was the inadequate Shepperton organisation.

Walked back with Graham C, who was fed and placated by that time. He looks tired, but that's to be expected. He's full of optimism about the rushes and, I gather from talking to people on the set, is doing well in his first sober acting role – probably in fifteen years.

As I got home, Terry J rang. I'd still not recovered from trouble-shooting at Shepperton and had had nothing to eat all day, so was not at my best when Terry asked if we could talk about acting in the three *Ripping Yarns* which we are about to write. Arranged to meet him for lunch tomorrow.

Then all the world and his dog either rang or turned up. Terry Gilliam and I had a long chat. I feel that he must get on with his next movie, because I think he's the only person I know who could make a better movie than *Close Encounters*.

Thursday, March 16th

Must spend some time this week reappraising the financial situation. The hopes raised and dashed by EMI leave me with a financial squeeze on. Might have to turn to commercials. The trouble is I have to spend another £10,000 on Redwood's new mixer very soon and £10,000 at least on our second house and the Python cash has stopped coming in.

To Pizza Express in Hampstead, where almost two years ago Terry and I were going through the difficult motions of rethinking our working relationship. The problem had to be faced again today, but was settled instantly and amicably. Since yesterday evening I had had enough time to decide that I must, as before, follow my instincts – and I told Terry, accordingly, that I felt it better not to change the structure of the *Yarns* at this stage. TJ, I think, was sad in one way, but much more relieved in another – and he says he can now plan to think of other projects whilst I'm away filming.

Friday, March 17th

In the evening we go to dinner with Anne Henshaw.[1] Meet there Basil Bunting, a 78-year-old with twinkling, kindly eyes and a well-worn beard. He's evidently a poet and writer, in London for the publication of a new collection by Oxford University Press.

In the Second World War he was in military intelligence and travelled a lot – in Persia, North Africa and the Russian borders. Most of his work consisted of 'getting people drunk'. He used to give scotch whisky to Russians, whilst he himself drank scotch-looking cold tea. A marvellous man, with such richness of experience.

Some things he wouldn't tell me, claiming they were still classified under the Official Secrets Act, but he was closely involved in diplomatic activity at the end of the Second War, when he wrote very strong recommendations to President Truman – 'not a very intelligent man … but …' – concerning the Russian threat to the West – in purely military terms. He thinks that much of his information formed the basis of Churchill's 'Iron Curtain' speech in Fulton, Missouri – and he says that's the only period of his life when he felt his actions could in any way have affected the course of world events. He reckons that the war could have been over three or four weeks earlier if the Allies hadn't agreed to stop their advance in order to let the Russians take Berlin.

Fascinating.

Sunday, March 26th

Anne rings on Easter morning, no less – with a problem I could well do without. Eric is back, full of *Rutles* success in the US. He's probably going to edit *All You Need is Cash* film into a 70-minute version for the cinema, and is strongly urging us to put his 40-minute compilation of the Python Bavaria material out, as a second feature. It would keep Python's name in the American eye whilst we are refinancing *Brian* and would, given the success of *Rutles*, be a sure money-earner.

---

1 By now separated from her husband Michael.

Apparently the two Terrys and John will hardly consider the idea at all.

Monday, March 27th

Watch the tape of the *Rutles* film, which went out earlier in the evening. A smoothly made piece. Elaborate, ingenious, fun. It's interesting to compare what two Pythons have done with half a million and three-quarters of a million pounds respectively – Gilliam created *Jabberwocky* and Eric imitated the Beatles.

Wednesday, March 29th

Ring Neil I and congratulate him on *Rutles* – his music and performance both eminent. Then I ring Eric and get Tania, who is cheerful, but sug-gests that Eric is not in an expansive or chatty mood – and it's his birthday.

Decide to forsake my evening of work at home and go round to cheer him up. Take a couple of bottles of champagne and an old book on cricket (complete with the tantalising chapter – 'Making a Young Wicket-Keeper').

We all ended up having a good drink, chat and so on. Eric was rather low earlier, I think because he felt he had tried to do something with the German film and been sat on by the rest of us without even a chance to explain it at a meeting. But I didn't really need to tell him how jealous the Pythons are of each other's material. How ruthlessly and subjectively biased they are against anything which any individual in the group tries to do – and that's probably at the root of their/our unwillingness to throw 40 minutes of Python in with the *Rutles*. I personally think Eric was a little slow not to anticipate this reaction, but then he's not really living in the real world at the moment.

Phone calls from the States pour in for him.

Thursday, March 30th

The next two days I must pack in nine hundred and one things before leaving for the US Saturday morning. Nancy has booked me on Concorde – so I will arrive in NYC two hours earlier than I left London. I don't really approve – but it's got to be worth the experience. Once.

Drive down through sunny London to collect our Broadcasting Press Guild Award. The new Press Centre in Shoe Lane is depressingly smart – and several of the journalists there complain about this shiny-smooth monster which has replaced the smoky dens where journalists used to meet.

A rather small and touchingly simple ceremony. Present are Tom Stoppard and Peter Barkworth – collecting awards for *Professional Foul*.

Talked to Peter Barkworth. He remembered my sister Angela from the days they worked together in Sheffield.[1] 'Trim girl …' He's also a diarist and writes for an hour every morning. Of *Professional Foul*, in which he was first-rate, he said 'I was so depressed – I woke up one morning and said "It's not me … I can't do it … I'll never be a Stoppard actor".' He talks in a clipped, but unselfconsciously theatrical style. Like Noël Coward without the 'my dears'. A very likeable man.

Derek Jacobi was there to collect an award for *I Claudius*. He left early for *Henry IV* rehearsals. 'I must dash off and be deposed,' quipped he.

Saturday, April 1st, New York

Concorde check-in smooth, no waiting, your very own special escalator and colour scheme, whilst the boarding room – normally that feature-less little box where passengers gather and gaze silently past each other, very often in a state of delay – is, for Concorde, a well-equipped lounge, with phones. Glasses of champagne have to be warded off, so liberal are they with the freebies on this hugely expensive flight. (Concorde return to NYC – £920. Freddie Laker Skytrain return to NYC – around £90.)

Word comes through that Concorde will leave late as the automatically extending jetty has stuck, four feet from the aeroplane. They apologise for the delay, but when we do board we will board up a mobile ramp, which will be drawn up to the catering hatch entrance.

It transpires that Concorde is too high for the ramp, and the only way to lower it is to fill the nose – the famous Concorde droop-snout – with as many British Airways employees as possible. This wonderfully manic piece of improvisation still doesn't quite work, for as I'm half-way up the ramp, about to make my inelegant way into this beautiful, pencil-slim plane through the catering door, we are all shooed back – as the plane (by now filled up with many passengers)

---

1 She was an assistant stage manager at the Sheffield Playhouse for a time.

had sunk below the top of the steps. It was nearly midday when the last of us completed this ignominious boarding. Before take-off the captain, clearly very grumpy, urged us to write to British Airports Authority and complain!

Due to a combination of the free champagne and mean toilet space, several passengers, myself included, are queuing for a pee when the sound barrier is finally breached. Fifty-eight thousand feet and the digital counter hovering at 1.99 – with free Dom Perignon and a five-course meal to look forward to – is as heady and exhilarating a feeling as I've experienced.

The American coastline arrives with the last sips of Napoleon brandy, and we are down at Kennedy by 9.50 US time, having left Heathrow just after midday.

I ring Al and Eve and am soon in a cab round to their small, welcoming little flat in Gramercy Park. I think I'm still suffering a post-Concorde high and gabble on unrestrainedly.

Sunday, April 2nd, New York

Nancy and I go over to an ABC TV studio at the Elysee Theater, off Seventh Avenue – within spitting distance of City Center – where I am to make a brief appearance in a show being recorded for one of the several new cable TV outfits springing up. It's called Home Box Office, and the show is a special featuring comedy teams, or partnerships. They're showing a Python clip and want me to introduce it.

I suddenly find myself on the bill alongside hosts Rowan and Martin and such great and famous names as Sid Caesar – whose *Show of Shows* was one of the most influential American comedy programmes of all time. Meeting this rather shy, thin, drawn man who appears not to have aged, I think I probably poleaxed him with my effusiveness.

Rowan and Martin and everyone there seem very honoured to have me around. Dan Rowan – very smooth, on and off the camera – remembered his favourite Python line – the line in the 'Proust Competition' about giving the prize to the girl with the biggest tits.

Throughout the evening, the staff are overbearingly and unreasonably bossy. I am required to be at the ready, dressed and in the wings half an hour before the recording starts and once the recording does start I am to wait in the wings – not in my dressing room – despite the fact that I am not on for two hours.

The audience assembles, the live band starts to play and suddenly I'm part of an evening of American music hall, exchanging nervous back-stage pleasantries with the likes of The Flying Volantes.

In a makeshift dressing room, Senor Wences, a small, lined, balding little man, who was busy making up his left hand in preparation for his celebrated – and brilliant – ventriloquist act.

I was, apart from The Flying Volantes, easily the youngest person in the show – and I was, after much draughty waiting, finally announced by Dan Rowan, and ran out to spontaneous applause – cued up on the 'applause' signs which flashed above the audience.

My little piece went well, but not as surely and confidently as at the run-through. They didn't have the Python film clip ('Soft Fruit') to show, so I was left with some egg on my face after the announcement. All I could think of to do was eat the postcard which I was using as a prop. This at least had the effect of corpsing Rowan and Martin as they walked on later.

As it transpired, the evening belonged to the Ritz Brothers, two sharp old men who I'm afraid I had to admit I'd never heard of, but who evidently were legends in American showbiz for 50 years. Films, theatre … etc … they danced nostalgically and everyone loved them.

So, in the final line-up, as the audience were herded into endless applause, I found myself in the same jeans I'd worn since yesterday morning, shaking hands with these great men of American showbiz as this special drew to a close.

I was taken round, with Nancy and the others, to Charley O's, where a sumptuous cold buffet had been laid on for all concerned with the show. The producer's son was a frightful pest. He buzzed around the table constantly making alternately fawning and facetious Pythonic references. 'I mean, wow – oh, I get to shake the hand of Michael Palin, *the* Michael Palin …' And so on and so on and so on. Ed Goodgold, who I was talking with, finally lost patience with the boy. He called him over.

'Hey,' says Ed, 'are you Jewish?'

'Half,' returns the gawky acolyte quickly.

'Well, it's your worse half.'

Monday, April 3rd, New York

At five over to NBC – in the RCA building at 30 Rockefeller Plaza. One of the old-fashioned skyscrapers, soaring sixty or seventy storeys above the skating rink in the Plaza, with the flags billowing all around it.

The décor of the foyer is New Deal Inspirational. 'Wisdom and Knowledge Shall be the Stability of Thy Times' is picked out in bold relief above the doors, whilst inside murals – in oils and what looks like gold stucco – mix airliners with naked maidens.

A bewildering variety of lifts, from which I was eventually spilled out at the seventeenth floor.

Magnificent views – the Empire State Building dominating to the south-east and, to the north-east, the twin gothic spires of St Patrick's cathedral on Fifth Avenue, guarded by sweeping skyscraper blocks on all sides. A classic New York panorama.

Lorne Michaels was not in his office when I arrived. I got to know the room a little first. It was small and individually furnished – not at all like the usual American executive office, more like a rather trendy Oxford don's room. Along one wall were framed mementoes of *Saturday Night Live* – the show Lorne created and has guided through three years and eighty-seven shows. Pictures of the cast meeting President Ford, numerous jokily inscribed photos from Chevy Chase,[1] letters from the White House, Emmy awards. On the facing wall, two wood-framed cabinets full of video cassettes of the shows labelled according to their host – 'Steve Martin', 'Anthony Perkins', 'Lily Tomlin', 'Richard Pryor', 'Eric Idle', 'OJ Simpson', 'Kris Kristofferson', 'Paul Simon', 'Art Garfunkel' and so on.

Lorne ambled in. Small, unremarkably dressed, with a bright, intelligent face and disproportionately large head. An attractive, easy confidence as he shook hands. A lack of calculated effusiveness, but no lack of warmth in the welcome. I knew I was going to get along with him and felt suitably relieved.

I felt like a new boy at school with Nancy Lewis chaperoning me, and the sensation increased as Lorne took me around the offices and then down to Studio 8H, the legendary RCA studio where Toscanini recorded. Showing me the studio was a shrewd move, which I appreciated later, for from Thursday lunchtime until one o'clock Sunday morning it was home – the hub, centre and focus of the colossal outpouring of nervous energy that creates *Saturday Night Live*.

There are about fifteen writers who assemble in Lorne's office, five or

---

1 Catch phrase, 'I'm Chevy Chase and you're not,' he originally joined as a writer, became the star and left after one year to be replaced by Bill Murray.

six of them women. All, bar one – a venerable, white-haired father-figure[1] – look younger than me. Mainly scruffy. A rather earnest, college boy look about them.

The meeting is a curiously stilted affair. Lorne presides gently, analyses the ideas that come up and shows encouragement for the good and half-good, and firm but diplomatic discouragement for the bad. But no one sounds energetic. No ideas are put forward with great conviction. It's as though this first meeting is part of a formula which has to be gone through – the real ideas will form tomorrow.

Lorne invites me to a party to be thrown at the fashionable disco, Studio 54, by Truman Capote and Andy Warhol.

Outside huge arc lamps are directed at the entrance to the club. A crowd, probably hired by Warhol and Capote along with the lamps, clusters around the entrance and I'm ushered quickly through the ropes and into the club.

There's a broad passageway in, and cameras are pointing at us as we go down it. 'Smile,' somebody says. As we push in through double doors, I catch sight of the black-cloaked figure of T. Capote. In the bright light he looks like a mole or a badger, appearing briefly, immaculately ... then gone. Inside, the club is like any other heaving mass of bodies. Strobing lights, helpful darkness for those who want it – strategic pools of bright light for those who want it.

Almost immediately brush up against Mick J and Jerry. Jagger is at his most inelegantly slurry, and warns me against the poofs here. He greets me with congratulations on the film, which I dopily don't comprehend. He is referring, of course, to the *Rutles* film. I compliment him on his performance – and he is lost, borne away on the crowd.

The party was ostensibly to watch the 50th Academy Awards Ceremony live from LA and at the same time show off Polaroid's video-beam technique – by which a TV picture can be projected by means of three light sources onto a flat screen. The lights and cameras on the way in were to demonstrate the new instant film techniques. So we were all being used in a way – either for Capote and Warhol's ego, or simply Polaroid's salesmanship.

A glorious mixture of people. On one journey through the crowd I passed Dick Martin and Salvador Dali (not together). The model girl,

1 Herb Sargent, the head writer, brother of Alvin, the screenwriter (*Ordinary People, Spider-Man*, etc).

Brooke Shields, who plays the twelve-year-old whore in Louis Malle's shortly to open *Pretty Baby* was sitting beside us.

They bayed at the Academy Awards, especially when Vanessa Redgrave gave her short and rather mistimed speech about anti-semitism and fascism and they roared with exultation at the three awards for *Annie Hall*. It was quite exciting in a wasteful way – for in the end the home crowd won. The starched and trim bronzinos of the West Coast, with their showbiz smiles and oozing wealth, were routed by the forces of the East Coast – by the critical, introspective, tasteful Mr Woody Allen. Woody, who was not even at the Hollywood awards, but was playing clarinet in Michael's Pub in Greenwich Village. As Lorne said, 'Woody always has taste, and not being at the awards demonstrates taste at its highest.'

After the awards everyone headed either to the bar or to dance – ignoring glasses on the dance floor, which were smashed and trodden underfoot. At the bar the epicene bar boys held court. They pulled off their tight black T-shirts and swayed and swished and showed off. It was hard and aggressive and not at all friendly. The place was filling up and there was a growing compulsion to decadence – as if it was expected of the audience here to be outrageous, egomanic, wild and uncontrolled. I found it horribly depressing – almost a nightmare, and was relieved when we left just before one.

Tuesday, April 4th, New York

Woke, frightened, after about two and a half hours' solid sleep. Lay there – aware I had been losing sleep at the rate of four hours a night over the last five days and wondering how it would affect the rest of the week.

At five in the afternoon round to NBC, to the well-worn sprawl of offices – like a very liberal arts college, with Professor Michaels presiding. Unlike England, where writing is largely a domestic industry, here in the States they assemble in a suite of offices and start to tap out ideas.

Around ten, Lorne and Jean Doumanian – the assistant producer – wander down and across Broadway to eat at Wally's. Another unpretentious restaurant, which seems to be Italian despite the name. We join a table of Lorne's friends (he seems to have friends everywhere he goes), comprising Paul Simon, Shelley Duvall,[1] David Geffen,[2] Diana Ross, her

1 Actress girlfriend of Paul Simon. Favourite of Robert Altman's. About to start filming on Kubrick's *The Shining* with Jack Nicholson.
2 Agent, record producer, co-founder of Dreamworks in 1994.

escort – a handsome, but taciturn young Nordic chap – and a lady called Diana Von Furstenberg,[1] who's just seen and 'adored' *Pretty Baby*. She looks like Cher's grandmother, but is clearly something of a NY society lady.

The talk turns to the Oscars. Paul and Shelley were in *Annie Hall*, so are obviously pleased. There is much talk of John Travolta, the newest and most instant Hollywood star on the strength of one movie – *Saturday Night Fever*. All except Paul Simon are unqualified in their praise of him – or rather of what he represents – instant, assured, powerful glamour. Lorne, who talks easily, volubly, and on the whole wisely, reckons *Saturday Night Fever* is the movie of the '70s – the same way as *Easy Rider* was the movie of the '60s. Some truth. Paul S bemoans the passing of the '60s. He regards the '70s as dull and derivative – in the '60s everything was fresher. I agree with him that issues seemed clearer, sharper then.

Wednesday, April 5th, New York

The phone wakens me at ten past eight. 'Where's Eric Idle?' enquires a girlish voice – and it's some while before I can assure her that I don't know. 'Did I wake you?' the voice turns on me provocatively. 'Yes …' 'Well, I hope you can go back to sleep, because I *never* can after I wake up …' I put the phone down. Aw hell, four hours.

Over to the restaurant somewhat heavily named 'Sea-Food of the Aegean', where we are dining with Bob Osterberg and Ray Brodie – our lawyers in the Python versus ABC case. Osterberg is straight, Ray Brodie the gushing enthusiast. Very good to see them and pay back some of our thanks.

Then half an hour of still pictures for continuity on the show and at 3.15 ready for the read-through. This takes place in the Green Room on the ninth floor (this is to become one of the landmarks of the building over the next few days). Bowls of salad, coffee and beers are provided and the room is crammed with twenty or thirty people.

My feelings after the read-through were that I was reading an awful lot of narrator/link man parts and would have preferred to have done more characters.

The writers sensed and appreciated this and went off to rewrite,

1 She was known as New York's Fashion Queen.

whilst myself, Dan Aykroyd, Bill Murray[1] – grim-faced and unshaven – and Garrett Morris – the neat, chirpy black member of the cast – began first rehearsal for our Chilites dance routine. Sometimes I find it hard to figure out quite how Lorne's mind works. He loves the Chilites' song 'Have You Seen Her' – a hit of eight years ago – and wants to see it on the show. However, since that time two of the Chilites have been imprisoned and one is dead. Lorne still has the lead singer – Eugene Record – and hopes that the rest of us, in Afro wigs, will be able to recreate the Chilites behind him. I'm sceptical, dear diary.

Decline Lorne's invitation to dine with Paul at Wally's and am just heading east to the Essex House when Laraine[2] and a group of the writers ask me to eat with them. Well, I am hungry, and it's good to take any opportunity to get to know them better, so I find myself up on W91st at Marvin Gardens – huge but cheap plate of turkey salad and a couple of bottles of wine with Laraine, Bill Murray, Al Franken,[3] Brian Doyle-Murray[4] and others.

In the cab on the way back Al F says how easy people are finding it with me – which I take as a compliment – and fall into bed, tired but grateful, just after one.

Thursday, April 6th, New York

To NBC and Studio 8H, for the first day of 'blocking' the sketches.

I have to do a series of visual promos between four o'clock and five o'clock, which go smoothly and in their small way give the studio crew confidence in me. We work on with blocking, rehearsing our Chilites number, which is fast becoming my bête noire of the week – it's musically quite complicated.

That night I eat with Lorne at Charly O's. He's inquisitive, but not prying. We talk about marriages, kids, relationships. His marriage (to one of the present writers) lasted ten years. He thinks kids would have

1 Bill Murray had joined the cast three months earlier.
2 Laraine Newman was one of the regular cast, who called themselves The Not Ready For Prime Time Players.
3 Al was also in *All You Need is Cash*, and now he has since made a lucrative career out of protest. He has his own show on TV and wrote the bestseller *Lies and the Lying Liars Who Tell Them*.
4 Writer and cast member, brother of Bill Murray.

saved it. He's a Canadian, won his spurs with CBC, trained for the law, but never practised, wrote for the 'Laugh-In', etc. He's a very effective, rather stylish leader of men and, though his own ego is clearly a thing of pleasure to him, he does give as well as take. I like him more and more.

It's at two in the morning that myself, Lorne, writers Al Franken and Tom Davis, stumble eventually onto what is to become the shape of the opening monologue – my own proving-piece. I am to play my manager and come on and apologise for Michael not having arrived.

The ideas fall thick and fast and I suggest that the manager should talk about his other acts, and then possibly end on an act of his own. This fits neatly in with an idea of James Downey, one of the young, new writers, who said he's always wanted to see someone dancing with ferrets down their trousers. I adapt this to dancing to 'The White Cliffs of Dover' whilst putting sea-food salad and two cats down my trousers. Great is the nocturnal hilarity. I just hope it wears well in the morning.

Friday, April 7th, New York

There is a lift operator at Nancy Lewis's apartment building on Central Park South who is genuinely, creatively loopy. The last time I saw him he told me in some detail, with a perfectly straight face, that he is currently making replicas of New York public buildings out of false teeth. 'I have a lot of dentists in this block, you see.'

Now I understand why Python can be so successful in the US. And it is prestigious. It is repeated endlessly – currently on Mondays on Channel 13 in New York and five nights a week in Los Angeles, five nights a week in New Orleans, plus numerous other regional showings one hears of, in Pennsylvania and North Carolina, etc, etc.

Such is the respect for Python, that Lorne confided to me today that he felt it has adversely affected some of the writing on this week's show. Some of the newer writers, he feels, have become self-conscious and forsaken their own style and their own instincts in favour of attempts to supply me with Pythonic material.

There is one sketch in particular, which has changed from a lecture on drama and a 'What's wrong with this scene from Chekhov?' idea to a fully fledged RADA-trained actor escaping from chains, locks, padlocks and a trunk whilst performing *The Seagull*. All this grew from an observation of mine that the narrator needed brightening up and couldn't one possibly begin by, say, breaking out of a trunk, before going into a perfectly straight introduction?

Finish blocking around nine. But then there's wardrobe fittings and yet another dance rehearsal – and it's nearly eleven by the time I'm relaxing in Lorne's office. Lorne is staring up at the order of sketches pinned on cards to one wall of his office – 'Holmes', 'What's Wrong?', 'Nerds', 'Cold Opening', etc, etc. And when we leave for a meal half an hour later writers are still writing in smoky offices.

Dan Aykroyd (Watson), Bill Murray and myself (Holmes) watch an old Basil Rathbone movie in order to check on our voices and performances for tomorrow's sketch. Then Lorne and I go up to the Japanese restaurant.

Lorne says he wants to tell me – before tomorrow night so anything said will not be affected by the show – that he would like to work with me again. Ideally he would like to set up a Michael Palin show, which would be financed by NBC, but co-produced by Lorne and myself, so that we would retain overseas rights. Like the *Rutles*, in fact.

All this profession of confidence sweeps over me, but almost fails to make contact in reality. I can't really believe it can be as easy as this. Am I really being offered *at least* one 90-minute show of my own on NBC? I think that my failure to connect must come across as either diffidence or supreme confidence.

Saturday, April 8th, New York

Shave, select clothes that will be seen across the nation tonight – and I think that's probably the last time today that I consciously stop and think about the awesome accessibility of TV. The number of homes all over America who will be looking at me, tonight, in these jeans I'm just hauling myself into. The number of friends whom I may never see again, who will see me, after their dinner party, or as they row, or because they can't sleep. The number of film stars I idolise, sports heroes, ex-Presidents of the World Bank, Watergate conspirators (Dean), authors I'm reading at the moment (Bellow), boxers, test pilots, Mick Jaggers, Senators, Congressmen, criminals, who may be looking at this shirt, or these white sneakers, before this day is out, is a thought too colossal to comprehend.

So I don't. I get going. My philosophy of the day is that this is a cabaret. And the words are all on cards.

To the studio around lunchtime. Almost the first person I see is John Belushi – he is a regular member of the team and probably the best-known now Chevy Chase has left. He has flown in overnight from LA, where he has been working on a movie, and he returns tomorrow.

The Chilites dance routine does not please Lorne and is cut just before the dress rehearsal. 'You'll thank me in years to come,' says Lorne. I'm thanking him now.

My main worry centres around a Sherlock Holmes sketch which is not just a rather long one joke item, but which requires a certain amount of playing and elaborate use of cue-cards. I find it hard and unrewarding work. Lorne said yesterday that it's a sketch which will not work until the show. Brave words.

We still have sketches unblocked when the audience come in for a full-house dress rehearsal at 7.30. For the first time today I feel nervous.

At eight we roll – the cold opening – an encouragingly funny retrospective look at the Academy Awards with Vanessa Redgrave (Jane Curtin) introducing a splendid Yasser Arafat from Belushi. Then titles – my name in lights on an electric billboard in Times Square (oh, Lorne the showman), the cast and then the rich, trusty tones of announcer Don Pardo – 'Your host for tonight … Michael Palin.'

This is the moment of truth. For the next five or six minutes it's just me. The monologue goes averagely. The show speeds on – no major boobs, but a poor audience. However, I appreciated the psychological boost of a full-audience dress rehearsal. Most of the terrors are gone now. From now on there's no time to think.

First there is a meeting of technical staff in Lorne's office. Briskly, but unhastily, Lorne runs through the show. Two sketches disappear altogether. 'Holmes' is still there and didn't go too well at dress. Lorne remains confident. Writers are sent scurrying off to rewrite material. By 10.15 a smart, new, typed running order is issued. Decisions on material that have taken three days of the week are reversed or replaced by other decisions in the space of 30 minutes.

Then to the dressing room – and Nancy and Al Lev and telegrams from Terry and Eric – 'Please Stay In America' – and into the wonderful, baggy, shiny grey suit with the specially protective cat lining in front. It could be a Python recording. I feel strangely and completely at home as 11.30 nears.

I'm moved into position by Joe Dicso, the dependable, refreshingly un-camp floor manager, and at 11.30 we're off. The cold opening, the big build-up – 'And now your host …' – and out I go – into America.

A warm reception, the monologue intrigues them, but I can't wait to get to the dance with the cats and sea-food salad. All is going well, but the cats have stage fright and, as I gyrate and at the same time try and coax these pussies into my trousers, I become aware of a frightful smell, and a warm, brown mess all down my arm. Even as I am grinning man-ically and pushing it down, the cat is shitting more violently. I can't hear the audience reaction above the band, but I know that the worst is happening. This is going to be tele-embarrassment on a monumental scale.

The offending cat leapt away, and I was left stroking the other one's little marmalade head as it peeked out of my trousers. I caught sight of myself on the monitor and it looked nightmarishly obscene. But the red light of the camera shone unblinkingly at me – revealing to the entire US a man who looked as if he was masturbating with an arm covered in shit. Awful. An awful, monumentally awful, moment.

No time after it to stop, think, question – I had to run into a one-minute costume change (the show could never work without commer-cial breaks) to become an RC priest in a confessional. I reached the confessional with five seconds to spare, slid back the partition and sud-denly realised my arm was still stained with cat nerves. In a split second I changed arms – which must have greatly thrown the director – and the stink in the cramped little confessional grew by the minute.

Even after the confessional there was no time for the scrub I needed, for I had to be raced the length of the studio, tearing off my soutane as I rocketed through the audience, in order to make a change into a Very Famous Actor. This time I was locked in a trunk with my smell.

Half an hour of high-pressure insanity had gone by before I was able to stop and think and gauge reactions to the hideous occurrences during the opening monologue. Lorne, who was on the floor throughout the taping, was the first to try and convince me that the opening had been hilarious – and I realised that nobody knew the hell of embarrassment I'd been through. After all, you can't smell on TV and the camera was never close on my arm – and anyway, it all looked like sea-food salad. No … it was great, they all said.

The 'Holmes' sketch came to life – or as much life as it'll ever come to – which was especially rewarding as we approached one o'clock. Lorne was cutting and changing and reshaping even as we were on the air, and we lost a sketch before one, and the farewells and thank yous and it was all over.

Nancy had a huge magnum of champagne ready, but I hardly had time to drink any. Many congratulations, but I think mainly just the joy of relief – of having done it. Completed this 'dangerous' show, as Lorne called it. 'Come and meet a fan', I was asked, and rushed from my champagne, which everyone else was drinking anyway, to meet a scrawny, freckled youth in loose clothes, who was introduced as Jeff Carter, the President's son.

Up to Lorne's office to see the tape. It did look monstrously funny. Bill Murray thought it was the best show this year. Everyone very happy.

Sunday, April 9th, New York

Woke just before seven. Head and senses centrifugal. My condition brings to mind Yeats – 'Things fall apart the centre cannot hold'. Shower, Alka-Seltzer, and I sleep again until ten. Amazing how resilient is the human system.

There are two fans outside my room. Yesterday one of them tried to reach me posing as an NBC cameraman. Now, as I first venture out, they're there. A big fellow and a girl. Unattractive, damp-handed. They look frightened. In the lobby a tall, elegant girl with dark glasses approaches and hands me a picture she's drawn of myself and Rachel (taken from a photo in a Central Park playground nearly two years ago).

Around five, people start arriving for a small party which I felt I should give for production team and cast. Partly because my suite needs filling up. Now they arrive, I'm feeling low on energy and would really rather be sitting in an aeroplane. But the place fills up. Nancy has brought wine, Laraine N brings hot bagels and cream cheese, and I try to make the superhuman effort to bring together the disparate elements of my own friends, who have only me in common, and the *Saturday Night Live* folk, who have each other in common.

John Belushi has flown back to complete his movie, but his wife is at the party, and Dan, Bill, Laraine and Gilda and a lot of the writers turn up. Many of them bringing presents. Tom Schiller (he who was wont to tap on my dressing room door and shout '258 minutes please, Mr Palin!') has brought me *Saturday Night and Sunday Morning*.

The cast end up smoking in the bedroom and watching a TV programme on airline hijacks. Ed Goodgold was not impressed by last night. His angle seemed to be that I was too good for the show and shouldn't soil my hands. I like Ed, but sometimes I think he's away in a too-private world. When I spoke to Lorne on the phone he said he had heard good reactions. Paul S had rung especially to say he liked it.

The Essex House party is still in uproarious form as I leave for the plane. Dan, Bill and I perform our Chilites routine and I am given a send-off at the lift, at the front desk and at the limousine.

At the airport the check-in girl complimented me on the show, as did a couple of passengers.

Unspeakable joy of sinking into an aircraft seat and being served champagne and a meal as I let my mind drift happily over the extraordinary week. Next to me a burly young man reads *Chocolate Production and Use*. Very seriously.

Thursday, April 13th

General resurgence of fortunes continues. Anne rings with positive news on John Goldstone's meetings with Denis O'Brien,[1] our latest, and probably last, hope for *Brian* backing. Apparently O'Brien has okayed the budget, but is negotiating over above the line costs. So *Brian* is on the way to a resurrection.

Cleese rings, no, sorry, Cleese's secretary rings to ask me if I would like to go with him to see Alan Bennett's play *The Old Country* tonight. I accept (in the absence of my secretary!).

Terry Hughes is going to speak directly to Bryon Parkin, head of BBC Enterprises, over the *Ripping Yarns* and Lorne. Great excitement, atmosphere of things happening. Probably quite illusory.

I fall asleep easily these days – the legacy of New York. I reckon I still have ten hours' sleep at least to catch up. Managed to stay awake for most of *The Old Country*, but neither John nor I rated it very highly. Full of surface wit, some elegant lines and well-turned phrases, and many funny moments, but, with the exception of Guinness, it was woodenly played by a cast which seemed to have less energy than the audience. This had the effect of leaving the mellifluous and gently confident Guinness high and dry, giving a Great Performance.

We walked across Shaftesbury Avenue and into Gerrard Street. The

---

1 American merchant banker introduced to us by George Harrison. He'd been Peter Sellers' financial adviser.

warm, bright lights and hanging cooked ducks in the windows brightened us against the unseasonable cold. Ate at a Szechuan restaurant.

We talked about America. When I described to him the day of recording, John grimaced and said he could feel his stomach tightening even as I spoke. I told him he ought to be out doing a decent movie part. He's always landed with poor roles in movies which doubtless make him money, but end up either getting cut or making no impact at all.

John is defensive – he's happy at the moment, writing new *Fawlty Towers* with Connie, though he says each script takes a month's hard work, but he gets a great deal of satisfaction from them. He makes money from 'hack work', as he calls it. Easy-money training films for Video Arts, commercials, films in which he has little involvement.

So John has polarised his life into earning (routine, no great pleasure) and non-earning (creative and artistically satisfying). A dangerous set-up, I would say. I believe the only sane and satisfying way to live is to fuse the two and avoid, wherever possible, cheapening yourself for money. In that way talent gets eradicated.

Tuesday, April 18th

Jill Foster rings to say that the Pascall Bon-Bon commercial may be on next Thursday.

In a weak moment in darkest March, when it looked as though we would be begging on the streets this summer, I came as near to agreeing to consider doing a commercial as I have done for years. My present confusion is the result. But they still haven't let me see a script.

Wednesday, April 19th

Arrival of the Pascall Bon-Bon script over breakfast. I read it and straightaway felt slightly nauseous. Jill had mentioned a figure exceeding £20,000 for this commercial, or possibly two, and what I had just read was a 30-second piece of trivia – worthless, unoriginal and banal. It looked as though it had been written in four minutes after a drunken lunch. Yet again my mind boggles at the huge discrepancy between money and talent.

I could so easily pick up the phone to Jill and say yes. Yes, I will ignore all my creative and artistic instincts, I will get an injection from the doctor on the morning of the commercial which will render me intellectually numb for the period of a day – at the end of which I will have done the horrendous deed, and be thousands of pounds better off.

Quite a temptation. But I realise that if I did this script I would be committing a crime against all the principles that concern me – honesty, value, integrity – all would be totally compromised. Helen reads the script and agrees. So I have to phone Jill and withdraw my toe from the seductive waters of advertising yet again.

Fortunately Jill has seen a script and is equally unimpressed, so the problem of hurting her doesn't arise. She phones the agency. An hour later the director calls back and asks if I would still be interested if the script were entirely rewritten.

Friday, April 21st

In the afternoon drive down to Anne's for a meeting with John Goldstone and the Pythons to discuss the new *Brian* deal.

This has been put together by Denis O'Brien and his company, EuroAtlantic. He will collect £400,000 from four rich folk and then borrow the rest, on their behalf, from the bank. The £2 million borrowed can then be written off against taxes.

Nearly everything we asked for is granted – and they seem less worried about controls than EMI. They *do* want to work closely with John on all distribution deals and we are being asked to put up £200,000 of our (and John Goldstone's) fees to cover the completion guarantee and £177,856 of our fees for the contingency money.

If we are all good boys and the weather's nice and there are no revolutions, we will make more money upfront than the EMI deal. But if we overrun or overspend then, by the terms of this deal, Python stands to be hit harder.

We talk on for two hours. Eric is aggressive – sometimes quite outrageously awkward over small points – but it's very good to have someone in the group stirring it up, when the rest of us are really happy to accept this stroke of good fortune.

Wednesday, May 3rd

The BBC ring to say that they cannot get the 'resources' for two *Ripping Yarns* this summer, and can record only one in July and the other two will have to wait until March/April 1979. Once more I feel the dead weight of BBC bureaucracy and mentally resolve to do without them for a while. Maybe I will use July/August to prepare a special for NBC. That is, if Lorne's still keen.

Friday, May 5th

Half-way to seventy today.

We signed the contract with EuroAtlantic, which gives us £2 million to make the next Python movie.

When Anne asked if there were any points in the contract we wished to discuss, there were unanimous shouts of 'Get on with it!' and 'Give us the money', so the signing went ahead with due irreverence for this vast sum we are acquiring. A magnum of champagne was opened and Anne produced a birthday cake for me, so everyone had to sing 'Happy Birthday'.

At this point Oscar Beuselinck,[1] the lawyer we have approached to help us on the Bernie [Delfont] front, arrives in the champagne and chocolate cake-stained salon. He sits himself down comfortably and confidently – a marked contrast to most people's behaviour when first confronted by the massed Pythons – as if preparing for a performance.

Oscar, who is only slightly less obsessed with being Jewish than Edwin Goodgold, clearly relishes the case. In his opinion, Bernie can't take the Otto bit about Jews putting people into 'little camps' – too near the truth about the West Bank, etc.

The upshot of Oscar's jolly visit is that we are, on his advice, going ahead with plans to sue Delfont for the money we had to pay out, and for loss of earnings due to rearrangement of our activities – on the basis that there was an oral contract, and with the moral point that we should do everything legally possible to react against this blatant act of personal censorship as being detrimental to us, good business and the British film industry … Amen.

Python has always enjoyed a fight – and with the heads of ABC and Time-Life on a charger already, we're now spoiling for action nearer home.

---

1 Much-sought-after entertainment lawyer. Known for ringing up his opponent and saying 'I'm Oscar, what's your best point?'

Saturday, May 6th

Pull myself from slumber by nine and wake myself up by driving down to Old Compton Street for croissants and newspapers.

Time to clear up and clean up before Danny Aykroyd, Rosie Shuster and friend Margot Kidder drop in ... 'What a well-vacuumed house,' Danny comments. Danny and Rosie have come over on Laker's Skytrain, and say it's grim but cheap.

Margot Kidder is playing Lois Lane in the *Superman* movie (which is still shooting, over a year after they pulled out of Shepperton).

Apparently most of her work involves hanging in harness alongside Christopher Reeve whilst people do strange things to them. They have to fight an eagle on the top of the Empire State Building. The first 'eagle' they got was from Taiwan and looked so un-eagle-like, with a funny red crop on its head, that it was sent home and it was decided instead to use large falcons. The falcons would only fly after chicken bones, so Margot and *Superman* were suspended, with wind machine blowing them, between one man hurling falcons towards another man holding chicken legs.

As Superman perspired heavily, leaving tell-tale patches around the armpits of his costume, one member of the crew was standing by to blow-dry his armpits.

The length and design of Superman's cock was the subject of much controversy, which culminated in Superman appearing at a photo-session with a large metal dong down his tights. Margot said she got so fed up with this thing digging into her leg that she took to flicking it with her fingernail, causing a light but noticeable metallic ting every time she touched his shorts.

The Salkinds are not the most conventional businessmen, she readily admits, but she thinks the movie will be great and confirms the rumour I heard at the Shepperton board meeting that it will be premiered at the White House.

Monday, May 8th

To Devonshire Place to face Dr Kieser and the dreaded world of gingivectomy.

Debbie is there and bucks me up in the waiting room with enthusiastic words about the *Ripping Yarns* – had I seen Celia Brayfield's piece in the *Standard* last Friday saying that the *Yarns* were the only things worth staying in for on Friday evenings ... ? These crumbs of comfort are gobbled up eagerly.

The surgery, which involves one half of my mouth, top and bottom, begins just after six and goes on for two hours, almost without a break. Kieser is thorough, but much more gentle than Robin Powell, constantly congratulating me on being a model patient and doing everything to make sure I'm as comfortable as it's possible to be with someone slicing into your gums and scraping away at the exposed bone.

I'm stitched up and sent away with a reassuring collection of mouth-washes, extra-strong aspirin, should I need it, swabs, should bleeding recur ... and the plaudits of the cheery, extrovert South African ringing in my ears.

Thursday, May 18th

Just like the old days. Up at 7.45 for an hour's work, then down to Terry's around ten for a day's writing that lasts until seven. With a great effort of concentration we have completed a typescript of the 'Potter of the Punjab' tale, now called 'Roy of the Raj'. It will go to the BBC tomorrow and I have a feeling that we shall be filming it in July.

Saturday, May 20th

Wonderful start to the day – a letter from Spike Milligan saying simply '*Ripping Yarns* are super – more please.' What an accolade. For me it's like Pelé telling you you're a good footballer.

Gilliam and Terry J dropped in – though at different times. TG has finished his film script, he says. I asked what he was going to do now. 'Write it,' quipped the paranoid animator.

Sunday, May 21st

To a lunch party at Tom Stoppard's in Iver Heath.

It's a marquee do – with lots of noise and clinking of opinions.

Miriam greets us effusively. Her two – or two of her several children – are great *Ripping Yarn* fans. I'm getting worried by all these children who love it – not by them, but by the lack of corresponding enthusiasm amongst grown men and women. Tom asks what it's like to be everybody's favourite children's programme.

Talk to Prunella Scales and husband Tim West. Pru says she was not really happy doing the first series of *Fawlty Towers* – she was so concerned with getting it right and lacked confidence in her part. But I think this is a touch of theatrical modesty.

Clive James, looking very pallid – as if trying deliberately to throw off the bronzed Aussie image – heaves over to our table, plonks himself down beside Prunella and declares 'I'm Clive James, I've come to lionise you.'

After finishing with Prunella, he turns to lionise me. Says he liked 'Stalag Luft' and had not seen it the first time round, when he first wrote his *Ripping Yarns* review in *The Observer*. He would have re-reviewed it, but ... He said two revealing things. One being that the arts pages of most Sunday papers go to press on Friday afternoon – so programmes on Friday night (on which the *RY* repeats currently are) stand less chance of review than almost any other slot in the week.

I asked him why comedy got such short shrift in TV columns – and why Alan Coren should be so dismissive of *Ripping Yarns* after raving about *Tomkinson*. James put it down to jealousy. 'We all want to be doing your job,' he says. 'We can write and talk, but we're frustrated because we can't perform.' Interesting.

I take the plunge and ask Stephen Frears if he would be at all interested in directing a comedy special for NBC with me. To my intense enjoyment he says yes ... and I think the idea appeals to him.

Monday, May 22nd

With Spike's card facing me at my writing desk, and Stephen Frears' interest in the NBC special, I start this week with a stirring sense of optimism. So much could go wrong – the NBC special is still not a firm offer – but so much could, if it goes right, be some of the most exciting work I've done.

Today, after checking out my body – Alexander class at 8.50 – and my teeth at 11.30 – I drive over to the BBC to hear the verdict on our *Yarn* for July. Fairly predictably, 'Roger of the Raj' (as it's now known) is the one they're keen on. John Howard Davies, now Head of Comedy, doesn't like the 'child-molester' references, I hear.

Talk over the script with Jim F and the various points of rewriting to be done. It's a big cast, and I find myself stuck with Roger ... another juve lead!

Wednesday, May 24th

In to the BBC at 2.30 to help Jim audition young lads for the part of Roger as a young boy. One had a black eye, the other a sore throat and a magnificently irretractable Cockney accent, and only one was any good at all ...

Then more casting chat with Jim, mainly involving desultory turning of *Spotlight* pages. I want to aim high and suggest we try for someone like Ralph Richardson for the father. BBC Artists' Bookings are amazingly unimaginative as usual, and say Ralph Richardson will cost £1,000. The booker said, 'You know, he's almost ga-ga.' Anyone who can command £1,000 for a half-hour can't be entirely ga-ga.

Sir Michael Redgrave, another possible, is £200 cheaper than Sir Ralph, but Peter Lovell, the PA, said that when Sir Michael was doing a one-liner on Morecambe and Wise, he took eight takes to get it right. And there's a suggestion that he's 'not awfully well'. I stall Jim into letting me make my own enquiries. Refuse to be put off by BBC Artists' Bookings.

Back home, ring Tom Stoppard to check out Sir Ralph. Tom doesn't know him, but will ring Michael Codron, who put on Sir Ralph's last play, and test the water for me. So hopes are still high.

Thursday, May 25th

John Howard D is persisting in his objections to the words 'child molester' in the 'Roger of the Raj' script. Jim says I'll have to go and see him tomorrow. Also every avenue of exploration into the Sir Ralph situation seems fraught with money and Jim sounds as if he would rather drop the whole approach. Shall have to try and rally the troops tomorrow.

Friday, May 26th

Hot again. Into the sizzling silly season for the newspapers. The *Mirror* is pulling every stop out – even the weather – to try and boost Callaghan and the government before the election (not yet announced, but everyone thinks it's October). Callaghan is personally very popular at the moment and Thatcher is not. I think anyone with any information of substance must realise that Jim's good news basket is a very small one and all the signs are that the present drop in inflation (now down to 7.8%) and unemployment figures cannot be maintained.

Still, I'm better disposed to letting the present Labour government run my country for me than any other group – apart, perhaps, from Pan's People – and I feel better governed (in a moral, rather than material sense) than at any time for many years.

Over to the BBC. At least JHD doesn't attempt the economic argument to convince me why 'child molester' should be omitted. He tries hoary old chestnuts like 'What happens if a child is attacked that evening?' He tries the power approach, '*I* really can't let this sort of thing go out.' I absorb everything cheerfully and can only plead that every line is part of the creation of a vital character and is used in innocent reflectiveness for the purposes of getting a laugh. Which it will get. JHD cannot pull experience on me either. We are almost the same age. So he capitulates with, I think, mock-crossness, and I think he's not so bad after all. He's just frighteningly competitive, that's all.

Monday, May 29th

A thoroughly pleasant, though I suppose at times awkward, canal trip on Chris Orr's converted ice-breaker 'Scott'. The 'voyage' had been arranged by Robert, in order to get Chris and I talking about 'Arthur', his latest project, a story with lithograph illustrations. Chris needs up to £5,000 to get the project under way. The Arts Council and the Fraser Gallery have been approached – unsuccessfully.

I've read the book over the last week and am very disappointed. I found it loose, undisciplined – in short a mess of good ideas, bad ideas, in about 40–60 proportion. Am I getting old? Why do I feel exasperation with this 'experimental' style? If only Chris would pare it down to essentials – but I fear that the very diffusion of style is what's important to him.

Tuesday, June 6th

Ring Laurence Evans, Sir Ralph R's agent one last time. A lady assures me that he has all the details and has been trying to get in touch with Sir Ralph. This game has gone on for well over a week, and I still haven't even spoken to Laurence Evans.

I ring Lindsay Anderson. Lindsay is at his most charming and cheerful and, fortunately, helpful. He is interested to hear of my lack of success with Richardson's agents. 'They're shits,' he says, with feeling, 'and I should know – they're my agents as well.' He himself will ring Sir Ralph (an old friend) and mention my interest.

A little breakthrough. Lindsay calls back. He's spoken to Sir Ralph, who sounds to be available, and he has asked me to drop a script at Sir Ralph's house in Regent's Park.

Lindsay suggests that I give Sir Ralph a ring before dropping round – 'His wife will probably answer, but if you can get through her you're alright' – so I'm relieved but momentarily shaken to hear the familiar voice of Sir Ralph himself at the other end of the line. Would he mind if I brought him a script … ? 'No … no … by all means. I have my plaque up … "Actor available, no waiting …"' the great man assures me genially. 'I'll read it … Put your phone number on the bottom and I'll give you a ring.'

It's not often one speaks to a Living Legend – there aren't many left – and it takes me a while to come down from a slightly sweaty tremble of excitement. But in a cooler, more rational moment I remember what Lindsay had said – don't be apologetic, if you've got a good script, an actor will jump at it.

So, armed with a good script, and William, who's come along for the ride, I make my way to No. 1 Cumberland Terrace, the residence of Sir Ralph and Lady Richardson. It's on the end of one of Nash's impressive, classical terraces – full of ambassadors and burglar alarms. Lady Richardson answers the door and I hand her the script. Exchange of charming smiles and the door shuts.

Wednesday, June 7th

A crisp and efficient two-hour production meeting at the BBC. After we've been through the show and Jim is politely grumbling about the BBC, Sir Ralph phones and asks for me.

His voice has a chuckle in it. 'Yes … Yes …' says the Great Man. 'He's rather a nice old chap isn't he … rather charming …' He chuckles again. It's as if he's talking about himself, but I realise he's communicating cautious approval, enjoyment even, of the character of Lord Bartlesham. I mutter something solidly flattering (to both myself and Sir Ralph) about the character working on two or three different levels and that's why we need the best player we can get. He mutters and grunts and makes noises of distinct pleasure, but then says he's off to watch the Derby and we'd better ring his agent, who will be expecting a call. 'You see, I'd like to take my wife with me.' He promises to read the script again tonight and asks who will be Lady B. With that, our goodbyes.

It's not a great surprise when Jim rings a few hours later to say that despite the BBC stretching all its resources (!!) Laurence Evans has turned down the offer, explaining that, 'He likes a bit of luxury, you know.'

Thursday, June 8th

A patchy day of sun and cloud. Patchy in achievement too. John Le Mesurier evidently likes the 'Roger of the Raj' script so much that he's very happy to do a small part (Runciman). This encourages me, because I know he will be brilliant.

More encouragingly, I find that 'The Wreck of the Harvey Goldsmith' looks in good shape – an abundance of funny material (but an expensive show) and I start a new tale, 'Dracula at St Dominic's'.

TJ tells me Diana Quick can't do Judith in the *Life of Brian*, as she is committed to the RSC in the autumn. We are seeing a girl called Sue Jones-Davis tomorrow morning.

Friday, June 9th

Regent's Park bathed in sunshine as I drive down to Park Square West for the Python meeting. Terry J and John Goldstone are present. Eric didn't think it was worth coming. John is out of the country, evidently playing cricket in Corfu! Gilliam is still in France.

So TJ, myself and a very much slimmed-down Dr Chapman, meet Sue Jones-Davies. A tiny, boyish little Welsh lady with an upturned nose. Dressed in jeans and shirt – no frills. She reads Judith in a delightful Welsh accent. She's quite a tough and sparky little girl, and has a strong, open face, which should come across well in all the Judith v Brian close-ups. Not a versatile comedy lady like Gwen Taylor, but a good Judith we all think.

John Le Mesurier's agent rings to say he wants his full *Dad's Army* fee for playing the one-day cameo in 'Roger'. Jim will sort this out, though he's puzzled and rather cross about it.

Wednesday, June 14th

Have been reading extracts from Virginia Woolf's *A Writer's Diary*. How hard she worked at writing. What impossibly high standards she always seemed to set herself.

Sylvia Plath – another lady whose depth of perception and whose shining intelligence seemed to render her always more vulnerable than secure – expressed this in *The Bell-Jar*: 'I feel like a race horse in a world without race tracks.' In *Christopher and His Kind*, Isherwood expresses a less fraught attitude: 'Christopher said to himself that only those who are capable of silliness can be called truly intelligent.'

I'm with Isherwood.

Friday, June 16th

Complete a reading of the *Brian* script this morning, then drive down to Park Square West.

Keith Moon is unanimously voted into the rep company. John Young, the Historian in *Grail*, is unanimously voted in as Matthias, the largest single non-Python role in the movie. We can't agree yet on a Judith.

Eric's two songs – 'Otto' and the 'Look on the Bright Side' crucifixion song – are rather coolly received before lunch.

My suggestion of Ken Colley as Jesus is accepted nem con – thus solving quite a long-term problem. And the title is to be *Monty Python's Life of Brian* – not 'Brian of Nazareth' as GC and I liked, or 'Monty Python's Brian', as TJ suggested.

Thursday, June 22nd

Down to Donovan at lunchtime to surrender my false teeth, which will be 'reworked and reordered' for me to collect them tomorrow. Toothless, out into chill London.

Drive to a reception at the National Book League (again), this time for contributors to *The Writers' Book of Recipes*, which I had evidently replied to about fifteen months ago. At the cocktail party my letter is included in a hastily assembled display case – right next to one from Jan Morris.

I sauntered over and was, hopefully rather discreetly, glancing over my letter of 16th March '77, when a soft, rather deep, voice charmingly insinuated on my private gloat. Looked up to find myself confronted by a large lady with rather dry and unkempt wispy grey hair, which sat unsatisfactorily on a bold, square head. Kind, warm eyes, a generous mouth. An interesting, but rather disturbing face – fine and strong in the features, but messy in detail.

This was Jan Morris, who, as James Morris, wrote one of the travel books which most affected me – in fact one of my favourite books of all – that on Venice.

Jan said how much she'd enjoyed 'Across the Andes by Frog' – especially remarking on the way development heaped on development. I in turn gave a quick rave about Venice – the book.

Had this comfortable, tweedy lady really climbed the Himalayas as a man *and* written for *Rolling Stone* as a woman? This encounter was the high point of the cocktail party for *Recipes*, which seemed ironic as I had no teeth in.

Saturday, June 24th

TG drops by for some more chit-chat. He's more worried than ever about the words – the dialogue in his films, which he's always had an inferiority complex about – and is thinking of trying to make his new film tell its own story – like his animations – and be less 'written'. His dream sequence ideas sound great – especially the brick skyscrapers with no windows.

Wednesday, June 28th

Lorne Michaels called from the Savoy mid-afternoon. He'd arrived from New York just before lunch. Now recovered, he was making arrangements to meet. I would have liked to talk privately, but there were various people who wanted to have dinner with him, so we agreed to meet up at the Savoy around nine.

To the Savoy, where I find Lorne in a comfortable, but a little colourless suite with an impressive panoramic bay window view of Waterloo Bridge, the Thames, St Paul's and the City.

He thinks that I should consider spending six to eight weeks in the US each year and bring family, etc. This is the difficult area in our plans. It's one thing to do a special with freedom and money, but this freedom is going to be compromised in many little ways – and I fear the American exposure bit is one of them.

Thursday, June 29th

It's raining heavily as I set off for the Arlecchino restaurant in Notting Hill to meet Terry Hughes and Lorne Michaels for lunch. Lorne hasn't slept all night – but looks exactly as he always does and he talks rather more than usual, relishing a new audience. He drinks coffee, but little else.

Almost on cue, an American girl and her friend come across the restaurant and tell me how much they loved 'Across the Andes by Frog' – and with Terry there too. What timing.

About 3.30 we cram into my Mini and drive through the rain to the TV Centre. In Terry's office Lorne produces a tape of a Steve Martin *Saturday Night* show, which he's putting in for an award. Terry H disappears, and some time later, when we've finally got the BBC machine to work (this takes four or five people, secretaries, window cleaners, etc), Terry emerges from Jimmy Gilbert's office and, in an urgent whispered aside, tells us that Bruce Forsyth has just signed for ITV, and that Jimmy is in a state of utter confusion and trying to write a press release.

Eventually Lorne and I leave. I can't help finding it remarkable that, even with the Forsyth saga going on, the head of BBC Light Entertainment doesn't have time even to shake hands with one of the US's top LE producers – or top producers, period.

To the house Shelley Duvall has rented in Avenue Road, while she's working on *The Shining*. It's furnished like a luxury penthouse in a bad English 'B' movie, and I find myself feeling little envy for the sort of life which results in having to live for six months in such colourless, characterless transitory surroundings. Shelley says the ambassador for Ceylon lives next door, so she's alright for tea.

Shelley I like more and more. She's humorous, silly almost, direct and accessible and defiantly un-glamorous – and she loved 'Escape From Stalag Luft 112B' and my *Saturday Night* show!

Friday, June 30th

Drive to Shepperton for lunch with Graham Ford and Paul Olliver. The catering manager, whose guts I'm after at every board meeting, is most obsequious – offers me cod 'fresh caught from Grimsby' and whispers loudly how very much he enjoyed the *Ripping Yarns*.

Saturday, July 1st

A Python read-through at Anne's. We begin by trying to do the quiz in the 'Complete Monty Python' fan book. The questions are incredibly hard, and the entire team scores only 60% – on our own material!

Read-through a little stilted to start with. Graham has a long list of suggestions and each scene is rather heavily post-mortemed. Then we suddenly find three hours have gone by and Terry J hurries us all through. The state of the script isn't bad, but doubts are voiced about Judith's role (by Terry G) and Brian's. The usual arguments that they're rather dull parts – and as soon as we start to work on the Brian/Judith relationship we lose the comedy.

Indecision still over the casting of Judith. Gwen is good, but I feel Judith needs to be tougher, stronger, more dangerous than Gwen could ever be. We need a stroppy feminist with a sense of humour to play the role.[1]

Tuesday, July 4th, The Bull Inn, Bethersden, Kent

'Roger of the Raj' shoot begins. Meet Richard Vernon and Joan Sanderson at breakfast as well as Jim and co.

Richard and Joan haven't rehearsed together and it's only when we're in and sitting round the dining room table in this beautifully furnished Elizabethan manor house, with the sparks rigging the lights, that they have a chance to play the scene together. Joan tends to overplay, Richard to underplay, but they are both very willing listeners and extremely gentle, approachable folk.

Happy to be working again with this tight, efficient little unit and with the increasing feeling that the series now has acquired a much greater prestige than I thought (Joan Sanderson was telling me of its high reputation among 'the profession'), I feel as easy, confident, optimistic and relaxed as I can ever remember on filming.

---

1 After a few more auditions Sue Jones-Davies was confirmed in the role, and was brilliant.

Friday, July 7th, Bethersden

The pattern of filming now well established. Up at a quarter to eight, down to breakfast (coffee and grapefruit juice only) at eight o'clock. Various ablutions and bodily functions, then a ten-minute drive through Kentish fields to High Halden and down the long avenue of trees that leads to Harbourne Hall.

Here we have ensconced ourselves comfortably. The BBC has taken over, installing wires and cables and new shutters and blinds on the windows and palm trees and Edwardian lamps and cane tables and chairs. This is India for two weeks.

Today is the Regimental Dinner, for which several actors, including John Le Mesurier, have been imported, and the dark back room in the servants' quarters which houses Make-up and Wardrobe is overflowing.

John Le Mes, it transpires, is a great friend of Derek Taylor's, and Derek, who was taking a short break over here from his irksome life in Warner Bros, LA, had reassured John Le Mes that he was a great fan of the *Yarns*. So maybe Derek was instrumental in securing John.

The scene works marvellously. All the performances are strong and first rehearsal brings the house down. Of course the volume of laughter never greets the scene again, as we plod through it during the day, but the actors work hard to keep the freshness, despite all the technical delays and waits.

John Le Mes wears his slippers for the last shot. He doesn't drink any more now – after a bout of hepatitis – but chain-smokes instead. He looks physically frail, but his eyes are sharp, bright, lively and humorous.

Monday, July 10th, Bethersden

The last of our day shoots. From tomorrow until the end of the week we work all through the night.

Catch up a little today. But I feel that some of the ensemble work between Roger Brierley, Richard Vernon and Joan S lacks something – some spark. It's almost as though they're finding it too easy. So I'm up and jumping around and giving hints and encouragements whenever I can.

Jim is very good here and lets me work with the actors as much as I like. But I have the first feelings of irritation that the camera and lighting have once again set the pace, so that the actors tend to be forgotten –

expected to just turn on the right performance after waiting an hour for a shot to be lit. The priorities are becoming muddled. The show ultimately stands or falls on how good the actors are – and they need as much work as the lights.

Wednesday, July 12th, The Brecknock Arms, Bells Yew Green, East Sussex

I'm sitting alone in the small back garden of this unassuming little pub. There is no muzak, there are no coloured lights, or chairs and tables crafted crudely to the shape of bent tree bark. Just an iron table and comfortable but inelegant iron chairs, slatted with wood. And a pint of Harvey's best Sussex bitter, brewed in Lewes and looking very friendly with the sun shining through it. A blackbird or a song thrush, something very melodious, trills in the tree above me. Peace and solitude.

Last night's filming was hard work. Neighbours complained about rifle fire in the middle of the night and threatened us with an injunction (they know their rights down here) and this was even *before* Joan Sanderson opened up with her 1914 Lewis machine gun – the crack echoing around the whole of Kent, so it seemed, to such an extent that after the third or fourth round there was an impassioned cry from the black depths of the woodland – 'Shut up!' We finished at ten past four this morning.

Friday, July 14th

The final day of shooting on 'Roger'.

Back to Harbourne Hall for the last time. The Major and his wife appeared every now and then – the Major ruddy-faced, obviously enjoys a drink. I became aware, talking to him, of the pathos of their situation – both married for the second time – the children belong to Mrs F, not him – 'So we don't always see eye to eye.' He was in tanks at Alamein, the kids are on motorbikes in Tenterden. He looks blearily round at the huge, red bulk of the unattractive house behind him – 'It's always been a happy home.' He repeats this sadly, shaking his head. It's very moving.

At dawn we're gone, packed up, the cables stowed away and the house returns to normal. On Wednesday this 'happy home' is up for sale by auction. Major F talks of a bungalow in Bethersden they've got an eye on.

Wednesday, July 19th

Python medical today. More thorough than usual. Begins with a chest X-ray, then a visit to Dr Ronald Wilkinson, who holds my testicles and asks me to leave my urine in his bathroom. A girl takes a sample of my blood and a man sticks electrodes all over me for an electro-cardiograph test. Wilkinson reassures me that this all means I'm a much bigger property than when he last held my testicles.

The ECG man purred happily as he unravelled my reading. 'A very nice heart,' he pronounced.

Thursday, July 27th

Off to Ealing full of anticipation. My first look at the two weeks of pictures from 'Roger'. Instant disappointment on almost every front, except the look of it – costumes, colour, design, the house, etc. The performances of Lord and Lady B only adequate, the whole tale seems flatly paced and humourlessly edited. My role as Roger is another of those irritating, ingenuous younger sons which are in danger of becoming a real bore.

Even the regimental scene, a sure-fire winner, seems to be misfiring. There's a great deal of re-editing to do, and the first task is to establish a rapport with Dan Rae, the editor. He's tall and taciturn and rather likeable, but he begins by appearing to resent my suggestions.

This turns out to be defensiveness on both our parts. As we go systematically through the film (Jim F is away on holiday, so I have a free hand), both of us ease up. I realise that it was a shock to all my carefully nurtured pre-conceptions of the piece to see it for the first time through [cameraman] Reg Pope's and Jim Franklin's eyes, and Dan Rae has realised I am neither an unnaturally lugubrious old bugger, nor a stroppy writer who can't stand to see any editor touch his work. We carry on after lunch and when I leave at four Dan reckons he has four more days to do on tightens, corrections, re-positioning and finding new shots. Fingers crossed it will work then.

Friday, July 28th

First progress of any sort on the NBC special. Work on outlines for a new Robin Hood tale – the story of an insecure, nightmare-ridden, ex-hero, trying to live with his legendariness. At least there's a character there I'd like to play.

But writing up in my room today is like resting on an anthill. The children, plus friends, are all at home, there are four builders in No. 2 and, after lunch, Helen trying to grab some of the hot sunshine out on my balcony. I like my house and my family, but today the attractions of a quiet hotel room with just a bed and a typewriter flashed briefly, but poignantly across my mind.

Off to play squash with Terry and try to rid myself of this inability to produce brilliance. The game revives me.

Afterwards we pay a visit to Michael Henshaw.[1] Michael is anxious to talk over a tax-avoidance scheme to deal with the estimated £82,000 in foreign-earned money which we should be receiving as our full share of the performance fee on *Brian*.

An endearingly frank middle-aged man with greying hair and a lisp explains the scheme. It would involve Terry and me becoming a partnership, based on the island of Guernsey, with the aid of a Guernsey partner whom this man would find for us.

He was disarmingly open in acknowledging that there were risks. 'The worst that can happen is that after six years you may have to pay it all back,' he told us. 'What if it's all been spent on the houses and swimming pools it will enable us to have?' asked I. His reply was equally cheerful. 'You can always go bankrupt.'

A hot evening, but two pairs of cold feet as we left Michael's.

Friday, August 4th

To Dog's Ear Studio in Wapping, where Chris Orr was having an open day party to celebrate the completion of printing of the *Arthur* lithographs.[2]

London Docklands is a weird and wonderful place – a desert of empty warehouses and forlorn cranes frozen for ever in semi-tumescence. Dog's Ear is on the third floor of one of these warehouses. Dark and solid buildings where your footsteps echo from stout stone floors and ring through empty stairwells. Then the delight of the studio

---

1 Despite his separation from Anne, he was still, officially, the accountant for Terry and myself.
2 I'd decided, despite my earlier reservations, to publish *Arthur* through Signford Ltd.

itself – a long thin room of quite unusual scale, almost seventy yards long.

Chris is at the end of the room, setting bottles of wine out on a white-clothed table, and, as I walk down the room to him, my customary sense of proportion and perspective is quite thrown. I never normally spend this amount of time crossing a room.

At the far end and beyond the table is the wide river access and, three floors below, with no walkway or garden or patio to interrupt access, is the green-brown slosh of the Thames. A stunning location – and a more dramatic London setting for a studio it would be hard to imagine. I feel that the docks are, must surely be, about to undergo a renaissance. Already hotels are creeping down from Tower Bridge, and these strong, spacious warehouse buildings with the immeasurable asset of direct river access, will, in ten or twenty years, be full and busy again.

To add to the pleasure of the place there was also the satisfaction of seeing the fruits of Chris and friends' careful craftsmanship in the production of the lithographs. The end results were sharper, clearer and had much more impact on me than the original proofs.

Drove to the Savoy and there met Lorne (discreetly behind shades).

Lorne, en passant, muses on what it would be like if J Cleese and I were to do a show together … Now that would be a world-beater, he says, ever so gently.

Tuesday, August 8th

Out to dinner this evening with Anne Beatts – a *Saturday Night Live* writer who is over here – and Shelley Duvall, with whom she's staying. Helen came along too, reluctantly at first, for this was to be a rare evening at home. Shelley is good company, though, tells a good tale and has an effortlessly appealing warmth which wins over one's confidence easily. She's very sharp and intelligent – except for buying a very small and cross dog, which leaves little pools all over the carpet.

She's just had sixteen days off from *The Shining*, whilst Jack Nicholson's back recovered, but is now back on the 8.15 to 8 routine at Elstree. She very much wants to borrow my tape of 'Eric Olthwaite', which she raves about, to show Jack and Stanley. Now there's a thought.

Wednesday, August 9th

What a silly business I'm in. In what other walk of life would a 35-year-old company director be signing his tax return for the year whilst dressed as a Jewish shepherd? This was my first full fitting of the costumes for *Brian* – the project which will affect my tax bill more than anything else in the next couple of years.

Friday, August 18th

At the TV Centre for the dub of 'Roger of the Raj'.

A depressing day. The show still lacks the humour of 'Tomkinson' or the impact of 'Olthwaite', or the good old reassuringly familiar territory of 'Murder at Moorstones'. 'Roger' is quite an ambitious little script and needs to be very tight to work. It still is loose and lazy in vital areas – the acting, some of the lighting and the serious dearth of close-ups, which could have been used to great effect.

So today needed patience, time and tolerance. None of these seemed to be forthcoming from the dubbing editor. He was brisk, rather curt, and gave the whole session an unenjoyable and uncreative tension.

But the faster and less patient he became, the more I dug my heels in, voicing every suggestion and every tiny idea. Then at eight in the evening – after nearly ten hours' solid dubbing – it became obvious we'd need more time and, as the show wasn't due to go out until probably 1980, it seemed that such a thing wouldn't be out of the question! The editor suddenly brightened, admitted he was tired, and made various constructive suggestions that we should all have talked over at ten this morning when we started.

As had now become an almost annual event, we escaped for a few days to Mary and Edward's rural retreat in the Lot Valley.

Wednesday, August 30th, France

Woke at a quarter to eight and creaked my way downstairs as noiselessly as possible and pulled open the big, old, well-weathered wooden front door of the house.

The grass and the surrounding fields were in shade, as the sun does not mount the trees on the hill behind until nearly ten o'clock at this time of year. But it was dry, as it has been every day, and crisply cool. Not a breath of wind stirs the trees. The only sound is a distant dog barking and a very cod cock crowing. Everything feels fresh, clean and renewed.

Monsieur Crapaud, as we have christened the warty-backed toad who lives down in the bathroom, is easing his way around the shower floor – and we gaze at each other for a moment as I sit on the lavatory. Then he makes his stretched, rubbery way towards the door, where he hangs a sharp right turn and crawls under the washing machine.

Then into my white shorts, socks, gym shoes and 'Central Park' T-shirt from Macy's and begin my last pre-breakfast run. Up through the woods – an uphill start and very vicious – through gorse bushes on the path with freshly spun spiders' webs catching at my face. But the nearer I get to the top of the hill, the nearer I get to the sun and to the open ground.

Finally out of the gloom of oak and sweet chestnut saplings, beneath tall pines and into a sun-filled field of maize in hard red earth. Three times round this uneven rustic race-track (with three sprints), then down the far side of the hill and across a ridge covered in blue anemones, with copses and small, irregularly shaped, irregularly stocked fields of maize and vines and weeds and pasture, where sheep with bells graze on either side. And hillsides empty of buildings stretch away to the north-east and south-west, their colours softened by the subtle haze of morning sunshine.

I drank it all in today – my last run through this Elysian countryside for a year or more.

We've been in France for eight and a half days. The weather so warm, dry and settled that I estimate we spent 16 hours every day in the open air. They were commonplace and unremarkable holiday days. I wrote nothing and revelled in the complete lack of any vital tasks apart from those involved with day-to-day living.

Back home, it's very cold and there's a letter awaiting from Bryon Parkin[1] – the carbon of a letter to Lorne confirming that there is no way two of the *Ripping Yarns* can be sold to NBC for a special, as the contract with PBS has gone ahead.

1 Head of BBC Enterprises – sales arm of the BBC.

Thursday, August 31st

Down to 2 PSW for all-day session of rehearsal. Feel drained physically by five, when we break.

In the evening I try to rally my flagging resources to write letters, etc, and to think sensibly about the consequences of Bryon Parkin's letter about the *Yarns*. Lorne rings – he's equally depressed at the news, will call again in a week's time … We confirm once again the 'intent to work together'. Though when I stop and think about it, I've altered my perspective slightly after the stay in France. My scheme to retire at 40 and write and travel (write travel books – but decent, original, bright, funny ones) has been thrust well to the fore, the BBC has gone right to the bottom of the list and Python and Lorne float somewhere in between.

Saturday, September 2nd

I take William down to Covent Garden, where they're holding a two-day street festival. A genial, scruffy bunch of folk selling a lot of wholemeal bread and entertaining noisily and a little desperately in the shadow of the two big new office blocks that are rising up around them – showing that money, not good intentions, is still boss in Covent Garden, as in any other part of London.

But for the moment what's left of the Alternative Society is all here today, and I even catch a nostalgic whiff of grass – a smell of ten years ago, when people like this had never really been seen on the streets of London before. The middle classes letting their hair down and coping, in one way, with all the guilt their parents left them.

Thursday, September 7th

To Redwood by eleven to record a radio commercial – the first I've done for a couple of years. It was an anti-smoking radio commercial made (on a pittance, of course) for the Scottish Health Council. I had asked Charles McKeown[1] to come along and do it with me. Tony Herz of Radio Operators had written and was producing it. It's one of several in the campaign, part of an impossibly uphill struggle to try and make non-smoking as glamorous as smoking appears to be.

1 A versatile actor and writer who I'd met through David Leland. He appeared regularly in *Ripping Yarns*, as well as in a variety of roles in *Life of Brian*.

From Redwood down through Covent Garden and along Fleet Street to the offices of Methuen.

I talked myself rather rapidly into a one week book-signing, radio and TV promo-tour at the end of November. Suggested that we had a theme for the tour that was pertinent to the book – something like an expedition. This was eagerly taken up by Jan Hopcraft [the publicity manager], and hardened into Round Britain By Frog – the Palin/Jones expedition to British bookshops 1978. I hope this won't sound too wet by November. But I made them promise to avoid extreme efforts at wackiness.

Saw some proofs of the book (artwork included) – enough to give me encouragement that at least we will be publicising and signing a well-made article. Will anybody come along, though? Nightmare vision of sitting in bookshops waiting for someone, having to resort to low methods of accosting passers-by.

To Robin Simmons for a quick Alexander reminder. Already feel myself tending to stiffen up in anticipation of the excitement of Tunisia, so must remember what I've learnt.

Sunday, September 10th

As a result of having time last week to plan for Le Grand Depart, this morning's leave-taking is easier, emotionally and physically, than some I can remember.

It's almost a psychic phenomenon, my departures, for some sixth sense seems to inform the 'villagers' that something is about to happen and, as I try discreetly to slip away, doors open and cars drive up and the place is soon like a stadium. Today they weren't let down. An enormous American limousine, of the low, interminably long, black New York variety, swung into the village, and out stepped Dr Chapman in immaculate light grey suit, and matching it, and creating the final and complete effect of flamboyant elegance – nay, even stardom – was a light grey fedora. Never, outside of a sketch, have I seen the Doctor looking quite as dashing.

My last memory of the children is of Tom, Willy, Rachel (in Helen's arms), Holly, Catherine, Louise and Helen Guedalla forming a tableau in the back window of the Cadillac. It felt like an archetypal image of the native son off to the big city to find fame and fortune. Except he wouldn't have left in a Cadillac.

We went on to Eric's, and I realised that these vast cars are designed to make the occupants look important, rather than to take on goods and chattels. So, despite being twice as long as any other non-goods vehicle on the road, we still had to go through a minor comedy routine with the cases.

Graham had by this time taken his hat off, and looked less jaunty. Through growing clouds of pipe smoke he told me, a little apologetically, that he'd only bought the suit because he was going to take a tax year out of the country (and this was the first day).

Eric has equally positively decided to move out of London, though only as far as the outer commuter countryside – Oxfordshire, possibly – 'to be near George [Harrison] and near London'. He talks of the country wistfully now, as if drawn to it as the next inevitable step in his development.

I had nothing to equal such hefty decisions.

Graham and I talked of Keith Moon, who was to have been in the movie and flying out soon to join us, but who died some time on Thursday night, after a party. Graham, whose abstention from alcohol has increased his appeal a hundred per cent – he now sounds like, as well as looks like a very wise old owl – told me that Keith was trying to cut down his Rabelaisian appetite for booze, and had some pills called Heminevrin to help out, but these should be taken under carefully controlled conditions and never with alcohol – for they act to increase the strength of anything you *do* drink.

So Keith had just gone too far and, although his whole life was lived constantly up to the limits, this time, like an adventurous schoolboy on a frozen pond, he'd stepped a little too far out. What a waste. But GC reckons both Peter Cook and Ringo S are also in trouble with booze.

A long taxi drive from Tunis to Monastir as night fell. Impressions of aridity, emptiness, scrubland stretching away on either side of the road. A camel train tottering, or rather swaying, in that peculiarly restful camel motion, along a dried up river bed.

The villages we pass through are reminiscent of Ireland or Cyprus – not neat and tidy Best Kept Village candidates as in France, Germany or Britain, but collections of houses built as basically as possible to provide shelter for men, women, children and their animals. No time or money for grass verges or floral clocks here.

To the Hotel Meridien by eight. It's large, new and comfortable – as different from those villages as England is from the moon. An international standard of comfort and atmosphere, protecting the Overdeveloped from the Underdeveloped.

The bed is comfortable and the room has no fewer than three balconies with views out over the sea – which sounds near. Unpack and drift off to sleep about two o'clock. Almost my last memory is of Rachel sitting in my bed this morning and asking 'Where are you going today, Daddy?'

'Africa, darling.'

Monday, September 11th, Hotel Meridien, Monastir, Tunisia

Looking through the script, it strikes me, not for the first time, that the schedule is very full indeed. A long and ambitious film to be squeezed into the eight-week shoot we have planned. Can't help but feel that some scenes will be trimmed or cut altogether.

Lunch on the terrace of the Sidi Mansour Hotel, where TJ, TG and most of the crew are staying. Terry J was struck down by some metabolic demon in the night and is still in a very delicate state. The art director, Roger Christian, is in bed with sunstroke, and Doctor Chapman, with his napkin draped over his head as an improvised sunshield, has already been called upon to dispense from the apothecary's treasure trove he brought out with him yesterday.

Graham claims to have seen a hoarding advertising a film about my old school called 'The 12 Salopians'. It turns out to be *Les Douze Salopes, The Dirty Dozen*.[1]

In the afternoon we walk around the Ribat – the old fort of Monastir, now a public monument. It's built of very light, almost golden, local sandstone, and the innumerable dark passageways and steep stone stairs leading to doorways and more stairs and passages is reminiscent of Doune Castle. Terry J shows us as many of the locations as he can before his bowels seize up again and he is rushed away by Graham.

To the Café de la Plage at Coq Égyptien – known to all as the Coq. This is local, not international, and lacks air-conditioning and imitation leather carte des vins and other trappings of international hotel life.

---

1 Gung-ho US war film of 1967, directed by Robert Aldrich and starring Lee Marvin and Charles Bronson. It was marketed with the tag-line, 'Train Them! Excite Them! Arm Them! … Then Turn Them Loose on the Nazis.'

Instead it has peeling, pink-painted walls, decorated with rather shrine-like devotional pictures.

Fish were brought round on a tray and we selected those we wanted. As usual with any group of eight foreigners in an ethnic stronghold like the Coq, we probably made the waiter's life unbearably complicated, but he was tolerant about the whole thing.

Wednesday, September 13th, Monastir

The Meridien has an atmosphere of almost eerie spaciousness. Lights are lit around empty swimming pools. Wide new tiled corridors, discreetly lit and elegantly dotted with well-chosen chairs and sofas, lead into empty hallways where immaculately turned-out staff can be found at doors and behind desks. It's a perfect relaxation from the Sidi Mansour, though, and I enjoy an hour's guilt-free read of a Kingsley Amis (*The Green Man*).

A phone call from John Goldstone and Terry J to see if I could exert pressure on John to agree to shooting the stoning sequence on Saturday. Tim Hampton had suggested we start two days early as all the crew were here and ready to go, and it would give us an invaluable extra day in the packed schedule.

John stuck to an awkward stance – that we could indeed do the day, but he wasn't going to endanger a 'major' comedy scene like the stoning on a first day. Some sense there. But, as we rehearsed it today, it seemed not only easier to shoot than perhaps we'd feared but, even at this stage, very funny. I don't think delay will help it. Anyway, I told Goldstone to ring John himself.

At dinner John told me of the call and expounded what he called The Cleese Theory of Convenience. I think, roughly précised, it means that everyone will do only what's most convenient for them – and if you want things done your way you must not appear too agreeable or easy to please, or you will be the victim of other people's desire for convenience.

John and I consumed a bottle and a half of a fine, big Tunisian red wine, then back in John's room – seemingly full of underpants and duty-free bottles of spirits – we took a slightly woozy, but thorough, look at the Pilate scenes.

Thursday, September 14th, Monastir

Woken at 8.15 by Terry Gilliam who, with a construction team waiting, was anxious to have the latest on whether JC was prepared to do the stoning scene – for stones and rocks have to be made today. Able to reassure him that John was only pursuing the Cleese Theory of Convenience.

After rehearsals we go up to the Ribat for a photo-call for a *Variety* ad to herald the start of shooting. Nostalgia time. John was dressed in his Pacamac as Praline,[1] complete with dead parrot. Terry had drag on and a huge lipstick smudge across his lower face. Graham C was in his Colonel's outfit – which hangs off him now he's lost weight! Eric was in spangly jacket and I was in knotted handkerchief. And here we were photographed against mosques and palm trees. The past catching up with the present.

Saturday, September 16th, Monastir

The first day of filming.

Woke early, listening for JC rising early in the room above. He was called for seven, after a decision reached last week that we should start early and have as much time off as possible in the heat of the middle of the day. We have to finish before six, when we lose the light.

Went for a swim in the hotel pool – which was cool and invigorating – and shaved close (I have to play a woman today) with great care, packed an (Indian) bag full of script, towel, swimming trunks, black notebook and 1930 Macmillan edition of Hardy's *Tess of the D'Urbervilles* (part of my cultural survival kit) and drove in my little grey Renault 5 along the road across the salt flats, past Monastir Airport, past Bourguiba's summer palace, through the plywood triumphal arches, taking great care to avoid bicycles, wandering old men and dozens of women, bottle-shaped in their white chadors. Finally turned sharply left in the direction of the bright, white, elegantly simple and unadorned lines of the Ribat – and its false sister building (built by Zeffirelli for *Jesus of Nazareth*), which stands rather impertinently beside it.

A take has just begun, and John Young, dressed in loin cloth, is being

1 Mr Praline was the name John gave to his man in the plastic mac.

dragged to the stoning yard beneath the outer walls of the Ribat by a wonderfully dressed, swirling crowd. It's an impressive, exciting, authentic Biblical crowd – and more than anything today gave me a sharp boost of confidence. This film really could be impressive.

A crowd of ladies in beards has been assembled from a nucleus of our rep company, Tunisian actresses, Tunisian non-actresses and several people from Manchester who are on holiday.

John C is a little stiff in his early performances, but loosens up as he realises it's going to be rather good. John Young is wonderful. As JC says, though, at the end of the day, considering this is the first day of principal photography on a 'major motion picture', there's no sense of occasion, we just get on with it. Terry J hops about in a businesslike way, and doesn't exude any of the egomania of the Great Director. Peter Biziou[1] and John Stanier (camera operator on *Midnight Express*) are equally efficient and unflamboyant.

Then later in the afternoon the camera breaks down. Could this become a traditional feature of Python first days?

I change and, while a huge stone is being dropped on John Cleese, go into the Ribat and work over my words for the Pilate scene on Wednesday. Then I sit in the rather calming air-conditioned comfort of the caravan and learn some of the Shepherds scene.

In the evening back to the Meridien to change, then out to eat at the Coq with Terry J, Peter and Cristina [Peter's partner] and Gwen [Taylor] and Andrew McLachlan.[2] Drink rather a lot of wine and end up plunging into the sea starkers at midnight. A small but lecherous crowd of Tunisians gathers to watch and, as we walk away, a young boy offers us 40 dinars for an English girl who happens to be the girlfriend of Garth Marshall, our sound recordist. Then later offers me the services of a young man 'only just down the road'.

Sunday, September 17th, Monastir

Breakfast out on my balcony. Early light cloud disperses by mid-morning. Write various postcards and ring Helen and talk to the kids. Of course I miss them, but because of the holiday in France and the fact that this was all planned so long ago, I think we're all adjusted to being

1 Director of Photography – also for, among others, *Bugsy Malone*, *Mississippi Burning* and *The Truman Show*.
2 Friend of Terry J's from Oxford and another of our rep. company.

apart, so it's just good to hear them – not at all painful – apart from Willy, whose chief topic of conversation is that he's just been hit on the head by Rachel.

A walk up the beach and a swim before lunch. Then afterwards feet up and an hour's read of *Tess of the D'Urbervilles*. Hardy travels well. His stories especially suit Tunisia, a country with still much of the slow pace and time for social intercourse that Hardy regretfully saw passing in Dorset.

In the evening, two friends of Eric and Tania – Anjelica Huston and Nona Summers – arrived from London, bringing Sunday papers, which we grabbed from them avidly. Wine up on the balcony in Eric's suite and briks (local speciality – a crispy pancake enclosing usually egg and tuna – a sort of Tunisian equivalent of the hamburger).

Monday, September 18th, Monastir

Woke early – around seven – but snoozed fitfully until 8.30, having, in wonderful solitude, read *Tess*, and tried some Pilate oratory for Wednesday. I can really bellow here, and am happily screaming something like 'This man wanks as high as any in Wome', when, out of the emptiness, a young Arab on a bicycle appears. He cycles, slowly, warily, past me for a moment, then, after he's put in a suitable distance, he takes one last look and cycles off like a man possessed.

Enthusiastically closing the day with some press-ups, feel a muscle go in my back. Curse my luck.

Tuesday, September 19th, Monastir

Called today to be Francis crawling through tunnels on the way to capture Pilate's wife, but late enough for me to have a swim, breakfast and a read before going in. My pulled muscle, or whatever, was still painful enough in the night to jolt me awake two or three times, but seems no worse this morning.

What finally cures my back is two or three hours of very uncomfortable work in the tunnels.

We filmed on until seven, when the last platoon of Roman soldiers had tramped over our heads. Back at the hotel Graham gave me some back rub – but it all feels much better after the mini outward-bound course.

Graham is rapidly becoming a saint. He's been treating so many people in the unit – and now he's stopped drinking he has time to do his medical work properly, and the ability to do it without shaking or dropping whatever he's about to stick in you. In the evenings Graham does his rounds, with pills and rubs and words of reassurance.

Apart from his medical activities, he's sharp on his words and, from being a rather disconcerting influence on previous Python epics, he's now become a model of co-operation and efficiency, and his avuncular presence is calm and reassuring. In fact John today suggested that Graham was reminding him more and more of a vicar.

Wednesday, September 20th, Monastir

Up at six, and on the road to Monastir by six-thirty. My first really testing day – the Pilate Forum speech.

I know that I have to beware of factors such as being overawed by the scale and size of this particular movie. I have to try and forget previous successes or failures. I have to feel light and bright and free of any diversionary anxieties.

Well today, as I drive across the salt and mud flats, with the sun low above the eastern horizon, casting a bright golden glow hard into my eyes, I feel good and prepared and just downright happy to be performing again. So the morning goes well, except that it is possibly the hottest, least windy day yet and out on our rostrum it becomes almost unbearable.

But we cover everything bar John's close-ups, then bring in the Tunisian crowd, whom we have heard outside the walls of the Ribat learning to shout 'We want Wodewick!'

They are marvellous and it's a tremendous confidence boost for the rest of the filming, for at one time the difficulties of teaching Python techniques to a crowd of Tunisians seemed almost insuperable. However, today, Terry J has this mixed bunch of Arab students, peasants, grandmothers, mothers with babes in arms, old men with missing noses, middle-aged men with almost leprous skin, lying on their backs and waggling their feet in the air. They find no trouble in jeering at the posturings of the Roman Empire, and seem to enjoy it immensely.

I talked yesterday with Mahomet, who is one of our Tunisian extras, and was one of the raiders in the tunnel. He belongs to a theatre group in Mahdia, and much of their work is critical of the status quo in

Tunisia. 'Anti-Bourguiba?' I asked. He shushed me quickly. 'You can end up in prison saying things like that.'

Mahomet is a Tunisian nationalist of a different sort from Habib Bourguiba, whose likeness adorns the road into the town in twenty-foot-high posters. Mahomet wants Tunisia to be independent on its own terms and by virtue of its own resources. He's not a pan-Arab, and he certainly does not approve of independence based on dependence on America, Europe or Russia.

We took a late lunch – I managed a swim at the Sidi Mansour pool – and were back at three for more crowd reactions. Terry J won them over with a masterly display of co-suffering. He ran and jumped and grinned and lay on his back for them, and I could feel a great Celtic–Tunisian bond being formed.

In an excess of zeal tonight I crack the top of my dental plate whilst cleaning it.

Thursday, September 21st, Monastir

Back on our imperial rostrum again this morning.

One of the great delights is playing with John on his close-ups. John is, on a good night, one of the world's great corpsers, and today I have the rare luxury of being able to try and corpse him absolutely legitimately. On one take he is unable to speak for almost half a minute.

Drive back with JC. We take a bedtime Armagnac in my room and I bore him with a monologue about my novel. JC doesn't think he could write one. His mind tends to the factual and informative, he says – he feels he can't reproduce or create atmosphere.

Friday, September 22nd, Monastir

At the location by eight to provide off-camera lines for the crowd at Mandy's house, which is located in a busy corner of the Ribat, dressed to give the feeling of a Jerusalem tenement block of AD33. Lots of Gilliam detail. Full of Arabs, it really looks amazingly good.

Graham gives us a few full-frontals early on. He does pose rather well – probably an unconscious result of many years' absorption in gay mags.

As well as our ever-enthusiastic crowd of Arabs, we also have some English tourists, rounded up from nearby hotels and referred to by various collective nouns – the 'Clarksons', the 'Cosmos'.

I was asking our patient, hard-working Arab assistant director, who has the unenviable task of explaining Terry's instructions, how the locals were assembled. Apparently some are students and others just villagers, recruited after a tour of the surrounding areas in which the assistant director, as he told me, 'explained Python to them'. That must be worth some sort of award.

Terry J's method of teaching an Arab crowd to speak English is quite a phenomenon ... He was pressed for time, admittedly, but the Jones technique went something like this ...

'Let's try it then ... "We are all individuals".'

The good-natured, completely baffled Arabs mimic Terry as best they can.

Terry: 'Good ...! Good ... you've nearly got it ... Once more, "We are all individuals".'

Arab noise.

Terry: 'Very good! Now let's try "Yes, we must decide everything for ourselves".'

Economic note: the Arab extras get 3 dinars per day (£3.50), plus a loaf of bread and a tin of sardines at lunchtime. We are getting about a thousand pounds per filming day, plus accommodation at a first class hotel and a lunch from the Italian caterers which will be a choice of spaghetti, ravioli, steak, veal, omelette, salad and fresh fruit. At the Hotel Meridien, pride of Air France's new hotels, the Arab who comes to turn my bed back in the evening gets one dinar 500 millimes per day.

Avoid an invitation to a spaghetti party this evening – Signor Memmo, the caterer, is challenging Achmed, our Arab production head, to a spaghetti-making contest. My voice is strained after two days as Pilate and today's efforts, so I will rest it before the Ex-Leper tomorrow.

Eat in the gloomy Meridien restaurant. But food good, and fall to talking with John about relationships. John has been going to therapy groups for two or three years. Says he finds most of those present are Jewish couples. He seems to be very conscious of the fact that his mother gave him very little affection. He was always close to his father.

However, he has a very good relationship with the head waiter. I found that the reason was that John had given him ten Mogadon, as the man hadn't slept properly for a month. Now he's eating out of JC's hand.

Saturday, September 23rd, Monastir

At the make-up house at seven to prepare for the Ex-Leper. He's supposed to look golden, tanned, muscular and fit, and I must say, as a result of my recent sun-bathing, plenty of swimming and running through French woods and along Tunisian beaches, I don't look too bad. Certainly in better shape than for a while, and mentally congratulating myself for having coped with the food over these first two weeks without any recourse to pills, potions or other medicaments. This seems to be an increasingly rare thing on the unit.

On the set, I realise how much of an ivory tower I am in at the Meridien – and such detachment surely does not behove a diarist. I missed, for instance, the scenes after Pilate's filming. Apparently there were near riots as people struggled to make sure they got their 3 dinars. On Friday morning Terry J's car was chased by hopeful extras as he left the hotel.

Also I missed (thankfully) the sparks' excesses at the spaghetti party, when a specially prepared giant cake was thrown at the wall. They can't stand any form of lack of excess.

This evening we are invited to a cocktail do by the Tunisian Minister of Tourism. Drive round to the Skanes Palace Hotel at 7.30. Cosier decor than the Meridien, but still in the International Modern Airport style. First thing I see is one of the chippies with a sticker across his forehead and the word 'English' on it, looking dangerously provocative, but it all passes off without incident.

Monday, September 25th, Monastir

Up at 7.30. Swim, breakfast in room. See John C leaving. He says, ominously, that although he's not in today's scenes, he is going to 'help out' behind camera. John Goldstone is worried about TJ's unshakeable commitment to full-frontals in the Mandy/Brian bedroom scene. Says he's talked to John about it. So that's why John's gone in.

Arrive on set to find a harassed Terry J. He's not pleased at John's interference today – words have been changed at the last minute. By the pool at the Sidi M, over lunch, TJ, GC both feel very tensed up by John's presence 'behind the camera'. The first sign of any serious split in the Python ranks.

There's little danger from Eric, who keeps himself very much to himself and will not get into costume unless he's absolutely certain that he will be seen. The lengths to which he has to go to preserve this elusiveness would seem to me hardly worth the strain.

I actually enjoy a fairly unrewarding afternoon as a revolutionary creeping up smoky passages – and have pleasant chats with Bernard [McKenna] and Andrew and others. We shoot till six in conditions of increasing discomfort.

Tuesday, September 26th, Monastir

Long, complicated, but unusually vivid dreams these nights. Last night I was in a jumbo jet flying from Australia to London, in which there were rooms, pillared, columned and lavishly spacious – rather like those of Heron Bay. I wasn't feeling well, and Graham diagnosed measles. I remember thinking it could be a three- or four-week break in the schedule – but Graham said he'd give me some special stuff, which, provided I kept out of everyone's way for a few days, would put me right. I was then confined to the bulbous interior of a cargo aircraft's nose, surrounded by blocks of ice.

Was promised a day off today and, after a swim, settle to a longer than usual breakfast in my room of two very tastily fried eggs, fruit juice, croissant and coffee. Talk briefly to the dear, dark-eyed lady at reception, who always replies to one's 'Thank you' with a disturbingly cheery 'Never mind'.

Then I'm called in and sit in the caravan in a full beard and wig make-up until lunch, when, still not used, I strip it all off and take to the pool, where GC is relaxing after his usual busy morning. Medical work is running acting very close as Graham's chief activity these days – even at the poolside today he was approached by the stills photographer's wife with a raging sore throat, Terry J with a sore throat and Peter Biziou on behalf of Cristina, who is ill in bed.

This afternoon hang around, but am still not used. However, finish *Tess of the D'Urbervilles* and begin *Vile Bodies* before a rather cool and buffeting wind drives me off the poolside and down to the bar of the Sidi.

For the first time since our arrival, found myself drinking out of sheer laziness and, as more and more people wandered into the bar, I could hardly be bothered to get out of the way of about four beers and, two hours later, a group of us spilled over to the Coq for briks and things.

Today has shown signs of strain in the unit. Terry G is worried that TJ is driving everyone along at such a frenetic pace that he isn't leaving enough time to get the best shots. Gilliam is especially irked that the elaborately splendid detail of his market place is not being seen. He keeps muttering that this might as well have been done at Shepperton for two million less.

Thursday, September 28th, Monastir

Boring Prophet morning for me. Quite exhilarating as had to ad-lib most of the dull, droning speech. We did four or five takes and I tried to, or rather felt compelled to, make it a little different each time. Terry G spends most of the day coated in mud and does another of his extraordinary and grotesque gargoylical performances – this time as a Blood and Thunder Prophet.

I'm through by three and, feeling oppressed by the layers of dirt – mainly fuller's earth and the less wholesome aerosol spray – which attend nearly all my characters, I soak some of it off in the sea. A fresh north-west wind has blown everyone off the beaches and left empty deck chairs whose canvases now flap and slap violently in the wind, as if repelling unseen occupants.

Tonight at rushes (one and a half hours' worth) my chief worry is the Ex-Leper. The dancing, prancing, gum-chewing character seems to go down well enough, but he looks like a cross between Tarzan and Geronimo – and somehow this detracts from the impact of the scene. As TJ says, he's the only character so far who has looked out of period. The Terrys agree, and a reshoot of this end part of the scene is scheduled for tomorrow.

Dinner at the Sidi Mansour with the British Ambassador and his wife. A special menu, fresh flowers, champagne and lines of various shaped glasses adorn the table. No ethnic music, fortunately.

Sit next to Mrs Ambassador. A plummy-voiced, not unattractive lady a hand taller than her husband. She speaks with lazy confidence and I marvel at how very British she is – she manages to sound and look more like a bishop's wife on a four-day visit to Tunisia, than someone who's been here a year. Not a trace of tan, or any real enthusiasm for things Tunisian.

She was not unkind, but the very nature of her language and way of expressing herself produced some treasured lines … 'Do you know, our gardeners, every night, whenever they go home …' I wait with bated breath for the revelation, '… always take a little bunch of weeds with them.' She was referring to the Tunisian habit of not wasting anything. She was also good on not 'spoiling the local people'. Her example was not giving them the best Fortnum and Mason tea, 'which they probably wouldn't like anyway'.

Friday, September 29th, Monastir

A hard last day of the week. Into the small Ribat today, where a hypocaust has been constructed which is even harder to walk through than the tunnel. It's very hot, too, and besides being encumbered with extraordinarily clumsy props, there's an almost stifling smell of incense[1] inside the tunnels.

A BBC film unit arrive to shoot us. They look a sad little group – white and flabby and rather down at heel. Makes me aware how well we all must look after three weeks of sunshine out here.

Swim in the sea at lunchtime. Re-do the Ex-Leper ending afterwards. All sorts of things go wrong – a plane flies over, the BBC camera crew get in shot, the Ribat lavatory attendant gets in shot, an extra called Mahomet wanders in and out of shot at unpredictable moments, as no one takes the trouble really to explain things to him.

Terry G keeps strewing the ground where I'm standing for the Ex-Leper with scatterings of sheep's legs, squashed water melons and foul-smelling water around which the flies gather.

Then back to crouch in the tunnel again as Francis. John Stanier, the operator, says it isn't nearly as bad as filming forty feet down in a water-filled sewer in *Midnight Express*. This cheers me a little. It's now after seven and darkness has fallen on the Ribat. Final massive shot of the wall being cleaned at night. Comradeliness of night-shooting compensates for feeling of discomfort caused by dirt, very uncomfortable gear and cold wind.

Sunday, October 1st, Monastir

Beside the sea an Arab boy is striking a recalcitrant camel with a stick. Big, swinging blows directed at the head. Have noticed before that there

---

1 At this time, church incense smoke was regularly used by directors to create a diffused light. Later it was proved to be dangerous to health.

are some quite vicious camel and donkey punishers plying the Corniche. Tania once saw an elderly man striking an even more elderly and wretched horse with such force that it fell on to its side, whereupon he began to kick it. Tania (ex of Bronx Zoo, and as fine an example of how to treat God's creatures well as you could wish to find) ran up and remonstrated with him.

The hotel is quiet. Tim Hampton [our line producer] arrives at five to eleven with his four-year-old son Piers to play tennis with me in the Python competition.

Our tennis match, on a rough-textured, dusty court, surrounded by palms and reminiscent of Barbados, lasted for nearly one and a half hours in punishing heat. Neither of us could serve very well, but we played comfortable, if unexciting rallies – and took almost every game to deuce. Tim, an awfully pleasant and well-mannered chap, was a gallant loser – and I a winner only by consistent mediocrity and once holding my serve.

Woken at a quarter to one by flashes. A violent storm passes down the coast. Almost continuous blue, yellow flashes and hotel-splitting cracks of thunder. And torrents of rain.

Monday, October 2nd, Monastir

Wake at six. Today we're at Sousse, filming outside the city walls, where Zeffirelli filmed his crucifixion scenes. The day doesn't look promising. Though it's not actually raining, the countryside is waterlogged and the sky much cloudier than usual. It's cooler too.

The opening shot (of Mandy and Brian) seems to take forever, and I sit around, half-naked, made up as the Ex-Leper. I've even been evicted from my caravan, which is being used as a make-up base for extra lepers. An hour and a half before I'm used – leaping up, bronzed and fit, from a crowd of lepers at the city gates. Eric is quite impressed by my Steve Reeves-ish torso.

No sooner is the leper shot done, than the heavens open and a steady, unspectacular rainfall begins. The clouds merge into a single leaden sky, and Sousse, and its ancient and impressive castle walls, becomes Yorkshire or Scotland or Dartmoor.

I share Eric's caravan. Gwen, Eric and I natter. Eric takes a cluster of health pills – a small handful from a little pill box with compartments. Discover Gwen has three names – Allsop, Blount and Taylor. The first her real one, the second her married name, the third her adopted stage name. She worked in a bank for eight years before going to Stratford East Drama School, married a toolmaker called Fred Blount, who had a habit of obsessive hand-washing, and whom she divorced partly for this reason.

Eric told of his father, who was killed in the war when Eric was two. He was an RAF gunner – killed in a car accident whilst on Christmas leave. Which was why Christmas was never a very happy time at the Idles'.

Jonathan Benson (our genial, well-bred assistant director, who is writing a screenplay about the Lord Lucan affair) chimed in here, without a trace of anger or even malice, 'I went to the pictures the night my old man died. He was a judge. We were glad to get rid of him ...'

John Cleese was judging a flower show near Weston-super-Mare as his father was dying. He didn't know whether to cancel or not – and felt he couldn't let them down.

Tuesday, October 3rd, Monastir

The schedule has been rearranged and much of my heaviest work will now be when Helen and the children are here. The weather seems to be more settled this morning, but it rained again in the night.

After rushes last night I sat up talking with Anjelica Huston who told me of their experiences down in the desert. It sounds depressing – things you don't expect, like the oases, which look beautiful, but on closer inspection are littered with plastic detritus and cotton wool swabs. And flies which cluster at nose and mouth and every other orifice within a matter of seconds.

We talked over Armagnac for a couple of hours. She's one of those people I feel instantly at ease with. She's articulate, but has a certain quality of apologetic nervousness.

She talked about her dad, John Huston, and the childhood in Ireland – which sounded almost perfect – not only comfort and space and horses to ride, but also a steady stream of visitors like Brando and William Wyler and Katharine Hepburn – many of whom used her to get through to her father.

Then father and mother split and she didn't see a lot of him and, for a while, was 'kind of scared of him'. Now he's living in Mexico, still making plans for movies, though he's had a serious operation. He acts, but has great contempt for actor's bullshit. He likes Jack [Nicholson], she said with a smile, and would quite like her to marry him … She laughed, as if appreciating the thought, but having no intention of acting on it.

Then there was more lightning to entertain us and more Armagnac and I began to talk about Python. Then she suddenly got up and said she ought to go – and we exchanged a polite kiss – the Armagnac had not altogether overcome a hint of attractive awkwardness in her as we said goodbye.

First thing this morning, the BBC filmed Eric, John and myself getting ready. John shows them his hair transplant and I show them how my dentures no longer seem to fit.

Then a rather jolly day inside Matthias' room as plotting revolutionaries. Everyone on good form and much improvised joking. At lunchtime a meeting with John G and Anne H.

The subject of EMI's settlement came up. They are talking of offering us something by way of recompense but would probably insist on a secrecy clause. John C resisted this idea for a bit, but when told that the alternative was a possible two-year wait for a court hearing, he agreed quite sharply.

Drove back to the hotel with JC. I took him a silly route through the car park which he enjoyed so much I had to drive him round again – in and out of narrow gaps, tightly round trees, almost on two wheels. He really enjoyed it and seemed genuinely impressed that I could drive like that! I know John can only drive automatics, but I didn't know he couldn't go round corners.

No rushes tonight as the projector has broken down, so avoid the rather cloying atmosphere of the unit-filled bar at the Sidi and go out to the Coq with the two Terrys and Anne and Rachel Henshaw.

The quiet shattered by the arrival of Spike Milligan! Spike is staying at the Skanes Palace for a two-week holiday, revisiting Second World War battlefields.

Relaxed a little by the wine, he starts to treat the assembled throng – Chris Langham,[1] Carol Cleveland, Andrew McLachlan, Anne H, Rachel and myself – to Milligan's potted précis of 'Tomkinson's Schooldays' (he's another fan of the school leopard line – which must be one of the most enduring last-minute ad-libs I ever came up with!), and the

---

1 Chris Langham, another of our rep. company and partner of Sue Jones-Davies who played Judith.

Yorkshire tale, and then 'Parrot Sketch' (the Norwegian Blue becomes the Arctic Grey, as Spike tells it).

Wednesday, October 4th, Monastir

A long and arduous morning in Matthias' house. John Stanier is strapped into his Steadicam harness, which makes him look like a walking dentist's console.

John C takes Reg at a frenetic pitch, which loses all the nuances that had us rolling about in rehearsal. John becomes hot, tired and rather touchy as he tries to relax into the performance.

We slog on for three hours solid. There are no tea breaks as such out here, but Cristina and other unit ladies regularly do the rounds of crew and actors with water, Coca-Colas, coffees, etc, rather like the WVS or Meals on Wheels. By lunchtime it's finished and John stays on to do the Centurion and Matthias in the afternoon.

Helen rang later, but the line can be so indistinct I really can't wait to see her and talk without crackles.

Thursday, October 5th

A rather touching reminder from Kim H Johnson[1] in my pigeonhole at the hotel this morning – a card showing the Ribat and reminding us it's nine years to the day when the first Python show was transmitted.

Out to the location in Sousse. Clouds hamper progress today. On the slopes outside the impressive city walls, a huge, nude statue of me as Pilate is hauled towards the city on an oxen-drawn cart.

Almost every hour, on the hour, one of the donkeys has sexual intercourse – which entertains the unit, extras and citizens of Sousse marvellously.

At one point I find myself standing beside the lady donkey with Eric. 'How many times do you think she's been banged today?' I asked …

'Including the crew?' says EI. The wag.

The BBC crew are still at work. They do seem to favour John, and John, who's been strangely ill at ease performing, laps it up and is constantly to be found giving interviews behind caravans.

---

1 Python super-fan from Chicago, who had been given various parts in the movie. He later wrote one of the first histories of Python.

Spike Milligan turns up to do a part. He over-plays thoroughly and becomes very testy when asked to wait for the clouds to pass for a retake. Mind you, I rather feel for anyone who arrives to help out and is asked to do a role which involves saying 'Let us pray' before being trampled by 300 Tunisian extras.

Sunday, October 8th, Monastir

Take a long walk up the beach and, feeling well fatigued, get back to my room and enjoy the incomparable sensation of being quite mentally adjusted to doing nothing more than putting my feet up and steeping myself in Paul Scott's *The Raj Quartet*.

The phone rings. It's JC. 'Have you got a couple of minutes, Mikey … ?'

So I find myself spending the next hour or so rewriting the legendary, oft-written Scene 62 again.[1] Actually it turns out rather well, and we make each other laugh – and it is a lot better than what was there before.

John and I eat together at the Skanes Palace (international wine list and waiter syndrome) with John's secretary, Joan Pakenham-Walsh. Joan's cheery, extrovert company together with two bottles of very good red wine make for a happy evening.

Spike Milligan, white suit matching his fine, close-cropped white beard, wanders rather morosely into the dining room to ask us if Eric is usually more than five minutes late picking people up. He's evidently eating out with them.

John is rather short-tempered about Spike. His self-righteousness is what irks JC. The self-righteousness of a man who one day is protesting against the killing of eels in biological experiments, and the next moment is shooting air gun pellets at kids who climb into his garden.

Monday, October 9th, Monastir

Start of week four. The nineteenth day of filming. We'd have shot almost two *Ripping Yarns* by now.

At the make-up house by 7.30. Tunisians, eager for work, cluster

---

1 In Mandy's kitchen, in which Judith tells the revolutionaries to stop talking and do something about it.

round the wrought iron gates of the two-storey villa lent to us as a wardrobe and make-up base. I have to shoulder my way through. They stare at me, unblinking stares.

Emerge three-quarters of an hour later as Pontius Pilate, in short grey wig and long white under-toga and, thus attired, pile into my Renault, under the half-smiling gaze of a beautiful dark-haired, dark-eyed little boy working with his father, who is building a wall from a dusty pile of rubble.

A delay for lighting, then a very gruelling day shooting the first Pilate scene. The need to keep the vital giggling ingredient fresh and spontaneous made it a little bit harder to play than an ordinary scene with set words and reactions. The success of this scene will depend on the genuineness of the guard's reaction to Pilate. It can't all be acted, it must be felt.

So I have to do a great deal of ad-libbing at the end of the scene – and by the end of the day I must have thought up over twenty new names for Biggus Dickus' wife – ranging from the appallingly facetious Incontinentia Buttox to the occasional piece of inspiration which resulted in breakdown from the guards. Bernard McKenna in particular did the nose trick spectacularly – once right down my toga.

Tuesday, October 10th, Monastir

My two busiest days of filming are complete now – and so is Pilate, my hardest part. So I feel pleased. I think I managed to keep on top of it in quite trying circumstances – endless retakes for noises off, lighting, curtains flapping, Graham's hat, etc. Last thing I remember: JC on Jonathan Benson, the assistant director, after one of his barked instructions for silence, or 'skirt' in Arabic: 'That's what a sergeant major would sound like if he'd been to Eton.'

Wednesday, October 11th, Monastir

The rushes include a liberal amount of copulating donkeys and some good stuff at the gates of Sousse. But I find myself becoming very angry now whenever I see John wearing his tiny beard and moustache make-up – which was designed for him when he complained about the discomfort of full beards. So the rest of the crowd look wonderful – absolutely convincing Biblical figures – and there, looming large on left of frame, is John looking like a sort of fourth-rate Turkish illu-sionist advertising on the back of *Stage*.

Dine with Eric, Elaine [Carew], Tania and Spike Milligan and his lady Shelagh. They hold hands lovingly. Eric is nodding off towards the end of the meal. A huge and tasty fish couscous is specially prepared and served up for us in a big china bowl – they do take trouble.

Spike relaxes quite quickly and becomes genial, slightly nostalgic and almost expansive. Notice that his eyes have a great expressive sadness in them. He could be a very moving tragic actor.

Some nice silly ideas come up – such as a trick bow tie which stays still whilst the entire body revolves – and Spike is genuinely touched when I remember sketches and ideas from *Q5* and his other shows. He too is generous in his appreciation – in particular he compliments me on my pet-shop owner. Spike says he tends to identify with the fall guy or feed man in a sketch.

Thursday, October 12th, Monastir

Down in the lobby when a travel-stained bus pulls into the almost deserted car park and disgorges three Palin children, one wife, Chris Miller [Eric's PA], Eric's son Carey (almost indistinguishable from William).

Their arrival virtually doubles the occupancy rate of the entire Meridien and for a couple of hours the lobby and lifts are full of rest-lessly energetic English nippers bringing more life to the place than I've detected in five weeks.

Friday, October 13th, Monastir

A grey, overcast ride in at a quarter to seven for a one and a half hour make-up session in preparation for Ben's cell.

About 7.15 on this cold and unfriendly morning the heavens open and Elaine's whitening of my body seems awfully symbolic. The rain is relentless; there's no break in the clouds. Spirits sink. After three-quar-ters of an hour of make-up the decision is taken to abandon Ben for the day and to go into Matthias' House for our weather cover scene.

Feeling suitably Friday thirteenth-ish, I trudge through the rain to the Sidi M, and wash all the grease off in Elaine's bath. A good part of my gloom is disappointment at the thought of the family all waking to streaming rain and grey skies on their first morning in Tunisia.

Change into Francis and drive myself up to the Ribat. It's a quarter to nine, the rain is heavier than ever, and the place is almost deserted. Rush into the nearest caravan, which happens to be Eric's. Eric and I watch the rain soaking the scaffolding and threadbare plaster walls of what remains of Zeffirelli's temple.

'This is filming,' Eric says, with a certain air of satisfaction.

At rushes this evening, I watch my endless takes of the first Pilate scene. Have never seen myself working so hard. Take after take – with instructions thrown out from behind the camera during the scene, making me seem like the dog at a sheep dog trial.

Monday, October 16th, Monastir

Up early (after three sessions on the loo during an eight-hour night). This time the weather looks more settled and the Ben cell scene goes ahead. Aided by a bicycle saddle and two wooden pegs for my feet, I'm able to hang from real iron handcuffs, ten feet up a wall.

The first take sounds tight and unfunny and this, allied to the discomfort of doing it, makes me feel rather depressed. But the problem is that my movements are so restricted if my arms are *directly* above my head, that I'm mainly concerned with surviving rather than performing.

Anyway, the camera breaks down at this point, so we have pause for consideration. Decide to lower the manacles. This makes a tremendous difference and, though it's never very easy, I manage several takes full of the sarcastic vehemence that makes Ben funny.

The children and Helen come to the location for lunch. Rachel is quite frightened by my appearance and will not come near me.

Tuesday, October 17th, Monastir

I'm off by 3.15 in the afternoon and back to the Meridien for a swim, a run up the beach, a brief lie in the sun, a look at the *Sunday Express* for news of the Sheffields (both uninspiring draws) and a chance to see Rachel leaping into the pool – this time with no arm-bands – and swimming along under the water. So she becomes the youngest of all the Palins to learn to swim. She's on marvellous form here now.

Sunday, October 22nd, Monastir

Hotel Meridien, twenty to five in the afternoon. It's a sombre Sunday – heavy grey clouds have built up since this morning, locking in most of the sky.

Elgar plays on the tape recorder. *Enigma Variations.* The suite is painfully quiet now Helen and the children have gone. It's back to being my comfortable cell.

The presence of Helen and the children had set a very different pace to this last week. The children swam as much as possible, Helen took Connie Booth to Sousse and was very proud of her achievement in getting her to haggle. Helen definitely was cut out for the cut and thrust of Tunisian market techniques. One man wanted to come back to the hotel with her, until he discovered she had three children – then he said he wouldn't come after all.

On Saturday, after they'd all come in for a taste of Signor Memmo's lunches, Tom decided he would like to appear in the afternoon's filming, so he was supplied with a long robe and turban and looked very handsome. He was the only one of the Python children to have a go, but was very proud of himself. The room was packed and it was definitely one of the less comfortable scenes, but graced by the presence of the visiting George Harrison, who took the part of Mr Papadopolous, the impresario in charge of the Mount.

At least Tom could say he'd been in a scene with Beatles and Pythons.

Couldn't really face the empty rooms of the suite – with traces of breakfast and freshly crumpled beds – so I walked along the beach, then played my tennis match with John C. Playing solidly rather than cleverly I rattled him enough to take the first set 6–2. Great elation. But I relaxed and the wind began to strengthen (favouring the technically proficient player who could control his shots), John recovered his confidence and began to play me solidly, if not spectacularly, off the court.

Then Terry J dropped by – we drank a beer each then went into Sousse for Sunday lunch at the Lido. As cheerful and restorative to the spirits as ever. Body and soul brought together with grilled prawns and sole and perch and goat's cheese, washed down with Tunisia's best white wine – Domaine de Karim. We sat next to two Tunisian couples who work on the film, who insisted on sharing various of their dishes with us, giving us a taste of harrissa (the hot sauce), pomegranate, and showing us how to eat dates with butter.

After a leisurely lunch, we walked out onto the quay where two or three Russian cargo boats were unloading (Sunday being a half working day here), feeling all was very well with the world. Walked up through the narrow streets of the souk – the smell of leather mingling with the sweet aroma of the many confectionery stalls. Watched a cow's head being skinned and cut up in a butcher's – you'd never see that in England – past kids playing football (very well) and men hammering patterns onto brass plates for the tourists. Took mint tea in a café, then back to the docks. Decide that I feel safer in cities with the sea on one side …

I've just placed a call to London to see if they've arrived. Six thirty-five, they have … It's raining in London. Feel a bond with them as I listen to the angry windswept sea in the darkness outside.

Monday, October 23rd, Monastir

Walking on the beach after breakfast I frame an idea for a *Ripping Yarn* – 'Golden Gordon', a soccer tale. It feels good, as the surge to write returns after all these weeks. I sit at a table in the sunshine and scribble away for a couple of hours. Then, having reached an impasse, lie in the sun by the pool and read through 'Whinfrey' to get a timing on it.

Eric and Tania – buoyant – join me and we have lunch together. Eric reads in the *Daily Express* that Nelson's last words were in fact 'Don't throw me overboard, Hardy.'

In the afternoon I run along the beach, then write a couple of letters to Al L and my ma – and by a quarter to six it's dark.

Eric, Tania, Charles McK, Terry J, Andrew M, Bernard and the Hamptons fill a table at the Café de la Plage et Coq. There is much singing of old English music hall numbers and First World War songs – at full voice, utterly drowning anyone else in the restaurant. A fine display of selfish and high-spirited behaviour. A release of a lot of tensions. The Coq treat us to a very tasty eau de vie-like liqueur and we toast the World's Greatest, Most Long-Suffering and Least Flappable Waiter – Ali – with a rising chorus of 'Ali, Ali, pride of our Sally'.

Tuesday, October 24th, Monastir

Farewell to Monastir.

I'm going to miss the place. I've shared a lot of experiences with the

Hotel Meridien. The intense feelings of preparation for the movie and the five weeks of performing – with all the various degrees of tension, stress and strain which the peace of the Meridien has helped to smooth and minimise. In all its grand emptiness, it's like leaving an old family home. The staff probably account for these feelings of sadness at departure. They have been universally friendly and good-natured. Yes, I shall miss them.

Gabès a nice, muddled town, at first glance, and the Hotel L'Oasis is down by the beach. The decoration is Russian twentieth century luxurious, but the two rooms I have (and two bathrooms) are pleasantly proportioned and have vaulted, white-painted ceilings.

Ate at the Ex-Franco Arabe Café de L'Oasis, to give it its full title, with John C and friend Charlotte. It turned out that most of the crew were in there, as well as dozens of locals, so we took an age to get served – despite JC breaking a plate on the floor to attract the waiter's attention.

Sunday, October 29th, Hotel L'Oasis, Gabès

Toy with the idea of treating Gabès as a series of abstract impressions – 'Sea, smell of seaweed, spreading sands … hotel continuously alive with jarring sound of chairs on marble floors, tiredness, tat, two toilets, infinitely slow emptying baths, locals quick to laugh and equally quick to take offence – '.

Long to return to England and really concentrate on writing. Urge to work carefully and thoroughly on a second novel grows daily. Together with a curiosity about Jill's reaction to my first one – and a growing frustration with the tedium of film-acting.

Friday's filming of the Sermon on the Mount was difficult – mainly because we had a crowd of 600 local extras. Prouder, more independent, less malleable folk than up in Monastir.

Ken Colley performed marvellously as Jesus – using a modern translation of the Beatitudes, which we'd decided on in preference to the St James version, because it felt less like a set up for a joke, and more of an attempt to portray Jesus as honestly as possible.

After the early takes, stunning in their recreation of the image of the Bible story, the extras started getting restless. It turned out that many of them had left their homes at 2.30 in the morning and had had neither food nor water since then.

At one point the crowd thought they were finished, and streamed from the Mount down towards the coaches, whilst Hammeda, one of our Tunisian assistants, pursued them screaming and shouting. The womenfolk had to be taken back early, because if they arrived back after sunset there would be hell to pay from the male villagers. All very different from the jolly, co-operative crowd who rolled on their backs at Monastir.

So to this Sunday. I sit listening to my latest favourite tape – Kate and Annie McGarrigle's 'Dancers with Bruised Knees' – sipping a Glenlivet from the litre bottle which Helen brought two and a half weeks ago and which is half gone, and looking out onto the darkening sky and sea.

This morning I looked through an assembly of the film – from Pilate's forum up to the crucifixions – and was greatly encouraged.

I'm not quite sure that I'd go along with TJ, who last night ventured to me that it was going to be 'a masterpiece', but, having seen the stuff this morning, I feel closer to his judgement than to Terry Gilliam, who spread gloom and despondency over me on Friday morning, as we motored out to Matmata, with his analysis of shortcomings and missed opportunities.

But more of this later. Night has fallen on the end of our seventh week in Tunisia. I feel optimistic about the film tonight and less depressed at the thought of being trapped here for two more weeks. All I have to decide now is which of my two baths to use …

Tuesday, October 31st, Gabès

The violence of the downpour is increasing as I listen. The prospect of an enforced day off tomorrow looks ominously likely.

Yesterday morning I was hauled up on the cross. It wasn't an unpleasant sensation, but I was stretched out for half an hour or so whilst various takes of Big Nose were done and, as I write, I've numbed a nerve in my left arm and lost some control of my muscles, so the arm keeps rising involuntarily – rather like Peter Sellers' rogue limb in *Dr Strangelove*.

Thursday, November 2nd, Gabès

Wake to sunshine. Give Cleese a lift out to the location. Have to wait five minutes at a shop whilst he buys honey and almonds for his breakfast.

John is sharing a caravan with TJ and me at the moment, so that make-up can have extra space. As a result I have Cleese, who has a cold, and his girlfriend, Charlotte, who arrives around lunchtime and smokes.

Today we spend most of our time and effort on the final song, which twenty-four crucifees sing as the climax of the film.

I'm in one of the front-row crosses. There's a slightly heady feeling – a tiny rush of vertigo as I clamber up onto the racing bicycle saddle (which protrudes absurdly anachronistically from an otherwise convincing cross). There's a certain sense of camaraderie amongst us all as we clip our nails over the top of our hands and push aching arms through the ropes.

Among the few compensations is a wonderful view over the hills of Matmata.

Saturday, November 4th, Gabès

Wake up to grey skies again. The weather is being really unkind these days.

Drive out to the location at Matmata with sinking spirits. Prospects for a return to England on the 13th look in jeopardy as the rain comes down and we wait for half an hour as the water pours across the road so fast no one dares venture across. One loony tries to get across in a Peugeot taxi, skids in the mud and bounces off one of our Renault 5s.

Sitting in one of the caravans waiting for us to be called, the talk turns to discussion of tomorrow's rest day. Roy Rodhouse, chief electrician, maintains this film has been a doddle – and anyone who's feeling the pressure ought to try 'a day or two with bloody David Lean – then they'll know what slave-driving is'.

Charles Knode reckons it's been the hardest picture he's worked on – mainly because he feels his work isn't used. For instance this week he's been up early to dress seventy-five extras each day, and the most they've eventually used is six of them.

There's no consensus of discontent, but from the attitudes of everyone I reckon the most disruptive element in any operation like this is lack of diplomacy – and that means regular attention to every department to make sure they're given time to air their grievances and lashings of appreciation. In a big unit like this there doesn't seem to be time to look after everyone like that.

Monday, November 6th, Gabès

Out to Matmata for the last time. Still cloudy, but dry. Much running about, sometimes carrying Terry aloft, sometimes followed by 150 Arabs.

One long chasing shot has to be done all over again after one extra, wearing leather shoes, Terylene socks and smoking a cigarette, stops and looks straight into the lens, before being attacked with angry howls by Habib, Hammeda and the massed Anglo-Tunisian assistant directors.

Friday, November 10th, Carthage

Carthage is a comfy, bourgeois suburb – the Beverly Hills of Tunisia – and there is no centre of the old town and precious little on display to show for the years when people from this shore dominated the Mediterranean. The Roman Empire has been put away, as it were, and the Punic is under the ground.

John dropped in for breakfast. We looked through Three Wise Men together – the steady, unrelenting rain gave us the thought of doing a play about an English holiday called 'It's Clearing Up'.

John Goldstone and Tim are of the opinion that we should aim to leave on Monday whatever happens – and that the amphitheatre close-ups and the Three Wise Men can be shot in London. The weather forecast offers no cause for hope.

At three we travel down to the location beside the sea, where amidst the bulky ruins of a Roman baths we are to shoot the Three Wise Men.

The roof of the stable drips occasionally as a welcome reminder that it *could* have been raining on Jesus' birthday. The costumes are excruciatingly hard to bear. My headdress is like having a sixty-pound haversack on one's skull, and both Graham and I have immense trouble with long, swirling trains – as we make an impressive exit, Graham's train catches on the door, rips down the middle and pulls the door off its hinges.

Saturday, November 11th, Carthage

At the amphitheatre at eight.

The consistent sunshine keeps us moving steadily forward, and my last shot of the movie (witnessed by the British Ambassador, who appears mid-afternoon in the ruins of Carthage and is observed by T

Gilliam tapping tentatively on solid rock to ascertain whether it's false or not) is myself as one of the Revs 'flitting' through the streets. Then John, Eric and myself are finished.

Succumb to the temptation of the cool, calm sea and take what is probably my last Tunisian dip. A chill, fresh edge to the water – not a day for drying out on the beach. Instead back into my chalet for a long, lingering hot bath.

November's connotations seem the same whether in foggy England or sunny North Africa – warm fires, warm baths, protection and shelter are the order of the month.

A fine sunset – a great final curtain. Dinner at the Gulf restaurant with TJ, after rushes. He's pushed through thirty-six shots today and only the wide-shots of the amphitheatre, with Neil running away from the giant gladiator, remain to be done.

Sunday, November 12th, Carthage

I left the chalet at a quarter to seven.

Eric is outside already, standing on the sea-shore, looking towards the sunrise. A canopy of small, white, grey-edged flecks of cloud dot the sky, changing from rich red to deep gold as the sun slowly rises.

Bernard McK leapt out of his chalet and intercepted me with the joyful news that he had been writing his *Robin's Nest*[1] episode since three o'clock in the morning and the end was in sight!

Left the cheery Bernard and reflective Eric and climbed up the path, past good, fresh smells of early morning – pine and grass and the hint of soft, sweet scents from bougainvillea and camellia.

Back in London by twelve, but Helen was over at Mary and Ed's with the children for lunch. Drove over there in the Citroen, and had not gone one mile before I was hit a glancing blow on the back wing from a careering Triumph Herald. I could hardly believe it. After nine weeks' driving in Tunisia without a scratch (despite all TJ's warnings about manic Arab drivers) I return to Kentish Town and wham! The driver, a dapper young man with untrustworthy eyes, actually tried to make a fight of it, accusing me (who had been stationary at a junction) of taking up too much road. I refused to argue, but I was shaking with anger by the time I eventually reached my family.

1 *Robin's Nest*, starring Richard O'Sullivan, was a big ITV comedy hit.

Tom played me in with a clarinet fanfare. Rachel was shy at first and pretended not to notice and Willy bounded up and nearly bent me double.

Later in the day the man who had thudded into the back of my car appeared contritely at our door to apologise and admit full responsibility! He turned out to be a very frightened, newly qualified young barrister. His girlfriend had recognised me and given him a frightfully guilty conscience all afternoon. He had finally found my address by ringing up a couple of policeman 'friends' who gave him information from the police computer!

Monday, November 13th

Start to dig through the oceans of mail and assorted papers. Appeals from Birkdale Preparatory School, Shrewsbury School, the ETC [Experimental Theatre Club] at Oxford – my past seems to have run out of money.

Otherwise there are those who want a name to boost appeals or appear at concerts – a concert for racial equality in Oldham, Fair Play for Children in Kentish Town, The Association of Boys' Clubs, Sheffield University Medical Society, The Dog-Lovers' Club of Northern Kent. One-Parent Families want me to do a Christmas show.

In the evening watch the third of the Monty Python repeats. Shows as old as this diary. Capering around as Cardinal Ximenez in the 'Spanish Inquisition'.

Tuesday, November 14th

Confirmation of my suspicions that the BBC will not commission any more *Yarns* after April, on grounds of cost. Jill quotes a letter from John Howard Davies saying that the shows 'though prestigious', are 'beyond the BBC's resources'.

I am greatly relieved by the news, for the go-ahead on three more would have stretched my/our ideas, would have filled up next year – which is now left tantalisingly clear for any involvement with Lorne M.

Mind you, you could say they let us go without much of a struggle.

Friday, November 17th

One of the odd things about the Tunisian trip is that it's very easy to believe it didn't happen. It's as though I've been in a time-warp, and I feel as if there has been absolute continuation of my time in England, and that this is mid-September. The Tunisian episode is like the hour a drunk cannot account for.

I suppose this is partly because of today's summery sunshine, which matches September quite well, if you don't look at the trees, but mainly because my life in Tunisia was such a neat and self-contained entity. It was nine weeks of creating fantasy – and it's easy now to see it all as a fantasy anyway. A complete break, in dress, food, habits, climate and surroundings, held together by a story set 2,000 years ago.

Monday, November 20th

To the Hemdale Preview Theatre in Audley Square at four to see the assembly of all the *Brian* material. Apart from the Python team – all looking a lot more like pale-faced Englishmen after a week of British November – Tim Hampton and John Goldstone, Anne Henshaw, George Harrison and Denis O'Brien were there.

After cups of tea and a 15-minute wait for Dr Chapman, the film starts. The whole preparatory assembly runs two hours and eight minutes.

General consensus is that it's a most encouraging viewing. Some scenes provoked gales of laughter – including the latter half of Ben and Pilate's audience chamber, the Hermit's hole, Brian's bedroom when the crowd arrive, and the Centurion and Matthias at the door of Matthias' house (the searching). There was a consistent level of interest and no embarrassments, though I confess to finding Otto dangerously like a cameo sketch.

The raid on Pilate's palace could be cut down too, by five or six minutes.

Round to Langan's for a drink, then John Cleese, Anne, John G, myself and Gilliam stay for a meal. We discuss Richard Ingrams (briefly) and his pairing of *Citizen Kane* and Monty Python in his *Spectator* TV column last week. He was talking about over-estimated phenomena and thought *Citizen Kane* quite useless and Python, now he had finally seen it, junk. Quite a refreshing bucket of water after the almost unqualified critical praise which Python has had to endure these last few years.

Tuesday, November 21st

Late in the afternoon, to Robert Maas[1] to hear the latest on the Signford tax saga, which broke last August with the issuing of precepts. Maas, admirably downbeat in style, told me that Signford's status with the tax authorities was still not settled.

If Maas succeeds in persuading the Inspector of Taxes that Signford was not set up with intent to trick or defraud, and that the time gap between the setting up of the company and the performance of the services from which the company derived most of its income was permissible and done in good faith, then Signford will have succeeded.

If not, there could be a bill of £26,000 to pay straightaway, in addition to a personal tax bill up to the end of August '78 of between £15,000 and £20,000.

But Maas is competent and efficient and very sharp, so I have some hope. At the very worst I still have two cars and two houses and the best-equipped 8-track recording studio in London to show for nine years of Python!

Thursday, November 23rd

Up to Suffolk. The peace and pause for reflection worked almost immediately. As the Ipswich–Darsham train swayed up from Wickham Market to Saxmundham, with still green fields and rapidly emptying oaks and ashes and elms on either side, I suddenly felt very clear about the next year. I would complete the *Yarns* in March and April, then work from May 5th (a symbolic starting date: 36th birthday) until December 31st on a new novel.

The prospect brightened me, as we passed through Saxmundham and alongside dark, rich, fresh-ploughed fields south of Darsham. By the time I reached Darsham and saw the smiling, diminutive, almost gnomic little figure of my Ma, I knew it was the right decision.

Saturday, November 25th

Embark for George Harrison's in the Mini.

Arrive at Friar Park as the sun has just set. It must be two years since I

---

1 My new accountant.

came here with Eric to complete the mixing of 'Lumberjack Song' (or was it three?). There's a blazing log fire in the galleried hall and George has just come in from planting bulbs in the garden. He seems very relaxed and settled into the role of a country squire – his face has fleshed out a little, he looks less frail and tortured.

We have tea and talk about the house and Sir Frank Crisp, the eccentric lawyer who built it.[1] And died penniless as a result. My mother remembers Sir Frank hiding behind bushes in the garden and jumping out on her and her sister when they visited the place as little girls.[2]

Saw George's four-month-old boy, Dhani, then his other recent enthusiasm, his book. Called *I Me Mine*, it's an expensively leather-bound collection of his songs with his own hand-written notes and corrections.

We find out that George is just older than me. He was born February 1943. He is quite struck by this and, as a memento of him being just older, gives me one of the glass eyes made for his Madame Tussaud's dummy!

Derek Taylor and Joan arrive later and we eat a superb Indian meal cooked by Kumar. Quite delicious and delicate.

Derek tells of the horrors of LA that have driven him back to England – to a farmhouse in Suffolk. So humourless and depressing were his colleagues in Warner Records, that Derek took great pleasure in puzzling them by eccentric behaviour. He would insist on playing Hollywood record moguls a tape of Violet Bonham-Carter[3] being interviewed. They sat there polite but utterly bewildered. 'Twenty minutes' peace,' Derek recalled with feeling.

Monday, November 27th

Taxi arrives when I'm half-dressed, just before eight. Half a cup of tea, then leave for the BBC at 8.15. To Studio 4A at Broadcasting House for *Start the Week*, with Richard Baker – a jolly, harmless, middle-of-the-road therefore well-liked chat show, which goes out live.

RB frightens me with quick asides like 'We'll be talking travel … oh,

1 Crisp (1843–1919) bought Friar Park in 1895. He, like George, was a keen horticulturalist. Unlike George, he was a fully paid up member of the Royal Microscopical Society.
2 My mother was born and brought up on Hernes Estate, which borders Friar Park.
3 Extremely English upper-class daughter of former Prime Minister, H. H. Asquith; leading figure in Liberal politics.

and bicycles ... so if you'll get some travel and bicycling stories together ... Right, we're on air.'

Not as hair-raising as I thought. I manage to hold my own, though Sandra Harris, who interviews me, is another of those people who feel the need to describe me as a 'nice middle-class boy'.

Drive over to Gough Square. It's nearly half past three and the shafts of sunshine are few as the buildings of London block out the low November sunshine. The city seems all in shadow. I tape a pre-recorded interview for London Broadcasting. Catch a glimpse of a visitors' book which is lying open – the last name is M Thatcher, H of C. Think of writing G Rarf, London Zoo, but refrain.

Before Christmas the Ripping Yarns *book was published and my signing tour began, as they still do now, in Scotland.*

Tuesday, November 28th, Stirling

Leave King's Cross at 11.55 on the Aberdonian.

Arrive in Stirling at a quarter to seven. Met by student organisers who say they have had to move the audience to a larger lecture theatre. I'm told the Literary Society (whom I am addressing) usually expect 80 or 90 for a visiting speaker, but 250 have turned up.

Give my talk eventually to a full house, ranged in front of and above me along steeply-banked rows of desks. Analysis of my method of writing doesn't go down well, but any jokes or sketches are rapturously received.

Wednesday, November 29th, Stirling

Up at a quarter to nine. Comfortable night in excellent, clean and well-equipped hotel. Breakfast alone with a *Scotsman* (the newspaper). Then walk down to Allanwater, away from the main road and along a path which follows the river. The air is clean, fresh and cold. It's marvellous to be in Scotland. I relish the short walk inordinately, gratefully drinking in the air and the sight of a quiet, full river flanked by bare-branched beech trees.

I still am affected by a post-Tunisian euphoria. A delight in being wherever I am, provided it's not Tunisia.

To Grant's Bookshop in Stirling for my first signing session.

Despite a big window display, the attendance at the signing session is not good. I console myself with the fact that thirty books were signed after last night's talk and publication isn't really till tomorrow. But I sit at my table with embarrassingly large piles of books beside me and sign less than twenty in one-and-a-half hours. At one point an irate lady who obviously thinks I work here, comes across and complains that a book about angling she bought for her nephew has two pages stuck together.

John Lennie, the Methuen rep for Scotland, drives me to Edinburgh. Terry J arrives. He and I go for a nostalgic walk up to the Royal Mile. We nose around the Cranston Street Hall in the traditional manner. TJ remembers the thrill of seeing the feet of a forming queue through a small window down in the toilets … That was fifteen years ago.[1]

We find ourselves in a wonderful, small, grubby, friendly bar in Young Street – the Oxford Bar. This is the glorious opposite of all the carpeted 'lounges' where drinks are now taken. It's small and gossipy and quite uncompromising with regard to comfort and décor … definitely a new 'must' when visiting Edinburgh.

Thursday, November 30th, Caledonian Hotel, Edinburgh

Publication day for *Ripping Yarns* and St Andrew's Day for Scottish people. Terry and I are hurrying along Queen Street. It's a quarter past seven and still dark.

Arrive five minutes late for live interviews.

We're out by 8.30. Time for an appalling breakfast at the otherwise splendid Caledonian, then we're running along the gracious streets – this time to Radio Forth, where we record a one-hour chat programme with a man called Clark Tate. The chat is easy and comfortable and the time passes fast.

By grubby train to Glasgow. Through countryside thick with snow.

From Radio Clyde to Grant's Bookshop. Heads turn as we enter. People look up uncertainly from their books. Bookshops are rather like churches – any incipiently flamboyant behaviour is rather discouraged.

---

1 The Cranston Street Hall, then head office of the Edinburgh Parks and Burials Department, was where he and I first performed together at the Festival in 1964. It was the first time in my life that I had the slightest intimation that there might be a living from comedy.

We settle down at our table and sign for an hour. Sixty books here, they reckon. Good reactions from people to the book and the series. Many want to know when there will be more …

A group of students attach themselves to us, one of them carrying the frog box[1] to the Albany. One of them makes a perceptive remark when he observes 'You're just kids really …'

Wednesday, December 6th

At six o'clock I go down to John Goldstone's office in D'Arblay Street. He has a two-page ad for *Variety* to announce the completion of filming. John takes all this side of the publicity very seriously. It's odd, such a quiet man setting such store by making a noise, but I'm assured it's essential with million dollar epics. *Superman*, I notice, has a ten-page ad in the latest *Variety*!

We both walk over to the Sapphire Theatre for the (much discussed and, for TJ, slightly feared) viewing of Julian Doyle's *Life of Brian*![2]

The film ran two hours and the reaction was very encouraging. The laughter (in scenes like Pilate's first audience chamber and the Gaolers in the cell) was long and loud. The song at the end worked and there was plenty of quite unequivocal applause.

Julian has done a good job and provided TJ with a well-shaped, well-structured cut on which he can work to lighten up all the details. It was a very good reaction tonight and the film can only get better.

Friday, December 8th

Collected Rachel from school at twelve and she and I walked into Kentish Town to have lunch at a new McDonald's there. Instead of seats they have perches – sloping plastic padded shelves which give you the feeling that they are trying to tip everyone out of the restaurant. Not entirely untrue, either – they're obviously designed to discourage quiet sitting and reflection and increase cash-flow.

Schoolkids hiss 'Who is he?' amongst themselves after a couple of the staff have asked me to sign autographs. I maintain a stoic display of unconcern and attend to Rachel – who is a lovely companion.

1 The box, as used in 'Across the Andes by Frog', was one of the props to enliven our book-signing tour.
2 Julian had assembled an early working cut of the film, more or less on his own.

A thought struck me as I left – the bags in which you are given food at McDonald's are almost identical in texture, shape and size with the vomit bags tucked in the seat pockets of aircraft.

After a couple of hours of profitable writing on 'Whinfrey's Last Case', drove down to St Pancras and took the 4.16 to Sheffield. Was able to work on the train. Took a taxi up to the Cutlers' Hall, where the Medical Society of Sheffield University were holding their 150th Annual Ball.

I speak for 20 minutes or so and despite, or perhaps because of, there being five speeches before me, mine is well received.

Afterwards I'm presented with a special brick and sign endless autographs. I have to stay and judge the cabaret acts, which is an impossible task as I can't hear or see anything. About 12.30 they're mercifully over and I make my judgement and present the winner with his trophy – a stainless steel bedpan with a plastic turd in it.

To think our life is in their hands.

Monday, December 11th

Visit the Royal Geographical Society, of which, thanks to Peter Luff,[1] I am now a Fellow. Complete peace and quiet, in a very avant-garde house, built in 1874 by Norman Shaw facing Hyde Park.

To me, the place was like Nirvana – for my earliest ambition, which endured for many years, was to be an explorer. And here I was, Fellow of a society set up in 1830, which has on display Charles Darwin's application for membership dated 1838.

Tuesday, December 12th

Down to Neal's Yard. Hive of activity. Val Charlton[2] and Terry Gilliam are making Martians upstairs for the interior of the Flying Saucer in *Brian*, next door Terry J is editing and in the studio André has put together a demo of the new *Brian* song.

Walk through rainwashed Leicester Square. Pick up tickets for the *Superman* film on Saturday and Dame Edna's new show, which opens tomorrow night.

1 Producer of the early Amnesty shows.
2 Modelmaker and partner of Julian Doyle.

Home to work on the *Yarn* with TJ.

Then Chris Orr arrives and I'm discussing with him the arrangements for further work on his 'Arthur' book (the revised, shorter version of which I like very much), when Roger Wilmut, a BBC sound engineer who's doing a book on the Oxbridge revue and comedy Mafia, arrives.

Juggle all these people around and cope with a constant barrage of phone calls and am finally left talking to Wilmut about How It All Began. I've never felt less like talking about How It All Began – the whole madhouse here is more indicative of How It All Will End.

Sunday, December 17th

Ian and Anthea and Clemency and growing, toddling Grace,[1] come round for roast lamb and apple crumble lunch. In the interval of one Barry Humphries show last week, Ian was up in the bar and overheard snippets of conversation between two people. One was accusing the other of 'sighing'. 'I wasn't sighing.' 'Yes you were, you were sitting there sighing all through it.' The other then produced the sharp rejoinder 'Don't be so combative.' Ian noted the whole exchange and, when he went back to Barry's dressing room, told him of it.

He couldn't believe his ears when, half-way through Edna's monologue to a packed 1,500-strong house, Edna told of how she couldn't take Norm to the theatre because he'd just sit there and sigh, and eventually become very 'combative'. Afterwards Barry said he'd slipped it in because of his enjoyment of the effect it would have on just two people. As Barry put it, it would make, for them, a truly 'uncanny' night in the theatre.

Wednesday, December 20th

Morose, east wind weather. Grey and with drizzle just this side of snow.

A power-cut yesterday blacked out the whole of France (bar Alsace).

London is full of queues at petrol stations because of rumours that there will be a tanker drivers' go-slow in January. All in all it's siege conditions again …

As the days get shorter and colder and darker a sort of pessimistic gloom descends. The next three months are low points for everybody,

---

1 The expanding Davidson family.

when our technology can't quite cope and our 'civilised society' shows alarming cracks.

I cheer myself up writing copy for J Goldstone's *Variety* ads for *Brian*. Re-read the 'Whinfrey' script and tighten. It looks good, but I wish the uncertainty over the rest of the *Yarns* and the director could be sorted out, for I feel like writing now and yet if it's to be top priority I need to know *who's* doing them and when.

Thursday, December 21st

Goldstone rings. He's very pleased with the *Variety* ad copy – it's going into early Jan or mid-Jan issue. His plan is to create as much of a stir as possible inside the US before showing the assembly to distributors in late January. It's essential to arrange a US distribution deal at least six or seven months in advance in order to have any chance of booking up cinemas.

He has a strange snippet of info – the film about Hitler called *Hitler – A Career* is attracting so many National Front supporters in the West End that they're thinking of taking it off. First time I've ever heard of a film being taken off for being too popular.

By two this afternoon it's almost dark. The sky is low and leaden grey and there's rain and sleet and a chill wind. The sort of day which sends wise men to the travel agents.

Tuesday, December 26th

A return to the greyness – and not just outside, where a blanket of slow-spattering rain covered London. At about ten Overseas Telegrams rang – news from New York. 'Not too good, I'm afraid,' said the faceless man at the other end. 'Eve died on Christmas Day,' he reads.

The outcome, which Al feared for a long time, but which he only resigned himself to in a letter to me last September, of Eve's recent severe depressive bouts (twice hospitalised) has finally come to pass.

At midday in NYC, I rang Al. Spoke to his son, John, who sounded tight and tense, but said it would mean a lot to Al that I rang. An hour later I spoke to Al himself. His voice cracked as soon as he spoke, though he said he'd been trying to keep himself together. Eve had committed suicide – no details – but John was asleep and Al had gone out for a walk. He returned to find an ambulance waiting there.

Now Al wanted to get away for a while. The apartment, which Eve found, Sag Harbor, which she adored, all were now an intolerable sorrow. The only thing that could in any way lighten the pain was that he had seen it coming. It was almost inevitable. As I said to Al, Eve had a terminal illness.

Friday, December 29th

The toyshop in Malden Road opens for the first time since the holiday, and is visited largely by parents returning malfunctioning goods. Kindly, middle-aged women with headscarves can be heard at the counter asking for advice ... 'I pressed the auto-destruct and the bit came off ...' or 'Every time it goes round a corner all the missiles fall out.'

I take Willy's Scalextric controls, which have been such a headache over the last few days. It turns out I've got a new model on which the controls have been improved. He gives me some old ones, and the whole thing works perfectly.

I then drive down to Dulwich, collect Granny for the day and drop in our Christmas presents to the Joneses. (They took Terry's father and Norah, his new wife, to see TJ editing. They showed Norah some of the film, and according to Alison she was most offended! But then she's from Welsh Fundamentalist stock and it's as likely that a Welsh Fundamentalist will laugh at people cracking jokes on the cross as it is that Snowdon's made of pâté.)

Over lunch at the Barque and Bite I try to allay my mother's fears about the film – aroused by the indexing of our film on totally specious grounds by the Festival of Light.[1] I hope she doesn't feel she's in for a rough year. Despite being a regular *Telegraph* reader, she's still tough and bright and with a mind of her own, so I'm not too worried.

Sunday, December 31st

Helen and I were watching *Top Hat* last night before a blazing coal fire and Helen was forever parting the curtains and looking out in glee as the powdery snow, driven by a sharp, south-easterly wind, covered Oak Village.

As we drive down to Dulwich I listen to the car radio and hear tales

---

1 A Christian pressure group.

of horror from all over the UK. Edinburgh is almost cut off from the rest of Scotland (a fact which the weather only confirms!) and Scotland is almost cut off from the rest of the UK. The police are advising only 'essential' journeys.

The result is a wondrously empty London. Even the streets of the West End are white with caked snow.

More bad Christmas news – this time that Veryan's mother died in a fire at her home early this morning. But Angela and Veryan want our visit to carry on as normal, and possible gloom is dispelled by pre-lunch cocktails with two neighbours and their three daughters, who bring with them a game called Twister, which involves participants in a grapple on the floor and, in the immortal words of Eric's joke salesman, 'Breaks the ice at parties'.

Driving back across Westminster Bridge at a safe and stately pace just before seven, with the Houses of Parliament floodlit and the bridge still uncleared of snow.

Al Levinson rings to wish me a Happy New Year. There was a memorial service for Eve yesterday and 150 people turned up. Which is very heartening, but only seems to emphasise the crippling irrationality of the condition that destroyed her. She was loved and she will be missed.

1978 passes – perhaps the swankiest year yet for me, what with two-week writing sessions in Barbadian luxury and elegance, a Concorde flight to the US, a week in New York with my own personal limousine (which I never used), and nine weeks of star treatment in Tunisia.

I feel that in the last year my work rate has slackened, but the slack has been largely taken up by increasingly complex business arrangements, more meetings and by a slowly, inexorably increasing number of memberships, demands for money, speeches or introductions to rag magazines – all the impedimenta of notoriety.

Next year we will have to live with the impact of the film. I know that, although now it seems that we just had a great deal of fun, both writing and performing, there is going to be something of a sensation when the subject matter is finally revealed.

1979

Monday, January 1st

1979 comes in cold. Very cold. Minus 7° centigrade.

Walk across the crackling snow to a party at neighbours. He's in advertising and has gathered a collection of 'hangover killers' from an article in *The Guardian*, which he's displayed like some alcoholic's stall at a Bring and Buy. Each with instructions. So you can have Fernet Branca, Bovril and vodka – known as a Russian Bison – Prairie Oysters – raw eggs are laid on – and a drink which Kingsley Amis christened 'The Final Solution': one spoonful of ground coffee, one spoonful of sugar wrapped in a slice of lemon, sucked and, in mid-mastication, swept through with a tumblerful of brandy. I tried it and I think I blame it for a consequent feeling of elation and a loss of all sense of time.

After a Final Solution and a couple of Buck's Fizzes, we slithered across to the Guedallas for lunch. Present were the Maliks, the Taylors. (Mary, very jolly, told us the latest Jeremy Thorpe stories. What's the similarity between Jeremy Thorpe and William the Conqueror? They're both fucking Normans.)[1]

Thursday, January 4th

Jimmy Gilbert rings to tell me his suggestion for the new director for the *Yarns*. Turns out it's Alan J W Bell[2] – the PA who should have been a director, who came in to help out with *Yarns* when we were arranging audience screenings. I'd forgotten about him – but he fits the bill rather well. He knows the *Yarns*, I know him, he's keen on film and, not identified with any particular programme so far, he could be very keen to make his mark.

Lunch at the San Carlo in Highgate to meet 'fellow speakers' at the Barclays Bank Northern Managers' binge next Thursday week. I'm doing it because the Highgate manager, Brian Kemp, is one of the organisers and is a bright, humorous, intelligent sort of bloke – met through Graham Chapman.

1 See footnote, page 623.
2 Later to direct the *Last of the Summer Wine* series.

Graeme Garden, who's also speaking, is there, which avoids the conversation becoming utterly stodgy. The other bank representatives look very English macho, rugby club rednecks, and not really the sort of people I would spend more than 12 minutes with if possible. My heart sinks as Brian (whose wife is, rather neatly, called Judith) tells me that there will only be two or three women there so we can be as filthy as we like.

Graeme is going back to theatre acting in the next couple of weeks. He's going to do Charles Dyer's *Rattle of a Simple Man* for Johnny Lynn and the Cambridge Theatre Company. He's only going on tour though. He hated the West End run of *Unvarnished Truth* and claims that the provinces provide much more enthusiastic audiences.

Saturday, January 6th

A party at Anne Henshaw's.

Talk to Richard Loncraine,[1] who says the BBC never asked him about directing the *Yarns*, and he would now almost certainly have been available.

Loncraine says he would have liked to have worked on the *Yarns*, which, he said with characteristic directness, always scored eight out of ten with him. He felt they all peaked at a certain point and the endings were a little disappointing. I agree. I don't think Terry and I ever quite got the measure of the 30-minute format. We always had too much to cram in.

Monday, January 8th

Alison[2] finishes typing 'Whinfrey's Last Case' and I collect it at lunchtime. Most garages are closed and the roads probably full of cars, like me, wasting petrol looking for a garage that's open. Plenty of petrol in Bantry Bay, however, where an unloading tanker blew up killing fifty people.

At four, in to the BBC to take the script and meet the new director and executive producer.

---

1 One of Anne's other clients. Successful commercials director who started Loncraine-Broxton, a novelty toy company. I'd suggested him to the BBC for the *Yarns*. We eventually worked together on *The Missionary* in 1982.
2 Alison Davies, our PA at Anne's office.

The talk is all positive. They are expecting a second script by January 17th and hardly a word is written yet. But at the same time they seem curiously uncertain as to their intentions. When I ask them what they'll do with these three *Yarns* it's as if they've never thought about it before.

Tuesday, January 9th

Write in the afternoon. Pleased to be away from 'Whinfrey' and on to something with a little more soul – and a good part for yours truly – namely the 'Golden Gordon' northern football saga. I do hope it works. I will dedicate it to the Meridien Hotel, Monastir, if it does – for that's where it began.

In the evening Willy and I join another 37,985 people at a chilly Highbury Stadium to watch the replay of Arsenal v Wednesday's Cup Tie. High up in the stands we get a good clear view and for once Sheffield give their supporters plenty to be proud of. They tackle fast and accurately, mark, move and even shoot much more tightly and efficiently than Arsenal. And just before half-time they score.

Willy and I drink our Thermosful of hot chocolate at half-time, well pleased. Wednesday even manage to hold out in the second half. We cannot bear to look at the clock. Terrific excitement – as gripping as any theatrical event I've ever seen. With four minutes to go, Arsenal hustle an equaliser. Everyone around us is up on their feet. But Wednesday survive what should have been Arsenal's surge of confidence until the end, and also through 30 minutes of extra time. So, still 1-1 and another replay in sight.

Willy and I feel like kings as we join the sea of people flooding down the neat residential streets, away from the ground. Passing groups of 10- to 18-year-olds waiting for 'Old Bill' to go so they can have a fight with Wednesday's equally pugnacious 10- to 18-year-olds.

Wednesday, January 10th

An unexpected boost, when Alan Bell rings to tell me how much he likes 'Whinfrey's Last Case'. Syd Lotterby, the executive producer,[1] finds the

---

1 Legendary BBC comedy producer and director (*Porridge, Butterflies, Last of the Summer Wine*). John and Graham particularly liked the sound of his name, and I seem to remember a sketch on *At Last the 1948 Show* in which every character was called Sydney Lotterby.

script funny and the only criticism is from Jimmy Gilbert about the 'non-ending'.

I take a pinch of salt and breathe a sigh of relief. Now we can go ahead. The work will be hard – the two new *Yarns* will have to be filmed back-to-back throughout March.

Thursday, January 11th

Round to a buffet supper at J Cleese's. John, who starts next week on a set of six new *Fawlty Towers*, saw the *Brian* film tonight at a showing laid on for him at the Audley Square Theatre. He'd asked me over to gauge reactions from his friends, most of whom had been in the audience.

Ronnie Eyre, a theatre director who recently completed an epic series on world religions called *The Long Search*, thought the film funny and important. He felt the script was at most points saying things and making thought-provoking observations – only occasionally, as in the Pilate's Wife raid scene, did it become one-dimensional.

Michael Rudman, looking, if possible, younger than when he was at Oxford fifteen years ago, said he only saw five films a year, but felt that this was going to be a big success. Jim Beach was greatly impressed – especially with Pilate – and I received many flattering remarks about my various hammy performances. Humphrey Barclay was full of praise and Michael Peacock,[1] who didn't like the haggling sequence because of its lack of urgency and wasn't keen on Otto, thought both script and performance were on the whole stronger than the *Grail*. He also thought Terry's direction was better than the *Grail*.

Saturday, January 13th

Terry J rang from a dubbing theatre at half past nine and, as in a call yesterday, referred to his paranoiac feeling of being 'ganged up' on by Julian and others at Neal's Yard during the editing. Terry G and Julian had sat together at the viewing and at a meeting afterwards Terry G had demolished all of the work Terry J had done.

Purposely try to avoid taking sides with either Terry. It won't help. Terry J must just be allowed to work as uninterruptedly as possible in

---

1 Along with John Cleese, he was one of the founders of Video Arts, who, very successfully, made training films for industry, many of them written by and starring Cleese.

order to make the film ready for the January 19th viewing. In a way TJ's call was a cry for help and support and I said I was prepared to go in and look at any edited film if it will help to get things ready any faster – but if it's merely to help TJ make a point, I said I felt that may be a waste of time at this stage.

Rachel's birthday party got under way at 3.30. Six or seven children. Alison brought Sally. They are at the age when a party is still very exciting and quite a new experience. Willy helped to entertain them – playing monsters in a very avuncular fashion. At one point I saw him leading them all upstairs for a puppet show. But within five minutes they were down again, leaving Willy sadly reflecting that only Sally Jones had really wanted to watch.

Wednesday, January 17th

J Goldstone tells me that the Warner Brothers chief – John Calley – is very enthusiastic about the movie, thinks it could be one of the greatest comedies ever, but the only part they all seemed to find offensive was Graham's brief protestation, after his mother tells him he's the illegitimate son of a Roman, that he's a 'Hebe, a Kike, a Hooknose, a Yid, a Red Sea Pedestrian and proud of it!' Memorable words, written almost a year ago to the day by TJ and myself in Barbados, and now the only section of this deeply controversial film which offends every member of Warner Brothers' Board of Directors!

It's still sleeting as I drive out to the BBC. The dull, harsh, uncomfortable weather seems to reflect the spirit of the times. More people are on strike at the moment than at any time since February 1974, when Heath confronted the miners and the country was put on a three day week.

I still regard the strikes and the disruptions that seem to hit British industry so severely every now and then as a healthy sign. A sign that there are people out there, amongst the computers and the rationalisations, concerned to defend their quality of life by shouting out in indignation rather than submitting Claim Form No. 478B to be heard at the Arbitration Committee's Headquarters by some faceless civil servant in eight months' time.

But there are still plenty of instances of the most wasteful and debilitating lack of personal trust and co-operation. The rail strikes this week seem to be a prime example. The two rail unions, ASLEF and the NUR, hate each other, with the result that, whilst many of the country's road hauliers are on strike, the railways, far from benefiting and offering an uninterrupted service in these cold, grey days – which would win them enormous goodwill – are going on strike too.

But amidst all this gloom there is a golden ring of light – the heroic, titanic struggle between Arsenal and Sheffield Wednesday in the third round of the FA Cup.

Tonight they face each other for the fourth time to try and break the deadlock. We have the radio on in the kitchen but I can hardly bear to listen. One-nil to Wednesday – heart surges. Arsenal miss a penalty – heart practically bursts. Then a minute later Arsenal equalise – numbness. Then Arsenal draw ahead – feeling of resignation, pulse rate almost down to normal. Then Wednesday equalise two minutes from the end! Extra time again. Over seven hours of football and still tied. Then an extra goal apiece in extra time. Another heroic evening. And they play again – in Leicester next Monday.[1]

Friday, January 19th

Brian screening. Terry Hughes, Michael White, George H, Jill Foster. John Goldstone issues us with clipboards and little torches to make notes. Just before time, Graham and Eric – our foreign exiles – arrive.

The showing does not go that well. Long periods of audience silence. But afterwards we all meet (mafia-like) in a private room above the Trattoria Terrazza. General feelings are that the movie works 75%. Disagreement on cuts, however. TJ wants to lose stoning. Eric feels that the Ex-Leper should go before the stoning. All are agreed to cut Haggling and most of the raid. I suggest cutting Mandy's last speech. TJ agrees. Eric is worried about Otto – we all feel that it half works. There are many instances of jokes half working, which disappoints me.

It's a good, workmanlike session, though people about to make earth-shattering points about the movie tend to be interrupted by waiters asking whether they'd like some aubergines.

1 Some readers of the diary may find it confusing that I appear to support both Sheffield football teams (a crime punishable by disembowelment in Sheffield itself). Living in London I'm always glad to hear of any Sheffield success. When I lived in Sheffield I was always a United fan, so that's what I've had to settle for.

My first appearance on Saturday Night Live *had gone well enough for me to be courted again. I was scheduled to guest host at the end of January and quite an adventure ensued.*

Saturday, January 20th

Managed to cope with a packed couple of days on Thursday and Friday, in order to make the 11.15 Concorde to NY this morning for my second guest hosting of *Saturday Night Live.*

About 40 minutes outside London, with the first cocktails flowing and freeing the traveller's brain from the numbing buzz of a hundred other conversations, the pilot's voice comes over the PA and, in bold, almost reassuring tones, advises us that there is 'bad news'. Momentarily visions of the worst sort flash through my mind, but the facts are quite mundane. There is a malfunction with the cooling system in one of the engines and 'transonic' flight will not be possible. We have to return to London.

So I find myself back in the lounge.

As the delay in repairing our aircraft grows longer (the airline even has a term for it – 'creeping delay'), I'm stuck for two more hours with a roomful of over-achievers. And no brunch.

Sunday, January 21st, The Hospitality Inn, Enfield, Connecticut

8.00 A. M.	Outside my room drizzle falls out of grey skies onto snow. Thin, spiky bare birch woods away to my right. Below me a man is clearing his car window of three inches of snow – the result of the storm that eventually ensured our progress across the Atlantic was nearer 22 hours than the three and a half Concorde proudly boasts.
	I kept a note of the lost day – January 20th – which surely will go down in the annals of supersonic flight.
12.15–	We wait in the departure lounge for five and a half hours
5.45 P.M.	whilst a new part is found for the aircraft. By then it's too late for the old crew to work, so a new crew has to be found.
5.50 P.M.	BA 171 starts take-off six and a half hours behind schedule. Take-off aborted as anti-skid warning light fails to function. We taxi back to ramp.
5.50–	Two hours' wait in the aircraft (more champagne) for new
8.00 P.M.	part to be installed and fuel tank topped up – 'Only three

tons,' says the captain cheerfully, though this may be a reference to the Dom Perignon.

8.00 P.M.	Successful take-off from Heathrow eight and a half hours late.
12.00 A.M.	Land at Bradley Field Airport, Connecticut, as there is congestion at JFK due to a snowstorm and Concorde, with its gargantuan fuel appetite and lack of big enough tanks, cannot afford to go in the stack.
1.30 A.M.	We leave the aircraft in a swirling snowstorm and wait in a baggage collection area (we cannot go through into the restaurant or even to the toilets because we have no immigration or customs men to clear us).
12.00– 1.30 A.M.	We wait as the decision is taken to put 82,000 gallons more fuel into the aircraft.
1.30– 2.45 A.M.	Wait in limbo at Bradley Field International, an airport that seems to be run entirely by students between the ages of 18 and 21.
2.45 A.M.	Board Concorde for the third time today. This time with a film crew to capture our every indignity.
4.00 A.M.	Pilot decides not to take BA 171 into JFK tonight owing to bad weather.
5.00 A.M.	We disembark for the third and final time.
5.45 A.M.	As we wait in the no-man's-land – now into our nineteenth hour in airports – news that the doors of the luggage bay are iced up.
6.00 A.M.	Our baggage is retrieved.
6.10 A.M.	Board our coach.
7.10 A.M.	Our coach arrives at Hospitality Inn, Enfield.
8.30 A.M.	Bed.

Still some doubt as to whether JFK or La Guardia are open. The remnants of flight BA 171 are now splitting into smaller groups to find their way to their final destination.

At ten, four of us – Pat, a stocky, young paper salesman, Nancy, a slim, wide-eyed New York model, and the white-haired, ruddy-faced, cherubic director of a Minneapolis-based agricultural foodstuffs corporation – set off, crammed tight into a yellow cab.

Even the cab drive is something of an ordeal. The driver is

short, squat, off-hand and incompetent. At one point, on the outskirts of Hartford, we find a road blocked by flooding and have to turn back.

An uncomfortable hour brings us to Hartford Station. An almost empty, long booking hall, of a vaguely classical design. It's shabby and run down. The poor relation of US transport – the railroad. But, full of hope, we board the 11.30 for New York via New Haven.

On the outskirts of New Haven, the line is submerged for about half a mile and we move slowly through the water, to arrive at New Haven ten minutes late, at 12.35. Another transfer of heavy bags and baggages to the New Haven–Penn Station train.

The station at New Haven is still well below the standards of British counterparts, but the Amtrak 'Parlor' Car – a First Class service – is comfortable, with modern, expansive armchair seats and a bar which serves food and drinks. My spirits rise.

However, the train does not move and the Awful Rumours begin. There is a derailment on a flooded line, further up the track, a power sub-station in the Bronx is out of action due to flooding, so none of the electric locomotives can function.

At one point the Parlor Car empties as we are advised that another train will be leaving for NY before us. This proves to be a false alarm, and everyone reboards. But fifteen minutes later, as I am about to settle down to a cool glass of Inglenook Californian Chablis, the word comes again that a train will definitely be leaving for Grand Central Station right away on Track 6. So everyone, apart from one man who remains because he can't bear the thought of standing all the way to New York (Wise and Shrewd Traveller) makes their way once more up the long platform, down the subway and up to the Connecticut Railway platform.

There's still a ten-minute wait, but the good news is that we do have the satisfaction of being the first train to leave New Haven since early morning. The bad news is we're squashed into a crowded open coach without lights or heating. There are gloomy predictions that the ride could take up to two hours.

In the end it takes over five hours. During that time we spend nearly an hour in darkness, with no fresh air, at a standstill somewhere in the outer suburbs of New York. The compartments have become fuller and fuller, and we have even suffered the indignity of seeing the Amtrak train – with my freshly opened half-bottle of Inglenook undrunk beside a broad and empty armchair – hurtle past us two hours before our arrival.

What makes it worse is that the train is full of Python devotees, who cannot believe that this crumpled ruin, with a once-fresh Concorde label on his bag, is to be the host of their favourite TV programme of the week.

Finally we reach Grand Central Station – it feels like rounding Cape Horn – but there is one final twist. Before we all split up we find that one of the cases we have been dragging around for the last nine and a half hours does not belong to any of the four of us. And it's the heaviest.

Wednesday, January 24th, New York

The read-through slowly fills up. There are thirty or forty people packed in the room to get the first inkling of what the show may be like. Belushi, as crumpled and unkempt as Aykroyd, is given 'Happy Birthday'. He's 30 today – and has a No. 1 film – *Animal House* – and No. 1 record to celebrate it. He's a big, fat boy made good. He eats like a Bunter and grunts and sniffs and emits continuous breathy groans.

The material is plentiful – the result of a three-week lay-off for the writers. There is one quiz game – 'Name the Bats' – written by Brian McConachie, which has one of the best receptions of any sketch at a first reading that I've ever heard. Myself, Belushi and Gilda can hardly read it. An absolute winner. A masterpiece of absurdity.

At the end of a read that lasts over two hours, Lorne declares that he thinks this is some of the best material he's heard for a show, and hastens to add that he never says things like this on a Wednesday. So everyone goes away pleased, apart from the few whose material died, and possibly Laraine and Jane[1] and Gilda, who never have enough material to suit their talents.

Thursday, January 25th, New York

Spend the morning working on the monologue and take it in with me to NBC at a quarter to one.

Bill Murray drops by the dressing room. He's making a movie (his second since I last told him he should be doing at least as many as

---

1 Jane Curtin – original cast member and very funny lady. Later starred in *Kate & Allie* and *Third Rock From the Sun*.

Danny and John), in which he plays Hunter S. Thompson, with Peter
Boyle as Thompson's lawyer, who hasn't been seen for five or six years.
They were the narrators of *Fear and Loathing in Las Vegas* – a twentieth-
century masterpiece.

He knows Hunter quite well now. A dangerous man, says Bill, in the
sense that he loves to live on the brink of excitement and the limits of
human stamina and ingenuity. His wit and humour works even better,
Bill maintains, because one's response to it is in part sheer relief that he's
still alive.

Friday, January 26th, New York

Sleep until 8.30 – an eight and a half hour stretch or more, punctuated
only by an early morning alarm call which wrenches me awake at six. It's
for a Mr Malone. Wrong number, I protest. 'You sure you don't have a Mr
Malone with you?' Her tone is such that I have for a moment to think
very clearly as to whether I might have a Mr Malone with me after all.

To NBC at two.

Reading the sketches there are some real gems – including a long
'What If Superman Had Been a German', in which I play Hitler.

We start blocking about three and make slow progress until eleven
when we have to stop, with one and a half sketches still untouched. One
encouraging thing is that from all around I'm picking up good word, not
only on this show, but on the last we did together. Bill Murray, over an
hour's supper break at Charley O's, still reckons it was the most
consistently funny show they did last year.

Bill is very flattering in his serious, downbeat way, which makes
cynical Englishmen, unused to accepting praise, worry a little in case
they're being sent up. Still, he's very surprised that I have had no outside
offers after *SNL* – he thinks I would be a cert for American movies!

I must say, one feels a very poor cousin hearing of all the movies
these people are doing. Belushi and Dan A are both in Spielberg's *1941*
and return to LA Sunday to continue shooting.

Saturday, January 27th, New York

Walk down to NBC with Nancy. She tells me Eric has arrived on this
morning's Concorde. I find I now wince involuntarily whenever I hear
that name (Concorde, not Eric).

My major problem of the afternoon is that the much improved and carefully honed monologue, in which I refer casually to a lack of proper socks (when everything else is perfect) and gradually build it into an obsession, just isn't working. It raises hardly a laugh (except from Bill Murray – my greatest fan!) and I return to the dressing room in a state of some despondency. How I could do with the security of the cat routine now!

After the meal break, and as the audience are beginning to file in for the dress rehearsal, I tell Lorne that I feel that a possible salvation for the monologue would be to lose the cards and do it ad-lib. Lorne agrees and I wait for the start of the dress rehearsal with added adrenaline output – knowing that I have to make up four or five minutes of spiel.

The monologue founders at dress rehearsal. I stumble on painfully. The whole of the rest of the show seems to sag too.

Various suggestions for cut-down monologues. Lorne says it may be best to be straight, sincere, say we have a fantastically full show and get off after 30 seconds. But someone – I think it may be director Davy Wilson, with his solid, dependable good humour – decides me to go with it.

11.30 – again the wait backstage, the very successful Carter cold opening, then the music builds and Don Pardo's classic American announcer's voice builds with stomach wrenching speed up to the climax – 'Michael Palin!' And out I come. And I know I'll survive. They're listening and I sense they're not embarrassed. In fact it begins to get a few laughs, I enjoy playing it, and it comes to an end with applause I'm very happy with. Not a great monologue – for it was always a slight idea – but I feel immeasurably happier throughout the show because it had worked – I had saved it.

The show, predictably perhaps, really takes off. Sketches, cut only within the last half-hour, work better than ever, performances are all tweaked up, the live magic works and even during the show, but certainly by the end, word gets around that it's a good one.

It's a nice, silly time of one's life, this hour or so after hosting a successful show. For a while you're King of the Castle.

The air of unreality continues at the after-show party at 1 Fifth Avenue, when half-way through our meal a waiter arrives, announces a telephone call for me and leads me off through the kitchens to the back of the restaurant where stand huge, evil-looking basins full of clogged washing-up. I'm told that one of the washing-up staff has always wanted to meet me, and was shown the man, who rather sheepishly turns round and breaks into a grin. It's Alan Bennett, a friend of the restaurant owner, hands in the sink. He immediately goes into profuse self-deprecation, saying what a fool he's felt waiting for me for an hour!

Eventually he comes to the table and I ask if he's going back to London for the press showing of the last of his Frears/London Weekend plays. Alan doesn't think he is. He likes New York. Stephen wants him to write a play about it, but he just enjoys being here and can't put his mind to work.

Monday, January 29th, New York

Lunch, organised by PBS, with TV critic Marvin Kitman, an eager, talkative, spongy-faced character, who's full of bounce and one feels is used to sharp, quick one-liners, which I can never supply very well. But we had a good talk. He noticed a difference between my two shows. In the first one my own contribution resulted, he felt, in two pieces which broke new ground for the show – one was the cats down the trousers, and the other was the escape from the box during *The Seagull.*

This time, he felt, the show was within itself and lacked a unique edge. Which I had to agree with. I should have registered my feelings more strongly to Lorne perhaps, but I did want to play a character – or at least do something original enough to top the cats.

Kitman told me of George Carlin, American comic, who once did a spot like that on a show and simply came out, said nothing for four minutes, then walked off again. And it worked!

Friday, February 2nd

To Neal's Yard this morning. Pick my way through piles of uncollected garbage piled up in the passageway from Monmouth Street. At least we've had heat and light, but we don't have any dustmen at the moment.

At six I'm in De Lane Lea's basement for a preview of *Brian.*

The audience is three or four times the size of the last showing I attended, the night before I left for New York. And, although the film is shorter, with Shepherds and a large part of the raid removed, I think it's the size of the audience that makes all the difference. They are much noisier in their appreciation and the end section goes particularly well.

I end up in the Carlisle Arms with Anne H, John G and Terry G and

Julian. Julian is finding it almost impossible to spend any time on his own fine-cutting the movie without constant interruptions from Terry, over small points which Julian now regards as of secondary importance to getting the movie completed on time.

I am appealed to, almost as if they'd tried everything else, to talk to Terry and impress upon him the need to keep away from Julian for the next few days.

Saturday, February 3rd

A clear, bright, sunny morning. My first weekend with the children since Rachel's fourth birthday on the 13th but I have to spend today at Neal's Yard, trying to patch up the wretched PR problems between editor and director. Gilliam arrives on his bicycle with a list of points on the film – 'A Few Hopefully Helpful Hints in the Pursuit of Perfection', which I take down with me.

I get to the editing rooms by 10.15. Terry is already there and Julian has been in since six!

Terry, Julian and myself sit and work amiably and constructively through the entire film, raising all the points from yesterday's viewing. Terry G's as well. TJ is amenable to most of the suggestions and some good cuts are agreed on.

Drive TJ back up to Hampstead at four and as we go he tells me of the difficulties of working with Julian. Terry acknowledges in one breath that Julian is an excellent editor, but at the same time bitterly accuses him of not taking a blind bit of notice of any of TJ's suggestions. I urge TJ to take a breather from the film – at least for twenty-four hours. He looks as baggy-eyed as Julian is red-eyed.

Tuesday, February 6th

Completed a rewrite on the end of 'Whinfrey' this morning.

Drive into Soho for one o'clock viewing of *Brian* – mainly for Eric who arrived back from LA last night. He has to leave the country again on Friday – for tax reasons. The showing is a good one and confirms my feeling after last Friday that the movie is consistently funnier than the *Grail*, but without the high points of visual and verbal felicity such as Trojan Rabbit and Black Knight fights.

Sandy Lieberson is at the viewing. He warns us that it will be 'X' rated because of the full-frontal nudity and that's about all. I feel we must not compromise on the 'full-frontal' (what an absurd phrase anyway). It's a very funny scene, and Graham's reaction as he appears stark naked at the window, only to find 500 'followers' waiting to worship him, is one of the biggest and best laughs of the film.

Eric looks unhappy. He feels both Haggling and Ex-Leper should go. He is dissuaded from this, at least until they're dubbed – the general feeling being voiced by Julian, who claims that they are both scenes which people listen to and appreciate rather than roar with laughter at.

Clash over 'Brian of Nazareth' *Life of Brian* title suggestions. Eric says everyone in America he's talked to will be very disappointed if it's not 'Nazareth'. TJ and I maintain it's inviting a misleading comparison with *Jesus of Nazareth*. Eric says we could lose a million dollars or so with a flat title like *Life of Brian*. Eric's sharpness makes me sharp in return. A pity, because we need to listen to each other a bit more.

David Leland and Stephanie come round to dinner this evening. We have a chat over the 'Northern Yarn' ('Golden Gordon') and he gives me a lot of useful casting suggestions for the small but vital parts in it. I persuade – not that it takes much doing – David himself to play the Football Manager. He rather likes the idea of wearing long shorts and old-fashioned boots with the huge toe-caps that curl round like Arab slippers.

Saturday, February 10th

Drive to Soho to get *Variety* and croissants. The piles of uncollected rubbish are now being blown apart by the wind and central Soho looks like a tip from which buildings emerge.

Gilliam tells of the latest *Brian* saga. Paramount Pictures are now the most likely distributor, and to further the deal Julian was to be sent over to Hollywood with the cutting copy of the film to show them the latest progress. All was well until it was discovered that Julian, in filling out his visa application form, had felt bound to note that he was a communist. America will not let in communists, so there was great commotion. However, after application to some special US department at Frankfurt, Julian was given permission to go. So the self-confessed communist travelled First Class in a Jumbo and will be staying at the Beverly Wilshire.

TG and I consoled ourselves with a *Variety* clipping which shows that *Jabberwocky* has out-earned *Rocky* and *Looking for Mr Goodbar*, in Spain!

Wednesday, February 14th

Terry tells me the latest on the American viewing of *Brian*, which Graham rang him so gloomily about at the weekend. It transpires that Graham had attended, not *the* viewing in LA, but a later, less well-attended overflow viewing. He had arrived late and the sound had been very bad. But GC still feels that 'an alien force' (his words) has been at work on the editing and he is flying back to England at the weekend with his thoughts and criticisms.

I don't think anyone is going to listen very sympathetically. John C thinks that Graham is being an old woman and anyway he's too busy putting *Fawlty Towers* together to attend any meetings. T Gilliam will not, on principle, attend any meetings unless we're all there. So the prospects for Chapman's Flying Visit don't look too hopeful.

A meeting at the Lamb with John Gorman and Chris Tarrant to discuss what TJ and I are expected to do on the ATV Saturday morning program *Tiswas*, which we are guesting on in a couple of days. Everything's left delightfully vague, but they're expecting two or three sketches from us, so it won't be a complete doddle.

Take Helen to the ICA to see Victoria Wood's play *Talent*, which was originally directed by David Leland for the Crucible – and two or three of the actors in it have been highly recommended by David for parts in the *Yarns*. I'm impressed by the cast, but also by the earthy, untheatrical directness of the play. It's not profound, but a very funny, well-observed slice of life ...

And obviously a cult success – Michael Codron and Humphrey Barclay are in a packed audience of 200 or so. Talk to Humphrey afterwards. He tells me he lives at the bottom of Derek Jacobi's garden, and gives a naughty smile.

Saturday, February 17th

Coffee at the Monmouth Coffee House, then across to the Bijou Theatre for another viewing of *Brian*. Sit next to Graham, who looks trim and healthy. Altogether a new, meek Graham. Then I remember he has got us here for a viewing no one particularly wants (and John Cleese and Terry Gilliam have refused to attend anyway).

Afterwards, at a meeting at John Goldstone's office, Eric, Terry J, myself and Graham have a rather efficient, direct and radical appraisal of the movie. I now feel that the Ex-Leper sketch, funny though it ought to be, isn't getting the right reaction, and is structurally holding up progress of the story at that early stage in the movie. Eric has always felt that and he feels Otto should go for the same reason. There is still a split on the title of the movie, however, between *Life of Brian* (John, Terry J and myself) and 'Brian of Nazareth' (the others).

Graham's fears about the pace of the film, of the 'alien force' in the editing, are all rather predictably more bark than bite and, apart from a couple of fairly tiny points, he makes no fight over the present look of the movie. If I were really uncharitable, I might think that this whole 'Graham Is Unhappy With The Film' scare of the past week was GC's way of getting a free ticket over to the UK to see his home again. But I'm not uncharitable.

Monday, February 19th, Penzance

Woke, seconds before production assistant John Adams' alarm shattered the peace of the Longboat Hotel at six. Easily caught the 6.31, and I was almost sorry to leave the attractive, atmospheric chunkiness of Penzance Station, after a whirlwind scouting of locations for 'Whinfrey'.

At Plymouth, two hours later, the train filled to the brim with eager south-western businessmen. We ate breakfast and I read the treatment of Terry Gilliam's new film, *Brazil*.

Marvellous effects and stupendous graphic ideas in TG's story – but with such stunning sets and surroundings the story needs to be very straight and simple or utterly fantastic. It isn't comfortably either.

Arrive at Paddington at half past twelve. No let-up for location hunters and Alan [our director] insists that we take a cab over to the Turf Club to see one of our London locations for 'Whinfrey'.

The club is in Carlton House Terrace and we meet our designer, Gerry Scott,[1] outside. The suave and elegantly pin-striped club secretary is thrown into frightful confusion by our arrival. He looks us up and down and then very reluctantly lets us in.

We have broken all the rules – especially bringing Gerry, quite

---

1 Production designer on 'Whinfrey's Last Case' and 'Golden Gordon', she went onwards and upwards to design some of the BBC's great period dramas, including *Pride and Prejudice*, *Clarissa* and *The Way We Live Now*.

manifestly a female, into these hallowed quarters – but there has been no revolution or mass resignations, so he's happy. I think he quite enjoys the frisson of naughtiness which letting us in involves. When it boils down to it, there are not many places we have visited whose head isn't turned by the BBC's name and the BBC's money.

Monday, February 26th, Southwold

My long-delayed visit to Southwold.

The weather continues fine, clear and sunny – the countryside up in East Anglia emerging from its most severe winter since 1947. Mother has survived the worst that this harsh winter can bring – and on her own as well. She looks a good colour and seems very bright and vigorous.

After lunch, a walk on the front to survey the damage of the gales – breakwaters smashed like matchsticks and the pier, landmark of my courting days with Helen, lies truncated, a mass of bent and twisted metal curving up from the sea.

Watch a marvellously constructed, very funny *Fawlty Towers*. It's so good it makes me want to give up!

In bed by eleven.

Tuesday, February 27th, Southwold

After breakfast, I work for a couple of hours, bringing the diary up to date and rewriting (again) D Leland's speech as the Football Manager. I think it should be a nervous breakdown, Alan Bell doesn't. Difficult to decide, but I think I must follow my own instinct. Dictate new nervous breakdown speech to the office over the phone.

Ring JC on impulse and congratulate him on last night's disgustingly funny *Fawlty*. JC worried that three jokes out of the still to be broadcast *Fawltys* have appeared in films he's seen over the last couple of weeks. Particularly worried that a scene of Fawlty talking to a dead body, which he wrote a year ago, has just cropped up in Altman's *A Wedding*.

He is very anxious to be in one of the next two *Yarns*. He says he will do anything silly for expenses only – provided 65% of his body is in shot.

Friday, March 2nd

Woke early – rewriting my words for the day over in my mind. The excitement and peculiar nervous tension involved in the first day of any new acting project does not lessen as the time goes on. Instead one grows to learn to accept it and how to deal with it, but it's still there. Tight stomach and loose bowels.

Today is the first day on the first of the two remaining *Yarns* – with a predominantly new crew and with scripts patched and sewn together more rapidly than the others.

Helen dropped me off at Russell Square, after I'd taken Rachel to playschool, and we set to on the single-shot, virtually one-take sequence in which the Orson Welles Introducer is consistently interrupted by everyday life when attempting to introduce a film in the centre of London.

Of course life imitated art. At one point a van drew up exactly where our van was due to draw up – and Alan exactly re-enacted the script when he dashed across the road and shouted at the van driver to move on. At times it seemed quite farcical – a man detailed to stop any traffic impeding the progress of our van ended up stopping our van as well.

Then an hour and a half with an affable, weather-beaten jack-of-all-trades called Reg Potterton, who interviews me for a Python *Playboy* interview. I like him, but an accident-prone day continues when he finds that he's recorded my interview over Terry Jones's!

Finally back home at six. Plenty of letters and phone calls and words to learn for a more gruelling filming day tomorrow – when we start at 8.30, on interior scenes, with actors I don't really know. A baptism of fire for all of us.

Saturday, March 3rd

The first problem of the day is to sort the set out – make suggestions about the look of the office without hurting the designer's feelings too much. There isn't much to do – a few adjustments – replacements of old maps for the recent ones of Europe which the props buyer has inexplicably provided with a great lack of historical sense.

More formidable a task is to tone down the performance of two of the actors – Jack May and Gerald Sim – who are delivering caricatures.

I watch the scene play through, rather anxiously, and constantly have to step in to adjust the actors' performances. I've given up doing this through the director as it just wastes time, and Alan seems very happy for me to talk to them whenever I want.

We complete the scene in mid-afternoon, but the weather is grey and dull beyond the windows and we shall not get the full value of our priceless, unchanged London skyline in the background.

Sunday, March 4th

Quick Sunday lunch, then on to a packed Penzance-via-Bristol train at Paddington. Work on the script – incorporating adjustments suggested by Terry at our meeting on Friday lunchtime.

Maria Aitken[1] and Edward Hardwicke (Otway and Girton) are the only other members of the unit on the train, which reaches Penzance a little after a quarter past nine. The Queen's Hotel, predictably and with some relish, greet us with the news that we can't eat there.

Maria is very complimentary about the script and says her husband (Nigel Davenport) laughed aloud whilst reading it, which is, she tells me, a rare thing. All this helps as I feel rather defensive about 'Whinfrey'.

Monday, March 5th, Penzance

Our luck is in. Awake to fine, almost cloudless skies. The location – around Cape Cornwall – is superb, and can be seen and used today to real advantage. An excellent first day – spent clambering up precipitous cliff sides and in and out of caves wearing dressing gown and pyjamas. Weather remains immaculate, though the wind is so strong I have to have my trilby hat stuck onto my head with double-sided tape.

Wednesday, March 7th, Penzance

The gods are with us. The sea on this side of the peninsula is millpond calm, Penzance quiet and settled once again in its own particular brand of out-of-season silence.

By a combination of eliminating our second cliff location today, good weather, and pushing a reluctant cameraman into an hour's extra

---

1 Maria later played John C's wife in *A Fish Called Wanda*.

shooting, we catch up all we lost yesterday. The sun is bright again – and the cliffs are well displayed. The wind has shifted to the north and is obligingly whipping up the sea below us and crashing it against the cliffs to spectacular effect.

Sunday, March 11th

Eric writes from the Chateau Marmont, thanking me for the *Life of Brian* book material and brimming over with facts and figures about the vast numbers of copies we'll be selling of this book we know nothing about. He's also floating the idea of an LA stage show in September.

Monday, March 12th

Supposedly a day off before completing 'Whinfrey' on the Ealing stages, but the continued strike of riggers and drivers has changed all that. At the moment we can do no more filming until the dispute is settled – and I hear that the last *Fawlty Towers* episode has been cancelled altogether.

Graham Chapman rings from LA. Mainly to voice anxiety over a page of the book he has seen, which, he says, reads like the story of how Eric Idle put the *Life of Brian* together. GC is much concerned with this interpretation of Python history – probably because he's not mentioned at all – but it does increase my own concern that this book is becoming Eric's fait accompli, and we simply must see what is and isn't in it.

Wednesday, March 14th

Cold and wet. North-easterly winds roll the clouds across and I'm glad we're not down in Devon trying to pick up shots. In fact the *Yarns* remain immobilised. Word is that the terms on which the BBC will climb down over the strike are settled, but the strikers have to meet and are unlikely to start the transport moving again until tomorrow morning. So two more unexpected days of peace lie ahead.

One of the many tests of my resolve to write a book this year – when Frank Dunlop rings and asks me if I would like to play in a new West End production of *Rookery Nook*. Ben Travers revivals are all the thing now, and Dunlop, who sounds straightforward, friendly and totally without bullshit, reckons *Rookery Nook* is his best.

I'm so looking forward to writing that it would take something very important to sway me. Farce in the West End would be delightful, but I don't think I really want to make my mark as an actor of farce. Still, can't put the phone down without pangs of regret.

To dinner with the Davidsons. Sheila Pickles is there. Much talk of LA, from which she has just returned. She stayed with Zeffirelli, who is reported to be very cross with the Tunisians for letting Pythons use his sets, and has threatened to decline Bourguiba's offer to make him Minister of Culture!

Sunday, March 18th, Black Horse Hotel, Skipton

Drive to the hotel in Skipton where I'll be staying for most of 'Golden Gordon'. A short back and sides to turn me into Gordon Ottershaw. A drink and a meal at the hotel – cooked by a chef who has seen the *Holy Grail* five times and who approached me, with trembling hands, clutching one of our LPs and five or six of our cassettes for signing. He and his wife will look after us well, I think …

Then to the elegant, tasteful portals of Kildwick Hall, by whose mighty fireplaces Laurence Olivier stood in the film *Wuthering Heights*, and on whose frieze mouldings are the letters W and C – C signifying the Currer family, friends of Charlotte Brontë, and from whom she took her pen name Currer Bell.

Sitting amidst this unretouched history, knocking back scotches in fairly rapid succession, is Bill Fraser, with whom I play the Foggen (scrap merchant) scene tomorrow, and a rather narrow-faced ex-tax inspector, who appears to be the hotel's only other resident.

Bill F looks older, rounder and a little smaller than I remember him.[1] But he is 71 and he has this day completed recording of the Trevor Griffiths' play *Comedians* for the BBC. He finished at 5.30 and was driven straight up here. So no wonder he's winding down.

A joke for bedtime – clamber into my pyjamas, only to find they're Thomas's. I laugh out loud and feel very silly with the little jacket half on before I realise.

---

1 He starred in *The Army Game* and *Bootsie and Snudge*, two of the few television programmes which united my father and myself in helpless laughter.

Monday, March 19th, Skipton

Today the last of the *Ripping Yarns* gets underway. I've no regrets that it is the last one, and yet I'm looking forward to putting it together almost more than any of them.

Bill is quieter this morning – and a little crustier – but he's good on his lines and turns in an effective performance, though not quite as dominating as I'd hoped. But by half past six we have four and a half to five minutes in the can.

Dickie Betts, the lighting gaffer, specially made a point of coming up to me and saying what a good piece of writing the scene was. This I take as a very high compliment, and I hope it will bode well for the rest of the filming.

For myself I found the day hard work and I was very happy to have cleared my own private hurdle – the rattling-off of two complete football teams, both with slightly different players' names. In a strange way the last week's enforced lay-off made it harder to start again. Still, now the wheels are turning once more and Gordon Ottershaw is beginning to come to life.[1]

Bad news at the end of the day – Richard Beckinsale has died: a heart attack at 31. Salutary perhaps. He had been working incredibly hard over the last two or three years, and especially recently. Didn't know him really, but Judy Loe, his missus, was in 'Claw' and a lovely person to work with.

Meal at Kildwick with a relaxing Bill. He's been very professional all day, not touching a drop, but he's now downing scotches with indecent haste and being charming and cantankerous.

Talks wryly of working at the RSC with Trevor Nunn. 'Well, we didn't really see eye to eye … you know, we'd all be in rehearsal and asked to think ourselves into being someone else, and they'd all crouch down on the stage and I'd go off in a corner and if anyone came along and asked what I was I'd say "A piece of shit" and they'd leave me alone.'

---

1 Gordon Ottershaw was the super-fan who smashed up his living-room every time the team lost. Which was most weeks.

Tuesday, March 20th, Skipton

In the evening we shoot some 24 carat gold exteriors at Kildwick Hall. The fine Jacobean façade illuminated by one single 250 amp arc light on a 120 foot hoist. Dickie Betts is in his element, strutting squat and small, with his Alaskan trapper's fur hat on and talking into his radio – 'Bring the moon round, Ron,' and other classics.

Friday, March 23rd, Skipton

A real bonus – a heaven-sent reward for our dogged perseverance. Sun shone all day and we moved to the football pitch at Saltaire to shoot arrivals of Bill Fraser (who'd patiently waited in solitary splendour at Kildwick for two or three days, waiting for the weather to clear) and Teddy Turner (a marvellous piece of casting by Syd Lotterby).

Then it was over to David Leland and his group of footballers – all cast at David's suggestion, and mostly from 'Talent'. David was excellent – efficient and very funny. The whole scene played beautifully and David did his long speech in one take. The crew and onlookers applauded as he raced off into the distance with his trousers down. Four and a half minutes in the can in a couple of hours. A reviving and morale-boosting day.

Sunday, March 25th, Skipton

Today the rain comes – and today is our only day off. Breakfast, buy *The Observer*, read hardly any of it, and retire to my low-ceilinged room looking out over the High Street to read through page proofs of the *Brian* book, which Eric has sent over.

Vaguely unsettled by the balance/bias of the book. Tendency to hagiolatry of Python – as well as an overbalance into the more specific, less subtle, Biblical parodies. Not a book I feel warm to so far.

No chance of working above the noisy bar of the Black Horse, so I drove on to a pub called the Cross Keys at West Marton, which sells Theakston's beer on draught. Bought a pint, found a table and settled to write some material for the Python book. But trying to be as anonymous as possible doesn't really work. People kept coming up with lines like 'Excuse me, but we've got a bet on – are you Eric Idle?' One kind lady bought me a beer – she had watched and enjoyed all the *Yarns*, especially 'Eric Olthwaite'.

To bed unusually early – about 11.15 – after watching heroes of mine, the Joint Stock Theatre Co, made to look pompous and very pretentious in a TV documentary. God save us from TV arts documentaries. Oh, and help *Ripping Yarns* with the weather next week …

Tuesday, March 27th, Skipton

Our second attempt at the football match is rained off after two shots. Two to three thousand pounds in cancelled fees, etc. Gwen Taylor summoned from her day off, etc, to go back to shoot interiors at Brontë Street.

This evening eat at Oats with Gwen and Syd Lotterby – Syd's status enhanced by his collection of a BAFTA award for Best Comedy Series last week – *Going Straight* – Barker, Clement/La Frenais. We will need to use all this status too, as the 'Gordon' costs look like escalating almost to 'Whinfrey'-ish heights.

Leave at ten to collect John Cleese from the 10.20 train at Skipton. Arrive at my car to find fans clustering around. 'Oh, sign this.' 'I can't, I have to meet a train.' Visions of Cleese standing on a cheerless station whilst I sign autographs causes me to be uncharacteristically abrupt with the fans. 'Well, give us a kiss then,' they say, as I slam the car door and search frantically for keys. Then I hear one say 'John Cleese is in there, you know' and point to the hotel I've just come out of.

Out of the car, across to the Black Horse – the downstairs bar, full of young and younger folk, is buzzing with excitement. I push through people looking for the normally unmissable Cleese. Everyone grins – they think it's a Python sketch. I'm directed upstairs, where more excited fans are clustered. It's like a scene out of the *Life of Brian*.

Finally track him down in Ron, the manager's, sitting room. He had reached Leeds by train, then been given a lift to Ilkley, and had taxied on from there to Skipton. Ron, the manager, a rather overweight, round-shouldered fellow with a thick head of red hair that I'm told is not his own, became conspiratorial and told me which button to press on the telephone in order to summon him, and at a moment's notice he would smuggle us out via a special back route.

So a few minutes later buttons were pressed, back stairways descended, back doors opened and John and I walked out into Skipton High Street, feeling like newly released prisoners.

Drove JC over to Kildwick Hall, where the Davises[1] greeted us and Hassan, the Moroccan waiter, hovered, mouth half-open, waiting to be introduced – a perfect echo of Manuel. After a few minutes the temporary excitement subsided and John and I talked for an hour or so.

At one in the morning, I drive back into Skipton, only to find the door of the Black Horse firmly bolted. Knocking won't raise anyone, no windows are open and they don't answer the phone.

Drive back to Kildwick and put up for the night there in conditions of extreme comfort – yet I have to sleep in my shirt and they don't supply toothbrushes.

Wednesday, March 28th, Skipton

Wake early as usual. So many thoughts streaming through my head. Filming a *Yarn* requires not just enthusiasm but stamina. Feel like a coachman controlling fiercely energetic horses, straining to go forward – a crew of fifty or sixty, extras, actors like Bill F, John C, David Leland and Gwen – lots of egos to be harnessed then turned in the right direction. And the weight of it all ultimately devolves on me – I'm the one holding all the pieces together. Only three or four more days to hang on.

It's very jolly working with John at Brontë Street. He looks fine in 1930s gear and wide felt hat. A good-humoured, happy atmosphere. Smash up Brontë Street and by six we are finished there.

Sunday, April 1st

Back home for a while now. Work out that I've been away four of the last nine months.

Today we meet with Denis O'Brien. Eric brings the mock-up of the book, which looks wonderful and allays most of my fears. Everybody approves. Denis O'Brien then fills us in on distribution information. Paramount, MGM, Twentieth Century Fox and Universal have all turned the film down. Paramount after being incredibly keen, until one powerful man on the board said no. Paramount and Universal both took offence at the unsympathetic Jews in the film (e.g. Otto, etc).

Warner Brothers – or rather John Calley, one of their top men – are keen and Denis and George are happy to go with Calley although he is

1 Owners of the hotel.

not offering them an enormous advance, or indeed any advance at all. But they like him. In passing Denis tells us that in fact there is more of his personal money at stake in this movie than George's – but then he smiles when we become solicitous and says 'Well, if it bombs, it's just a couple of houses.' I must say he's the nicest rich man I know.

We talk about the stage show. Eric is like the Top Scholar of the Year at the Dale Carnegie School of Positive Thinking. A powerhouse of ideas, projects, facts – all very impressive.

He sees the stage show in LA as a glorious celebration of Python – and Denis comes in with fervent enthusiasm. It'll be a sell-out, at whatever price, at whatever place. It's all rather like a revivalist meeting. America the Promised Land, wrapped up in contracts and million dollar bills and stuffed down the throats of the recalcitrant, thankless English members of the group.

John C is most vocal in resisting the idea of an expensive, big theatre show. He wants to do it well in a smaller place. But I'm afraid Eric is right – we *could* fill the Hollywood Bowl.

Monday, April 2nd

Back to the Bijou Theatre for another viewing, with some of yesterday's adjustments made. A tiny audience, but I enjoyed the showing much better. 'Ben's Cell' scene is a strange phenomenon. It appears to be very delicately balanced at the opening. If it starts well, then there is great laughter all through, but if something goes wrong at the beginning (God knows why), it can go in silence.

Peter Cook, with frizzed and hennaed hair, is amongst the audience. He seems to enjoy it. It must hurt, because he is so funny himself and yet has had so little success (apart from Derek and Clive records) in the last few years.

Tuesday, April 3rd

At the end of the day I have another Python session. This time to cover as much general ground as we can before Graham returns to Los Angeles tomorrow.

I get to 2 Park Square West by 6.30. They're just discussing the day's film viewing. 'Leper' is back in. It just hadn't worked without it. 'Otto' see-saws between condemnation and popularity. At the moment it's in favour. When discussion comes round to appropriately silly music to be played behind JC's dance, Graham suggests bagpipes and I suggest the bagpipes play 'Hava Nagila'.

The meeting now rattles on with decisions coming thick and fast. I agree to supervise the making of the soundtrack album, JC will put together a short to go out with *Brian*. Eric is keen to go into the merchandising, but his visionary commercial delights appeal not at all to JC, and to a lesser extent TJ, and I must admit I myself baulk at the idea of Python 10 Year mugs, which have the Queen's face crossed out on them.

One good and promising idea of his, though, is that Python set up its own label for the world-wide marketing of Python video cassettes – and also Python-related video cassettes, such as *Yarns*, *Rutland Weekend* and *Fawlty Towers*.

To round off the evening, Iain Johnstone brings his Python documentary (shot in Tunisia) to show us. It's ten o'clock and we're tired, but a little high on all our discussions and decisions and dreams of the future, and Iain's film goes down a treat. It manages to make every one of us look articulate and quite amusing, but wittily avoids being pretentious itself or allowing us to be pretentious.

An odd therapy to all sit round and hear ourselves saying things about each other on screen which we'd never say directly!

Wednesday, April 4th

In the evening (free of Python meetings for once), to dinner with J Cleese. Ronnie Eyre present with JC's psychiatrist's wife, and Christopher Falkus of Weidenfeld's plus wife. Superb meal of asparagus mousse and Jerusalem artichoke salad and roast beef with magnificent trimmings.

Ronnie Eyre, blunt, sane, humorous and down to earth. An effective debunker of pretension and a man whose combination of sharp intelligence, honesty and lack of deviousness makes him a joy to listen and talk to. He says that every religious group was in part offended by his TV programme *The Long Search*, except for the Moslems, who took it rather well.

I end up chatting to him about the *Brian* movie. He's not surprised to hear that the Festival of Light are almost daily ringing the censor's office. He could be a great ally if it ever came to public debate.

Monday, April 9th

Am up in my work-room by seven to look through the *Brian* book proofs and try to unblock some of the problem areas. Terry G is unhappy with the cover and wants me to try and bend Basil Pao's[1] ear on this, but TG is away in Cornwall having a week's break with Maggie. Cleese is in Jamaica, Eric seems to have washed his hands of the book now and is in Nice, and GC's in Los Angeles. So changes, if any, and improvements, are down to what I can think up and work out with Basil between now and lunchtime – when I have to take myself off to Devon for a day's 'Whinfrey' shooting.

Fortunately I'm feeling in quite a relaxed and creative mood and have written enough by the time Basil arrives at midday to satisfy me on several of the more problematical areas of the book. Basil, in turn, seems to be enjoying the book a little more now, after what sounds like an horrendous working experience in LA. I'm glad that Basil agrees with me on the changes – which will involve a week's more work, but which should still enable him to make the deadlines.

He and I leave in a cab at half past one. I to Paddington, Basil to go to the British Museum. Both of us, I think, rather pleased with ourselves.

Tuesday, April 10th

Drive out to Staverton Station. Heavy rain, maybe, but conditions exactly match those of March 10th (a month ago precisely), when we were last here. The shot in the train goes well. Smoking a cigar, leaning back on a soft, plush seat in a railway carriage made for Queen Victoria whilst being paid, filmed and drawn through pretty Devon villages by a steam engine is one of the perks of the job, I must say.

Back to London by half past ten.

Wednesday, April 11th

At 7.30 down to Soho for a viewing of *Brian* (this must be around the twentieth public viewing). Terry J, with a heavy cold and semi-flu, and I are the only Pythons. But, in a small audience, Barry Took (whom it's

---

1 Basil Pao, then working for Warner Bros in LA, designed the book. Now a writer and stills photographer, he has worked with me on six of my BBC travel shows and books.

reassuring to see, considering his part in the birth of Python) and Yves
de Goldschmidt, our natty, suave, French distributor, who greets me
very warmly with the news that *Grail* is still running in Paris.

'Otto' has been cut entirely from the movie for this showing. An
enormous improvement. Tightens the impact of the film, confines it
beneficially to the major characters without going off into extraneous
areas.

Barry liked it and Goldschmidt says afterwards that he reckons it a
much more intelligent film than the *Grail* – but posing many and
greater problems for a translator.

Out to London Airport, which is delightfully empty, and meet Al Lev
off the New York flight. I've taken along a couple of bottles of Penrhos
porter, which we crack sitting in the Mini in Car Park 3.

Thursday, April 12th

To Robert Maas [accountant] for a meeting at two o'clock. Oxford
Street and the main West End roads swollen with people. Pre-Easter
influx I suppose.

Walk through Soho. Despite the crowds, I love its grotty eccentricity
– the sex shops next door to the Chinese restaurants, the boiled duck
looking very similar to the artistes on display in the strip clubs.

John Goldstone says the censor has been along to see *Brian* and
reckons it would be an AA, and he liked it, but he is concerned about
licensing a movie against which there could be legal proceedings. He is
sure that the Festival of Light will try and use the blasphemy law
(upheld in the *Gay News* case) to try and stop the film. Lord Justice
Scarman's judgement in the *Gay News* case[1] gives them a ridiculously
wide area to play with. JG wants to be sure of the church's attitude and
so does the censor.

Friday, April 13th

Nancy rings from NYC. Apart from wanting me to do another *Saturday
Night Live* stint on May 12th, she says that the *Yarns* are due to air on
May 6th. Following an interview with me which appeared in *Publishers'*

1 Scarman upheld the ruling under the Blasphemy Act of 1697 that *Gay News* had offended
by claiming that Christ was homosexual.

Weekly in the US, the op-ed page of the *New York Times* wants me to write a 750-word piece on the state of the English and the elections in particular. A nice little project to take on.

Tuesday, April 17th

I took Anne Henshaw, Jonathan,[1] Al Levinson and Helen to Leith's Restaurant for our thirteenth anniversary meal. With wine from vines just starting to bud when we got married at Abbotsley in April 1966 – and very good food – it set me back £132, but was very jolly. Al in good form, and he and I got the giggles over Dusty Wesker's[2] quite serious offer to Al of 'unattached Canadian girls'. We laughed long and loud over our Calvados.

I think these two weeks will help Al's rehabilitation no end. He has a naturally warm and sunny side and this warm and sunny Easter is bringing him out of a dark and gloomy winter shell.

Anyway, we left Leith's in high spirits. Would say Helen and I are as together as we've ever been. (This could be the beginning of the end – ed.)

Friday, April 20th

After some early work on letters, etc, I took Thomas and Louise over to Shepperton Studios.

Alexander Korda[3] would turn in his grave if he could see the first sight that greeted me as I turned into the front gate of the studio – half the lawn outside the big house has been torn up and the cedar tree – symbol of the comfort, space and style of Shepperton – now ringed by a preserving fence and standing forlornly marooned as the builders hustle around it.

Inside the studios, on the other hand, Korda would feel quite at home. Every available piece of space is being utilised.

We watched the *Titanic* being sunk on H Stage, which had been flooded all over to a depth of five feet with one and a quarter million gallons of water – direct from the nearby reservoir. Polystyrene ice

1 Jonathan James, her new partner, whom she later married.
2 Arnold Wesker's wife.
3 Hungarian-born film producer who founded Shepperton in the 1930s.

floated on freshwater sea, ruffled occasionally by wave machines. Props boys and chippies in rubber diving suits busied around in the water, and dozens of extras looked convincingly tired and cold as they waited in the lifeboats for something to happen.

Then we were shown a wonderfully elaborate space set for *Saturn Three*, and Louise sat in Farrah Fawcett Major's chair.

The movies being made here are now American or Lew Grade[1]-financed blockbusters – there's nothing small about them – and the telegrams pinned to the *SOS Titanic* noticeboard in the production office chilled me to the marrow. They were from Hollywood and ran on the lines of: 'Have just seen the 15-minute assembly. I was moved, awed and excited by the tremendous brilliance of the material. You are creating a true masterpiece …' etc, etc. The schmaltz and sincerity dripped onto the floor like cream from an over-filled cake.[2]

Saturday, April 21st

Talk with TJ on the phone. Last Wednesday night he was attacked by an old gent in Soho who asked him where Charing Cross Station was. When he told him, the old man called our director 'a lying bastard' and belaboured him with his stick. TJ's head was cut and bleeding. A 'passer-by', who TJ thinks may have been a plainclothes man from the Metropolitan force, leapt on the old bloke and hauled him off to the nick. Apparently he had just attacked someone else further up the street.

Sunday, April 22nd

Long sleep. Rise just before ten. But a long recuperative day is not on the cards. TJ rings to ask me if I could spare time today to have another look at the 'Ben's Cell' scene. Although I bridle at the idea of endless re-editing, I think this is useful. There is something about 'Ben' which seems to hold it back from being as funny as it should and could be.

Collect Al L from Jack Cooper's house in Hampstead.[3] Jack, as I am

---

1 Lew Grade and his brothers Bernard Delfont (who abandoned *Life of Brian*) and Leslie Grade pretty much ran popular entertainment at the time.
2 A year later Lew Grade went on to make *Raise the Titanic*, which was such a flop that he famously said it would have been cheaper to lower the Atlantic.
3 Jack and Liz Cooper were famous Hampstead figures. Jack, who knew Al before I did, looked like the Laughing Cavalier.

discovering rapidly, is the Very Life Force itself. Last night he was grinding Al through a guided tour of six or seven malt whiskies. By Al's account Jack went to bed quite blotto, but was up at seven for three hours' birdwatching on the Heath. He spotted a Greater Crested Grebe and was delighted. This afternoon he's taking us to Lord's – he's a member of the MCC, of course.

I take Al home to unload, then we go on to Covent Garden. It's lovely and quiet around the Garden this Sunday morning – a good time to show it off. Al is impressed. We choose new takes of 'Ben', which improve the scene, I think.

Monday, April 23rd

Builders, phone calls, electrician. One of those all too frequently frenetic days at No. 4. I race around the house like a mad scientist trying to prevent the destruction of the world. Al, over in No. 2, gets some writing done. Unblocks that creative side which he has kept tight closed since Eve's death. So he's in good form.

At lunchtime, after I've taken Rachel up to the swings, a lead-grey sky suddenly opens up. Hailstones, leaky kitchen – the works.

J Goldstone tells me that EMI are re-releasing *Holy Grail* on a nationwide basis with *Blazing Saddles*. Fifty-fifty at the box office, and the whole double-bill could be worth £400,000. So EMI are backing Python after all.

Tuesday, April 24th

Work on my *New York Times* article on the election. It gradually comes together during a spotty morning's work. It's not easy to cut oneself off and concentrate during school hols.

Nancy sends me a telegram telling me that, with my Concorde track record, I should embark on a boat for NYC now to arrive in time for *Saturday Night Live* on May 12th. So they do want me. I accept the news with a few misgivings. Something deep down says don't do it.

Thursday, April 26th, Southwold

Buckle down to another journalistic task – this time 750 words for *Variety* – they want a Python piece to go in their Cannes Film Festival issue. Write it between nine and eleven. It comes easily, whereas the *NYT* article kept trapping me, by its status and 'importance', into trying to be heavy and significant.

I had spent an hour in bed this morning contemplating my *SNL* appearance, and had decided that I should begin my novel on May 5th as planned, and that *SNL* would not be progress forward, but a repetition of something I'd done as best I could anyway.

Armed with all these and other supportive arguments, I rang Nancy this evening to ask her to get me released from the show. There was a long and pregnant silence and Nancy finally desperately told me that she couldn't get in touch with them. Lorne and Jean and everyone had settled everything then left for European holidays.

Funnily enough, Nancy's decisiveness must have struck on some equally deep desire of mine to go to New York. I suddenly thought, well, if I have to do it, I'll do it and be positive about it. Armed with this new frame of mind, I don't feel nearly as bad about my volte-face! My 'conversion' was helped by a talk with Howard Goldberg of the *NYT* who was very happy with the article and is leading the op-ed page with it tomorrow – Friday 27th.

Friday, April 27th

Joe McGrath phones early, as I'm typing up the *Variety* piece. He's hustling me to do a commercial. Uses many techniques when I say no – 'They wanted either you or Peter Sellers or Stanley Baxter. I wanted you.' Etc, etc. Eric has recently done one for their company … But I stand firm and he uses his last card, which is loot. He'll still, if I don't mind, get the agency to ring my agent. What persistence.

Meal at Anne Henshaw's. She's 38 today.

Home to find Kelly, our baby-sitter, has been rung by John Cleese, who was stuck in Hull without a *Good Food Guide*! Kelly had to look through and find him somewhere. No luck!

Saturday, May 5th

Rachel is the first one to remember my 36th birthday. Shyly she potters into our bedroom around eight. Helen gives me the new Joseph Heller book, *Good as Gold*, as well as 'The Book of Lists' and a hammer.

Simon Albury arrives with a cake and forty candles just in case. SA announces his intention of trying Gestalt therapy – just once. Then Terry Gilliam arrives and I have an impromptu birthday party. Simon A is busily trying to sell Gilliam his idea for a 'Gilliam World' park – like Disneyworld, only nastier.

I leave for New York tomorrow for yet another *SNL* – and rather wearily start packing just before midnight.

Thursday, May 10th, New York

Down to NBC Studios. Reassuring old 8H. Big, clumsy and un-modern – it's a joy in the middle of all these glass and steel air-conditioned silences. NBC is going through rough times in the ratings war, but this is considered to be a 'good' process, which will lay bare the waste and reveal it as the only network with some soul and independence.

Tape, and write, my promotional announcements. I never enjoy being stuck up there in a vast empty studio at midday, having to say *Saturday Night Live* very fast many times. It's the selling bit of the week.

They're finished by two and suddenly I feel a surge of well-being and in a buoyant mood I begin to write the sort of monologue I wanted to write last January, and for most of this week, but couldn't. Now a nice fantasy forms itself, with good jokes and one liners – more like the Oxford or Cambridge Union speeches.

Belushi, big and panting like a steam engine at a station, sprawls round my dressing room. We talk about groupies. Belushi blows, wheezes, scratches his crotch and confides that 'I'm only fucking my wife now'. I concur and we agree only to fuck each other's wives.

The work in progress on the monologue is brought to a temporary halt by more media exposure. I'm driven over to some studio somewhere for a show hosted by an actor called Robert Klein – a brisk, dark, intense-looking man who has just picked up a Tony nomination. He's talking to three guests on his one and a half hour (with commercials) show: Jerry Garcia of a seminal and long-lasting West Coast group called the Grateful Dead, Clive Davis of Arista and myself. There is an audience of forty or fifty kids packed in a small studio, in which the air conditioning has failed.

Jerry Garcia is big, bearded and looks and sounds deep and rich. He freely bandies words like extrapolate and seems to need no help so I slope off to a small back studio and continue to scribble the monologue.

I do a 20-minute chat with Klein. He's easy, informed and intelligent with a good sense of humour. One of the two or three best people who've ever interviewed me on Python matters.[1]

Saturday, May 12th, New York

Sleep well. I don't suffer from nerves on account of the show quite so much now. I think my experience with the monologue last January at least convinced me that even if the worst happened there would always somehow be a show. Breakfasted – for the first time this week – on the full works – eggs and bacon, etc.

At dress rehearsal the show is well over half an hour too long and feels heavy and much more hit and miss than my previous two shows. With less than an hour to go before air, Lorne begins his selection process. Two or three sketches are cut (one, a Nerds piece about Mr Brighton arriving with a Pakistani wife, I had never liked) and cuts are made within a long pirate spoof, 'Miles Cowperthwaite'.

I do not react well when Lorne sends Al Franken down to my dressing room to cut the monologue. Lorne's touch, however positive, is nearly always delicate, and to send poor Al down with 55 minutes left before I have to go on – and to have him put his pencil through whole chunks of what I spent most of the later part of the week writing, is a most uncharacteristic and tactless move.

At 11.35, after Belushi's cold opening, as I wait behind the tacked-up scenery flats, only a half-inch of plywood separating me from the Great American Public, Lorne threads his way through the old scenery and counsels me to take it easy. 'Look them in the eyes – they'll like you because you're nice.'

The monologue starts well, but half-way through some part of my brain closes off and I'm not wholly riveted to the task of communicating my jokes to the Great American Public. Instead a voice in my head queries the importance, or indeed the necessity, of what I'm doing and why I'm standing here, and suddenly I'm conscious of the silence between the laughs, rather than the laughs themselves.

But the rest of the show swings along merrily. The miracle happens again. Lorne and others are complimentary about the monologue, and I cheer up considerably.

1 Klein later interviewed all the Pythons (bar Graham who was represented by an urn containing his ashes) on stage at the Aspen Comedy Festival in March 1998.

When we get to the goodnights, James Taylor, the week's musical guest, and Billy Murray hoist me on to their shoulders. As one of the stagehands told me later, 'It's not every host they put on their backs.'

3.30 a.m: to Danny's Bar – more drinking, dancing and, as dawn breaks outside, Belushi and two others start playing live. Strong, fine, noisy music. People have to spill out of the tiny bar onto the street to talk. It's six or six thirty – a remarkable sight. The tatty bar in a storehouse and factory area, with a line of limousines waiting outside in the odd white light of a New York dawn.

Thursday, May 17th

Back to my writing room for the first time in two weeks. At the desk by a quarter to eight. And then three hours after breakfast. The novel turns into a play – which seems to rattle very easily off the typewriter – so I will blow with this wind for a while.

Saturday, May 19th

In the p.m. I have to open a fete at William Ellis School. Usually try to avoid public appearances in the local area – once you start they all want you – and anyway, the less conspicuous I am around here, the more comfortable life is. But W Ellis is the most likely school for Tom and William to go to, so I'm interested to see it. It's on the edge of the Heath, was a boys-only grammar school, now a voluntary aid school within the comprehensive system (though still boys-only).

We are collected, en famille, by a car at a quarter to two and don't get home until after five. I give a short opening speech, then have to walk around like the Duke of Edinburgh, with various members of the 'committee' at a discreet distance behind me, whilst I smile and sparkle and fail to hit anything with seven balls on the smash the crockery stall!

Tea with the headmaster in the middle of all this. He's a short, unflashy, rather serious man, who I'm sure does his job well. I think there'll not be much problem getting the boys in. He practically kidnapped them on the spot.

Sunday, May 27th

Take Ma to see the Tate extension. Enjoy the Rothko room this time. After a bit Ma, who has been patient, says rather touchingly 'Before we leave, we will go and see some nice pictures, won't we?'

Home for Sunday lunch, then a trip to the zoo between showers (all except Willy, who won't come because it's cruel).

To help convince Warner Bros that they were doing the right thing in backing Brian, *Denis O'Brien corralled most of the Pythons into a marketing trip to Los Angeles.*

Friday, June 1st

Taxi collects me soon after ten. Another Oak Village send-off, as the children cluster out in the street to wave and Tom announces to Mrs B and any others who may be around that Daddy is going to Hollywood!

The plane takes off an hour late – they've had to change aircraft as the first one was faulty – and we head off on a route I'm not accustomed to – straight up England, past Gospel Oak. Soon after which the pilot makes the momentous announcement that we are flying over Sheffield. He must have relatives there.

At LA Airport meet Graham and Bernard McKenna. Graham is at the wheel of a long, grey Cadillac, which is in itself an astonishing sight – I've never seen GC behind the wheel of a car in my life. But here he is, with his leased Cadillac, heading us through heavy traffic – eight lanes of cars on either side of the freeway making rather a mockery of the hair-tearings over the world fuel shortage.

The weather is dull and cool as we pull up to GC's bungalow in Brentwood – a most salubrious-looking area of extensive houses and gardens. He pays $3,000 a month for this pleasant abode and, sitting out in the garden, sipping a Perrier and watching humming birds darting about and pointing their long noses into hibiscus and honeysuckle, it looks almost worth it.

Graham drives us back to the crumbling Chateau Marmont. It's quite a reasonable time in LA – before midnight. But it's dawn in England as I nod off over Evelyn Waugh's diaries.

Saturday, June 2nd, Chateau Marmont, Los Angeles

No one seems to have slept very well. Potter in my room until mid-morning, then go with a group of us to the Egyptian Theater, Hollywood Boulevard, to see *Alien* – the Shepperton-shot, British-directed, space monster movie that is the latest to do record-breaking business in this film-hungry country.

The Egyptian Theater is a wonderful piece of extravagant decoration in itself – a lot brighter and more cheerful than the movie, which is very well directed and very creepy, up to a point, and loses its way in the last half-hour, by which time all the best shocks have happened.

Out into Hollywood Boulevard. There is nothing of the breathtaking beauty of New York about this city. Low, flat, sprawling and laid-back – like a patient on a psychiatrist's couch.

As Basil the elegant Pao says, people come out here to Hollywood and lease a lifestyle. Here the problem is not how to cope with the difficulties of living, it's how to cope with the ease of living.

A meeting at 5.30. People wander in about six. Graham arrives in dark suit and tie, in extraordinarily voluble form. It gradually dawns on the assembled gathering that he is 'speeding'. Whatever he has taken has turned him into a parody of Ian MacNaughton agreeing and disagreeing without discrimination or information, but with enormous enthusiasm. It's an extraordinary phenomenon and renders the meeting quite useless.

Two limousines arrive to take us to the Bruin Theater in Westwood where *Brian* is to be 'sneak previewed'. At the theatre we find a full house and 1,000 people turned away. Meet the Warner's executives who are, understandably, grinning pleasurably.

John Calley, our greatest supporter and second in command at Warner's, turns out to be a very soft-spoken, pleasant-faced, tweed-jacketed 45–50-year-old, more like an English public school headmaster than a Hollywood mogul. In fact, none of the people I'm introduced to from Warner's are in the least bit mogulish. Not a cigar in sight in the foyer and jeans and soft jackets are the order of the night.

Mike Medavoy – head of Orion Pictures, a chunky redhead with compellingly smiling eyes – takes Terry J out to look at the line (or queue, as we would say in the UK), stretching round the building.

Eric and Graham, meanwhile, are lurking in their limousine, waiting not to get mobbed. They eventually rush out of the limousine, heads down, and race for the door across a, by now, virtually deserted sidewalk.

But inside the theatre are sights and sounds to glad our hearts. A full house – 800 strong – and a tremendous air of anticipation. Cheers and applause as the lights eventually dim.

It's a marvellous showing. Great laughs and applause on a scale we have not yet seen for *Brian*. At the end Eric leads the rush out – and gets into the wrong limousine – whilst Terry and I stand on the sidewalk and talk to one or two of the audience and those waiting – who are not of the tear-your-clothes-off fan type and want to talk quite unsensationally about the movie.

Back at the Marmont for a party (with Thai food) in Basil's room, it's clear that the viewing was a good one. A few people at the party. Harry Nilsson, looking very white and unhealthy by any standards, especially LA, is a father today.

Later in the evening TJ gets woken in his room by a present from Harry in the shape of a Los Angeles naughty lady.

Sunday, June 3rd, Los Angeles

Out to Graham's long, low Brentwood residence. Still cloudy and overcast. A meeting arranged for 11.30, but no one seems to want to get down to anything, application seeming a bit of a crime in this balmy, West Coast atmosphere.

Denis O'Brien, benign as ever, arrives with some lunch – and can hardly contain his excitement over last night. He returns to it with awe and wonder, and even he, who is one of the most level-headed men I've met, comes out with such assurances as 'You know, none of your careers will be the same after last night ... the way they were talking in that foyer ...'

Eventually we start the meeting and become a little more down to earth discussing what is still wrong with the movie. Warner's are worried about the stretch from 'Leper' to 'Ben'. There is nothing but agreement for the 'Otto' cut. Graham is down from yesterday and more gently avuncular.

We discuss our attitude to censorship, on which there is total agreement within the group that we do not and will not change anything because we're told to, unless we happen to agree that it isn't funny anyway. We're all happy to go to court in defence of the movie.

The day drags on into a party, which Graham has arranged for us. None of us is on best partying form. Timothy Leary, he of the drug culture, is there smiling and laughing and seeming very jolly – and again looking like a public school master. A marvellous advert for drug use.

Monday, June 4th, Los Angeles

I slept until four, then woke and stayed awake on a hard bed, streams of thoughts going through my mind – what to do with the *Ripping Yarns*, *Saturday Night Live*, what to say to Warner's today … Then the birds started. It's like sleeping in an aviary. Gorgeous trilling sounds, dozens of different voices – including one bird with a broad American accent calling 'Dor*een*! Dor*een*! Dor*een*!'

Well, it's 8.35, I'm washed, dressed, bathed and going to meet John, Terrys J and G and Anne for breakfast at Schwab's.

At the moment I feel as though I'm stuck fast in some awful enervating dream. Being slowly flattened by the insidious luxury of Hollywood life – and ready for some enormous creature to come and remove my brain and other vital organs. I must get home. It's dreadful here. To add injury to insult my room smells of gas and I've been bitten quite severely by some maliciously hungry LA flea.

We drive out to Burbank Studios to talk to a small contingent (eight or nine) of Warner Bros marketing people. They are all now solidly behind the movie and have decided to give it the treatment.

Some of us, TJ especially, are concerned over the American fundamentalist Baptist backlash – after all, George Harrison, as producer, has already had letters threatening never to buy his records again – but Warner's dismiss all this.

GC comes up with an excellent idea for Python movie No. 4 – 'Monty Python's World War II'. I think it could be a marvellous format for more of a sketch-type film – which everyone seems to want.

So Hollywood can be creative.

A bright end to a day that started for me in quite considerable gloom.

Tuesday, June 5th, Los Angeles

No further bites tonight and a much better sleep.

At Burbank we go first to Warner Records – a lovely, entirely wood and glass-framed low, long building.

Their marketing strategy, developed since we met yesterday, is to concentrate us all in New York for nine days – with all the press coming in from across the US to see the movie (which will have been running in NYC for two or three weeks) and climaxing with a big party.

But all their ideas and enthusiasms fuse into one great howl of approval when Eric suggests using Jeanette Charles (the Queen's double) to spearhead a Royal 10th Anniversary of Python celebration in New York. They all absolutely love this, but, I must admit, using J Charles fills me with little enthusiasm. Eric's used her on *Saturday Night Live*, and she is a rather easy, tacky option for us. Still, if handled quite straight it could be fun.

Back to Warner Records' wooden shack for chats with Denis in an office walled with G Harrison's gold discs. I remember, as I admire again this pleasant working environment, that this is the place which drove Derek Taylor back to England on the verge of madness.

Business chat with Denis – merchandising and the like, then out to the airport with a rather unpleasant cab driver, who admits to his dislike of black people. 'They're bad drivers and bad people and that's that.' He looks Mexican and drives appallingly.

Must get back to the novel. Eric says he's writing a play which has turned into a novel, whereas I have a novel which has turned into a play.

Friday, June 8th

The idea of a full-length *Ripping Yarn* movie, based on the existing films, is crystallising in my mind. Must draft a letter to John Howard Davies and to Bryon Parkin at BBC Enterprises.

In the evening go with Helen and Willy to see Tom play recorder in the Gospel Oak concert. Large orchestra and choir; audience crammed in at the back. Fair share of laughs – someone sick at the back of the orchestra just after a child had announced that she would play 'Variations on Theme of a Lark Song'. 'Hava Nagila' by the massed violins and recorders was wonderfully silly and reminded me to make sure that Python's bagpipe version of the same song should not go unnoticed.

Tuesday, June 12th

The '£1 a gallon petrol' having arrived, I decide to walk Rachel to play-group for ecological reasons. So she and I, hand in hand, trip lightly through the dirt and dog shit down Grafton Road, dodge the lorries turning fiercely and uncompromisingly out of the Building Depot and into the little oasis of tiny people – the Camden Playgroup.

In the evening Mikoto, Helen's Japanese badminton friend, comes to cook us a Japanese meal. The preparation is a painstaking and delicate business – as indeed is communication with Mikoto. The food – tempura I think they're called – vegetables in batter – is quite delicious. We drink sake with it. The kids rave.

I end up eating too much. The food, the sake and the strain of four hours with someone who doesn't speak your language or you his, is perhaps to blame for a colossal drowsiness which numbs my senses about midnight.

Stay awake long enough to see that I and other rich folk are the chief beneficiaries of the first Thatcher–Howe Tory Budget. The top rate of tax is down from 83 to 60%, dividend restraint is lifted, tax thresholds are all lifted. In short, I'm probably £10,000 a year better off after today. There is some inescapable lack of social justice in all this. But it doesn't keep me awake.

Thursday, June 14th

Another viewing of *Brian*. Small audience at the Bijou Theatre – all Pythons there, bar Graham. John Mortimer[1] and Oscar Beuselinck represent the law – Mortimer is to give us his opinion afterwards.

He's a nice, friendly, disarming man, with small, but not at all humourless, eyes, and a ready smile. He's clearly chuffed to be amongst such humorous company. He loves the film and reckons that we are quite safe. The chances of a jury convicting Python of blasphemy on the basis of this film are very remote, he believes – but not impossible. However, should an action be brought, Mortimer thinks it would take at least a year to come to court, by which time we'll have hopefully made our money and our point.

Friday, June 15th

Slow journey over to Chelsea, where I arrive 25 minutes late at chic French seafood restaurant Le Souquet, for lunch with Iain Johnstone,

---

1 Barrister, playwright, novelist, creator of *Rumpole*.

producer of *The Pythons*,[1] who has a proposition for me. It turns out to be the offer of host on a new BBC2 chat show which Iain is hoping to produce from October onwards for thirteen to twenty-six weeks.

My first reaction is fear – how could I cope with this world of wit and repartee? Iain tries to assuage my doubts by telling me that Brian Wenham, head of BBC2, and other BBC luminaries were all very pleased that he'd suggested my name. So I feel a bit wanted, I suppose, but still doubtful. Iain talks of it bringing me 'real fame'. But I think if I have to have 'real fame', I would rather it came from acting or writing, rather than hosting a chat show.

Saturday, June 16th

Spend the morning buying bikes – one each for Tom and Willy, who are now thoroughly enjoying cycling round Gospel Oak, and one for Helen and myself to use as a family workhorse. Equipped like a tank, with voluminous wicker basket on the front and a child seat for Rachel on the back.

In the evening to a party at Eric's – given by Chris Miller[2] (Eric having returned to France) for Carrie Fisher (the heroine of *Star Wars*), who is renting EI's house whilst she works on a *Star Wars* sequel at Elstree.

Carrie looking very small and delicate, her soft, pale skin a refreshing change from the butch aerosol-spray health look of most Los Angeleans. She doesn't know anyone, but is straight and funny at the same time, and we have a mutual line of chat – both belonging to the select band of *Saturday Night Live* hosts. She is currently 'going with' Paul Simon, so sees a great deal of Lorne. Lorne the Great Catalyst – whose name is the criterion for meeting sympathetic people.

The two heroes of *Star Wars* are also there – Mark Hamill (Luke Skywalker) and Harrison Ford.

Hamill is chirpy and is dressed like a delivery boy. Harrison Ford looks young and alienated. He would look over his glasses at us if he had any. As it is he moves broodingly around – like a famous man might do if he knew how famous he is.

---

1 A documentary, made for BBC1 to mark the tenth anniversary of Python's birth.
2 Chris looked after the house while Eric was away.

Monday, June 18th

Collect Rachel from school on the new bike. She laughs and giggles all the way home as we cycle over the bumpy, pitted roads beside the garment factories and under the railway. Definitely a successful purchase.

In the mid-afternoon, Cleese comes round with a small, slim, handsome, trim-faced girlfriend called Suzanne.

We sit in the garden and John eats fruit and talks me into doing a few sketches for the Amnesty shows next week. Nothing terribly exciting. 'Custard Pie Lecture' again. 'Cheese Shop' to look forward to.[1]

Sunday, June 24th

Midsummer's Day. To Her Majesty's Theatre for rehearsal of the second Amnesty Show [*The Secret Policeman's Ball*]. John being very serious and efficient as director. Like a character in a sketch who one expects to suddenly crack into uncontrollable comic spasms – but it never happens.

Meet Rowan Atkinson and Buckman and Beetles[2] for the first time. I suppose we (i.e. the Pythons) are the senior team now – the 'famous ones'. But Eleanor and Pete Cook are there – comforting figures from *our* past.

Helen applies coat after coat of bronzing cream to recreate Tunisian tan on my white body ahead of a *Brian* reshoot tomorrow.

Monday, June 25th

Drive out to Shepperton soon after eight to shoot a new opening to the much-filmed 'Ex-Leper' sequence – a last ditch attempt to try and salvage a piece which everyone (with the possible exception of Eric) thinks ought to be in, but are not quite happy with.

It's over seven months since we last shot 'Ex-Leper' – I've put on a few pounds, but make-up does a pretty good job (Elaine and Maggie).

1 One of my favourite sketches with John. I don't think once, either on television or on stage, was I ever able to get through it with a straight face.
2 Rob Buckman and Chris Beetles carried on the tradition of doctor/comedians (Jonathan Miller, Graham Chapman, Graeme Garden) with *The Pink Medicine Show* in 1978. Buckman remains a doctor, Beetles runs an art gallery.

Shepperton depresses and embarrasses me – the dressing rooms are uncleaned, the place looks shabbier and more down-trodden than ever. The canteen, now partitioned off with hideous paint and a huge, unsightly, unfriendly expanse of plastic sheeting, is unspeakably grim.

We shoot at the main gate of the old *Oliver* set – in itself a sad and crumbling place, with memories, for me, of *Jabberwocky*. The shooting, between showers and aeroplanes, goes along well and we even do some hand-held dialogue shots.

At one point, a strange occurrence. The catering manager shuffles up to me and asks if he might have a word. Is this the moment of truth, when he will at last confess to the appalling service he has inflicted on Shepperton these last few years? Not a bit of it. He tells me he is going to Los Angeles with a film script *he has written* and slips an envelope containing said script into my Ex-Leper's palm, for my perusal – and could I give a copy to Mr Galsworthy (John Goldstone). Game, set and match to him.

Afterwards, over a drink and a very acceptable sandwich in the 'executive' canteen, I talked to David Munro[1] and was astounded to be told by him that he resigned five weeks before, and is only staying on for another month.

On the way home I drop in at Cleese's mighty ex-Bryan Ferryish pile in Ladbroke Road and we rehearse 'Cheese Shop' together. I notice John has all the books I see reviewed, covet and never buy, in his shelves, in pristine condition. 'For my retirement,' John tells me.

Wednesday, June 27th

First night of *The Secret Policeman's Ball*. The shows have all been sold out since Monday and they've been selling standing tickets.

A motley crowd assembles at Her Majesty's about 10.30. The pattern of the evening is set by the first sketch, an E L Wisty piece involving Cook and Cleese and a park bench, which is down on the running order as three minutes, but by the time John C has finished corpsing and Peter ad-libbing, is well past nine.

We take a book on the time of final curtain (curtain up being 11.15). I plump for 1.53 and am nearly an hour out. By the time we pull sweaters up over our heads for Peter Cook's *Beyond the Fringe* 'End of the World Sketch', it's just passing 2.30 – we finally take our bows at 2.35.

1 The successor to Graham Ford as manager of Shepperton.

Saturday, June 30th

Drive over to Anne Henshaw's for a meeting with Denis O'Brien, only to find that the meeting is at Denis's place in Cadogan Square. Dense traffic down Piccadilly, the carbon monoxide fumes filling my lungs as bitter anger fills my rapidly wearying brain.

Finally reach Denis's. John C, Terry G and Terry J – the 'Home' Pythons – are all there. John G and Anne as well. They've been waiting for me. For once I cannot raise a smile in acknowledgement of the usual abuse which any late Python arrival has to endure.

Then Denis pitches in. He's never aggressive, never boorishly arrogant, but by God he's persistent. He would like to take on Python and any individuals in Python. He claims that his organisation (EuroAtlantic) will be able to minimise our UK tax liability on the money we earn from *Brian* – which could be substantial.

So, after very little hard talking, Denis has managed to persuade the four of us that we should let him 'structure' our earnings from *Brian* right away. I suppose this is the thin end of the wedge and I expect that Denis and EuroAtlantic are with Python to stay.

Drive back across London. The parks look green and pleasant, and the Gay Pride March, which caused the traffic build-up which nearly resulted in my death from carbon monoxide poisoning four hours earlier, has dispersed.

Can't get in till late at Her Majesty's as *Ain't Misbehavin'* has come down late. A relaxed show – usual, very warm, very appreciative audience.

Mike Brearley[1] beats up Terry J in the 'Celebrity Sketch' rather well, and Peter Cook's judge's summing-up of the Thorpe court case, which he wrote yesterday, is the small triumph it deserves.[2] Sad it is for the country that political satire, or just satire of important people, has been so effectively stamped out of the media in the last ten years. Good for P Cook.

A huge crush of folk in the stalls bar for a party afterwards.

Home by four. Dawn is breaking over Gospel Oak. Richly satisfying 'after the ball' feeling ...

1 Captain of the England cricket team that won the Ashes in 1981. Now a psychoanalyst.
2 Jeremy Thorpe, the Liberal leader, had just been acquitted on charges of involvement in the attempted murder of his gay lover, Norman Scott. The judge's summary was seen by many to be blatantly biased in Thorpe's favour.

Monday, July 2nd

Ate lunch at an empty but excellent Indian restaurant in Berwick Street with Clive Hollick and put to him as clearly and forcibly as I could the extent of my dissatisfaction with Shepperton's progress over the last year. He would not at first accept that things were as serious as I made out – as indeed they are not from the point of view of the balance sheet – but I was talking about the guts and soul and down-to-earth human appeal of the studio, which has suffered disastrously.

He began to take this in, I think, and I persuaded him that things were urgent enough for us to pay a visit within the next week to the studios, as a Board, and inspect it, and I think I dissuaded him from accepting Charles Gregson's recommendation that we should not employ a replacement for Munro, but busk along with two girls. This was contrary to all I felt was needed.

Shepperton needs someone with a spark of fight in them – someone who will be fiercely proud of the studio, who will not be intimidated, who will not be a forelock-tugger to the Board. Ideal sort of man would be Simon Albury, I suggest, almost flippantly, but the more we think about it, the more of a possibility it becomes.

Back into London for some dubbing and post-synching on *Brian*. The new work on the 'Leper' last week does seem to make the speech clearer, but I see-saw on the effectiveness of the sketch. Terry J is the greatest champion of the 'Leper' at the moment. I think Denis O'B would rather see it out. (Have noticed his artistic and creative participation increasing slowly but surely as he and we have got to know each other better.) I dub George Harrison's voice on – another to add to my collection.

Wednesday, July 4th

To the Camden Swimming Gala at Swiss Cottage Baths. Tom P wins the third-year crawl against six other schools, makes up ground in the relay and helps Gospel Oak to the overall and the boys' trophy – and they only just missed a clean sweep in the girls'. A terrific occasion. I feel wonderfully proud. Tom does not brag or boast and is quietly over the moon.

Thursday, July 5th

To John's for a writing session and discussion on film posters and publicity generally in preparation for the Warner launch. JC says he'll chair
the meeting, as he's written a film on how to chair meetings – he means
it half in fun, but mostly seriously.

Eric is in France and has sent a letter with suggestions. GC is in Los
Angeles and has sent a request for another loan from Python. TJ bears
gloomy news about our post-*Grail* tax situation. The authorities are
getting tougher and could interpret our tax position in such a way that
we fork out at least £60,000 of our *Grail* earnings to the government.

But it's a sunny day and we are brought cups of coffee by John's lady
retainers and we spread out over his huge dining table (originally in
Holloway prison) and churn out the sort of easy drivel which gives
much pleasure and does not have to follow plot, story or character. JC
works upstairs, writing heavily sardonic biographies of us all, and TG
looks through photos.

I read out a long and inaccurate synopsis of the film which brought
tears to assembled eyes (there is no better moment in one's creative life
than hysterics at a first read!).

Wednesday, July 11th

I go to Neal's Yard and yet my heart is not really on the [*Life of Brian*
soundtrack] album – it's somewhere else, with the children in the sun. I
find myself gazing at pictures of the countryside, looking at maps,
reading novels – all the paraphernalia of getting away seems much more
important than the paraphernalia of getting on.

In the back of my mind plans turn towards all the things I want to
do, but keep postponing – learning Italian again, going on walking
weekends with the boys, travelling to India – getting out on a limb
again, taking a few risks, facing a few unknowns.

*A new kind of summer holiday for the Palins this year. Instead of Europe,
we stayed for almost a month at Al Levinson's house in the old whaling
port of Sag Harbor on Long Island.*

Sunday, July 29th, Sag Harbor

Here in the middle of this cosy, little New England town (they all call it a village, but it's Southwold size), I have, for almost the first time in a week, a few moments free of my family and Al, who is taking the boys for a swim, and my first urge is to get to the diary.

In the mornings I rise good and early and each new day is greeted with elation – a run through sweet-smelling gardens and woods – breakfast is jolly, and our mornings, spent on the beach at Bridgehampton – a huge, broad, clean sweep of sand with a big clear sea and Atlantic rollers to add to the entertainment – are unequivocally fine – cool in the water, hot in the sunshine, full of invigorating physical activity.

The holiday so far has been a helter-skelter of happiness and frustration. Great ups and downs of pleasure and irritation. I'm afraid that I cannot get France or Italy out of my mind and keep making unfair comparisons between their sophistication and the naïvety of America.

Sag Harbor *is* a beautiful little town, with delightful clapboard houses, all comparatively well-kept, all architecturally consistent, nothing new and horrendous. It's attractive to walk around, full of trees and the scent of flowers and yet … and yet … What is it? What is this gloss with which the American Way of Life coats everything? Is it trying too hard to impress?

Is it that the freshness of America has been near-suffocated by the materialism of the place – by the vast wealth of the country, which pours forth a million products, where a thousand would do?

Standards of food and television are appallingly low, and yet there are lots of both. Yet the standards of kindliness and consideration amongst the people are high – though they are sometimes made fools of by their over-sufficiency. See the size of so many over-fed citizens of all ages. Human incarnations of the economy of waste.

Tuesday, July 31st, Sag Harbor

At about six – when my resources were not at their best after a long, hot, tiring day – the phone rang. It was Anne H, from London, ringing to say that Warner's go to press on the posters in two hours.

They have finally rejected our unanimous Python ad-line 'He Wasn't the Messiah, He Was a Very Naughty Boy', and have suggested three alternatives – all of which are dreadful and tend to accentuate the 'outrageousness' of the movie.

Wednesday, August 1st, Sag Harbor

Al's 'guru', the poet and writer Norman Rosten, has arrived. Like Jack Cooper, he is the sort of charming, slightly roguish, loquacious, salt-of-the-earth character that Al seems to attract to him. One of the Brooklyn writers' group that included Mailer, Arthur Miller, James Jones, Joe Heller – a real group of literary giants.

Rosten is respected, but never achieved world status. He wrote a nice little book on Marilyn and he reminisces easily and unselfconsciously about her. His friend was Arthur Miller, and he remembers Miller going to meet Marilyn at the penthouse in the Barbizon Plaza. 'He was scared stiff … I mean, Arthur was a good Jewish boy … he asked me to go up with him because he was literally afraid of going up there on his own.'

Rosten is wonderfully dry and self-deprecating and wittily obser-vant. Marilyn really wanted to be a housewife, and she ended up with Miller and Di Maggio, both 'very religious men' – Rosten called them the two high priests, Jewish and Catholic, presumably to stress the irony of their association with a lady of such profane associations.

Rosten talks of Nixon's revival – of his threatened return to active life and New York. R reckons Nixon one of the two 'diabolic' forces in America. I can't remember the other one. Norman advises me to read De Tocqueville's observations on America as providing some of the best insights on the US, albeit 140 years ago.

Thursday, August 2nd, Sag Harbor

Up at half past seven. Run along the quieter roads, full of a wonderful mixture of scents – musty, sweet, poignant, sharp – rising from the woods and gardens. It's a very sticky, close morning again.

Rachel and I saw a middle-aged man wearing a T-shirt: 'More people died in Ted Kennedy's car than at 3 Mile Island'.

Thursday, August 9th, Sag Harbor

Cooler, clearer sunshine on the way.

Am dripping with sweat on the patio after my fourth run this week when the phone rings. It's Denis O'Brien, to apologise for his sudden indisposition and to renew the invitation to Fisher's Island. Although he has fathers, mothers, children and hordes of relatives arriving and departing, he says we *must* come. 'We'll try and break house records,' he promises cheerfully.

I take a call from Nancy. She has some request for the two Terrys and myself to go to Toronto during our film publicity in September. This 'publicity binge' rears menacingly close. God, it's then I shall miss these superb, drifting, timeless, sunny days. This Thursday is near-perfect – sunlight bright, sky royal blue, all the countryside lit as if God was showing round prospective buyers.

Friday, August 10th, Sag Harbor

Shopped for presents, then took an early lunch and drove in search of Easthampton Airport. At the airport we waited for a single-engined Piper Cherokee Six to float in like a butterfly over the low surrounding woodland and taxi up to the little suburban bungalow with sun-deck, which served as the airport office building, refreshment room and control tower. This was our Yankee Airways flight to Fisher's Island.

The entire Palin family filled the little plane, with one spare seat for the pilot. Weather was good and we turned north and then east in a circle to avoid some restricted area over Plum Island where 'they do experiments on animals' (said the otherwise taciturn pilot, darkly), then within 20 minutes we were turning over Fisher's Island and down onto an overgrown strip surrounded by what looked like a scrap yard.

Brian, Denis's 'man', who is from Huddersfield (with a Yorkshire accent tempered weirdly by fifteen years in Vancouver), meets us and drives us the length of the island (about six miles) to what he calls 'The Castle', but Denis calls 'The Farm'. This confusion is understandable, the house on the point is a hybrid of Scottish baronial and French fortified farmhouse. Built in the middle of the Depression (1930) by a man called Simmons – a bed magnate! – who spent money on a grand scale.

We sat after dinner in the long, dark room, and Denis turned the lights so low that at one point (his wife) Inge thought Helen had gone to bed, although she was in fact sitting in a chair opposite.

We went up to our brass four-poster bed soon after ten. Rachel's rubber lilo kept deflating and we had to improvise a bed for her. Eventually, and slowly, I drifted off to sleep, surrounded by a cacophony of nocturnal seagulls and buoys making a variety of doom-laden, bell-tolling rings out on the Sound.

Saturday, August 11th, White Caps, Fisher's Island

After breakfast, Denis and I adjourn to the long room, sinking into their comfortable sofas and looking out towards the not-too-distant Connecticut shore and the bevy of fishing boats come to snatch bluefish from the rich waters off the headland. Denis and I talk about his taking over my financial affairs – everything will be looked after from holidays to contracts, all of which will be personally negotiated by Denis himself. He wants to give us 'flexibility' – that is to take all possible measures to ensure that we control as closely as possible the commercial exploitation of all our work.

After a good talk, Denis suggests that he and I go over to see John Calley, who lives mid-way down the island.

John Calley, friend to the talented (viz Kubrick, Lorne Michaels), genial face full of neatly cropped beard and big, black-rimmed spectacles, is wearing a colourful, light wool topcoat over a *Superman* T-shirt and green striped slacks with shoes and no socks.

He takes us through endless sitting rooms and libraries until we settle on a room to sit in – the size of the coach house where eight of us are living at Sag Harbor! It turns out that he is only on Fisher's Island for a month of the year. Denis confirms that the summer population may be 3,000, but in winter it shrinks to 300 all-year residents.

Denis goes to phone the airline, leaving me with Calley. Decide to go in at the deep end and ask him if he will look at the three new *Ripping Yarn* films I've brought over and advise on whether they may be combined as a theatrical movie in the US.

As soon as we start talking 'business', I find myself talking easily and constructively to him, rather as I can with Lorne. Calley does not react in any stereotyped Hollywood way – he muses, reflects and suggests, gently and amusingly, not playing the mogul. I felt contact being made on a sensible and sensitive level and I will be very interested to hear his reaction to the *Yarns*, which he promises to view next week.

From Calley's we drive in the Black Bronco down the road (mostly unmade, with occasional strips of tarmac) back to White Caps. The weather is holding firm, but overcast – the flights are going. The Palins are lifted off Fisher's Island in two planes – Helen, Willy and Rachel first, then myself and Tom a few minutes later.

A useful visit, but I'm glad to be back in the cosy, crowded warmth of Sag Harbor and the coach house. I still feel uncomfortable and a little uneasy in enormous houses. For me they are still like living in museums. It sets me to thinking about our little home and 'living in the community' – as Al puts it.

Enough philosophising. This short trip and the talks of August 10th/11th with Denis and Calley could alter all our circumstances within a year. We may just have to spend, throw away or give away an awful lot of money – being accepted on Fisher's Island seems to mean that.

Sunday, August 12th, Sag Harbor

It sounds to be raining every time I wake in the night and there's a strong wind too. All rather cosy inside our house.

Al comes in at ten – I'm just looking at the first Python poster of the *Brian* campaign, which appears this morning in the *New York Times*. Al looks worried and says a 'North-Easter' has set in and high wind and rain could persist all day. Temperatures must have dropped almost 30 degrees over the weekend and I roll on my sweater for the first time.

It's the day, suddenly, amazingly, for a log fire. And where else but America would you *buy* a log at the local delicatessen. Smoked salmon and a log, please. It comes ready-wrapped with instructions on how to unwrap and light it. Extremely – dare I say – sensible and a Godsend on a rip-roaring wet day when you have no other dry wood to burn. So, what with our instant log fire, our resident screaming wind and lashing rain, we settle into our (now) traditional lox, bagels and champagne Sunday lunch, which the last two weeks have been eaten sweatily, in shorts, trying to avoid the heavy, omnipresent heat.

Monday, August 13th

Try to make farewells as quick and impermanent as possible, for I know Al will miss all the life at the coach house.

This has been a great children's holiday, and they have been generally easy company too. Though perhaps my list of books read – one Anthony Powell, ninety pages of a Steinbeck, fifty pages of a Levinson work in progress – testifies to the way they dominated the holiday. I feel good, though, and I am looking forward to home and writing.

The New York–London flight passes unmemorably. It's efficient and notable only for the sight of very high seas and white caps and breaking waves on the approach to Cornwall. I've never seen the sea in such turmoil.

Tuesday, August 14th

Within a quarter hour of arrival at Gospel Oak, the phone contacts begin. A series of quite important calls. Bryon Parkin from BBC Enterprises calls to say that 'his colleagues' at TV Centre have assured me that there would be insurmountable problems from unions in the way of a theatrical release for the *Ripping Yarns*.

What a complete Beeb man is Parkin. He seems to have about as much drive as Rachel's tricycle and has consistently failed to come up with the goods on anything I've asked him.

Alan Bell calls to confirm dates for the three new *Yarns* – beginning Monday, September 24th at 9.25. He tells me that John H-D has viewed the three shows and recommended laugh tracks on them all. Alan Bell softens this other bit of BBC recalcitrance by saying that he, too, watching them on TV, felt the audience helped. Back to square one there. But, again, I don't feel angry or even disappointed. The holiday helped.

Terry Gilliam tells me that Eric was so unhappy with the Python soundtrack album André and I had produced, that he is working on a replacement. The objection was, I'm told, basically to the live album, audience idea. I feel not bitter, but just frustrated. I was never wholly keen on the live album, Eric was away and quite inaccessible for quick decisions and Warner's wanted the album quick. So my work was wasted. I'm quite glad it at least stirred other Pythons into some sort of action, and I shall send back £1,000 of the £1,500 fee I took for my work on it. An episode in my creative career that I shall happily forget.

Thursday, August 16th

The jet-lagged Palin household (still living in US time) finally rose around ten. I see from the paper that the white-capped waves which I noticed on the approaches to Cornwall on Tuesday morning have so far claimed seventeen lives. As we sat rather comfortably in our First Class lounge, dabbing

Cooper's Oxford on dull croissants, the yachtsmen in the Fastnet Race were directly below us, fighting huge storms, forty-foot waves and the worst conditions the race has ever run into.

My cold is still heavy, but after a morning's work on letters and phone calls I drive down in sunshine and scudding cloud to Neal's Yard.

Eric arrives heavily bearded. His land in the Var has been razed to the ground by a forest fire, poor bugger. Graham is here too, and Terry G. We listen to the 'new' album – which is the stereo soundtrack *without* laughs, which evidently all the Pythons prefer. I must say the selection sounds lifeless, but Eric and Graham's ad-libbed links are funny.

At the end, all present OK the new album, but without enthusiasm. André does not look happy at the prospect of working for two more days – and probably nights – to complete this one. Eric and Graham will have to supervise the work. I refuse.

Friday, August 17th

Opening day for *Brian* in New York and Los Angeles. It seems difficult to grasp that we will actually be starting to get our money back, as from this evening.

Terry J rang from New York to say that there was a queue of *one* at the Cinema One at first light this morning – and he had a copy of the *Ripping Yarns* book.

But Canby's review in the *New York Times* was a rave and that the 'Post' and 'News' too were good. So far a clean sweep of reviews.

Saturday, August 18th

At lunchtime I cycle up to the Freemasons for a drink with GC, John Tomiczek and Bernard McKenna.

They all came down to inspect No. 2. Graham quietly pottering and muttering about all the bills he still has to face from *Odd Job*. Still, he's driving a hired Mercedes, which EuroAtlantic found for him, and seems well, though a little quiet since he gave up the booze. Bernard as big and warm as ever. A lovely man. Rachel takes to him immediately.

I take the boys to St Martin's Lane Odeon to see *The Spaceman and King Arthur* – jolly tiring Disney wholesomeness sticks in the gut of a true cynic, but by the end its sort of charm won even me over. John Le Mesurier playing an exact replica of his *Jabberwocky* role – standing just behind the king and getting wonderful laughs from beautifully thrown asides.

Sunday, August 19th

A call from Denis on Fisher's Island to tell me that the audiences are rolling into *Brian*. Warner's hoped for an $8,000 take at Cinema One on opening day and took $13,000. In Los Angeles all the movie houses showing *Brian* are good. In the Python stronghold of Orange County, one movie theatre took as much on opening day as it did in a week of *Grail*.

Wednesday, August 22nd

I have endeavoured, to help Anne and everyone else, to try and bring the five Pythons present in the UK together for a chat. After many time-consuming phone calls, a meal is arranged for tonight.

At L'Etoile by 8.30. When I arrive Cleese is waiting.

JC and I talked of future plans. Once again, as so often in the last few months, I caught the feeling that Python had come full circle. After ten years, climaxed by what sounds to be a successful opening of *Brian* in the US, John is telling me how he would like to work together on something. A real April '69 conversation between us. It's nice to feel, as John says, that we do work well off each other. No conclusions were reached when Graham, then Eric and TG finally arrived.

JC made the point that in the next Python film we should perhaps stick less to our rigid writing combinations and write with more fluidity. He thought this would help Eric, who always wrote by himself. 'I like writing by myself,' Eric countered, rather defensively.

I said I would rather not work on a new Python script for a full year, JC having proposed that we should all 'go somewhere very nice and just talk for two or three weeks about the subject'. I was called selfish by Eric. JC accused him of bullying. TG came in, as he said, to 'bale me out', by stating that he was not interested in working on another Python movie until he had completed something of his own. Graham said nothing.

But there is remarkable agreement thus far on the main points – that we should do another movie, that it should be completed within three to three and a half years from now, and that World War II is a good area to start thinking in.

Thursday, August 23rd

Drive out to Shepperton for a board meeting.

An efficient meeting, followed by a walk around the site. There have been radical improvements in almost every area which so depressed me six weeks ago. The canteen is cleaner and better equipped, the toilets cleaned, the on-site mess has been drastically reduced and, with the smart new gatehouse and opening of 'Studios Road' as a symbol of this regeneration, the place is suddenly well on the way to looking an attractive and exciting place to work.

Great news that we will probably be able to rent 'H' Stage back, for a very reasonable fee of £92,000 for five years, from the council – impoverished by Thatcher's local spending cuts. At present a *Flash Gordon* forest set, full of swirling tendrils and rubber lianas, fills the place, at a cost of over $1 million in construction fees.

Friday, August 24th

T Gilliam arrives. He's been writing *Brazil* with Alverson[1] all week. He looks a bit unwell. I think he feels their writing combination is not working as well as it should. He's also in the middle of a debilitating hassle with Warner's over the poster. They are determined to use their own wacky in-house ads that they first showed us in LA in June, and which we all immediately and instinctively disliked. But TG and Basil have been unable to produce our own strong alternative. Basil has now given up and Denis O'B, who really doesn't know quite why we're making a fuss over the Warner's poster, is trying to heal the gap.

Saturday, August 25th

Get up a little earlier than I should to buy *Variety*. *Brian* is 'Big 65G' in New York. There is a full-page ad extolling our opening grosses and an editorial piece headed 'Is Holy Screed Fair Game For Hokum?' – which is a fine example of the mid-twentieth century *Variety* style, and to which the answer is – all together now – if it makes money, yes!

I think that Python has actually stolen a march on the critics with this one. As one admitted, he really didn't know how to begin a critical

---

1 Charles Alverson, American thriller writer, and friend of TG, Terry J and myself.

assessment of the movie. Similarly, trade press, though obviously liking the movie, are still a little wary – like children in a playground who've just found a huge, unopened box of chocolate and aren't quite sure how much to enjoy it.

Monday, August 27th

Just musing with Helen over our supper that we have not had one phone call all day, when the instrument of terror tinkles. It's Anne to say that some Jewish groups in the US are offended by *Brian* and are counselling their followers not to see the movie.

There are worse things going on in the world. Today the Provisional IRA took 'credit' for blowing up Lord Mountbatten's yacht, killing Mountbatten, his fourteen-year-old grandson and another young boy, and wounding four others. Two hours later they killed fourteen soldiers in an ambush.

The Mountbatten thing makes me feel almost physically sick.

Saturday, September 1st

The hot, dry weather continues.

Helen tidies the house like a maniac as soon as she hears Uncle David[1] is coming, and it gleams and sparkles by the time the Vice-Chancellor of Loughborough arrives.

A lunch for ten, then we sit around for a while. I do not bring out the copy of *Variety* I bought this morning, which has one entire page devoted to the condemnations of various religious groups. 'Catholic Org Rap Orion For Brian', 'Rabbinical Alliance Pours On Condemnation of *Life of Brian*', 'Lutheran Broadcast Slam at *Life of Brian* – Crude, Rude'. It looks as though we may become a major force for ecumenical harmony.

The next page shows that there are as many of open mind as there are of closed – we are the 21st top-grossing movie, despite playing at only three sites.

Uncle David has a habit of pointing to various domestic improve-ments we've had done at great expense and enquiring heartily 'You've

1 David Collett was Helen's uncle. When I first set eyes on her, in Southwold in 1959, she was last in a column of sisters and cousins being led out behind Uncle David for an early-morning dip in the North Sea. Something about her obvious reluctance appealed to me.

made this, have you, Michael?' I plead incompetence and feel very much the flaccid aesthete in his company.

Monday, September 3rd

Up at seven and out and running down Oak Village by ten past.[1] A quiet, windless morning with much cloud. Straight up to the crest of Parliament Hill, then through beech and oak woods to Kenwood. A half dozen other runners and as many people again walking their dogs.

I do feel much better prepared for the day. This should be the start of the 'new work' season.

Wednesday, September 5th

Attack Parliament Hill in the gleaming early morning sunlight, a haze of warmth to come, through which trees and spires can be glimpsed from across broad fields. The very best morning so far – the freshness of the air and the shafts of sunlight piercing the dark ceiling of oaks and beeches are quite dazzling.

Mind you, I can only move with difficulty for the rest of the day.

George Harrison calls. He has just come back from appearing in court in his continuous saga of the fight for Allen Klein's Beatle money. He said he was very nervous before taking the stand (he went to the lavatory three times before he even left for the court-house). He went to see *Brian* – found a one-third black audience and a row of orthodox Jews – all enjoying it.

But he does tell me of an exquisite piece of justice. Whom should George find himself in the first class lounge at Kennedy with, but Bernard Delfont – the man who turned down *Life of Brian*. George was not backward in going forward and in an informal way enquired whether or not Bernie was acquainted with the fact that Python had taken $1 million already. George thanked him profusely. A heartfelt thanks – echoed by us all.

With Brian *storming the US box office, Denis was increasingly keen to fly the Pythons to America to discuss our future together.*

1 After regular running at Sag Harbor I decided to make it part of my regime in London.

Thursday, September 6th

Up to 80 today as the hot weather continues. A poem from Norman Rosten – 'Good news, about spokesmen for Catholics and Jews' – inspired by the ecumenical outcry.

Denis O'Brien calls. He is assiduous in his efforts to make us all want to come over next week and anxious to assure me, whom I think he sees as chief opposition, that it will be worthwhile.

This evening all the Pythons meet at Anne's to discuss it. As we sit around, it's John who asks 'Isn't there someone missing?' We all agree that we have this sensation whenever the Python group assembles nowadays. The unknown Python. The present 'seventh' Python (taking over from Neil Innes) arrives a moment or two later in the person of George Harrison.

To Odin's for a nice meal and too much wine. Eric, over a glass of champagne, checks round the table, revealing that three Pythons are broke – himself, GC and TJ – and three aren't. George tells tales of the Beatles – of the hugely dominant Yoko who has reduced J Lennon to a housewife, of George's liking for Paul and his 'ego', and Ringo who's … 'You know, very simple'. Other little glimpses into the lives of the rich and famous – like the fact that George admits (with a smile acknowledging the absurdity) that he doesn't buy clothes any more. Clothes come to him.

And, having once again outlasted all other diners, we meander back to Park Square West. It's a full moon and the entire kerb is taken up with Python cars – George's little black Porsche, John's dirty Rolls, my Mini, Terry J's yellow Volkswagen Polo, Gilliam's mighty yellow Volkswagen tank and G Chapman's rented Mercedes.

Loud farewells, door slams, car tyres reversing on the road and the Python fleet heads off in the moonlight to find a way out of Regent's Park.

Wednesday, September 12th, Plaza Hotel, New York

Fixx would have been proud of me.[1] Knowing from previous experience that I would not sleep much after six this morning and spurred on by

---

1 James E Fixx wrote the influential *Complete Book of Running* (1977), which used to inspire me whenever I felt like giving up. The author, rather unfortunately, died of a heart attack in 1984, whilst out running.

the gradually expanding pink-gold rim around Central Park, promising another clear, hot day, I did my ten minutes' warm-up and forsook the thickpile carpets and the marble halls of the Plaza for the worn and scruffy herbiage of Central Park.

It was worth the effort, for I ran well and easily and enjoyed passing the Guggenheim and the Frick and the Met before most New Yorkers were up. But as the time neared seven joggers poured in from all the entries and exits. Very different to the solitude of the Heath.

Rang Al in Sag Harbor – a bleary, but heroic voice. He has Terry's two French lady friends staying with him,[1] and has fallen passionately in love with one of them. As Al says, 'As soon as she slipped her top off when we went bathing in the ocean, I knew she was the girl for me!' So, stirrings at Sag.

Denis O'B, eyes sparkling like a child with a new toy, buttonholes each of us with the good news that 600 cinemas throughout the US will be taking *Brian* by early October and, because of the performance and reputation of the movie so far, Warner's have been able to do deals split 90–10 with the exhibitors (90 to Warner's, 10 to the exhibitors). The *Grail*'s deals were 50–50 usually.

Thursday, September 13th, New York

Another early-morning run. It's becoming addictive. Up to 96th Street and back by 7.35. The good weather goes on.

To the Navarro for an interview (me and TG) for *Chapter One*, a publishing magazine. Then at twelve I stand in for Eric in an interview for the *Washington Post* book column.

We chat for a half-hour, but I take a while to settle, having been far more rattled than I should have been by EI's outburst over our Tom Snyder *Tomorrow* show interview. Eric, who has become far more obsessed with the interviews than I would have expected from such a press-hater (he's already looked at our *Good Morning America* on tape twice), berates me for mentioning the *Gay News* blasphemy case and the Jorgen Therson *Sex Life of Christ* in the same breath as *Brian*.

The Snyder interview was not just about *Brian* – that got good plugs – it was also about censorship, and that's why I instanced the two cases.

---

1 One had been an au pair at the Joneses' in London. They were on a budget trip to the US so Terry had asked Al if he could put them up.

It's a one o'clock in the morning show, it was a relief to be able to talk about our concerns in some detail – and it now turns out that Eric is in favour of censorship – at least in interviews, which I can't accept.

Back to the Navarro – this in itself quite an exciting little trip, as The Who's fans are thick outside the hotel, and word has gotten around that Pythons *and* George Harrison are also in there. George walks with practised skill, firmly ahead and steadfastly refusing to even see anybody. 'Pretend they're invisible, it's the only way.'

At Terry Gilliam's apartment, with fine views of the New York canyons below, a party develops. Eric is by now utterly mellow and a quite changed man. He apologises for this morning's episode and says he has since rung a friend in LA, who thought the *Tomorrow* interview was very good.

A photographer from the *Post* has now joined Cindy Stivers, the *Post* reporter. We pose for photographs outside the restaurant – all lying slumped on the pavement with empty gin bottles. Will we regret it in the morning?

Friday, September 14th, New York

This morning I passed a paper on the newsstand called *Home Reporter*, with a banner front page: 'Clergy Ban Python Film'. Inside a massively misinformed report of the movie (Brian is Christ, of course), being banned in England and how a new group calling themselves Citizens Against Blasphemy are planning a demonstration on Sunday to try and get the film taken off here. Also notice that the *New York Post* carries a spread of drunken Pythons lying on the sidewalk outside a New York restaurant.

Finish reading TG's *Brazil* script. Rather dull characters complicate an otherwise quite striking visual feel. Later in the evening, when we are all taken to Elaine's by Denis and George, TG and I talk about it. He's near desperation on the script – knows what needs to be done, but can't do it himself.

Champagne in my suite with Al Levinson and Claudie, the French lady to whom he has lost his heart. She is indeed lovely – slim, long dark hair framing a small face with lively eyes. She is obviously quite taken aback by the champagne and Plaza style – and when George H comes down to join us for a drink, her smashing eyes widen to 70 mill. George, so nice and so straight, disarms her.

He brings a tape of some Hoagy Carmichael[1] songs – one of which he's thinking of recording – whilst the remains of Hurricane Frederick finally reach Manhattan with a brief but impressive display of lightning and sheeting rain outside.

Sunday, September 16th

By limousine to the 59th Street helicopter terminal, where the Warner Bros chopper awaits to take us to Fisher's Island.

As we whirl up over the East River and over La Guardia Airport, read the visitors' book. It's headed by Frank and Barbara Sinatra.

Below, a perfect day. Hundreds of yachts fill Long Island Sound and we keep at a 120-mph speed and a height of 2,000 feet and maintain course up the mainland shoreline, with a clear view of the Good Life of America below us. Sailing boats, swimming pools, houses on the water – a huge, middle-class commuter belt stretches, unbroken by farmland or parkland, right up the NY and Connecticut coast as far as New London, where we turn and head across the untroubled blue waters to Fisher's Island.

Up the length of the island, swing round over the point and then down onto the gravel pathway right outside Denis' front door.

In the evening, after dinner, George and Eric bring guitars out, and we sing the oldies – including many Beatles songs which George can't remember.

Monday, September 17th, White Caps, Fisher's Island

A leisurely breakfast – banana bread and corn bread and nut, honey and cream spreads, and good, fresh fruit and tasty coffee – discreetly provided by the two girls in the kitchen.

Then to business. Denis had softened us up the night before, when we had a pre-meeting meeting to discuss agendas, etc, so it was no surprise to us when he began his pitch this morning by strongly advising a sooner-rather-than-later schedule on the new movie. The argument being that he would like to strike while *Brian* is hot and likely to get hotter with the 600-cinema release this coming Thursday.

---

1 Hoagland Carmichael (1899–1981) was a jazz musician and composer who wrote some all-time classics such as 'Georgia on My Mind' and 'Up a Lazy River'.

Warner's want a deal, and Paramount too. Denis reckons at the moment he can, with a few trimmings, go to Warner's and get a percentage of gross deal. Something like 10 or 15% of gross – which means 10 or 15 cents of every dollar paid at the box-office. (Usually this would be a percentage of distributor's gross.) He would like to try and prise *Grail* away from Cinema 5 and give it to Warner's together with our German film as a double-bill pot-boiler for next summer.

Enthused by Denis' evangelical approach, and in good spirits because of *Brian*'s success here, there is little opposition to a tighter schedule to the new movie than that discussed at L'Etoile in mid-August. In fact, by the end of the morning session we have agreed to a delivery date for the finished movie in November 1981. Shooting would be in March/April 1981.

Before lunch we held a Monty Python Walking on the Water competition in the swimming pool. I got slightly further than Terry.

Tuesday, September 18th, Fisher's Island

After breakfast we spread out on Denis' impeccably well-chosen sofas and armchairs and begin our first group session on the fourth film.

It's rather a desultory affair.

I think that JC brings up the same sequence that he did when we first began *Brian*. In which a spacecraft with alien beings looking just like us lands. The beings emerge, give a stirring message of hope to the world, turn to re-enter their ship and find they've locked themselves out.

Other suggestions are a sci-fi movie of a vision of the future where everything's almost exactly the same. Or a state of war – but a war which is always in the background. Or a vision of hell, or Monty Python's 'Utopia'.

Denis, walking by the pool, looks anxiously at us for signs of A Great Breakthrough or A Hugely Commercial Idea, or at the very least some outward and visible sign that genius has been at work.

After lunch we desert the sun reluctantly and listen to Denis describing the 'structuring' of our future earnings.

In a scenario which is more like what one reads in the back of *Private Eye*, Denis tells us of the bizarre odyssey that some of our earnings will make, via Holland, Panama and Switzerland. Denis speaks of all this with the zeal of a fiendishly clever scientist who cannot help but be light years ahead of governments and bureaucracy and officialdom.

Not that Denis is sensational as he tells us of this wonderland of vastly increased wealth. He is dependable Denis – with his reassuring eyes, balding, domed head and affectionate bear-like presence. But occasionally John and I have to laugh when he strays into the satirisable. He talks of a company called Ganga Distributors: 'An old-established company – a company which we have representatives with … and … and I would gladly let the world know that.'

When we re-emerge into the dwindling sunlight around the pool at 5.30 this afternoon, we have all become accomplices in something most of us don't understand.

Terry J and I bathe in a brisk, bracing, choppy sea below Henry Luce's house. There's a fine sunset.

Drinks are a little quieter. After dinner there is Calvados, but no sing-a-long. Terry J becomes voluble over politics, over progress and the lack of it since the fourteenth century, and Denis joins the rest of us, until he receives a quite gratuitously shrill attack from TJ during the 'debate'. Denis' eyes momentarily widened, as if to say 'Is he often like this?'

Wednesday, September 19th, Fisher's Island

Last run. This time 45 minutes non-stop with sprints. The island seems empty. I frighten hen pheasants, rabbits, crows and water rats as I pad by. The sun warms me and when I get back to White Caps there's only Brian, the major-domo, around. Bathe, then luxuriate in the jacuzzi.

As if a symbol of our new life under O'Brien, we leave the States majestically. Fresh and tingling from the massage pool, we're served fresh fruit and coffee breakfast, then a helicopter lifts us off from outside the front door, heads us over Long Island, passing over and around Sag in which I was running a little over a month ago, along the sun-filled shoreline into JFK, where a coach transfers us to the Concorde lounge, then across to darkening London in three hours, sixteen minutes.

Sunday, September 23rd

Terry G comes round in the evening and gives me the first 'unofficial' inkling of *Brian*'s progress in the States. Apparently one and a half million dollars were taken in the first couple of days (Thursday/Friday) and Warner's are now looking beyond a $25 million gross.

Rain comes down from heavy, darkening skies as I sit in my work-room talking with TG about his future plans – *Brazil* or *Theseus*.

Apparently John Calley liked *Jabberwocky*. TG is caught. He has stated that he will and must do his own movie in the next two years. He only wants to do animation and a bit of performing for Python. Can he do both and resist Eric's suggestion that he alone should direct Python 4?

Tuesday, September 25th

Yesterday morning I began my new 'finish the play' schedule. Up in my work-room by nine o'clock. Unplug the phone and concentrate solely on the play until one.

Good progress yesterday and today. It's taking a more serious turn, which I'm happy with.

Wednesday, September 26th

Morning's work curtailed in order to get to Shepperton for a board meeting. Arrive there soon after 1.30. All sorts of men in green tights with leafy costumes and panto-style helmets wandering about. A group of dwarfs, smoking. Charles Gregson is about the first person I see in modern dress. *Flash Gordon* is filming crowd scenes today.

I am extremely happy that we choose Hall Ellison as the best of the three catering bids. They are independent. The other two are subsidiaries, of Trust House Forte in one case, and Grand Met in the other.

Both THF and Grand Met emphasise economy, cost-effectiveness and profit maximisation and hardly mention food at all. Hall Ellison propose to pay their chef a weekly salary of £115.00 and their manager £120.00. THF would pay the chef £75.00 and the manager £134.00.

To Methuen for a preliminary meeting on the launch of *Monty Python's Scrap Book* on November 15th. So good to be amongst publishers who actually sell books. I feel very well-disposed towards Geoffrey, Jan H and David Ross. They've stood by us well. Geoffrey gives TJ and me a copy each of a new edition of Noël Coward's plays, because one of the plays in the collection was said to have had its first performance at Oflag VIIB and lists the POWs who made up the cast.

Thursday, September 27th

Talk to Denis O'B after breakfast. He says he's almost 'too embarrassed' to talk about *Brian* figures, but on the first three days of our 'break' in the US (this is film-man's jargon for first nationwide exposure), we have broken nine house records and done 250% better business than Warner's next best this summer – *The In-Laws*. He confirms the figure of one and a half million dollars taken in the first three days in 120 cinemas.

Work on with the play – keeping my feet on the ground until 2.30-ish.

At four down to Donovan's for a check-up and I record him doing a radio commercial for *Brian* – 'Hello, I'm Michael Palin's dentist' – to the effect that Michael requires all the money he can get to pay for expensive dental treatment. This is an extension of the 'interviews with our mothers' idea, which has produced at least one gem – from John's mother, in which she shows immaculate comic timing in pleading for money to keep her in her old age.

Friday, September 28th

Variety calls *Brian* variously 'Swell', 'Fat', 'Potent', 'Brawny', 'Loud', 'Smash', 'Booming' and 'Hot' – and it looks like the biggest-grossing film in the US this last week in September.

Visit EuroAtlantic in mid-afternoon. I meet Mark de Vere Nicholl, Philip McDanell (frighteningly young, like an elder brother of Tom) and others of benign Denis's rather Kensingtonian staff. The offices and the building in Cadogan Square are clean-limbed, neat, elegant and cool without forcing any effect of dynamism or modernity.

Denis talks first of *Jabberwocky*, which both he and Calley feel is a small masterpiece. Denis feels bound to ask me why Terry G, after proving his directorial ability so clearly in *Jabberwocky*, didn't get to handle *Life of Brian*. So I try to fill him in on a little Python folklore.

From Denis' I drive to Shepherd's Bush to John Jarvis' cutting rooms, where JC is on the final stages of preparation of the Pythonised travelogue[1] which will make up the complete all-Python bill when the *Life of Brian* opens in London.

---

1 It was a traditional, bland piece about Venice, made special by John's commentary – 'gondolas, everywhere fucking gondolas'.

John is in his element with the slowly building rant, which he can take to hysteria and beyond like no one else I know. Suggest a couple of cuts which he seems happy with.

Wednesday, October 3rd

Python's *Life of Brian* has made No. 1 on the latest *Variety* chart. One year to the day since we were packed in a tiny upper room of the Ribat in Monastir, ours is the film most people in America want to see.

Maybe subconsciously this reassuring state of affairs propels me to the end of the second act of my play.

Thursday, October 4th

Out in the evening with Denis O'B, Inge and John Calley, who is in town for a couple of days.

Calley asked a few leading questions of the 'what next for you?' variety as we ate in the cosily sumptuous surroundings of Walton's restaurant. Denis steered him towards the 'Roger of the Raj' *Ripping Yarn* and I told Calley of my fondness for Indian subjects – and the British in India – eccentricity developing there quite splendidly. He seemed very keen for me to do a *Ripping Yarn* movie, which was nice.

But he was tired and popped into his waiting Rolls after the meal.

Friday, October 5th

Talked to Denis in the morning. He said that John Calley had called him before leaving Heathrow to tell me or any other Python that any recce to India would be paid for by Warner Brothers.

Saturday, October 6th

Drop in on George at Friar Park. He's about to have his breakfast (onions, egg and peppers (green)). I apologise for arriving too early, but George (half-way into a new beard) assures me that he's been up a while, and out planting his fritillaries.

He takes the gardening very seriously and has a bulb catalogue, which he refers to now and then in between telling me of the $200 million suit the Beatles are bringing against the management of *Beatlemania*, a live show in the US using their look-alikes.

He hasn't heard that *Brian* is No. 1, but is greatly chuffed at the news and shakes my hand.

'Now you can all have one of these,' says George, nodding round at Friar Park.

'The trouble is,' I have to say, 'I'm really happy where I am.'

'Nonsense, Palin,' replies the Quiet One, 'you'll have a mansion and like it!'

I enjoy George's company and I think he mine. Despite all his trappings he's a down-to-earth, easy-to-please character.

Have promised to take Tom and some friends on a pre-eleventh-birthday treat. We drive down to South Ken and visit the Science, Geology and Natural History Museum (which has a worthy ecology exhibition) and then to Wolfe's in Park Lane for highly expensive hamburgers. The children delight in telling me in large stage whispers how pricey everything is … 'Cor! Coca-Cola 50p!' 'You can get a can in the shops …' and so on. It's like the Young Consumers' Club.

Sunday, October 7th

Into the sixth week of dry, warm and sunny weather. I am much lifted by the Sunday press previews of the new *Ripping Yarns*. All papers carry extensive details and are uniformly glad to see the series back. 'Topping treat of the season so far' says Purser, and *The Observer* are very nice. All helps to counter *Time Out*'s 'return of this desperately disappointing series'.

Feel tired, but rally to take the family down to Dulwich. Family lunch with all the Herberts (Jeremy just about to go up to York University for first term). Conker hunting along past Dulwich Picture Gallery in the afternoon.

Monday, October 8th

Begin work on the third act of the play. I feel committed to it now and am writing eagerly and easily – as if I'm now warmed-up, loosened up to the task and the end is in sight. I think I might actually make the self-imposed deadline of the end of October.

Over to Cadogan Square to talk to Denis O'B. He is off to the US on

Wednesday to begin negotiations with Warner's for the next Python movie. He wants 15% of the gross for the Pythons. Unheard of.

This afternoon in Denis' small, rather endearingly cramped upper-room office, with bottles of Penrhos Porter on the table, we talk about Redwood and the future. Denis is hard. He says that he wouldn't really mind if everyone involved with the studio left tomorrow – he could put people in to run it. He wants to protect and to use my £80,000 involvement in the studio to give me control and a steady profit – and to stop the rather generous but disorganised drift in the running of Redwood's affairs.

All good sound business sense, but I have to fight hard for the consideration of the personal side and the relationships and obligations I feel I have with André, which cannot be easily commercially quantified.

I drive home feeling a little oppressed, knowing that all this will not be easy and feeling that Denis is being more destructive than constructive and is in danger of putting the whole spirit of Redwood and Neal's Yard – the fun and the enjoyment – in jeopardy.

Tuesday, October 9th

To lunch at the Trattoria San Angelo in Albemarle Street with Aidan Chambers, who wants me to write a children's book for Macmillan.

He brightens my day considerably. We are both northerners; he has a very blunt and untwee attitude to children's books. He's always fighting publishers for the right to be as open as possible with kids and to avoid either patronising or pretentious writing. I agree, for a tiny sum, to write one of the three new books for 8–11-year-olds. He's trying to get Joyce Grenfell to do the other one.

Denis calls with another incredible piece of news. Before leaving for the US he was collating all the info on *Jabberwocky*, saw the agreement with me and was shocked. He could not believe that I was only getting 1½% and told John Goldstone that he would not dream of speaking to Warner's on *Jabberwocky*'s behalf unless the percentages for me and TG were greatly improved. Within a couple of hours Denis had upped my percentage from 1½ to eight!

Wednesday, October 10th

More extensive coverage of tonight's *Ripping Yarn* first episode. I really couldn't have believed when I came back from Sag Harbor in mid-

August to find that all the ITV channels had been off the air for over a week, that they would still have found no solution by mid-October. So 'Whinfrey's Last Case' rivals only *Sportsnight* – boxing – for the TV viewers' attention tonight. And it follows twenty-five minutes of *MASH*, which is the most successful (*only* successful) US comedy import.

Watch 'Whinfrey' with Nicky[1] and Helen. Do not enjoy it at all, but then I never do when watching coldly at home – and especially not after two big-screen showings at BAFTA with laughter and great appreciation. The selective replaying of the audience track is neither honest nor successful.

Thursday, October 11th

It's a warm and benign morning – and sunshine rather appropriately streams in the window of All Hallows open-plan church, into which Helen and I troop at a quarter to eleven for the Gospel Oak School Harvest Festival Service. As we leave, the vicar beams at me: 'If they're all as good as last night, I shall cancel my engagements *every* Wednesday.'

Terry J rings to say that the show was approved of very much in Camberwell. So the day is bright.

Drive to Notting Hill to buy a birthday present for Helen. Wander about. To BAFTA by 2.30 to do an interview with Ivan Waterman of the *News of the World*. I'm thankful of being warned by Maggie Forwood of the *Sun* on Tuesday that Waterman was 'very keen' and always muttering 'must make it dirtier ...' He seems to be quite bright.

But I have to guffaw when, at about ten past three, as burly BAFTA ladies are hoovering under our feet he asks 'And finally, sex?'

At nine the phone rings. It's Al from Sag Harbor. He's decided to marry Claudie. He wants me to investigate the possibility of a register office wedding in Hampstead in mid-November. He would like a gathering of 'just a very few people' and he and Claudie want to come and stay at No. 2 for a while after the wedding. 'We're a couple of old romantics, Mike. She's rung her sister, and I've rung you. You're the second to know.'

I am unaccountably depressed by the news. Why he should feel he has to marry her, I cannot totally understand. Lovely girl though she seemed. It's Al's huge, warm, lovely, romantic soul welling out of him

---

1 Nicky Boult, Helen's niece and a newly qualified teacher, who was staying with us.

with happiness. And as such I don't think he is in a fit state to decide on marriage. He is not yet back in life. He may think he is, but his affair with Claudie is still too much like a dream, I fear, for the reality to be anything other than anti-climax. I would rather big A had got back into the mainstream of life – a job, an interest, a project that brought him back amongst people – than pursuing so single-mindedly a relationship which can only isolate him further.

I may be wrong in all this.[1]

Friday, October 12th

Up at seven to prepare for departure to Gordonstoun to address the sixth form and the Preparatory School before this day is out.

In the queue for the Inverness flight, meet Les Megahey.[2] He's off to the Highlands to do a week's research for a film on Landseer. He's second in command to H Burton at BBC Music and Arts. Later on the plane – a reassuringly plodding Viscount crossing the country at 320mph – he mentions that if TJ and I, or either one of us, have any ideas for films we might like to do, he does control twenty of them a year, and has a very good relationship with crews and technicians.

On arrival at Gordonstoun, was taken on a tour of the school site by Graham Broad – the brother of David, my classmate at Shrewsbury in 1960–61. He walked me up the Silent Walk – a mile-long stretch of isolated school site, where boys have to walk in silence as a punishment. Graham assured me, quite seriously I think, that it was alright for *us* to talk. The trouble is anything he said on the Silent Walk was drowned out by the screaming roar of Nimrod and Jaguar fighters, taking off in pairs from RAF Lossiemouth – about three-quarters of a mile away!

Tea with the headmaster. A young, bright, effective-looking man, four years my junior. G Broad seems very scared of him. Two sixth-form girls and two sixth-form boys – one with hairy legs protruding from shorts – are also present. A cake is passed around. I feel I must consume my slice. It's given in that sort of spirit. Everyone dutifully eats their slice.

At 6.30, as dusk is falling, I leave Gordonstoun and, with the 16-year-

1 And I was. They lived together very happily until Al's death in 1989, and had a daughter, Gwenola.
2 Friend and fellow thespian at Oxford.

old daughter of the prep school headmaster as my guide, drive over to Aberlour House – the prep school of Gordonstoun.

I arrive just as the smallest boys (many of them, inexplicably, blond, blue-eyed and yet from Peru) are squatting on the floor engaged in some ritual prior to being packed off to bed.

The headmaster was a quite different character to the steely Mr Mavor of Gordonstoun. Tall, rambling, with that air of slightly disreputable elegance which speaks of nights, rather than days, well spent. Even the name, Toby Coghill, is straight out of le Carré.

Soon after arriving I'm taken in to talk to a roomful of about fifty boys and girls. They're all so young – most of them younger than my eldest son – and only a very few put their hand up when I ask who's heard of *Ripping Yarns*. But it makes for an easy, jolly, relaxed talk. They're fascinated by how we nailed the boys to the wall in 'Tomkinson'. 'First we select three really naughty boys,' I began, and they all titter.

Saturday, October 13th, Gordonstoun School

Dozed until 8.15, when Mrs M left a cup of tea and orange juice outside my room.

Thumbed through a book on Gordonstoun School as I sipped tea. Influence of Plato's *Republic* on Kurt Hahn's original philosophy of the school – preserved in the houses, where housemasters are Guardians and heads of house Helpers. But what stuck most in my mind was the reason why one of the Gordon family built the fine stone dovecote in the grounds mid-way through the nineteenth century. It turns out that there is a highly improbable Scottish saying 'A new doe'cot means a death i' the family'. He hated his wife, and built four of them.

Aberdeen by 11.30. Checked car in, walked through drizzle around grey granite squares. A man nearly scared me to death with a bellow of greeting –'You're my *hero*!' Neither of us had pencil and paper for autograph, so I gave him my Municipal Arts Society of New York membership card.

Thursday, October 18th

Speak to both Jack and Liz Cooper, who are as concerned as I am by our mutual friend Levinson's precipitate leap into wedlock. Jack wrote him quite bluntly advising that they think a lot more carefully – and just live

together. What a fine reversal of the traditional social and moral position
– advising someone not to marry but to live together. But, as Jack says,
'We're in this together.'

As I'm sitting trying to look at a rather good TV play by Stephen
Lowe, there is a knock on the door and a man from the flats behind our
house comes round to see if his escaped owl has taken refuge in our
garden. We can't find it, and he's rather in despair because it's one of a
breeding pair. Nice to meet an owl enthusiast.

Tuesday, October 23rd

T Gilliam is round to borrow a bicycle pump. We end up talking for an
hour. Last night TG saw Denis, freshly returned from LA, but found him
strangely low. None of the deals he'd gone to the States to make had
been made – the main reason being a 30–35% dive in *Brian* business on
the very weekend Denis arrived in the US. So Warner's were not falling
over themselves to sign on any of Denis' dotted lines. He's chatting up
Paramount now.

I gather we are now banned in South Carolina – the first *state* to pro-
hibit *Brian* – thanks to the activities of that great fighter for human
rights, Governor Strom Thurmond. Someone told me of a news item
about a cinema in Oklahoma being sued for showing the movie.

So the backlash has finally hit and Denis is now trimming his esti-
mates about the gross. No longer are we on the upward spiral towards
40 million and beyond; he now seems to be happy to settle for a total of
24 or 25 mill, across the US, which would leave a distributor's gross of 15
mill. Still way above anything the *Grail* did, but nevertheless bigotry,
prejudice and intolerance – or pure and untarnished ideals – have at last
shown there is a limit to *Brian*'s heady progress. The Promised Land of
the dollar millionaires is way beyond us after all. Actually both TG and I
breathed a sigh of relief.

Wednesday, October 24th

ITV returns, the weather changes, grows colder and wetter. The *Ripping
Yarns*, which have been so well received and have seemed to highlight
the sunny, gentle, equable days of early October, end tonight.

The news of *Brian* seems to set the heady, warm, jacuzzi-lounging,
golf course running days in the sun at Fisher's Island firmly in

perspective. Then Python and *Brian* were unbeatable, set to be the biggest, and Denis was making plans accordingly. Now the brakes are on.

Even Shepperton suddenly faces an end to the volume of activity which has kept the place full for eighteen months. After *Flash Gordon* there is not a single movie lined up. Elstree and Pinewood also reflect this lack of activity. The BBC's plans to hire Shepperton to make films for a year (which would have been excellent for the studios) have been shelved owing to lack of money and union co-operation. The 1980s look bleak – here, as elsewhere.

Owing to my cold, I've put off a proposed curry evening with TJ and Alison at Veeraswamy's to celebrate 'Roger of the Raj' and the end of the *Yarns*.

So happily watch at home, with Helen and a half bottle of champagne – and thoroughly enjoy it. 'Roger of the Raj' is now, in my book, quite restored to top status. It's been a long process of rehabilitation after the depths of gloom into which I unaccountably sank over it last summer. It's now up there with 'Tomkinson' and 'Olthwaite' as one of my three greats.

T Gilliam, who is very restless at the moment since 'Brazil' has not been accepted unequivocally by anybody, was round again this morning, bubbling over with a mixture of excitement and embarrassment. He has a new plan for a subtle sort of Gilliam/Palin link-up. I will write my children's book for Macmillan and he will film it! Simple – except that I'm writing a book, not a film script, and I won't be putting thoughts to paper until January.

TG is only slightly daunted by this. He still thinks that for the two of us to collaborate on a children's film – me the basic script and characters, TG with the visual fireworks – would be an unbeatable combination and manage to solve the problem of his almost all-consuming urge to do his own movie in the next two years. Otherwise, he says, he will go mad.

Thursday, October 25th

Taxi takes me to King's Cross to catch the 7.45 to Leeds. Dawn only marginally lighter than the pitch darkness of an hour ago has rather resentfully broken as we move out of the station, as if God didn't really want today to happen.

The restaurant car is packed. I sit with David Ross, whom I like more and more each time I see him. Droll Scottish humour. Breakfast as we nip along across a flat landscape, dimly lit by a sullen sky, to whatever awaits us at the *Yorkshire Post* literary lunch.

To the Queen's Hotel. Only Steve Race, a fellow speaker, in evidence. A soft-spoken, humorous man, much concerned with being polite – in the best way. I liked him and had to tell him that he was one of my earliest television heroes. He and Hank on *Whirligig*.[1] It was satisfying to share pure nostalgia with the man responsible for it.

Into a sort of large public ballroom with windows boarded up. A sea of faces at long tables – maybe 400 people out there. About 10% were what one might call 'young people' – under 35. But mostly they were middle-aged, generally female, wearing hats and there to be seen to be there, without exuding any obvious signs of literary curiosity.

They gave us grapefruit segments, beef in a brown and unexciting sauce, good Brussels sprouts and a trifle which looked like the remains of an unsuccessful heart-swap operation.

Donald Carroll, an American, spoke first. He mumbled, was a little pissed and his confidence dried up in the face of this monstrous regiment of women. Jilly Cooper, nervous, but attractive because of this, showed that it *was* possible to make them laugh, particularly if you quoted someone else. I spoke third and delivered a bit of half-farce, half-fantasy which I thought deserved a lot better than it got. There were many laughs, but it was impossible to get this audience to just enjoy itself – presuming, that is, that many of them would know how to go about enjoying themselves in the first place.

Katharine Whitehorn spoke with the cool, poised, assurance of one who knows exactly where her appeal lies. Quite shamelessly disdainful and Hampsteadian, and she has the profile of a rather beautiful cow. Steve Race was nice and clean and funny.

Afterwards we signed. An embarrassing moment, this, if you're not a favoured author. Donald Carroll had not a single taker. I can quite understand how, on the train back, he could refer to today as 'the worst day of my life'.

---

1 A fortnightly children's show in the 1950s, probably my first favourite programme. Hank the Cowboy was a ventriloquist's dummy and Steve Race accompanied his adventures on the piano.

Friday, October 26th

Anne H has asked to have a meeting with me. She doesn't look cheerful and what she has to say is disturbing. Her 'relationship' with Denis has crumbled to nothing. After various attempts to acquire information (on our behalf) about matters such as copyright of Python material – songs, etc – Denis became very sharp with her and they haven't spoken for two weeks.

I had fears that this transition would not be easy, but I am a little worried by the uncompromising toughness that Denis is showing to those who are our friends and those whose value and service to us is proven – Anne and André, to name but two.

Monday, October 29th

The weekend at Abbotsley unblocked the system most successfully. Worked in the garden picking apples on Saturday and quite heavy work clearing the banks of the pond on Sunday. But my cold lingers on and I feel uncertain about my *Desert Island Discs* recording. I know it's daft to worry, but once you have agreed to do the show you're committed to a half-hour's fairly intensive study of yourself and your taste, so it's worth working on it.

I spend much of this morning, then, thumbing through my record collection and redigesting ideas for my eight records. Eventually come up with a pleasingly Catholic selection: Ellington, Elvis, Elgar, the Beatles, 'Lullaby of Broadway', a song from *Oh What a Lovely War*, some brass band and a *Goon Show*. And, after many second thoughts, plumped for Thackeray's *Vanity Fair* as my book, even though I haven't yet read it, so impressed and cheered am I by the first forty pages!

Armed with these decisions, I took a run on the Heath, greatly enjoyable because of the sunshine, and, after a bath, took a cab down to the Garrick Club to meet Roy Plomley for lunch.

Lovely, rather dusty atmosphere, with fine rooms and above adequate menu. Smoked eels, very tasty and uncluttered kidneys and bacon, a rather average cheeseboard and good house wine. Plomley keeps referring to the club as 'we'. I think he's a bit of a snob and not frightfully exciting company. I feel tired and find the effort of making conversation harder than usual.

Considering he does fifty-two programmes a year and has done for the last twelve years, it's not surprising, though a little disappointing, that once on air Plomley clicks into a routine. He doesn't listen all the time and, having confessed he has only seen two Python shows and no *Ripping Yarns*, there is little chance of a similarity of interests. So it's a touch formal, but he seems very happy.

Taxi home and within an hour leave with Helen for a party at the ICA and a showing of *Brian* for the crew. About 300 people there – all the old faces of those who were either hoisting me up on crosses, or making the crosses, or filming me being hoisted up, one year ago today.

Afterwards a drink and eats. Much good-mouthing of *Ripping Yarns* – Chris Miller says that John Osborne raves about me and the *Yarns*.

And Helen enjoyed much of the movie. Very praiseworthy of GC's central performance.

Wednesday, October 31st

To an Oak Village Residents' Association meeting.

The chairperson took me aside at the start of the meeting, before I went in, to warn me about certain 'activists' on the Association and their dangerous work. Armed with these fears, and ever watchful, I approached the hall to find about six people sitting there. None of them really seemed to fit the bill as 'activists'.

Anyway, I spoke up, rather insistently, about the appalling state of Lismore Circus and have undertaken to gather signatures about it. I was almost voted on the committee at one point, when Bruce Robertson proposed me, amidst uproar, after one lady had questioned the necessity for a committee at all and the chairperson had been accused of 'intolerable restriction of debate'.

All excellent entertainment. I made a good friend out of the admirable Bruce Robertson, and I've also lumbered myself with the job of organising next summer's street party.

Thursday, November 1st

A large Jaguar picks me up after lunch and takes me down to a BBC interview at Broadcasting House, this time with Gerald Priestland for the networked *Today* programme. John C is also on with me.

Priestland is enormous – he's actually *taller* than John, but amiable and donnish. They play back his review of the film, which swings from great praise –'very funny … Pythons at their best' – to a note of distinct criticism for our handling of the 'Crucifixion' sequences – or for the 'Crucifixion' sequence period. He equates it with 'whistling at Auschwitz' and to him it appears that we are condoning suffering.

JC answers smoothly, as if he's rehearsed. I become a little tongue-tied faced with Priestland's penetrating stare and huge bulk – and the always disconcerting sight of soundless technicians behind the control room glass, gazing impassively at me as if I were a goldfish gasping for breath.

But the interview seems to pass off well. Priestland is not huffy or offended, and we part good friends. 'Here's a sex manual for you, Michael,' he jokes at one point, handing me a paperback by some theologian, titled *The Orthodox Way*.

Friday, November 2nd

Am working on the play in the solitude of No. 2 when Mrs B buzzes on the intercom, which she really can't figure out very well, so I have to leave the brief progress I've made on the work anyway and cross over into No. 4. Here I find Mrs B talking to Spike Milligan on the telephone.

Poor Spike, who tried to phone after 'Roger', but Jill Foster Ltd would not give him my phone number, is now being given the cold shoulder by Mrs B, who, quite rightly, is trying to respect my privacy – as instructed. I apologise profusely to the great man, who tells me rather pitifully that he had only wanted to say how bloody marvellous 'Roger of the Raj' was, whilst his enthusiasm was white-hot. Now, as he says, it's two weeks later and he thinks it's bloody awful!

To hear Spike thus praise the show and tell me that there are only two people who make him laugh these days – myself and John Antrobus – is wondrous music to the ear. Only on Monday was I telling the listening millions on *Desert Island Discs* of how I used to race home from school, running two miles if there was no bus, pushing myself to the limits of physical endurance, just to get back in time to hear *The Goons*. Now, twenty-four years later, the creator of Eccles, Moriarty and Henry Crun is asking me to dinner.

This was worth interrupting a morning of interruptions for. Already, over breakfast, I was forced to read TG's latest treatment for a new TG movie – this time just for kids.

I was still reading his synopsis on the lavatory at 9.30 when he called to hear what I thought. As I saw it, there were two courses of action open to me in the face of the Gilliam treatment. One was to agree, and the other was to agree instantly. After a half-hour's chat I threw in my lot – cautiously – with what I feel is a much stronger movie for TG than *Brazil*.[1]

Tuesday, November 6th

Work on the play rewrites. Alternate feelings of elation and despair about its contents. Run on the Heath in light drizzle.

Drove over to JC's for co-interview with a lady from LBC. JC expressed disillusion with the Labour Party – for whom both he and the lady once used to work. Inability to deliver is, JC feels, their main drawback.

Out in the evening to dinner with Spike, at his request, with Terry and Al as well. Everyone, apart from Helen and myself, seemed to be ill.

Spike quite subdued, but the kind, gentle and generous side of his nature was well to the fore. Shelagh said he's very vulnerable and easily hurt and a meal like this boosts his confidence. They recently had dinner with Graham, who didn't say anything. I rather enjoyed myself and was quite loud and ebullient.

Wednesday, November 7th

Heard from TG that Denis has told him to start work on his kids' film – the money will be there! So within two weeks TG has written a synopsis from nowhere, sort of persuaded me into co-writing and has finance for an April/May shoot! He says as soon as he heard the news he went home and panicked.

Helen goes out to badminton, I put the children to bed and placate my mother, who is literally counting the hours until *Brian* is unleashed on the British public. She really does fear public outcry, picketings and general national anger and whatever I say can't really calm her. I was able to tell her that the Festival of Light are now taking a much saner view of the movie and come to the conclusion that 'it is extremely unlikely that the film would sustain a successful prosecution in English law'.

1 Its working title was *Time Bandits*.

Really I feel just very tired. Tired of talking, tired of endlessly having to justify the film – to defend it against a controversy that will probably never happen. At least opening day is now less than twenty-four hours away.

Friday, November 9th

I go for a run across the Heath. Tonight is our confrontation with Muggeridge and the Bishop of Southwark [on BBC2's *Friday Night, Saturday Morning*] and, as I squelch through the now leafless beech-woods and around West Meadow, with Kenwood House a glittering white symbol of order and reason in the background, I sort out my thoughts about *Brian*, and the points that the movie tried to make seem to be all to do with power – its use and abuse by an establishment.

As I work in the afternoon on committing to paper some of my morning's thoughts, I find myself just about to close on the knotty question of whether or not I believe in God. In fact I am about to type 'I do not believe in God', when the sky goes black as ink, there is a thunderclap and a huge crash of thunder and a downpour of epic proportions. I never do complete the sentence.

Look for the last time at my notes and drive down through Aldwych and across Waterloo Bridge to the Greenwood Theatre. Over drinks we meet Tim Rice, the presenter – tall, open, unassuming and quite obviously a sensible and sympathetic fellow – then little gnomic Muggeridge – great smile and sparkling eyes – and Mervyn Stockwood, the Bishop of Southwark – big, impressive, avuncular, cradling the second of his whiskies and complaining gently that he'd been told the wrong time of the film and had missed 'some of it'. But his chaplain had told him all about it, he assured me. I found him quite amenable.

JC was, and always is, nervous at first and had asked Tim Rice to direct his early questions at me! As I found Tim so easy to talk with this was quite an easy task and I felt that I was being as fluent and as relaxed as I'd ever been. We must have talked for ten to fifteen minutes, getting a few laughs, making very clearly the point about Brian not being Jesus and the film not being about Jesus, and I think keeping the audience amused.

Then Stockwood and Muggeridge joined us and were asked for their opinion of the film. From the moment that Stockwood, resplendent in his purple bishop's cassock, handsome grey hair, fingering his spectacles and his cross with great dexterity, began to speak, I realised his tack. He began, with notes carefully hidden in his crotch, tucked down well out of camera range, to give a short sermon, addressed not to John or myself but to the audience.

In the first three or four minutes he had brought in Ceauçescu and Mao Tse-tung and not begun to make one point about the film. Then he began to turn to the movie. He accused us of making a mockery of the work of Mother Teresa (a recent Nobel prize-winner), of being under-graduate and mentally unstable. He made these remarks with all the smug and patronising paraphernalia of the gallery-player, who believes that the audience will see he is right, because he is a bishop and we're not.

'If there'd been no Jesus, this film would not have been made,' crowed Stockwood. I wanted to say 'If there had been no Jesus, we wouldn't have needed to make the film.'

Muggeridge, in his odd, obsessive way, accused us of denigrating the one man responsible for all the first works of art ever and made other thoroughly irresponsible digs. Vainly did John try and remind him that there were *other* religions in the world, that there *was* a civilisation before Jesus, that there have been artists who have *not* painted the Crucifixion or written about the Incarnation, and the world's religions have never been above a bit of torture if it suited them.

No, Malcolm was gone, set on a bizarre course, armed with his own navigational guides, and nothing we could do could prevent him going straight for the rocks. But the Bishop was meanwhile throwing himself off the cliffs. Outrageously dismissing any points we made as 'rubbish' or 'unworthy of an educated man', he posed and preened and pontifi-cated. And he ended the long 'discussion' by saying he hoped we would get our thirty pieces of silver.

In the hospitality room we were surrounded like heroes returning from a war. I was introduced to Raymond Johnston of the Festival of Light – always our most arch-enemies.[1] Instead I found myself con-fronted with a thin, rather nervous man, a committed Christian, who had been embarrassed at the display of the Bishop. He (Johnston) *had* seen the film. He had found it quite clear that Brian and Jesus were sep-arate people. He had many differences of opinion with us, but he

---

1 They had called for the film to be banned. 'Though not in itself blasphemous, it will tend to discredit the New Testament story of Jesus in confused semi-Pagan minds.'

thought the film not malicious, not harmful and, furthermore, he saw and appreciated that we were making very valid points about the organised religions which told you what to think, in the same way that Stockwood tonight had used the cheapest and most dishonest methods to tell people what to think.

Later I watched it go out and fortunately the Bishop's 'performance' came over as badly on air as it did in the studio. TG rang as the last words of the interview faded and ranted with anger for a full half-hour. He thought that the programme was Python's finest hour since the ABC trial.

Saturday, November 10th

I had only just got up this morning when my mother rang – quite incensed by the behaviour of Stockwood last night. At last I feel she realises what *Brian* is saying and perhaps feels that we *do* have a point, that religion *can* be criticised without malice or spite. She saw the Bishop as an Inquisitor – smug, fat and well-fed. Angela was with her, fortunately, and I think they both went to bed quite disturbed.

Sunday, November 11th

The Sunday reviews – the last main batch, thank God – are very favourable. *The Observer* is a rave, as are most of the popular papers (from whom I expected more disapproval). Once again the *Telegraph* shrinks from enthusiasm – as if unwilling to endorse us, which I regard as a sign that we may have hit the Establishment quite hard on the nose. But they positively state that the film will not harm anyone, and there should be no 'shades of the Ayatollah' over *Brian*.

Monday, November 12th

Final work through the play. Though I have misgivings about the ending, I deem it typeable – and Monday, November 12th goes down as the finish date of 'The Weekend'. (I've gone for the simple title – either this or a totally silly one; had toyed with '4 Letters Beginning With H'.)

Tuesday, November 13th

Thankfully it's a good day. Bright, dry and clear. To Heathrow to meet Al and Claudie off the 9.10 Pan Am from New York and Detroit. Then bring them back to Hampstead and the delightful Willow Hotel in Willow Road, which Jack Cooper has found for them. It's wonderfully decorated with lacquered wood, pot plants, bamboo blinds à la Somerset Maugham, and a big, brass bed for the newly-weds on their 'lune de miel'.

Wednesday, November 14th

Letter in *The Guardian* from the Vicar of Hampstead, very critical of Stockwood and Muggeridge, thinks that the church needs its pretensions pricking by such as Cleese and myself.

To Pizza Express in Hampstead for lunch with T Gilliam. TG has expanded his film well and wants to hear my views on the various episodes and once again to confirm my availability to write some material. I hope I will not regret saying yes.

Denis O'B rings to say that the first-week take at the Plaza is £40,000. 'Forty thousand *pounds!*' Denis incredulates in tones of almost religious fervency. It is impressive and has beaten the previous highest-ever take at the Plaza (which was for *Jaws*) by £8,000, with seven fewer performances. So all the publicity has had maximum effect.

Monday, November 19th

Started work on the new Python movie. A bright, crisp morning. Cycled to the meeting at 2 Park Square West and arrived about tennish.

Then a general chat about the world. The Anthony Blunt spy story[1] is top news at the moment. America is about to indulge in its own maudlin fascination with power and privilege now that Ted Kennedy is running officially for President. We in beleaguered England, continually battered by stories of our imminent economic collapse, at least have one of our own scandals to keep us happy.

---

1 Blunt, son of a bishop, Professor of Art History at London University, Surveyor of the Queen's Pictures, had been found to be spying for the Soviets for many years. Though he had been unmasked in 1963, he had been allowed to retain all his posts to avoid scandal tainting the Royal Family.

Have we not become as established as the Establishment we seek to kick? Are we not really licensed satirists? Keepers of the Queen's Silly Things, enjoying the same privileges as the Keeper of the Queen's Pictures who has been revealed to have been a very naughty boy – but will be given the full protection of a Cambridge man in an English Establishment that is still Oxbridge-controlled?

JC thinks war is a limiting subject. EI and myself both see it in wider terms. The talk then shifts, or is shifted, by TJ who is lobbying indefatigably for World War III, to a science fiction world of the future. Where very little has changed. Possibly a benevolent and very well-meaning society in which everything is attended to, but it is quite unworkable. Enormous queues to complain everywhere. Everyone born into this society, I suggest, is handed a raffle ticket on birth which gives him or her the chance of being PM eventually.

Some good chat – generally concerned with revealing the idiocy of many of our rules and regulations, hardly a new area, but there is a certain satisfaction in the combined strength of all our input.

We walk in the park, then lunch at our 'regular' round table by the window at Odin's. Over Primeur, Muscadet, walnut and lettuce salads and liver, we become very happy and it's decided that we shall not shackle ourselves with too much discussion – we shall go away for a couple of days and write *any*thing. We pledge ourselves, like the Three Musketeers, that we will do all in our power to bring about a silly film. JC warns, splendidly, that 'We'll show them how silly a film can be.'

Wednesday, November 21st

At 3.30 to the Mornington Foot Clinic to have my corn attended to by Mr Owen. A small, distinguished, elderly man working in a small, undistinguished, elderly room. But he's quite a character. Prophesying doom and the collapse of the world (at the hands of KGB-inspired anti-American Muslim rioters), as he slices into my corn and cauterises it most expertly.

Actually there does seem some cause for his concern as we approach 1980. Read in the paper today that armed men are holding hostages in Mecca – the most holy mosque in the whole Muslim religion 'violated'. And the Ayatollah Khomeini still holds American hostages in Iran. All rather worrying. But my foot feels better!

Thursday, November 22nd

Drive down to TJ's, stopping off at Henry Sotheran in Sackville Street – my favourite London bookshop – to buy a birthday present for T Gilliam, who is 39 today. At Terry's it's like old times, writing together up in his top room as darkness falls. TJ has written a classic piece about soldiers presenting their officer with a clock under fire. Really funny. We complete that and by 5.45 find ourselves with a large output – maybe 20 or 25 minutes, for the meeting tomorrow.

Up to T Gilliam's for his 'surprise' birthday party, which isn't really a surprise. Chris Miller is there and Elaine Carew and Richard Broke.[1] Richard tells me that at the BBC Programme Review Board after the *Friday Night, Saturday Morning* epic the Head of Religious Broadcasting, Colin Morris, castigated the BBC for presenting two such 'serious and brilliant' performers as JC and myself with such 'geriatric' opposition!

Friday, November 23rd

Up at 8.10. Leave the house at 9.15 to drive to JC's for writing session.

A very angry, abusive letter to *The Times* from a man called Allott in Finchley, who clearly doesn't like the *Life of Brian*, but admits he hasn't seen it. It is proposed to send a Python reply to *The Times* saying 'We haven't seen Mr Allott, but we don't like him.'

Finally we start to read the first sketches of the new movie. Eric has a couple of quite tart monologues, then I read the first of our two blockbusters. It's received with much nodding and the '*Some* good bits' line. JC reads a long and rambling and not awfully funny piece about Kashmir and sex and male brothels, which doesn't go down very well. It's our second effort (mainly TJ's), including the clock presentation, which is the one big hit of the session.

Sunday, November 25th

This is the day I *should* be looking forward to but am not. I have to give a party for Al and Claudie – or rather I want to give a party for Al and Claudie – but, as it turns out, I've rarely felt more in need of a Day of Rest.

1 He and fellow-producer Mark Shivas had produced *Secrets* by Terry and myself in 1973.

Al is very morose, though tries his best. He has done little on his trip but stay in or on bed at the Willow Hotel and lately make several frustrating trips to the US Embassy, to find that he has serious problems with Claudie's visa – if she tries to enter the US as Al's wife. Al really should have checked all this out before he left, but that's Al – we love him for his romantic enthusiasm, not for his practical knowledge of the immigration system of the US. But he is down in the dumps.

Fortunately the combination of the champagne and Gilliam and Simon A and the Coopers all get to work on him. We have a little speech from yours truly and Willy presents Al and Claudie with portraits of them!

My mother survives, indeed flourishes, on all of this. The fire crackles. Clare [from next door] makes a superb theatrical presentation of two dressed salmon. The French contingent smoke themselves silly and a good time is had by all.

Al and Claudie are the last to leave. Al, with a few nips of Laphroaig and a good chat under his belt, steps out into the wet streets at seven.

Take my mother to see *Life of Brian*. The Plaza is packed. A sell-out. I think she enjoyed it, except for a few qualifications about the 'Crucifixion' ending. But the fact she's awake at all at the end of a day like this, says a lot for her strength and stamina. Remain virtually incognito and afterwards we slope off to the Dean Street Pizza Express.

Tuesday, November 27th

A grey, unprepossessing day. Damp and quite warm. Take Al and Claudie out to Heathrow to catch the two o'clock Pan Am return to NYC. Al, leathery tough though he may look, is a softie at heart, and confesses that he is very frightened of what might happen when they arrive at NYC immigration. But I try to cheer him up and give him and Claudie a small book of Bewick's woodcuts with careful and finely drawn vignettes of an idyllic and calm rural world – long before US immigration regulations and Kennedy Airport.

I hear Mervyn Stockwood announced his resignation today. I also hear that he has cancer and drinks heavily to douse the pain.

Wednesday, November 28th

As November, and our two-week Python writing period, draws to a close, I find myself fighting for time. Suddenly everyone wants me for something or other. Quite apart from TG's film looming, I'm also contacted by a BBC Manchester TV features producer, who wants me to do a programme on railways for him; four or five managements have written expressing interest in my play.

Mel Calman is almost daily in touch, like a sheepdog trying gently to bring me into the fold of his new humour mag. I have a book review for *New Yorker* magazine, which I must do by December 1st and today I have to present the *Melody Maker* pop awards at lunchtime and talk to Hunter Davies for a piece in the *Sunday Times*.

A hired car smoothes me down to the Waldorf Hotel in the Aldwych, where I spend the next three hours, drinking and talking and only for about twenty minutes mounting a stage and presenting eighteen or twenty 'trophies' to the *MM* readers' favourites.

Met Bob Geldof of the Boomtown Rats – the current articulate pop idol, just down from a tour of Scotland. He was unshaven, slouched and wore a loose-fitting yellow velour suit that looked as though it had been slept in since Carlisle. An anti-hero for the times. Nothing spruce, no bright eyes, needed here. He's a very rude man and shows his bottom at the coach window to passing old ladies. I liked him a lot.

Friday, November 30th

Collect Terry and Maggie and we drive out in the Citroen to George H's for a Python dinner. George scuttles around putting records on the juke-box, playing silly pieces on the piano and generally trying to make everyone feel at home – whereas all the guests are of good bourgeois stock and far more ill at ease with George's unpredictable caperings than with standing sipping champagne and making polite conversation.

Cleese and I decide that the house would make a superb set, for a period film. We agree to write a farce together set in Friar Park. 'Ripping Towers' suggests JC's blonde and lovely girlfriend (whom I've not seen before).

The table in the dining room is set splendidly. Table seating has been worked out by Olivia, who clutches a piece of paper as nervously as George earlier pottered with the juke-box. I end up sitting next to George, with Joan and Derek [Taylor] and Eric up our end. Excellent food, especially the salmon, and 1966 claret which was virtually on tap.

George confesses to feeling uncomfortable with a 'posh' evening like this, which I find reassuring – all the glitter and glamour that money can buy, all the success and adulation, has only affected our George very superficially.

Monday, December 3rd

To JC's, via the bank. Coffee, a chat. JC very indignant over decision of Southend and Harrogate councils to ban *Brian* from their towns. It's suggested we take big ads with all the good reviews and paste them up on hoardings in the aforementioned towns with big stickers like 'Banned In Southend' across them.

Then to reading of material. JC and GC, some very funny material (at last) of the British Raj sort. Gilliam has a wonderful idea for a cartoon in which the town fights the countryside – and one marvellous idea of Central Park in NYC spilling its banks and flooding the city with green.

All in all we have about 30 minutes of a very good TV show to show for our two weeks on the film. But morale is high – we seem to be getting on together well. TJ harries and hurries, but the rest of us seem moderately un-panicked.

An over-sybaritic lunch at the Pomme D'Amour in Holland Park rather flatters us. TJ suggests Benn is one of the best politicians around, which makes JC twitch uncontrollably. 'Why is John so afraid to be left-wing?' pleads TJ, ingeniously.

Tuesday, December 4th

I have been offered a one-hour documentary on a railway journey through England after a mention of my railway enthusiasms on *Personal Call*[1] and I've had a letter from Weidenfeld and Nicolson who want to read my novel after a chat with Hunter Davies!

Wednesday, December 5th

Work at Ladbroke Grove. John is half in pyjamas, half in clothes and dressing gown. He says he's not very well, but we sit in his kitchen and a list is made up of the first two weeks' certs. Kashmir and army are strong, but there is no coherent theme yet.

---

1 A radio phone-in, chaired, as I remember, by Simon Bates.

We break up soon after four after John threatens to call the police to have us removed.

To the school carol concert at All Hallows Church. Willy is the percussionist and Tom and Holly are the two clarinettists. Tom sits so straight and blows so hard it brings tears to my eyes. Sing 'Once in Royal David's City' lustily.

Thursday, December 6th

Another grey, unreal awakening. It's ten past eight and feels like the middle of the night. Complete the Oxford Union speech on the motion 'That civilisation ends at Watford'. I'm quite pleased with it.

Sit in a half-mile-long, three-lane jam from White City to Acton. Little to do but sort out the cassettes in the glove compartment, listen to tapes and buy an evening paper, from kids who walk amongst the stationary, helpless cars selling *Standards* with the headline 'Garages Running Dry'. Yes, there's another dispute featuring the country's top blackmailers – the poor, oppressed tanker drivers, who realise the enormous power they hold and are putting the screws on for the second Christmas running.

Decide to call in at Stanton St John as I'm early and, if I've learnt one thing from regular debating at Oxford and Cambridge it's to avoid the pre-match meal. So I find myself stumbling, in the dense and unaccustomed darkness, up the driveway of Robert H's little cottage. I see a light is on and, sure enough, Robert is inside, with a bottle of wine warming on the mantelpiece, a small wood fire, Radio Three simmering away with some piano concerto, going about his business of being a writer.

I do like and admire Robert's self-contained world. I couldn't honestly see myself sitting alone in a cold Oxfordshire cottage, without carpets, midst a slight smell of damp, working. It seems so cut off. Cut off from my sort of life, I suppose.

We talk over his proposal to write an official Python biography, which was turned down by the chaps – for the moment anyway. I don't think people could face any more interviews about the past. But I will press for Robert to be made chronicler of the *Brian* struggle. I think there is a useful book to be done on the whole controversy and its various manifestations.[1]

1 This was eventually commissioned by Geoffrey Strachan at Methuen and came out as *Monty Python: The Case Against* in 1981. It is the first, best and last word on the history of Python's run-ins with the censor.

Arrive at the Union at 8.10. The usual collection of rather smug, self-important little poseurs and meek women with them who look much more interesting.

I rise to speak at 10.35 – having sat for two and a quarter hours on the hard bench. Peter Sissons of ITN sat next to me and I whispered to him as ten o'clock struck that this is the moment when I always decide never to do another debate.

Walk round the Radcliffe Square for old times' sake.

Home by five past one. Read *Decline and Fall.* Asleep by two.

Saturday, December 8th

Drive up to a party in Hampstead at half past nine.

I get talking to a lady – a forceful, well-preserved middle-aged lady (who might have been Mrs Foot) – who knew all about the Gospel Oak Redevelopment Scheme. I asked her if it was just a combination of a genuine desire to house as many people as possible as decently as possible, as quickly as possible, and to do this according to new Corbusier-esque principles which the architects had eagerly espoused.

She said that the scheme was a result of these two 'forces', but added, most positively, a third – corruption. T Dan Smith of Newcastle was just unlucky to be caught out, she reckoned – the corruption in awarding of contracts in schemes was widespread throughout Britain, and Bruno Schlaffenberg – the planner of Gospel Oak, who once said 'Ze English must learn to live in flats' – was not immune.

Later in the evening I was introduced to James Cameron, one of my great living heroes. He has only been out of a long hospital spell for three days. Like Michael Foot, he seems to be cracking up physically, but on great form mentally. He tried to write in hospital, but reckoned it was impossible – 'Every ten minutes people are coming to stick something up your bum.'

We talked of Malcolm Muggeridge, and Cameron, with his peculiar, hissing, rather blurred delivery (caused, I'm told, by having to work hard to keep his teeth in), said he hadn't seen the interview but 'One must remember that Malcolm was, for many years, a promiscuous, drunken bum.' He said this cheerfully, with no malice.

I was able to express my admiration for the man and his work. He brushed the compliment aside – '... Well, ten years ago *perhaps.*'

Monday, December 10th

A run is a must today. Rewarded with warm, refreshing sunshine. To lunch at the Barque and Bite with Ken Stephinson, BBC Manchester producer who wants me to do the *Great Railway Journey* with him.

I like Stephinson immediately. He's easy company and straightforward. He knows what he wants – he wants to make this journey the best of the lot (and there are others written and presented by such luminaries as Ludovic Kennedy, Julian Pettifer, Michael Frayn and so on). He has ambitious plans for shooting – and clearly loves film and filming. It seems hardly likely to be *un*pleasant work, but whereas he says all the other presenters are on twelve-week contracts, he would be happy to adapt as much as he could to my needs.

Thursday, December 13th

Work on Gilliam film until midday then down to Covent Garden – to be bought yet another lunch. This time at Poons, by Peter Luff.

Peter, eager and enthusiastic as ever, had sent me some ideas he's been mulling over for a TV series on Values – contrasting the unity of tribal values in the primitive tribes he and his organisation, Survival, are trying to protect, and the complex structure of values based on a split between the intuitive and the empirical which characterises our own society. Good basic questions are asked. I have to be strict with myself and express great interest but, looking at my diary, appear to have no time for any major involvement for one and a half to two years. Peter says he's rather glad he doesn't find himself in that position.

Friday, December 14th

Determined to produce a sizeable slice of *Time Bandits* script for TG to read later today, I worked hard on 'Napoleon' and 'Robin Hood' scenes throughout the morning. The still clear skies lured me out on a run, instead of lunch, then, after a bath, I committed a rather rushed song called 'I Was Born Sir Keith Joseph's Double' to tape as my only contribution to this afternoon's 'Python Sings' record meeting.

Round to E Idle's in Carlton Hill at 2.30. Terry J had written ten songs or fragments of songs. All rather sweet – sung into his pocket tape-recorder in Terry's delightfully doleful voice, which wanders occasionally into areas of deep tunelessness.

Take Willy and Tom to the school. The concert is not quite as enjoyable as previous years'. W plays Sir Lancelot and it's rather touching watching him mouth the other actors' lines before he speaks. Tom is 'Sloth', one of the Seven Deadly Sins, but they have to sing some endlessly tedious sub-Elgarish song by Malcolm Arnold. Needless to say the audience is ecstatic.

Sunday, December 16th

On our own until midday, when TG comes by with David Rappaport, who we both hope will be the leader, Randall, of the dwarf bandits. He must be in his thirties and is about the same height as Rachel.

He is wonderful company – articulate, bright, extrovert, immediately easy and likeable. He's grumbling about his part in *Cinderella* in Newcastle – everyone takes the panto so seriously (in the cast, that is), that he feels that his and Sylvester McCoy's anarchic, spontaneous, disciplined lack of discipline is not being sufficiently used.

He eagerly accepts an invitation to lunch and has a rather chaotic Sunday repast with us. Then I take him up to TG's again. I'm very encouraged, meeting him, that he will be our man.

Wednesday, December 19th

No business lunch today – in fact after this afternoon business at Palin Ltd will be closing down for nearly two weeks, until the 1970s have been tidied away and January – which is nose to the grindstone month – heralds in nose to the grindstone year.

Run in celebration across the Heath. The balmy westerlies, which somehow skewed round warm air destined for the Med onto the Heath in early December have been replaced by biting, piercing easterlies, which will have Londoners filling the pubs and wine bars and reaching for the second bottle of ginger wine if they continue over Christmas.

Thursday, December 20th

First really cold morning for a while. The Mini won't start, which makes me want to kick it, but the Simca, the French alternative, purrs instantly into action.

Take Tom, Willy and Tom's friend Glen to a lecture by David Fanshawe at the Royal Geographical Society at 2.30. They're televising the lecture and the first person I recognise is the burly, barrel-like, uncompromising figure of Ted, the lighting rigger who I remember most from the night-shoot party in Kent on 'Roger of the Raj'. 'You must be a millionaire by now Mike,' he says cheerily. I laugh. But I know he's keenly aware of the fact that I might be.

Lord Hunt introduces the lecture. Fanshawe is quite a jolly character. Typical British explorer type and it's good to see they're still making them. 'This is the hut where I recorded this priceless music, the chap outside's got leprosy – you can see that there.'

But always unexpected touches – he shows us the simple rush mat he always sleeps on, saying that the mat is all he needs, that and four sleeping pills. He then gets the kids to hold up the box of Mogadon as evidence of the sort of thing the modern explorer carries.

He's keen, enthusiastic about life, music, the world – his motto is 'Every day is a day of praise and history'. He records African tribal music and harmonises it with Western choirs into a mass he calls African Sanctus – and it is exciting, stirring, powerful music.

Friday, December 21st

Drive up to Southwold to collect Ma. An unexpected white Christmas scene at Reydon. A shower of snow followed by sharp, bright sunshine makes the countryside look beautiful. But on the way back a storm replaces the showers and it's hard going on the A12. No one is gritting or clearing the snow and sometimes I feel as though I'm going into a black hole as I push on past the massive, terrifying, hurtling bulk of forty-ton super-trucks, hurling mud and slush at the windscreen.

Sunday, December 23rd

Deep in the murky depths of pre-Christmas. Flat skies. Chill, damp, grimy weather. The newspapers forecast a white Christmas for the south of England. The colour supplements are flaccid and empty – all advertising budgets spent. The recession is just around the corner, but seems to be being staved off for the moment. *Brian* is top film in London yet again and the *Life of Brian* book is up to No. 3.

Next door to an excellent little party at Clare's. Oak Villagers do give good parties and it's marvellous not to have to drive. Hugh Latimer, Clare's father, a wonderful, extrovert theatrical, tells me a story of how Yvonne Arnaud had once had 'too many greens' at lunch and in the matinee farted so severely that the curtain had to be brought down early.

Thursday, December 27th

Rain throughout the day. Great weather to be indoors before a roaring fire.

Helen's mother reminisced over supper about H's eccentric relations, including Norah Gibbins who, among other things, tried to raise money for orphaned German boys during the First War and slept outside all year round in her garden at Seaford, under a cover of parachute silk. I must say Rachel has inherited the genes of a remarkably strong set of maternal grandparents.

Sunday, December 30th

A cold, dry day. Light the fire in the morning and sit beside it with Ma, reading Sunday papers.

Decade spotters seem to be rather disappointed with the 1970s. The decade of selfishness, narcissism, introversion, etc, etc. I suppose for me it's been a 'decade' of general upward progress – in status, work, earnings, freedom and enjoyment of life. Personally I'm well pleased. The 1980s will be interesting. Python has established itself and we are now in an almost unassailable position of respect and comfortable living – and we now have to face up to the prospect of what the hell we do with this respect, freedom and comfort. They're not always the bedfellows of creativity.

In a sense I feel my big creative push has been and gone – and yet I'm writing as fluently as ever and taking on as much work as in those heady days between '68 and '75 when we did *everything*. Will the next direction be into more personal, solitary writing, using Python still as a base? Will

Python wither and die of natural causes? John will be 50 in ten years' time. But then Spike Milligan is well past 50 and still being very silly.

This extraordinarily pleasant, settled interlude beside the fire lasts only an hour or less and then I'm walking up to a party at Jack and Liz Cooper's. Full of Hampstead folk.

Met portly Ian Aitken – *Guardian* political correspondent – who's lost his eye. 'I think the cleaner must have put it somewhere.' He has a host of wonderful false-eye stories – including the time when he was bathing off Guadeloupe (covering a summit meeting of Callaghan, Giscard and Carter) and his eye fell out whilst diving. Two or three days later an American walks into the press centre and shouts 'Hey, anyone here lost an eye?' He had found it whilst swimming.

Monday, December 31st

Last day of the 1970s. Clear, dry, fine, cold. Up in time to read work so far on the Gilliam film before taking Granny to Broad Street on the Gospel Oak line to catch the 11.30 to Suffolk. On the way back to Hampstead Heath a magnificently cheery black ticket-collector waived my offer of the extra 16p for my ticket with great bonhomie. 'Happy New Year,' he shouted. It was like the end of *A Christmas Carol*!

Friends come round in the evening and we eat Chinese take-away and play games and half watch a poor compilation of the 1970s from BBC TV. As midnight strikes and the first chimes of the 1980s are met by the obligatory cheers of well-oiled Scotsmen on the box, we take photos of ourselves in celebration and agree that whatever happens – barring the work of the Grim Reaper, of course – we will look at these pics together on December 31st 1989!

Index

Read on for an exclusive extract from Michael Palin's
Travelling to Work: Diaries 1988–1998

1988

Wednesday, September 28th: Espresso Egitto *on the Adriatic*

I've just got up, washed two pairs of socks and pants and considered what to wear for the day. As we have shots that are continuity with last night, I have to settle for the trousers I've worn since leaving London on Sunday morning and my second shirt of the voyage.

The sea is calm, my cabin, which is one of the more comfortable, has two beds alongside each other and a shower and loo. A porthole looks onto the deck and a lifeboat hangs above.

The journey has been fast and furious until now. Yesterday we were up and filming at first light in Venice – we left the city yesterday evening.

I still find the nights a problem. Last night I slept six hours, but that was with the help of a pill which I took in a panic about two. I swear not to take them again except in extremis. They do so little anyway.

Occasionally the realisation that this whole project is supported on my shoulders and demands not just my survival but my wit, energy, exuberance and enthusiasm quite terrifies me. It is going to be a supreme test, and now, only onto my fourth day and feeling low on all levels, I just can't contemplate the same continuing for two and a half more months.

But I'm determined to pull this off. Failure is unthinkable.

Thursday, September 29th

It's nearly one o'clock and clear skies outside over the Saronian Gulf. We've just completed the quite dramatic navigational feat of the passage of the Corinth Canal – a man-made gorge it took us an hour to pass through.

Feel in good spirits today after a long sleep.

Phone Helen after breakfast and, despite the crew crouching and filming every word, it is one of our better phone calls and Helen sounds clear and very pleased to hear me – and surprised too. I don't think she'd expected a call from the ship. These boat journeys will, I think, be a necessary interlude between periods of intense rush and activity.

The crew of the boat are treating us nobly, though I suspect they could turn ugly if they're not enjoying themselves. Today I got up in my *Adriatica* T-shirt, which pleased them – I was promptly given a sailor's hat.

It's hot outside now – the scrub-covered mountains of Greece are all around. Glad of the air-conditioning on the *Egitto*.

Friday, September 30th

This boat trip has been restorative. I'm eager and receptive to places – especially glad I stirred myself from bed this morning to run into Heraklion. I don't suffer, as yet, from seasickness or homesickness.

Fears about my adequacy for the journey persist. I don't think now that I shan't make it, as I did that gloomy first morning on the *Egitto* – my worries now are what I shall make out of it.

My style is friendly, humorous and laid-back. It isn't best suited for revealing things about people – whose right to privacy I respect, as I would want them to respect mine. How much of the time should I be acting?

Saturday, October 1st

Slept fitfully until finally rising at 6.20 to watch us approach Alexandria.

A thorough break with Europe, which I suppose could have been disturbing, but which I find exhilarating and energising. So the day dazzles and everything, all the hard work and the rushing around from location to location and city to city, encourages and stimulates me.

All we need at the end of our first week is sleep. We've filmed well and interestingly on the whole – though it is hard to get people on camera to be as easygoing and informative and anecdotal as they are off.

Sunday, October 2nd: Cairo

Sour taste of tourism at the Pyramids, and back to film two interviews in the bar of the Windsor[1] (where many stars of Egyptian theatre and opera gather!). Conscious of asking easy questions, not probing enough, being almost too respectful. Always after the interview I think of the one question I should have asked.

Monday, October 3rd: Suez

Seven o'clock at the Red Sea Hotel – the silence outside on the straight, empty avenues is quite a shock after Cairo. So is the hot water, even though it's only a shower – no bath since Venice. The room is quite characterless and depressing, as is Suez. Can't wait to get on a boat tomorrow and get moving.

This morning we completed various shots in and around the hotel and I didn't have to go out. As in New York City, one has to be fit and strong to go out into the streets of Cairo, and a two-hour lay-off in the morning to write cards and ring the office was much needed and appreciated. *Wanda* is over 50 million in the States now. [The film *A Fish Called Wanda* had been released in the USA on July 15th.] Terry J starts *Erik the Viking* in Malta on the 19th.

The journey by taxi to Suez was pretty grim. The heat, dust, traffic and fumes of Cairo for the first half-hour were as uncomfortable as anything I've experienced so far on the trip. Once out of Cairo we were in desert – relics of war, barracks and endless rubbish tips.

The hotel is dry and we're all meeting at 7.30 to seek out a place for beer.

Wednesday, October 5th: Aboard the Saudi Moon 2, *on the Red Sea*

As of today the journey has become quite an adventure. Information reaching us from Jeddah indicates that all our options must be reconsidered. I might have to drive across Arabia – but our visas, we think, confine us to Jeddah. I may be dropped from a container boat to go

---

1 The Windsor Hotel. Eccentric city-centre hotel. The air-con unit was noisier than the traffic outside. 'I now know why they laughed at me when I'd asked for a quiet room' (*Around the World in Eighty Days*).

ashore at Muscat, or we may be in Jeddah for four or five days, losing precious time.

The Arab world was always to be the most difficult, Clem Vallance had warned. Even he is now lost for answers. So we move on a rolling sea towards Jeddah and uncertainty on a considerable scale. It will be very hot, we shall have our patience tested to the limits, and we shall have to work a hard and long day.

What's more, we have been eleven travelling and filming days in succession and a day off would be an orgasmic pleasure. None beckons. Add to this poor food on the boat and a delicate situation in my stomach. Still, thanks to Allah – *Insh-Allah*! – it'll be the longest time I've been without alcohol for decades!

Out on deck as I write (ten p.m.) are sleeping, like corpses, hundreds of Egyptian workers, many of whom are leaving everything behind for a year or more.

Friday, October 7th: Red Sea Palace Hotel, Jeddah, Saudi Arabia

Day 13, country number 9. Outside my fourth-floor windows to the left it is a modern cityscape that looks back at me, dual carriageways, roundabouts, traffic moving in plenty of space, tall, featureless concrete high-rise clusters. Move a little to my left, say, to pick up an apple from the complimentary basket, and I look down on a beleaguered, ill-kempt quarter of older houses, four storeys at most with balconies of wood and screens and carved details about the windows.

First thing to be said about Jeddah is that it has been a rest and renewal stop. Our arrival on an uncluttered dockside, even our efficient clearance through customs, thanks to Ahmed and the presence of young Nick from the embassy in Riyadh, was much less of a strain than doing anything in Egypt.

The hotel – affluent, international, but really conforming to American standards of comfort and service – may be nothing to do with the real Saudi Arabia, but it has provided hot water and a bath and space and service and laundry and room to move and gather wits.